D1480396

Studies of Labor Market Intermediation

**A National Bureau
of Economic Research
Conference Report**

Studies of Labor Market Intermediation

Edited by **David H. Autor**

The University of Chicago Press

Chicago and London

DAVID H. AUTOR is professor in the department of economics at the Massachusetts Institute of Technology and a research associate of the National Bureau of Economic Research.

The University of Chicago Press, Chicago 60637
The University of Chicago Press, Ltd., London
© 2009 by the National Bureau of Economic Research
All rights reserved. Published 2009
Printed in the United States of America

18 17 16 15 14 13 12 11 10 09   1 2 3 4 5
ISBN-13: 978-0-226-03288-7 (cloth)
ISBN-10: 0-226-03288-4 (cloth)

Library of Congress Cataloging-in-Publication Data

Studies of labor market intermediation / edited by David H. Autor.
        p. cm. — (National Bureau of Economic Research conference report)
    Includes bibliographical references and index.
    ISBN-13: 978-0-226-03288-7 (cloth : alk. paper)
    ISBN-10: 0-226-03288-4 (cloth : alk. paper) 1. Labor market—Congresses. 2. Employment agencies—Congresses. 3. Temporary help services—Congresses. 4. Manpower planning—Congresses. 5. Manpower policy—Congresses. 6. Job hunting—Computer network resources—Congresses. 7. Consorzio interuniversitario AlmaLaurea—Congresses. I. Autor, David H. II. National Bureau of Economic Research. III. Series: National Bureau of Economic Research conference report.
    HD5701.8.S88 2009
    331—dc22
                                                            2008047515

♾ The paper used in this publication meets the minimum requirements of the American National Standard for Information Sciences—Permanence of Paper for Printed Library Materials, ANSI Z39.48-1992.

Relation of the Directors to the Work and Publications of the National Bureau of Economic Research

1. The object of the NBER is to ascertain and present to the economics profession, and to the public more generally, important economic facts and their interpretation in a scientific manner without policy recommendations. The Board of Directors is charged with the responsibility of ensuring that the work of the NBER is carried on in strict conformity with this object.

2. The President shall establish an internal review process to ensure that book manuscripts proposed for publication DO NOT contain policy recommendations. This shall apply both to the proceedings of conferences and to manuscripts by a single author or by one or more co-authors but shall not apply to authors of comments at NBER conferences who are not NBER affiliates.

3. No book manuscript reporting research shall be published by the NBER until the President has sent to each member of the Board a notice that a manuscript is recommended for publication and that in the President's opinion it is suitable for publication in accordance with the above principles of the NBER. Such notification will include a table of contents and an abstract or summary of the manuscript's content, a list of contributors if applicable, and a response form for use by Directors who desire a copy of the manuscript for review. Each manuscript shall contain a summary drawing attention to the nature and treatment of the problem studied and the main conclusions reached.

4. No volume shall be published until forty-five days have elapsed from the above notification of intention to publish it. During this period a copy shall be sent to any Director requesting it, and if any Director objects to publication on the grounds that the manuscript contains policy recommendations, the objection will be presented to the author(s) or editor(s). In case of dispute, all members of the Board shall be notified, and the President shall appoint an ad hoc committee of the Board to decide the matter; thirty days additional shall be granted for this purpose.

5. The President shall present annually to the Board a report describing the internal manuscript review process, any objections made by Directors before publication or by anyone after publication, any disputes about such matters, and how they were handled.

6. Publications of the NBER issued for informational purposes concerning the work of the Bureau, or issued to inform the public of the activities at the Bureau, including but not limited to the NBER Digest and Reporter, shall be consistent with the object stated in paragraph 1. They shall contain a specific disclaimer noting that they have not passed through the review procedures required in this resolution. The Executive Committee of the Board is charged with the review of all such publications from time to time.

7. NBER working papers and manuscripts distributed on the Bureau's web site are not deemed to be publications for the purpose of this resolution, but they shall be consistent with the object stated in paragraph 1. Working papers shall contain a specific disclaimer noting that they have not passed through the review procedures required in this resolution. The NBER's web site shall contain a similar disclaimer. The President shall establish an internal review process to ensure that the working papers and the web site do not contain policy recommendations, and shall report annually to the Board on this process and any concerns raised in connection with it.

8. Unless otherwise determined by the Board or exempted by the terms of paragraphs 6 and 7, a copy of this resolution shall be printed in each NBER publication as described in paragraph 2 above.

Contents

Studies of Labor Market Intermediation: Introduction

David H. Autor

Labor Market Intermediaries (LMIs) are entities or institutions that interpose themselves between workers and firms to facilitate, inform, or regulate how workers are matched to firms, how work is accomplished, and how conflicts are resolved. In the textbook competitive model of the labor market, LMIs do not exist—nor is there any need for them. If information is complete and markets are competitive, theory suggests that decentralized, atomistic labor markets are hard to improve upon.

Economists have long recognized that labor markets deviate substantially from this neoclassical benchmark. Sumner Slichter (1950) observed more than fifty years ago that the "law of one price" did not appear to hold in labor markets; seemingly identical workers earned markedly different wages depending upon what industry they labored in.[1] H. Greg Lewis (1986) demonstrated in the 1970s that membership in a labor union conferred substantial wage benefits, underscoring that atomistic wage setting is far from universal. Akerlof (1970) showed that a small amount of private information in markets may be sufficient to thwart trade entirely. Shortly thereafter,

David H. Autor is a professor of economics at the Massachusetts Institute of Technology and a research associate of the National Bureau of Economic Research.

The twelve papers in this volume were prepared for and presented at the NBER Conference on Labor Market Intermediation in May of 2007. The Labor Market Intermediation conference and resulting volume were generously supported by the National Bureau of Economic Research and the National Science Foundation (CAREER award SES-0239538). I am particularly grateful to James Poterba, Marty Feldstein, and Richard Freeman for their intellectual guidance and moral support in the development of this endeavor. In addition, David J. Pervin of the University of Chicago Press, Helena Fitz-Patrick of NBER, and two anonymous referees provided invaluable input on the manuscript. I finally thank Carl Beck of NBER for his superb coordination of all aspects of the conference.

1. This finding was corroborated by, among others, Krueger and Summers (1988) and Katz and Summers (1989).

Spence (1973) identified a set of conditions under which employers might reward workers for acquiring costly credentials that have no productive value. During the 1980s, Diamond, Mortensen, and Pissarides formalized the observation that decentralized labor market search typically leads to a market equilibrium with both unfilled jobs and unemployed workers.[2] This body of theory and evidence suggests that labor market information is not usually complete or symmetric, workers are not typically commodities, firms are not always price takers, and in general, there may be scope for third parties—LMIs, in particular—to intercede both to improve the operation of the labor market and to profit from its imperfections.

The goal of this volume is to offer a conceptual foundation for analyzing the roles that these understudied economic actors play in the labor market, and to develop a qualitative and, in some cases, quantitative sense of their significance to market operation and worker welfare. The twelve chapters in this volume, prepared for and presented at the National Bureau of Economic Research Conference on Labor Market Intermediation in May of 2007, offer novel empirical analyses of a diverse array of LMIs, including online job search engines, criminal records providers, public employment offices, state regulatory bodies, labor unions, centralized job matching markets, and temporary help agencies. Although heterogeneous, a central theme of this volume is that these intermediaries serve a common role, which is to address a set of endemic departures of labor market operation from the neoclassical benchmark. The intellectual challenge taken up by the volume is to identify and systematically classify these departures, and to consider how market and nonmarket actors—workers, firms, public officials, nongovernmental organizations—adapt to them to improve or to exploit the decentralized outcomes that result.

The parsimonious and (I hope) encompassing taxonomy offered by this introductory chapter highlights three major deviations of labor market operation from the neoclassical benchmark and considers how LMIs potentially address—and in some cases, exploit—them. These deviations are costly information, adverse selection, and (failures of) collective action. This chapter develops this three-part taxonomy and uses it to illustrate the underlying economic forces that connect the twelve chapters in the volume. A unifying observation that emerges is that participation in the activities or services of a given LMI are typically *voluntary* for one side of the market—workers or employers—and *compulsory* for the other. I argue that this pattern of voluntary and compulsory participation is largely dictated by the nature of the market imperfections that LMIs address, and thus can tell us much about the roles that intermediaries play in the market. Table 1, which categorizes LMIs by market function and the nature of worker and firm participation in their activities (voluntary/compulsory), provides a roadmap to the main arguments of the chapter.

2. Diamond (1982), Mortensen (1982), Pissarides (1986).

Table 1   Categorizing labor market intermediaries by market function and nature of participation

	Primary function				Nature of participation		
	Information provision/ search costs	Worker-side adverse selection	Firm-side adverse selection	Collective action	Voluntary for workers and firms	Voluntary for firms not workers	Voluntary for workers not firms
Traditional job boards	✓				✓		
Comprehensive job boards (e.g., AlmaLaurea)		✓				✓	
Criminal records providers		✓	✓			✓	
Public employment offices			✓				✓
Labor standards regulations			✓				✓
Centralized medical job match				✓		✓	
Labor unions				✓			✓
Temporary help agencies	✓				✓		

Costly Information

In the benchmark neoclassical model of the labor market, it is costless for workers and firms to search for each other. In reality, search is costly. Workers pay directly for search, through the monetary and psychic costs of applying and interviewing for jobs, and indirectly, through foregone work or leisure. Employers likewise incur search costs directly—through help-wanted advertising, job fairs, and applicant screening and interviewing—and indirectly through foregone output while vacancies await workers. Since information about job vacancies and job-seekers is in large part a public good—in particular, each firm would like to be aware of all job-seekers, and each job-seeker would like to be aware of all vacancies—this information is likely to be undersupplied by the market.

The first chapters of this volume portray a set of LMIs that serve as "information-only" intermediaries—entities whose near-exclusive function is to aggregate, package, and sell information about job-seekers and job vacancies. The leading example of an information-only intermediary is the online job board, which serves as a clearinghouse for workers seeking jobs and jobs seeking workers. The chapter by Nakamura, Shaw, Freeman, Nakamura, and Pyman provides an analytic perspective on how the business of online job search functions—how firms use it, how workers use it, and how online search firms profit from the process.

While at their most basic level, job boards merely post lists of job-seekers and job vacancies, Nakamura et al. outline how the business of online job boards has evolved greatly from this rudimentary help-wanted function. Large job boards—like Monster.com, CareerBuilder.com, and Hotjobs. yahoo.com—increasingly provide an outsourced personnel recruitment function for large employers, hosting the employment sections of their corporate websites, contacting potential candidates en masse, accepting and prescreening resumes, tracking applications, and providing access to an exclusive set of candidates. For example, students of elite universities are given privileged access to these sites as they near the completion of their studies.[3] A key point made by Nakamura et al. is that, by making it easier for employers to identify potential candidates among those currently employed ("passive seekers") and simultaneously lowering workers' costs of engaging in on-the-job search, job boards may particularly advantage employed relative to nonemployed job-seekers.[4]

The chapter by Stevenson complements this analytic overview by providing an initial empirical analysis of how the Internet may be changing job

3. A related paper by Kroft and Pope (2007) provides evidence on the degree to which online job engines, Craigslist in particular, have displaced the traditional newspaper help-wanted business.

4. Kugler and Saint Paul (2004) consider how the imposition of firing costs in the presence of worker adverse selection differentially disadvantages nonemployed relative to employed job-seekers.

search behavior in the United States. Stevenson documents that the variety of job search methods used by unemployed U.S. workers has increased significantly over the last decade, coincident with the rapid rise in Internet penetration. Moreover, in U.S. states where Internet penetration has risen the most, the unemployed appear increasingly likely to use job advertisements for seeking and contacting employers directly—suggesting that online and offline search may be complements. Consonant with the observations by Nakamura et al., Stevenson shows that the vast majority of workers using the Internet to gather information about employment are those who are already employed. Logically, workers who use the Internet for job search are more likely to leave their current employer. It is plausible—though far from certain—that online job search may increase the rate at which workers change jobs.[5]

Mitigating Adverse Selection

While pure "information-only" intermediaries address an important public goods problem, this category of LMI is relatively narrow and, I would argue, less consequential than the bulk of the LMIs discussed in the following. The reason is that where information is costly, the central economic problem is typically not exclusively costly information but also asymmetric information. Specifically, if information about the quality of workers or jobs is incomplete, better-informed market actors have an incentive to exploit their informational advantage to the detriment of less-informed market actors. As first outlined by Akerlof (1970), these information asymmetries readily generate a market equilibrium where lower quality market actors (workers or firms) exert negative externalities on their higher quality counterparts, depressing both the quantity and quality of trade.

While job boards might appear to offer a powerful mechanism to bolster aggregate labor market efficiency, qualitative and quantitative evidence suggests that job boards do not reach this potential. An analysis of U.S. job search data by Kuhn and Skuterud (2004) finds that workers who use the Internet to search for jobs fare no better—and perhaps worse—than observably similar workers who do not search for jobs using the Internet. Their analysis suggests that either Internet job search is ineffective at reducing unemployment durations or Internet job searchers are negatively selected on unobservables. One recruiting executive, quoted in Autor (2001b), lends informal support to the latter hypothesis, asserting that job boards are populated by four adversely selected pools: "The unhappy (and thus probably not a desirable employee); the curious (and therefore likely to be a 'job-hopper');

---

5. If the Internet provides incumbent workers with better information about their outside opportunities, these workers do not need to change jobs to benefit. Websites like greedyassociates.com, for example, which publicize the salary offers made to newly minted attorneys, may serve to homogenize the distribution of law firm associate wages.

the unpromotable (probably for a reason); and the unemployed (probably for a worse reason)" (32).

The core problem facing job boards—reflected in the preceding quotation—is that workers posting their resumes and credentials online face a strong incentive to conceal or slant information to make themselves more attractive to potential employers. Recognizing this, employers are likely to treat information posted to job boards with skepticism. If in equilibrium, employers view the information on job boards as untrustworthy, these boards can do little more than provide employers with names and numbers, leaving them to discover essential information about worker skills and qualifications through other mechanisms such as interviews, background checks, and job references.

A natural solution to this asymmetric information problem is compulsory disclosure; if job-seekers can be compelled to reveal information that they would not necessarily disclose voluntarily, this could substantially improve the efficiency of job search and matching—though clearly not all workers would benefit. Though compulsory disclosure sounds difficult to achieve in real world labor markets, chapters 3 and 4 study two labor market intermediaries that perform exactly this function: reducing worker-side adverse selection by, implicitly or explicitly, compelling job applicants to reveal information that they might otherwise conceal.

A key piece of information that employers may seek to ascertain is criminal history. As chapter 3 by Keith Finlay reveals, almost 20 percent of black males and more than 10 percent of white males in recent U.S. youth cohorts have been incarcerated by age twenty-four. Historically, criminal background checks have been comparatively expensive to perform and not particularly reliable. Between 1998 and the present, however, more than a dozen U.S. states placed their criminal history records databases online for use by employers and other interested parties. Implicitly, job-seekers applying for jobs in "open records" states are now compelled to submit to a criminal background check at the employer's discretion. The opening of criminal records therefore functions as a publicly operated LMI that may in theory reduce worker-side adverse selection.

How does this opening affect labor market operation in practice? Working from a simple statistical discrimination framework, Finlay hypothesizes that if employers do not initially observe applicants' criminal histories and instead attempt to infer them based on other observable characteristics (such as education, age, gender, and race), the opening of criminal records should diminish the labor market prospects of ex-offenders while potentially *benefiting* non-offenders who might otherwise be viewed as potential criminals. Using data from the National Longitudinal Study of Youth (NLSY) 1997 Cohort, Finlay finds support for the first proposition. Young adults with criminal histories face reduced employment odds and lower wages after states make criminal histories available online. There is less evidence, however, that young adults *without* criminal records who appear demographically similar to potential criminals fare *better* once criminal records are opened. This result may indicate that employers underestimate the prevalence of criminality in the absence of open criminal records—and hence, opening of criminal records impedes applicants who are revealed to be offenders without benefiting those who are revealed to be non-offenders. As Finlay cautions, however, the relatively small NLSY 97 sample provides insufficient power to detect the diffuse benefits hypothesized to accrue to the non-offender population. What appears unambiguous is that opening of criminal records does diminish the labor market prospects of ex-offenders.

Although both online job postings and online criminal records potentially serve to reduce search costs in labor markets, the crucial distinction between these LMIs from the perspective of this chapter lies in the nature of information disclosure. Users of job boards may reveal, disclose, or simply fabricate information at will. Job applicants in "open records" states have no say in whether their criminal backgrounds are made publicly available. It appears plausible that this distinction explains why open records have real bite: they credibly supply information about worker credentials that applicants might otherwise conceal.

The chapter by Bagues and Labini studies an unusual job search engine, *AlmaLaurea,* which also has this compulsory revelation feature. Founded in 1994 by an interuniversity consortium of Italian universities, *AlmaLaurea* was set up to increase the frequency of successful school-to-work transitions among Italian university graduates, which have been astonishingly low in recent decades. What distinguishes *AlmaLaurea* from most electronic job boards it that it provides detailed *administrative* records on participants' courses of study, grades obtained, and rank in class. Moreover, it provides this information for almost the entire set of students currently graduating from the universities in the consortium. In effect, *AlmaLaurea* offers the university equivalent of open records for job applicants: a college transcript, a class ranking, and, implicitly, a comparison of each applicant to his or her immediate peers.

A thoroughgoing empirical analysis by Bagues and Labini offers compelling evidence that *AlmaLaurea* reduced the nonemployment rate of graduates of *AlmaLaurea* member universities. Specifically, comparing changes in the nonemployment rate of graduates of universities joining *AlmaLaurea* over 1998 to 2001 relative to graduates of universities that had not *yet* joined during this period suggests that *AlmaLaurea* reduced the nonemployment rate of *AlmaLaurea* graduates by several percentage points, which is considerable. Because Italian labor market conditions were rapidly improving during the time period studied, there is room for concern that the difference-in-difference approach employed might be unreliable. Bagues and Labini do much to allay this concern, including conducting placebo tests of the

AlmaLaurea treatment in the pretreatment period, and exploiting a second wave of *AlmaLaurea* roll-outs to confirm the main finding.

The *AlmaLaurea* study leaves open two questions that subsequent research will want to address. First, did the reduction in unemployment of *AlmaLaurea* graduates come in part at the expense of other potential workers? Intuition might suggest yes, but initial analysis by Bagues and Labini suggests otherwise. Alternatively, if *AlmaLaurea* primarily expanded the total employment roster, what does this imply about the magnitude of search costs or adverse selection in the Italian labor market absent *AlmaLaurea*? A second question ripe for study is whether *AlmaLaurea* resulted in a redistribution of opportunities among job candidates within member institutions. Since *AlmaLaurea* was built to facilitate direct comparisons among candidates from member universities, it is plausible that it produced both winners and losers—improving opportunities for the most distinguished students and reducing them for the least distinguished.[6]

Adverse selection is not, of course, limited to the worker side of the labor market. Firms may equally face incentives to exploit asymmetric information, to the detriment of workers and customers. The chapter by Woong Lee confronts the problem of adverse selection of firms—in particular, firms that are themselves LMIs. Lee's chapter provides an original empirical analysis of the rise of U.S. Public Employment Offices (PEOs) at the turn of the twentieth century. At that time, the services of private, for-profit employment agencies were widely sought by job-seekers, particularly by unskilled workers and migrants. The lack of sophistication of these job-seekers, however, left them vulnerable to exploitation. Some of the abuses perpetrated by for-profit employment agencies included sending job-seekers to distant locations where no work existed, colluding with employers to provide applicants with only temporary work stints followed by summary discharge, and (occasionally) sending unwitting female job-seekers to brothels. Thus, for-profit employment agencies appear to have heavily exploited precisely the information asymmetries they were purported to resolve.

For U.S. state governments facing this predicament, several remedies were conceivable, including regulating and licensing for-profit employment agencies or banning them outright. The approach pursued by the states, however, was ingenious. Rather than attempting to directly curtail the behavior of abusers, states chose to effectively compete them out of business by offering high-quality employment assistance services at Public Employment Offices at no cost to job-seekers. This response seems to reflect a pinpoint diagnosis of the market failure and its remedy. By introducing competition between for-profit LMIs and reputable public sector LMIs, states likely drove many of the lowest-quality PEOs out of business. What was left behind, presum-

6. This outcome would also be consonant with the reasoning of the Finlay study.

ably, were PEOs that offered sufficient value-added to justify a positive price despite the presence of a reputable, zero-cost competitor.

The chapter by Dick Todd and Morris Kleiner considers another example of a public response to a perceived failure of intermediation, in this case by mortgage brokers. Mortgage brokers are for-profit agents (individuals or firms) that match potential mortgage borrowers with lenders and assist borrowers in completing the loan origination process. These brokers were insignificant in the mortgage market in 1980, but by 2004 were involved in approximately 68 percent of all mortgages originated. Coinciding with their rapid growth was a rise in public concern that market failures prevented competition from effectively disciplining brokers' quality of service.[7] As mortgage brokering grew, numerous states passed laws requiring brokers to post surety bonds or maintain a minimum net worth in order to operate. These requirements potentially work to ensure that borrowers have financial recourse if brokers are malfeasant. In addition, because sellers of surety bonds would be expected to charge risky brokers a higher price, bonding requirements create an entry barrier that is potentially more onerous for low-quality than high-quality mortgage brokers.

Consistent with this reasoning, Kleiner and Todd show that bonding requirements reduced mortgage broker employment, curtailed subprime loan originations, and increased the observed qualification levels (measured by education and experience) of brokers operating in the mortgage broker occupation. Interestingly, however, Kleiner and Todd also find that bonding requirements increased mortgage foreclosure rates and raised the probability that newly originated loans were high priced relative to other loans with similar characteristics. While Kleiner and Todd advise caution in interpreting these adverse impacts, they note that they are consistent with the influential arguments of Friedman (1962) that occupational licensing requirements dampen market discipline and produce artificial scarcity, leading to higher fees for providers and lower quality for consumers.[8]

While mortgage brokers are arguably *product* market rather than labor market intermediaries, they have much in common with the for-profit employment offices studied by Woong Lee. Both employment offices and mortgage brokers serve to match individuals on one side of the market (workers or borrowers) to sellers on the other side (employers or mortgage lenders). The role played by these intermediaries is a natural market response to the problem posed by costly search. There is, however, an adverse selection problem that intrinsically arises in this setting: intermediaries that are in the

---

7. This concern was exacerbated by the fact that mortgage brokers dominated the origination of so-called subprime mortgages—that is, loans to borrowers who would not be considered creditworthy by traditional lending standards.

8. For an extensive treatment of this topic, see Kleiner's (2006) monograph on occupational licensing.

business of selling information are, by nature, better informed about information they sell than are the customers they serve. A wealth of theory and evidence suggests that markets are unlikely to operate optimally when sellers and buyers are not equally informed. As the chapters by Lee and Kleiner and Todd suggest, some subset of intermediaries will use their informational advantage to exploit rather than to assist customers.

These parallels suggest some general lessons on the mixed role that intermediaries play in reducing information costs in labor markets. Since the public good of labor market information is likely to be underprovided by the free market, a set of LMIs will find it profitable to collect and sell information at a cost that job-seekers could obtain by their own efforts. These intermediaries mitigate the underprovision problem. But their informational advantage also potentially gives rise to another market failure, which is information asymmetry and the attendant risk of adverse selection. Whether this asymmetric information problem is moderate or severe depends in part on the market structure in which intermediaries operate. In the case of private employment agencies at the turn of the twentieth century, these abuses were apparently profound. But a change in market structure, fostered by competition between public and private-sector providers, substantially mitigated the problem. In the case of mortgage brokers, it is less certain that the regulatory remedy—creating barriers to entry—provided the structural change needed.

In both cases, it is significant that the policy response to adverse selection included forcible public intervention in the market: an injection of competition in the case of Public Employment Offices and the imposition of bonding requirements in the case of mortgage brokers. These examples reinforce the general observation that, to address significant market imperfections, LMIs must be capable of changing the incentives faced by at least one set of market agents, typically workers or firms.

Solving Collective Action Problems

Providing information—even compelling it—is not necessarily sufficient to resolve market failures. Notifying a bank's deposit holders that the institution faces a small risk of insolvency does not make a run on the bank less likely—rather, it spurs each depositor to withdraw his or her funds, thus ensuring collapse. In such cases, rational agents acting with full information and accurate expectations about one another's actions make decisions that are privately optimal yet collectively suboptimal. There is potential in such settings for market intermediaries to improve on competitive outcomes. But this is only feasible if these intermediaries have teeth—or, more specifically, the power to change payoffs so that the maximizing choices of actors on one or both sides of the market also serve the common good.

The chapters by Muriel Niederle and Alvin Roth and by Richard Freeman and Marit Rehavi consider two such intermediaries. Niederle and Roth analyze the labor market for medical fellowships (post-residency training) in the specialty of gastroenterology. Unraveling is widespread in entry-level labor markets for highly specialized positions, including legal clerkships and medical specialties. Candidates in these fields often sign binding employment contracts one or more years prior to the start of work—well before the quality of job matches can be reliably assessed. And job offers are frequently made with short (exploding) decision deadlines and substantial professional penalties for reneging. The allocative efficiency of such a matching process is likely to be poor.

The Niederle and Roth chapter offers a diagnosis of the market failures in entry-level specialty markets and a quantitative analysis of how these problems were manifest and subsequently resolved (at least for some time) by the LMI of a centralized fellowship match. Niederle and Roth argue that the underlying cause of market unraveling is congestion. In occupations where most entry-level candidates enter the labor market simultaneously (i.e., as a cohort completes its studies), there is typically insufficient time for employers to evaluate and make offers to all relevant candidates before competing offers have already been made and accepted. This congestion spurs employers to make time-limited (exploding) offers to candidates to reduce the risk that, should their initial offers be declined, they are left to hire from the residual candidate pool. When exploding offers become commonplace, employers quickly recognize that they can employ them strategically to make job markets artificially thin for their preferred candidates. Specifically, by forcing a candidate to make a binding decision before his or her alternative offers are known, an exploding offer turns the candidate's simultaneous decision problem into a sequential decision problem. Such strategies naturally lead to unraveling: anticipating that their competitors will make exploding job offers, each employer has an incentive to accelerate its own offers.

A primary implication of Niederle and Roth's diagnosis is that market unraveling could potentially be checked if job offers were effectively delayed (or made nonbinding) until candidates and employers had sufficient time to search over their relevant choice sets. The National Resident Matching Program (NRMP), studied by Niederle and Roth, performs this function. The NRMP provides a centralized clearinghouse where applicants and employers submit rank-ordered lists representing their preferences. Applying a set of deferred acceptance algorithms, the NRMP allocates candidates to fellowships.[9] Candidates participating in the match are, in theory, not bound by job offers initiated prior to the resolution of the match—thus nullifying the power of exploding offers to constrain their choices. Employer participa-

---

9. As the chapter discusses, the results of such a match are stable—that is, there exists no applicant-employer pair, not matched to one another, who would prefer each other to their current match. Moreover, it is generally (though not always) incentive-compatible for applicants to submit their true preferences to the clearinghouse.

tion in the match is voluntary, however, and the value of participation will depend positively on the fraction of competitors who are also participating.

A compelling feature of Niederle and Roth's quantitative case study of the gastroenterology (GI) market is that the profession adopted a centralized match in 1989 in response to widespread signs of market malfunction, but participation in the match began to decline after six years, and the match was formally abandoned in 2000. This set of events yields two prepost contrasts for quantitative study, one prior to the match's adoption and the other subsequent to its demise. The available evidence suggests that the centralized match mitigated some clear market maladies, dramatically compressing the highly dispersed timing of job offers (which led to artificial thinness) and increasing the mobility of GI residents out of the hospitals where they performed their residences (suggesting that the match reduced monopsony power among incumbent employers). The chapter also examines the contentious question of whether the centralized match depressed fellowship salaries below competitive levels. Niederle and Roth find essentially no difference in salary levels between specialties that use a match and those that do not, suggesting that centralized matching does not dampen salaries per se. Equally remarkable, however, is that the data reveal almost no economically significant variation in fellowship salary levels or dispersion across the fourteen specialties considered. This absence of variation raises the question of whether, in addition to congestion, the maladies of the fellowship market are in part explained by other noncompetitive factors.

The GI matching market example underscores the potential of a Labor Market Intermediary to resolve collective action problems—in this case, restraining employers from making early offers. The demise of the GI match in 2000, however, suggests that something was amiss. Niederle and Roth trace the breakdown of the match to a sudden and substantial falloff in the supply of GI fellows spurred by a policy change by the Gastroenterology Leadership Council. When the number of fellows fell below the number of available fellowship slots in 1996, the temptation for employers to circumvent the match to guarantee their supply of labor may simply have become overwhelming. And because employer participation in the match was voluntary, the matching intermediary had no teeth with which to discipline defectors. The match therefore unraveled as initial defections spurred further defections, rendering the match irrelevant by 2000. The GI case again demonstrates that the ability to compel participation by at least one side of the market—and perhaps by both—is a necessary requirement for an LMI to redress a market failure—in this case, a collective action failure. The GI fellowship match appears to have had this power when the labor market was slack, but not when it was tight.

The Freeman and Rehavi chapter, which offers an innovative study of the changing shape of labor unions, provides a compelling point of comparison to the GI case. While the National Resident Matching Program is an LMI with the power to change market payoffs (at least some of the time), labor unions are an LMI adapting to the loss of this power. Unions have historically solved collective action problems among atomistic workers by organizing collective bargaining, sanctioning employers for misconduct, and regulating employers' hiring and dismissal policies. A key to their ability to perform this function in the United States is the National Labor Relations Act of 1935, which compels employers to bargain collectively with a labor union if a majority of the firm's employees votes for union representation. Thus, once a union is established, it holds an effective monopoly on bargaining.

While survey evidence suggests that worker demand for union representation has increased with time, union density in the United States has fallen to almost negligible levels (7.4 percent in 2006). Labor unions have also lost their efficacy in the United Kingdom, where the range of issues subject to collective bargaining has narrowed. If unions can no longer generate sizable member benefits, their ability to build membership and levy dues diminishes, reducing their power further. This threatens their viability as an LMI.

Against this backdrop, Freeman and Rehavi study an alternative organizing model for unions, which they refer to as "open source." In the open-source model, unions are decoupled from workplaces and do not collectively bargain. They attract members by offering a package of services such as legal advice, group employment benefits (e.g., health insurance), and political lobbying on labor issues. Two features of this open-source model represent a radical departure from the traditional labor union mode. First, open-source unions lack what is certainly the most effective tool that traditional unions possessed for generating member benefits: collective bargaining. Second, many of the services that open-source unions purportedly provide, such as lobbying, are nonexcludable public goods. This leaves them highly vulnerable to free-riding, which was essentially impossible when union membership and compulsory dues paying were preconditions for participation in collective bargaining. This open-source model will sharply limit the membership fees that such unions can charge.

Despite these threats, Freeman and Rehavi see reasons for tempered optimism about unions' prospects in the current era. A first is that the Internet has greatly augmented the capability of unions to communicate with potential members outside of the workplace, and at much lower cost than door-to-door canvassing. Moreover, the set of union services that can be provided over the Internet has proven to extend beyond mere online replication of traditional direct-mail and fundraising operations. Freeman and Rehavi's creative analysis of question-and-answer postings (threads) on the Web site of unionreps.org provides a compelling example of a union successfully using the Internet to provide a set of tangible, individual-level member services—most significantly, legal advice on workplace matters.

Freeman and Rehavi also consider the success of a non workplace-based union, Working America (a "community-affiliate" of the AFL-CIO union), which enrolled two million workers between 2004 and 2007 by canvassing at homes and over the Internet. Working America's success in drawing membership suggests, consistent with survey evidence, that there is considerable latent demand for organized labor as a political movement. Working America's direct membership benefits are, however, quite limited relative to a traditional labor union, and its fee structure is accordingly modest.

If unions are successful in reconstituting under the open-source model, my expectation is that this will reflect a profound change in their core function as Labor Market Intermediaries. Whereas traditional labor unions primarily served, in the taxonomy of this chapter, as enforcers of collective action, open-source unions appear poised to serve primarily as information-provision intermediaries—more akin to job boards than to the medical match studied by Niederle and Roth. If the power to compel participation is the sine qua non of LMIs that move the market equilibrium, the potential of open-source unions to generate worker benefits that approach those of unions of an earlier era is likely to be limited.

Temporary Help Agencies: What Do They Do for Workers? What Do They Do to the Market?

More than any other Labor Market Intermediary, the temporary help industry has been the subject of intensive recent debate. This is in part due to its spectacular growth. In the United States, the temporary help industry accounted for 10 percent of net job creation during the decade of the 1990s (Autor 2003). In continental Europe and the United Kingdom, temporary help agency employment increased its share of average daily employment from 1.0 to 1.8 percent between 1986 and 1996. In the same interval, the number of workers employed by temporary help agencies more than tripled in Germany, Denmark, and Ireland. In Japan, temporary help employment grew fourfold following significant deregulation (International Confederation of Private Employment Agencies [CIETT] 2007).

Accompanying the growth of temporary help employment has been a qualitative change in the type of jobs filled by temporary help agencies. Historically, temporary help agency jobs were synonymous with clerical and office work. By 2005, a larger share of temporary help jobs in the United States was found in production, transportation, and material moving jobs than in clerical or sales occupations.[10] As temporary help jobs have moved into blue-collar occupations, the industry has become an increasingly

---

10. Bureau of Labor Statistics, http://www.bls.gov/news.release/conemp.toc.htm, accessed 1/20/2008 (based on Current Population Survey February 2005 Contingent Worker Supplement).

important employer of less-skilled workers. Although it accounts for less than 3 percent of average U.S. daily employment, U.S. state administrative data show that 15 to 40 percent of former welfare recipients who obtained employment in the years following the 1996 U.S. welfare reform took jobs in the temporary help sector (Autor and Houseman 2005). Alongside their traditional role of filling short-term staffing needs, temporary help jobs are increasingly used by employers to screen workers for direct-hire positions at arm's length (temp-to-hire) without the attendant risk of litigation should the match end badly.

The rapid growth of temporary help employment among low-skilled workers and the increasing prevalence of temp-to-perm arrangements has spurred an academic and policy debate as to whether temporary help jobs facilitate or hinder labor market advancement of job-seekers. Numerous researchers have hypothesized that stints in temporary help employment enable workers to develop skills and contacts that eventually lead to stable, long-term employment. Moreover, because temporary help firms face uniquely low marginal costs of hiring and firing, these firms may be willing to audition candidates who would otherwise have difficulty finding direct-hire jobs (Abraham 1988; Katz and Krueger 1999; Autor 2001a and 2003; Houseman 2001; Autor and Houseman 2002; Houseman, Kalleberg, and Erickcek 2003; Kalleberg, Reynolds, and Marsden 2003). But these hypothesized benefits are uncertain. Scholars and practitioners have also argued that the unstable and primarily low-skilled positions available through temporary help agencies provide little opportunity for workers to develop human capital or engage in productive job search (Parker 1994; Pawasarat 1997; Jorgenson and Riemer 2000; Benner, Leete, and Pastor 2007). If spells with temporary help agencies also inhibit workers from engaging in productive job search—after all, job search takes time—temporary help employment might hinder workers from obtaining stable jobs.

Distinguishing between these competing hypotheses is a significant empirical challenge. It is inherently difficult to differentiate the effects of holding, given job types from the skills and motivations that cause workers to hold these jobs initially. Four chapters in this volume take steps in this direction by studying the role that temporary help jobs play in the labor market advancement of job-seekers in Portugal, Germany, and the United States.

Before discussing the findings of these chapters, it is useful to consider the temporary help industry through the conceptual lens applied to other LMIs—that is, as institutions that potentially redress market imperfections arising from decentralized job matching between workers and firms. The market imperfection to which temporary help firms primarily address themselves is the *fixed cost* of job search. Identifying, screening, and hiring workers is a fixed cost that must be sunk before actual paid work gets done. This cost may not be worth sinking if the job to be filled is brief or has a short shelf life; for example, substituting for an employee who falls ill for a week. Temporary help firms sink these fixed costs up front by prescreening workers and clients. They defray these sunk costs by introducing a wedge between the hourly wage billed to the client firm and the hourly wage (and other payroll costs) paid to the temporary worker.

Unlike most of the LMIs considered earlier, temporary help agencies function on a two-sided voluntary participation model; neither workers nor firms are obliged to use their services unless they see gains from doing so. From the firm's perspective, the gain to temporary help arrangements is that they convert their fixed job search costs into marginal costs by providing a ready supply of prescreened workers. From the job-seeker's perspective, temporary help agencies potentially offer immediate short-term, hourly employment with almost no initial, fixed investment in job search.[11] In addition, temporary help arrangements facilitate arm's-length screening by allowing firms to audition workers without the attendant fixed costs of hiring and the legal risks of firing. The possibility of a temp-to-perm transition also makes temporary help positions more attractive to workers, many of whom report using temporary help as a means of job search (Autor 2001a).

These observations—in particular, the fact that temporary help agencies rely on voluntary two-sided participation—immediately suggest that their potential to *substantially* change labor market outcomes for *individual* workers or firms is likely to be limited; if this were not so, these arrangements would either be much less common or much more prevalent. This does not imply that temporary help firms neither help nor harm workers (or firms) at the margin. Indeed, Autor and Houseman (2005) provide quasiexperimental evidence that low-skilled former welfare recipients in the United States placed in temporary help agency jobs receive no lasting earnings or employment benefits from these placements, whereas ex ante identical individuals placed in direct-hire positions accrue substantial earnings gains over the course of two to three years following placement. Nevertheless, if temporary help agency employment exists in equilibrium alongside other employment forms, it is unlikely that temporary help jobs are either strictly dominant or strictly dominated by either employment arrangement.

The evidence presented in the final four chapters of the volume appears to corroborate this reasoning, though with many nuances. The study by René

11. Why, given these efficiencies, are the majority of jobs not found through temporary help firms? A likely answer is that, due to their informational advantage on both the supply and demand side of the labor market, temporary help firms find it optimal to charge a relatively high markup on their services. This markup, estimated at 40 to 60 percentage points above the hourly wage paid to the worker (Autor, Levy, and Murnane 1999), provides workers and firms with an incentive to circumvent temporary-help arrangements for longer-term matches. Similarly to mortgage brokers and for-profit employment agencies, temporary-help agencies hold an informational advantage relative to their clients, and, as seen in other examples, this gives rise to its own difficulties—here, monopsonistic pricing.

Böheim and Ana Rute Cardoso uses uniquely detailed, linked worker-firm data from Portugal to analyze whether workers suffer a wage penalty either while working for temporary help firms or in the two years following entry into temporary help employment. As a descriptive matter, their analysis confirms that workers in temporary help jobs earn about 10 percent less than observationally similar workers in nontemporary help (direct-hire) jobs. But once person fixed-effects are included to account for unobserved worker heterogeneity, this wage penalty disappears or becomes positive. These results imply that there is negative self-selection of workers into temporary help jobs in Portugal, a pattern also documented for the United States (Segal and Sullivan 1997).[12]

While Böheim and Cardoso focus primarily on earnings in temporary help jobs, the chapters by Carolyn Heinrich, Peter Mueser and Kenneth Troske, Frederik Andersson, Harry Holzer and Julia Lane, and Michael Kvasnika study the question of whether temporary help jobs augment or inhibit labor market advancement over the longer term. Using employment register data from Germany, Kvasnicka analyzes whether unemployed job-seekers who take temporary help jobs are more likely to later obtain direct-hire employment than observationally similar workers who do not take temporary help jobs. The analytical tool used in this study is a matching estimator, which identifies pairs of workers who are observationally similar *up to the point* where one member of the pair obtains a temporary help job. From this point of divergence forward, the estimator compares the trajectory of the two workers to estimate of the impact of temporary help employment on the "treated" relative to the "nontreated" worker over the subsequent four years.

Contrary to many studies of temporary help employment in European countries, Kvasnicka's analysis finds no evidence that temporary help employment increases job-takers' subsequent rate of direct-hire employment over four years. However, the data clearly show that workers who enter temporary help employment from unemployment are substantially more likely to remain in temporary help jobs over the subsequent four years. Kvasnicka concludes that temporary help jobs increase workers' employment and earnings in the temporary help sector without causing any crowd-out of their advancement into direct-hire employment. As with all studies based on observational (i.e., nonexperimental) data, one must also consider the possibility that the results are in part driven by unobserved differences in skills and motivations among different groups of workers. Ultimately, the validity of this approach hinges on the assumption that the treatment variable (temporary help job employment) can be treated as randomly assigned, conditional on the observable variables used for the matching estimator.

---

12. Böheim and Cardoso also estimate that workers who have previously held a temporary-help job suffer no measurable wage penalty when entering direct-hire employment. Interpretation of this result deserves particular caution, however, since the analysis is conditioned on remaining in employment (wages are not otherwise observed).

Similar in spirit to the Böheim and Cardoso study, the chapter by Andersson, Holzer, and Lane estimates a model of worker earnings that includes both worker and firm-fixed effects. Distinct from Böheim and Cardoso, the fixed-effects model in this chapter draws on earnings data from an earlier time period, thus making the fixed effect more akin to a measure of workers' permanent earnings and firms' average salaries than a conventional fixed-effects estimator. A particular strength of the Andersson, Holzer, and Lane chapter is its rigorous analysis of the trajectory of employment by sector. The chapter explores not only whether workers in temporary help jobs later obtain direct-hire employment, but also whether these jobs are found in high-wage industries and with high-wage employers. The key result of this analysis is that, although workers earn comparatively low wages while in temporary help jobs, their subsequent earnings are often relatively high— but only if they succeed in gaining stable work with direct-hire employers. Consistent with the view that selective firms use temporary help arrangements to screen workers for desirable direct-hire jobs, the chapter documents that temporary help workers who successfully transition to stable, direct-hire employment often end up employed by relatively high-wage firms.

A question left open in part by the Andersson, Holzer, and Lane chapter is the role played by worker heterogeneity. In particular, for workers who successfully transition from temporary help employment to stable, direct-hire jobs, it is difficult to know whether their spells in temporary help employment were the cause of these successful transitions or primarily a waypoint on the route that these workers were navigating. The chapter by Heinrich, Mueser, and Troske makes an ambitious effort to assess the importance of such self-selection in this context, drawing on recent econometric techniques developed by Altonji, Elder, and Taber (2005). Altonji, Elder, and Taber show that it is feasible to assess the likely extent of bias stemming from self-selection on *unobserved* variables by measuring the extent of self-selection on *observed* variables. The key to their approach is the maintained hypothesis that self-selection on observables and unobservables is positively correlated. Concretely, imagine that in estimating the effect of temporary help employment on subsequent employment outcomes, a researcher finds that including a worker's educational attainment in the statistical model leads to a substantial increase in the estimated benefits from temporary help employment. This pattern would indicate that there is significant negative self-selection into temporary help employment based on education (an *observable* variable).[13] Under the assumptions of the Altonji, Elder, and Taber framework, this would further imply that selection on *unobserved* variables, such as latent

13. Specifically, we take as given that education is strongly positively correlated with earnings and other positive labor market outcomes. If adding education to a wage regression raises the coefficient on temporary-help employment, this implies that temporary-help employment and education are negatively correlated; that is, there is negative self-selection into temporary-help employment based on education.

human capital or taste for effort, is also likely to be important. By contrast, if the estimates were found to be largely invariant to the exclusion of all subsets of observable variables, this would serve as evidence that self-selection on unobservables is unlikely to be important.

Heinrich, Mueser, and Troske put these ideas into practice by studying the employment and earnings trajectories of individuals in the state of Missouri who sought employment assistance or cash support through one of several federal assistance programs. Consistent with prior research by the authors (Heinrich, Mueser, and Troske 2005), the temporary help industry plays a uniquely important role as a transitional source of employment for low-skilled job-seekers. A key finding of their chapter is that stints in temporary help employment have little measurable effect on subsequent earnings or employment. Yet, consistent with Andersson, Holzer, and Lane, Heinrich, Mueser, and Troske observe that successful transitions from the temporary help sector are critical to workers' labor market advancement; workers who remain in temporary help employment experience long-run earnings that are substantially below those of workers in other sectors.

The major contribution of the Heinrich, Mueser, and Troske chapter is their application of the Altonji, Elder, and Taber method to assess the likelihood that the causal effects estimated from the observational data are spurious. This analysis presents a nuanced picture. For earnings, the Altonji, Elder, and Taber test is frequently consistent with the null hypothesis that the causal effects estimates are *not* spurious. For employment, this is less often the case. Though these results present a somewhat ambiguous picture, one cannot fail to be impressed by the rigor, clarity, and intellectual candor of the Heinrich, Mueser, and Troske analysis. Economic knowledge and credibility would be well served if more researchers subjected their findings to equally rigorous sensitivity testing.

In net, these four chapters, using disparate data sources from three different industrialized economies, have a clear commonality of conclusions. None suggests that temporary help jobs have any lasting negative effect on the workers who obtain them. Whether holding these jobs has *positive* effects on worker outcomes relative to what they would have obtained in the absence of temporary help employment is less certain. As a descriptive matter, many temporary help workers transition from temporary help to direct-hire jobs at higher wages. Simultaneously, those who stay behind fare relatively poorly. It is a certainty that those who stay behind over the longer term are on average adversely selected—that is, their unobserved skills or motivation put them at a disadvantage relative to other workers. By the same token, those who leave temporary help employment for higher-paying and more durable direct-hire positions are likely positively selected. These countervailing forces of selection make it difficult to conclude with certainty if the causal effect of temporary help employment is positive, or merely neutral, for the subset of workers making successful transitions from temporary help to direct-hire employment.

This set of findings suggest a relatively benign labor market role for temporary help agencies. Yet there exists substantial suspicion among policymakers and social scientists (particularly outside of economics) that temporary help jobs are exploitative, offering below-market pay and limited opportunities for advancement. From where does this suspicion arise? One possibility is that because temporary help agencies are *for-profit* LMIs—unlike, for example, labor unions, public employment agencies, or university job placement consortia—they face a pecuniary incentive to minimize wages and benefits, and to inhibit workers from obtaining other, potentially superior, positions. In this respect, however, temporary help agencies appear not significantly different from other employers, and so it is hard to credit this viewpoint.

Perhaps a more compelling argument is that widespread use of temporary help agencies, even if beneficial to individual workers and firms, may exert a negative externality on the aggregate labor market—that is, it is a "public bad." One case in point for this argument is that temporary-agency workers cannot vote in union certification elections at client firms since, for legal purposes, the temporary help agency is their employer of record. Moreover, temporary help workers are nearly impossible to organize at their temporary help agency offices since they do not perform work at these sites. Temporary help arrangements may therefore inhibit collective action that would otherwise benefit workers. Indeed, anecdotal evidence suggests that some firms use temporary help agencies to illegally screen out potential union organizers.[14]

More broadly, some scholars have argued that the availability of temporary help agencies encourages employers to pursue a high turnover, low skill-investment human resources strategy (see, in particular, Benner, Leete, and Pastor 2007, chapters 1 and 6). Were the LMI of temporary help unavailable, this argument suggests that employers would offer better job opportunities with greater opportunities for skill acquisition and labor market advancement.[15]

Because they operate exclusively at the general equilibrium, macroeconomic level, these hypotheses are extremely difficult to test—even more so than person-level effects of temporary help employment studied by the four chapters in the volume. Moreover, alongside these arguments, one must alternatively consider that temporary help agencies may increase aggregate labor market efficiency and reduce unemployment by diminishing the time

14. Reflecting the natural tensions between temporary help agencies and labor unions, Houseman, Kalleberg, and Erickcek (2003) document specific union prohibitions on the use of temporary help agency workers at the auto parts manufacturers and hospitals that they study.

15. Kaushik Basu (2003) provides a rigorous discussion of how laissez-faire bargaining among competitive workers and firms over the terms of employment can result in a market equilibrium that is not necessarily socially desirable.

workers and firms spend in unproductive search (Katz and Krueger 1999).[16]
At this point, one can only confidently state that the question of how temporary help employment affects aggregate labor market efficiency and the quality of jobs available in general equilibrium is of first-order importance. A compelling answer to this question, however, awaits a suitably ingenious research design.

Conclusions

The labor market depicted by undergraduate textbooks is a pure spot market, characterized by complete information and atomistic price taking. Labor economists have long understood that this model is highly incomplete. Search is costly, information is typically imperfect and often asymmetric, firms are not always price takers, and atomistic actors are typically unable to resolve coordination and collective action failures. In this second-best of all worlds, there is scope for third parties to intercede, both to improve the operation of the labor market and to profit from its imperfections.

One might have speculated that in an era of rapid information flows and substantial job mobility, the importance of labor market intermediaries would wane. Indeed, the most prominent LMI—the traditional labor union—has been in secular decline for decades. Yet the decline of labor unions as an LMI is the exception rather than the rule. Three of the LMIs studied in this volume—online search engines, criminal records providers, and open-source unions—have only recently emerged. And a fourth—temporary help agencies—has risen from relative obscurity to international prominence over the last two decades.

Though recent technological advances have made market information more abundant and less expensive, cheap information alone is rarely sufficient to solve the fundamental problems posed by costly and asymmetric information, adverse selection, and failures of collective action.[17] Ultimately, the imperfections endemic to decentralized labor markets generate demand for institutions that can variously compel disclosure of hidden information, coordinate the actions of members of a congested market, or solve collective action failures among parties with complementary interests. The Labor Market Intermediaries studied in this volume perform these functions, though always imperfectly, and not without attendant costs and abuses. Despite widely heralded advances in the technology of job matching,

16. This positive aggregate benefit, if present, does not preclude the possibility that individual workers who use temporary-help agencies fare worse on average than those who do not; that is, the public good and the private good may have countervailing effects on individuals, even if the public good dominates, on average.

17. Indeed, cheap information can in some cases exacerbate adverse selection by eliminating the signaling value of formerly costly actions such as submitting job applications (Autor 2001b).

it is my strong contention that Labor Market Intermediaries will continue to arise to address, ameliorate, and exploit the imperfect environment in which workers and employers interact.

References

Abraham, K. G. 1988. Flexible staffing arrangements and employers' short-term adjustment strategies. In *Employment, unemployment, and labor utilization,* ed. R. A. Hart, 288–311. Boston: Unwin Hyman.

Akerlof, G. A. 1970. The market for "lemons": Quality, uncertainty and the market mechanism. *Quarterly Journal of Economics* 84 (3): 488–500.

Altonji, J. G., T. E. Elder, and C. R. Taber. 2005. Selection on observed and unobserved variables: Assessing the effectiveness of Catholic schools. *Journal of Political Economy* 113 (1): 151–84.

Autor, D. 2001a. Why do temporary help firms provide free general skills training? *Quarterly Journal of Economics* 116 (4): 1409–48.

———. 2001b. Wiring the labor market. *Journal of Economic Perspectives* 15 (1): 25–40.

———. 2003. Outsourcing at will: The contribution of unjust dismissal doctrine to the growth of employment outsourcing. *Journal of Labor Economics* 21 (1): 1–42.

Autor, D., and S. N. Houseman. 2002. The role of temporary employment agencies in welfare to work: Part of the problem or part of the solution? *Focus* 22 (1): 63–70.

———. 2005. Do temporary help jobs improve labor market outcomes for low-skilled workers? Evidence from random assignments. NBER Working Paper no. 11743. Cambridge, MA: National Bureau of Economic Research, November.

Autor, D., F. Levy, and R. J. Murnane. 1999. Skills training in the temporary help sector: Employer motivations and worker impacts. Unpublished Manuscript. MIT Press, September.

Basu, K. 2003. The economics and law of sexual harassment in the workplace. *Journal of Economic Perspectives* 17 (3): 141–57.

Benner, C., L. Leete, and M. Pastor. 2007. *Staircases or treadmills? Labor market intermediaries and economic opportunity in a changing economy.* New York: Russell Sage Foundation.

Diamond, P. A. 1982. Wage determination and efficiency in search equilibrium. *Review of Economic Studies* 49 (2): 217–27.

Friedman, M. 1962. *Capitalism and freedom.* Chicago: University of Chicago Press.

Heinrich, C. J., P. R. Mueser, and K. R. Troske. 2005. Welfare to temporary work: Implications for labor market outcomes. *Review of Economics and Statistics* 87 (1): 154–73.

Houseman, S. N. 2001. Why employers use flexible staffing arrangements: Evidence from an establishment survey. *Industrial and Labor Relations Review* 55 (1): 149–70.

Houseman, S. N., A. J. Kalleberg, and G. A. Erickcek. 2003. The role of temporary help employment in tight labor markets. *Industrial and Labor Relations Review* 57 (1): 105–27.

International Confederation of Private Employment Agencies (CIETT). 2007. The agency work industry around the world. Available at http://www.ciett.org/file admin/templates/ciett/docs/Ciett_Economic_Report_2007.pdf.

Jorgenson, H., and H. Riemer. 2000. Permatemps: Young temp workers as permanent second class employees. *American Prospect* 11 (18): 38–40.

Kalleberg, A. L., J. Reynolds, and P. V. Marsden. 2003. Externalizing employment: Flexible staffing arrangements in U.S. organizations. *Social Science Research* 32 (4): 525–52.

Katz, L. F., and A. B. Krueger. 1999. The high-pressure U.S. labor market of the 1990s. *Brookings Papers on Economic Activity* 0 (1): 1–65.

Katz, L. F., and L. H. Summers. 1989. Industry rents: Evidence and implications. *Brookings Papers on Economic Activity, Microeconomics*: 209–90.

Kleiner, M. M. 2006. *Licensing occupations: Ensuring quality or restricting competition?* Kalamazoo, MI: W. E. Upjohn Institute for Employment Research.

Kroft, K., and D. G. Pope. 2007. The effect of the Internet on matching markets: Evidence from Craigslist. Wharton School Working Paper, November.

Krueger, A. B., and L. H. Summers. 1988. Efficiency wages and the interindustry wage structure. *Econometrica* 56 (2): 259–93.

Kugler, A., and G. Saint-Paul. 2004. How do firing costs affect worker flows in a world with adverse selection? *Journal of Labor Economics* 22 (3): 553–84.

Kuhn, P., and M. Skuterud. 2004. Internet job search and unemployment durations. *American Economic Review* 94 (1): 218–32.

Lewis, H. G. 1986. *Union relative wage effects.* Chicago: University of Chicago Press.

Mortensen, D. T. 1982. The matching process as a non-cooperative bargaining game. In *The economics of information and uncertainty,* ed. J. J. McCall, 233–58. Chicago: University of Chicago Press.

Parker, R. E. 1994. *Flesh peddlers and warm bodies: The temporary help industry and its workers.* New York: Rutgers University Press.

Pawasarat, J. 1997. The employer perspective: Jobs held by the Milwaukee County AFDC single parent population (January 1996–March 1997). Milwaukee: Employment and Training Institute, University of Wisconsin–Milwaukee.

Pissarides, C. A. 1986. Unemployment and vacancies in Britain. *Economic Policy* 1 (3): 500–559.

Segal, L. M., and D. G. Sullivan. 1997. The growth of temporary services work. *Journal of Economic Perspectives* 11 (2): 117–36.

Slichter, S. 1950. Notes on the structure of wages. *Review of Economics and Statistics* 32 (1): 80–91.

Spence, M. 1973. Job market signaling. *Quarterly Journal of Economics* 87 (3): 355–74.

I

Reducing Search Costs

1

Jobs Online

Alice O. Nakamura, Kathryn L. Shaw,
Richard B. Freeman, Emi Nakamura, and
Amanda Pyman

1.1 Introduction

In his 2001 *Journal of Economic Perspectives* article, David Autor wrote:

The reasons that job boards have proliferated are clear. They offer more information, are easier to search, and are potentially more up to date than their textual counterpart, newspaper help wanted ads. (Autor 2001, 26).

Autor is describing the first generation job boards that were used much like the help wanted and position wanted sections of newspapers. He also notes the appearance, already by 2001, of other e-recruiting services, including employment sections on corporate websites, online application forms, and

Alice O. Nakamura is a professor of management science at the University of Alberta. Kathryn L. Shaw is the Ernest C. Arbuckle Professor of Economics at Stanford University, and a research associate of the National Bureau of Economic Research. Richard B. Freeman holds the Herbert Ascherman Chair in Economics at Harvard University, and is director of the Labor Studies Program at the National Bureau of Economic Research. Emi Nakamura is an assistant professor of economics at Columbia University and a research associate of the National Bureau of Economic Research. Amanda Pyman is Lecturer in Industrial Relations and Human Resource Management and Director of the Kent MBA Programme in Athens.

The authors thank David Autor and three anonymous referees for comments that greatly improved this chapter. They also thank Yannis Ioannides and other participants in the May 17–18, 2007 conference, "Labor Market Intermediation," organized by David Autor, for comments on an earlier version of this chapter. And they acknowledge exceptional help of various sorts, without which this chapter would not exist, from Denis Capozza, Jason Carter, Paul Davenport, Erwin Diewert, Rod Fraser, Shulamit Kahn, Karl Kopecky, Kevin Lang, Peter Lawrence, Masao Nakamura, Mike Percy, Martha Piper, Marc Renaud, Alan Russell, Kathy Sayers, and Ging Wong. All errors are the sole responsibility of the authors. The corresponding author is Alice Nakamura. In addition to being a professor with the University of Alberta School of Business, she is the volunteer president and a founding board member (along with Paul Davenport, president of the University of Western Ontario, and Karl Kopecky, a chemistry professor at the University of Alberta) of the nonprofit Canadian jobsite www.CareerOwl.ca.

searchable resume databanks. The use of e-recruiting has grown in volume and variety since 2001. This chapter seeks to provide insight into the nature of e-recruiting services as these have evolved in the United States, thereby laying a better basis for further research on the use and efficacy of different types of e-recruiting services and the importance for the United States (and other nations) of a U.S. lead in the provision and use of these services.

We first explain and document key features of the e-recruiting industry and the interrelationships among its service products. There is a large literature on information exchange in labor markets,[1] but relatively little has been written about how e-recruiting works and its providers. In writing about the e-recruiting industry, we draw on business reports, on interactions with employers in business discussion groups and classes, and on case example experiences from the operation of www.CareerOwl.ca, a Canadian e-recruiting company in business since 1998 that provides custom online job application products for companies in addition to operating a job board that Autor mentions by name in his 2001 *Journal of Economic Perspectives* article.

We then examine the Freeman Worldwide Job Search Survey data. The survey data confirm that educated, employed workers from around the globe are online and checking English-language material about jobs. Most respondents report not only that they are using general jobsites, but that they are using multiple such sites and also that they are checking the employment sections of company websites. Many of the respondents are living in lower-wage countries where U.S. businesses are involved via foreign direct investment and outsourcing. After building a factual and institutional foundation, we then share our thoughts on how the growth of e-recruiting can be expected to affect wage trends for various sorts of work.

1.2   Industry Basics and Five Key Facts about E-Recruiting

Both job-seeker and employer search and selection activities are referred to as recruiting. E-recruiting services for employers include:

- *Advertising job ads* on general jobsites (e.g., http://www.monster.com).
- *Construction and operation of custom employment sections for corporate websites* (e.g., http://www.wendys.com/careers/ on *Wendy's* website), often including the construction and management of *custom online application forms for job openings* and the associated databases for these forms.
- The collection via jobsites and online application forms of qualifications and contact information for job-seekers and the operation of *searchable resume databanks.*

1. See, for example, Autor, Katz, and Krueger (1998); Brunello and Cappellari (2008); Fallick, Fleischman, and Rebitzer (2006); Ioannides (2007); Katok and Roth (2004); Kuhn (2003); Lang (2000); Leamer (2001); Mortensen (1986); Quah (2002a, 2002b); Rebick (2000); and Roth (2002).

Regardless of who they are, those viewing job ads on general jobsites like Monster.com must usually register to use the full features of these sites. Registration on jobsites typically is free and involves providing a contact phone number, a working e-mail address, basic demographic information, information about current student or work status, and educational qualifications information. This information is termed a *resume,* without an accent on either "e."

Registered job-seekers can also fill out profiles about the types of jobs of interest to them. When a job ad is posted that meets the profile of a registered user, this triggers an e-mail *job alert.* The job alert service is believed to be popular with both students and employed jobsite users who are not actively looking for work at that point in time (the so-called passive job-seekers).

We focus on the three commercial U.S. jobsites—Monster, CareerBuilder, and HotJobs—and on three other U.S. jobsites operated according to not-for-profit principles. The e-recruiting providers that we examine are listed in table 1.1 alongside the prices charged for the publication of a single regular job ad and for search for a year over the jobsite's resume databank.[2] The commercial e-recruiting companies we discuss were chosen because they are the three largest ones. We refer to these hereafter as "the Big 3." As for the nonprofit providers, America's Job Bank was once America's largest e-recruiting site. Craigslist seems to be the best known by now of the nonprofit e-recruiting sites. And JobCentral is interesting because, as explained subsequently, it was started by and continues to be owned by a large nonprofit association of U.S. employers, including some companies that reportedly are also big users of e-recruiting services provided by commercial companies, including Monster.

Being large has network scale advantages for a jobsite. As Bolles (2007) explains:[3]

"[I]t makes sense that the more popular a site is, the more likely that both job-hunters and employers will find what they are looking for there."

In addition to potential network scale effects for both job-seekers and employers, those who make their living helping job-seekers, from writers of job search guides to counselors in schools, must decide what services to recommend. It stands to reason that those who earn a living helping job-seekers would tend to prefer larger jobsites because they seem unlikely to close down. Also, there are probably increasing returns to scale effects for establishing jobsite brand names.[4]

Third party estimates of website size can be produced in different ways. One way is via counters installed on the computers of users, as for

2. See Brenčič and Norris (2008) for information about how these costs have changed over time.
3. See also Quah (2002a, 2002b) for more on network scale effects.
4. On returns to scale in advertising, see Kaldor (1950); Comanor and Wilson (1967, 1974); McCloskey and Klamer (1995); and Mullainathan, Schwartzstein, and Shleifer (2006).

Table 1.1   Six U.S. E-recruiting providers

Jobsite	Launch year	Price of a single job posting	Price for year-long, nationwide search over job-seeker resumes for regular business
		Providers with for-profit operating principles	
Monster.com	1995	$395	$9,995
		http://hiring.monster.com/products/BulkJobPostings.aspx	http://hiring.monster.com/products/CandidateSearch.aspx?
CareerBuilder.com	1996	$419	$9,553
		http://www.careerbuilder.com/jobposter/products/ postjobsinfo.aspx?sc_cmp2=JP_HP_JobLearn	http://www.careerbuilder.com/jobposter/products/ searchresumesinfo.aspx?sc_cmp2=JP_HP_RDBLearn
hotjobs.yahoo.com	1997	$369	Resume search prices provided individually to employers based on their needs
		http://hiring.hotjobs.yahoo.com/hjss/ss-select-location. html?error=noState&City=	
		Providers with not-for-profit operating principles	
America's Job Bank (AJB)	1995	$0 (for 1995 through July 2007, when AJB was discontinued)	$0 (for 1995 through July 2007, when AJB was discontinued)
Craigslist.org	1995	$0 to 75, depending on the city[a]	Not applicable; Craigslist has position-wanted ads, but no resume bank
JobCentral.com	2001	$25	$25

Note: These prices were collected on October 25, 2007.

[a] For San Francisco Bay Area (https://post.craigslist.org/sfo/J) job postings now cost $75. For NYC, LA, DC, Boston, Seattle, and San Diego, the charge for a job posting is $25. Elsewhere the job postings, like all the other Craigslist services, are free.

Nielsen/NetRatings (column [1] of table 1.2) and Alexa (column [2]).[5] A second way is through agreements with Internet Service Providers (ISPs), which is the Hitwise way (columns [3] and [4]). And a third is from phone interviews or other surveys of job-seekers. The Jupiter Media Metrix comScore figures (columns [5] through [9]) are based on a continuous telephone survey using Random Digit Dialing. Table 1.2 shows that, for all data collection methods and all years for which results are shown, the rank ordering for Monster, CareerBuilder,[6] and HotJobs is the same, with Monster first.[7]

Employer surveys provide insight into the substantial usage that companies now make of e-recruiting. According to the 2007 report of the U.S.-based Society for Human Resource Management (SHRM), the private and public sector organizations that responded to the March 2007 SHRM survey attributed, on average, 44 percent of their new hires the previous year to e-recruiting (SHRM 2007, table 6b).

As noted previously, in addition to providing jobsites where job ads can be posted and building resume databases, e-recruiting companies often provide custom services to companies, such as the construction and hosting of employment pages for company websites. The annual surveys on the use of e-recruiting by the Global 500 companies are of special interest in this regard. Table 1.3 shows that, in 1998, 14 percent of Global 500 companies[8] did not have a corporate website, whereas by 2000, all did. And, in 1998, only 29 percent of Global 500 companies with corporate websites also used their websites for recruiting purposes whereas by 2003 this usage rate had increased to 94 percent.

North American companies adopted e-recruiting more rapidly than companies based elsewhere, as can be seen from table 1.4.[9]

Large U.S. retailers are especially heavy users of e-recruiting. For example, the figures in table 1.5 show that the employment sections of the

5. We only had access to 2004 rating figures for Nielsen/NetRatings, but this rating service has continued to state in press releases that Monster, CareerBuilder, and HotJobs are the top three career Web sites, in that order. Alexa has changed their reporting methods so that their earlier ratings are not comparable with more recent years, and Alexa stopped reporting figures for HotJobs separately from parent company Yahoo!.
6. Hitwise states that CareerBuilder is the most visited jobsite. They arrive at this conclusion by treating separately the figures for monster.com and for my-monster.com, which we combine.
7. The raw data are corrected by the rating companies for suspected bias problems (e.g., user deletion of cookies) to produce the reported traffic estimates. Processing details are considered proprietary and are only partially disclosed.
8. The Fortune Global 500 list, often referred to simply as the Global 500, is a ranking of the top 500 corporations worldwide measured by revenue. The list is compiled and published annually by Fortune magazine. As listed in Fortune Magazine in the first quarter of 2003, the regional percentage distribution of the Global 500 companies was 42.8 in North America, 24.4 in Asia-Pacific, 31.2 in Europe, and 1.6 in the rest of the world.
9. In 2007, the United States was home to 162 of the Global 500 companies; Canada was home to sixteen. The 2007 Global 500 list was published in the July 23, 2007 issue of *Fortune* magazine, and can be found online at http://money.cnn.com/magazines/fortune/global500/2007/countries/US.html.

Table 1.2   Jobsite traffic metrics

Jobsite name	Nielsen/NetRatings unique site visitors for June 2004 (millions) (1)	Alexa: reach per million on Internet, 3-month avg. as of Sept. 4, 2005 (2)	Hitwise: market share week ending April 15, 2006 (%) (3)	Hitwise: market share week ending Jan. 6, 2007 (%) (4)	ComScore: unique site visitors for Sept. 2004 (000) (5)	ComScore: unique site visitors for Sept. 2005 (000) (6)	ComScore: unique site visitors for Jan. 2006 (000) (7)	ComScore: unique site visitors for Sept. 2007 (000) (9)
Monster	9.6	4,515	18.73	15.64	18,331	25,792	27,283	25,615
CareerBuilder	9.3	2,950	16.09	15.05	14,329	18,648	21,247	22,507
HotJobs	7.1	1,650	5.53	5.33	—	—	—	—
America's Job Bank (AJB)	—	294	1.86	1.90	—	—	—	—
Craigslist.org	—	33			—	—	—	23,124
JobCentral	—				—	—	—	—

Note: For Hitwise, the figure for Monster is the sum of the Hitwise figures for www.monster.com and my.monster.com; the figure for CareerBuilder is the sum of the Hitwise figures for www.careerbuilder.com and msn.careerbuilder.com. For America's Job Bank, the Hitwise figure includes only traffic for the domain www.jobsearch.org, whereas the Alexa reach figure covers that plus http://www.ajb.dni.us/. The ComScore figure for Monster is for Monster Worldwide, and similarly for CareerBuilder.

Table 1.3   **Corporate website use for global 500 companies**

	1998	1999	2000	2001	2002	2003
Corporate website employment section	29	60	79	88	91	94
Corporate website, but no corporate website employment section	57	31	21	12	9	6
No corporate website	14	9	0	0	0	0

Source: iLogos Research (2003).

Table 1.4   **Percent of global 500 companies with employment sections, by region**

	2000	2001	2002	2003
North America	92	93	95	96
Asia/Pacific	68	88	90	96
Europe	73	83	92	94

Source: iLogos Research (2003).

Table 1.5   **Market shares for employment sections of company websites (for the week ended January 6, 2007)**

Name	Domain	Market share (%)
Careers at Target	careers.target.com	1.05
USAJobs	www.usajobs.gov	0.45
Wal-Mart Hiring Center	hiringcenter.walmartstores.com	0.30

Source: January 10, 2007 http://www.hitwise.co.uk/presscenter/hitwiseHS2004/us-11012007
careersites.php. Data is based on market share of U.S. Internet visits from a sample of 10 million U.S. Internet users.

corporate websites for Target and Wal-Mart receive large amounts of traffic compared even with the traffic figures for the USAJobs employment site for *all* U.S. federal government jobs.

1.3   E-Recruiting in the United States

Having outlined some of the basics for the e-recruiting industry, in section 1.3.1 we introduce the main commercial e-recruiting companies and five facts about commercial e-recruiting. Then, in section 1.3.2, the three selected U.S. nonprofit e-recruiting providers are introduced as well. And in section 1.3.3, we raise the question of how large commercial e-recruiting providers could coexist and grow alongside the nonprofit e-recruiting companies.

1.3.1   The Commercial Big 3: Monster, CareerBuilder, and HotJobs

The Big 3 commercial e-recruiting companies all sell recruiting services to employers. They all advertise that they are successful in attracting job-seekers of the sorts that employers most want. A persistent theme in the business press is that most employers prefer not to hire those who are out of work for fear that there are hard-to-detect reasons why many of them are in this employment state. In this context, the empirical finding of Kuhn and Skuterud that the use of e-recruiting by unemployed job-seekers did not shorten their jobless spells is unsurprising.[10] In general, no one is paying commercial e-recruiting companies to help the unemployed find jobs.[11]

Among the Big 3, we pay the most attention to Monster because it is the largest of the commercial e-recruiting providers. Also, CareerBuilder and HotJobs, in many ways, have evolved following the Monster lead.

Monster Global was launched in 1995 by the Telephone Marketing Programs Company (TMP Worldwide), an established marketing company and a recruiting agency that was in a position to ensure a steady flow of job postings onto the Monster site from the start.[12] In 2000, Monster acquired the college and university e-recruiting market leader, JobTRAK, and renamed this service MonsterTRAK. Employers can use MonsterTRAK for institutionally targeting job postings. Only students and alumni of Harvard, say, get direct access to job postings on MonsterTRAK targeted to Harvard users. Employers can also pay to have messages e-mailed directly to designated pools of MonsterTRAK users, and can pay to search over the resumes of students registered with MonsterTRAK who have opted to have their resumes available to employers. In addition to ushering in native-born users, the MonsterTRAK feeder system draws in foreign students, including many who subsequently move back to their home countries and continue using Monster. MonsterTRAK provides recruiting services tailored to the needs of students and campus career offices, and has partnerships with leading educational institutions including Harvard, MIT, Princeton, and Berkeley.

If a job-seeker submits a resume via the online application form or a website managed by Monster, that resume can then be conveniently used for other purposes via the Monster system. If the job-seeker subsequently activates this resume while using the Monster system, it may then be made available as well in the main Monster resume bank.[13] In other words, Monster makes it especially easy for job-seekers to put their resumes into the

10. See Kuhn (2003) and Kuhn and Skuterud (2004).
11. Advertising revenues on an Internet site will tend to rise with increases in user traffic, but even advertising rates are affected by the online purchases that site users make and those out of work would not be expected to be high online spenders.
12. In line with this view, Bolles (2007) notes that: "Many of the job listings on Monster . . . are . . . placed by agencies."
13. See http://www.wendys.com/legal.jsp. As of November 3, 2007, a Google search for the exact phrase "powered by" followed by each of the relevant company names yielded 160,000 items for Monster and 110,044 items for CareerBuilder. HotJobs had few listings under its own name, but HotJobs parent Yahoo! had by far the most, though most of those are for other types of sites.

Monster resume bank. The following passage from Wendy's website illustrates this point:

> A portion of the Careers section of this website is powered by Monster. . . . [Y]our information and your resume are hosted on a segregated area of Monster's servers. . . . In the future . . . if you activate your resume on Monster's website, such activation will be treated as if you had originally registered with Monster and posted your resume in its searchable database for viewing and downloading by Monster's employer and agency clients.

Employers are sometimes interested in recruiting experienced workers as well as (or rather than) new graduates. Military.com was an important addition to the Monster family in this regard. Military personnel reentering the civilian workforce typically have technical skills, teamwork and leadership experience, and security clearances.[14] By 2003, Monster Global had built up a vast network of local content and language Internet sites throughout North America, Europe, and the Asia Pacific Region.[15] This global network of websites enables Monster to help U.S. companies doing business in foreign locations to find the workers they need, and is also valuable for businesses looking for workers in other countries to bring into the United States to meet skill shortages there or for outsourcing contract work.

CareerBuilder, launched in 1996, was developed as a complement to the classified advertising activities of media giants: Tribune, Knight Ridder, and Gannett. CareerBuilder has had an assured flow of job ads from the classified sections of affiliated newspapers. By the end of 2003, CareerBuilder also had achieved a global reach via partnerships in the United Kingdom, Ireland, Italy, Spain, France, Belgium, the Netherlands, Latin America, India, Australia, Malaysia, the Philippines, and Singapore.

HotJobs, the youngest of the Big 3, was launched in 1997, and is now owned by Yahoo! Yahoo!'s central objective is to increase the size and engagement of its portal user base, so as to increase the revenue from the online sale of goods and services by partnered merchants.

In going through the rest of this chapter, it is helpful for readers to keep in mind the following facts about commercial e-recruiting in the United States:

Fact 1: The main commercial jobsites are run by corporate giants with multiple complementary lines of business.

---

14. In her studies with various collaborators, including Andersson et al. (2008) and Lazear and Shaw (2007, 2009), Shaw argues that firms that are commercially successful innovators try to hire workers with histories of prior success as evidenced by being *employed* and what their employers have been willing to pay them. Andersson et al. (2008) show empirically that innovative firms grow by searching more and attracting star workers.

15. Over these years, Monster.com entered into partnerships and executed buyouts and takeovers that brought into their network large numbers of e-recruiting companies started by others, ranging from Flip Dog to China HR.com.

The Big 3 jobsites are not stand-alone operations. As already noted, Monster was started by a company selling advertising and corporate recruiting services. CareerBuilder is owned by media companies. And HotJobs is part of the Web portal Yahoo!.

Fact 2: E-recruiting can help increase the reach and reduce the costs of hiring.

E-recruiting services can help employers find and consider more, and more widely located, job candidates in the early phases of the recruiting process. (See Appendix A for a case study example.) Also, it is widely reported in the business press that the use of online application forms and applicant database software systems can substantially reduce the variable costs of recruiting. In other words, e-recruiting can allow businesses to search more widely, while decreasing certain applicant processing costs.

Fact 3: Big businesses enjoy returns to scale in using e-recruiting.

The cost of advertising a job posting on a commercial jobsite like Monster is usually the same whether the employer is looking for one new employee of a given type, or ten or 100. However, learning investments are required for employers to make good use of e-recruiting services like search over resume databanks, and these costs can usually be spread over larger numbers of hires by large companies. Other fixed costs are also involved in the making of custom employment pages for company websites and custom job application forms and their associated databases.

Fact 4: e-recruiting services indirectly promote search for employed workers

E-recruiting services can make it easier for recruiters to find and contact employed workers with suitable skills. Workers who passively look at job ads on jobsites like Monster typically must register to make full use of the jobsites, and this often results in their making their e-mail and other contact information available to the employers who pay for search over the resume databanks run by the large commercial e-recruiting firms. Virtually all employers that we have heard discuss the topic assert that they do not want *their* employees looking for work elsewhere while working for them. And yet, when employers go looking for experienced workers, many clearly state that they prefer to hire workers employed elsewhere. *Fast Company* contributing editor Scott Kirsner (2005) quotes Auren Hoffman, founder of the referrals company KarmaOne,[16] as stating: "A vast percentage of the people who are looking aren't the people you want. . . . It's extremely hard to get to the people who aren't actively looking, and generally, that pool is much better."[17] This is a candid statement of what we feel is a ubiquitous subtext in

---

16. KarmaOne has now been acquired by http://www.spotajob.com/us/, another referral company.

17. http://www.boston.com/business/technology/articles/2005/10/03/its_a_scary_time_for_monstercom/?page=2.

the trade literature on recruiting. This is also a position that employers using CareerOwl have made comments about to the CareerOwl Call Center staff.

Above the entry level, one might presume that problem workers could be reliably detected by checking references from past employers. However, employers sometimes ask unwanted workers to leave "voluntarily," offering these workers promises of good references if they comply. This alleged practice reportedly leaves many employers worried about hiring lemons[18] if they select from the pool of currently unemployed workers. The use of e-recruiting can augment fears of hiring lemons because less of the information about individuals found using e-recruiting is rooted in personal acquaintance, a key traditional strategy for employers to detect workers with hidden flaws.

Fact 5: The U.S. is the global leader in the provision of e-recruiting services

Many e-recruiting sites for other nations are run by U.S. companies.[19] The U.S. dominance in e-recruiting parallels U.S. dominance in other areas of Internet-related business.[20]

1.3.2   Nonprofit E-recruiting in the United States

We now introduce three selected nonprofit e-recruiting providers.[21] From the lower panel of table 1.2, it can be seen that these providers have nominal or no charges for employers. The existence of these services thus directs attention to functions the large commercial e-recruiting companies provide for employers that the nonprofit providers do not provide.

America's Job Bank (AJB) was launched in 1995 by the U.S. government.[22] The early success of AJB was noted, for example, in the 1999 testimony to the House Committee on Veterans' Affairs by Robert Gross, the President of the Interstate Conference of Employment Security Agencies:[23]

America's Job Bank, the public workforce system's Internet-based job bank, is the largest job bank on the Internet with over one million job openings—far surpassing other job banks like Monster.com and HotJobs.

18. See Akerlof (1970, 2003); Spence (1973); Aigner and Cain (1977); Altonji and Pierret (2001); Milgrom and Oster (1987); and Gibbons and Katz (1991) on the "lemon theory" and its labor market applications.

19. For example, research on the Internet in Mexico revealed popular "Mexican" e-commerce sites that were hosted on computers in the United States (Curry, Contreras, and Kenney 2004).

20. Kenney (2003) argues that four features of the U.S. system led to this U.S. success: (a) research strength that provided first-mover advantages; (b) the flat rate local phone tariff and the competitiveness of the U.S. telecommunications sector; (c) the willingness of U.S. shoppers to switch to ordering online; and (d) U.S. venture capital, which funded vast numbers of experiments.

21. We include in the nonprofit category e-recruiting companies that, legally, are for profit, but have pledged to hold prices down and use any profits for stated good causes (e.g., Craigslist.org).

22. Alice Nakamura was given a briefing in 1995 by AJB officials as part of a fact-finding mission for Canada.

23. See http://veterans.house.gov/hearings/schedule106/oct99/10-28-99B/gross.htm.

America's Job Bank was the responsibility of the U.S. Department of Labor (USDOL).[24] All services were free. America's JobBank allowed job posting and job search by zipcode as an alternative to searching by state or city, so it was useful for rural as well as urban users. It also had a resume bank that employers could search. Effective July 1, 2007, the USDOL closed AJB. The reason given was that "the technology and markets have developed in such a way that government sponsorship is no longer needed."

Craigslist.org was launched in 1995 by an individual, Craig Newmark. By now, this is the best known of the surviving nonprofit jobsites. However, this service, by design, only meets the needs of job-seekers and employers looking locally. Craigslist is a collection of no-frills online community bulletin boards offering classifieds and forums for 450 cities, with most of the services being free. At the top of the page on Craigslist.org where employers must enter the information for their job postings, there is a message in red that states: "Please post to a single city/site and category only—cross-posting to multiple cities or categories is not allowed." In 2004, eBay acquired a 25 percent stake in Craigslist. However, Craigslist continues to operate as a collection of free and low cost community bulletin boards.

JobCentral.com is the jobsite of the DirectEmployers Association.[25] Once the Internet was available, employers began adding employment sections to their company websites. Employers soon discovered that most of their own websites do not attract enough traffic of the sort needed for recruiting. Big companies became the biggest customers of third party e-recruiting providers like Monster.

Over time, some big companies began to resent the fees and requirements of the e-recruiting companies. Hence in 2001, a group of big U.S. companies founded the DirectEmployers Association, which created JobCentral.com, and recruited William Warren (see Warren 2005), a former president of Monster, to run JobCentral. According to Ann Harrington (2002):

> [M]ajor clients like IBM, GE, and Lockheed Martin, which spend six figures—sometimes seven—per year on online job boards, are . . . joining together to create a nonprofit, no-frills career portal . . . And although none have torn up their Monster contracts just yet, some of the charter members suggest the big job boards' raison d'etre is no longer assured.

Owing to his years as president of Monster, Warren was aware of the importance to Monster of MonsterTRAK as a talent-feeder system. Thus,

---

24. Expected benefits to the United States had included the saving to the overall system from returns to scale in providing job posting and resume databank services along with the returns to the economy from improved decision making enabled by the information about the talent needs of employers and the skill sets of job-seekers that such a system could provide.

25. As of July 2007, 165 U.S. companies had joined DirectEmployers. Member companies include industry leaders such as Abbott Laboratories, Accenture, Cingular Wireless, GE, H&R Block, IBM, Kindred Healthcare, Lockheed Martin, Mellon Mutual of Omaha, Raytheon Company, Sprint, Union Pacific, and Xerox Corporation.

soon after taking charge of JobCentral, Warren set about trying to create a talent feeder system for JobCentral, too: NACElink, built in collaboration with members of the National Association of Colleges and Employers (NACE). Warren also sought to link Job Central to the U.S. state employment services. He created the JobCentral National Employment Network, consisting of fifty state jobsites and over 6,200 cities and communities.

1.3.3 Given the Nonprofit Competition, What Exactly Do the Big 3 Do for a Living?

The continued existence and growth of the commercial Big 3 along with low-cost services like Craigslist and JobCentral is prima-facie evidence that the commercial companies provide services of value to companies that the nonprofits do not. Based on our observations, services that largely satisfy this criterion include: (a) support for U.S. company recruiting that is worldwide; (b) well developed, searchable resume banks; (c) cooperative working relationships with established third party recruiters for large companies; (d) for-hire services for the construction and operation of the employment sections of corporate websites; and (e) for-hire services for the construction and operation of online job application forms and their databases.[26] Monster and CareerBuilder have also developed special feeder systems for experienced workers, and claim that their resume databanks are valuable resources for employers searching for experienced workers.

Thus far, none of the main U.S. nonprofit e-recruiting providers has engaged in heavy outreach activities aimed at building global networks or at aggressively building resume databases for experienced jobseekers.[27]

1.4   The Global Outreach of E-Recruiting

We turn our attention now to the issue of the sorts of job-seekers who can be reached via the Internet. For commercial e-recruiting to be able to provide global recruiting and outsourcing support for U.S. companies, there must be educated job-seekers in countries where U.S. businesses reportedly are interested in hiring. To find out about this, we examine data from a recent survey of online job search. Over the period of February through April of 2007, Richard Freeman ran his own online job search survey. The usage of e-recruiting has been rapidly changing. The recentness of the Free-

---

26. Commercial e-recruiting services try to ensure that *experienced, employed* workers are well represented in their user pools and resume databanks. Moreover, Stevenson (2005, 2007) finds that employment-to-employment flows have risen in the United States. See also Fallick and Fleischman (2004).

27. However, Bagues and Labini (chapter 4, this volume) write about a nonprofit e-recruiting provider that runs an extensive resume bank in Italy with the stated goal of helping the employers of the nation connect more cost effectively with the talent their tax dollars helped to train in the universities of the nation. The service that Bagues and Labini describe is actively supported by government and the educational institutions involved.

man survey is important, since the longest established of the e-recruiting firms were founded in 1995. When the results of this survey are considered alongside the growth of the e-recruiting industry, some interesting tentative conclusions emerge.

Freeman used the English language Google AdWords and AdBrite international advertising options to invite the job-seekers of the world to fill out his job search survey. The ads were shown to Internet users entering the key word "job search" and also on what the advertising agencies describe as "content sites," which are simply other Internet sites that the advertising agency personnel deemed likely to generate hits on the ad given the text of the ad itself. The only statistical information we have about those who saw the ad is based on the responses of those who opted to take the survey. Nevertheless, we would argue that fielding an international survey using online ads is one reasonable way of reaching the job-seekers we most want information from. In our view, this survey data should be thought of and used like case study data: evidence to be weighed alongside other available evidence.

Two inducements were offered to encourage people to fill out the survey. One was being entered in a draw for $1,000 in U.S. currency. The other was an offer of free job search advice:

IF YOU COMPLETE THE SURVEY, you will receive, for FREE, an e-book with tips about what works for finding work.

The population of people who would see the ads is a population of people that e-recruiting could also hope to reach: job-seekers who frequent the Internet. There were twenty-eight questions in the Freeman survey (see appendix C), referred to in the text and tables as Q1–Q28.

Of course, any survey that offers inducements to survey takers could potentially attract some respondents who proceed to take the survey multiple times, though the directions say each person can only take it once. In processing the data, steps were taken to eliminate multiple and other bogus responses.[28] Also, the job survey contained a text box at the end where survey takers could enter a message for professor Freeman. We are reassured by the fact that many survey takers entered messages asking questions about job search and only one also mentioned something about her need for winning the prize money.

1.4.1   Who Are the Freeman Survey Respondents?

As can be seen from table 1.6, the Freeman survey pickup was much higher in lower wage countries in Asia and also Africa than in countries like

---

28. The Freeman survey is long and asks questions that make it unlikely that any two individuals would have identical responses on all questions. From an analysis perspective, the elimination of completed duplicate surveys that provide correct information would be less harmful than the retention of bogus completed surveys. Thus we eliminated all duplicate submissions. Also, multiple bogus entries would almost surely have different age and sex distributions than good data, and would tend to cause aberrations in the response patterns for some of the survey questions. Regular patterns by age and sex, and patterns that fit well with other available evidence, are circumstantial evidence that the data are of reasonable quality.

Table 1.6   **Number of respondents by country group**

	All	16–19	20–24	25–34	35–44	45–64
All countries	1,603	113	459	626	250	155
N. and S. America	221	9	45	55	49	63
All E.U.	203	24	50	70	37	22
Australia and N.Z.	183	36	43	54	26	24
All Africa	273	13	121	179	58	11
All Asia	609	31	199	256	79	35

Note: This table is based on the responses in the master file for all those who answered Q18 (country), Q20 (age), and Q21 (sex).

Table 1.7   **Age distribution of respondents**

	Men				Women			
	16–19	20–24	25–34	35–64	16–19	20–24	25–34	35–64
Full master data set	6.1	29.9	39.4	24.6	9.5	27.8	37.8	24.9
($N = 1,717$)	(57)	(281)	(370)	(231)	(74)	(216)	(294)	(194)

Notes: The full data set consists of the responses in the master file for all those who answered questions Q20 (age) and Q21 (sex). Thus it includes the 114 survey takers who did not answer the question about what nation they were currently living in. The numbers in parentheses are sample sizes that apply for the percentage figures shown.

the United States and Canada and the United Kingdom and other higher income nations. The pattern of pickup on the survey supports the hypothesis that there are workers in lower wage countries who can easily be reached by employers via the Internet and via jobsites.

Jobsites can facilitate employer advertising for job candidates provided that the right workers are checking jobsites. The vast majority of the Freeman survey takers reported that they are checking jobsites. In this section, results are shown by age group and are usually shown separately as well by sex. Also, we focus on groups with at least 100 respondents. In each of the designated age groups except the youngest, from table 1.7 we see that somewhat more men than women took the survey. The distributions by age are quite similar for both sexes.

The vast majority of respondents state they are employed. Question Q2 asks respondents if they "worked as an employee" or if they were "self employed" the previous week. The responses are summarized in table 1.8.[29] From row 1, we see that most of the respondents were working. Presumably, those who are not working have more incentive to be interested in the

29. The sample sizes in the last row of table 1.8 are somewhat larger than the sample sizes shown in row 1 of table 1.6 (for all countries) since we have included in the tabulations for table 1.8 (and henceforth) the responses to other questions of respondents who did not specify their country. The country question involved a drop-down menu. Some respondents may not have understood how they could view that menu.

Table 1.8   **Work status by sex and age group (%)**

	Men			Women		
	20–24 (1)	25–34 (2)	35–44 (3)	20–24 (4)	25–34 (5)	35–44 (6)
1. An employee and/or self employed	58.2	72.2	82.8	47.1	70.3	61.0
2. Self employed, and not an employee	10.7	9.0	13.1	4.4	7.6	11.9
3. Employee and also self employed	8.0	5.5	6.2	1.5	4.8	3.4
4. Not working	41.8	27.7	17.2	52.9	29.7	39.0
Number of observations	261	346	145	206	290	118

Note: This table is based on the responses in the master file for all those who answered questions Q20 (age), Q21 (sex), and Q2 (activity last week).

Table 1.9   **Internet use (%)**

	Men			Women		
	20–24 (1)	25–34 (2)	35–44 (3)	20–24 (4)	25–34 (5)	35–44 (6)
1. Have ever made a purchase online[a]	60.5 (271)	55.8 (353)	55.2 (145)	66.2 (213)	63.9 (288)	72.6 (117)
2. Have ever looked/used jobsites[b]	82.5 (268)	87.6 (356)	86.3 (146)	85.0 (214)	93.8 (290)	86.4 (118)

Note: The table is based on the responses in the master file for all those who answered questions Q20 (age), Q21 (sex), Q4 (Internet purchase status), and Q6 (jobsite user). The numbers in parentheses are sample sizes that apply for the percentage figures shown.
[a]Checked "sometimes" or "often" on Q4.
[b]Selected "yes" on Q6.

tips for finding work that were offered for free to survey takers, more time for survey taking, and a higher need for winning the $1,000 draw. Thus, we would expect the proportions in row 4 of table 1.8 (those not working) to be higher than for the general population of Internet users.

Consistently high percentages of the survey takers report that they are checking jobsites (row 2, table 1.9): higher percentages than for those who have made an online purchase. Of course, the use of the Internet for making online purchases would be expected to be less common in lower income countries since the prices of the goods and services offered for sale on the Internet are set by companies focused mostly on selling to those in higher income countries.

1.4.2   How Are the Respondents Searching?

The respondents are not only using the jobsites to search for work, but it can be seen from table 1.10 that the majority are checking multiple jobsites. For those twenty-five to thirty-four and thirty-five to forty-four, the propor-

Table 1.10   **Jobsite users by number of sites used (%)**

	Men			Women		
	20–24	25–34	35–44	20–24	25–34	35–44
The number of jobsites used:	(1)	(2)	(3)	(1)	(2)	(3)
Percentage over 10	16.2	32.4	34.0	17.4	19.4	22.2
Percentage for 2–10	57.8	45.3	54.0	52.3	62.0	66.7
Percentage for 1	16.2	17.3	10.0	22.1	15.7	11.1
Number of respondents	142	139	50	86	108	36

Note: This table is on the responses in the master file for all those who answered questions Q20 (age), Q21 (sex), Q6 (jobsite user), and Q15 (no. of sites).

Table 1.11   **Jobsite uses (%)**

	Men			Women		
	20–24	25–34	35–44	20–24	25–34	35–44
	(1)	(2)	(3)	(4)	(5)	(6)
1. Check job postings	44.0	47.5	47.3	50.0	54.1	46.6
2. Upload or send an online resume	26.9	32.3	38.4	29.0	35.9	35.6
3. Enable employers to find their resume	20.5	27.0	35.6	22.9	30.7	25.4
4. Get salary or wage information	22.0	28.4	32.9	24.8	29.7	23.7
Number of respondents	268	356	146	214	290	118

Note: This table is on the responses in the master file for all those who answered questions Q20 (age), Q21 (sex), and Q6 (jobsite user).

tions who report checking over ten jobsites are significantly higher for men than women. In addition, the proportion checking ten or more jobsites rises with respondent age.

Those who use jobsites were asked about what they do on these sites. The most prevalent use is checking job postings, as can be seen from row 1 of table 1.11. About a third of the respondents in each age-sex group also report uploading or sending their resume using a jobsite. Moreover, the percentages are almost as high for those who note that they put their resume on a jobsite so that employers would be able to see it.

It is often said that personal contacts are of importance for finding employment. The respondents to the 2007 Job Search Survey mostly agree that personal contacts and referrals are useful (row 3, table 1.12).[30] Newspapers are selected as useful for job search by even higher percentages of respondents (row 2). However, Internet recruitment sites (i.e., jobsites) are

30. These response rates are similar for men and women, so we pooled over sex to focus attention on the age patterns.

Table 1.12   Respondents by age who found each method useful (%)

	20–24	25–34	35–44
1. Internet recruitment sites	77.0	80.1	85.8
2. National/local newspapers and/or trade magazines	74.2	76.1	80.9
3. Personal contact/referrals	63.8	68.1	74.7
4. Recruitment consultants/headhunters	43.2	53.4	58.6
Number	326	423	162

Notes: This table is based on the responses in the master file for men and women combined for all those who answered questions Q20 (age), Q21 (sex), and Q1 (methods of job search).

Table 1.13   Percentage of survey respondents who used the Internet for finding current or most recent work

Men			Women		
20–24	25–34	35–44	20–24	25–34	35–44
(1)	(2)	(3)	(4)	(5)	(6)
56.1	41.8	35.0	43.9	39.3	31.0
(255)	(340)	(143)	(198)	(277)	(116)

Note: This table is based on the responses for all who answered questions Q20 (age), Q21 (sex), and Q14 (used Internet to find most recent job). The numbers in parentheses are sample sizes for the percentage figures shown.

selected as useful for job search by the highest percentage for each of the age groups (row 1). More than three-fourths of the job-seekers in each age group indicated that jobsites are useful for job search.[31] In addition, more than 40 percent of each age group of respondents report that recruiters and headhunters have contacted them and have been useful (row 4). The proportions rise with the age group, with the adjacent pairs of proportions for the different age groups being significantly different at the 95 percent level of confidence. What this pattern suggests is that, over the prime working years of twenty to forty-four, job-seekers learn the advantages of searching via multiple channels.

The percentages of respondents in different groups who report they found their current or most recent work using the Internet range from 31 to 56 percent, as shown in table 1.13, which seems impressively high to us. These percentages decline with age, in contrast with the table 1.12 percentages in row 1. This makes sense. Many respondents are, in fact, employed, and reportedly have been with the same employer many years, and hence may have found their current job before e-recruiting became prevalent.

31. Also, Stevenson (2007) is surely right in noting that a difficulty in judging the meaning of responses to questions about the job search methods that job-seekers view as worthwhile is that neither they nor we can know what their counterfactual experiences would have been had they looked in ways other than what they each tried.

Table 1.14   Percentage who used the Internet for finding current or most recent work, grouped by whether they have some university or college

	Men		Women	
	20–24 (1)	25–34 (2)	20–24 (4)	25–34 (5)
Some university or college	57.44 (195)	42.18 (275)	47.44 (156)	42.86 (224)
No university or college	50.88 (57)	37.93 (58)	32.50 (40)	25.00 (48)

Note: This table is based on the responses in the master file for those who answered Q20 (age), Q21 (sex), and Q14 (used Internet to find most recent job). The numbers in parentheses are sample sizes for the percentage figures.

Table 1.15   Percentage of respondents using the Internet to search for work who also search on company websites

Men			Women		
20–24 (1)	25–34 (2)	35–44 (3)	20–24 (4)	25–34 (5)	35–44 (6)
75.9 (141)	84.2 (139)	73.5 (49)	80.2 (86)	83.3 (108)	83.3 (36)

Note: This table is based on the responses in the master file for all those who answered questions Q20 (age), Q21 (sex), Q14 (used Internet to find most recent job), and Q16 (used company websites for job search). The numbers in parentheses are sample sizes that apply for the percentage figures shown.

In table 1.14, the responses to the table 1.13 question are shown separately for those who have some university or college education versus those who do not (i.e., for those who answered "yes" versus those who answered "no" on Q25: "Have you attended some university or college?"). The differences between the education group pairs for each age group are significant, with a 95 percent level of confidence. Thus, university- and college-educated workers are significantly more likely to have used the Internet for finding work than less educated workers.

We were curious about whether those using jobsites also check for work opportunities on employer websites. From table 1.15, we find that the answer is "yes" for roughly 75 to 85 percent of the respondents in each age group.

General jobsites are good for helping job-seekers discover when various companies have job openings. It takes a job-seeker considerable time to visit, site by site, company websites, checking for postings of new job openings. However, job-seekers who are experienced at using the Internet to look for work can use general jobsites to make a list of the companies that are recruiting, and then can visit the websites of those companies directly to view the job ads and apply if interested. One reason why a job-seeker might benefit from visiting company website employment pages is that companies sometimes post more positions on their own websites when they are recruiting than they publish on the general jobsite, and companies sometimes do a better job of updating information about positions that have been filled on their own websites. Secondly, it is often more convenient for job-seekers to apply for open positions on the employer websites because, in so doing, they only need to deal with the requirements of the employer rather than a combination of the employer's requirements and the information sought by the general jobsite for that company's operating and commercial purposes.

Finally, table 1.16 shows results for regressions using as the dependent variable a dummy variable set equal to 1 for those who selected "yes" on Q16 in answering: "Have you ever checked work opportunities on company or other employer websites?" The explanatory variables are all dummy variables. For the first variable, the dummy is set equal to 1 for those who selected "employee" on Q2. For the second variable, the dummy equals 1 if the respondent selected "often" on Q5 about the frequency of their use of general search engines like Google. For the third variable, the dummy equals 1 for respondents who answered "yes" for having completed high school or secondary school. For the fourth variable, the dummy equals 1 for a respon-

Table 1.16   Coefficients for regression of dummy for job search using company websites

	20–24 (1)	25–34 (2)	35–44 (3)
1. Intercept	.54	.50	.43
	(5.02)	(5.33)	(2.77)
2. Employee dummy	.02	−.02	−.03
(= 1 if "employee" selected on Q2)	(.50)	(.48)	(.49)
3. Frequent search engine user	.15	.15	.15
(= 1 if "often" selected on Q5)	(3.35)	(4.51)	(2.56)
4. High school completion dummy	−.00	.01	.11
(= 1 if "yes" for Q24)	(.04)	(.07)	(.67)
5. University education dummy	.11	.23	.14
(= 1 if "yes" for Q25)	(2.08)	(5.23)	(1.80)
6. Sex dummy	.01	.01	.01
(= 1 if "male" for Q21)	(.36)	(.28)	(.24)
Number of observations	447	593	246
R^2	.035	.082	.051
F-statistic	3.2	10.6	2.6

Notes: The dependent variable is a dummy set equal to 1 if the respondent selected "yes" on Q16. The regression data samples consisted of the responses in the master file for all those who answered questions Q20 (age), Q21 (sex), Q2, Q5, Q24, and Q25. The numbers in parentheses are the absolute values of t-statistics. Heteroscedasticity-corrected standard errors have been used.

dent who answered "yes" for having at least some university education. And the fifth variable is a sex dummy set equal to 1 for men.

From row 3 of table 1.16, we see that those who use general search engines frequently are more likely to report also checking company websites for job ads. Having some university or college education raises this probability. In row 6 of table 1.16, the sex dummy coefficients are insignificantly different from zero, like the coefficients for the employee dummy in row 2.

1.5   Discussion of Likely Labor Market Effects of the Growth of E-Recruiting

The use of e-recruiting services has grown greatly since Monster, the first launched of the Big 3, got its start in 1995. There is interest in trying to foresee how the continued growth of e-recruiting will affect wages for various sorts of work and workers.[32] We speculate on this issue here, drawing on information that is far from sufficient to prove our conjectures.

The job titles in table 1.17 are used to illustrate our ideas about how job attributes can be expected to shape the way the growth of e-recruiting will affect pay rates for different sorts of work. The columns of table 1.17 are defined in terms of differences in how contestable the jobs are for outsiders.

Table 1.17 also contains three panels, defined in terms of the required education levels for jobs. The education requirements for a job can affect how contestable it is. The three levels of education in table 1.17 were chosen to facilitate finding job descriptions on Monster.com with the stated educational qualifications. These levels are: (a) high school diploma, (b) a bachelor's degree, and (c) a bachelor's degree plus a PhD, MD, or JD degree.

In parentheses following each job listing in table 1.17 we show the number of job ads of that sort that were listed on Monster.com for New York City and vicinity (a twenty-mile radius) as of November 11, 2007. For each job listing, the median base salary is given, too, taken from the salary wizard on the Monster site[33] for that sort of work in New York. The figures on the number of listings for each job type demonstrate that Monster is being used by employers to search for all of these types of workers. As would be expected, the median pay levels for the various types of jobs rise as the education level rises, moving down each column.

Column (1)-type jobs must be locally carried out and locally staffed. We conjecture that small-sized classified advertisements in newspapers, which have always been low cost, and other mechanisms like posting notices in customary public places, gave employers adequate means for getting out the word about column (1)-type jobs long before the advent of e-recruiting.

---

32. Other related research on wage trends includes Autor, Katz, and Kearney (2005); Autor, Katz, and Krueger (1998); Autor, Levy, and Murname (2003); Bresnahan, Brynjolfsson, and Hitt (2002); and Kirkegaard (2005).

33. See appendix B for details of the Monster Salary.com salary wizard on the Monster site.

Table 1.17 Job types likely to be affected differently by globalization: Median base salary (number of positions advertised on Monster.com)

Work that must be locally carried out and locally staffed (G1)	Work that must be carried out locally, but that outsiders can apply for and can come in to do (G2)	Work that potentially can be carried out anywhere in the world (G3)
Panel 1—Education level I: high school or less		
(C1)	(C4)	(C7)
Plumber I—$44,802 (7)	Janitor—$28,657 (2)	Accounting clerk, level I—$32,787 (213)
Electrician I—$46,877 (18)	Bus driver—$21,147 (4)	Call center, inbound representative, level I—$32,822 (640)
Panel 2—Education level II: bachelor's degree		
(C2)	(C5)	(C8)
School teacher—$56,665 (99)	Medical technician, emergency—$32,292 (239)	Tax accountant I—$54,430 (31)
	Dental assistant—$37,036 (2811)	Applications systems analyst I—$59,388 (199)
Panel 3—Education level III: PhD, MD, or JD		
(C3)	(C6)	(C9)
Lawyer II—$134,110 (2)	Postdoctoral scientist, 10+ years experience—$49,192 (12)	Scientist II, biotech—$104,929 (152)
Dentist—$151,483 (42)	Surgeon, cardiothoracic—$496,497 (1)	

Source: The numbers in parentheses are the number of positions of the given sort that were advertised on Monster.com for New York, and the twenty-mile commuting area around that city on November 11, 2007. The search terms used for counting the number of job listings were somewhat broader than those used for obtaining the median salary figures from the Monster.com salary wizard (http://monster.salary.com/salarywizard/layoutscripts/swzl_keywordsearch.asp). For example, instead of a cardiothoracic surgeon, we searched for positions for a heart surgeon.

E-recruiting services like online application forms might bring down hiring costs for some employers for column (1)-type jobs, but the savings would not necessarily be passed on to workers. We feel that the growth of e-recruiting and an increased ability of outsiders to find out about these sorts of job openings is not likely to affect the demand-and-supply conditions for column (1)-type jobs (directly at least)[34] since outsiders cannot be hired for these jobs.

Column (2)-type jobs must be locally carried out, but can be staffed by any qualified workers able to work in the United States (e.g., nannies). In contrast to the column (1) situation, for most column (2) sorts of jobs, we would expect the growth of e-recruiting to increase the supply and exert downward pressure on relative wage rates. For similar reasons, we would expect the growth of e-recruiting to put considerable downward pressure on *most* column (3) sorts of jobs: jobs that could be performed almost anywhere (e.g., call center services).[35]

However, we would expect the growth of e-recruiting to put *upward* pressure on wage rates for column (2) and (3) jobs requiring individuals with globally rare skills. As with a Rembrandt painting, when there is no way of quickly making more of something people want and would be willing to pay more to have immediately, then wider advertising will tend to cause the price to be bid up. Cardiac surgeons may well be an example of such a case.[36] Several people we have talked with in large businesses reported that their companies are mining resume databanks and using other forms of e-recruiting to seek out globally scarce skills needed by their companies.[37] There is no

34. Of course, legislators or the courts can overturn licensing and other restrictions on labor market competition. For example, many states once required foreign physicians to be U.S. citizens in order to obtain licenses. Also, from 1976 to 1991, foreign-born physicians were barred from obtaining temporary working (H-1B) status for performing direct patient care, but this situation changed in 1991. Mullan (2005, 1810–11) reports in the *New England Journal of Medicine* that, as of 2004, about 25 percent of physicians in practice in the United States were international medical graduates.

35. Welsum and Reif (2005), in an OECD report, use official statistics to examine the impact of offshoring on national labor markets. They list occupations where jobs are being offshored from developed nations and also list occupational characteristics of the jobs being offshored. See also Mann (2006) and Mann, Eckert, and Knight (2002). Freeman (2006) and Autor (2007) are among those who point to the growing cadre of educated workers outside the United States as a potential resource for addressing domestic skill shortages as these arise.

36. Mullan (2005, 1810–11) notes that international medical graduates constitute between 23 and 28 percent of physicians in each of the four developed nations he examines: the United States, the United Kingdom, Canada, and Australia. Mullan (2005, 1814) notes also that a heavy reliance of the four developed nations on international medical graduates from poor nations does not preclude them also drawing on each other, and that the United States is the clear net winner in this exchange while Canada is the biggest net loser.

37. The companies making this sort of use of e-recruiting are probably mostly very large companies that are in a position to pay for globally scarce talent when they succeed in locating such individuals. However, some smaller companies are also in a position to spend large amounts on hiring, as documented by Andersson et al. (2008), but the large companies are the mainstay revenue source for the large e-recruiting companies.

readily observable indicator for globally scarce worker skills. However, these skills tend to be developed by advanced post-graduate education programs.

1.6   Concluding Remarks

The matches that employers and job-seekers make determine the makeup of companies for generations to come as surely as the love matches of men and women do for family trees. Understanding developments affecting the nature of these matches is of the utmost importance for the future of a nation and its companies and workers. E-recruiting by now has evolved into a suite of services that employers can use for finding and connecting with job candidates: job posting, resume search, and online job application forms and their associated applicant tracking systems. We speculate that commercial e-recruiting companies like Monster have continued to grow alongside cheaper nonprofit e-recruiting providers because the commercial companies provide services not available from the nonprofits, including global recruiting support.

We take an initial step in empirical analysis of how job-seekers from nations around the globe are using e-recruiting services by reporting results for the 2007 Freeman Worldwide Job Search Survey. Most of those who took this survey were employed. The survey asked respondents about how they search for work, and what they do on jobsites. It asked about respondent perceptions of the relative usefulness of jobsites compared with other employment information sources such as newspapers, and about how the respondents found their present or most recent jobs. We find that 82 to 94 percent of the survey respondents are checking jobsites. Indeed, most are checking multiple jobsites. About a fourth are aware that employers are searching over resumes on jobsites, and a substantial proportion reported being contacted by recruiters. A high 73 to 84 percent of those using the Internet for job search also reported that they are checking the employment sections of company websites, revealing a more sophisticated understanding of how e-recruiting services can be used to find work. Respondents with some university or college education are significantly more likely to be using the Internet for job search, and more likely to also be checking the employment sections of company websites.[38]

In concluding, we also share our vision of how the growth of e-recruiting over the coming decades might be expected to affect wage growth for different types of jobs and workers. We anticipate downward pressure on wage rates for types of jobs that outside workers can compete for and for which the numbers of qualified workers are globally plentiful. However, we anticipate upward pressure on remuneration for types of work that require workers

---

38. About 68 percent are in the prime working ages of twenty to thirty-four, and 81 percent of these have some college or university education.

with skills for which there are global shortages. We believe that e-recruiting is likely to be especially helpful for U.S. multinational companies that need to hire in multiple nations. We believe that the U.S. dominance in e-recruiting might be a part of the explanation for the relative success of U.S. multinational companies in lines of business where recruiting is an ongoing activity because of workforce churning, or because survival demands ongoing innovation.[39]

Appendix A
One Company's Transition to E-Recruiting

Here we describe the transition of one company (company X hereafter) from traditional to e-recruiting. The specifics illustrate more general points made in the body of the text.

The old recruiting process for company X for their entry-level management track positions began each year with the drafting of a description of their job openings. The description of the job openings at company X was sent to the career and placement services (CAPS) offices at five large universities where company X traditionally recruited. Next, an interviewer traveled from one university to the next, conducting initial interviews and collecting hard copy resumes at each campus. About 200 initial interviews were conducted. Some students who got initial interviews turned out not to have taken the required courses specified in the job ad, but the company found enough qualified candidates each year.

After the initial interview round, the recruitment director went through the collected resumes and interviewer notes and chose twelve or so of the students for follow-up phone calls and reference checks. Two to six were then short listed and invited for interview trips to the company headquarters. Usually two or three of the short listed candidates were subsequently hired. *The company reported a high retention rate and believed this was largely due to confining their search to the selected five universities.* However, company X had no information to back up the belief that confining their search for job candidates to just five universities produced better results because they never tried searching more widely prior to switching to e-recruiting. What was certain was that adding more universities to their field of search would have increased their recruiting costs because of increases in interviewer costs.

After company X adopted e-recruiting, the first phase of the recruiting cycle still began with the drafting of a description of the job openings. Company X also drafted the questions for an online application form, and arranged to

---

39. See Feldstein (2003) and Freeman (2002).

have an e-recruiting company build, host, and advertise the online application form and the associated applicant tracking database.[40]

When the application period closed, company X had more than 1,000 complete files for applicants with the required qualifications. These files were automatically sorted according to prescreening questions embedded in the online application form. Scanned-in transcripts were included as part of each applicant file. The recruitment director shared the applicant files with the directors whose groups had the openings. The director explained it was now far easier for the files to be shared than before because they were now electronic. Those who went through the files entered notations for the candidates that interested them most. The recruiting director went through the files and notations and about 320 applicants were selected for initial phone interviews—sixty-two of these applicants were chosen for initial in-person interviews. Those chosen for the in-person interviews were at eight different locations. A trip for the recruiter was mapped out and the initial in-person interviews were carried out with much more prior information than in past years. After the initial interviews, the process proceeded essentially as it had in the years before the adoption of e-recruiting, and two candidates were hired that year. The experiences of that first year have basically been replicated each of the subsequent years.

With the switch to e-recruiting for company X, a bigger number of students and grads at more universities and colleges found out about the job openings and applied. The two-year retention rates for new hires have been high since the switch to using e-recruiting, but they were high before as well. Company X believes that it is more likely that they will sometimes be able to find and recruit star employees with their new recruiting approach compared with their old one. But so far, the only clearly demonstrated outcome from the adoption of e-recruiting is that the total cost per hire is lower. The savings in recruiting cost were achieved primarily through a reduction in paperwork for handling the files of applicants and a reduction in interviewer travel costs.

Appendix B

Salary.com

The Salary.com service offered on the Monster website uses purchased information from surveys conducted by compensation consulting firms. The fol-

---

40. This contract was won by the CareerOwl Institute, a nonprofit e-recruiting company for which Alice Nakamura is the volunteer president. The information about the experiences of company X is used with permission, with some details changed to protect the identity of the company. For more on the CareerOwl Institute, see Nakamura and Lawrence (1994); Nakamura et al. (1999); Nakamura and Pugh (2000); Nakamura, Wong, and Diewert (1999); Warburton and Warburton (2001); and Nakamura and Bruneau (2002).

lowing explanation is given: "Salary.com does not use any salary information from individual site users, placement agencies, job postings, nor any other sources that would traditionally be characterized as 'unreliable' by compensation or human resource professionals." Salary.com states that the results provided are arrived at using the ongoing analysis of their experts and their proprietary mathematical model. Salary.com attempts to validate and adjust their salary information using comparisons with other market indicators such as government data (e.g., the Bureau of Labor Statistics, though these data are typically older than the commercially available survey data and the results for these validation exercises are proprietary). The Salary.com wizard lets the user specify a metropolitan region and applies a geographic differential to reflect differences in pay levels in different cities or geographic areas. The national median salary for a job (which is returned if the user does not enter a zip code or region) is given a weight of 100.0, and salaries in other regions are expressed in relation to the national median based on cost of living and purchasing power adjustment factors. In table 1.17, we report pay results for New York because we needed to choose a location for counting the available job openings posted on Monster.com.

Appendix C

The 2007 Freeman Job Search Survey

2007 Worldwide Job Search Survey
(February 15, 2007 version)

Learn what works for finding work!
Complete this survey, and you'll be entered into a $1,000 US cash prize draw!
(some conditions apply click <u>here</u> for details)

This survey is being conducted by Dr. Richard Freeman, a professor at Harvard University and the London School of Economics. To learn more about Dr. Freeman, click <u>here</u>.

IF YOU COMPLETE THE SURVEY, you will receive, for FREE, an e-book with tips about what works for finding work.

** Your information will only be used for statistical analyses about job finding methods and outcomes. No personal information will be released. **

---

1. In your experience, which of the following are useful methods of looking for work? (Check ALL methods you feel are useful. For each one of these, choose a term from the drop down menu to indicate HOW useful you found that method.)

☐ National/local newspapers and/or trade magazines ▢

☐ Internet recruitment sites ▢

☐ Personal contact/referrals ▢

☐ Recruitment consultants/headhunters ▢

☐ Networking or word of mouth ▢

☐ Careers office/graduate recruitment ▢

☐ Career fairs/exhibitions ▢

☐ Other (please specify) ▢

☐ Not relevant; never looked for a job

---

2. Check *all* of the following that describe your activity last week?

☐ worked as an employee

☐ self employed

☐ unemployed

☐ on strike

☐ attended school/studied

☐ kept house, caring for children or others ☐ inactive due to illness, injury or disability
3. Which of the following places do you use the computer? Check *all* that apply. ☐ work ☐ home ☐ school ☐ library ☐ other (specify) [＿＿＿]
4. Have you ever made a purchase over the Internet? ☐ sometimes ☐ often ☐ never
5. Do you ever use search engines (such as Google) to look for information on the Internet? ☐ sometimes ☐ often ☐ never
6. Have you ever looked at or used Internet job sites? ☐ Yes ☐ No If yes, why? (Check ALL answers that apply. For each one of these, choose a term from the drop down menu to indicate HOW useful you found Internet job sites for the stated purpose.) ☐ To check job advertisements [＿＿▼] ☐ To find out about specific companies/potential employers [＿＿▼] ☐ To obtain information about industry sectors [＿＿▼] ☐ To access career tips/advice [＿＿▼] ☐ To get salary or wage information [＿＿▼] ☐ To create an online resume [＿＿▼] ☐ To upload or send an online resume [＿＿▼]

(continued)

☐ To enable potential employers and recruiters to find your resume

[dropdown]

☐ To access employment news [dropdown]

☐ To access research or reports [dropdown]

☐ For career planning [dropdown]

7. Do you have work now?

☐ yes

☐ no

If yes, are you satisfied with your current job?

In terms of pay ☐ yes ☐ no

In terms of benefits ☐ yes ☐ no

In terms of the type of work that you do ☐ yes ☐ no

In terms of relations with supervisors ☐ yes ☐ no

In terms of relations with co-workers ☐ yes ☐ no

If yes, how much longer do you intend to stay at this job? (choose the answer that best describes your expectations)

☐ Less than another month? ☐ 1-11 months ☐ 1-5 years ☐ 6-10 years

☐ more than 10 years

8. If you are not working now, when did you last work?

☐ never

☐ within the last 12 months

☐ prior to the last 12 months

9. Are you looking for work now?

☐ yes

☐ no

If you are *not* looking now, do you plan to look for work in the coming 12 months?

☐ yes

☐ no

If you are *not* looking for work now, have you ever looked for work?

☐ yes

☐ no

10. When you last looked for work, what was your main motivation?

☐ wanted to find a first job

☐ needed work because of losing or quitting the work I had before then

☐ was working, but wanted to find a new job

☐ needed to show evidence of job search as a requirement for collecting income support benefits like unemployment insurance

☐ just curious about the jobs available

☐ not applicable; never looked for work before

11. How did you find the work you have now, or that you had most recently?

☐ Through friends or other people I knew

☐ Through a newspaper ad

☐ Through an ad I saw on a bulletin board

☐ On an Internet recruitment site

☐ On a company web site

☐ I was contacted directly by the employer

☐ Union/professional organisations

☐ Recruitment agency/headhunters

☐ Through a school career or employment office

☐ Other; please specify [＿＿＿＿＿]

☐ Not relevant; never worked before

12. Have you ever filled out a job application on the Internet?

☐ yes

☐ no

13. How long did it take you to find your current or most recent work?

☐ No time; they came to me

☐ Less than 6 months

☐ 6 months to a year

☐ More than a year

☐ Not relevant; I never worked so far

(*continued*)

14. For finding your current or most recent work, did you use the Internet?

☐ yes

☐ no

If you used the Internet, how important was this as a means of job search?

☐ very

☐ somewhat

☐ not very

☐ not at all important

15. Approximately how many online recruitment sites did you visit while looking for your current or most recent work?

☐ 0

☐ 1

☐ 2-10

☐ more than 10

☐ not relevant; never looked for work before

16. Have you ever checked work opportunities on company or other employer web sites?

☐ yes

☐ no

If yes, was this useful?

☐ very

☐ somewhat

☐ not very

☐ not at all

17. While you were looking for your current or most recent work, which of the following best describes what you were doing?

☐ working at another job for the same employer

☐ working at another job, for a different employer

☐ doing contract work or working in my own business

☐ working in a family business

☐ ill or recovering from an accident

☐ unemployed

☐ studying

☐ homemaker; caring for others

☐ other; please specify [＿＿＿＿＿]

☐ not relevant; never worked

18. What country are you living in now?

[Choose One...   ▾]

19. Which of the following best describes where you live? (choose one of the following)

☐ big city (more than one million people)

☐ smaller city or town

☐ rural or other non-urban place of residence

20. How old are you?

☐ < 16 years of age

☐ 16-19 years of age

☐ 20-24 years of age

☐ 25-34 years of age

☐ 35-44 years of age

☐ 45-64 years of age

☐ over 64 years of age

21. Are you:

☐ Male

☐ Female

22. Which of the following best describes the industry of your current or most recent work?

☐ Not relevant; never worked

☐ Biotech/pharmacy

☐ Education

☐ Engineer/Applied sciences

☐ Finance

☐ Health care

(*continued*)

☐ Hospitality/tourism

☐ Human resources

☐ Insurance

☐ IT or e-commerce

☐ Legal

☐ Manager/Administration

☐ Marketing

☐ Natural sciences

☐ Primary industry such as mining, oil or gas, forestry, farming or fishing

☐ Production management

☐ Public service

☐ Recreation/culture

☐ Retail

☐ Trade or Transportation

☐ Other (please specify) [   ]

23. For your current or most recent work, what type of organisation is/was this for?

☐ Public sector/government

☐ Private business

☐ Volunteer organization

☐ Myself, or a family business

24. Have you completed high school or secondary school?

☐ yes

☐ no

25. Have you attended some university or college?

☐ yes

☐ no

If yes, list any degree(s) you completed?

26. Do you have technical school or trade training or certification?

☐ yes

☐ no

If yes, what training or certification do you have?

[   ]

27. Were you a student at any time over the last 12 months?

☐ yes

☐ no

If yes, were you a full time student?

☐ yes

☐ no

Were you studying by correspondence or in a distance learning program?

☐ yes

☐ no

If yes, when will you finish your program of study?

☐ already finished

☐ within the next 12 months

☐ more than 12 months from now

28. How much did you earn from work in the last full year (12 months)?

☐ Earnings for last year: [   ][▼]

☐ Not relevant; did not work for pay or profit

29. If you could give some advice to others like you who are looking for work now, what would that be?

[   ]

(*continued*)

If you wish to be entered in the draw for the $1000 US prize and to receive a job search e-mail address: [   ]

(For details concerning the prize draw, click here.)

If you have any questions or concerns about this survey, or suggestions to make, or if you wish to send a message to Professor Freeman, please enter your remarks here:

Thank you for taking the survey!

Submit Survey

References

Aigner, D., and G. Cain. 1977. Statistical theories of discrimination in labor markets. *Industrial and Labor Relations Review* 30: (2): 175–87.

Akerlof, G. A. 1970. The market for "lemons": Quality uncertainty and the market mechanism. *Quarterly Journal of Economics* 84 (3): 488–500.

———. 2003. Writing "The Market for 'Lemons'": A personal and interpretive essay. Available at: http://nobelprize.org/nobel_prizes/economics/articles/akerlof/index .html.

Altonji, J., and C. Pierret. 2001. Employer learning and statistical discrimination. *Quarterly Journal of Economics* 116 (1): 313–500.

Andersson, A., M. Freedman, J. Haltiwanger, J. Lane, and K. L. Shaw. 2008. Reaching for the stars: Who pays for talent in innovative industries? Available at: http://www.indexmeasures.com/dc2008/finalprogram.htm.

Autor, D. H. 2001. Wiring the labor market. *Journal of Economic Perspectives* 15 (1): 35–40. (A Working Paper version of this paper can be found at http://web.mit .edu/dautor/www/papers.html.)

———. 2007. Structural demand shifts and potential labor supply responses in the new century. Paper presented at the Federal Reserve Bank of Boston Conference on Labor Supply in the New Century. 19–20 June, Boston, MA.

Autor, D. H., L. F. Katz, and M. Kearney. 2005. Trends in U.S. wage inequality: Reassessing the revisionists. NBER Working Paper no. 11627. Cambridge, MA: National Bureau of Economic Research, September.

Autor, D. H., L. F. Katz, and A. B. Krueger. 1998. Computing inequality: Have computers changed the labor market? *Quarterly Journal of Economics* 113 (4): 1169–1214.

Autor, D. H., F. Levy, and R. Murname. 2003. Skill content of recent technological change: An empirical exploration. *Quarterly Journal of Economics* 118 (4): 1279–1333.

Bolles, R. N. 2007. What color is your parachute 2007: A practical manual for job-hunters and career-changers. Berkeley, CA: Ten Speed Press.

Brenčič, V., and J. B. Norris. 2008. Online job boards as an employer recruitment tool. Available at: http://www.indexmeasures.com/dc2008/finalprogram.htm.

Bresnahan, T., E. Brynjolfsson, and L. M. Hitt. 2002. Information technology, workplace organization and the demand for skilled labor: Firm-level evidence. *Quarterly Journal of Economics* 117 (1): 339–76.

Brunello, G., and L. Cappellari. 2008. The labour market effects of Alma Mater: Evidence from Italy. *Economics of Education Review* 27 (5): 564–74.

Comanor, W. S., and T. A. Wilson. 1967. Advertising, market structure, and performance. *The Review of Economics and Statistics* 49 (November): 423–40.

———. 1974. Advertising and market power. Cambridge, MA: Harvard University.

Curry, J., O. Contreras, and M. Kenney. 2004. The Mexican Internet after the boom: Challenges and opportunities. *Berkeley Roundtable on the International Economy,* Paper BRIEWP159.

Fallick, B., and C. A. Fleischman. 2004. Employer-to-employer flows in the US labor market: The complete picture of gross worker flows. FEDS Working Paper no. 2004-34, May.

Fallick, B., C. A. Fleischman, and J. B. Rebitzer. 2006. Job-hopping in Silicon Valley: Some evidence concerning the microfoundations of a high-technology cluster. *Review of Economics and Statistics* 88 (3): 472–81.

Feldstein, M. 2003. Why is productivity growing faster? NBER Working Paper no. 9530. Cambridge, MA: National Bureau of Economic Research, March.

Freeman, R. B. 2002. The labour market in the new information economy. NBER Working Paper no. 9254. Cambridge, MA: National Bureau of Economic Research, October.

———. 2006. People flows in globalization. *Journal of Economic Perspectives* 20 (2): 145–70.

Gibbons, R., and L. Katz. 1991. Layoffs and lemons. *Journal of Labor Economics* 9 (4): 315–89.

Harrington, A. 2002. Can anyone build a better monster? *Fortune,* May.

iLogos Research. 2003. Global 500 website recruiting: 2003 Survey, iLogos Research, Division of Taleo. Available at: www.ilogosresearch.com.

Ioannides, Y. M. 2007. Empirics of social interactions. Tufts University Discussion Paper no. 0611. Tufts University Economics Department.

Kaldor, N. V. 1950. The economic aspects of advertising. *Review of Economic Studies* 18 (1): 1–27.

Katok, E., and A. E. Roth. 2004. Auctions of homogeneous goods with increasing returns: Experimental comparison of alternative "Dutch" auctions. *Management Science* 50 (8): 1044–63.

Kenney, M. 2003. The growth and development of the Internet in the United States. In *The global Internet economy,* ed. B. Kogut, 69–108. Cambridge, MA: MIT Press.

Kirkegaard, J. F. 2005. Outsourcing and skill imports: Foreign high-skilled workers on H-1B and L-1 visas in the United States. Working Paper no. 05-15, Peterson Institute.

Kirsner, S. 2005. It's a scary time for monster.com. *Boston Globe,* October 3.

Kuhn, P. 2003. The Internet and matching in labor markets. In *New economy handbook,* ed. D. C. Jones, 508–23. Amsterdam: Academic Press.

Kuhn, P., and M. Skuterud. 2004. Internet job search and unemployment durations. *American Economic Review* 94 (1): 218–32.

Lang, K. 2000. Panel: Modeling how search-matching technologies affect labor markets. Paper presented to IRPP and CERF Conference on creating Canada's advantage in an information age. May, Ottawa.

Lazear, E. P., and K. L. Shaw. 2007. Personnel economics: The economist's view of human resources. *Journal of Economic Perspectives* 21 (4): 91–114.

———. 2009. Wage structure, wages, and mobility. In *The structure of wages: An international comparison,* ed. E. P. Lazear and K. L. Shaw, 1–57. Chicago: University of Chicago Press.

Leamer, E. 2001. The economic geography of the Internet age, NBER Working Paper no. 7959. Cambridge, MA: National Bureau of Economic Research, August.

Mann, C. L. 2006. *Accelerating the globalization of America: The role of information technology.* Washington, D.C.: Peterson Institute for International Economics.

Mann, C. L., S. E. Eckert, and S. C. Knight. 2002. *Global electronic commerce: A policy primer.* Washington, D.C.: Peterson Institute for International Economics.

McCloskey, D., and A. Klamer. 1995. One quarter of GDP is persuasion. *Rhetoric and Economic Behavior* 85:191–95.

Milgrom, P., and S. Oster. 1987. Job discrimination, market forces, and the invisibility hypothesis. *Quarterly Journal of Economics* 102:453–76.

Mortensen, D. T. 1986. Job search and labor market analysis. In *Handbook of labor economics,* ed. O. Ashenfelter and R. Layard, 849–919. Amsterdam: Elsevier Science Publishers.

Mullainathan, S., J. Schwartzstein, and A. Shleifer. 2006. Coarse thinking and persuasion. NBER Working Paper no. 12720. Cambridge, MA: National Bureau of Economic Research.

Mullan, F. 2005. The metrics of the physician brain drain. *New England Journal of Medicine* 353 (17): 1810–18.

Nakamura, A. O., and J. Bruneau. 2002. The global talent hunt and the growth of e-recruiting in Canada. In *Renovating the ivory tower: Canadian universities and the knowledge economy,* Policy Study 37, ed. D. Laidler, 80–104. Toronto: C.D. Howe Institute (www.cdhowe.org).

Nakamura, A. O., and P. Lawrence. 1994. Education, training and prosperity. In *Stabilization, growth and distribution: Linkages in the knowledge era,* ed. T. J. Courchene, 235–79. Kingston, Ontario: John Deutsch Institute for the Study of Economic Policy, Queen's University.

Nakamura, A. O., M. Percy, P. Davenport, R. Fraser, and M. Piper. 1999. The genesis of CAREEROWL: The story of how SSHRC funded university research led to an on-line electronic hiring hall for Canadian post secondary students and alumni. Vancouver.

Nakamura, A. O., and T. Pugh. 2000. Our governments should stop freezing out smaller Canadian e-recruiters. *Policy Options* 21 (8): 48–52.

Nakamura, A. O., G. Wong, and W. E. Diewert. 1999. New approaches to public income support in Canada. *The local dimension of welfare-to-work: An international survey,* ch. 11, 297–337. Paris: Organization for Economic Cooperation and Development.

Quah, D. 2002a. Digital goods and the new economy. LSE Discussion Paper. Available at: http://www.strategic.gr/publications/NewsAlert/2004/03/03/TL/Thought Leaders1.pdf.

———. 2002b. Spatial agglomeration dynamics. *American Economic Review* 92 (2): 247–52.

Rebick, M. E. 2000. The importance of networks in the market for university graduates in Japan: A longitudinal analysis of hiring patterns. *Oxford Economic Papers* 52:471–96.

Roth, A. E. 2002. The economist as engineer: Game theory, experimentation, and computation as tools for design economics. Fisher-Schultz Lecture, *Econometrica* 70 (4): 1341–78.

Society for Human Resource Management (SHRM). 2007. 2007 Advances in e-recruiting: Leveraging the .jobs domain. Alexandria, VA: SHRM.

Spence, A. 1973. Job market signaling. *Quarterly Journal of Economics* 87:355–74.

Stevenson, B. 2005. The Internet, job search. Paper presented at the 2005 Meeting of the American Economics Association, Philadelphia, Pennsylvania.

———. 2007. The Internet and job search. Paper presented at the conference on Labor Market Intermediation. 17–18 May, Cambridge, MA.

van Welsum, D., and X. Reif. 2005. *Potential offshoring: Evidence from selected OECD Countries.* Paris: OECD, July.

Warburton, R. N., and W. P. Warburton. 2001. Canadian-made e-solution proves cheap and effective. *Canadian Business Economics* 8 (3): 37–39.

Warren, W. 2005. New national online job board JobCentral to launch with more than 310,000 listings. Available at: http://www.jobcentral.com/JClaunch4_05.asp.

The Internet and Job Search

Betsey Stevenson

2.1 Introduction

As dot-coms proliferated and at home Internet use skyrocketed, many economists began to speculate on how this new technology would change the labor market. In 2000 Alan Krueger wrote that "The Internet is rapidly changing the way workers search for jobs and employers recruit workers . . . [with] significant implications for unemployment, pay, and productivity." Autor (2000) outlines several of the ways in which the Internet might improve matching and provides evidence on the use of the Internet for job search. In the ensuing years the Internet has become an important part of people's lives and jobs: in 2004, 73 percent of households had access to the Internet and 58 percent and 28 percent of adults used the Internet at home and work, respectively.[1] Yet we still know very little about how the Internet has impacted job search and employment.

Betsey Stevenson is an assistant professor of business and public policy at The Wharton School, University of Pennsylvania, and a faculty research fellow of the National Bureau of Economic Research.

This project has drawn on the advice of many generous friends and colleagues, including Susanto Basu, Peter Cappelli, Stefano Della Vigna, Chris Foote, Richard Freeman, Claudia Goldin, Austin Goolsbee, Caroline Minter Hoxby, Lawrence Katz, Ulrike Malmendier, Todd Sinai, and Justin Wolfers. Thanks also to seminar audiences at the American Economic Association meetings, the European Summer Symposium in Labor Economics, the Society of Labor Economists, Harvard University, Stanford GSB, The Federal Reserve Banks of San Francisco and St. Louis, and Kellogg. Rohak Doshi and Adam Isen provided excellent research assistance. All remaining errors are my own. Generous funding from the Wharton eBusiness Initiative (WeBI) and the Zell/Lurie Real Estate Center is gratefully acknowledged. And a special thanks to Michael Gazala, Charlene Li, and others at Forrester Research for providing access to their confidential data.

1. Data calculated from Forrester Research's 2005 Technographics Benchmark. Eighty-six percent of those who use the Internet at work also use the Internet at home; however, the majority (59 percent) of those who use the Internet at home do not have access at work.

This research focuses on how the Internet may be changing job search activities. For workers, the Internet may reduce the cost of acquiring information about jobs both by impacting how workers learn about job openings and how they respond to openings. Job posting boards are one of the clearest ways in which the Internet has increased information about available jobs; however, these boards are a small part of the Internet's impact on employment information. Beyond learning that a job opening exists, it is possible for a job-seeker to glean information about the characteristics of the job and the firm. Information exists not only in a job posting, but through company websites and other external sites that provide information about the industry or even the particular firm. Websites such as vault.com provide detailed information about salaries and work environments, including salary ranges for various positions at specific companies. In addition, many sites allow current and former employees to anonymously discuss or provide information about corporate culture and work life. Beyond the web, e-mail is a vital part of how the Internet has potentially changed job search. Indeed, through the use of e-mail, personal networks may be a complement to the Internet, allowing workers to learn about openings or let others know that they are seeking a new position. Having learned about a position or a company, the Internet facilitates applying for openings and communicating with potential employers, as these things can be done twenty-four hours a day, without ever leaving one's home or work desk.

Workers have turned to the web to take advantage of this new wealth of employment information, with more than one in four online adults visiting job or career information sites in 2004.[2] And workers believe that the Internet is helping them find jobs. Figure 2.1 shows that among those that began a job in mid-2002, 22 percent credited the Internet as the primary means by which they found their job. A little over half of those citing the Internet pointed to a posting on a general job board, while the rest said that specialty job search engines or company websites had been their primary source for finding their most recent job. Furthermore, over half of those surveyed felt that the Internet was an effective method of job search (however, this is still fewer than those selecting newspaper ads and personal referrals as effective).

These survey responses indicate that workers are integrating online job search into their regular search process. This research examines how job search behavior has changed in the wake of the Internet. The chapter proceeds as follows: the first section starts by examining growth in online usage and Internet-based job search using data from the 1998, 2001, and 2003 Cur-

---

2. Data are from Forrester Research's 2005 Technographics Benchmark. Individuals who use the Internet were asked how often they use certain types of websites. This data is comparable to that found using the 1998, 2000, and 2001 CPS Computer Supplements, which finds that among those with Internet access, online job search is used by a fifth of the employed and over half of the unemployed.

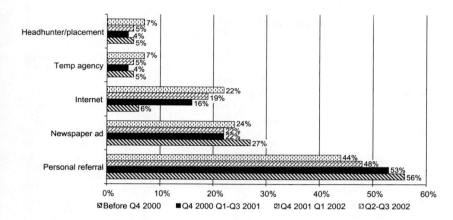

Fig. 2.1   Primary method used to find current job
Source: Forrester Research survey (November 2002). Question was only asked to those who were currently employed and use the Internet. Individuals are divided by when they started their current job.

rent Population Statistics (CPS) Computer and Internet Use Supplements. The next section considers how the availability of the Internet has impacted the type of job search activity undertaken by the unemployed, examining trends in these activities over time. This research demonstrates that over the past ten years the variety of job search methods used by the unemployed has increased. We then turn to examining the relationship between changes in state-level annual Internet penetration rates and Internet job search activity by the unemployed. The latter approach demonstrates that the Internet is associated with a reallocation of effort among various job search activities and that job search activity grows as a state's Internet penetration rate expands. In particular, higher Internet penetration is associated with a significantly higher probability of contacting an employer directly—potentially highlighting the role of e-mail in job search. The last section considers the relationship between Internet job search and employment outcomes for on-the-job online job searchers. Using the longitudinal aspect of the CPS, I follow employed workers in the CPS Computer Supplements and find that those using the Internet to search for a job online are more likely to have left their employer one month later. Examining access to the Internet rather than job search per se reveals that, conditional on observable predictors of Internet use, those who use the Internet are more likely to have changed jobs.

2.2   Descriptive Statistics

The December 1998, September 2001, and October 2003 CPS Computer and Internet Use Supplements ask respondents about their and their households' computer and Internet use in addition to the usual battery of employ-

Table 2.1   Online job search from 1998 to 2003

	Year	Employed	Unemployed	Not in the labor force	Total
Panel A: Percent searching for jobs online					
Total population	1998	7.2	14.0	1.9	5.7
	2001	11.4	31.2	3.3	9.4
	2003	13.7	37.8	4.3	11.5
Those who use the Internet	1998	17.1	52.6	11.2	16.9
	2001	17.2	58.8	9.6	16.9
	2003	19.1	65.1	11.4	19.0
Panel B: Descriptive statistics: Internet use and online job search in 2003					
Percent online from home		57.3	46.5	33.2	49.2
Percent online from anywhere		71.7	58.0	37.8	60.3
Proportion of adult population		64.3	3.3	32.4	100
Share of online job searchers		76.8	11.0	12.2	100

Source: Data are from the Current Population Statistics Computer and Internet Use Supplements conducted in December 1998, September 2001, and October 2003.
Note: Online are individuals who access the Internet from any location.

ment questions. These data reveal that online job search has grown rapidly among the employed, unemployed, and even those not in the labor force. Panel A of table 2.1 shows that in 1998 5.7 percent of adults searched online for jobs, rising to 11.5 percent by 2003.

Much of the increase in online job search during this period was due to the rise in access to the Internet: the total share of those online using the Internet to search for a job was unchanged between 1998 and 2001. In both 1998 and 2001, among those online, over half of the unemployed, one-sixth of the employed, and around 10 percent of those out of the labor force engaged in online job search. Between 2001 and 2003 the increase in online job search activity was somewhat greater than the increase in Internet usage overall, and in 2003 nearly a fifth of those online reported engaging in job search activities on the Web, including nearly two-thirds of the online unemployed and a fifth of the online employed.

Panel B of table 2.1 shows descriptive statistics for home and total online usage among the employed, unemployed, and those not in the labor force for 2003. Total access to the Internet is greater than home access for all groups. The nonhome access comes from a variety of sources and raises access for the unemployed and employed by 12 and 14 percentage points, respectively. It is worth noting that access to the Internet through work drives very little of the difference between the Internet access of the employed and unemployed. More than 80 percent of the employed in 2003 who have regular Internet access at work also have access at home; however, the opposite is not true: many people who get access through home do not have access at work.

Among those employed, 57 percent used the Internet at home and 14 percent searched for a job online. While only 47 percent of the unemployed have online access at home, they are much more likely to search for work online (38 percent). However, the large difference in the stock of the employed relative to the unemployed means that the unemployed are a very small share of online job searchers. In 2003, the unemployed represented only 11 percent of those searching for a job online, a similar share to those not in the labor force (who comprised 12 percent). The majority, 77 percent of those searching for a job online, are currently employed. These descriptive statistics illustrate the importance of the employed in assessing the potential overall effect of the Internet on job matching.

Once we have conditioned on who uses the Internet, among Internet users there is surprisingly little heterogeneity between demographic groups in the tendency to search for a job online. Table 2.2 shows the proportions of different demographic groups searching for a job online both among the total population and among those with Internet access. While there are differences in online job search by income, age, race, and gender differences among the unemployed, these differences are more muted when conditioning on those with Internet access. In contrast, there are greater differences in online job search by age among the employed who use the Internet, with online job search falling with age. Similarly, among those not in the labor force the percentage using the Internet to search for a job falls sharply with age. These differences likely reflect the desire to find a job, and thus differences in general search activity, with the value of changing employers, or entering the labor force, falling with age. For instance, among those aged twenty-five to thirty and online, 28 percent of the employed and 15 percent of those out of the labor force were searching for a job online. These proportions fall to only 4 percent and 1 percent, respectively, among those over age sixty-five.

Those with more education and income have greater access to the Internet; as such, Internet job search rises with education and income. However, after conditioning on access to the Internet, there is little relationship between income and job search. Among the online employed, job search falls slightly with income; that pattern is not seen among the online unemployed, perhaps suggesting that higher-income employed individuals are less likely to use the Internet to search for a job because they are more likely to be in a better match or to have built up job-specific human capital. In contrast, a positive relationship remains for Internet job search and education among those using the Internet, perhaps indicating that the Internet is more valuable as a tool for job search among the highly educated. However, it may also be that those with more education have a greater underlying tendency to engage in job search activities whether online or off. Finally, it is worth noting that blacks who are employed or not in the labor force are more likely than employed whites to search for a job online, conditional on having access to the Internet.

Table 2.2   Percent searching for a job online among demographic groups: 2001

		Percent searching for jobs online total population			Percent searching for jobs online among those online		
		Employed	Unemployed	Not in the labor force	Employed	Unemployed	Not in the labor force
Gender	Women	11.8	31.1	3.4	16.8	54.9	9.2
	Men	10.9	28.6	3.1	17.0	54.7	8.5
Race	White	11.2	32.2	3.1	16.2	54.8	8.1
	Black	11.3	20.0	4.2	21.8	52.3	16.9
	Asian	13.9	43.9	5.2	19.8	65.5	10.2
Education categories	High school drop-out	3.2	8.3	1.6	9.5	23.5	6.2
	High school graduate	6.9	20.1	2.3	13.1	45.7	8.3
	Some college	12.6	40.1	5.7	17.1	60.9	11.3
	College	19.3	68.8	5.8	21.6	77.5	9.7
	Post graduate	16.4	66.6	4.7	17.9	75.2	8.1
Household income categories	Less then $20K	9.2	18.0	2.0	24.2	54.1	12.4
	$20K to $40K	11.4	30.4	2.9	21.2	58.7	9.1
	$40K to $60K	11.9	32.4	4.4	17.1	48.6	8.5
	Above $60K	13.9	49.5	5.5	15.3	59.0	7.8
Age categories	18–25	16.6	28.7	9.9	24.3	46.8	15.0
	26–30	19.3	36.0	7.7	27.5	66.0	15.6
	31–35	14.8	34.7	7.6	20.9	67.7	14.3
	36–40	11.5	31.0	6.5	16.6	63.1	13.7
	41–45	10.0	33.5	4.9	14.5	68.2	11.4
	46–50	8.9	32.8	5.4	13.1	69.6	12.8
	51–55	6.1	36.2	2.4	9.4	71.2	6.5
	56–65	4.0	25.7	1.1	7.2	59.1	3.6
	Over 65 years old	1.4	9.4	0.2	3.9	31.6	1.4

Source: Data are from the Current Population Statistics Computer and Internet Use Supplement September 2001.

2.3 Job Search by the Unemployed

We now turn to asking whether job search activity has changed as a result of the Internet. By making it cheaper to apply for jobs and to find job ads, the Internet should cause people to engage more frequently in these activities. As such, we should expect an increase in search intensity for job search activities that are made cheaper by the Internet. However, while "search intensity" has a clear meaning in matching models, we lack a good empirical counterpart for this concept. Theory has less clear implications for easily measured job search metrics. For instance, time spent searching for a job may either increase or decrease, depending on the elasticity of substitution between job search and other activities. The most readily available data covering the period of rapid Internet adoption measures job search activity at the extensive margin—the number of search activities in which a person engages. Whether the Internet causes individuals to search more or less extensively depends on the relative price changes of the different job search methods. For example, if e-mailing friends and contacts is now much easier than before, individuals may decide to forgo another activity, such as contacting a union or professional organization.

Over the relevant time period—1994 through 2003—the monthly CPS consistently captures the types of job search activities undertaken by the unemployed. Specifically, the unemployed are asked to list all the things that they have done in the previous four weeks to look for a job. The categories do not include Internet job search, but they do not exclude them, either. For example, the category "submitted resume" could apply to electronic or postal submission, and those who "looked at job ads" could have done so via the Internet or newsprint advertisements.

The Internet is likely to have changed job search at the extensive margin if either Internet search makes methods more complementary—for example, if reading job ads online makes you more likely to submit resumes because it can be easily done electronically—or if Internet search changes the relative costs of different job search methods. Looking at the United States as a whole, figure 2.2 shows that there has been a steady and significant increase in job search by the unemployed—at least at the extensive margin—over the past decade. The national unemployment rate falls through much of the period, hitting a low point in 2000 and rising for the next few years. In contrast, the average number of search methods rises not only through the recent downturn but also through the long boom.[3] In contrast to what would be expected, given the changes in the broader economy over the period, the percentage of the unemployed who sent out a resume in the previous four weeks rose from 36 percent in 1994 to 48 percent at the peak of the boom

---

3. Blau and Robbins (1990) show that individuals search more extensively with high unemployment.

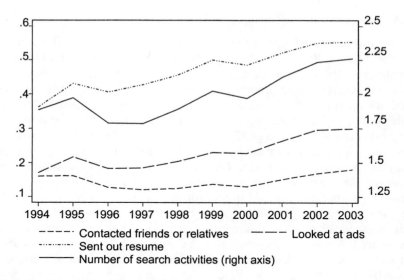

Fig. 2.2   Job search methods of the unemployed

Source: Monthly Current Population Statistics annual averages of the job search methods by those who are unemployed and looking for work in the four weeks prior to the interview. National unemployment rate is from the Bureau of Labor Statistics.

in 2000, and continued to rise to 55 percent in 2003 as unemployment rose. Similarly, the proportion looking at job ads rose from 17 to 23 percent and ultimately 30 percent over the same period. Moreover, the anonymity of the web does not appear to be replacing traditional networking, as the percentage of the unemployed contacting friends or relatives went from 16 to 19 percent over the period.

To gain further insight into whether the growth in the Internet was associated with these changes in job search behavior we turn to examining how job search behavior changed across states as Internet penetration in states grew. States adopted the Internet differentially, with some states growing quickly early on, while others had larger growth several years later. Proprietary data obtained from Forrester Research provides data from large annual surveys on whether an individual is actively online (defined as accessing the web at least three times in the past three months). While the online usage rates calculated from the Forrester data are quite similar to online usage rates calculated from the CPS Computer and Internet Use Supplements, the Forrester data provide a longer time period over which to examine online access and to look at job search behavior. The Forrester surveys commenced in 1997 and contain roughly 100,000 respondents per year through 2001 and 60,000 per year thereafter. Additionally, Forrester captures retrospective information about when a person first went online, allowing data to be constructed back to 1994. I combine current and retrospective data from these surveys to

Table 2.3   **State online penetration rates**

	Mean	Standard deviation	Minimum	Maximum
1992	2	1	1	3
1993	4	1	2	7
1994	7	2	4	12
1995	12	3	7	18
1996	20	4	12	27
1997	30	5	19	39
1998	44	5	31	54
1999	56	5	41	65
2000	65	5	50	74
2001	68	5	54	77
2002	70	6	53	80

Source: Online penetration numbers are from Forrester Research's proprietary data, where online is defined to be "online at least 3 times in the last three months" from any location. State-year penetration numbers are calculated from five years of survey data including retrospective data on how long the respondent had been online. For example, state data for 1999 is calculated by combining current reports in 1999 and retrospective reports in 2000–2003. Data for 1992 and 1993 is interpolated following Brown and Goolsbee (2002): by scaling 1994 online usage by the overall rate of growth of domain names. I applied their scaling to my estimates of 1994 online usage.

measure annual state online penetration rates.[4] Measurements for 1992 and 1993 are interpolated following Brown and Goolsbee (2002).[5] Prior to 1992, Internet penetration, while unmeasured, is effectively zero. Table 2.3 shows the mean, standard deviation, minimum, and maximum of state online penetration rates defined to include those who regularly used the Internet.[6] By 2002, 70 percent of the United States used the Internet, but this varied from 53 to 80 percent across states.

Using the growth in the Internet over time and across states, we can examine the relationship between changes in job search behavior in a given state-year with changes in access to the Internet in that state-year as measured by the change in the proportion of the population using the Internet in that state-year. Table 2.4 reports the results of the following regression run for each search method:[7]

4. Forrester provides data for forty-eight states plus the District of Columbia, omitting Hawaii and Alaska from their surveys.

5. Brown and Goolsbee (2002) calculated rates for 1992 and 1993 by scaling 1994 online usage by the overall rate of growth of domain names. I applied their scaling to my estimates of 1994 online usage; my estimate differs from theirs because I obtained access to a larger set of surveys.

6. Those who regularly use the Internet can do so either at home or work, but much of the variation occurs because of differences across states in home use.

7. State demographic characteristics include the proportion of the population who are white, female, married, ages eighteen to thirty, ages thirty to fifty, ages fifty to sixty-five, over age sixty-five, and the share by years of education completed for those with less than twelve, twelve, thirteen to fifteen, sixteen, and seventeen to twenty.

Table 2.4   **Job search methods: The effect of the internet on the extensiveness of job search**

		Effect of the Internet on the probability of using each method			
		OLS results		IV results	
Dependent variable	Mean (A)	(B)	(C)	(D)	(E)
Contacted employer directly	63%	.070***	.164***	.058**	.174
		(.024)	(.064)	(.025)	(.137)
Contacted public employment agency	21%	.075***	−.016	.097***	.273*
		(.021)	(.060)	(.022)	(.148)
Contacted private employment agency	6%	.069***	−.011	.079***	−.026
		(.011)	(.028)	(.011)	(.065)
Contacted friends or family	13%	.114***	−.072	.144***	.062
		(.019)	(.049)	(.021)	(.124)
Sent resume	48%	.097***	−.159**	.144***	.212
		(.030)	(.077)	(.032)	(.206)
Contacted union or professional org	2%	.011**	−.016	.016***	.027
		(.006)	(.015)	(.005)	(.031)
Placed ad or answered ad	15%	.105***	−.162***	.139***	−.230**
		(.023)	(.050)	(.024)	(.109)
Looked at ads	23%	.147***	.111	.152***	.124
		(.024)	(.070)	(.026)	(.132)
Other form of active search	5%	.078***	.079***	.078***	.105*
		(.010)	(.026)	(.010)	(.058)
Number of methods used	2.0	.681***	−.090	.927***	.712*
		(.058)	(.175)	(.079)	(.413)
	Controls				
Current and lagged state unemployment		✓	✓	✓	✓
Logged state per capita personal income		✓	✓	✓	✓
State demographic characteristics		✓	✓	✓	✓
Percentage of state workers in large firms		✓	✓	✓	✓
State-fixed effects		✓	✓	✓	✓
Year-fixed effects			✓		✓

Sources: Job search data reflect annual data from 1994 through 2003, created from the monthly Current Population Statistics by aggregating over twelve months, with the exception of 2003, for which only the first nine months were available. Online penetration numbers are from Forrester Research's proprietary data, where online is defined to be "online at least 3 times in the last three months" from any location. State-year penetration numbers are calculated from five years of survey data including retrospective data on how long the respondent had been online. Data on online use gathered in December were matched to job search behavior in January through December of the following year.

Notes: Robust standard errors are in parentheses. State-level demographic characteristics include the fraction of the state's total population who are white, married, ages eighteen to thirty, ages thirty to fifty, ages fifty to sixty-five, over age sixty-five, and the share by years of education completed for those with high school, some college, college, and more than college. The percentage of state workers in large firms is the percentage of the employed who work in a firm with more than 1,000 employees. The first stage of the IV is available in appendix table A2.1. The IV estimates online penetration each year as a function of the year-fixed effects interacted with the percentage of a state that had telephones in 1960 and the year-fixed effects interacted with the percentage of a state that had automatic washing machines in 1960.

***Significant at the 1 percent level.
**Significant at the 5 percent level.
*Significant at the 10 percent level.

(1)   Percentage of unemployed using job search method $j_{s,t}$

$$= \beta \text{ Online Penetration}_{s,t} + \sum_{i=0}^{2} \mu_i \text{ unemployment rate}_{s,t-i}$$

$$+ \sum_k \varphi_k \text{ State demographic characteristics}_{s,t}^k$$

$$+ \psi \% \text{ of workers in large firms}_{s,t} + \sum_s \eta_s \text{State}_s + \varepsilon_{s,t},$$

where β is the coefficient of interest and online penetration is a measure of annual average online usage across states. These regressions show that as online penetration grew across states, so did the use of each type of job search method. All methods show large, statistically significant increases that coincide with the growth in Internet penetration across states and years. For example, a state-year with a 10 percentage point higher Internet penetration rate is associated with: a 2 percent increase in the probability of sending out a resume, a 7 percent increase in the probability of looking at job ads, a 10 percent increase in the probability of contacting a private employment agency, and a 1 percent increase in contacting an employer. Summing all search methods shows that on average, the unemployed have used two of the methods queried and that a 10 percentage point higher Internet penetration in a state-year is associated with an increase in the number of search methods of .07. All told, the tremendous growth of the Internet—from 0 to 70 percent—over this period is associated with large increases in search activities. Figure 2.2 showed that search increased both during the boom and following the bust. A similar result is found by estimating the regressions shown in column (B) separately for the period before 2000 and after 2000.[8]

The analysis thus far considered variation coming from both the growth of the Internet over time and from differences in that growth across states. In order to control for other trending factors that might have also led to changes in job search behavior over time, we can instead consider only the variation that comes from differences across states while controlling for the aggregate trends through the inclusion of year-fixed effects. Column (C) of table 2.4 thus reports the results of estimating equation (1) with the inclusion of year-fixed effects. While states vary in the timing of growth in Internet penetration, this specification necessarily involves less variation, as it holds constant the aggregate growth in Internet penetration in a given year. Not surprisingly, many of the coefficient estimates are now imprecisely estimated—standard errors triple or quadruple in most cases. The within-state variation yields a less clear story but suggests that perhaps relative prices of the different search methods have changed.

Using variation in states' adoption of the Internet over time raises questions about what is driving the variation and with what else it might be correlated. For example, if people get access to the Internet at home as a

---

8. Results are available from the author.

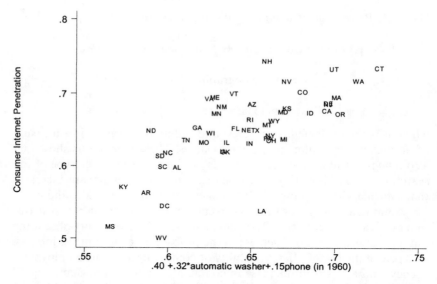

Fig. 2.3   Consumer Internet penetration predicted by 1960, phone and automatic washing machine ownership rates

Source: Online penetration is from Forrester Research's proprietary Technographics Benchmark 2001 data. Online is defined to be "online at least three times in the last three months" from any location. Automatic washer and phone penetration data are from the Public Use Micro Sample (PUMS) of the 1960 Census of Population.

Notes: The graph compares actual online penetration measured in 2000 (shown on the y-axis) with that predicted by the following regression shown on the x axis:

$$\text{Online}_{s,t=2000} = \alpha + \beta \cdot \text{Own Phone}_{s,t=1960} + \delta \cdot \text{Own Automatic Washing Machine}_{s,t=1960} + \varepsilon.$$

spillover from firms adopting the Internet in their area, then job search activity may change along with Internet growth simply as a result of labor market changes associated with industry technology adoption. Similarly, states' business cycles may drive variation in the growth of Internet penetration, and thus, any relationship between Internet growth and job search behavioral changes may simply reflect variation in regional business cycles.

Stevenson (2009) addresses the first concern by comparing the adoption of the Internet by consumers with that by firms and finds that while adoption by both consumers and firms has occurred at a rapid pace, the adoption patterns have not been at all similar.[9] The second concern is partially addressed by the control variables; however, an alternative is to instrument for Internet growth. Following Stevenson (2009), I use a linear combination of state ownership rates of automatic washing machines and telephones in 1960 interacted with year effects to instrument for online access. Automatic washing machine and telephone adoption rates in 1960 are a powerful predictor of Internet penetration rates in 2000, as can be seen in figure 2.3.

9. Data on firm Internet use refer to the measure of commercial participation developed in Forman, Goldfarb, and Greenstein (2002).

While the characteristics in states that lead to these different adoption patterns might themselves be correlated with employment outcomes, the fact that these characteristics have been stable over the past forty-five years suggests that the inclusion of state-fixed effects will control for this endogenous relationship. Plausibly exogenous identification of states' Internet growth rates comes from the *interaction* of the fixed-state characteristics predicting adoption and the annual average diffusion.

Columns (D) and (E) of table 2.4 replace the ordinary least squares (OLS) estimates in columns (B) and (C) with instrumental variables estimates. The first stage uses the ownership rates of automatic washers and telephones in the 1960s interacted with year-fixed effects as a plausible exogenous predictor for state online penetration growth, the results of which are shown in appendix table 2A.1. Instrumenting yields estimates that are qualitatively similar. As in column (C), the specification including year-fixed effects is less precisely measured and, in most cases, we can reject neither a zero effect nor the large effects estimated in columns (B) and (D). However, in both specifications there is an economically and statistically significant increase in the number of search methods used by the unemployed. Overall, the IV regressions provide some suggestive evidence that the Internet has led the unemployed to increase total job search activity, at least at the extensive margin, while it also led the unemployed to reallocate effort among various job search activities.

2.4 Employment Flows for Job-Seekers

While the previous section explored the job search behavior of the unemployed, most online job search is done by the currently employed. Unfortunately, data do not permit a similar analysis for job search activities among the employed. However, the longitudinal component of the CPS allows employment outcomes to be examined following the reporting of using the Internet to search for employment. I followed all people who were employed in the August 2000 and September 2001 Supplements into the September 2000 and October 2001 monthly surveys, respectively.[10] The CPS (since 1994) employs a dependent interviewing technique in which interviewees are read back their employment details from the preceding month and asked to confirm them. These questions allow employment flows to be calculated, including identifying those who switched employers.

Table 2.5 shows the one-month employment flows of those employed in August 2000 and September 2001 broken into those who had searched for a job online in the previous month and those who had not. The first column reports results for the 88.7 percent who had not searched for a job online

10. While the survey is designed to be able to follow 75 percent, roughly 95 percent of the 75 percent can actually be matched from one month to the next. For more information on matching in the CPS see Madrian and Lefgren (1999). Details about the match used in this chapter are available from the author by request.

Table 2.5   **Employment flows by previous months on-the-job search status for online and offline search (%)**

Employment status one month later	2000 and 2001 CPS Computer Supplements		2001 CPS Contingent Worker Supplement	
	No online on-the-job search	Online on-the-job search	No traditional on-the-job search	Traditional on-the-job search
Total employed in the first month (%)	88.7	11.3	94.4	5.6
Same employer	93.3	91.2	95.3	84.0
New employer	2.7	4.5	1.8	9.1
Unemployed	1.0	1.9	0.9	4.4
Not in the labor force	2.9	2.4	2.0	2.4

Source: Data for columns (1) and (2) are generated using the August 2000 and September 2001 CPS Computer and Internet Use Supplements matched with the September 2000 and October 2001 monthly CPS, respectively. Data for columns (3) and (4) are generated using the 2001 February Contingent Worker Supplement matched with the monthly March 2001 CPS. Flows represent employment status one month later for those employed in the original supplement month.

in the preceding month: 93.3 percent are employed in the same job one month later, 2.7 percent are employed with a new employer, 1.0 percent are unemployed, and 2.9 percent are no longer in the labor force. The second column shows the employment flows for the 11.3 percent of workers who were looking for a job online in the first month: 91.2 percent are employed in the same job one month later, 4.5 percent are employed with a new employer, 1.9 percent are unemployed, and 2.4 percent are no longer in the labor force.

Comparing the first two columns in table 2.5 reveals that those who were searching for a job online were more likely to change jobs and more likely to become unemployed. However, this comparison ignores the counterfactual of offline job search. To compare online on-the-job search to the counterfactual of any on-the-job search we turn to the February 2001 CPS Contingent Worker Supplement.[11] Workers in the February 2001 supplement are matched to the March 2001 CPS and their employment status one month later is shown in the third and fourth columns of table 2.5. The third column shows employment flows for the 94.4 percent of workers who were not engaged in on-the-job search: 95.3 percent are employed in the same job one month later, 1.8 percent are employed with a new employer, 0.9 percent are unemployed, and 2.0 percent are no longer in the labor force. While these results are similar to those found for workers who had not engaged in online on-the-job search, striking differences arise in the fourth column when examining employment flows for the 5.6 percent of workers who were

11. Fallick and Fleischman (2004) use the Contingent Worker Supplements to examine the difference in employer flows for those who engage in offline on-the-job search. This table follows their examination in table 6 of the 1997 and 1999 Contingent Worker Supplements.

seeking a job the previous period.[12] Among these seekers, only 84.0 percent remained with their previous month's employer, 9.1 percent were employed with a new employer, 4.4 percent were unemployed, and 2.4 percent were no longer in the labor force.

More than twice as many workers engage in online on-the-job search compared with traditional measures of search; however, a smaller percentage of those engaging in on-the-job search have left their employer one month later, compared with those engaging in traditional on-the-job search. The outcomes for both online and traditional on-the-job seekers indicate that workers who are searching for a new job while employed have a preference for changing jobs. They may have personal reasons for wanting a change or have private (or at least unobservable to the econometrician) information about the likelihood of their job continuing. Indeed, the large percentage of those engaging in traditional on-the-job search who end up unemployed suggest that some of these job-seekers are adversely selected in that they are more likely to experience an unemployment shock than is the average worker. This increased likelihood of unemployment is also seen for the online on-the-job searchers, although to a smaller extent.

The difficulty with looking at workers who are searching online is that there is no direct way to measure the counterfactual, what would have happened had they not been able to search online. Indeed, while the previous comparison did not rule out online job search for those engaged in traditional job search, it is not possible to identify those who are using the Internet to search separately from those who are not. Ideally, one would want to measure both offline on-the-job search and Internet-based on-the-job search and compare employment outcomes for the two groups. One way to get around this is simply to compare employment outcomes for those who use the Internet with those who do not. To the extent that Internet use is itself uncorrelated with the unobserved characteristics that cause on-the-job search (such as private information about current match quality or personal preference to change jobs), then comparing employment outcomes among Internet users with nonusers (controlling for observables) will capture the effect of the additional search induced by the Internet on employment outcomes. However, this introduces a similar selection problem if those who use the Internet are more (less) likely to change employers for reasons unrelated to the Internet—in this case, the coefficient will be biased upward (downward).

An additional benefit of comparing Internet users with nonusers is that it captures the total net effect of using the Internet on employer-to-employer flows, regardless of whether a worker perceives him- or herself to be actively

---

12. The contingent worker surveys use similar definitions as the monthly CPS uses to assess unemployed job search activity. The questions are not designed to capture method of action (for instance, e-mailing versus postal mailing of resumes).

searching online (those who communicate by e-mail with a friend about a potential job lead and then submit applications online may very well be more likely to change jobs as a result of the Internet, but may not answer "yes" to a survey question regarding online job search).

To test whether Internet use is itself associated with a change in the probability of changing employers, we follow workers in the 2001 and 2002 CPS Computer Use Supplements and assess whether the probability of moving from one employer to another employer in the subsequent month (EE) depends on Internet use in the previous month (I) controlling for observed characteristics such as current age, age-squared, marital status, race, education, gender, income, family type, industry and occupation, along with state and year fixed effects. That is, probit regressions were run for:

$$(2) \quad EE_{i,t} = \alpha + \beta I_{i,t} + X_{i,t}\phi + \sum_{k}\chi_{k}\text{Occupation}_{k} + \sum_{p}\varphi_{p}\text{Industry}_{p}$$
$$+ \sum_{s}\eta_{s}\text{State}_{s} + \sum_{t}\lambda_{t}\text{Year}_{t} + \varepsilon_{i,t},$$

where EE is a dummy variable equal to one if the worker changed employers in the subsequent month, I is a dummy variable equal to one if the worker uses the Internet, and X is a vector of demographic variables. The parameter of interest is β.

The regression results are reported in table 2.6. Column (1) reports the results for the entire sample of those who were employed in the Supplement surveys. The coefficient on Internet use represents the change in the probability for a discrete change from no Internet use to using the Internet evaluated at the mean of the dependent variable. The coefficient evaluated at the predicted mean implies that those who use the Internet are 15 percent more likely to have changed employers the following month.

In addition to individual behavior, the CPS Computer and Internet Use Supplements ask respondents about the use of computers and the Internet by anyone in the household. This allows one to examine Internet use within households that have a computer and those that have Internet access. Seventy-five percent of the employed in households with a computer use the Internet, while 83 percent in households with Internet access do. The last two columns in table 2.6 show coefficients that are larger than, albeit not statistically different from, those shown in the first column. Evaluating the effect of Internet use at the mean of the dependent variable shows that Internet use is associated with a 28 percent increase in job changing among households with computers and among households with Internet access. While the last two columns potentially reduce selection problems at the household level, they also potentially exacerbate individual selection issues.

This section illustrates that the Internet has the potential to affect worker flows in many dimensions. While previous work by Kuhn and Skuterud (2004) showed little effect of the Internet on unemployment duration, this

Table 2.6   **Probit estimates of employer changes and Internet use**

Independent variable	All workers	Households with computers	Households with internet access
Individual internet use dummy	.003***	.005*	.004**
	(.002)	(.002)	(.002)
± b			
Pseudo R^2	.036	.042	.045
Number of observations	88,681	61,136	52,673
Mean of dependent variable	.024	.023	.024
Percent effect of Internet use on job changing evaluated at X bar	15%	28%	28%

Source: August 2000 and September 2001 CPS Computer and Internet Use Supplements matched with the September 2000 and October 2001 monthly CPS, respectively.

Notes: Each column is a probit regression evaluating the probability that a worker changes jobs between the two months conditional on Internet use in the first month and control variables. The dependent variable = 1 if the respondent uses the Internet. Coefficients represent the change in the probability for a discrete change from no Internet use to use evaluated at the mean of the dependent variable. Robust standard errors are in parentheses. Controls include state- and year-fixed effects, occupation and industry, and demographics. Demographic controls include age, age squared, marital status, race, family type, income, education, and gender.

***Significant at the 1 percent level.
**Significant at the 5 percent level.
*Significant at the 10 percent level.

finding relies on the assumption that the Internet had no impact on the flow into unemployment. Stevenson (2009) examines employment flows more fully, considering that the Internet may have impacted employment-to-employment flows, as shown here in table 2.6, as well as employment-to-unemployment flows and unemployment-to-employment flows.[13]

2.5   Concluding Remarks

In the past ten years Internet usage has risen from effectively zero to 70 percent of the population. This rapid rise in information technology has the potential to dramatically alter labor market outcomes. The Internet is perceived to have made job search more efficient for workers, yet research has lagged popular perception. This chapter examines how job search activity has changed in the wake of the Internet and traces the effects of using the Internet to search for a job—while employed—on employment outcomes one month later.

I find that over the past ten years the variety of job search methods used

13. Kuhn and Skuterud (2004) find unemployment durations for Internet job-seekers that are similar, or perhaps longer, than those not using the Internet to search for work. Stevenson (2009) finds that this partially reflects a higher probability of an employment-to-employment spell without having a spell of unemployment.

by the unemployed has increased and job search behavior has become more extensive. Furthermore, the Internet appears to have led to reallocation of effort among various job search activities. The unemployed are now more likely to have looked at ads and to have contacted an employer directly—however, there is some evidence that the unemployed are becoming more selective about the jobs to which they ultimately apply. Perhaps not surprisingly, the amount of information available about a given job increasingly allows the unemployed to better target his or her job search activities. While there is little evidence that the unemployed have experienced shorter unemployment durations as a result, the Internet's ability to reduce the cost of on-the-job search may have changed the likelihood that a worker ends up unemployed.

The vast majority of workers using the Internet to gather information about employment are those who are already employed. As such, the Internet potentially provides a large shock to the rematching market, as those currently employed are better able to assess opportunities in the marketplace. This research has shown that workers using the Internet are more likely to leave their current employer and that, compared with traditional on-the-job search, online on-the-job search may increase the rate at which employees change employers—at least in the short run. Employees who are better calibrated about their outside options are not only more likely to change employers, but they are in a better position to negotiate with their current employer. Thus, future research should consider whether the Internet is affecting wage compression within occupations.

Appendix

Table 2A.1   **First stage: instrumental variables approach**

Online Penetration$_{s,t}$ = α + $\sum_t \eta_t$Year$_t$ · Phone + $\sum_t \eta_t$Year$_t$ · Automatic Washing Machines + $\varepsilon_{s,t}$

	(A) First stage without additional controls	(B) First stage with all controls included in second stage
Phone · Year = 1995	.015	.017
	(.039)	(.041)
Phone · Year = 1996	−.009	.019
	(.039)	(.044)
Phone · Year = 1997	.009	.014
	(.039)	(.043)
Phone · Year = 1998	.039	.009
	(.039)	(.042)
Phone · Year = 1999	.239	.060
	(.039)	(.054)
Phone · Year = 2000	.316	.082
	(.039)	(.055)
Phone · Year = 2001	.478	.108
	(.039)	(.056)
Phone · Year = 2002	.502	.064
	(.039)	(.057)
Phone · Year = 2003	.628	.188
	(.039)	(.061)
Washer · Year = 1994	.086	.088
	(.073)	(.043)
Washer · Year = 1995	.076	.089
	(.073)	(.042)
Washer · Year = 1996	.186	.175
	(.073)	(.049)
Washer · Year = 1997	.309	.273
	(.073)	(.052)
Washer · Year = 1998	.510	.401
	(.073)	(.068)
Washer · Year = 1999	.490	.359
	(.073)	(.068)
Washer · Year = 2000	.578	.386
	(.073)	(.077)
Washer · Year = 2001	.536	.319
	(.073)	(.088)
Washer · Year = 2002	.438	.206
	(.073)	(.073)
Adjusted R^2	.97	.99

Source: Online penetration numbers are from Forrester Research's proprietary data. Telephone and automatic washer data are from the Public Use Micro Sample (PUMS) of the 1960 Census of Population.

Notes: Robust standard errors are in parentheses. First-stage regression for instrumental variables results presented in table 2.4. For control variables included in column (B), see table 2.4.

References

Autor, D. H. 2000. Wiring the labor market. *Journal of Economic Perspectives* 15 (1): 25–40.

Blau, D. M., and P. K. Robins. 1990. Job search outcomes for the employed and unemployed. *Journal of Political Economy* 98:637–55.

Brown, J., and A. Goolsbee. 2002. Does the Internet make markets more competitive? Evidence from the life insurance industry. *Journal of Political Economy* 110 (3): 481–507.

Fallick, B., and C. Fleischman. 2004. Employer-to-employer flows in the US labor market: The complete picture of gross worker flows. FEDS Working Paper no. 2004–34, May.

Forman, C., A. Goldfarb, and S. Greenstein. 2002. Digital dispersion: An industrial and geographic census of commercial Internet use. NBER Working Paper no. 9287. Cambridge, MA: National Bureau of Economic Research, October.

Krueger, A. B. 2000. The Internet is lowering the cost of advertising and searching for jobs. *New York Times,* July 20.

Kuhn, P., and M. Skuterud. 2004. Internet job search and unemployment durations. *American Economic Review* 94 (1): 218–32.

Madrian, B., and L. Lefgren. 1999. A note on longitudinally matching current population survey (CPS) respondents. NBER no. 247. Cambridge, MA: National Bureau of Economic Research.

Stevenson, Betsey. 2009. The impact of the Internet on worker flows. Unpublished Manuscript.

II

Mitigating Adverse Selection

3

Effect of Employer Access to Criminal History Data on the Labor Market Outcomes of Ex-Offenders and Non-Offenders

Keith Finlay

3.1 Introduction

At the end of 2001, an estimated 5.6 million U.S. adults had served time in state or federal prison, including 4.3 million former prisoners and 1.3 million adults in prison. Each year, more than half a million state and federal prisoners are released from correctional institutions and may attempt to reenter the civilian labor force (Harrison and Beck 2006). As these ex-offenders seek employment, they face employers averse to hiring applicants with criminal records. Until recently, it has been difficult for hiring officials to verify an applicant's criminal history. Since 1997, states have begun to make criminal history records publicly available over the Internet, which has lowered the cost and increased the scope of the criminal background checks that can be conducted in those states. This chapter exploits this previously unexamined variation to measure the effect of expanded access to criminal history data on the labor market outcomes of ex-offenders and non-offenders. Since an employer's decision to conduct criminal background checks is likely a function of his or her applicant pool, using policy variation in record openness should provide estimates closer to the direct effect of greater information available to employers during hiring.

Employers are apprehensive to hire ex-offenders, so opening criminal

Keith Finlay is an assistant professor of economics at Tulane University.

I am grateful to David Neumark and David Autor for extensive comments. I have also benefitted from the suggestions of Marigee Bacolod, Francesca Mazzolari, Bob Michael, Anne Polivka, and seminar participants at the 2007 Society of Labor Economists Meetings, the NBER Labor Market Intermediation Conference, the 2007 Southern Economics Association Meetings, the Public Policy Institute of California, and the NLSY97 Tenth Anniversary Conference.

history records is expected to worsen their labor market opportunities. But economic theory predicts effects for non-offenders as well. Employers have imperfect information about the criminal records of applicants, so rational employers may use observable correlates of criminality as proxies for criminality and statistically discriminate against groups with high rates of criminal activity or incarceration. In the absence of open records, non-offenders from groups with high incarceration rates would be adversely affected. When accurate criminal history records become easier to obtain, the labor market outcomes of these non-offenders should improve, as employers can determine with greater certainty whether applicants have criminal records.

This chapter tests these hypotheses, using detailed criminal and labor market histories from the 1997 cohort of the National Longitudinal Survey of Youth (NLSY97). The criminal history variables in this survey allow me to distinguish ex-offenders from non-offenders. I also use the criminal histories to model employer perceptions of criminality, assuming that they are based on rational expectations of incarceration probabilities. I find evidence that labor market outcomes are worse for ex-offenders once state criminal history records become available over the Internet, which demonstrates that employers have imperfect information about criminal histories. Non-offenders from highly offending groups do not appear, however, to have significantly better labor market outcomes. The sign of the non-offenders estimates are consistent with the predictions of the statistical discrimination model, but the estimates are not significantly different from zero. It is important to note that these estimates may be confounded by a short sample period and ongoing human capital investments.

This study makes two important contributions to the empirical literature on the labor market effects of employer use of preemployment screening technologies: it exploits an exogenous change in the employer's information set to identify the effect of that information and it uses observed criminal history data to distinguish effects for less desirable applicants (offenders) from more desirable applicants (non-offenders). The research design makes use of technological changes in the amount of criminal history data available to employers. This strategy contrasts with research that uses variation in employer decisions to conduct criminal background checks, since these decisions are likely endogenous to the composition of applicant pools. For example, Holzer, Raphael, and Stoll (2006) use establishment data on employer use of criminal background checks and preferences toward hiring ex-offenders. They find evidence that employers who are averse to hiring ex-offenders are relatively more likely to hire black men if they conduct criminal background checks. Since black men are more likely to be incarcerated than white men, they argue that this is evidence of statistical discrimination in the absence of background checks. The authors control for some observable characteristics of the applicant pool, but the employers that choose to use criminal background checks do so because of the potential of hiring an ex-offender, which generally is a quality unobservable to researchers using firm-level data. In order to get estimates that are closer to the causal effect of criminal background checks, my analysis identifies the effect of employer access to criminal records using variation that is unrelated to the proportion of ex-offenders in the affected labor markets or the hiring preferences of employers.

The research design used in this chapter is similar to one used by Autor and Scarborough (2008) to study the diffusion of preemployment personality tests at a national retail chain. They find that the relative hiring of blacks did not fall after the introduction of the tests, despite the fact that blacks in general perform worse on the tests, and they suggest that managers were effectively statistically discriminating before the tests. Both that paper and this chapter use technological changes in the employer's information set to study how more information affects groups who do poorly on the preemployment screen (e.g., personality tests or criminal background checks). This chapter also builds on this approach by exploiting longitudinal criminal history data to distinguish ex-offenders from non-offenders (or more generally, undesirable from desirable applicants). Using this information, I explicitly model employer perceptions of the criminality of potential employees using characteristics observable to both the employer and the researcher. These data allow me to estimate separate effects of expanded access to criminal histories for ex-offenders and non-offenders, which allows for a unique test for statistical discrimination.

In addition to providing an empirical test of statistical discrimination, the results of this chapter are important for understanding the transition of ex-offenders back into the legitimate labor force. As the flow of released prisoners increases over the next ten years, the issue of reentry into the legitimate labor market will force policymakers to consider the unintended consequences of open criminal history records. Legitimate employment is a strong predictor of criminal desistence (Sampson and Laub 1993; Needels 1996; Uggen 2000), so expanded use of criminal background checks has the potential to increase recidivism and the long-term fiscal costs of criminal punishment. But there may also be some beneficiaries from open records. All else equal, individuals who do not have criminal records but come from highly offending groups stand to benefit from a more transparent criminal records system.

The chapter is structured as follows. First, I outline recent changes in the availability of criminal background data and how I use these changes for this study. Then, I consider how more open criminal history records may affect ex-offenders and non-offenders, review the literature related to the labor market outcomes of ex-offenders, and review some literature on the labor market effects of preemployment screening. Next, I describe the individual-level data. Then, I discuss the empirical strategy, regression results, and conclusions.

3.2   Expanded Availability of Criminal History Data

A criminal history record positively identifies an individual and describes that person's arrests and subsequent dispositions relating to a criminal event. Until recently, they have been used primarily for law enforcement purposes. Criminal history records have been legally available to the public since the 1976 case *Paul v. Davis,* in which the Supreme Court ruled that the publication of official acts, including arrest, conviction, and incarceration records, were not protected by privacy rights.[1] Widespread use of criminal background checks as a preemployment screen is a relatively recent phenomenon that stems from expanded legal availability and technical improvements that have made records more accessible.

Employer demand for criminal background checks is driven by their aversion to hiring applicants with criminal records. Criminal offenders may have fewer skills or be more likely to commit crime at the workplace, which can expose employers to negligent-hiring lawsuits.[2] In a 2001 survey of employers, more than 60 percent would "probably not" or "definitely not" hire an ex-offender (Holzer, Raphael, and Stoll 2006). The U.S. Equal Employment Opportunity Commission (1987a, 1987b) has declared that employers may violate Title VII of the Civil Rights Act of 1964 if they broadly deny employment to applicants with criminal records, but that employers can ban applicants who have committed particular offenses if employers demonstrate these offenses are directly related to job functions. Some states have more severe restrictions, but there is little evidence of active enforcement.

Given the risks of hiring ex-offenders and the relatively low cost of conducting criminal background checks, human resource practitioners now recommend conducting checks on all hires (Andler and Herbst 2003; Rosen 2006). Evidence from employer surveys shows a large increase in the last two decades in the use of criminal background checks during the hiring process. Holzer, Raphael, and Stoll (2007) report responses from surveys of Los Angeles employers in 1992 to 1994 and 2001. In the 1992 to 1994 sample, 32 percent of employers reported that they always conducted criminal background checks. In the 2001 sample, 46 percent said they always conducted criminal background checks. In 2004, the Society for Human Resource Management surveyed its members about preemployment screen-

---

1. *Paul v. Davis,* 424 US 693 (1976).
2. Negligent hiring can occur when an employee causes injury to a customer or coworker and the employer failed to take reasonable action in hiring that could have prevented the injury. A 2004 survey of human resource managers found that 3 percent of their firms had been accused of negligent hiring in the three years before the survey (Burke 2005). Although the incidence of negligent hiring suits can be small, the potential monetary costs can be substantial. Wider availability of criminal background checks may be an important cause of increased attention to negligent hiring, since it lowers the cost of "reasonable" due diligence. See Odewahn and Webb (1989), Johnson and Indvik (1994), and Connerley, Arvey, and Bernardy (2001) for a background on negligent hiring.

ing practices. In this national sample, 68 percent responded that they always conduct criminal background checks. These samples are not directly comparable, but they suggest that employer use of criminal background checks has increased substantially over time.

Employers who conduct criminal background checks must decide who to have conduct the search and over what jurisdictions to search.[3] Private providers of background checks are plentiful, but the accuracy of their searches is not guaranteed to be any better than if an employer conducts the check on his or her own (Bushway et al. 2007). In reality, employers have no access to a *national* criminal background check. The Federal Bureau of Investigation maintains the only national repository of criminal records, known as the National Crime Information Center (NCIC), but it is not accessible by the general public. In lieu of a national search, most employers settle for a localized search of criminal records, which have historically been conducted by couriers at local courthouses. Employers seeking a wider search of criminal history data can use state databases that aggregate local and state arrest, conviction, and incarceration records.

Until the mid-1990s, there were few state-level resources for criminal background checks, but state-level databases are increasingly the most comprehensive sources of criminal history data.[4] Automation of records by the states was facilitated by the National Criminal History Improvement Program, which was mandated by the Brady Handgun Violence Prevention Act of 1993.[5] The Act imposed a five-day waiting period for firearm purchases and required that prospective gun owners clear background checks during that waiting period. The Act also stipulated that within five years of its effective date such checks should be performed instantaneously through a national criminal background check system maintained by the Department of Justice (which became the FBI's NCIC system), and allocated funds for states to automate their records. Since 1995, states have received approximately $400 million to improve data quality and speed the time between a criminal history event and when it is entered into a state-level database (Brien 2005). As a result of the Brady Act, states began to have the technical capability to make criminal history records more accessible. In the late 1990s, some states began to make these records available over the Internet. Internet-based criminal background checks are significantly more convenient than any other method and state-level aggregation increases the geographic scope of background checks, so provision of criminal history

---

3. See Rosen (2006) and Hinton (2004) for thorough discussions of criminal background check sources and reliability.

4. From 1993 to 2001, the number of individuals in state criminal record databases increased from 47 million to 64 million (SEARCH 1994, Brien 2005). Over the same period, the proportion of all criminal history records that were automated increased from 79 to 89 percent (SEARCH 1994; Brien 2005).

5. Public Law 103-159, Title I, 30 November 1993, 107 Statute 1536.

records over the Internet is one of the most significant changes in the accessibility of records since the Supreme Court declared them public records in 1976. For these reasons, I use the provision of records over the Internet as the policy variation to identify the effect of record openness on labor market outcomes of ex-offenders and non-offenders.

A state is classified as having open records if, in a given year, it provides online access to the criminal histories of individuals released from its prisons. I collected this panel of policy data directly from state departments of correction or state police agencies, starting with a cross section of policies reported by the Legal Action Center (2004). Officials were asked when their state first provided criminal history records of released prisoners over the Internet. These websites allow any member of the public to search for ex-offenders who served their time in that state's prison system. In general, this will not be all prisoners, but rather prisoners who were sentenced to a year or more of prison time in local or state (but not in federal) courts. Although this is a subset of all prisoners, it is the majority of the incarcerated population. The sites provide personal information—such as name and aliases, birthdate, physical characteristics, and race—that allow a searcher to positively identify an ex-offender. The searches also detail the offenses for which time was served, lengths of the sentences, and release dates for each offense. Some systems only identify current offenders, but this information is not useful to employers, so these states are not coded as having open records.

Figure 3.1 is a map of the United States showing the states that provide access to criminal records over the Internet, and the first year that information was available online. Between 1997 and 2004, sixteen states began to make their criminal records available over the Internet.[6] The map shows that the expansion of access to criminal history records at the state level has been geographically and temporarily dispersed—an important feature of my identification strategy. To account for time-invariant unobservable differences across states that adopt open records versus states that do not adopt open records, all empirical models include state fixed effects. All models include year fixed effects to account for the overall relative employment trends of ex-offenders. Then, the effects of opening criminal records are identified if there are no contemporaneous trends in labor market outcomes for ex-offenders relative to non-offenders in states that open records versus states that do not. If these conditions hold, this research design will yield estimates of the causal effects of greater information for employers about the criminal histories of their applicants.

6. Florida was the first state to open records in this way in 1997. It was followed by New York and Washington in 1998; Michigan and South Carolina in 1999; Georgia, Indiana, New Mexico, and Wisconsin in 2000; Kansas, Nebraska, and North Carolina in 2001; Montana and Oklahoma in 2002; and Vermont in 2003.

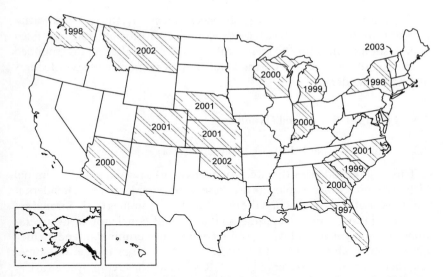

Fig. 3.1   States that distribute criminal history records over the Internet (and the first year they did so)
Source: Data collected by author, starting from a cross section available in Legal Action Center (2004).
Notes: States are shaded if they distribute the criminal history records of released prisoners over a publicly accessible Internet site.

One threat to identification of a causal effect is if states choose to make records available online based on legislative decisions related to employer preferences toward hiring ex-offenders. Fortunately, state adoption of Internet-based records searches was primarily a function of administrative decisions and the removal of technological hurdles. Of the sixteen states distributing criminal history records to the public in my sample, eight states responded to a survey by SEARCH (2006) of their governments' criminal records practices.[7] Of these, seven states were providing records over the Internet because of an administrative decision that relied on some preexisting statute. Only one state (Oklahoma) was opening records by a direct order of legislation. This evidence suggests that the timing of record openness was not primarily a result of specific legislation. In another survey by SEARCH (2001), state officials responsible for criminal history records emphasized the importance of technical issues in determining when records went online. The statements of these officials support the argument that the limiting factor in the public provision of criminal history data over the Internet was

7. SEARCH, the National Consortium for Justice Information and Statistics, has conducted surveys of criminal records systems on behalf of the Bureau of Justice Statistics.

technology rather than political preferences.[8] Therefore, the temporal variation in introduction of open records, combined with state and year fixed
effects, should allow for the identification of the causal effect of expanded
access to criminal records on the labor market outcomes of ex-offenders
and non-offenders.

3.3   Literature Review and Hypotheses

3.3.1   Labor Market Effects of Incarceration

This chapter addresses the effects of changes in the availability of criminal
history records. Since employers use these records to identify ex-offenders, it
would be useful to first discuss the literature that examines the labor market
effects of incarceration. Determining the effect of conviction or incarceration on employment and wages is nontrivial, since criminal offenders may
have unobservable qualities that affect both their labor market outcomes
and their propensities to commit crime. Researchers have employed a variety
of methods to identify unbiased estimates of the effect of incarceration on
employment and wages. Grogger (1995) compares the labor market outcomes of offenders before and after periods of incarceration. Kling (2006)
uses variation in judge sentencing to instrument for individual sentence
length. Another strategy is to use more homogeneous samples, such as
those that will ever be convicted or incarcerated, an approach used by Grogger (1995), Western (2002), and Kling (2006). This literature tends to find
small, negative, statistically significant effects of incarceration on wages and
employment without sample restrictions. Once less heterogeneous samples
or fixed-effects strategies are used, estimates attenuate and commonly
become insignificant.[9] Following this literature, some of the specifications
in this chapter use individual fixed effects to account for unobservable het-

---

8. For example, Dave Sim of the Kansas Bureau of Investigation alludes to a learning process
in administrative agencies with respect to providing criminal history data over the Internet:

> Kansas maintains a prototype system that provides select non-criminal justice entities with
> Internet access to criminal history record information. The State will expand access to all
> users when it migrates from the prototype to its final design later in 2001. The system was
> designed primarily for criminal justice agencies but Kansas provided limited non-criminal
> justice access as it gained experience with Internet operations. (SEARCH 2001)

In the same survey, Ruth Lunn of the Maine State Police reported that Maine had not even
begun the automation process necessary to provide records over the Internet (SEARCH 2001).
Her responses do not mention statute as the limiting factor in providing records, but rather the
technological issues. David Dishong of the Nebraska State Patrol also suggested that the timing
of public access to records over the Internet was a function of "programming and procedural
issues" (SEARCH 2001).

9. Almost all prisoners are male, so most studies of the labor market effects of incarceration
use only samples of men. But in a recent study of women incarcerated in Illinois, Cho and
LaLonde (2008) find some positive effects of incarceration on earnings.

erogeneity. My research also complements this literature by exploring how employers learn about the criminal records of potential employees.

3.3.2 Labor Market Effects of Criminal Background Checks

Since employers have a strong aversion to hiring ex-offenders and since criminal history records have recently become more accessible, it is not surprising that the use of criminal background checks has increased at the same time the number of ex-offenders has increased. Given the large racial differential in incarceration rates, the small literature on the labor market effects of criminal background checks has focused on how greater use of or access to criminal records affects the relative hiring or employment rates of black men. While the theory of statistical discrimination predicts that open records will worsen the outcomes of black ex-offenders and improve the outcomes of black non-offenders, the theory is ambiguous about the net effect for blacks relative to whites. None of the existing studies of criminal history records rely on data that distinguishes ex-offenders from non-offenders, so the authors focus on the net effect for blacks relative to whites.

Holzer, Raphael, and Stall (2006) use establishment data on employer use of criminal background checks and preferences toward hiring ex-offenders. They argue that firms that prefer not to hire ex-offenders will be more likely to hire black applicants if they also conduct background checks. Employers who state an aversion to hiring ex-offenders are more sensitive to asymmetric information with respect to the criminal records of job candidates. Therefore, these employers have a stronger incentive to statistically discriminate, and so the relative hiring of blacks should be more positively affected once these firms conduct criminal background checks. The authors find evidence that supports this hypothesis and indicates that employers do statistically discriminate. But employers who conduct criminal background checks may also have applicant pools with a higher proportion of applicants who are black or have criminal records. Some of the estimated parameters of interest are not significantly different from zero once the authors control for the composition of each firm's applicant pool. Nonetheless, the study is an important look at the effects of criminal background checks and the results provide some evidence that opening records may lead to net benefits for individuals from highly offending groups.

In the first attempt to examine the availability of records across states, Bushway (1996) finds that the weekly earnings of young black men with a high school degree were higher in states that had more of their criminal history records automated—a measure he argues can serve as a proxy for record accessibility. In other work, Bushway (2004) uses a composite record openness score generated by the Legal Action Center (2004). He finds that the ratio of black to white wages was higher and the ratio of black to white employment probabilities was lower in states that had higher openness scores, although neither estimate is significant. The estimated effect on wages is consistent with large drops in employment if it is primarily low-skilled black men that are dropping out of the labor market. While Bushway is the first to use state variation to measure the labor market effects of criminal background checks, his work is cross-sectional, so it does not control for unobserved differences in labor markets across states particular to black men that are correlated with criminal records automation or accessibility. My research design builds on Bushway's work by using a panel of state policies regarding criminal history records, which should better isolate the direct effect of employer access to records on labor market outcomes.

In a very different research design, Pager (2003) conducted an audit study of the effect of criminal records. In the study, four male, college-educated auditors each applied to low-skill job listings in Milwaukee. One pair was black, one pair was white, and one of each pair identified himself as having a criminal record. The callback rate for ex-offenders was less than half of the callback rate for non-offenders. Pager also finds that the callback rate for the black, ex-offender applicants was lower than the callback rate for the white, ex-offender applicants, controlling for a lower overall callback rate for all black applicants, although the interaction estimate is not significantly different from zero. Pager's results suggest that the labor market effects of incarceration are tied to the effects of race in the labor market. The results also highlight the difficulty that ex-offenders have in gaining employment after release.

While these studies have examined the net effect of access to criminal histories on blacks relative to whites, economic theory predicts more nuanced effects for non-offenders and ex-offenders that may result from statistical discrimination by employers. If employers are averse to hiring ex-offenders, then they have an incentive to use observable correlates of criminality or incarceration as proxies for those qualities. Using these proxies, employers can classify individuals as coming from groups with low rates of incarceration (or low perceived criminality) or high rates of incarceration (high perceived criminality). In the absence of open records, one would observe an averaging of the labor market outcomes for individuals within either group. For example, black men who are high school dropouts have very high incarceration rates. If employers statistically discriminate, then the outcomes for black non-offenders that have not completed high school will be relatively worse than they would have been without statistical discrimination, but ex-offenders from that group will have relatively better outcomes. Similarly, white ex-offenders should benefit from statistical discrimination because they come from a group with relatively low rates of incarceration.

Now suppose that criminal history records become publicly available. If employers can directly observe criminal history records, they no longer need to rely on statistical discrimination. This will cause a separation in the labor market outcomes of ex-offenders and non-offenders within highly offending groups. Specifically, ex-offenders should do worse and non-offenders should

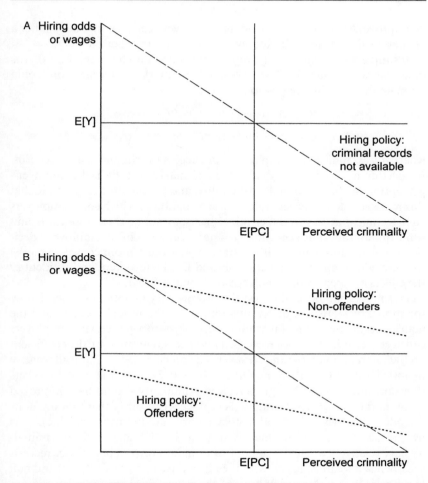

Fig. 3.2   Statistical discrimination model with criminal history records: *A*, Criminal records not publicly available; *B*, Criminal records available

have improved labor market outcomes. Figure 3.2 illustrates the main features of the model. Each panel shows a plot of labor market outcomes (hiring odds or wages) against an index of perceived criminality. Perceived criminality is an index created by the employer using observable proxy variables as a substitute for observed criminality. Panel A shows the hiring policy when criminal records are not available to employers. The dotted line shows that labor market outcomes are decreasing in perceived criminality. Panel B shows the hiring policy when criminal records are available to employers. In this case, there would be a bifurcation from the hiring policy under closed records. Now that employers can distinguish offenders from non-offenders, the labor market outcomes of non-offenders with high perceived criminality improve. Also note that offenders with low perceived criminality suffer a greater decline in labor market outcomes relative to other offenders.

A simple empirical model can capture the main characteristics of the model shown in figure 3.2. For a relevant labor market outcome Y, one could estimate the following regression:

$$(1) \quad Y = \beta_0 + \beta_1 PC + \beta_2 Access \cdot Inc + \beta_3 PC \cdot Access$$
$$+ \beta_4 PC \cdot Access \cdot Inc + \beta_5 PC \cdot Inc + \beta_6 Access + \beta_7 Inc + \varepsilon,$$

where *Access* indicates if employers have access to criminal history records, *Inc* is a dummy for an individual's own criminal record, *PC* is the employer's perception of the individual's criminality, and ε is an error term. Note that this model could apply generally to any situation in which some employers have technical access to the criminal history data of their applicants and some do not (and this accessibility is not a function of an employer's decision). For the moment, I will abstract away from a more complete model that includes the individual controls and fixed effects required to identify the effects of open records in my institutional context.

This model can be used to test the two primary hypotheses generated by the model of statistical discrimination. First, the model predicts that the main effect of true criminality should become more negative when employers can access criminal history records. This effect is captured by the coefficient on the interaction of *Inc* and *Access,* so it can be tested with the alternative hypothesis $\beta_2 < 0$ and null hypothesis $\beta_2 \geq 0$. Second, the model predicts that non-offenders with high perceived criminality should have improved labor market outcomes if potential employers can verify that they are non-offenders (i.e., when criminal history records are publicly available). This hypothesis mirrors one in which ex-offenders with high perceived criminality have relatively worse outcomes from similar non-offenders once records are open. This can be tested with the alternative hypothesis $\beta_3 < 0$ and null hypothesis $\beta_3 \geq 0$. Note that both of these hypotheses test relative and not absolute effects of employer access to criminal history data.

This statistical discrimination framework will guide the empirical approach that follows. First, I discuss the individual data on criminal and labor market histories that will be used to estimate the model suggested earlier.

3.4   Data

This chapter uses the criminal and labor market histories from the 1997 cohort of the National Longitudinal Survey of Youth (NLSY97). The NLSY97 includes a nationally representative sample of all youths aged twelve to sixteen years by the end of 1996, and an oversample of black and Hispanic youths meeting the same age restriction. Currently, the NLSY97 has released eight rounds of data, covering interviews from 1997 through

Table 3.1   Number of NLSY97 respondents aged eighteen years or older, by age and survey year, 1997–2004

Ages	1997	1998	1999	2000	2001	2002	2003	2004	Total
18	21	1,407	1,618	1,648	1,597	1,613	113	0	7,996
19	0	109	1,380	1,595	1,587	1,583	1,497	52	7,803
20	0	0	67	1,381	1,560	1,638	1,597	1,444	7,687
21	0	0	0	133	1,318	1,576	1,583	1,508	6,118
22	0	0	0	0	108	1,322	1,559	1,551	4,540
23	0	0	0	0	0	111	1,291	1,524	2,926
24	0	0	0	0	0	0	79	1,288	1,367
25	0	0	0	0	0	0	0	97	97
Total	21	1,516	3,065	4,757	6,170	7,843	7,719	7,464	38,555

2004. The NLSY97 is an excellent sample for this project because it has information about both the criminal activity of respondents and their labor market outcomes. This is a rare quality for a nationally representative survey, and the NLSY97 is especially useful because the sample period coincides with the introduction of Internet sites for accessing criminal history records. The criminal records policies discussed previously are matched with individual respondents using the state geocodes available in the private-release version of the NLSY97. There are a few drawbacks of using the NLSY97 for this research. This is a very young sample, when the first states make their records available online. While young people are the most likely to be incarcerated, many of the survey respondents are still completing their schooling at or near the end of the sample period. This limits the extent to which the labor market outcomes of NLSY97 respondents can reasonably be affected by changes in criminal records openness. Table 3.1 shows the number of NLSY97 respondents aged more than eighteen years, by age and survey year. It shows the small range of adult ages available in Round 8 of the NLSY97, the most recent survey year. The oldest survey participants have aged twenty-five years, but few individuals have reached this age in the sample period.

The sample I use in regression analysis consists of men and women aged at least eighteen years, covering survey years 1997 to 2004. Because of the particular importance of clearly identifying race and ethnicity for this analysis, the sample is further restricted to respondents who are either non-Hispanic white, non-Hispanic black, or Hispanic. I use both the representative sample and the minority oversample with sampling weights.[10] Table 3.2 shows how the sample restrictions affect the number of individuals and panel observations. Up to Round 8, the NLSY97 is composed of 64,336 completed interviews from 8,984 survey participants. With the age, race, and ethnicity

10. Custom sampling weights for NLSY97 respondents in any survey year come from http://www.nlsinfo.org/web-investigator/custom_weights.php.

Table 3.2   NLSY97 sample restrictions

Iterative sample restrictions	Panel observations	Individuals
Completed interviews	64,336	8,984
	−25,781	−325
Aged 18 or more years	38,555	8,659
	−1,439	−325
White, black, or Hispanic	37,116	8,334
	−2	−2
Nonzero sampling weights	37,114	8,332
	−427	−28
Not incarcerated during interview	36,687	8,304
	−359	−359
More than one interview (effective variation for individual fixed effects models)	36,328	7,945

Note: The last two sample restrictions apply only to the samples for the regressions of labor market outcomes.

restrictions, the analytic sample is reduced to 37,114 observations on 8,332 respondents.[11] In regressions of labor market outcomes, I also exclude individuals who are incarcerated at the time of their interviews since those incarcerations might mechanically determine employment and earnings in a way that is unrelated to employer decisions. This restriction leaves 36,687 observations from 8,304 individuals. In regressions that exploit within-individual variation in labor market outcomes, identification effectively comes from the 7,945 individuals who have at least two interviews (36,328 observations).

I use three labor market outcomes as dependent variables: employment status, the natural logarithm of hourly wage, and the natural logarithm of annual earnings. Employment status is equal to 1 if the respondent was employed at the date of the interview. Hourly wage is the maximum of the NLSY-created hourly wage variables for each job held since the last interview. The earnings variable is the total income from wages and salary in the calendar year before the interview.[12] Employment status is observed for all respondents (36,687 observations), while there are only 30,145 positive observations for wages and only 27,137 positive observations for annual earnings.

The NLSY97 also has extensive information on interactions with the criminal justice system.[13] Incarceration information comes from two types

11. In addition, two observations are dropped because they have sampling weights equal to zero.
12. Wages and earnings are inflated to 2005 dollars using the All-Urban series of the Consumer Price Index.
13. The criminal history data in the NLSY97 is used by Lochner (2007) to study how young people update arrest probabilities and by Hjalmarsson (2008) to study the effect of conviction and incarceration on high school completion. These papers focus on criminal justice interactions as a minor, while this chapter focuses on adult interactions.

of questions. First, if the interview was conducted at a jail or the respondent classified his or her dwelling as a correctional institution, this was noted. Second, an iterative round of questions addressed any arrests and whether they led to conviction or incarceration. I created indicator variables for whether the respondent was incarcerated at the time of the interview or since the date of the last interview. Since this research is about criminal history records that are limited to adult offenses, I also constructed incarceration indicators that are restricted to adult offenses.[14] Finally, a variable was created to indicate whether the respondent had ever been incarcerated as an adult by the date of the current interview.[15]

I also include a number of other variables as controls. To control for labor market experience, I use the years of accumulated labor market experience from age thirteen. Education controls include accumulated years of school attended since age thirteen and a set of dummies for highest degree received as of June 30 of the survey year (namely, whether the individual has a general equivalency diploma [GED], a high school diploma, an associate's degree, or a bachelor's or postgraduate degree). To account for macroeconomic conditions, the state-level unemployment rate is also included as a control. In regressions without individual fixed effects, the Armed Services Vocational Aptitude Battery (ASVAB) test score and race, ethnicity, and gender indicators serve as controls.

3.4.1 Descriptive Statistics

Table 3.3 shows selected descriptive statistics for labor market outcomes, incarceration, and other covariates from the last survey round in which NLSY97 respondents participated. The employment rate at the end of the sample is 72 percent. The average wage is $12.15 and the average annual earnings are about $10,400. Four percent of the sample has been incarcerated as an adult. The average age in the last reported interview is almost twenty-two years. Respondents report average work experience of about seven years, which includes work experience as a minor. Average completed schooling is almost thirteen years, although 30 percent of the sample is still enrolled in school at the end of the sample.

Table 3.3 also details how ex-offenders and non-offenders differ across observable characteristics. Ex-offenders are significantly less likely than non-offenders to be employed (59 percent versus 72 percent, respectively). Despite the employment differential, the hourly wages of ex-offenders are not significantly different from the hourly wages of non-offenders (although

---

14. It is difficult to determine in which state each respondent experienced his or her conviction or incarceration, so I cannot make a clean determination if an individual's records are definitely available to employers in his or her state of residence if he or she has moved across states. Luckily, there are relatively few interstate moves.

15. Studies of post-incarceration employment have found no significant effect of longer sentences on labor market outcomes (Needels 1996; Kling 2006), so I focus on the binomial characterization of past incarceration.

Table 3.3   **Selected descriptive statistics of variables from the last survey round in which each NLSY97 respondent participated, by adult incarceration history**

Variable	All respondents	Incarcerated as an adult	Not incarcerated as an adult
Employment status	0.72	0.59	0.72
	8,304	369	7,935
Hourly wage	12.15	11.85	12.16
	(6.54)	(5.80)	(6.57)
	6,744	290	6,454
Annual earnings	10,402.22	7,304.67	10,546.74
	(12,010.67)	(8,824.73)	(12,120.02)
	8,166	364	7,802
Ever incarcerated as an adult	0.04	1.00	0.00
	8,304	369	7,935
Age	21.74	22.22	21.72
	(1.57)	(1.52)	(1.57)
	8,304	369	7,935
Highest grade completed	12.80	11.21	12.87
	(1.90)	(1.61)	(1.88)
	8,304	369	7,935
Currently enrolled in school	0.30	0.08	0.31
	8,304	369	7,935
Has GED	0.06	0.19	0.05
	8,304	369	7,935
Has HS diploma	0.67	0.32	0.69
	8,304	369	7,935
Has associate's	0.03	0.01	0.03
	8,304	369	7,935
Has bachelor's or more	0.08	0.04	0.08
	8,304	369	7,935
Years of school attended since age 13	8.70	9.17	8.68
	(1.55)	(1.49)	(1.55)
	8,304	369	7,935
Years of labor market experience since age 13	6.78	6.81	6.78
	(2.29)	(2.74)	(2.26)
	8,304	369	7,935
Armed Services Vocational Aptitude Battery score	45.05	27.61	45.79
	(29.18)	(24.52)	(29.13)
	6,642	270	6,372
Lives in state with criminal records Internet site	0.37	0.39	0.37
	8,304	369	7,935

Notes: Cells contain the mean, standard deviation (where applicable), and number of nonmissing observations for each variable within the given sample. The sample used to generate these descriptive statistics excludes individuals who are incarcerated at the time of their interviews. See table 3.2 for a complete description of the sample restrictions.

Table 3.4   **Percentage of NLSY97 respondents who report having been incarcerated as an adult since the date of their last interview, by age, gender, and race/ethnicity, 1997–2004**

	Respondent age						
Subsample	18	19	20	21	22	23	24
White males	1.80	2.18	2.13	1.82	2.34	1.98	0.96
	$n = 1,996$	$n = 1,969$	$n = 1,925$	$n = 1,537$	$n = 1,111$	$n = 708$	$n = 312$
Black males	4.51	5.92	7.03	7.85	8.18	6.38	7.82
	$n = 1,043$	$n = 1,014$	$n = 981$	$n = 790$	$n = 599$	$n = 376$	$n = 179$
Hispanic males	2.25	2.57	2.75	4.40	2.94	3.11	1.37
	$n = 844$	$n = 818$	$n = 800$	$n = 659$	$n = 476$	$n = 322$	$n = 146$
White females	0.32	0.21	0.49	0.41	0.28	0.15	1.01
	$n = 1,903$	$n = 1,866$	$n = 1,829$	$n = 1,458$	$n = 1,089$	$n = 687$	$n = 298$
Black females	0.56	0.49	0.38	0.50	0.32	0.48	0.43
	$n = 1,076$	$n = 1,023$	$n = 1,053$	$n = 807$	$n = 625$	$n = 421$	$n = 231$
Hispanic females	0.12	0.74	0.37	0.77	0.42	0.65	0.00
	$n = 833$	$n = 815$	$n = 807$	$n = 648$	$n = 477$	$n = 307$	$n = 147$

Notes: Each cell contains the proportion as a percentage of respondents who are incarcerated as an adult sometime in the given age and the sample size. Age twenty-five is excluded because of small sample sizes.

the mean is lower for ex-offenders, the difference is not significantly different from zero). This might be explained by the higher rate of school enrollment of non-offenders (31 percent of non-offenders are enrolled, but only 8 percent of ex-offenders are enrolled). Ex-offenders also have fewer years of completed schooling and less labor market experience. Finally, the table shows that the proportion of individuals who live in states that provide criminal history data over the Internet is qualitatively similar across offender status. In the analytic sample, 39 percent of respondents who have been incarcerated live in such a state, while 37 percent of the other respondents live in open-records states.

Table 3.4 shows the age profiles for adult incarceration rates of NLSY97 respondents, broken down by gender, race, and ethnicity.[16] The differences in incarceration probabilities across both gender and race are stark. Black males are about four times as likely as white males to be incarcerated at any particular age. Hispanic males are somewhat more likely to be incarcerated than white males, but not to the same extent as blacks. For example, of males aged twenty-two years, 8.2 percent of black respondents were incarcerated, while 3.0 percent of Hispanic males and 2.3 percent of white males were incarcerated. Males of any race are significantly more likely to be incarcerated than their female counterparts. These incarceration rates are qualitatively similar for men of these ages from other data sources, although the rates are somewhat lower. Using data from the 2000 Census, Raphael

16. Age twenty-five is excluded because of small sample sizes.

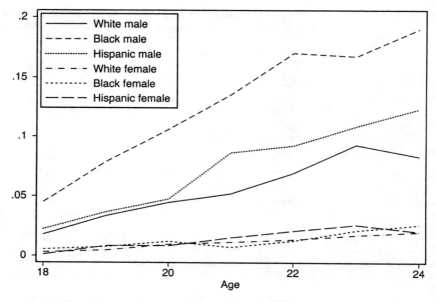

Fig. 3.3   Cumulative proportion of NLSY97 respondents who have been incarcerated as an adult by age, gender, and race/ethnicity, 1997–2004

Notes: Plot shows the cumulative proportion of each subsample that has been incarcerated as an adult by the appropriate age. Age twenty-five is excluded because of small sample sizes. Lines are not all monotonic because not all respondents reach twenty-four years of age by the end of the sample, some respondents miss interviews, and some respondents attrit.

(2006) reports that 11 percent of black men aged eighteen to twenty-five years and 2 percent of white men aged eighteen to twenty-five years were incarcerated. This suggests that incarceration is somewhat underreported in the NLSY97.[17]

Figure 3.3 and table 3.5 show the cumulative age profiles for adult-incarceration rates of NLSY97 respondents, broken down by gender, race, and ethnicity. The gender and racial patterns of the age-specific incarceration probabilities are also seen in the cumulative rates. (Note that the cumulative rates are not monotonic because of the age structure of the respondents and survey non-response and attrition.) By age twenty-four, almost 19 percent of black men have been incarcerated as an adult, while about 8 percent of white men and about 12 percent of Hispanic men have been incarcerated as an adult. These cumulative rates are qualitatively consistent with published rates from the Bureau of Justice Statistics (Bonczar and Beck 1997; Bonczar 2003).

17. Survey respondents are known to underreport criminal activity, and these underreports tend to be larger for blacks (Hindelang, Hirschi, and Weis 1981; Viscusi 1986; Abe 2001).

Table 3.5　　　**Cumulative percentage of NLSY97 respondents who report having been incarcerated as an adult by interview date, by age, gender, and race/ethnicity, 1997–2004**

	Respondent age						
Subsample	18	19	20	21	22	23	24
White males	1.80	3.35	4.47	5.20	6.93	9.32	8.33
	$n = 1,996$	$n = 1,969$	$n = 1,925$	$n = 1,537$	$n = 1,111$	$n = 708$	$n = 312$
Black males	4.51	7.89	10.60	13.54	17.03	16.76	18.99
	$n = 1,043$	$n = 1,014$	$n = 981$	$n = 790$	$n = 599$	$n = 376$	$n = 179$
Hispanic males	2.25	3.67	4.75	8.65	9.24	10.87	12.33
	$n = 844$	$n = 818$	$n = 800$	$n = 659$	$n = 476$	$n = 322$	$n = 146$
White females	0.32	0.48	0.98	1.17	1.38	1.75	2.01
	$n = 1,903$	$n = 1,866$	$n = 1,829$	$n = 1,458$	$n = 1,089$	$n = 687$	$n = 298$
Black females	0.56	0.78	1.23	0.74	1.28	2.14	2.60
	$n = 1,076$	$n = 1,023$	$n = 1,053$	$n = 807$	$n = 625$	$n = 421$	$n = 231$
Hispanic females	0.12	0.86	0.87	1.54	2.10	2.61	2.04
	$n = 833$	$n = 815$	$n = 807$	$n = 648$	$n = 477$	$n = 307$	$n = 147$

Notes: Each cell contains the cumulative percentage of respondents who have been incarcerated as an adult by the given age and the sample size.

Age twenty-five is excluded because of small sample sizes. Proportions are not all monotonically increasing because not all respondents reach age twenty-four by the end of the sample, some respondents miss interviews, and there is attrition.

3.5　Regression Results

This section presents regression results of the labor market effects of more open criminal history records. First, I focus on the effects for ex-offenders. Then, I examine how more open criminal history records affect the labor market outcomes of both ex-offenders and non-offenders from highly offending groups.

3.5.1　Access to Criminal History Data and the Employment Effects of Incarceration

There are a number of reasons to believe that employer access to criminal history data may influence the labor market effects of incarceration. First, employers in states that do not have open criminal records may have trouble distinguishing ex-offenders from non-offenders, so adoption of open records should adversely affect the labor market outcomes of ex-offenders relative to non-offenders. Second, if employers are risk averse, the negative labor market effects of incarceration may last longer under an open criminal records policy. Moreover, even higher-productivity ex-offenders may have longer lasting employment problems if employer risk aversion prevents them from being hired in the first place. Finally, if employers also underestimate the degree of criminality among applicants, then greater employer access to criminal history records may also harm offenders, on average, without necessarily benefiting non-offenders.

The effect of wider availability of criminal history records on the labor market outcomes of ex-offenders is estimated in the following regression:

(2) $$Y_{ist} = \delta_0 + X_{ist}\delta_1 + \delta_2 Inc_{it} + \delta_3 Access_{st} + \delta_4 Access_{st}Inc_{it}$$
$$+ \gamma_s + \gamma_t + v_{ist},$$

where Y_{ist} is a relevant labor market outcome of individual i living in state s in year t, Inc_{it} is equal to 1 if individual i has been incarcerated as an adult by year t, and $Access_{st}$ is equal to 1 if state s has an Internet site in year t on which the public can search for the incarceration records of ex-offenders. State fixed effects γ_s account for any time-invariant differences across states that adopt open records and states that do not. Year effects γ_s account for any secular changes in labor market outcomes. The vector of individual controls, X, is discussed previously, and v is the error term. In order to meaningfully interpret the coefficient on $Access$, each continuous covariate in this vector is centered by its mean from each regression's respective sample. The parameter of interest δ_4 is the difference in the employment outcomes between ex-offenders in states with more open records versus ex-offenders in states with more closed records.

Table 3.6 shows the estimates from equation (2) for each labor market outcome, using two identification strategies. In the odd-numbered columns, the parameters are identified off of the state and time variation in the introduction of the provision of criminal history records over the Internet. These specifications treat the data as repeated cross sections and use state and year fixed effects for identification. In the even-numbered columns, the parameters are identified off of changes in both offender status and perceived criminality, in addition to the temporal and spatial variation in the introduction of open records. These specifications exploit the panel structure of the NLSY97 and include individual fixed effects and year effects, but exclude the state effects and time-invariant controls.[18]

Employment status is the dependent variable in columns (1) and (2). In columns (3) and (4), the dependent variable is the log of hourly wages. And in columns (5) and (6), the dependent variable is annual earnings. For each identification strategy, the table shows results with and without the open records variables included. I first replicate the basic results of how incarceration affects labor market outcomes. While a number of papers have considered these effects using other data, I know of no other papers that estimate labor market effects of incarceration using the more recent NLSY97. By first estimating the incarceration effects with this new data, we can interpret the estimated effects of background checks in the context of previous estimates

18. Given the small number of interstate moves, state fixed effects are not included in specifications with individual fixed effects.

Table 3.6 Regressions of labor market outcomes on incarceration and criminal records policy variables, NLSY97, 1997–2004

Covariates	Emp. (1a)	Emp. (1b)	Emp. (2a)	Emp. (2b)	LnWage (3a)	LnWage (3b)	LnWage (4a)	LnWage (4b)	LnEarn. (5a)	LnEarn. (5b)	LnEarn. (6a)	LnEarn. (6b)
Has been incarcerated?	−0.088	−0.082	−0.029	−0.010	−0.017	−0.005	−0.029	0.003	−0.152	−0.159	−0.192	−0.114
	(0.020)	(0.018)	(0.021)	(0.025)	(0.022)	(0.029)	(0.019)	(0.023)	(0.052)	(0.072)	(0.080)	(0.098)
Access × incarcerated		−0.015		−0.050		−0.029		−0.087		0.015		−0.187
		(0.040)		(0.035)		(0.040)		(0.024)		(0.099)		(0.104)
Access		−0.014		−0.024		−0.005		−0.025		−0.014		−0.056
		(0.017)		(0.013)		(0.016)		(0.010)		(0.037)		(0.025)
Has GED	0.070	0.070	0.006	0.006	0.052	0.052	0.008	0.008	0.348	0.348	−0.009	−0.008
	(0.018)	(0.018)	(0.016)	(0.016)	(0.016)	(0.016)	(0.018)	(0.018)	(0.057)	(0.058)	(0.059)	(0.059)
Has HS diploma	0.133	0.133	0.021	0.021	0.060	0.060	0.020	0.020	0.174	0.174	0.067	0.068
	(0.007)	(0.007)	(0.012)	(0.012)	(0.010)	(0.010)	(0.012)	(0.012)	(0.027)	(0.027)	(0.038)	(0.038)
Has associate's	0.216	0.216	0.008	0.008	0.138	0.138	0.078	0.078	0.316	0.316	0.067	0.066
	(0.026)	(0.026)	(0.027)	(0.027)	(0.034)	(0.034)	(0.029)	(0.029)	(0.079)	(0.079)	(0.055)	(0.055)
Has bachelor's plus	0.184	0.184	0.151	0.150	0.226	0.226	0.219	0.218	0.062	0.062	0.245	0.243
	(0.011)	(0.011)	(0.021)	(0.021)	(0.019)	(0.019)	(0.018)	(0.018)	(0.051)	(0.051)	(0.048)	(0.048)
Years attended since 1	0.016	0.016	0.043	0.045	−0.002	−0.002	0.103	0.106	0.097	0.097	0.335	0.345
	(0.011)	(0.011)	(0.024)	(0.024)	(0.011)	(0.011)	(0.017)	(0.018)	(0.032)	(0.032)	(0.031)	(0.033)
Years exp. since 13	0.002	0.002	0.006	0.006	0.004	0.004	−0.000	−0.000	0.010	0.010	−0.0003	−0.0003
	(0.002)	(0.002)	(0.002)	(0.002)	(0.002)	(0.002)	(0.002)	(0.002)	(0.005)	(0.005)	(0.0037)	(0.0037)
Age	0.075	0.075	0.238	0.238	0.100	0.100	0.138	0.137	0.977	0.977	1.115	1.114
	(0.039)	(0.039)	(0.032)	(0.032)	(0.033)	(0.033)	(0.031)	(0.031)	(0.127)	(0.127)	(0.096)	(0.096)
Age^2	−0.001	−0.001	−0.006	−0.006	−0.001	−0.001	−0.003	−0.003	−0.019	−0.019	−0.027	−0.027
	(0.001)	(0.001)	(0.001)	(0.001)	(0.001)	(0.001)	(0.001)	(0.001)	(0.003)	(0.003)	(0.002)	(0.002)

(continued)

Table 3.6 (continued)

Covariates	Emp. (1a)	Emp. (1b)	Emp. (2a)	Emp. (2b)	LnWage (3a)	LnWage (3b)	LnWage (4a)	LnWage (4b)	LnEarn. (5a)	LnEarn. (5b)	LnEarn. (6a)	LnEarn. (6b)
ASVAB	0.0002	0.0002			0.0008	0.0008			-0.0025	-0.0025		
	(0.0001)	(0.0001)			(0.0002)	(0.0002)			(0.0005)	(0.0005)		
Missing ASVAB	-0.003	-0.003			0.044	0.044			-0.078	-0.078		
	(0.008)	(0.008)			(0.013)	(0.013)			(0.037)	(0.038)		
Black male	-0.108	-0.108			-0.065	-0.065			-0.312	-0.312		
	(0.015)	(0.015)			(0.012)	(0.013)			(0.042)	(0.042)		
Hispanic male	0.017	0.017			-0.032	-0.033			0.020	0.020		
	(0.019)	(0.019)			(0.014)	(0.014)			(0.044)	(0.044)		
Female	-0.039	-0.039			-0.099	-0.099			-0.323	-0.323		
	(0.010)	(0.010)			(0.011)	(0.011)			(0.022)	(0.022)		
Unemployment rate	-0.004	-0.003	-0.005	-0.004	-0.007	-0.007	-0.012	-0.011	-0.029	-0.029	-0.022	-0.019
	(0.007)	(0.007)	(0.005)	(0.005)	(0.006)	(0.006)	(0.006)	(0.006)	(0.017)	(0.017)	(0.015)	(0.014)
Specification												
Year effects	x	x	x	x	x	x	x	x	x	x	x	x
State effects	x	x			x	x			x	x		
Individual effects			x	x			x	x			x	x
Observations	36,687	36,687	36,687	36,687	30,145	30,145	30,145	30,145	27,137	27,137	27,137	27,137
R^2	0.05	0.05	0.04	0.04	0.15	0.15	0.14	0.14	0.25	0.25	0.35	0.35

Notes: Heteroscedasticity-robust standard errors that are clustered at the state level are in parentheses. Sample consists of NLSY97 respondents aged eighteen to twenty-five years. See table 3.2 for a complete description of the sample restrictions. Each continuous covariate is centered by its mean from each regression's respective sample. Full regression results available from the author on request. Employment-status regressions are linear probability models.

of incarceration effects. This exercise will also verify the reliability of the incarceration variables from the NLSY97, which are used to distinguish ex-offenders from non-offenders.

For each labor market outcome, the first of the paired, odd-numbered columns in table 3.6 shows the effects of incarceration in a repeated cross-sectional model. In these specifications, ex-offenders are 8.8 percentage points less likely to be employed than non-offenders (column [1a]), have wages that are only 1.7 percent less than those of non-offenders (column [3a]), and have annual earnings that are 15 percent less than the earnings of non-offenders (column [5a]). The differences in employment probabilities and earnings are significantly different from zero, while the difference in wages is not. As mentioned before, the result for wages may be attenuated by the ongoing relative school enrollment rate of non-offenders. Since ex-offenders and non-offenders may differ systematically in unobservable ways, a second set of specifications in table 3.6 exploits the panel structure of the data with individual fixed effects. In these models, the effect of incarceration on employment is smaller in absolute value (−2.9 percentage points) and no longer significantly different from zero (column [2a]). In the panel setting, the wages of ex-offenders are 2.9 percent lower than those of non-offenders, but the estimate is still not significantly different from zero (column [4a]). Earnings are still lower for ex-offenders and the estimate is significantly different from zero (column [6a]).

I now turn to the estimates of the effect of the openness of criminal history records on the labor market outcomes of ex-offenders. These estimates can be found next to their respective models without the open records variables. In the repeated cross-sectional models, the sign on the estimated coefficient *Access · Inc* is negative for employment status and log wages, but positive for log earnings—indicating that ex-offenders are less likely to be employed, have lower wages, but higher earnings in states with Internet sites providing information about ex-offenders (columns [1b], [3b], and [5b]). But none of these parameter estimates is statistically significant, which suggests it is difficult to identify the relative effects of open records using only state and time variation in record openness. The specifications in the even columns additionally identify the effect of open records using individual changes in offender status. Each of these models includes individual fixed effects, but excludes the state effects and time-invariant controls. For all three labor market outcomes in the panel models, the sign of the estimated coefficient on *Access · Inc* is negative, indicating that ex-offenders are less likely to be employed, have lower wages, and lower earnings in states with Internet sites providing information about ex-offenders. In particular, the employment probabilities of ex-offenders are 5 percentage points lower in open-records states, but the estimate is not significantly different from zero (column [2b]). The wages of ex-offenders are 8.7 percent lower in open-records states, and this estimate is significantly different from zero (column [4b]). The earnings of ex-offenders are 18.7 percent lower in open-records states (column [6b]). This estimate is significantly different at the 0.1 level of significance. What is striking about these estimates is that they overshadow the main effect of incarceration in those regressions. In the wage regression (column [4b]), the main effect of incarceration is indistinguishable from zero and very small relative to the marginal effect of open records. This suggests that the availability of information about criminal histories plays a major role in determining the labor market outcomes of ex-offenders.

These results show that greater employer access to criminal histories is associated with worse labor market outcomes for ex-offenders. This evidence demonstrates the presence of imperfect information about criminal histories by employers. If employers had perfect information about the potential criminality of applicants, then greater access to criminal histories would not change the employment and wage outcomes of ex-offenders. The combination of imperfect information about applicant criminality and employer aversion to hiring ex-offenders is a strong motivation for employers to statistically discriminate. I now investigate whether such statistical discrimination occurs by examining the relative outcomes of non-offenders from highly offending groups.

3.5.2   Expanded Access to Criminal History Data and the Labor Market Outcomes of Ex-Offenders and Non-Offenders

In order to learn about whether employers statistically discriminate in the absence of criminal history data, one would like to compare the labor market outcomes of non-offenders from groups with high rates of incarceration with the labor market outcomes of groups with low rates of incarceration, and in states that have open records policies versus states that do not. In the empirical model that follows, I base that comparison on predicted cumulative probabilities of incarceration using variables that any prospective employer is likely to be able to observe and could use as a basis for statistical discrimination.

Suppose there is a vector of individual characteristics, given by $\mathbf{Z}$, whose elements are easily observable by potential employers and are known to be correlated with criminality or prior incarceration. If employers cannot directly observe criminality or prior incarceration, they can use these observable qualities to construct a measure of predicted or perceived criminality. One way they could do this would be to create a regression-weighted index of variables in $\mathbf{Z}$, and use this as a proxy for criminality in their hiring decisions. Since the base rates of prior incarceration are so different, I run these regressions separately for men and women. Since prior incarceration is a low-probability event, I focus on a probit model of the following form:

(3) $P(Inc_{it} = 1) = P(\alpha_0 + \mathbf{Z}_{it}\alpha_1 + \eta_{it} > 0) = \Phi(\alpha_0 + \mathbf{Z}_{it}\alpha_1 + \eta_{it}),$

where η_{it} is an error component and $\Phi[\cdot]$ is the cumulative distribution function of the standard normal distribution. After estimating this regression, employers can predict a measure of perceived criminality:

$$PC_{it} \equiv \widehat{P(Inc_{it}=1)} = \Phi(\hat{\alpha}_0 + \mathbf{Z}_{it}\hat{\alpha}_1).$$

The vector of characteristics observable to employers, $\mathbf{Z}$, could include many variables, and only some of these are observable in the NLSY97 (or any labor market survey, for that matter).[19] Given the racial and ethnic disparities in incarceration, I include dummy variables for race and ethnicity. There are also substantial education differences between the incarcerated and nonincarcerated populations, so employers might also try to use educational enrollment or completion as proxies for criminality. I include indicators for school enrollment and highest degree completed and a continuous measure for years of completed schooling. Employers may consider evidence of prior labor market experience as precluding much prior incarceration, so I include the number of years of labor market experience since age thirteen. Employers may also use other easily observable demographic or physical characteristics as proxies for criminality, such as age, body mass index, and central-city residence.[20] I include these in the incarceration regressions. Since some of the respondents in the sample are still in school, I interact age with the schooling variables. Incarceration probabilities vary significantly for men by race, so the control variables in the male equation are interacted with the black and Hispanic indicators.

Table 3.7 shows the coefficient estimates for equation (3) from probit regressions of the indicator for prior incarceration on the variables discussed earlier. I use all panel observations but do not exploit the panel structure, since those effects are unobservable to employers. Column (1) shows the coefficient estimates for men, broken down by the main effects and the racial and ethnic interaction effects. Column (2) shows the coefficient estimates for women. Current enrollment is a strong negative predictor of prior incarceration for both men and women. Black men, Hispanic men, and women who have completed high school are significantly less likely to have an incarceration record relative to those who do not finish high school. Years of labor market experience is a positive predictor of prior incarceration for black men and women, but for white and Hispanic men the coefficient estimates are not significantly different from zero. This labor market experience variable includes work as a minor, so the estimates for women and black men are

19. There may be very important characteristics that employers observe during the application or interview process, such as dress or speech, that may be correlated with criminality or incarceration.

20. The body mass index (BMI) cannot be constructed for all NLSY97 respondents because of missing data, so the BMI is demeaned and missing values are assigned a zero (i.e., the sample mean). Then a dummy is included that is equal to 1 if the BMI is missing for that observation, and zero otherwise.

Table 3.7   **Coefficient estimates from probit regressions of prior adult incarceration on variables observable by employers, by gender, NLSY97, 1997–2004**

	Dependent variable: Ever incarcerated as an adult			
	(1) Men			
Covariates	Main effects	Black interactions	Hispanic interactions	(2) Women
Enrolled	−0.435	−0.087	−0.032	−0.438
	(0.076)	(0.116)	(0.142)	(0.101)
Highest grade completed	−0.300	0.014	0.179	−0.140
	(0.027)	(0.040)	(0.047)	(0.026)
At least high school graduate	0.088	−0.160	−0.614	−0.353
	(0.093)	(0.135)	(0.151)	(0.104)
At least a BA	0.174	0.083	−0.505	−0.110
	(0.198)	(0.290)	(0.364)	(0.220)
Years of labor market experience since age 13	0.015	0.049	0.003	0.040
	(0.012)	(0.019)	(0.023)	(0.016)
Lives in central city of MSA	−0.026	0.189	−0.253	0.063
	(0.059)	(0.081)	(0.097)	(0.067)
Body mass index	−0.028	0.010	0.012	−0.006
	(0.005)	(0.005)	(0.009)	(0.006)
Missing body mass index	−0.594	−0.014	−0.001	−0.454
	(0.129)	(0.026)	(0.028)	(0.229)
Age	0.188	−0.032	−0.047	0.119
	(0.017)	(0.142)	(0.558)	(0.022)
Black	−0.047			−0.008
	(0.558)			(0.075)
Hispanic	−1.852			−0.083
	(0.670)			(0.080)
Pseudo R^2	0.18			0.14
Observations	18,657			18,457
Proportion ever incarcerated	0.06			0.01

Notes: Probit coefficient estimates are shown with standard errors in parentheses. Sample consists of NLSY97 respondents aged eighteen to twenty-five years. See table 3.2 for a complete description of the sample restrictions. Neither model exploits the panel structure of the data by including individual fixed effects, since those effects would be unobservable to employers. Rather, the data are treated as repeated cross sections. MSA = Metropolitan Statistical Area.

consistent with work as a substitute for schooling. Central-city residence is associated with higher cumulative probabilities of incarceration for black men, but lower cumulative probabilities for Hispanic men. A higher body mass index is associated with a lower cumulative incarceration probability, but the effect is less negative for black men. Finally, note that the coefficient estimates for the main effects of race and ethnicity in the male equation are not informative about the relationship between race and cumulative probabilities of incarceration. For women, the estimates are quite similar to the main effects for men. The exception is that there is no comparable difference

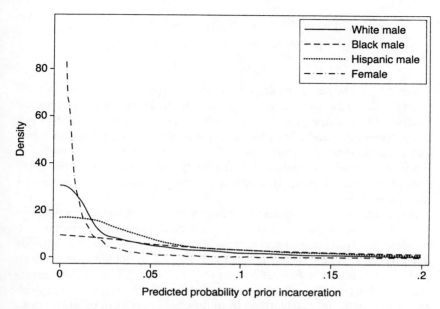

Fig. 3.4   Estimated kernel densities of predicted probability of incarceration, by race and ethnicity (for men) and gender, NLSY97 respondents aged eighteen to twenty-five years, 1997–2004

Notes: Densities are smoothed by the Epanechnikov kernel using boundary correction and the Silverman rule-of-thumb bandwidth. Predictions are from the male and female models in table 3.7.

in prior incarceration by race or ethnicity for women. In general, these estimates are consistent with the demographics of the incarcerated population.

Using the estimated parameters from table 3.7, predicted probabilities of incarceration are generated for each person-year observation. The predicted probabilities for men and women are combined into a single measure of perceived criminality. For white men, black men, Hispanic men, and all women, figure 3.4 shows the estimated kernel densities of the predicted probability of incarceration from the probit models.[21] Note that the distribution contains the cumulative incarceration probabilities for the entire range of ages in the sample. Thus, the cumulative incarceration probabilities for the oldest male respondents are located in the far right tail of the distributions in figure 3.4.

Using the constructed measure of perceived criminality, the effects of open records for ex-offenders and non-offenders can be estimated. For each labor market outcome Y, I estimate the following regression:

21. The densities are smoothed by the Epanechnikov kernel, using boundary correction and the Silverman rule-of-thumb bandwidth.

(4) $\begin{aligned} Y_{ist} = {} & \beta_0 + \beta_1 PC_{it} + \beta_2 Access_{st} Inc_{ist} + \beta_3 PC_{it} Access_{st} \\ & + \beta_4 PC_{it} Access_{st} Inc_{ist} + \beta_5 PC_{it} Inc_{ist} + \beta_6 Access_{st} \\ & + \beta_7 Inc_{ist} + \mathbf{X}_{ist} \beta_8 + \gamma_s + \gamma_t + \varepsilon_{ist}, \end{aligned}$

where PC_{it} is the perceived criminality index predicted from equation (3) for individual i in year t, and ε is an error term. Equation (4) embeds the relative effects of open records on ex-offenders and on non-offenders in a single framework and allows these effects to vary by the individual's predicted criminality. This equation is an extension of the one used earlier to examine the model of statistical discrimination (equation [1])—adding the control variables $\mathbf{X}$, state fixed effects γ_s, and time effects γ_t necessary for identification.[22]

As before, the effects of employer access to criminal history records can be identified in two ways. In the first research design, the parameters can be identified from spatial and temporal variation in the introduction of open records.[23] These specifications treat the data as pooled cross sections and use state and year fixed effects for identification.[24] The repeated cross-sectional design is the one shown in equation (4). In an alternative strategy, the parameters are identified from the changes in both offender status and perceived criminality, in addition to the state and time variation when states began to make criminal history records available over the Internet. This design exploits the longitudinal structure of the NLSY97 and includes individual fixed effects and year effects, but excludes the state effects and time-invariant controls. The pooled cross-sectional specification is somewhat difficult to interpret without additional assumptions about the effect of perceived criminality conditional on the elements of $\mathbf{X}$, which are standard covariates included in regressions of labor market outcomes. Even with the interaction effects of perceived criminality, the estimates could be identifying changes in the return to education, for example, rather than changes in how employers perceive the risk of hiring an applicant with a particular expected value of criminal activity. For this reason, the panel regression with individual fixed effects is the preferred model because it eliminates the need to make any identifying assumptions about how the covariates directly affect the outcomes. I include the cross-sectional models because the short

22. As in the first set of regressions of labor market outcomes, all continuous covariates in these specifications are centered by the sample means from each model's respective sample. This allows meaningful interpretation of the main effect of *Access*.

23. It is possible to identify the effect of opening records on the labor market outcomes of ex-offenders relative to non-offenders by using only data from states that change their policy toward criminal history records. In specifications that use this smaller sample of states, point estimates for parameters of interest are similar, but less precisely measured.

24. A pre-post effect may be confounded by time trends that are specific to adopting states. To account for this, linear time trends for Census regions were included in a set of specifications as a robustness check. The estimated parameters of interest were quite similar with those shown in table 3.8.

sample and youth of the respondents limits the variation available to identify an individual fixed-effect regression.

Table 3.8 shows the estimates from equation (4) using the two identification strategies for each labor market outcome. The odd-numbered columns show the estimates using the pooled cross-sectional identification strategy and the even-numbered columns show the estimates using the longitudinal identification strategy.

Now, recall the two primary hypotheses of the statistical discrimination model. The first hypothesis is that open records should increase the relative penalty that ex-offenders face in the labor market because they can be distinguished from non-offenders. This can be tested with the coefficient on the interaction of *Access* and *Inc* using the alternative hypothesis $\beta_2 <$ 0. The second hypothesis is that open records should improve the relative outcomes of non-offenders who have high levels of perceived criminality. Restated, this is equivalent to the hypothesis that open records should harm the relative outcomes of ex-offenders who have high perceived criminality. This can be tested with the coefficient on the interaction of *PC, Access*, and *Inc,* using the alternative hypothesis $\beta_4 < 0$.

First, focus on the estimates of β_2, which measures how open records affect the main effect of actual criminality. In the pooled cross-sectional models in the odd-numbered columns, the estimates of β_2 are positive, which is not as expected, but the estimates are very close to zero and statistically insignificant. Since there may be substantial unobservable differences between ex-offenders and non-offenders, the longitudinal models in the even-numbered columns may provide more informative results. In these specifications, the estimated coefficients on *Access · Inc* are all negative, which is consistent with the hypothesis that ex-offenders will do relatively worse in the labor market once criminal history records are easily accessible by employers. The estimate of β_2 is only statistically significantly different from zero, however, in the earnings regression. Although I hesitate to make strong statements given the lack of statistical significance, the signs of these effects are consistent with a statistical discrimination story in which employers continue to hire ex-offenders and non-offenders in similar proportions after criminal records become more available, but non-offenders do start to receive somewhat higher wages than ex-offenders when employers can verify their criminal histories.

The next hypothesis from the statistical discrimination model is that non-offenders from highly offending groups should have improved labor market outcomes once employers can verify their clean criminal histories. This is the same as saying that ex-offenders from highly offending groups should have relatively worse outcomes from non-offenders from highly offending groups. This is captured by the coefficient on the interaction of perceived criminality, open records, and actual criminality, β_4. If β_4 is less than zero, ex-offenders do increasingly worse than non-offenders as a function of their

Table 3.8 **Regressions of labor market outcomes on criminal records policy variables and perceived criminality, NLSY97, 1997–2004**

Covariates	Emp. (1)	Emp. (2)	LnWage (3)	LnWage (4)	LnEarn. (5)	LnEarn (6)
PC (β_1)	0.342	0.084	0.266	−0.078	1.759	0.735
	(0.095)	(0.119)	(0.067)	(0.083)	(0.213)	(0.298)
Access × Inc (β_2)	0.013	−0.028	0.036	−0.036	0.090	−0.319
	(0.038)	(0.043)	(0.044)	(0.042)	(0.170)	(0.136)
PC × Access (β_3)	−0.169	0.146	−0.246	−0.114	−0.185	0.047
	(0.159)	(0.143)	(0.097)	(0.123)	(0.352)	(0.356)
PC × Access × Inc (β_4)	−0.095	−0.258	−0.282	−0.298	−0.351	1.094
	(0.255)	(0.324)	(0.338)	(0.278)	(1.170)	(1.084)
PC × Inc (β_5)	−0.131	0.148	−0.179	−0.053	−1.591	−1.635
	(0.188)	(0.267)	(0.207)	(0.173)	(0.381)	(0.573)
Access (β_6)	−0.027	−0.030	−0.001	−0.021	−0.046	−0.059
	(0.015)	(0.014)	(0.015)	(0.011)	(0.043)	(0.030)
Inc (β_7)	−0.085	−0.033	0.003	0.011	−0.053	0.069
	(0.028)	(0.036)	(0.024)	(0.033)	(0.083)	(0.114)
Has GED	0.087	0.009	0.054	0.006	0.367	0.005
	(0.015)	(0.016)	(0.014)	(0.018)	(0.058)	(0.058)
Has HS diploma	0.162	0.022	0.070	0.020	0.277	0.067
	(0.007)	(0.011)	(0.009)	(0.012)	(0.026)	(0.039)
Has associate's	0.230	0.013	0.152	0.074	0.447	0.081
	(0.027)	(0.027)	(0.030)	(0.029)	(0.080)	(0.054)
Has bachelor's plus	0.210	0.155	0.234	0.214	0.213	0.258
	(0.014)	(0.020)	(0.017)	(0.017)	(0.052)	(0.047)
Years attended since 13	0.021	0.045	0.004	0.106	0.100	0.343
	(0.011)	(0.024)	(0.010)	(0.017)	(0.029)	(0.032)
Years exp. since 13	−0.002	0.006	0.001	0.000	0.001	−0.002
	(0.002)	(0.002)	(0.002)	(0.002)	(0.005)	(0.004)
Age	0.102	0.245	0.119	0.130	1.033	1.145
	(0.044)	(0.032)	(0.036)	(0.031)	(0.133)	(0.098)
Age^2	−0.002	−0.006	−0.002	−0.003	−0.021	−0.028
	(0.001)	(0.001)	(0.001)	(0.001)	(0.003)	(0.002)
ASVAB	0.0007		0.0011		−0.0009	
	(0.0001)		(0.0001)		(0.0005)	
Missing ASVAB	0.017		0.049		−0.010	
	(0.008)		(0.013)		(0.030)	
Black male	−0.118		−0.066		−0.359	
	(0.014)		(0.012)		(0.038)	
Hispanic male	0.032		−0.028		0.028	
	(0.017)		(0.015)		(0.033)	
Female	−0.045		−0.103		−0.287	
	(0.009)		(0.011)		(0.024)	
Unemployment rate	−0.004	−0.004	−0.011	−0.011	−0.021	−0.018
	(0.006)	(0.005)	(0.006)	(0.006)	(0.018)	(0.015)
Specification						
Year effects	x	x	x	x	x	x
State effects	x		x		x	
Individual effects		x		x		x
Observations	36,687	36,687	30,145	30,145	27,137	27,137
R^2	0.07	0.04	0.15	0.14	0.25	0.35

Notes: Heteroscedasticity-robust standard errors that are clustered at the state level are in parentheses. Sample consists of NLSY97 respondents aged eighteen to twenty-five years. See table 3.2 for a complete description of the sample restrictions. Each continuous covariate is centered by its mean from each regression's respective sample. Employment-status regressions are linear probability models. Full regression results available from the author.

perceived criminality. In the repeated cross-sectional models, the parameter estimates of β_4 are all negative, which is consistent with improved outcomes of non-offenders from highly offending groups. None of these estimates, however, are statistically significantly different from zero. In the panel models, the estimates of β_4 are negative for employment status and log wages, but positive for log earnings. In general, the estimates for this hypothesis are imprecisely measured but broadly consistent with the notion that employers statistically discriminate in the absence of criminal history records.

In summary, there is some evidence that expanded employer access to criminal history records has increased the difference in outcomes between non-offenders and ex-offenders, holding perceived criminality constant. There is some evidence that the labor market outcomes of non-offenders have improved in states that have made records available over the Internet compared with the change in outcomes for non-offenders in states that did not make records available over the Internet. This suggests that the expanded outcome gap between non-offenders and ex-offenders is primarily driven by the worsening outcomes of ex-offenders once records become available over the Internet.

3.5.3   Interpreting the Results

Evidence presented previously indicates that the employment effects of incarceration are more negative in states that provide criminal history records over the Internet than in states that do not. These results for ex-offenders are consistent with asymmetric information about criminal histories in labor markets. If employers had perfect information and could identify all potential criminals among applicants, then greater access to criminal history records would not cause a change in the labor market outcomes of ex-offenders.[25] And evidence of imperfect information suggests that employers have a strong motivation to statistically discriminate against individuals from highly offending groups. Another important finding for ex-offenders is that the estimated effects of open records on the outcomes of ex-offenders are relatively large compared with the main effects of incarceration on labor market outcomes. That is, the marginal effect of opening records on the labor market outcomes of an individual who has a criminal record is larger than the main effect of the incarceration itself. This suggests that the availability of criminal history data is an important determinant of the labor market outcomes of former prisoners.

While this research provides compelling evidence that increased availability of criminal background data is associated with worse labor market

25. This evidence is consistent with the audit study results of Pager (2003). She finds that auditors who signaled their own incarceration record during the application phase of hiring had call back rates that were half as large as the call back rates for the other auditor. The relative effect of information disclosure was similar for auditors from highly incarcerated groups (blacks) and auditors from less incarcerated groups (whites).

Table 3.9   Frequency of panel observations, by whether state of residence will ever
adopt the provision of criminal history records over the Internet, before
and after policy change, for ex-offenders and non-offenders

	Preadoption	Post-adoption
Adopting states		
Will ever be incarcerated in sample		
Not yet incarcerated	77	135
Already incarcerated	38	427
Will never be incarcerated in sample	1,627	11,505
Nonadopting states		
Will ever be incarcerated in sample		
Not yet incarcerated	148	279
Already incarcerated	35	653
Will never be incarcerated in sample	2,567	19,196

Notes: Adopting states are those that have ever adopted Internet sites with information on
ex-offenders. The synthetic cut-off for nonadopting states is 2001, the median year of adoption in adopting states.

outcomes for ex-offenders, evidence for its effects on non-offenders is less conclusive. Most of the estimated effects of open records on the outcomes of non-offenders are negative, as expected, but none are statistically significant. There are a number of explanations for the lack of clear results for non-offenders. First, as in most studies of the differences between ex-offenders and non-offenders, there is a limited number of observations on the ex-offenders. Moreover, few ex-offender observations occur in the time period before most states adopted Internet background checks sites. Table 3.9 shows the number of panel observations by whether respondents will ever be incarcerated and by whether their states of residence provide criminal history records over the Internet. This weakens the identification of any effects of open records, since the comparisons are primarily cross-sectional rather than longitudinal.

The short sample period available in the current release of the NLSY97 also makes it difficult to draw conclusions about the long-term consequences of wider criminal background checking by employers. There is evidence that some ex-offenders have improved labor market outcomes immediately after conviction or prison release since they tend to seek work in spot markets for labor that have little prospect of training or earnings growth (Nagin and Waldfogel 1995; Nagin and Waldfogel 1998). In the short run, non-offenders may also invest more in human capital and have temporarily lower employment odds and wages relative to ex-offenders. A short time frame exacerbates this problem, since estimates may give an incomplete picture of the labor market outcomes of ex-offenders relative to non-offenders. Future research should attempt to use a longer sample to investigate if estimates from the model are more consistent with statistical discrimination.

Another concern is that there is no information about the actual perceptions that employers have about who is likely to commit crime once hired.

In this chapter, perceived criminality is assumed to come from rational expectations based on current incarceration probabilities. That is, I assume employers are capable of making unbiased predictions of the likelihood that any applicant has a criminal record conditional on characteristics that are observable to both the employer and the econometrician. But employers may have other concerns than who has been incarcerated or they may be misinformed about the actual probabilities of criminal activity or incarceration. If employers estimate criminality with substantial error, then they are not effectively statistically discriminating, but rather they are simply discriminating against the groups for whom employers overproject a risk of crime. Economists generally argue that inaccurate forecasts should be driven out of the market by competition. But employers who face ex-offenders as applicants may be risk averse in light of negligent-hiring lawsuits, and so have little incentive to improve their forecasts of criminality. This is an area where ethnographic work or audit studies may be particularly informative to establish how employers perceive the potential risk of hiring ex-offenders. Further work could examine the sensitivity of these results once one accounts for measurement error and imperfect perceptions of incarceration probabilities.

Finally, the nature of criminal history systems may lead to Type 1 and Type 2 error rates that drive effects primarily for ex-offenders but not non-offenders. One possibility is that criminal background checks have very low probabilities of false negatives, but very high probabilities of false positives. There is some concern in the government agencies that manage criminal history data systems that name-based searches of records can yield high rates of false positives (of a criminal record) and false negatives. The System for the Electronic Analysis and Retrieval of Criminal Histories (SEARCH [1999]) reports that name-based searches made through the Federal Bureau of Investigation's National Crime Information Center yielded false positives at a rate of 7.5 percent. If false negatives are rare and employers have imperfect information about records, then greater access to criminal histories should lead to substantial negative effects for ex-offenders since it reveals damaging information previously unavailable. But if the rate of false positives is very high, then greater access to criminal histories may not cause an improvement in the labor market outcomes of non-offenders from highly offending groups, even if employers statistically discriminate. Employers may consider *not* finding a record of little consequence if they are aware of the imperfections in the criminal records systems, so they may continue to discount the productivity of individuals with high predicted criminality. This effect would be exacerbated if there is more similarity of names within narrow racial and social classes.[26] Therefore, this type of asymmetric preci-

---

26. The observation that some names are common within racial groups, but not across them, is the basis of Bertrand and Mullainathan's (2004) correspondence audit study of discrimination in hiring.

sion of criminal background checks is consistent with the evidence in this chapter but also with statistical discrimination by employers.

Some of the concerns discussed here apply generally to empirical studies of statistical discrimination, and their implications should be considered when researchers try to interpret the magnitude of estimated effects of statistical discrimination.

3.6   Conclusion

This chapter examines how expanded employer access to criminal history data influences the labor market outcomes of ex-offenders and non-offenders. I find evidence that employment effects of incarceration are more negative in states that provide criminal history records over the Internet than in states that do not. There is also evidence that ex-offenders in states with open records policies have lower wages and earnings than ex-offenders in states with more closed records policies. There is less conclusive evidence that labor market outcomes of non-offenders from highly offending groups are improved by greater employer access to criminal history data. While the estimates are consistent with the theoretical prediction, the estimated effects for non-offenders are not estimated precisely enough to draw strong conclusions about whether employers statistically discriminate to avoid hiring ex-offenders. One explanation for these results is that the sample period is too short to capture the long-term effects of opening criminal history records to the public. Another explanation is that the nature of false-positive and false-negative criminal check results generates significant effects for ex-offenders but not non-offenders. Nevertheless, the empirical methods used in this analysis are a fruitful way for examining the extent of statistical discrimination when there are changes in the information set available to employers during hiring.

This research is important for understanding why released prisoners experience poor labor market outcomes. The labor market outcomes of ex-offenders are a public finance concern because failure to gain legitimate employment after prison release is a strong predictor of recidivism, which is costly for prison systems. Regression estimates indicate that more widely available criminal history data worsens the labor market outcomes of ex-offenders. In fact, in some specifications, the effect of open records on ex-offenders trumps the main effect of being an ex-offender, suggesting that the information available to employers has a major impact on how ex-offenders reintegrate into the legitimate labor force. This research also highlights how the high relative rates of incarceration for black and Hispanic men may affect the employment outcomes of non-offenders from those groups. One of the expected benefits of an open-records system is that informational symmetry should help non-offenders from highly offending groups. I do not find statistically significant evidence of this effect, but further research should continue to address this potential side effect of providing criminal history records over the Internet.

A criminal background check is, however, just one type of preemployment screen that has become more convenient for employers to carry out because of technological changes. Our personal information is increasingly available over the Internet and some of this information can be used in the hiring process. For example, personal credit reports are used by some employers to gauge the financial responsibility of applicants (Arnoldy 2007). Some human resource managers also search peer-to-peer websites like MySpace for revealing information about potential employees, especially recent college graduates with little labor market history (Finder 2006). The productivity basis for some screens may be obvious, such as driving record checks for commercial truck drivers, but for other screens the connection to productivity may be less clear. The research design in this chapter could serve as a useful strategy for measuring the effects of these types of technologies that expand the information sets available to employers during hiring.

References

Abe, Y. 2001. Changes in gender and racial gaps in adolescent antisocial behavior: The NLSY97 versus the NLSY79. In *Social awakening: Adolescent behavior as adulthood approaches,* ed. R. T. Michael, 339–78. New York: Russell Sage Foundation.

Andler, E. C., and D. Herbst. 2003. *The complete reference checking handbook.* New York: American Management Association.

Arnoldy, B. 2007. The spread of the credit check as civil rights issue. *The Christian Science Monitor* 18 (January). Available at: http://www.csmonitor.com/2007/0118/p01s03-ussc.html.

Autor, D. H., and D. Scarborough. 2008. Will job testing harm minority workers? Evidence from the retail sector. *Quarterly Journal of Economics* 123 (1): 219–77.

Bertrand, M., and S. Mullainathan. 2004. Are Emily and Greg more employable than Lakisha and Jamal? A field experiment on labor market discrimination. *American Economic Review* 94 (4): 991–1013.

Bonczar, T. P. 2003. Prevalence of imprisonment in the U.S. population, 1974–2001. *Bureau of Justice Statistics,* NCJ 197976.

Bonczar, T. P., and A. J. Beck. 1997. Lifetime likelihood of going to state or federal prison. *Bureau of Justice Statistics,* NCJ 160092.

Brien, P. M. 2005. Improving access and integrity of criminal history records. *Bureau of Justice Statistics,* NCJ 200581.

Burke, M. E. 2005. *2004 reference and background checking survey report.* Alexandria, VA: Society for Human Resource Management.

Bushway, S. D. 1996. The impact of a criminal history record on access to legitimate employment. PhD diss., Carnegie Mellon University, Pittsburgh.

———. 2004. Labor market effects of permitting employer access to criminal records. *Journal of Contemporary Criminal Justice* 20 (3): 276–91.

Bushway, S., S. Briggs, F. Taxman, M. Thanner, and M. van Brakle. 2007. Private providers of criminal history records: Do you get what you pay for? In *Barriers to reentry? The labor market for released prisoners in post-industrial America,* ed. S. Bushway, M. A. Stoll, and D. F. Weiman, 29–79. New York: Russell Sage Foundation.

Cho, R., and R. LaLonde. 2008. The impact of incarceration in state prison on the employment prospects of women. *Journal of Quantitative Criminology* 24 (3): 243–65.

Connerley, M. L., R. D. Arvey, and C. J. Bernardy. 2001. Criminal background checks for prospective and current employees: Current practices among municipal agencies. *Public Personnel Management* 20 (2): 173–84.

Finder, A. 2006. For some, online persona undermines a résumé. *The New York Times,* June 11. Available at: http://www.nytimes.com/2006/06/11/us/11recruit .html.

Grogger, J. 1995. The effect of arrests on the employment and earnings of young men. *Quarterly Journal of Economics* 110 (1): 51–71.

Harrison, P. M., and A. J. Beck. 2006. Prison and jail inmates at midyear 2005. *Bureau of Justice Statistics* NCJ 213133.

Hindelang, M. J., T. Hirschi, and J. G. Weis. 1981. *Measuring delinquency.* Beverly Hills, CA: Sage.

Hinton, D. 2004. *The criminal records manual.* Tempe, AZ: Facts on Demand Press.

Hjalmarsson, R. 2008. Criminal justice involvement and high school completion. *Journal of Urban Economics* 63 (2): 613–30.

Holzer, H. J., S. Raphael, and M. A. Stoll. 2006. Perceived criminality, criminal background checks, and the racial hiring practices of employers. *Journal of Law and Economics* 49 (2): 451–80.

———. 2007. The effect of an applicant's criminal history on employer hiring decisions and screening practices: Evidence from Los Angeles. In *Barriers to reentry? The labor market for released prisoners in post-industrial America,* ed. S. Bushway, M. A. Stoll, and D. F. Weiman, 117–150. New York: Russell Sage Foundation.

Johnson, P. R., and J. Indvik. 1994. Workplace violence: An issue of the nineties. *Public Personnel Management* 23 (4): 515–23.

Kling, J. R. 2006. Incarceration length, employment, and earnings. *American Economic Review* 96 (3): 863–76.

Legal Action Center. 2004. After prison: Roadblocks to reentry: A report on state legal barriers facing people with criminal records. Available at http://www.lac .org/lac.

Lochner, L. 2007. Individual perceptions of the criminal justice system. *American Economic Review* 97 (1): 444–60.

Nagin, D., and J. Waldfogel. 1995. The effects of criminality and conviction on the labor market status of young British offenders. *International Review of Law and Economics* 15 (1): 109–26.

———. 1998. The effect of conviction on income through the life cycle. *International Review of Law and Economics* 18 (1): 25–40.

Needels, K. E. 1996. Go directly to jail and do not collect? A long-term study of recidivism, employment, and earnings patterns among prison releases. *Journal of Research in Crime and Delinquency* 33 (4): 471–96.

Odewahn, C. A., and D. L. Webb. 1989. Negligent hiring and discrimination: An employer's dilemma? *Labor Law Journal* 40 (11): 705–12.

Pager, D. 2003. The mark of a criminal record. *American Journal of Sociology* 108 (5): 937–75.

Raphael, S. 2006. The socioeconomic status of black males: The increasing importance of incarceration. In *Poverty, the distribution of income, and public policy,* ed. A. Auerbach, D. Card, and J. Quigley, 319–58. New York: Russell Sage Foundation.

Rosen, L. S. 2006. *The safe hiring manual.* Tempe, AZ: Facts on Demand Press.

Sampson, R. J., and J. H. Laub. 1993. *Crime in the making: Pathways and turning points through life.* Cambridge, MA: Harvard University Press.

SEARCH, The National Consortium for Justice Information and Statistics. 1994. Survey of criminal history information systems, 1993. *Bureau of Justice Statistics,* NCJ 148951.

———. 1999. Interstate identification index name check efficacy. *Bureau of Justice Statistics,* NCJ 179358.

———. 2001. Internet computerized criminal history survey. Sacramento, CA: Author.

———. 2006. State criminal history record information availability survey. Sacramento, CA: Author.

Uggen, C. 2000. Work as a turning point in the life course of criminals: A duration model of age, employment, and recidivism. *American Sociological Review* 65 (4): 529–46.

U.S. Equal Employment Opportunity Commission. 1987a. Policy statement on the issue of conviction records under title VII of the Civil Rights Act of 1964. Notice N-915.

———. 1987b. Policy statement on the use of statistics in charges involving the exclusion of individuals with conviction records from employment. Notice N-915-061.

Viscusi, W. K. 1986. Market incentives for criminal behavior. In *Black youth employment crisis,* ed. R. Freeman and H. Holzer, 301–52. Chicago: University of Chicago Press.

Western, B. 2002. The impact of incarceration on wage mobility and inequality. *American Sociological Review* 67 (4): 526–46.

4

Do Online Labor Market Intermediaries Matter? The Impact of *AlmaLaurea* on the University-to-Work Transition

Manuel F. Bagues and Mauro Sylos Labini

4.1 Introduction

The Internet and electronic technologies more generally have a great potential for changing the way employer-employee matches are made (Autor 2001). Since the mid-1990s there has been a well-documented increase in the number of Internet job boards and corporate websites devoted to job applications, and in the shares of job-seekers and recruiters using online resources. For example, according to Taleo Research, the incidence of Fortune 500 companies using their careers website as a corporate job board increased from 29 percent in 1998 to 92 percent in 2002. Moreover, the importance of online technologies may be underestimated, since the possible uses of the Internet in job search are multifaceted and go well beyond viewing advertisements or posting resumes (Kuhn 2000).[1]

However, it has been extremely difficult to assess the impact of online

Manuel F. Bagues is an assistant professor in the business department at Universidad Carlos III. Mauro Sylos Labini is an assistant professor at the IMT Lucca Institute for Advanced Studies.

We thank David Autor and Anne Polivka for very helpful comments. We also benefitted from comments from participants at seminars at University of Oviedo, University of Bologna, 4th IZA/SOLE Transatlantic meeting, Bocconi University, S. Anna School of Advanced Studies, University of Alicante, 6th Villa Mondragone Workshop, XI Spring Meeting of Young Economists, and the NBER Conference on Labor Market Intermediation. The usual disclaimers apply. The empirical analysis would not have been possible without the data and help provided by Giovanni Seri at ISTAT (the Italian Statistical Office). The econometric analysis was carried out at the ADELE Laboratory. We are grateful to Michele Rostan for providing the data from the European Project "Careers after Higher Education: A European Research Study." Corresponding author Mauro Sylos Labini: m.syloslabini@imtlucca.it.

1. In a recent report, the U.S. Congressional Budget Office pointed out that "internet job searching may also have played a role in reducing the natural rate (of unemployment)" (CBO 2002).

technologies on labor market outcomes. The Internet is believed to increase the amount of information available to recruiters and job-seekers and at the same time to improve their ability to screen online applications and opportunities. Both aspects are likely to decrease the cost of job search and, therefore, to improve matching productivity (Pissarides 2000).

Nevertheless, it has also been noted that even if searching online has private individual benefits, it does not follow that the equilibrium effects on labor market outcomes are socially beneficial (Autor 2001). In a recent empirical investigation, Kuhn and Skuterud (2004) also find that—once individual observable characteristics are controlled for—Internet seekers do not have shorter unemployment duration than other searchers and, in some specification, it may even be longer. As the authors acknowledge, these results may be contaminated by selection into Internet job search on unobservables that are negatively correlated with employability. However, it is also possible that Internet search is counterproductive at the individual level because of the negative signal it might send to employers. Workers may still use the Internet, the authors argue, because it is very cheap and they are not aware of this drawback.

Therefore, despite their rapid diffusion, whether online electronic technologies are capable of increasing the overall efficiency with which workers and jobs are matched or, conversely, are merely cheaper substitutes for more traditional means (e.g., newspaper ads or face-to-face intermediation) is still an open issue.

This chapter evaluates the impact of the availability of electronic labor markets on the university-to-work transition. In particular, we study the effects of a specific electronic intermediary, the interuniversity consortium *AlmaLaurea*, on graduates' unemployment, mobility, and matching quality. In a nutshell, *AlmaLaurea* collects and organizes online information concerning college graduates' curricula and, conditional on their permission, sells it to firms in electronic format. Hence, similar to other commercial job boards, it makes information about searching candidates available online. However, it also contains information on almost the entire universe of graduates from the institutions that it serves.

The present case study provides exceptional evidence on the effect of online labor market intermediaries for two main reasons: first, the impact of *AlmaLaurea* is observed during a time period when e-recruitment was almost nonexistent in Italy. *AlmaLaurea* was founded in 1994 and, to the best of our knowledge, until 1999 there were no major Internet job boards operating in Italy. Second, different timing of universities' enrollment in *AlmaLaurea* produces counterfactuals that allow us to tackle the problems faced by previous empirical investigations. Although today most Italian universities are members of *AlmaLaurea*, a smaller subset was in the consortium at the time our data were collected. We identify the average effect of *AlmaLaurea* on graduates from this initial subset—that is, the ones that might have used its services—comparing the dynamics of their employment outcomes with those of graduates from universities that were not members. Hence, we aim at estimating the effect of the *availability* of electronic intermediaries, not the private benefits of using them.

Formally, we measure the effect of *AlmaLaurea* using the difference-in-differences (DID) approach applied to a repeated cross-sectional data set. The data set is built by merging two distinct (but almost identical) surveys run by the Italian Statistical Office (ISTAT) on representative samples of two cohorts of university graduates interviewed three years after graduation. Given that *AlmaLaurea* intermediation activity only started in a subset of universities in the period between the graduation of the two cohorts, we split the sample into two distinct groups: graduates who completed their degree in a university that joined *AlmaLaurea* in 1996 and 1997 (the treatment group) and those who graduated from universities not members of *AlmaLaurea* during that period (the control group). The subtleties of envisaging participation of academic institutions in *AlmaLaurea* as a quasi-natural experiment are discussed in more depth in the following. Here, it suffices to say that, first, individual decisions concerning college enrollment were made before *AlmaLaurea* came into being; second, graduates and universities in the two groups are not statistically different in terms of observable characteristics; third, according to personal conversations with the consortium's director, initially membership in *AlmaLaurea* was fairly accidental and mostly based on informal relationships among a few faculties.

AlmaLaurea, as we discuss more thoroughly in the following, has a number of features that make it likely to be effective. First, it collects official information, which is partially disclosed to firms, concerning also those individuals who decide not to post their resumes online. Second, it achieves very high enrollment rates from graduates. We conjecture that these features are likely to reduce adverse selection.

According to our most conservative estimate, *AlmaLaurea* decreases the probability of unemployment by about 1.6 percentage points and has a positive effect on wages and two self-reported measures of job satisfaction. We also find that it fosters graduates' geographical mobility.

To check the robustness of these findings, we test for pretreatment parallel outcomes and find that graduates from the two groups of universities had similar employment dynamics prior to *AlmaLaurea*'s operation. Our results might also be affected by the adverse consequence of *AlmaLaurea* for graduates from universities, not members of the consortium. To control for this possibility, we build alternative treatment and control groups based on geographical proximity. We find no evidence of such a negative effect.

Our work is related to the growing number of studies that investigate the effect of the Internet and electronic technologies on the labor market (Autor 2001; Freeman 2002). Kuhn and Skuterud (2004) study the impact of Internet job search on the probability of the unemployed finding a job.

According to their analysis, there are no discernible differences between transition to employment of online and traditional searchers. They conclude that either online search is ineffective or that Internet job searchers are negatively selected. In a recent paper—methodologically similar to ours—Kroft and Pope (2008) exploit the uneven geographical expansion of the website Craigslist to assess the impact of online search on labor and housing markets efficiency. Although, consistent with Kuhn and Skuterud (2004), they find that online search had no effect on the unemployment rate, they did find that it lowered more traditional classified job advertisements in newspapers. Stevenson (2008) investigates the importance of online technologies on employed online job search and finds that in the United States, state-level rise in Internet penetration is associated with state-level rise in employer-to-employer worker flows. In this chapter, we focus on the impact of online search on a specific segment of the labor market—that is, transition of university to work.

Our study is also useful for policy evaluation and formulation: the consortium *AlmaLaurea* is cofinanced by the Italian Ministry of Education; therefore, clear evidence on its effectiveness is useful for evaluating how public money is spent.[2] Moreover, should *AlmaLaurea* prove to be an effective institutional arrangement, other European countries might learn from its example, improving public policy aimed at facilitating the university-to-work transition.

The rest of the chapter is organized as follows. Section 4.2 presents an overview of the university-to-work transition in Italy, provides an in-depth description of the *AlmaLaurea* consortium, and briefly discusses the economics of online labor market intermediaries. Section 4.3 outlines the identification assumptions needed to make our empirical strategy valid. Section 4.4 describes the data used in the analysis. Section 4.5 presents the main results. Sections 4.6 and 4.7 justify the validity of the results of our empirical approach, and section 4.8 concludes.

4.2   Background

4.2.1   University-to-Work Transition in Italy

Labor market functioning is deeply affected by different kinds of information imperfections and asymmetries. The education-to-work transition is particularly exposed to these imperfections: first-time job seekers typically lack work experience, and this negatively affects both their outlooks con-

---

2. Given that we do not know the magnitude of public funding invested, we are not able to measure whether *AlmaLaurea* is a worthwhile social investment; we can only measure whether students from *AlmaLaurea* member universities have benefitted from it.

Table 4.1   Employment rates of university graduates by age class—2004

Country	Age class		
	25–29	30–34	35–39
Denmark	79.7	87.7	91.2
Finland	84.4	86.7	87.9
France	80.1	85.0	87.5
Greece	72.2	85.5	87.9
Italy	58.0	81.9	89.4
Spain	76.3	85.9	86.7
Sweden	76.6	88.2	88.3
United Kingdom	90.5	98.1	90.1

Source: Eurostat.

cerning employment opportunities and job characteristics, and employers' screening options.

In most countries, unemployment rates are lower for university graduates than for the rest of labor force, and highly educated people experience a smoother entry into working life (Organization for Economic Cooperation and Development [OECD] 2007). As table 4.1 shows, however, international comparisons depict the university-to-work transition in Italy as one of the most problematic cases among industrialized countries.[3] There are three main possible explanations for this. First, there are frictions on the *supply* side: it might be that education provided by Italian universities is of such a low standard that graduates are obliged to undertake further training, either formal or informal, before getting into work. Second, the slow transition rates may be due to labor *demand* characteristics: the Italian industrial structure, compared to that of other developed countries, is biased in favor of small firms and low-tech industries that typically do not employ highly qualified workers. Third, there may be inefficiencies in the *matching* mechanisms caused by information imperfections and, possibly, by lack of intermediaries.

AlmaLaurea potentially improves labor market functioning for two reasons. First, it reduces search costs for both firms and workers by making accurate qualification, grade, and study data readily available. Second, it may mitigate adverse selection by making it possible to compare searching students with others in their cohorts.

Universities are often active actors in labor market intermediation. For instance, most academic institutions set up and manage placement offices and, in some cases, their faculties establish informal ties with firms.[4] However, when universities receive financial resources on a relatively egalitarian

3. See also the data in Mannheim Centre for European Social Research (2002).
4. See Rebick (2000) for an insightful account of the Japanese case.

Table 4.2   University graduates using university placement offices

Country	Utilization rates (%)	Used to get the first job (%)
Italy	10.3	1.42
Spain	39.3	3.96
France	18.1	3.21
United Kingdom	37.6	6.61
Germany	6.6	0.54

Source: Authors' calculation, based on the data set produced by the Project funded by the European Community under the Targeted Socio-Economic Research (TSER) "Careers after Higher Education: A European Research Study." Details on the project and downloadable material can be found at http://www.uni-kassel.de/wz1/tseregs.htm.2.

Notes: The relevant questions (asked in 1998 to graduates who obtained their degree between autumn 1994 and summer 1995) were: (a) "How did you search for your first job after graduation?"; (b) "Which method was most important for getting your first job after graduation?" Multiple options follow, among which "I enlisted the help of a careers/placement office in my higher education institution." The ratios displayed are computed, respectively, over graduates who have sought a job and over those graduates who have been employed at least once.

basis and their graduates' labor market performance does not affect their financial endowments, they may have little incentive to concern themselves with students' placement. In Italy, before *AlmaLaurea* was established, public universities were involved in minimal formal intermediation activity.[5] Table 4.2 refers to 1995 graduates and, for a selected sample of European countries, displays the share of graduates who used the services of their institutions' placement office (first column) and the share of graduates who got their first job through this channel (second column). It can be seen that Italy ranks low, higher only than Germany, in both respects.[6]

4.2.2   AlmaLaurea

AlmaLaurea was founded in 1994 and began online intermediation in 1995 at a time when, to the best of our knowledge, there were no other Internet job boards in Italy. Monster and InfoJob, the current most popular e-recruitment sites (according to Nielsen/NetRatings) started in 2001 and 2004, respectively.[7]

Initially run by the Statistical Observatory of the University of Bologna, *AlmaLaurea* is currently managed by a consortium of fifty private and public

5. There is anecdotal evidence that several departments on an informal basis provided unorganized, paper-based information on their graduates to recruiting companies.

6. Percentages are calculated using the data set built by a European Community-funded project under the Targeted Socio-Economic Research (TSER) "Careers after Higher Education: a European Research Study." See http://www.uni-kassel.de/wz1/tseregs.htm for details.

7. It ultimately proved impossible to establish with any precision the timing of the first Italian Internet job board. Nevertheless, according to personal communications with industry experts in the field the first was JobPilot, which was founded in 1999 and was acquired by Monster in 2005.

universities, with the support of the Italian Ministry of Education. Member universities pay a one-time association fee (ranging from 2,582 to 5,165 euros, according to the size of the university) and an annual subscription fee for the collection and the insertion of new data in the *AlmaLaurea* database (4.96 euros for each student in the database).

AlmaLaurea's institutional objectives are twofold. First, it provides member academic institutions with reliable information on their graduates. Second, it aims at facilitating graduates' labor market transition.

In terms of the first objective, *AlmaLaurea* manages a database that collects information on graduates, drawing it from three distinct sources. First, academic institutions provide official data on grades, course durations, and degrees received for their alumni. Second, undergraduates provide several pieces of information, including military service obligations, periods of study abroad, work experience, and a self-evaluation concerning foreign languages and computer skills. Finally, graduates have the option to upload and update their curricula online for up to three years after graduation.[8] In accordance with Italian privacy law, only a subset of the information in the database can be disclosed to third parties.[9]

With respect to the second objective, *AlmaLaurea* manages a service that gives firm electronic access to graduates' curriculum vitae (CV). The CV is an electronic file containing biographical information, age at graduation, university and high school grades, information on internships, experience abroad, postgraduate education, languages and computer skills, work experience, and work preferences (i.e., type of occupation desired, location, and contract preferred). Graduates may include additional information and a cover letter.[10]

The service is free for graduates. Firms and other institutions can browse individual curricula and observe populational aggregate information for free, but are required to pay if they want to contact a particular graduate. The price ranges between 0.5 and 10 euros per CV, depending on the type of subscription and the number of curricula acquired.[11]

Table 4.3 provides an overview of *AlmaLaurea*'s history and performance. It displays the number of universities enrolled, the share of graduates from *AlmaLaurea* universities, the numbers of resumes available to firms, and number sold by the consortium.

---

8. Recently, the option was extended to five years.
9. More information can be found online at http://www.almalaurea.it/eng/index.shtml.
10. A sample CV (in Italian) is available at: http://www.almalaurea.it/info/aiuto/aziende/esempio_cv.shtml.
11. Firms can choose between self-service or subscription. The so-called self-service involves payment of fifty euros, after which any number of CVs can be acquired at the cost of ten Euros per CV. Subscription allows a firm to prepay for a whole package of downloadable CVs, over a period of one year. The range is between 200 CVs for around 500 euros, and up to 5,000 CVs for 2,600 euros. More detailed information is available (in Italian) at http://www.almalaurea .it/info/condizioni/buono_ordine_abbonamenti.pdf.

Table 4.3   **Evolution of *AlmaLaurea***

	1998	1999	2000	2001	2002	2003	2004	2005	2006	2007
Number of universities	15	20	22	25	25	27	37	39	44	50
Share of graduates	.24	.31	.34	.39	.39	.37	.43	.51	.57	.67
Number of CV in *AlmaLaurea*	62,745	105,409	153,843	213,976	286,345	367,497	477,282	624,960	792,575	900,000
Number of CV sold	3,973	15,999	115,603	194,635	164,209	271,364	389,625			
CV sold in the same region (share)	.55	.72	.50	.37	.35	.30	.30			

Source: Authors' calculation based on data provided by *AlmaLaurea*. "Share of graduates" refers to the share of graduates in *AlmaLaurea* universities with respect to the entire population of graduates in Italian universities. Data on curriculum vitae (CV) sold for 2005, 2006, and 2007 are not available.

Note: Data for 2007 are estimates calculated in June 2007.

4.2.3   *AlmaLaurea* and the Economics of Electronic Labor Markets

The *AlmaLaurea* recruitment service turns out to be an insightful example concerning how online communication technologies—coupled with more traditional forms of intermediation—might ameliorate the way in which employers and employees match in the labor market. Online labor market intermediaries are expected to decrease the search costs for both employers and employees. Standard search theory predicts that, everything being equal, this should lead to better matches. Conversely, the effects on unemployment duration are ambiguous. In fact, although Burdett and Ondrich (1985) suggest that it is unlikely, online technologies might induce both job-seekers and employers to be more choosy and to increase their reservation wages and screening standards (Pissarides 2000). Finally, online labor market intermediaries are expected to weaken the constraints posed by geographical distance (Autor 2001). Consistently, in the *AlmaLaurea* case most graduates' curricula are bought by firms located in regions other than the one where the individual graduated (see table 4.3).

On the other hand, a likely consequence of lower costs in distinct job search channels is that job seekers, ceteris paribus, will apply for more jobs. And when employers perceive such *excess application* to be a problem, adverse selection is likely to undermine the effectiveness of cheap search methods (Autor 2001).

With the exception of time required to update personal information, *AlmaLaurea* is completely free for students and therefore is potentially exposed to the adverse selection problem referred to previously: employers might expect that individuals who upload and update their resumes online are somehow negatively selected. However, *AlmaLaurea*'s organizational features are likely to make its intermediation activity less exposed to this risk for two reasons.

First, as explained previously, some pieces of the information contained in the *AlmaLaurea* data set concern the entire graduate population and are provided directly by academic institutions. This information is organized by *AlmaLaurea* and made freely available online at its website.[12] For every member university and degree, the website provides information on average grades, share of students who completed their degree on time, and the share of individuals who studied abroad within an EU subsidized program. Therefore, employers who purchase a CV should be able to identify differences between the selected job-seeker and the entire graduate population, which considerably reduces the adverse selection problem.

Second, academic institutions that joined *AlmaLaurea* are able to enroll the vast majority of their graduates. For instance, more than 92 percent of 1998 graduates updated their CVs online at least once. High participation

---

12. See (in Italian) http://www.almalaurea.it/cgi-php/aziende/profilo/profilo.php.

rates have been very effective in building a good reputation for the service, and make adverse selection unlikely. To sum up, we expect that *AlmaLaurea*'s particular organizational features protect it from the disadvantages of online labor markets.

4.3 The Empirical Strategy

The basic goal of this chapter is to evaluate the impact of a treatment; that is, the availability of online labor market intermediaries on an array of labor market outcomes—that is, the probability of being unemployed, mobility, and matching quality. This section formalizes and explicitly discusses our empirical approach and outlines the strategies employed to assess its validity.

One of the most serious empirical problems that arises in assessing the impact of online intermediaries is that job-seekers and firms typically self select in the adoption of online technologies. It is therefore difficult to identify to what extent the correlation between their use and labor market outcomes stems from the technology itself and to what extent it stems from some important and difficult-to-measure individual characteristics.

In this chapter we can rely on a transparent exogenous source of variation; that is, the timing of universities' enrollment in *AlmaLaurea*. This heterogeneity allows us to apply the DID method to a repeated cross-sectional data set. This helps to overcome the previously mentioned problem.

The simple DID framework can be described as follows. The causal effect of a treatment on an outcome is defined as the difference between two potential outcomes (Rubin 1974; Heckman 1990). Of course, it is impossible to observe such an effect for a given individual. However, it is possible to identify an average effect if the population of interest is observed in at least two distinct time periods, if only a fraction of the population is exposed to treatment, and if we assume parallel paths over time for treated and controls. The main intuition is that, under this design, an untreated group of the population is used to identify time variation in the outcome that is not due to treatment exposure.

More formally, each individual i belongs to one group, $G_i \in \{0, 1\}$, where for convenience group 1 is the treatment group and 0 the control one. Moreover, individual i is observed only in time period $T_i \in \{0, 1\}$. Let $I_i = G_i \cdot T_i$ denote an indicator for the *actual* subministration of treatment.[13] Then $Y_i^N(t)$ and $Y_i^I(t)$ represent two *potential* outcomes: respectively, that achieved by i at time t if not treated and that achieved if treated before t.

The fundamental problem in identifying the treatment effect on individual i, defined as $Y_i^I(t) - Y_i^N(t)$, is that for any particular individual, it is not pos-

---

13. Note that in our simple setting I_i assumes the value 1 only for the treatment group ($G_i = 1$) in the post-treatment period ($T_i = 1$).

sible to observe both potential outcomes. What we do observe is the *realized* outcome, which can be written as $Y_i(t) = Y_i^I(t) \cdot I_i + Y_i^N(t) \cdot (1 - I_i)$.

If it is assumed that

(1) $\qquad E[Y_i^N(1) - Y_i^N(0) \,|\, G_i = 1] = E[Y_i^N(1) - Y^N(0) \,|\, G_i = 0],$

then it easily follows that

(2) $\quad E[Y_i^I(1) - Y_i^N(1) \,|\, G_i = 1] = E[Y_i(1) \,|\, G_i = 1] - E[Y_i(0) \,|\, G_i = 1]$

$\qquad\qquad - \{E[Y_i(1) \,|\, G_i = 0] - E[Y_i(0) \,|\, G_i = 0]\}.$

In other words, if the average outcomes for the treatment and control groups had parallel paths over time in the absence of treatment, then the so-called average treatment effect on the treated (ATT) can be expressed as something whose sample counterpart is observable; that is, as the average variation of the treatment group purged by the average variation of the control group.

Hence in the present study, it is assumed that in absence of *AlmaLaurea* the average occupational outcomes of graduates from early joining universities (hereafter *AlmaLaurea* universities) would have followed the same dynamics as those of graduates from universities that either joined later or did not join (hereafter non-*AlmaLaurea* universities). Thus the average effect of *AlmaLaurea* is obtained simply by subtracting the dynamics of the graduates of the control group from the dynamics of those in the treatment group.

The previous estimator is easily obtained as

(3) $\qquad\qquad Y_i = \mu + \gamma \cdot G_i + \delta \cdot T_i + \alpha \cdot (G_i \cdot T_i) + u_i,$

where α is the ATT and the assumption stated in equation (1) is equivalent to mean independence.

The validity of our approach faces a number of threats. As far as the so-called internal validity is concerned—that is, the causal effect within the context of the study—there are two main problems.[14] First, the compositional effect: the use of repeated cross sections is only valid when the composition of the target population does not change between the two periods; that is, $u_i \perp T_i \,|\, G_i$. Given that individual decisions concerning college enrollment were taken before the existence of *AlmaLaurea*, we can presume that, in our case, this problem is not very severe. Nevertheless, following standard practice, we shall test whether the means of relevant characteristics of the population within each group did change unevenly between the pretreatment and the posttreatment periods.

Second, the assumption of parallel dynamics in the absence of treatment between the two groups (equation [1]) turns out to be strong. It is, in fact, possible that the two groups have different trends for reasons other than

---

14. See Meyer (1995) for a comprehensive discussion of internal validity in this framework.

treatment. However, if nonparallel dynamics are due to observables, we can overcome the problem by including covariates. This analysis, as we discuss in detail in section 4.4, relies on a large array of individual and university covariates. Nevertheless, if the dynamics of the outcome variables of the two groups are affected by unobservables, identification breaks down.[15] In section 4.6 we try to overcome this important problem using data for an additional pretreatment period in order to test for nonparallel paths between the treatment and control groups before treatment.

Another issue concerns the unit of analysis of our ATT. It could be that *AlmaLaurea* might not be an appropriate individual level treatment, since member institutions are enrolled at once, and there are possibly important interactions among each university's students. If, for instance, the impact of *AlmaLaurea* on a given student depends on the characteristics of students in his or her cohort, we are measuring the effect on university rather than the individual graduate employment performance. Although in the present study we model *AlmaLaurea* as an individual level treatment, in future research we aim to investigate the possibility of within-university spillovers.

Similarly, to be valid, the DID approach assumes no interactions among the agents in the treatment and control groups. If, for example, *AlmaLaurea* graduates improved occupational outcomes harm non-*AlmaLaurea* graduates, our estimates have very different implications, especially in terms of informing policy. In section 4.7, we try to assess this problem by identifying additional control and treatment groups that include only graduates from those universities that are located in the same geographical region.

Finally, in order to generalize the results to different individuals and contexts, external validity is important. It is possible that *AlmaLaurea* would not have had an effect for graduates from those universities that chose not to join. This would also explain why they did not join. However, we do not think this is a major problem since, as mentioned in the introduction, membership tended to be accidental, at least during the first years. Nevertheless, in the following we test whether the observable characteristics of the universities in the two groups differ significantly.

4.4   The Data

Our data on graduates are drawn from two almost identical surveys— *Indagine Inserimento Professionale Laureati* (Survey on University-to-Work Transition) in 1998 and 2001 of individuals who graduated in 1995 and 1998, respectively.[16]

---

15. Given that decisions to enroll in *AlmaLaurea* are made by universities, we are mostly concerned with university unobservables.

16. The publicly available microdata do not include information concerning from which university the surveyed individual graduated. Therefore, we carried out the analysis at the ADELE ISTAT laboratory in Rome.

Table 4.4   **Universities enrolled in *AlmaLaurea***

1994	University of Bologna starts collecting electronic data concerning its graduates
1995	University of Bologna starts selling data
1996	University of Modena-Reggio Emilia, Ferrara, Parma, and Florence start selling data
1997	University of Catania, Trieste, Udine, Messina, Chieti, Trento, Molise, and Venice School of Architecture start selling data
August 1998	University of Turin and Eastern Piedmont start selling data

Note: The Venice School of Architecture started selling data on January 1. For consistency, it is included in 1997 group. The universities of Siena and Lecce joined in 1997, but did not start to sell CVs until 1999 and 2003, respectively. All the information is available on the *AlmaLaurea* website.

To implement the econometric approach described in section 4.3 we include in our main treatment group those individuals graduating from universities that joined *AlmaLaurea* in 1996 and 1997. As shown in table 4.4, this includes the universities of Modena-Reggio Emilia, Ferrara, Parma, Florence, Catania, Trieste, Udine, Messina, Chieti, Trento, Molise, and Venice School of Architecture. Students in the treatment group account for about 18 percent of the sample (see table 4.5).

In section 4.5.2, we exploit an additional source of variation. As shown in table 4.4, the Universities of Turin and Eastern Piedmont start selling graduates' CVs only after August 1998. Thus, we used graduates from these universities as an additional treatment group in a DID setting in which the "before and after" are the time of graduation before and after August 1998, and only graduates from 1998 are considered.[17]

Unfortunately, ISTAT does not provide information concerning the month of graduation for 1995 graduates. Therefore, graduates from Bologna are not considered in the analysis.[18]

The ISTAT target samples consist of 25,716 individuals in 1998 and 36,373 individuals in 2001. They represent, respectively, 25 percent and 28.1 percent of the total population of Italian university graduates. The responses were 64.7 percent and 53.3 percent, for a total of 17,326 and 20,844 respondents.[19] After eliminating individuals who did not respond to the question concern-

---

17. In Italy, graduates can complete their degree at different times in the same academic year, depending on when they finish their dissertation.

18. Bologna is also a very special case, the most self-selected one, given that it is the university where *AlmaLaurea* got started. However, results do not change qualitatively whether we include Bologna graduates in the control group or the treatment group.

19. Differences in response rates probably stem from the different interviewing techniques in the surveys: in 1998, ISTAT mailed paper-based questionnaires, while in 2001 the CATI (Computer Assisted Telephone Interview) was used. In principle, this change should affect universities in a homogenous way and therefore it should not represent a major problem for our analysis.

Table 4.5   Sample design and means of key variables

	All	AlmaLaurea	Non-AlmaLaurea
	1998 Survey		
Number of graduates	15,282	3,512	11,770
Weighted share		.188	.812
	2001 Survey:		
Number of graduates	18,181	3,515	14,666
Weighted share		.183	.817
	Means of selected sample characteristics in 1998		
Share of female	.527	.528	.527
	(.004)	(.010)	(.005)
Age	27.45	27.61	27.41
	(.038)	(.086)	(.042)
High school grade	48.38	47.87	48.49
	(.066)	(.151)	(.074)
	Means of selected sample characteristics in 2001		
Share of female	.551	.567	.548
	(.004)	(.009)	(.004)
Age	27.47	27.55	27.45
	(.028)	(.063)	(.031)
High school grade	48.96	48.62	49.04
	(.057)	(.130)	(.064)

Notes: Standard errors in parentheses. Shares, means, and standard errors are computed with stratification weights. High school grades range from 36 to 60. Only individuals that responded to the question about employment status are considered.

ing their employment status, those with missing values for key variables, and graduates from Bologna, Turin, and Eastern Piedmont, we are left with 15,282 and 18,181 observations, respectively. In both years the sample is stratified according to sex, university, and university degree, and in the following analysis all estimations are performed using stratification weights.

The surveys collect information on: (a) school and university curricula; (b) labor market experience; and (c) demographic and social backgrounds of graduates. Table 4.5 presents summary statistics for the key variables. In the following analysis, individual level right-hand variables are grouped into two subsets. The first includes characteristics that are predetermined with respect to college efforts and outcomes: sex, age, high school grades, fourteen dummies for high school type, one dummy for having two university degrees, five dummies for each parent's level of education, 104 dummies for province of residence before college enrollment, and 345 dummies for departments (university · field of study). The second contains indicators related to college curricula that could—at least potentially—be influenced by *AlmaLaurea:* university grade and number of years to graduation.

As table 4.5 shows, with the exception only of the share of women, which increased for both groups, the remaining variables show no notable varia-

Table 4.6   **Universities' characteristics**

	All	*AlmaLaurea*	Non-*AlmaLaurea*
Universities in 1995			
Number of universities	59	12	47
Average number of students	23,946	22,033	24,434
	(3,742)	(4,569)	(4,568)
Average number of students per professor	31.09	26.27	32.32
	(2.59)	(2.53)	(3.17)
Average share of delayed students	.288	.278	.291
	(.010)	(.026)	(.011)
Universities in 1998			
Number of universities	61	12	49
Average number of students	25,473	24,134	25,801
	(3,875)	(5,096)	(4,679)
Average number of students per professor	31.82	26.50	33.12
	(2.36)	(3.15)	(2.82)
Average share of delayed students	.362	.396	.354
	(.011)	(.029)	(.012)

Notes: Averages are computed at university level. Standard errors in parentheses.

tions within groups over time. Moreover, control and treatment groups present very similar characteristics for both years, reducing the possibilities of major interactions (beyond the treatment itself) at the individual level, of between being enrolled in a college member of *AlmaLaurea* and graduating in 1998.

In order to control for observable variations in academic institution quality, we use data on university characteristics provided by ISTAT in its annual *Lo Stato dell'Universitá* (University Indicators), for the academic years 1991 to 1998. In particular, we collect information at the level of the individual university, on numbers of students, professors, and delayed students.[20] Table 4.6 shows that universities in the treatment group enroll fewer students per professor than the universities in the control group. The difference, however, is not statistically significant. The two groups have very similar average rates of delayed students. Both indicators are generally considered proxies for university teaching quality.[21] Note, also, that the share of delayed students increased in both groups, but the increase is steeper for the treatment group. In terms of overall number of students, the two groups of universities have very similar averages.

Finally, to control for major economic shocks that may affect graduate labor market performance, we collect province-level information on per capita gross domestic product (GDP) and unemployment rates.[22]

20. In Italy, most students graduate after the official deadline.
21. As discussed in Bagues, Sylos Labini, and Zinovyera (2008), both indicators have drawbacks in a system such as the Italian one, where most universities cannot restrict entry and therefore the number of students per professor depends, among other things, on demand.
22. Italy is composed of 104 provinces, which correspond approximately to U.S. counties.

The present study considers three basic outcome variables measured three years after graduation: occupational status, which takes the value 1 if an individual is unemployed, and zero otherwise;[23] regional mobility, which takes the value 1 if the individual resides in a different region from the one where he or she graduated;[24] and wage, measured as net monthly wage expressed in euros and self reported by the interviewed. We also consider two additional proxies for matching productivity. The first is for the perceived level of adequacy of the knowledge acquired at university with respect to the content of the present job. The second is related to the perceived stability of the job. Both variables are self reported and take values from 1, not at all satisfied, to 4, very satisfied.

4.5   The Impact of *AlmaLaurea*

4.5.1   Universities That Joined in 1996 and 1997

A first picture of the impact of *AlmaLaurea* is obtained by comparing time differences in means of key outcomes within the two groups (treatment and control). Table 4.7 shows that unemployment rates decreased sharply from 1998 to 2001 for the whole target population.[25] Moreover, and most importantly for the present study, occupational status improved the most for those in the treated group: the rate of unemployment decreased about 3.5 points more than in the control group. Note also that the ranking between the two groups reverses. This means that the same qualitative result would be obtained if we used changes in employment logs as outcome variables.

For mobility, rates remained stable for *AlmaLaurea* students, and decreased for non-*AlmaLaurea* ones. Hence, for graduates in the treatment group, regional mobility increased by about 1 point relative to graduates in the control group. However, this difference is not statistically different from zero. Note also that graduates in the treatment group are more mobile than those in the control group. Finally, in terms of matching quality, monthly wages increased by some forty-four euros more for *AlmaLaurea* graduates than for the control group.

To interpret these results as being the sole effect of *AlmaLaurea* involves

---

23. Following standard definitions, we consider unemployed to be those individuals who declare not to having worked during the week before the interview and to be searching for a job.

24. Italy is composed of twenty regions.

25. Italian labor market conditions improved substantially between 1998 and 2001. According to ISTAT, standardized unemployment rates for the entire population were 11.7 in 1998 and 9.4 in 2001. The change was from 12.8 to 9.8 for university graduates aged between twenty-five and thirty-nine. It could be that our figures display a steeper decrease because individuals in the sample are younger and because of the changes made to the survey technique mentioned earlier.

Table 4.7   **Unemployment, mobility, and wages by year and *AlmaLaurea***

	1998	2001	Diff.
Unemployment			
AlmaLaurea	.228	.094	−.134
Non-*AlmaLaurea*	.205	.107	−.098
Diff.			**−.036*****
Standard error			(.011)
Mobility			
AlmaLaurea	.297	.292	−.005
Non-*AlmaLaurea*	.219	.203	−.016
Diff.			**.011**
Standard error			(.014)
Wage			
AlmaLaurea	899.7	1,118.4	218.7
Non-*AlmaLaurea*	980.9	1,155.1	174.2
Diff.			**44.5*****
Standard error			(16.8)

Notes: Unemployment rates are computed using stratification weights. We consider unemployed to be those individuals who did not work during the week before the interview who were looking for a job. Average gross monthly wages are expressed in euros and are calculated for the 20,838 individuals that provide this information. The bold differences are the results of a DID estimation, where Diff = $(Y^{01}_{Alma} - Y^{98}_{Alma}) - (Y^{01}_{non\text{-}Alma} - Y^{98}_{non\text{-}Alma})$. In parentheses are robust standard errors of regressions of the dependent variables on dummies for year, belonging to *AlmaLaurea*, and their interaction.

assuming that in the absence of the treatment the averages of the two groups would have experienced the same variation (equation [1]). This is a strong restriction when treatment (i.e., graduating from a university enrolled in *AlmaLaurea*) is not randomly assigned across individuals. In the remaining part of the chapter we use the approaches outlined in section 4.3 to assess the extent to which the observed changes may be interpreted as the effect of *AlmaLaurea*.

The basic identification assumption of the DID method (equation [1]) may be too stringent if treatment and control groups are unbalanced in covariates that are thought to be associated with the dynamics of the outcome variable. To begin with, we follow the traditional way to accommodate this problem and introduce a linear set of controls X_i in equation (3), which then becomes:

(4) $Y_i = \mu + \beta \cdot X_i + \gamma \cdot G_i + \delta \cdot T_i + \alpha \cdot (G_i \cdot T_i) + u_i.$

Tables 4.8, 4.9, and 4.10 report ordinary least square (OLS) coefficients of this equation where the outcome is, respectively, unemployment, mobility, and log wages. All standard errors are corrected for the nonindependence of employment outcomes of individuals graduating in the same region, degree,

Table 4.8   **The effect of *AlmaLaurea* on unemployment probability**

	(1)	(2)	(3)	(4)
AlmaLaurea	−.020** (.008)	−.021** (.008)	−.021** (.008)	−.016* (.008)
2001	−.101*** (.013)	−.103*** (.013)	−.099*** (.013)	−.073*** (.013)
Female	.060*** (.006)	.061*** (.005)	.061*** (.005)	−.061*** (.005)
Age	−.002** (.001)	−.004*** (.001)	−.004*** (.001)	−.004*** (.001)
High school grade	−.002*** (.0003)	−.001*** (.0004)	−.001*** (.0004)	−.001*** (.0004)
University grade		−.001** (.005)	−.001** (.001)	−.001** (.0006)
Students per faculty			−.002*** (.001)	−.002*** (.001)
Share of delayed students			−.018 (.073)	−.076 (.077)
GDP				−.001*** (.0003)
Provincial unemployment				.009*** (.003)
Dummies on year delay		YES	YES	YES
R^2	0.147	0.147	0.149	0.150
Observations	33,463	33,463	33,463	33,463

Notes: The results of four different specifications of a linear probability model are displayed. The dependent variable assumes the value 1 if the individual declares not to be working and to be searching, 0 otherwise. All specifications include university · department fixed effects, fourteen dummies for high school type, eleven dummies for having another university degree, five dummies for each parent's level of education, 104 dummies for province of residence before university enrolment. Column (1) includes only predetermined individual control, column (2) considers all individual controls, column (3) incorporates time-variant university characteristics, and column (4) includes Provincial GDP and unemployment rate. Robust standard errors in parentheses. All regressions are clustered at region · degree · year.
***Significant at the 1 percent level.
**Significant at the 5 percent level.
*Significant at the 10 percent level.

and year.[26] The analysis is structured along the classification described in section 4.4—hence four specifications are displayed: column (1) includes individual characteristics predetermined before university entry; column (2) presents also potentially endogenous individual controls; column (3) incorporates time-variant university characteristics; and column (4) displays the results of a regression that includes province unemployment and GDP per capita. Note that all specifications include university time department dummies.

Table 4.8 shows that, conditional on individual characteristics, if a university decides to affiliate to *AlmaLaurea* the probability that its graduates are unemployed three years after graduation significantly decreases by about two points. Potentially endogenous individual regressors (column [2]) and university controls (column [3]) do not significantly affect our results. Conversely, controlling for provincial unemployment rates and GDP (column [4]) reduces the magnitude of the coefficient to about 1.6 points, and also

26. If we cluster standard errors at university level, most of the coefficients are not statistically significant at the 10 percent level.

Table 4.9   **The effect of *AlmaLaurea* on mobility**

	(1)		(2)		(3)		(4)	
AlmaLaurea	.024**	(.011)	.024**	(.012)	.027**	(.012)	.024**	(.012)
2001	−.008	(.007)	−.008	(.007)	.007	(.008)	−.009	(.011)
Female	−.022***	(.004)	−.022***	(.005)	−.022***	(.005)	−.022***	(.005)
Age	−.001**	(.001)	.0004	(.0006)	.0003	(.0006)	.0002	(.0006)
High school grade	.001**	(.0003)	.0002	(.0003)	.0003	(.0003)	.0004	(.0003)
University grade			.0003	(.0006)	.0003	(.0006)	.0001	(.0006)
Students per faculty					.001	(.001)	−.001	(.001)
Share of delayed students					−.209***	(.001)	−.179**	(.077)
GDP							−.0005	(.001)
Provincial unemployment							−.005	(.004)
Dummies on year delay			YES		YES		YES	
R^2	0.282		0.283		0.283		0.283	
Observations	33,463		33,463		33,463		33,463	

Notes: The results of four different specifications of a linear probability model are displayed. The dependent variable assumes the value 1 if an individual resides in a different region from one where he or she attended university, and 0 otherwise. All specifications include university · department fixed effects, fourteen dummies for high school type, eleven dummies for having another university degree, five dummies for each parent's level of education, 104 dummies for province of residence before university enrolment. Column (1) includes only predetermined individual controls, column (2) considers all individual controls, column (3) incorporates time-variant university characteristics, and column (4) includes Provincial GDP and unemployment rate. Robust standard errors in parentheses. All regressions are clustered at region · degree · year.
***Significant at the 1 percent level.
**Significant at the 5 percent level.
*Significant at the 10 percent level.

reduces its statistical significance. However, the coefficient is still statistically significant at the 10 percent level. Quantitatively, this implies that, out of the 23,688 individuals that graduated from a member university in 1998, 379 graduates were out of unemployment as a consequence of *AlmaLaurea* adoption. Although we do not have direct evidence on the extent to which *AlmaLaurea* crowded out other search channels, this finding is plausible if one observes the high number of curricula sold by the consortium displayed in table 4.3.

Table 4.9 also shows that regional mobility rates have different dynamics for graduates in *AlmaLaurea* universities: depending on the controls used, *AlmaLaurea* has a positive and statistically significant effect on mobility, ranging from 2.3 to 2.8 points.[27] About 570 individuals, which without the consortium would have been resident in the region where they graduated, moved to a different one.

As mentioned, lower search costs are also expected to improve the quality

27. Similar results are obtained if we consider provincial mobility.

Table 4.10   The effect of *AlmaLaurea* on wages

	(1)	(2)	(3)	(4)
AlmaLaurea	.034* (.017)	.036** (.018)	.035* (.018)	.031* (.018)
2001	.222*** (.015)	.227*** (.015)	.227*** (.016)	.201*** (.020)
Female	−.153*** (.008)	−.157*** (.008)	−.158*** (.008)	−.158*** (.008)
Age	.013*** (.002)	.017*** (.001)	.017*** (.002)	.017*** (.002)
High school grade	.005*** (.0005)	.003*** (.0006)	.003*** (.0006)	.003*** (.0006)
University grade		.005*** (.0008)	.005*** (.0008)	.005*** (.0008)
Students per faculty			.003* (.001)	.002 (.001)
Share of delayed students			.020 (.100)	.055 (.102)
GDP				.002*** (.0005)
Provincial unemployment				−.011** (.005)
Dummies on year delay		YES	YES	YES
R^2	0.252	0.259	0.259	0.260
Observations	20,838	20,838	20,838	20,838

Notes: The results of three different specifications of an OLS model are displayed. The dependent variable is the logarithm of monthly net wages. All specifications include university · department fixed effects, fourteen dummies for high school type, eleven dummies for having another university degree, five dummies for each parent's level of education, and 104 dummies for province of residence before university enrollment. Column (1) includes only predetermined individual control, column (2) considers all individual controls, column (3) incorporates time-variant universities characteristics, and column (4) includes provincial GDP and provincial unemployment rates. Robust standard errors in parentheses. All regressions are clustered at region · degree · year.

***Significant at the 1 percent level.
**Significant at the 5 percent level.
*Significant at the 10 percent level.

of labor market matches. Table 4.10 shows that, according to our analysis, *AlmaLaurea* significantly increases monthly wages by about 3 percent.[28] Taking as a reference the average wage, this implies that working graduates made about thirty-five more euros per month. We also find that *AlmaLaurea* increases graduates' satisfaction with the adequacy of the knowledge acquired at university, and job stability.[29]

4.5.2   Universities That Joined in 1998

The previous findings may be driven by time-varying omitted university characteristics. To investigate whether this is the case, in this section, we exploit an additional source of exogenous variation. The universities of Turin and Eastern Piedmont joined *AlmaLaurea* in August 1998 and hence sold resumes online only for those 1998 graduates who completed

28. This result needs to be interpreted with caution because of the possible different composition of the two samples. In fact, wage regressions are run only for those individuals who are employed.
29. Results are not reported but are available upon request by the authors.

Table 4.11   **Effect of *AlmaLaurea:* The case of Turin and Eastern Piedmont**

	Panel A Unemployment		
	Pre-August	Post-August	Diff.
Turin and Eastern Piedmont	.038	.016	−.022
Non-Turin and Eastern Piedmont	.102	.104	.002
Diff.			**−.024****
Standard error			(.011)
	Mobility		
Turin and Eastern Piedmont	.165	.164	−.001
Non-Turin and Eastern Piedmont	.227	.228	.001
Diff.			**.002**
Standard error			(.026)
	Wage		
Turin and Eastern Piedmont	1,151.4	1,103.9	−47.5
Non-Turin and Eastern Piedmont	1,152.3	1,134.1	−18.2
Diff.			**−29.4**
Standard error			(32.1)

	Panel B		
	Unemployment	Mobility	Long wage
AlmaLaurea	−.025*** (.008)	.009 (.022)	−.016 (.018)
Female	.043*** (.005)	−.021*** (.007)	−.149*** (.009)
Age	−.002* (.001)	.0005 (.001)	.017*** (.002)
High school grade	−.001*** (.0002)	.0001 (.0003)	.002*** (.0006)
University grade	−.001** (.0006)	.0004 (.001)	.005*** (.001)
Dummies on year delay	YES	YES	YES
Dummies for month of graduation	YES	YES	YES
R^2	0.122	0.251	0.226
Observation	20,547	20,547	12,975

Notes: The analysis is on 1998 graduates. The treatment group is composed of graduates from the universities of Turin and Eastern Piedmont. Before and after is graduation before and after August. All specifications include university · department fixed effects. Robust standard errors in parentheses. All regressions are clustered at region · degree · year. The bold differences are the result of a DID estimation.
***Significant at the 1 percent level.
**Significant at the 5 percent level.
*Significant at the 10 percent level.

their degree after that date. In our alternative DID setting the new treatment group is composed of graduates from these two universities, with the before-and-after being graduation after August 1998. In this specification, only 1998 data are considered and dummies for month of graduation are included. As table 4.11 shows, *AlmaLaurea* significantly decreases unemployment probability by about 2.5 points, which is a similar magnitude to

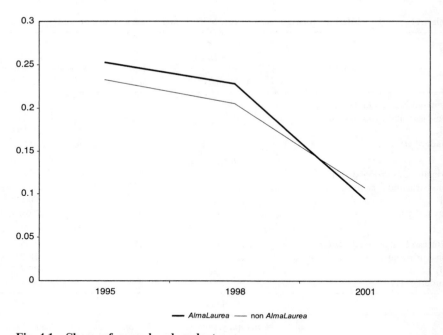

Fig. 4.1   Shares of unemployed graduates
Note: Only graduates from university departments that were in the database in 1995 are considered.

the effect achieved, as shown previously. However, there is no significant effect on either mobility or wages.

4.6   Unparallel Outcomes

Possibly the most important threat to the internal validity of the previously discussed results is the extent to which the "parallel trends" assumption stated in equation (1) is valid. One of the standard ways of assessing its plausibility is to use data from the pretreatment periods to check whether trends were parallel in the past. If this is the case, it is likely that the results achieved here stem from the treatment itself.

The Italian Statistical office conducted an earlier university-to-work survey on 1992 graduates, who were interviewed in 1995.[30] As depicted in figure 4.1, prior to 1998 the employment rate dynamics for the control and the treatment groups were remarkably similar. We apply the DID method with linear controls on data for 1992 and 1995 graduates; that is, before *AlmaLaurea* came into existence. Table 4.12 shows that the DID coefficient

30. Unfortunately, the 1995 survey does not include data on wages.

Table 4.12   **Pre-adoption falsification test of *AlmaLaurea***

	Unemployment		Mobility	
AlmaLaurea	.004	(.013)	.011	(.012)
1998	−.027***	(.008)	.005	(.006)
Female	.079***	(.008)	−.026***	(.005)
GDP	−.001**	(.0004)	−.003	(.003)
Provincial unemployment	.003	(.002)	.001	(.002)
R^2		0.150		0.322
Observations		27,373		27,565

Notes: In the first column the dependent variable takes the value 1 if a given graduate is un-employed, and 0 otherwise. In the second column the dependent variable takes the value 1 if a given individual resides in a different region from the one where he or she attended universi-ties. Only individuals that graduated in 1992 and 1995 are considered. *AlmaLaurea* takes the value 1 for 1995 graduates from universities that enroll in *AlmaLaurea* between 1995 and 1998. All specifications include university · department fixed effects. Robust standard errors in pa-rentheses. All regressions are clustered at region · degree · year.
***Significant at the 1 percent level.
**Significant at the 5 percent level.
*Significant at the 10 percent level.

for unemployment is positive, negligible, and not statistically different from zero. The result is similar for mobility: the *AlmaLaurea* coefficient is not sta-tistically different from zero. This reduces the likelihood that the coefficients in tables 4.8 and 4.9 stem from unparallel trends in the two groups.

Of course, these checks do not control for time-specific unparallel out-comes. In fact, possible interactions between *AlmaLaurea* enrollment and unobserved time-variant characteristics cannot easily be ruled out. One could argue, for example, that those universities that self selected in the treatment group are the ones whose unobservable teaching quality improved most. This might affect the occupational outcomes of their graduates.

To investigate this possibility we build a placebo treatment group com-posed of graduates from the universities of Siena and Lecce. According to *AlmaLaurea* official sources, these universities decided to join *AlmaLaurea* in 1997, but did not start selling their students' resumes online until 1999 and 2003, respectively. If these graduates also experienced an improvement vis-â-vis the others, the likelihood that *AlmaLaurea* enrollment proxies for something else is higher. We ran a regression similar to the one in equation (4), but with graduates from Siena and Lecce as the treatment group and non-*AlmaLaurea* universities as the control. Table 4.13 shows that this group experienced a slight increase in unemployment and wages and a decrease in mobility. None of these changes is statistically significantly different from zero. These findings provide evidence against the possibility that enrollment in the treatment group is correlated with unobservables that independently cause employment improvements.

Table 4.13   Effect of *AlmaLaurea* using a placebo treatment group

	Unemployment	Mobility	Log wage
Placebo *AlmaLaurea*	.024	−.017	.011
	(.025)	(.026)	(.036)
R^2	0.152	0.389	0.260
Observations	26,278	26,278	16,464

Notes: Placebo *AlmaLaurea* takes the value 1 for graduates for 1998 from the universities of Siena and Lecce, 0 otherwise. All specifications include the full set of controls used in the 4th columns of tables 4.8, 4.9, and 4.10. Robust standard errors in parentheses. All regressions are clustered at region · degree · year.

4.7   Alternative Treatment and Control Groups and Displacement Effect

The DID design can be further strengthened using alternative treatment and comparison groups. In fact, this is likely to reduce the importance of biases or random variation occurring in a single setting (Meyer 1995). In the ideal specification, treatment and control groups should face the same time-specific shocks: the more similar the two groups are, the better. Given that our dependent variables concern labor market outcomes and that (according to our data when the survey took place) more than 75 percent of Italian graduates reside in the region where they attended university (see table 4.7), a new sample is created including only graduates from regions that include both *AlmaLaurea* and non-*AlmaLaurea* universities.

Three Italian regions fit this criterion: Tuscany, Abruzzo, and Sicily. Graduates in these regions represent about 17 percent of the entire population and, within this group, about 57 percent of graduates are in the treatment group universities. As can be seen from figure 4.2, *AlmaLaurea* universities are Florence, Chieti, Catania, and Messina. Non-*AlmaLaurea* universities are Pisa, Siena, L'Aquila, Teramo, and Palermo. Table 4.14 shows that with respect to the general case, in this setting *AlmaLaurea* has a stronger effect on employment probability (3.5 points) and wages (5 percent) and about the same impact on mobility. The result for wages is not statistically significant. Overall, however, the general results are confirmed and even strengthened.

This control exercise is also helpful for checking for an additional potential problem in our analysis. As mentioned in section 4.3, graduates from nearby universities might be used to assess whether there is a displacement effect on non-*AlmaLaurea* students due to a reallocation of hiring. Interactions are in fact more likely for graduates' occupational outcomes from nearby universities. Hence, for example, the impact of *AlmaLaurea* might be exaggerated if individuals in the control group were negatively affected by *AlmaLaurea* itself. For instance, Pisa, in principle, is a better control group for Florence than Bari; nevertheless, the risk that its graduates' labor market performance is negatively affected by the presence of *AlmaLaurea* in Florence is higher. To control for this possibility, we perform a DID analysis

Fig. 4.2   Regions with both *AlmaLaurea* and non-*AlmaLaurea* universities
Note: Map displays only those cities that have a university.

with non-*AlmaLaurea* universities in regions where there are *AlmaLaurea* universities constituting the treatment group, with the control group being the remaining non-*AlmaLaurea* universities. From table 4.15, it can be seen that there are no significant differences in the trajectories of the two groups. This suggests that there are no major interactions among the graduates in the two groups and that *AlmaLaurea* does not have negative spillovers on universities located close by.

4.8   Conclusions

Since the late 1990s we have seen a large increase in the importance of online labor market intermediaries. While their diffusion may potentially

Table 4.14   Alternative treatment and control groups, based on geographic proximity

	Unemployment	Mobility	Wage
AlmaLaurea	−.035**	.024*	.053
	(.017)	(.026)	(.039)
R^2	0.149	0.492	0.263
Observations	6,225	6,225	3,521

Notes: Only graduates from regions that have both *AlmaLaurea* and non-*AlmaLaurea* universities are included. All specifications include the full set of controls used in column (4) of tables 4.8, 4.9, and 4.10. Robust standard errors in parenthesis. All regressions are clustered at region · degree · year.
***Significant at the 1 percent level.
**Significant at the 5 percent level.
*Significant at the 10 percent level.

Table 4.15   The effect of *AlmaLaurea* on nearby universities

	Unemployment	Mobility	Wage
AlmaLaurea	−.008	.006	.010
	(.012)	(.015)	(.023)
R^2	0.152	0.295	0.260
Observations	26,436	26,436	16,464

Notes: Only individuals who graduated from non-*AlmaLaurea* universities are included. The variable *AlmaLaurea* takes the value 1 if a 1998 graduate is awarded a degree from a non-*AlmaLaurea* university that is located in a region where there are also *AlmaLaurea* universities, and 0 otherwise. All specifications include the full set of controls in the 4th columns of tables 4.8, 4.9, and 4.10. Robust standard errors in parentheses. All regressions are clustered at region · degree · year.
***Significant at the 1 percent level.
**Significant at the 5 percent level.
*Significant at the 10 percent level.

improve labor market functioning, increasing the total quantity and quality of matches, solid evidence of their benefits is still missing. In addition, recent works have underlined the possibility of adverse selection in the use of electronic intermediaries among the unemployed (Kuhn and Skuterud 2004).

In this article we exploited the exceptional case study provided by the early adoption of the online intermediary *AlmaLaurea* by several Italian universities. The absence of other electronic intermediaries for those universities that had not adopted *AlmaLaurea* at the time of our study provides us with an adequate control group to estimate the effect of the treatment.

We employed the difference-in-differences method on a repeated cross-sectional data set. Given that enrollment in *AlmaLaurea* is not random, evaluating its impact is not trivial. However, assuming parallel outcomes between treatment and control group makes our estimation valid. The inclusion of time-variant indicators concerning individual and university characteristics and standard tests aimed at ruling out alternative explanations do not raise major concerns in relation to this important assumption.

The evidence shows that the adoption of the online labor market intermediary under study improved graduates' labor market outcomes three years after graduation. In particular, according to our most conservative estimate, *AlmaLaurea* decreased graduates' unemployment probability by about 1.6 percentage points.

Our study also suggests that online labor market intermediaries may have a positive effect on matching quality. In fact, in our case study, the wages of graduates from member universities increased by about 3 percent. Finally, we also observe an increase in mobility by about 2.4 percentage points.

The findings of this chapter are specific to a given segment of the labor market (i.e., university-to-work transition) and to a peculiar electronic intermediary. Thus, their external validity has to be carefully assessed. In particular, the single characteristic of *AlmaLaurea* that possibly made it a successful intermediary is also the most unusual: member universities certify the information contained in electronic curricula and also provide some information on the entire population of graduates. This important caveat helps to integrate our findings within the existing literature that does not find any effect of online search on the overall unemployment rates and duration (Kuhn and Skuterud 2004; Kroft and Pope 2008).

The results presented in this chapter also contribute to the policy discussion on the university-to-work transition. The poor labor performance of Italian graduates has been traditionally ascribed to demand-and-supply factors. We show that graduate labor market functioning can also be improved by the introduction of online intermediaries.

In future research we aim at exploring whether the positive impact of electronic labor market intermediaries affects the whole graduate population evenly. Also, while in this chapter we focus on average outcomes, the effect on outcome distribution remains an issue for further research.

References

Autor, D. H. 2001. Wiring the labor market. *Journal of Economic Perspectives* 15 (1): 25–40.

Bagues, M., M. Sylos Labini, and N. Zinovyeva. Forthcoming. Differential grading standards and university funding: Evidence from Italy. *CESifo Economic Studies.*

Burdett, K., and J. Ondrich. 1985. How changes in labor demand affect unemployed workers. *Journal of Labor Economics* 3 (1): 1–10.

Congressional Budget Office. 2002. *The effect of changes in the labor markets on the natural rate of unemployment,* April.

Freeman, R. B. 2002. The labor market in the new information economy. *Oxford Review of Economic Policy* 18 (3): 288–305.

Heckman, J. J. 1990. Varieties of selection bias. *American Economic Review* 80 (2): 313–18.

Kroft, K., and D. G. Pope. 2008. Does online search crowd out traditional search and improve matching efficiency? Evidence from Craigslist. Unpublished manuscript. University of California, Berkeley.

Kuhn, P. 2000. The Internet and matching in labor markets in *New economy handbook,* ed. D. C. Jones, 508–23. Amsterdam: Elsevier.

Kuhn, P., and M. Skuterud. 2004. Internet job search and unemployment duration. *American Economic Review* 94 (1): 218–32.

Mannheim Centre for European Social Research. 2002. Indicators on school-to-work transitions in Europe. Mannheim, Germany: Mzes.

Meyer, B. D. 1995. Natural and quasi-experiments in economics. *Journal of Business and Economic Statistics* 13: 151–61.

Organization for Economic Cooperation and Development (OECD). 2007. *Education at a glance.* Paris: OECD.

Pissarides, C. 2000. *Equilibrium unemployment theory.* 2nd ed. Cambridge, MA: MIT Press.

Rebick, M. E. 2000. The importance of networks in the market for university graduates in Japan: A longitudinal analysis of hiring patterns. *Oxford Economic Papers* 52 (3): 471–96.

Rubin, D. B. 1974. Estimating causal effects of treatments in randomized and nonrandomized studies. *Journal of Educational Psychology* 66:688–701.

Stevenson, B. 2008. The Internet and job search. University of Pennsylvania. NBER Working Paper no. 13886. Cambridge, MA: National Bureau of Economic Research, March.

Private Deception and the Rise of Public Employment Offices in the United States, 1890–1930

Woong Lee

5.1 Introduction

Public employment offices are nonprofit governmental organizations that match job-seekers and employers, one of their main purposes being to reduce job search costs in order to improve job-seekers' success in finding a job in the labor market.[1] As a labor market intermediary, public employment offices have existed in all of the Organization for Economic Cooperation and Development (OECD) countries since the 1950s (Walwei 1996). Recent trends in European countries have been to deregulate and privatize employment services since the 1990s (De Koning, Denys, and Walwei 1999). Interestingly, the opposite trend took place in the late nineteenth and early twentieth centuries. The establishment of public employment offices was a widespread phenomenon in both Europe and North America during this time.[2] Many countries also passed laws to abolish or strictly regulate private employment agencies (Martinez 1976; Finkin and

Woong Lee is a doctoral candidate at the Department of Economics, University of California, Irvine.

The author gratefully acknowledges the generous advice and guidance of his advisers, Dan Bogart (primary adviser), Jiawei Chen, Jun Ishii, and Gary Richardson. He also thanks Keith Finlay, Chen Feng Ng, Raaj Tiagi, and Kathleen Wong for their useful comments. In particular, David Autor and Susan Houseman gave invaluable comments and advice to improve this chapter. The author is indebted to Price Fishback, who shared his expertise regarding the data used in this chapter. All the errors and views in the chapter are the author's own.

1. There are other terminologies for public employment offices, such as public employment agencies, bureaus, or services. I use public employment offices in this chapter because historically it was the most frequently used.

2. Public employment offices were established in Belgium in 1870, Sweden and France in 1884, Britain in 1885, the United States in 1890, and Italy and Germany in 1897 (U.S. Employment Service 1935a).

Jacoby 2005).[3] As a result, the labor exchange market was monopolized by the central government in these countries. This institutional feature did not change until the late 1980s.

In this chapter, I provide a rationale for the establishment of public employment offices and explore the relationship between the development of public employment offices and labor market conditions in the United States in order to argue that public employment offices were effective in protecting job-seekers, who lacked information and networks with regard to the job search process, from malpractice by private employment agencies.

In the first part of this chapter, I propose a theory that exploitation by private employment agencies with respect to job-seekers resulted from asymmetric information between job-seekers and private employment agencies. Job-seekers who are uninformed cannot distinguish between high- and low-quality agencies, and this may cause them to not pay for high-quality services. This situation could give private employment agencies an incentive to exploit uninformed job-seekers (provide low-quality services) due to their profit-maximizing behavior, thus causing adverse selection. Consequently, the market may disappear—or only low-quality agencies may survive.[4] In theory, it is possible that introducing public employment offices may eliminate low-quality agencies that exploit uninformed job-seekers, increase competition in the labor exchange market, and thus improve labor market efficiency. The introduction of public employment offices may remove low-quality private employment agencies because such agencies cannot survive if uninformed job-seekers use public employment offices without charge and without the risk of malpractice, while informed job-seekers use public employment offices or high-quality private employment agencies. As a result, no one would use low-quality private employment agencies, which would cause them to eventually disappear. This implies that the introduction of public employment offices could resolve the problem of adverse selection, as they provide an alternative network to uninformed job-seekers in the labor exchange market.

In the second part of this chapter, I estimate the number of job-seekers using public employment offices as a percentage of the labor force to examine the development of public employment offices in the U.S. labor market over time. The data show that public employment offices grew substantially

---

3. The Canadian Labor Congress requested the complete abolition of private employment agencies in 1913. The German government began to abolish private employment agencies in 1922. Austria declined to issue any new licenses for new businesses after World War I. Finland, Romania, and Bulgaria completely eliminated private employment agencies by 1926 (Martinez 1976).

In the early twentieth century, state governments in the United States (e.g., Washington) tried to abolish private employment agencies, but the U.S. Supreme Court ruled their attempts to be unconstitutional (Finkin and Jacoby 2005).

4. In this chapter, private employment agencies that exploit uninformed job seekers are described as low-quality providers.

and became a major labor market intermediary concurrent with the U.S. involvement in World War I. The use of public employment offices by job-seekers as a percentage of the labor force was at least 4 percent between 1916 and 1940. This shows that public employment offices played an important role in the labor market, and thus could affect the behavior of job-seekers and private employment agencies.

In the third part of this chapter, I show that the majority of public employment office users were unskilled workers, immigrants, or migrants in the early twentieth century. These workers were also major clients of private employment agencies in this period. This finding suggests that these workers, who were most likely to be abused by private employment agencies, tended to utilize public employment offices for their job search.

Finally, I test the relationship between the use of public employment offices and changes in labor market conditions, which were related to asymmetric information such as proportions of immigrants, migrants, and unskilled workers. The key finding is that the relationship between the use of public employment offices and interstate migration is positive and significant in most specifications. This positive correlation may support the hypothesis that public employment offices contributed to lowering the degree of asymmetric information for interstate migrants who were most likely to lack information and networks with regards to the job search process, and thus the most vulnerable to exploitation by private employment agencies.

The rest of the chapter is organized as follows. Section 5.2 proposes a theory of public employment offices. Section 5.3 provides the background of public employment offices in relation to the labor market. Section 5.4 presents the analysis of public employment office users. Section 5.5 provides the empirical work. Section 5.6 concludes the chapter.

5.2   A Theory of Public Employment Offices

Economists have put forth theories about the existence of labor market intermediaries, including private employment agencies (hereafter referred to as "private agencies") and public employment offices (hereafter referred to as "public offices"), to explain why these intermediaries are necessary and how they help reduce transaction costs in the labor market (e.g., Pissarides 1979; Yavas 1994; Kübler 1999). The fundamental intuition behind these theories is that labor market intermediaries can increase the efficiency of the job matching process by reducing transaction costs (Pissarides 1979; Yavas 1994). It has also been suggested that the coexistence of public and private agencies may improve an employer's screening ability if there exists asymmetric information between job-seekers and employers (Kübler 1999). However, these theories do not explain why public offices were introduced to restrain private agencies from malpractices with respect to job-seekers. To explain this, I first describe how severe the abuses by private agencies were and why these were possible. Next, I propose a theory of how public offices served to limit the incidence of malpractices by private agencies.

Around the turn of the twentieth century, in response to the cries of job-seekers who were exploited by private agencies, social reformers and public officials tried to find a solution, one of which was to create public offices (Bogart 1900; Sargent 1912; Leiserson 1915; Herdon 1918).[5] Two examples, which support the notion that public offices were established to check on the actions of private agencies, are as follows:

> [T]he establishment of free public employment offices rests on the abuses which exist in the private agencies. . . . This point is made much of by the commissioners of labor in the various states, and their reports contain many instances of the deception and fraud practiced by these agencies on the unemployed. (Bogart 1900, 345)

> One of the influences making for the rapid growth in the number and importance of public employment offices has been the flagrant evils connected with these private employment agencies. (Herdon 1918, 5)

The most common malpractice by private agencies was the misrepresentation of characteristics on occupations to job-seekers (Commons and Andrews 1936). Sargent (1912, 36) summarizes common deceitful practices by private agencies, which took advantage of uninformed job-seekers in some of the following ways:

1. Charging a fee and failing to make any effort to find work for the applicant.

2. Sending applicants where no work exists.

3. Sending applicants to distant points where no work or where unsatisfactory work exists, but whence the applicants will not return on account of expense involved.

4. Collusion between the agent and employer (e.g., foremen), whereby the applicant is given a few days work and then discharged to make way for new workmen; the agent and employer divide the fee.

5. Charging exorbitant fees or giving jobs to such applicants as contribute extra fees, presents, and so on.

6. Inducing workers who have been placed, particularly girls, to leave, pay another fee, and get a better job.

In addition to these malpractices, several private agencies were found to have actually sent women to houses of prostitution (Muhlhauser 1916).

---

5. Establishment of public offices is an example of the Progressivism movement in the United States in the early twentieth century because they were introduced to eliminate the abuses by private agencies in response to the cries of job-seekers. Thus, this governmental intervention was a kind of social justice to help disadvantaged people.

Stewart and Stewart (1933), Edwards (1935), Commons and Andrews (1936), and Martinez (1976) report that many European countries also established public offices to prevent private agencies from exploiting their clients.

These abuses were possible because many job-seekers who used private agencies were immigrants, unskilled workers, or temporary workers (Sargent 1912; Commons and Andrews 1936; U.S. Bureau of Labor Standards 1962; Rosenbloom 2002). As such, they were most likely to be unfamiliar with the language and customs of the United States less educated, or had little legal recourse to recover damages from private agencies. Thus, I argue that exploitation by private agencies with respect to job-seekers resulted from information asymmetry between job-seekers and private agencies.

Private agencies that exploit job-seekers can be described as low-quality agencies. If job-seekers cannot distinguish between high- and low-quality agencies or if their search cost is very high, then high-quality agencies may have an incentive to reduce their service quality (if they stay in the market) because job-seekers who use private agencies cannot pay for high-quality services. Therefore, the market would disappear or only low-quality private agencies with severe abuses would prevail in the labor exchange market, meaning adverse selection. Furthermore, if private agencies exercise a high degree of market power, then the situation would become worse.

In general, there are two ways to reduce or eliminate asymmetric information that causes adverse selection in this situation: increase in search costs (for information gathering) by job-seekers, and signals by private agencies. Increase in search costs to distinguish between high- and low-quality private agencies is burdensome because job-seekers need to make additional effort. Moreover, it is very costly to those who are unfamiliar with a new environment, less educated, or needy (such as immigrants, unskilled workers, and temporary workers). Theoretically, signaling by high-quality private agencies is feasible, but there may be a possibility of a pooling equilibrium.[6]

The creation of public offices to provide job-seekers with placement services can be seen as a mechanism to eliminate low-quality private agencies, and thus resolve adverse selection caused by asymmetric information between job-seekers and private agencies in the labor exchange market. With the provision of public offices, low-quality private agencies may not survive because job-seekers who are uninformed can use public offices without charge and without the risk of malpractice, while job-seekers who are informed can use public offices or high-quality private agencies.[7] Under ideal conditions, job-seekers would be fully informed about the quality of the private agencies that they deal with, and thus could make a preferred choice along the quality-price locus. Public offices may help in this regard by driving

6. For example, low-quality agencies may charge high fees to their clients to imitate high-quality service providers because high fees are usually accompanied by high-quality services. This may result in a pooling equilibrium if both high- and low-quality agencies send high-quality signals to the clients.

7. An implicit assumption is that public offices are credibly high quality because services are publicly provided. Even if job-seekers are not sure about the credibility of public offices, they could provide an effective means to solve the information/quality problem faced by job-seekers because services by public offices are free.

deceptive private agencies from the market, allowing job-seekers to choose to use either public offices or credible private agencies. This implies that the creation of public offices can resolve the problem of adverse selection, as an alternative network is provided to job-seekers in the labor exchange market. Therefore, the introduction of public offices may inject competition that either causes low-quality private agencies to improve or drives them out of the market. Throughout this process, high-quality private agencies survive, and without monopolization of the labor exchange market by the government, both public and private agencies can exist together to improve the efficiency of the labor market.

Besides the introduction of public offices, state governments began to regulate private agencies even before public offices were established (see, for example, Bogart 1900). Some state or municipal governments required private agencies to pay license fees, deposit bonds, or both. In addition, several local governments imposed fines on private agencies or shut down their businesses when violation of the regulations was investigated.

Baldwin (1951) and the U.S. Bureau of Labor Standards (1962) insisted that before World War I, public offices did not function well and only restrictions on private agencies were effective in the labor exchange market. However, Devine (1909), Sargent (1912), and Leiserson (1915) argued that restrictions on private agencies were ineffective and the creation of public offices lessened the degree of malpractices, thus contributing to the protection of job-seekers. It is an open question as to which institution worked better to keep private agencies in check, since there is little evidence of specific statistics or detailed reports to compare these two institutions.[8] However, evidence supporting the effectiveness of public offices is as follows (State of Illinois Bureau of Labor Statistics 1906, 3):

> While the primary purpose in establishing these offices was to aid the common or unskilled laborers in getting work without cost to him or her, their influence has not been limited to that class. . . . From this it is shown that nearly 8,000 people, representing established skilled trades, including commercial and professional pursuits, have secured positions during the year. . . . The better class of private employment agencies will accept only applications for a certain service, mainly of a professional character.[9]

8. Fee and bond regulations could be effective because they are likely to raise costs by more for low-quality than high-quality agencies. But if there are no effective means of enforcement, then such mandates would be unlikely to work. For example, the U.S. Supreme Court ruled unconstitutional a New Jersey law regulating the fees that private agencies could charge their clients (Finkin and Jacoby 2005). In addition, inspection of private agencies could be very costly if there are many illegal (unlicensed) private agencies. Several states' labor bureaus reported violations of the license law (see, for example, State of Missouri Bureau of Labor Statistics 1913 and State of California Bureau of Labor 1923).

9. In 1905 the total number of job-seekers placed by Illinois public offices was 39,598 and the number of applicants was 45,323.

5.3   Background of Public Employment Offices

In this section, I provide evidence that public offices were a major labor market intermediary and thus could affect the behavior of job-seekers and private agencies in the United States in the early twentieth century. To do this, I estimate the number of job-seekers who used public offices (the use of public offices by job-seekers) between 1890 and 1940 (see figure 5.1).[10] I also measure the percentage of public office users in the labor force and compare this to the unemployment rate (see figure 5.2).

The first five (continuous) public offices established in Ohio in 1890.[11] Only fifty-one offices were operated in nineteen states by 1910 (Herdon 1918). The use of public offices by job-seekers as a percentage of the labor force also did not exceed 1 percent by 1910 (see figure 5.2). When immigration reached its highest point (1.4 million immigrants) in 1907, the federal government started to intervene in the labor exchange market (U.S. Employment Service 1935a). The Division of Information, the first federal employment agency, was created in the Department of Commerce and Labor. However, its role was restricted to disseminating to immigrants over the states up until World War I (Guzda 1983). Although both federal and local public offices contributed little to the labor market at that time, these organizations aimed to protect immigrants, who were unfamiliar with the urban environment in the United States, from the abuses of private agencies (International Labour Office 1955).

Many firms lost their foreign markets with the beginning of World War I, causing a serious unemployment problem, as shown by the relatively high unemployment rates in 1914 and 1915 (see figure 5.2). However, the problem of lack of labor demand changed to a shortage of labor supply upon the United States' entry into World War I, especially due to higher labor demand in war-related industries as well as demand by the military service (U.S. Bureau of Labor Statistics 1931). Accordingly, the Division of Information, renamed as the U.S. Employment Service (USES), was reorganized to serve as a nationwide labor market intermediary to assist the wartime emergency in 1917. Most public offices, which had the exclusive power of matching unskilled labor to industries, were under the control of USES during the nation's involvement in World War I (Kellogg 1933). The use

---

10. The first (continuous) public offices were established in Ohio in 1890, and the nationwide system of public offices as a permanent labor market intermediary was set in the United States in 1940 (the author's inspection). That is why the estimates in figures 5.1 and 5.2 range from 1890 and 1940.

11. There were a couple of trials to establish public employment offices before 1890. Examples are the Castle Garden Labor Exchange in New York City, opened in 1850 (Rosenbloom 2002), and the California Labor Exchange, established in San Francisco in 1868 (U.S. Employment Service 1935b). These public employment agencies were eventually discontinued due to a lack of funds.

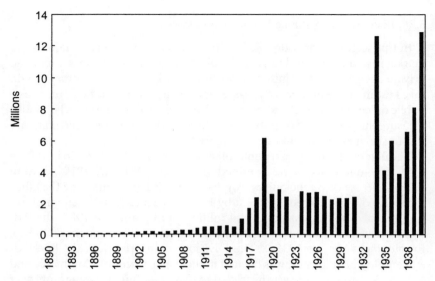

Fig. 5.1   Use of public employment offices by job-seekers

Sources: 1890–1914: Bogart (1900), Conner (1907), Sargent (1912), and various state governments' reports (State of Colorado Bureau of Labor Statistics 1903–1915; State of Connecticut Bureau of Labor Statistics 1902–1915; State of Illinois Bureau of Labor Statistics 1900–1915; State of Indiana Department of Statistics 1911–1915; State of Kansas Bureau of Labor and Industry 1901–1914; State of Kansas Department of Labor and Industry 1914–1915; State of Kentucky Bureau of Agriculture, Labor, and Statistics 1912–1915; State of Maryland Bureau of Statistics and Information 1904–1915; State of Massachusetts Bureau of Statistics of Labor 1904, 1907–1915; State of Michigan Bureau of Labor and Industrial Statistics 1906–1909; State of Michigan Department of Labor 1910–1915; State of Minnesota Bureau of Labor 1907; State of Minnesota Bureau of Labor 1907; State of Missouri Bureau of Labor Statistics 1900–1916; State of Montana Bureau of Agriculture 1902–1912; State of Montana Department of Labor and Industry 1913–1916; State of New Jersey Department of Labor. *Report* 1910–1915; State of New York Department of Labor 1901–1916; State of Ohio Bureau of Labor Statistics 1891–1914; State of Ohio Department of Investigation and Statistics 1915–1916; State of Oklahoma Department of Labor 1908–1915; State of Rhode Island Bureau of Industrial Statistics 1908–1914; State of Washington Bureau of Labor 1903–1916; State of West Virginia Bureau of Labor Statistics 1901–1915; State of Wisconsin Bureau of Labor and Industrial Statistics 1902–1916). 1915–1916: U.S. Bureau of Labor Statistics, January 1915 (Vol. 1, No. 1) to February 1918 (Vol. 6, No. 2). 1917–1919: U.S. Employment Service (1918, 1919, 1920). 1920–1921: Smith (1923), and Commons and Andrews (1936). 1923–1930: U.S. Employment Service (January 1924 to January 1932). 1933: U.S. Employment Service (1935b). 1934–1939: U.S. Employment Service, September 1934 (Vol. 1, No. 1) to December 1940 (Vol. 7, No. 12).

Notes: 1923, 1931, and 1932 are missing. The following states in each year indicate missing data by state and year: 1903 to 1906 (Kansas); 1907 (Colorado); 1909 to 1910 (New Jersey); 1912 (Kansas, Montana, New Jersey, Oklahoma); 1913 (New Jersey, Oklahoma, West Virginia); 1914 (California, Kentucky, Montana, New Jersey, Oklahoma, Texas, West Virginia). Data from 1915 to 1939 are reported for fiscal years (July to June).

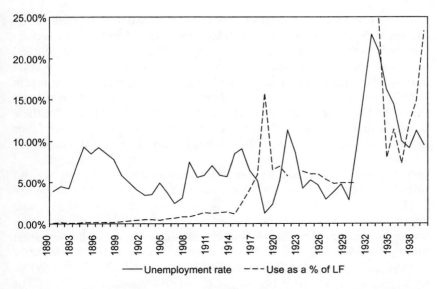

Fig. 5.2   Unemployment rate and use of public employment offices by job-seekers as a percentage of the labor force

Sources: Labor force (LF) and the unemployment rate (Wier 1992) and the use of public employment offices by job-seekers (same as figure 5.1).

of public offices soared during the 1918 fiscal year (see figures 5.1 and 5.2), mainly due to the massive number of returning soldiers and workers who had previously been transferred to war-related industries (U.S. Employment Service 1919). Soldiers and workers went back to their peacetime occupations after the war ceased, and public offices played an important role in reallocating them to their former positions and other places (U.S. Bureau of Labor Statistics 1931).

As the nation returned to normalcy, the use of public offices by job-seekers dropped substantially. The USES, the central authority of public offices during World War I, lost its power over the labor market due to huge budget cuts by Congress. Thus, a substantial number of offices were closed or turned over to state and municipal governments (U.S. Employment Service 1935a). The USES was a paper organization during the 1920s, meaning that the federal government's power over the labor exchange market was minimal. Most public offices were maintained and operated by states or municipalities independently of the federal government. Despite the decentralization of public labor exchange, the use of public offices was nontrivial. Most research and documents ignore public offices' contribution to the U.S. labor market in the 1920s (e.g., U.S. Employment Service 1935a; Commons and Andrews 1936; Adams 1969; Guzda 1983; Breen 1997). However, the evidence in figures 5.1 and 5.2 shows that more than 2 million job-seekers, or roughly 5 percent of the total labor force per year, used public offices during the 1920s. Public offices also made placements for 1.5 million job-seekers (approximately 3 percent of the labor force) during this period. Therefore, I argue that the role of public offices was also important in the labor market in the 1920s. One might think that public offices played an important role in the labor market only during times of emergency, such as World War I and the Great Depression, as public offices became centralized to resolve these chaotic situations. But public offices continued to serve as a major labor market intermediary in the 1920s, which was a time of peace and economic growth.

As the economy entered the Great Depression, the Wagner-Peyser Act of 1933 revitalized USES to be a nationwide employment service to control public offices across the nation. It was a joint system of federal and state governments.[12] As a main tool to perform New Deal relief programs for unemployment, public offices were influential over the entire labor market during the Great Depression. The substantial increase in the use of public offices by job-seekers in 1933 (as seen in figures 5.1 and 5.2) was mainly due to the public works provided by the Civil Works Administration (CWA). The Civil Works Administration hired more than 4 million people, and almost all placements for this administration were made by public offices. People who wanted to find jobs in the CWA had to use public offices (U.S. Employment Service 1935b).

Public offices also placed millions of unemployed in jobs created by the Works Progress Administration (WPA). High use of public offices since 1935 indicates this (see figures 5.1 and 5.2). The use of public offices was also directly related to the unemployment compensation between 1937 and 1939. The large increase in the use of public offices between 1938 and 1939 demonstrates this fact. Unemployment benefits were paid to jobless people, starting from January 1938, by the Social Security Act of 1935 (Atkinson, Odencrantz, and Deming 1938). People who wanted to receive these benefits had to register with public offices.

One point should be mentioned about the two spikes (around World War I and the Great Depression) in the use of public offices in figures 5.1 and 5.2, related to the argument in the previous section. The high use of public offices by job-seekers during the periods of World War I and the Great Depression is irrelevant to the hypothesis that public offices contributed to lowering the degree of asymmetric information between job-seekers and private agencies. Public offices performed employment services for wartime emergency during World War I and matched job-seekers and public work positions as a major tool to implement the New Deal policies in the Great Depression.

---

12. The federal government would provide up to 50 percent of the fund support, the remaining 50 percent being provided by the states to maintain and operate public offices (Ruttenberg and Gutchess 1970).

Given all the information provided in this section, it is clear that the impact of public offices on the labor market was not influential in the first two decades of its operation. However, the importance of public offices grew substantially, allowing them to be a major labor market intermediary with their involvement arising from World War I.[13]

5.4   Users of Public Employment Offices

In this section, I analyze users of public offices to test an implication of the theory proposed in section 5.2: The majority of job-seekers using private agencies in the nineteenth and early twentieth centuries were unskilled workers and immigrants who were vulnerable to the abuses of private agencies. If these job-seekers used public offices intensively, then this supports the hypothesis that public offices contributed to lowering the degree of exploitation by private agencies with respect to job-seekers (the degree of asymmetric information between job-seekers and private agencies) by providing an alternative network during their job search process. Therefore, I evaluate whether those who were vulnerable to exploitation by private agencies, such as unskilled workers and immigrants, actually used public offices more intensively.

To do this, I present the gender and occupations of public office users. I also construct the corresponding shares of workers in the population (the nation and state) from the Integrated Public Use Microdata Series or IPUMS (Ruggles et al. 2004) to see how public office users differed from other workers in the labor market in the early twentieth century.[14] In addition, I show other characteristics of public office users to analyze how they were related to the argument regarding asymmetric information.

First, I construct the shares of public office users by gender for a few selected states (Connecticut, Missouri, and Illinois) and compare them to those in the nation and the corresponding states in the early twentieth century (see table 5.1). In Connecticut and Illinois, the share of female public office users were much larger than those of female workers in the nation and in the states between 1900 and 1930, indicating that female workers used public offices more intensively than male workers in those states. In Missouri, the share of female public office users was larger than both the nation and the state female workers in 1900 (23.5 percent in Missouri public offices, 14.1 percent in the state of Missouri, and 18.0 percent in the nation), while this inequality was reversed between 1910 and 1920 (around 10 percent in Missouri public offices, 17 percent in the state of Missouri, and 20 percent

---

13. The use of public offices by job-seekers was at least 4 percent of the labor force between 1916 and 1940 (see figure 5.2).

14. The estimates for the nation and state workers in tables 5.1, 5.2, 5.3, and 5.4 are constructed from the working age population (aged between sixteen and sixty-five, inclusive) in the labor force.

Table 5.1   **Gender of public employment office applicants**

	Nation			State		Public employment offices	
Year	Men	Women	State	Men	Women	Men	Women
1900	82.0	18.0	CT	78.6	21.4	49.1	50.9
1910	79.1	21.0	CT	75.1	24.9	52.1	47.9
1920	79.4	20.6	CT	74.1	25.9	57.7	42.3
1930	77.7	22.3	CT	73.5	26.5	56.1	43.9
1900			MO	85.9	14.1	76.5	23.5
1910			MO	83.2	16.8	89.8	10.2
1920			MO	81.5	18.5	89.5	10.5
1930			MO	79.2	20.9	80.0	20.0
1900			IL	83.5	16.5	57.2	42.8
1910			IL	81.3	18.7	71.6	28.4
1920			IL	79.5	20.5	76.9	23.1
1930			IL	77.2	22.8	62.0	38.0

Source: See table 5.2.

Notes: The second and third columns present the percentages of male and female workers in the nation, respectively. The fifth and sixth columns present the percentages of male and female workers in the corresponding states, respectively. The seventh and eighth columns indicate the percentages of male and female job seekers registered in public employment offices in the corresponding states, respectively. All the percentages of the nation and states are calculated from the labor force of working age (i.e., aged between sixteen and sixty-five, inclusive).

in the nation). The shares of female workers in all cases (Missouri public offices, the state of Missouri, and the nation) were almost the same in 1930. Overall, female workers used employment services through public offices more intensively than male workers in Connecticut and Illinois, although this was not the case in Missouri.

Table 5.2 gives the proportions of public office users by occupation in the selected states over time. One clear pattern is that placements by public offices were biased toward service workers and laborers.[15] In Connecticut and Illinois, the largest proportion of public office users was service workers, while laborers formed the majority of public office users in Missouri (see the fourth, sixth, and eighth columns in table 5.2), respectively. As time went by, the importance of agriculture tended to dwindle in Connecticut (11.5 percent in 1900, 14.9 percent in 1910, 3.7 percent in 1920, and 2.7 percent in 1930), but in Missouri, the proportion of agricultural workers rose in 1920 (14.1 percent), declining in 1930 (8.3 percent). All three states' distributions of public offices show a concentration of service workers and laborers, but the degree of concentration was different. In Connecticut, approximately

15. Most of the public office applicants' occupations were also laborers and service workers in Connecticut, Illinois, and Missouri. I provide only the placements of public office applicants because more information on occupations is available.

Table 5.2   Occupations of male and female applicants placed by public employment offices

Occupation	Nation	CT State	CT Public offices	MO State	MO Public offices	IL State	IL Public offices
		1900					
Professionals and technical workers	4.5	5.0	0.2	4.7	0.2	5.6	0.0
Agricultural workers	33.4	10.3	11.5	39.5	3.2	24.2	2.5
Managers, officials, and proprietors	5.7	5.5	0.1	6.3	0.0	7.1	0.0
Clerical and kindred	3.4	4.0	2.2	3.8	8.3	5.3	0.4
Sales workers	4.5	5.2	8.0	5.2	4.0	6.1	0.7
Craftsmen and operatives	26.9	46.1	4.2	22.3	8.2	29.7	6.1
Service workers	9.3	9.0	66.7	8.6	24.4	9.9	40.3
Laborers	12.3	14.9	5.1	9.5	47.8	12.1	36.1
		1910					
Professionals and technical workers	4.9	5.6	0.1	5.0	0.0	5.6	0.0
Agricultural workers	28.6	7.4	14.9	32.8	5.8	18.7	1.6
Managers, officials, and proprietors	6.0	5.7	0.1	6.5	0.0	6.8	0.0
Clerical and kindred	5.6	7.1	0.4	6.4	0.3	8.7	0.6
Sales workers	4.7	4.9	4.0	5.6	1.4	5.8	0.9
Craftsmen and operatives	27.6	43.0	4.1	23.8	6.8	31.8	10.7
Service workers	9.5	10.8	61.1	9.1	35.5	9.5	43.7
Laborers	13.1	15.6	13.4	10.9	43.8	13.1	35.6
		1920					
Professionals and technical workers	5.6	6.3	0.0	5.7	0.1		
Agricultural workers	24.1	6.3	3.7	28.8	14.1		
Managers, officials, and proprietors	6.7	6.5	0.1	7.5	0.1		
Clerical and kindred	8.3	10.2	0.5	9.0	4.2		
Sales workers	5.0	4.3	2.8	6.0	0.2		
Craftsmen and operatives	30.8	46.0	7.1	25.0	14.5		
Service workers	8.1	7.9	71.8	8.0	19.4		
Laborers	11.5	12.6	13.6	10.0	46.9		

(*continued*)

60 to 70 percent of applicants placed were service workers, whereas more laborers were placed than service workers in Missouri (see the fourth and sixth columns in table 5.2). The differential between service workers and laborers was not large in Illinois relative to that in Connecticut (see the eighth column in table 5.2).

To investigate the types of public office users in more detail, I examine the occupations of male and female public office users over time, respectively. The data show that male public office users were largely laborers and the dominant occupation for females was service work, although there were some variations among states.[16] One clear fact is that the difference between

16. Tables for men's and women's occupational shares are available from the author upon request.

Table 5.2   (continued)

		CT		MO		IL	
Occupation	Nation	State	Public offices	State	Public offices	State	Public offices
		1930					
Professionals and technical workers	6.9	8.0	0.0	6.6	0.0		
Agricultural workers	20.1	4.6	2.7	24.3	8.3		
Managers, officials, and proprietors	7.3	7.4	0.0	7.7	0.1		
Clerical and kindred	9.2	12.2	1.3	10.0	1.3		
Sales workers	6.7	6.1	3.3	7.2	0.7		
Craftsmen and operatives	29.3	41.5	6.3	25.4	10.1		
Service workers	9.7	9.2	67.4	9.1	20.0		
Laborers	10.7	11.1	18.8	9.8	59.6		

Sources (tables 5.1 and 5.2): For 1900 occupation and gender distributions: State of Massachusetts Bureau of Statistics of Labor 1904. For 1910 occupation and gender distributions: Illinois and Missouri, Sargent 1912; Connecticut, State of Connecticut Bureau of Labor Statistics 1912. For 1920 occupation and gender distributions: Missouri, State of Missouri Bureau of Labor Statistics 1923; Connecticut, State of Connecticut Bureau of Labor Statistics 1922. For 1930 occupation and gender distributions: Missouri, State of Missouri Department of Labor and Industrial Inspection 1930; Connecticut, State of Connecticut Bureau of Labor Statistics 1931. For the nation and states' overall occupation and gender percents, IPUMS (Ruggles et al. 2004).

Notes: The first column is the classification of the occupations. The second column displays the percents of occupations of workers in the nation. The third, fifth, and seventh columns are the percents of occupations of workers in each state. The fourth, sixth, and eighth columns are the percentages of occupations of job-seekers placed through public employment offices in each state. The categorization of the occupations in table 5.2 is based on IPUM's 1950 occupation basis, which is the 1950 Census Bureau occupation classification system with some modifications. Agricultural workers include farmers (owners, tenants, farm managers) and farm laborers. Craftsmen and operatives are skilled and semiskilled workers in manufacturing. All the percentages of the corresponding states and the nation are calculated from the labor force of working age (i.e., aged between sixteen and sixty-five, inclusive).

public office users and other workers was not simply due to gender. Service work for women and common labor for men were the main types of occupations dealt with by public offices until 1930. Both service workers and laborers also made up the majority of private agencies' clients, who were vulnerable to the abuses of private agencies in the early twentieth century (Sargent 1912). Therefore, the intensive use of public offices by service workers and laborers supports the argument that public offices contributed to protecting job seekers from exploitation by private agencies. This means that the degree of asymmetric information between job-seekers and private agencies was lowered as an alternative job-matching service was provided by public offices at that time.

Besides the gender and occupations of job-seekers using public offices, interesting facts are revealed in Wisconsin and New York public offices in 1901. Table 5.3 shows some characteristics of public office applicants in Wisconsin for six months (July to December 1901). Approximately 40 percent of Wisconsin public office users were non-U.S. citizens, 80 percent were single,

Table 5.3   **Characteristics of Wisconsin Public Employment Office applicants
in 1901**

	Public offices	State	Nation
Place of origin			
U.S. born	63.8	63.1	77.1
Foreign born	36.2	36.9	22.9
Marital status			
Married	20.1	53.8	57.0
Single	79.9	46.2	43.0
Place of birth			
Wisconsin	26.3	49.4	54.3
Other U.S.	38.0	13.7	22.8
Other nations	36.2	36.9	22.9
Member of labor union			
No	95.9		
Yes	4.1		
Years in the U.S. for immigrants			
Less than 1	6.3		
1–5	15.0		
6–10	17.7		
11–15	17.6		
16–20	18.4		
21–25	10.2		
26–30	5.6		
Over 30	9.2		
Years of residence in Wisconsin			
Less than 1	30.1		
1–5	18.2		
6–10	8.2		
Over 11	18.1		
Since birth	25.7		

Sources: State of Wisconsin Bureau of Labor and Industrial Statistics 1902 and IPUMS (Ruggles et al. 2004).

Notes: Among 4,744 applicants in Wisconsin public employment offices from July to December 1901, 3,890 applicants filled at least one part of the application form. The first column describes personal characteristics of workers. The second column shows the percentages of the corresponding characteristics of public office users. The third and fourth columns are the corresponding percentages of the labor force of working age (aged between sixteen and sixty-five, inclusive) in Wisconsin and the nation in 1900, respectively.

and only 4 percent were labor union members. Compared to workers in the nation, the share of immigrants who used public offices in Wisconsin was higher by 13 percent. However, the difference in place of origin disappeared between public office users and the state workers. This may indicate that the share of immigrants using public offices was large because the immigrant share of state workers was also high. The share of single public office users was much larger than that of the nation or of state workers (approximately 80 percent for public offices, 46 percent for the state population, and 43 percent for the nation). One prominent feature was that only 26 percent of public office users were Wisconsin-born (about 49 percent for the state and 54 percent for the nation). In terms of residence, almost half of the job-seekers who used public offices had resided in Wisconsin less than five years (see the last part of table 5.3).

Table 5.4 describes several characteristics of public office applicants in New York State in 1901. One distinction is that table 5.4 also provides information on public office applicants separately by gender. Overall, 62 percent of the applicants in New York public offices were non-U.S. citizens (36 percent for the state). By gender, 52 percent of men and 68 percent of women public office users were non-U.S. citizens (versus 37 percent of men and 34 percent of women in the state population). Over 60 percent of the public office applicants were single and 4 percent were illiterate. In general, the share of single users was larger than that of state workers, although this inequality is reversed for women (the proportion of female public office users was 62.1 percent while the proportion of female workers in the state was 78 percent). About 60 percent of public office users were between twenty and forty years of age (see the last part of the second column in table 5.4). The common similarity between Wisconsin and New York is that many of the

Table 5.4   **Characteristics of New York State Public Employment Office applicants in 1901**

	Public employment offices			New York State		
	Overall	Men	Women	Overall	Men	Women
Place of origin						
U.S. born	38.0	47.9	32.1	63.9	63.3	66.1
Foreign born	62.0	52.1	67.9	36.1	36.7	33.9
Marital status						
Married	34.6	29.2	37.9	52.8	61.8	22.0
Single	65.4	70.8	62.1	47.2	38.2	78.0
Literacy						
Literate	96.3	99.4	94.0	94.8	94.6	95.7
Illiterate	3.7	0.5	6.0	5.2	5.4	4.3
Age of applicants						
Under 20 years	8.3	11.7	6.0			
20–30	37.9	45.1	33.6			
30–40	26.7	24.4	28.1			
40–50	18.8	12.8	22.5			
50–60	6.9	4.6	8.4			
Over 60	1.3	1.3	1.3			

Sources: State of New York Department of Labor 1902 for public offices; IPUMS (Ruggles et al. 2004) for New York State.

Note: The first column describes personal characteristics of workers. The second, third, and fourth columns show the percentages of the corresponding characteristics of overall, men, and public office users, respectively. The fifth, sixth, and seventh columns are the corresponding percentages of, overall, male, and female workers in the labor force of working age in 1900, respectively.

public office users were single around the turn of the twentieth century. In New York's case, it is clear that immigrants used public offices more intensively than U.S.-born workers for their job search.

It is striking that 38 percent of public office applicants in Wisconsin were interstate migrants (U.S. citizens who migrated from other regions in the United States to Wisconsin). Moreover, 50 percent of them had resided in Wisconsin for less than five years. The large proportion of recent migrants among public office users also supports the argument that public offices helped lower the degree of asymmetric information between job-seekers and private agencies because recent migrants from other states were more likely to be exploited by private agencies due to lack of information on the new environment. Even if the existence of public offices did not cause people to migrate to Wisconsin, I can argue that once people moved to Wisconsin, they were likely to look for jobs with the help of public offices if they could not rely on other networks, including private agencies.

In summary, most public office users were unskilled workers (service workers or laborers), immigrants, or migrants in several states' cases. These types of people were also major clients of private agencies in the early twentieth century. This fact, in part, supports the argument that public offices provided an alternative job-matching service for people who had low skills or were unfamiliar to their new environment, and thus more likely to be exploited by private agencies.

5.5   Empirical Work

Theoretically, job-seekers would be fully informed about the quality of private agencies as public offices drive low-quality private agencies from the market. Consequently, job-seekers could choose to use either public offices or reputable private agencies: the establishment of public offices can resolve adverse selection in the labor exchange market. Therefore, the most relevant empirical question from this theory is to explore whether the introduction or development of public offices resolved the problem of adverse selection.[17] However, testing this hypothesis presents difficulties because information on private agencies in the early twentieth century is scarce.[18]

Instead, I test the hypothesis that public offices helped lower the degree of asymmetric information for uninformed job-seekers. Even if this hypothesis is valid, it does not guarantee that adverse selection disappeared. However, it

17. Throughout this chapter, I frequently mention "lower the degree of asymmetric information" and "resolve the problem of adverse selection." Lowering the degree of asymmetric information is a process to resolve adverse selection because eliminating the asymmetric information problem is necessary to resolve adverse selection. Therefore, when information symmetry is achieved, low-quality private agencies are driven out of the market, and consequently adverse selection disappears.

18. To test the problem of adverse selection directly, detailed data on private agencies are required, such as fees charged by private agencies.

does tell us that public offices were directed to resolve the problem of adverse selection, because lowering the degree of asymmetric information between job-seekers and private agencies is a part of that process. This hypothesis was proposed in the last section and in part supported by the findings on the types of workers who used public offices. I extend this analysis to an empirical test by examining the relationship between the use of public offices by job-seekers (in terms of the number of job-seekers using public offices) and labor market conditions related to asymmetric information.

To test the hypothesis, a statistical model is constructed. The model describes the relationship between the use of public offices by job-seekers and labor market conditions, including proxy variables for asymmetric information. If the use of public offices and the asymmetric information factors are positively related, then the relationship may support the hypothesis. A positive correlation would indicate that the use of public offices increased as the number of people who were vulnerable to the abuses by private agencies due to lack of information increased. Hence, public offices contributed to lessening the degree of asymmetric information for uninformed job-seekers who were more likely to be exploited by private agencies.

I collected data for the use of public offices by job-seekers from annual reports and monthly bulletins published by the USES. I narrowed my empirical analysis to 1920 and 1930 because most of the labor market data at state or at lower regional levels are available decennially. Moreover, public offices were not influential as a labor market intermediary before World War I (see figure 5.2). I also limited the samples of explanatory variables to the labor force of working age (i.e., aged between sixteen and sixty-five, inclusive) in urban areas.[19] The regression model is as follows:

$$\ln(USE)_{it} = \alpha + \beta_1 \ln(WAGE)_{it} + \beta_2 \ln(EMPLOYMENT)_{it}$$
$$+ \beta_3 \ln(INCOME)_{it} + \beta_4 \ln(WOMEN)_{it} + \beta_5 \ln(SINGLE)_{it}$$
$$+ \beta_6 \ln(DSE)_{it} + \beta_7 \ln(ILLITERATE)_{it}$$
$$+ \beta_8 \ln(IMMIGRANT)_{it} + \beta_9 \ln(MIGRANT)_{it}$$
$$+ \beta_{10} \ln(SERVICE)_{it} + \beta_{11} \ln(LABOR)_{it} + D_t + X_{it}B + \varepsilon_{it}.$$

The dependent variable USE_{it} measures the use of public offices by job-seekers in terms of the number of applicants who used public offices. The subscripts i and t indicate state and year (1920 and 1930), respectively. *WAGE, EMPLOYMENT,* and *INCOME* are chosen to control for general labor market conditions.[20] For the data regarding the wage and employment

19. By definition, job-seekers using public offices are in the labor force and most of them are in the working age population. Most public offices before the Great Depression were located in major cities (Kellogg 1933; Breen 1997).
20. These three variables are not limited to working age population in the labor force in urban areas, unlike all the other explanatory variables, because of unavailability of data.

levels, "Estimates of Average Manufacturing Wages by State" and "Total Employment by State" are used, respectively (Fishback and Kantor 2000).[21] To control for level of income, I employ "Realized national income," which is an estimate consisting of "the total of payments to individuals by business and government in the form of wages, salaries, dividends, interest, net rents and royalties, and net profits withdrawn by unincorporated enterprises" (National Industrial Conference Boards, Inc. 1939, 114).

Other explanatory variables are selected based on the analysis of the types of public office users in the last section and constructed from Integrated Public Use Microdata Series (IPUMS) extracts (Ruggles et al. 2004) of 1920 and 1930 samples. *WOMEN* and *SINGLE* are estimates of the numbers of women and single workers. The last six variables (*DSE, ILLTERATE, IMMIGRANT, MIGRANT, SERVICE,* and *LABOR*) are proxy variables for asymmetric information. In the early twentieth century, immigrants, migrants, and unskilled workers were vulnerable to the abuses of private agencies due to lack of information about the area or less education. Variable *DSE* is the number of people who did not speak English and *ILLITERATE* is the number of people who were illiterate (i.e., cannot read or write) in any language. I add *DSE* and *ILLITERATE* for asymmetric information proxies because these workers were less likely to be educated and thus seemed to be vulnerable to exploitation by private agencies. The variable *IMMIGRANT* is the number of non-U.S. citizens; *MIGRANT* is the total number of migrants who were U.S. citizens; *SERVICE* is the number of service workers; and *LABOR* is the number of laborers. *MIGRANT* is a measure of interstate migration, which is estimated based on whether a person lived in the state in which he or she was born at the time of the Census (Rosenbloom and Sundstrom 2004). Variable D_t is a time dummy and X_{it} indicates the interaction terms between time and region dummies, to control for unobserved factors, in part, correlated with the explanatory variables over time or region.[22]

The summary statistics for the variables are shown in table 5.5 and the results of the regression analysis are provided in tables 5.6 and 5.7. First, I run cross-sectional regressions for 1920 and 1930 separately—the results are shown in table 5.6. Overall, signs of the key estimates are not significant in most specifications. However, the estimates for *MIGRANT,* which indicate the relationship between the use of public offices and interstate migration, are positive and significant. This pattern may imply that public offices helped migrants who were unfamiliar with their new environment and thus most likely to be abused by private agencies in their job search.

Table 5.7 presents the results for the unbalanced panel regressions with

21. "Total Employment by State" is the estimate of the number of employed workers of all kinds in each state.

22. The Census division is used for the regional classification in this chapter: New England, Middle Atlantic, East North Central, West North Central, South Atlantic, East South Central, West South Central, Mountain, and Pacific.

Table 5.5   Descriptive statistics

	1920			1930		
Variable	Observations	Mean	Standard deviation	Observations	Mean	Standard deviation
USE	49	52,861.9	85,955.8	44	54,707.8	72,237.6
WAGE	48	33.3	6.3	43	31.7	6.2
EMPLOYMENT	48	812,186.8	827,466.0	43	980,432.3	990,891.5
INCOME	49	1,398.1	1,780.3	44	1,606.5	2,276.0
WOMEN	49	115,384.6	174,173.1	44	165,598.7	226,613.4
SINGLE	49	189,663.1	297,903.9	44	225,468.7	350,049.2
ILLITERATE	49	19,242.1	29,545.0	44	16,841.8	24,218.5
DSE	49	12,205.5	25,143.8	44	7,618.6	15,561.4
IMMIGRANT	49	68,477.5	149,007.6	44	59,149.3	129,509.9
MIGRANT	49	114,209.6	116,875.0	44	170,187.3	203,006.5
SERVICE	49	49,039.0	68,972.4	44	76,454.7	102,278.1
LABOR	49	59,797.2	78,326.9	44	69,591.3	87,410.9

Sources: USE (for 1920, U.S. Employment Service 1921; for 1930, U.S. Employment Service January 1930 to December 1930). *WAGE* and *EMPLOYMENT* (Fishback, Price, and Kantor 2000). *INCOME* (National Industrial Conference Board Inc. 1939). Others (Ruggles et al. 2004).

fixed and random effects.[23] In general, as in the case of cross-sectional regressions, most of the signs for the estimates are not significant. However, the estimates are significant for *ILLITERATE* and *MIGRANT* but negative for *ILLITERATE* and positive for *MIGRANT.* The negative sign for *ILLITERATE* is understandable, since applicants of public offices had to fill out application forms when they registered and had to have interviews with the agents in public offices. Positive estimates for *MIGRANT* are consistent with the results in the cross-sectional analyses. The magnitude and significance of the estimates for *MIGRANT* increase after controlling for time and region-specific fixed effects.

This positive and significant relationship between the use of public offices by job-seekers and interstate migration reaffirms the hypothesis that public offices contributed to lowering the degree of asymmetric information, especially in favor of migrants who were most lacking in information and networks in their new environment.

5.6   Conclusion

Progressive Era (1890s through 1920s) social reformers viewed uninformed job-seekers as vulnerable to exploitation by private employment agencies. In response to the cries of these people, public employment offices

23. The balanced and unbalanced panel regressions produce nearly identical coefficient estimates.

Table 5.6   **Relationship between the use of public employment offices and asymmetric information-1: Cross section for 1920 and 1930 separately Dependent variable: ln (USE).**

Explanatory variable	1920 Coefficient (robust standard error)	1920 Coefficient (robust standard error)	1930 Coefficient (robust standard error)	1930 Coefficient (robust standard error)
Region fixed effects	No	Yes	No	Yes
ln(WAGE)	1.68***	1.17*	1.69	2.38
	(0.53)	(0.61)	(1.80)	(1.84)
ln(EMPLOYMENT)	−0.28**	−0.32*	0.25	−0.58
	(0.13)	(0.18)	(1.07)	(1.04)
ln(INCOME)	−2.32	−3.40*	−3.10	−4.24
	(1.54)	(1.68)	(2.80)	(2.65)
ln(WOMEN)	−1.05	−1.14	−1.83	−4.84***
	(0.72)	(0.85)	(2.06)	(1.80)
ln(SINGLE)	1.07	2.31*	0.43	2.51
	(0.87)	(1.13)	(1.90)	(1.78)
ln(DSE)	−0.27***	−0.22**	−0.16	−0.06
	(0.10)	(0.10)	(0.13)	(0.14)
ln(ILLITERATE)	−0.60***	−0.43	−0.11	−0.19
	(0.25)	(0.36)	(0.20)	(0.19)
ln(IMMIGRANT)	0.46***	0.35	0.37	−0.29
	(0.16)	(0.24)	(0.26)	(0.36)
ln(MIGRANT)	0.83**	0.93*	1.28***	1.74***
	(0.37)	(0.50)	(0.41)	(0.60)
ln(SERVICE)	−0.03	−0.34	−1.10	0.68
	(0.66)	(0.78)	(0.69)	(0.97)
ln(LABOR)	−0.50	−1.36*	0.64	−0.11
	(0.51)	(0.70)	(0.59)	(0.91)
Constant	−14.40***	−2.27	−12.79	−11.90
	(5.78)	(8.07)	(12.87)	(12.46)
R^2	0.86	0.91	0.75	0.86
Total observations	48	48	43	43

Notes: USE (dependent variable): the number of applicants who used public offices in a state in a year. WAGE: average manufacturing wages in a state in a year. EMPLOYMENT: total employment in a state in a year. INCOME: realized income in a state in a year. WOMEN: the number of women in a state in a year. SINGLE: the number of singles in a state in a year. DSE: the number of people who did not speak English in a state in a year. ILLITERATE: the number of illiterate in any language in a state in a year. IMMIGRANT: the number of non-U.S. citizens in a state in a year. MIGRANT: the number of migrants who were U.S. citizens in a state in a year. SERVICE: the number of service workers in a state in a year. LABOR: the number of laborers in a state in a year.

***Significant at the 1 percent level.
**Significant at the 5 percent level.
*Significant at the 10 percent level.

Table 5.7   **Relationship between the use of public employment offices and asymmetric information-2: Panel regressions (unbalanced). Dependent variable: ln (*USE*).**

Explanatory variable	FE coefficient (standard error)	FE coefficient (standard error)	RE coefficient (standard error)	RE coefficient (standard error)
Time dummy (1920)	Yes	Yes	Yes	Yes
Time*region	No	Yes	No	Yes
ln(*WAGE*)	−1.44	−1.50	0.93*	0.94*
	(1.30)	(1.69)	(0.52)	(0.57)
ln(*EMPLOYMENT*)	0.39	0.46	−0.19	−0.27
	(0.48)	(0.53)	(0.22)	(0.24)
ln(*INCOME*)	3.15	2.64	−1.10	−1.03
	(2.68)	(3.22)	(1.28)	(1.32)
ln(*WOMEN*)	−1.53	−1.82	−0.89	0.11
	(1.62)	(2.00)	(0.64)	(0.83)
ln(*SINGLE*)	2.49*	1.91	1.09	0.24
	(1.43)	(2.06)	(0.74)	(0.88)
ln(*DSE*)	0.15	0.18	−0.03	−0.03
	(0.12)	(0.14)	(0.08)	(0.09)
ln(*ILLITERATE*)	−1.70**	−1.82**	−0.68***	−0.69***
	(0.71)	(0.72)	(0.20)	(0.21)
ln(*IMMIGRANT*)	−0.16	−0.25	0.12	0.16
	(0.47)	(0.49)	(0.17)	(0.18)
ln(*MIGRANT*)	1.39	2.48**	0.68**	0.57*
	(1.07)	(1.23)	(0.29)	(0.31)
ln(*SERVICE*)	0.29	0.36	0.31	0.04
	(1.11)	(1.24)	(0.56)	(0.58)
ln(*LABOR*)	−0.07	0.76	−0.19	0.05
	(1.05)	(1.23)	(0.43)	(0.46)
Constant	9.28	1.16	−9.38*	−9.11
	(23.70)	(29.03)	(5.39)	(5.74)
R^2				
Within	0.36	0.56	0.14	0.25
Between	0.09	0.34	0.85	0.87
Overall	0.12	0.37	0.77	0.82
Total observations	90	90	90	90
Total group	47	47	47	47

Note: FE = fixed effects; RE = random effects.

***Significant at the 1 percent level.

**Significant at the 5 percent level.

*Significant at the 10 percent level.

were introduced to restrain private employment agencies from exploitation of job-seekers. I describe this situation as a case of asymmetric information between job-seekers and private agencies that could cause adverse selection in the labor exchange market. Creation of public employment offices can be viewed as a policy device to eliminate low-quality private employment agencies that were committing malpractices with respect to job-seekers.

My analysis shows that the majority of job-seekers who utilized public employment offices were unskilled workers, immigrants, or migrants, who were also major clients of private employment agencies at that time. One of the most interesting findings is a positive relationship between the use of public employment offices and interstate migration in 1920 and 1930. This supports the hypothesis that public employment offices lessened the degree of asymmetric information in favor of migrants in the labor exchange market. In other words, public employment offices were especially helpful for migrants who were most lacking in information and networks in their new environment.

Despite the importance of public employment offices in the early twentieth century, current trends are the reduction in public funding and privatization of public employment services in response to a decrease in their usage by job-seekers.[24] This could be in part due to inefficient operation of public employment offices in recent periods (De Koning, Denys, and Walwei 1999). However, the role of public employment offices is still relevant with respect to the asymmetric information problem in the labor exchange market. Autor and Houseman (2005) found that temporary help agencies provide low-skilled workers with jobs that have lower wages and shorter employment durations than do direct-hire jobs. There is a possibility that this ineffective outcome of temporary help agencies may result from asymmetric information between low-skilled workers and temporary help agencies. Temporary help agencies may have an incentive to make use of this information asymmetry to exploit their employees, which is an inefficient market outcome. In addition, services by public employment offices are always pertinent for certain groups such as illegal immigrants, very low-skilled workers, or low-educated workers who have little information about the labor market and little recourse to recover damages if exploited.

As a final remark, the focus of this chapter was on the supply side (job-seekers), but it is also important to investigate the demand side, the activities of private employment agencies, and their interactions with public employment offices. The direct test of adverse selection in the labor exchange market requires detailed information on private employment agencies such as fees charged by private employment agencies and the corresponding clients' characteristics. I plan to explore this in future work.

---

24. Approximately 19 percent of the unemployed used public employment offices in the United States in 2001, while 30 percent did in the 1970s (Eberts and Holzer 2004).

References

Adams, L. P. 1969. *The public employment service in transition, 1933–1968: Evolution of a placement service into a manpower agency.* Ithaca: New York School of Industrial and Labor Relations, Cornell University.

Atkinson, R. C., L. C. Odencrantz, and B. Deming, 1938. *Public employment service in the United States.* Chicago: Public Administration Service.

Autor, D. H., and S. N. Houseman. 2005. Do temporary help jobs improve labor market outcomes for low-skilled workers? Evidence from random assignments. NBER Working Paper no. 11743. Cambridge, MA: National Bureau of Economic Research.

Baldwin, G. B. 1951. Tulamusa: A study of the place of the public employment service. *Industrial and Labor Relation Review* 4 (4): 509–26.

Bogart, E. L. 1900. Public Employment Offices in the United States and Germany. *The Quarterly Journal of Economics* 14 (3): 341–77.

Breen, W. 1997. *Labor market politics and the Great War: The department of labor, the States, and the first U.S. employment service, 1907–1933.* Kent, OH, and London: Kent State University Press.

Commons, J. R., and J. B. Andrews. 1936. *Principles of labor legislation.* 4th ed. New York and London: Harper and Brothers.

Conner, J. E. 1907. Free public employment offices in the United States. *U.S. Bureau of Labor Bulletin* no. 68:1–116. Washington, D.C.: Government Printing Office.

De Koning, J., J. Denys, and U. Walwei. 1999. *Deregulation in placement services: A comparative study for eight EU countries.* Brussels: European Commission, DG for Employment, Industrial relations and Social Affairs.

Devine, E. T. 1909. Employment bureau for the people of New York City. *Annals of the American Academy of Political and Social Science* 33 (2): 1–14.

Eberts, R. W., and H. J. Holzer. 2004. Overview of labor exchange policies and services. In *Labor Exchange Policy in the United States,* ed. D. E. Balducchi, R. W. Eberts, and C. J. O'Leary, 1–31. Kalamazoo, MI: W. E. Upjohn Institute for Employment Research.

Edwards, G. W. 1935. Employment service of Canada. *Monthly Labor Review* 9 (2): 157–68.

Finkin, M. W., and S. M. Jacoby. 2005. An introduction to the regulation of leasing and employment agencies. *Comparative Labor Law and Policy Journal* 23 (1): 1–6.

Fishback, P. V., and S. E. Kantor. 2000. *A prelude to the welfare state: The origins of workers' compensation.* Chicago: University of Chicago Press.

Guzda, H. P. 1983. The U.S. employment service at 50: It too had to wait its turn. *Monthly Labor Review* 106 (6): 12–19.

Herdon, Jr., J. G. 1918. Public employment offices in the United States. *U.S. Bureau of Labor Statistics Bulletin* no. 241:1–100. Washington, D.C.: Government Printing Office.

International Labour Office. 1955. *National Employment Services, United States.* Geneva.

Kellogg, R. M. 1933. *The United States Employment Service.* Chicago: University of Chicago Press.

Kübler, D. 1999. Coexistence of public and private job agencies: Screening with heterogeneous institutions. *Public Choice* 101:85–107.

Leiserson, W. M. 1915. The movement for public labor exchanges. *The Journal of Political Economy* 23 (7): 707–16.

Martinez, T. 1976. *The human market place: An examination of private employment agencies.* New Brunswick: Transaction.

Muhlhauser, H. 1916. Public employment bureaus and their relation to managers of employment in industry. *Annals of the American Academy of Political Science* 65, Personnel and Employment Problems in Industrial Management (May): 170–75.

National Industrial Conference Board Inc. 1939. *National income and its geographic distribution 1919–1938.* New York: Conference Board Studies in Enterprise and Social Progress.

Pissarides, C. A. 1979. Job matching with state employment agencies and random search. *The Economic Journal* 89 (356): 818–33.

Rosenbloom, J. L. 2002. *Looking for work, searching for workers: American labor markets during industrialization.* Cambridge, England: Cambridge University Press.

Rosenbloom, J. L., and W. A. Sundstrom. 2004. The decline and rise of interstate migration in the United States: Evidence from the IPUMS, 1850–1990. *Research in Economic History* 22:289–325.

Ruggles, S., M. Sobek, T. Alexander, C. A. Fitch, R. Goeken, P. K. Hall, M. King, and C. Ronnander. 2004. *Integrated public use microdata series: Version 3.0* (Machine-readable database). Minneapolis: Minnesota Population Center (producer and distributor).

Ruttenberg, S. H., and J. Gutchess. 1970. *The federal-state employment service: A critique.* Baltimore and London: Johns Hopkins University Press.

Sargent, F. B. 1912. Statistics of unemployment and the work of employment offices. U.S. Bureau of labor Bulletin no. 109:5–140. Washington, D.C.: Government Printing Office.

Smith, D. H. 1923. *The United States Employment Service: Its history, activities and organization.* Baltimore: Johns Hopkins University Press.

State of California Bureau of Labor Statistics. 1923. *Twentieth Biennial report of the Bureau of Labor Statistics* 1921–1922. Sacramento: California Bureau of Labor Statistics.

State of Colorado Bureau of Labor Statistics. *Biennial reports.* 1903 to 1915. (Denver, CO 1903–1915).

State of Connecticut Bureau of Labor Statistics. Various issues. *Report of the Bureau of Labor Statistics.* 1902–1915, 1922, 1930. Hartford, CT: Bureau of Labor Statistics.

State of Illinois Bureau of Labor Statistics. Various issues (1900–1915). *Annual report of the Bureau of Labor Statistics of the Illinois Free Employment Offices.* Springfield, IL: Bureau of Labor Statistics.

State of Indiana Department of Statistics. *Biennial report.* 1910–1914. (Indianapolis, IN 1911–1915).

State of Kansas Bureau of Labor and Industry. *Annual report.* 1901–1912. (Topeka, KS 1901–1914).

State of Kansas Department of Labor and Industry. *Annual report.* 1913–1916. (Topeka, KS 1914–1915).

State of Kentucky Bureau of Agriculture, Labor, and Statistics. *Biennial report.* 1912–1915. (Louisville, KY 1912–1915).

State of Maryland Bureau of Statistics and Information. *Annual report.* 1903–1915. (Baltimore, MD 1904–1915).

State of Massachusetts Bureau of Statistics of Labor. Various issues. *Thirty-fourth, Thirty-eighth to Forty-fifth Annual reports.* 1904, 1907–1915. (Boston, MA 1904, 1907–1915).

State of Michigan Bureau of Labor and Industrial Statistics. *Annual report.* 1906–1909. (Lansing, MI 1906–1909).

State of Michigan Department of Labor. *Annual report.* 1910–1915. (Lansing, MI 1910–1915).

State of Minnesota Bureau of Labor. *Biennial report.* 1905–1906. (Minneapolis, MN 1907).

State of Minnesota Bureau of Labor. *Biennial report.* 1907–1914. (Minneapolis, MN 1915).

State of Missouri Bureau of Labor Statistics. *Annual report.* 1899–1915, 1920–1922. (Jefferson City, MO 1900–1916, 1923).

State of Missouri Department of Labor and Industrial Inspection. *Annual report.* 1930. (Jefferson City, MO 1930).

State of Montana Bureau of Agriculture, Labor, and Industry. *Annual report.* 1902–1912. (Helena, MT 1902–1912).

State of Montana Department of Labor and Industry, *Biennial report.* 1913–1914, 1915–1916. (Helena, MT 1913–1916).

State of New Jersey Department of Labor. *Report.* 1910–1915. (Trenton, NJ 1910–1915).

State of New York Department of Labor. *Annual report of Commissioner of Labor.* 1900–1906, 1915. (Albany, NY 1901–1916).

State of Ohio Bureau of Labor Statistics. *Annual report.* 1890–1913. (Columbus, OH 1891–1914).

State of Ohio Department of Investigation and Statistics. *Report.* 1914–1915. (Columbus, OH 1915–1916).

State of Oklahoma Department of Labor. *Annual report.* 1908–1915. (Oklahoma City, OK 1908–1915).

State of Rhode Island Bureau of Industrial Statistics. *Annual report.* 1908–1914. (Providence, RI 1908–1914).

State of Washington Bureau of Labor. *Biennial report.* 1901–1916. (Olympia, WA 1903–1916).

State of West Virginia Bureau of Labor Statistics. *Biennial report.* 1901–1915. (Charleston, WV 1901–1915).

State of Wisconsin Bureau of Labor and Industrial Statistics. 1902–1916. *Biennial Report.* 1900–1915. Madison, WI.

Stewart, A. M., and B. M. Stewart. 1933. *Statistical procedure of public employment offices.* New York: Russell Sage Foundation.

U.S. Bureau of Labor Standards. 1962. *Laws regulating private employment agencies.* Growth of Labor Law in the United States. Washington, D.C.: Government Printing Office.

U.S. Bureau of Labor Statistics. January 1915–February 1918. *Monthly Review* 1 (1–6): 2.

———. 1931. Public Employment Services. *Monthly Labor Review* 32 (1): 10–32.

U.S. Employment Service. 1919, 1920, 1921. *Annual report of the Director General US Employment Service to the Secretary of Labor, fiscal year ending June 30 1918, 1919, 1920.* Washington, D.C.: Government Printing Office.

———. January 1924–January 1932. *Monthly report of activities of state and municipal Employment Services cooperating with US Employment Service.* Washington, D.C.: Government Printing Office.

———. September 1934–December 1940. *Employment Service News* 1 (1–7): 12. Washington, D.C.: Government Printing Office.

———. 1935a. Historical sketch of public employment. *Employment Service News* 2 (2): 2–8.

————. 1935b. *Twelve and one-half millions registered for work 1934.* Washington, D.C.: Government Printing Office.

Walwei, U. 1996. Improving job-matching through placement services. In *International handbook of labour market policy and evaluation,* ed. G. Schmid, J. O'Reilly, and K. Schömann, 402–30. Cheltenham and Brookfield: Edward Elgar.

Wier, D. R. 1992. A century of U.S. unemployment, 1890–1990: Revised estimates and evidence for stabilization. *Research in Economic History* 14:301–46.

Yavas, A. 1994. Middlemen in bilateral markets. *Journal of Labor Economics* 12 (3): 406–29.

6

Mortgage Broker Regulations that Matter
Analyzing Earnings, Employment, and Outcomes for Consumers

Morris M. Kleiner and Richard M. Todd

6.1 Introduction

Mortgage brokers are intermediaries who both match potential mortgage borrowers and lenders and assist them in completing the loan origination process. Brokers have typically operated as independent service providers, not as agents or employees of either borrowers or lenders, and they are compensated by fees paid by the borrower and sometimes the lender as well.[1] Their role in the U.S. mortgage market has mushroomed from insignificant in 1980 to predominant in recent years. By 2004, about 53,000 mortgage broker firms were operating in the United States and were directly or indirectly involved in the origination of as many as 68 percent of all mortgages that

Morris M. Kleiner is a professor at the Humphrey Institute, University of Minnesota, visiting scholar at the Federal Reserve Bank of Minneapolis, and a research associate of the National Bureau of Economic Research. Richard M. Todd is vice president at the Federal Reserve Bank of Minneapolis.

We thank Hwikwon Ham, Patricia Haswell, Matthew Hendricks, Thomas LaMalfa, Alexander Lefter, Heidi Liu, Cynthia Pahl, Dan Rozycki, Michael Weisbrot, and J. W. Bond Consultants for their assistance with the chapter, and the staff at the Board of Governors of the Federal Reserve System for providing much of our data. We also thank David Autor, Richard Freeman, Alexandre Mas, and two referees for comments that greatly improved the chapter. In addition, we benefited from suggestions from Susan Woodward and participants at seminars hosted by the Aarhus School of Business, the Federal Reserve Board, the Federal Trade Commission, the London School of Economics, the National Bureau of Economic Research, Princeton University, and the University of Minnesota. The views expressed here are those of the authors, and not necessarily those of the Federal Reserve System or the Federal Reserve Bank of Minneapolis.

1. Some states have recently moved to enact or more strictly enforce laws that make the broker an agent of the borrower, but this was not a factor during our study period.

year (Wholesale Access 2005).[2] As the mortgage broker business grew, so did questions about the industry's role and its effects on consumer welfare.

From one perspective, the rise of mortgage brokering was just one part of a broader vertical disintegration of the lending business that is widely thought to have made mortgage credit more widely and cheaply available to many households (Jacobides 2005; Gerardi, Rosen, and Willen 2007). According to both the general theory of brokers (Yavas 1994) and mortgage market scholars (El Anshasy, Elliehausen, and Shimazaki 2005; U.S. Department of Housing and Urban Development 2002; Guttentag 2000), mortgage brokers have played a role in the evolution of the highly specialized and efficient mortgage market. In particular, brokers can make the complicated task of shopping and applying for the increasingly wide array of mortgage products more manageable and efficient for borrowers and lenders alike. Millions of households, including many affluent and sophisticated consumers, have arranged mortgages through brokers, frequently more than once. It seems likely that many, if not most, found value in the brokers' services, which is what we would expect in honest, competitive markets.

On the other hand, critics have argued that too many mortgage brokers are not honest or, more broadly, that market failures prevent competition from effectively disciplining brokers' profits and quality of service. According to these critics (Guttentag 2000; LaCour-Little and Chun 1999; Alexander et al. 2002; Kim-Sung and Hermanson 2003; Jackson and Burlingame 2007), market failures (chiefly in the form of information asymmetries) allow mortgage brokers to profit unduly at the expense of mortgage borrowers as well as lenders. These issues are said to be especially problematic in the subprime mortgage market, where mortgage brokers have dominated originations in recent years (Schloemer et al. 2006).

In response to these concerns, a range of policy measures have been discussed. One of the most common responses has been to increase the occupational licensing standards for mortgage brokers. Pahl (2007) documents how state licensing of mortgage brokers increased at both the extensive (more states) and intensive (more restrictions per state) margins between 1996 and 2006, and since then, a surge in mortgage foreclosures has provided political momentum for the enactment of further regulation. Policymakers seem to have concluded that a lack of market discipline and regulatory oversight has allowed many mortgage brokers to originate excessively expensive and risky mortgages (Gramlich 2007), and a more comprehensive system of mortgage broker licensing is often viewed as part of the solution (Kroszner 2007; Conference of State Bank Supervisors 2007; Shumer 2007).

2. By 2006, the number of firms had changed little but their share of originations was estimated to have declined to about 58 percent (Wholesale Access 2007). With the volume of subprime lending apparently falling significantly in 2007, mortgage broker numbers may be declining further, as brokers had originated the majority of subprime mortgages (Olson 2007).

Despite the growing attractiveness of mortgage broker licensing to poli-cymakers, both theory and empirical evidence suggest that licensing will not necessarily improve outcomes for consumers (Kleiner 2006). Even theories that emphasize the role of occupational licensing in enhancing the quality of services provided find that licensing tends to also raise the average price of the occupation's services, possibly to the detriment of consumers who prefer low prices to high quality. Some theories that focus on other aspects of licensing, such as its potential to serve as a vehicle for current practitioners to collusively impede the entry of new firms, may imply lower quality as well as higher prices. Empirical assessments of the effects of occupational licensing have often confirmed its potential to raise prices, sometimes with little or no gain in quality. However, the results differ widely by occupation, and we are not aware of any comprehensive assessments of mortgage broker licensing.

In order to fill this gap, we examine the relationships between mortgage broker licensing and market outcomes. We provide some background on the occupation and review theories of how licensing can affect outcomes in both the labor market for mortgage brokers and the consumer product market for mortgages. We introduce and summarize Pahl's recent compilation of mortgage broker licensing requirements from the fifty states and the District of Columbia for the period 1996 to 2006. We then use Pahl's data to analyze whether mortgage broker licensing or any of its components have significant relationships with labor or product market outcomes. We attempt to con-struct overall indices of the tightness of mortgage broker licensing but find that they are not significantly related to market outcomes. We then examine many of the separate components of state mortgage broker regulation and find that one component—the requirement in many states that mortgage brokers maintain a surety bond or maintain a minimum net worth—has a significant and fairly robust statistical association with fewer brokers, fewer subprime mortgages, higher foreclosure rates on subprime mortgages, and a higher percentage of mortgages carrying high interest rates.[3]

6.2   The Rise of Mortgage Brokering and the Issues It Raised

The evolution of mortgage brokering in the United States and the policy issues that arose with it have been well described in other sources;[4] we sum-marize them here to motivate and provide background for our analysis of

3. Some of the other components of mortgage broker regulation also are significant in some of our specifications and may deserve further research (see appendix D), but here we focus on the bonding and net worth requirements because they were more broadly and consistently significant.

4. For example, see U.S. Department of Housing and Urban Development 2002; Essene and Apgar 2007; Apgar, Bendimerad, and Essene 2007; Engel and McCoy 2002; El Anshasy, Elliehausen, and Shimazaki 2005; LaCour-Little 2007c; Jackson and Burlingame 2007; Guttentag 2000; Woodward 2003.

mortgage broker licensing. In particular, we note that mortgage brokering has become an economically significant industry, surrounded by controversy about the extent of benefits it provides to consumers and lenders, and we describe some of the key pricing and quality issues that policymakers try to address with licensing programs.

The National Association of Mortgage Brokers (NAMB) delineates the roles of the mortgage lender and the mortgage broker as follows:[5]

> The wholesale lender underwrites and funds the home loan, may service the loan payments, and ensures the loan's compliance with underwriting guidelines. The broker, on the other hand, originates the loan. A detailed application process, financial and credit worthiness investigation, and extensive disclosure requirements must be completed in order for a wholesale lender to evaluate a consumer's home loan request. The broker simplifies this process for the borrower and the wholesale lender, by conducting this research, counseling consumers on their loan package choices, and enabling them to select the right loan for their home buying needs. The mortgage loan process can be arduous, costly, and seemingly impossible to the consumer. The broker works as the liaison between the borrower and the lender to create a cost effective and efficient loan process.
>
> As an independent contractor, the broker allows wholesaler lenders to cut origination costs by providing such services as preparing the borrower's loan package, loan application, funding process, and counseling the borrower.

The services of mortgage brokers were not in great demand thirty years ago. At that time, the mortgage industry was made up almost entirely of large, integrated firms (banks and savings and loans) that managed the entire process of bringing borrowers and investors together. They located investors (depositors, in this case) and borrowers, recommended the appropriate type of mortgage (typically from a small set of options), analyzed borrowers' creditworthiness and the value of their collateral, closed the loans, serviced the loans, and made payments to the investors.

By 2000, the mortgage market had changed radically (Jacobides 2005; U.S. Department of Housing and Urban Development 2002). Technological change (fax machines, the Internet, etc.), financial innovation (credit scoring, automated underwriting, securitization of mortgages, etc.), and deregulation (e.g., repeal of state usury limits) abetted extensive specialization and

---

5. The quotation, from the NAMB's FAQ web page: www.namb.org/namb/FAQs1 .asp?SnID=1916912282, was downloaded on November 8, 2007. The term "broker" is generally used to refer to a firm offering mortgage brokerage services, while the term "loan officer" is commonly used to refer to an employee of a mortgage broker who actually performs these services. We adopt this common usage. However, terminology in the industry is not uniform (HUD 2002) and can be confusing, not least because the actual roles of brokers, loan officers, lenders, and others are not rigidly bounded and often blur. For a wry but useful summary of the overlapping roles and confusing jargon in the mortgage origination business, see "Mortgage Origination for UberNerds," a September 7, 2007, posting on the Calculate Risk blog, at http://calculatedrisk.blogspot.com/2007/09/mortgage-origination-channels-for.html.

vertical disintegration in the industry, so that separate firms could focus on particular steps in the process, such as loan marketing and closing (the brokers' origination specialties), underwriting, initial funding, servicing, pooling (for sale in the secondary market), and long-term funding. At the same time, the range of potential participants within each niche broadened; for example, nondepository mortgage banks competed with depository institutions to originate and sometimes service, pool, or fund mortgages. In addition, new types of mortgages (e.g., adjustable rate mortgages, or ARMs) and differentiated products aimed at a wider array of consumers (e.g., a variety of subprime mortgages with risk-based interest rates for high-risk borrowers) took significant market shares.

These developments both affected and were affected by the rapid growth of mortgage brokering. As the decision to grant credit became less based on subjective assessments of the loan applicant and more based on credit scores and other objective underwriting standards, underwriting moved to the back office, and loan officers employed by depository institutions focused increasingly on sales and loan closing services. Improved communications technology—fax machines and, later, the Internet—fostered the physical separation of the sales function from the underwriting function, and this, in turn, made it possible to outsource either or both. Mortgage brokers take outsourcing one step further, in that they work for themselves, as independent contractors dealing with multiple lenders. As such, brokers allowed both established mortgage lenders (the depository institutions) and new competitors (nondepository mortgage banks) to specialize and to rapidly scale up or down their sales efforts and loan origination volumes in response to market cycles and competitive opportunities (Apgar, Bendimerad, and Essene 2007; U.S. Department of Housing and Urban Development 2002).

Low overheads and the resulting ability to efficiently market within residential neighborhoods also helped brokers penetrate the emerging subprime market, which included many households who were somewhat unfamiliar with traditional mortgage lending institutions. The number of mortgage brokers and the number of subprime mortgage originations grew in tandem (figure 6.1), and mortgage brokers came to dominate the origination of subprime mortgages (Schloemer et al. 2006). Much of the growth of the mortgage broker industry took place on the extensive margin, by the addition of new firms, as the average size of firms remained small (about ten individuals) during most of our study period (Sichelman 2003).

On the consumer side of the market, the much wider array of lenders and mortgage contracts to choose from made mortgage shopping much more challenging (Guttentag 2000). Mortgage brokers, by consolidating information on multiple products from multiple lenders, offered consumers a convenient way to examine a variety of home loans for which they were financially qualified. The result was the creation of a viable intermediary role and rapid growth in the mortgage broker industry.

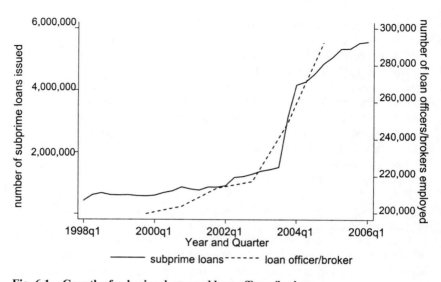

Fig. 6.1   Growth of subprime loans and loan officers/brokers

Sources: The Occupation Employment Survey and the National Delinquency Survey of the Mortgage Bankers Association of America (2007).

The transformation of the U.S. mortgage market after 1980 created significant benefits for U.S. consumers by increasing homeownership and improving the efficiency of mortgage processing (Gerardi, Rosen, and Willen 2007; U.S. Department of Housing and Urban Development 2002), and mortgage brokers can claim a share of the credit. They serve millions of customers from all parts of society, and their repeat business and the multiyear growth in their market share through 2006 suggest that many of their customers have been pleased with their services. Brokers have helped to shorten the loan closing process and to make it cheaper, and they have enabled the mortgage industry to meet enormous fluctuations in demand. However, the transformation of the mortgage industry created some new problems, and mortgage brokers are also blamed for some of these.

Critics of mortgage brokers generally focus on incentive problems stemming from the fact that the broker is an intermediary whose pay depends directly on the size and number of loans originated and only indirectly on whether the borrower got a good deal and also makes payments as expected (Schloemer et al. 2006). The incentive issues arise because of information asymmetries between the borrower, lender, and broker. Studies have repeatedly shown, for example, that borrowers are very confused by the language and terms of mortgage contracts and related documentation (Pappalardo and Lacko 2007; Woodward 2003; Guttentag 2000). Borrowers frequently fail to understand basic facts about the mortgages they have signed and are even more confused about the other mortgage options available to them.

Many are willing to follow the advice of a professional, such as a mortgage broker, even though they may be unable to verify the quality of the advice even after the fact (Pappalardo and Lacko 2007; Kim-Sung and Hermanson 2003). This creates an opportunity for professionals, including mortgage brokers,[6] to abuse that trust by, for example, recommending a mortgage that has a higher interest rate than the customer actually qualifies for, in order to obtain a higher fee. The following are among the most frequently cited consumer issues regarding mortgage brokers (and others with the same incentives):

1. Brokers steer borrowers "to mortgages that provide higher compensation to the broker but are not necessarily the lowest cost or most advantageous to the consumer" (El Anshasy, Elliehausen, and Shimazaki 2005, 4; also Apgar, Bendimerad, and Essene 2007; Essene and Apgar 2007; Schloemer et al. 2006), and they do so deliberately and disproportionately with subprime, minority, elderly, or poorly informed customers (Kim-Sung and Hermanson 2003; Jackson and Burlingame 2007; Ernst, Bocian, and Li 2008; Woodward 2008).

2. They market aggressively to maximize origination fees, in particular by persuading borrowers to take loans they cannot afford or to refinance too frequently (Kim-Sung and Hermanson 2003; El Anshasy, Elliehausen, and Shimazaki 2005).

3. They receive fees from borrowers and lenders that are more than commensurate with services rendered (Apgar, Bendimerad, and Essene 2007; Essene and Apgar 2007; Schloemer et al. 2006), especially from minority (Jackson and Burlingame 2007) or unsophisticated (Guttentag 2000) borrowers.

Asymmetric information also makes lenders concerned about the quality of mortgage brokers' services. Brokers' fees are usually paid only if and when loans are closed. Thus, brokers' immediate incentives are to earn their fees by getting lenders to approve and close loans, and they do not have a direct stake in subsequent loan performance. These incentives have been seen as raising the following major issues for lenders regarding brokers:

1. Brokers may corrupt the information about the borrower that is submitted for underwriting in order to increase the chances that the lender will approve the loan (Apgar, Bendimerad, and Essene 2007; El Anshasy, Elliehausen, and Shimazaki 2005), with the result that loans handled by brokers are more likely to default than loans processed by the lender's own loan officers (Alexander et al. 2002). The incomplete or inaccurate information

---

6. This potential is not limited to mortgage brokers, however. It extends to loan officers at mortgage lending banks when they are paid incentives based on the size and interest rate of the loans they originate.

can arise from either carelessness or deliberate misrepresentation or fraud (Schloemer et al. 2006).

2. Contrary to contractual agreements with their lender clients, they encourage the client's existing borrowers to refinance, so that prepayment rates on the lender's broker-originated mortgages are higher than on mortgages originated by the lender's own loan officers (LaCour-Little and Chun 1999).

In principle, private actions within the marketplace can mitigate these consumer and lender information and incentive problems and correct or alleviate the market failures that have been alleged. For example, over time, lenders can monitor the quality of the loans submitted by a given broker and either stop dealing with or pay lower fees to inferior brokers. Although some lenders began monitoring in this way, industry experts assert that, at least until recently, these efforts have not been sufficiently strict or widespread to significantly change aggregate outcomes (Alexander et al. 2002; Apgar, Bendimerad, and Essene 2007). Some lenders mitigated losses by pricing broker-originated loans differently, using higher interest rates on these loans to offset default risk or imposing prepayment penalties to offset higher prepayment risk (Alexander et al. 2002), but prepayment penalties became controversial in their own right. On the consumer side, confusion about mortgages contributed to enhanced efforts at homebuyer financial education, but with only limited results. Guttentag (2000) suggested a new contractual arrangement, the Upfront Mortgage Broker, under which mortgage brokers would serve as the borrower's agent in return for fixed, fully disclosed fees. So far only a small fraction of brokers work under this arrangement. In short, as of 2007 it appears that market responses have not eliminated concerns about bad outcomes caused by asymmetric information and incentive conflicts in the mortgage broker market. Partly as a result, many mortgage lenders have cut back on or ceased accepting broker-originated loans, exacerbating the steep decline in mortgage brokering since 2006.

6.3   Theory and Previous Studies of Licensing

With private responses not eliminating concerns about mortgage broker incentives and actions, public policymakers have entered the fray. The federal financial regulatory agencies have promulgated new guidelines and requirements regarding mortgage information disclosures and subprime loan underwriting and pricing. Many states and local governments have enacted so-called antipredatory lending laws that restrict mortgage interest rates, fees, and contract terms. In addition, state legislators and regulators, often with the support and help of mortgage broker trade associations, have broadened and tightened the requirements for mortgage broker firms and individual loan officers to obtain the licenses that they need to operate legally. Then, in the Housing and Economic Recovery Act of 2008, Congress established new minimum requirements for state mortgage broker registration and regulation. In this section, we review theories and previous empirical studies of occupational licensing. In the following sections we summarize the specifics of mortgage broker licensing in the United States and assess how state differences in mortgage broker licensing are associated with outcomes in the labor and mortgage markets.

6.3.1   Theories of Occupational Licensing

The simplest theory of occupational licensing draws more on a mechanical concept of administrative procedure than on economics. It envisions an essentially costless supply of unbiased, capable gatekeepers and enforcers. The gatekeepers screen entrants to the profession, barring those whose skills or character suggests a tendency toward low-quality output. The enforcers monitor incumbents and discipline those whose performance is below standards, with punishments that may include revocation of the license needed to practice. Assuming that entry and ongoing performance are controlled in these ways, the quality of service in the profession will almost automatically be maintained at or above standards.

We can add some economics to this otherwise mechanical model by noting that a key discipline on incumbents—the threat of loss of license—may not mean much if incumbents can easily reenter the profession, such as by moving to a new firm or state, or shift to an alternative occupation with little loss of income. For example, if sales skills are the key to both mortgage brokering and selling cars, then individuals may shift between these lines of work with little loss of income.[7] Under these circumstances, meaningful discipline may require deliberate steps to ensure that loss of license entails significant financial loss. Such additional steps could include imposition of fines, improved screening to prevent expelled practitioners from reentering the occupation, or requiring all incumbents to put up capital that would be forfeited upon loss of license.[8] To offset the possibility that incumbents could shift to other occupations with little loss of income, entry requirements could be tightened to limit supply and create monopoly rents within the licensed occupation. The threat of losing these monopoly rents could,

---

7. An experienced mortgage broker, quoted in McGarity (2001, 41), complains about "brokers who pop in and out of the market," claiming that they are often the ones who abuse borrowers and noting, "People think they can make a quick buck, but they're not in it for the long haul. We'll see every shoe salesman and photocopier salesman will all of a sudden be a mortgage broker, but come next year they'll all be gone."

8. Steps along these lines have been or are being taken by mortgage broker licensing authorities. Financial regulators from about forty states are currently cooperating on a new software application that will make it easier to track individual mortgage brokers and loan officers as they seek to change the firms or states in which they work (Conference of State Bank Supervisors 2007). Many states already require mortgage brokers to maintain a physical presence in each state in which they operate or to maintain a commercial surety bond. Potential loss of professional esteem may also be a deterrent (Kandel and Lazear 1992).

in principle, give incentives to incumbents to maintain standards. The rents also could motivate potential entrants to invest in high levels of training in order to gain admittance. This suggests that licensing can raise quality within an industry by restricting supply and raising prices.

Friedman (1962) questioned the assumption of unbiased gatekeepers and enforcers and viewed licensing's entry restrictions and monopoly rents as purely negative. He argued that licensing systems are almost always run by and for incumbents, so that gatekeepers and enforcers are, in reality, self-interested. Their vested interests lead them to not only create monopoly rents through restrictions on entry but also stifle complaints and disciplinary procedures against most incumbents. Weak discipline on incumbents, along with artificially high client-provider ratios, lead to a decrease in the overall quality of service that consumers receive. In other words, Friedman predicts that licensing reduces the size of an occupation and leads to a combination of higher fees for providers and lower quality for consumers. Friedman also stresses that the proper measure of quality is the overall quality of services received by consumers, not the average quality of services provided by licensed providers, because licensing, by raising prices within the licensed occupation, may cause consumers to seek substitute services from nonlicensed occupations that provide lower-quality output. Friedman's analysis led him to conclude that licensing had no useful role, except possibly in very limited circumstances involving externalities.[9]

In the 1980s, Akerlof's (1970) analysis of how information asymmetries about the quality of goods could lead to adverse selection and the predominance of low-quality goods in unregulated markets spurred the development of new theories of occupational licensing. The new models ignore Friedman's concerns about self interest and also largely disregard the disciplining of incumbents in order to focus on more realistic modeling of the capabilities of gatekeepers.[10] In particular, they assume that neither regulators nor consumers can directly observe the quality of producers ex ante. These models then explore how the theory of licensing changes when entry barriers depend only on information that might realistically be observed. The new models include not only unobserved heterogeneity in quality among producers but also heterogeneous tastes for quality among consumers. The new models yield a mixed perspective on the effects of licensing: licensing can increase the average quality of service within the occupation, but this

9. It is arguable that mortgage markets are subject to material externalities, to the extent that foreclosures impose significant costs on third parties, and these costs are not considered by the parties directly involved in originating risky mortgages (Apgar, Duda, and Gorey 2005; Gramlich 2007).

10. In fact, a common assumption of these models, as in Shapiro 1986 or Rogerson 1983, is that quality is chosen at the time of entry and cannot be changed thereafter, so that enforcement of standards on incumbents is meaningless.

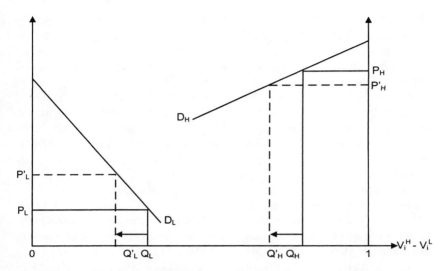

Fig. 6.2   An illustration of the possible effects of raising licensing requirements

Notes: Key: V_i^L = the ith consumer's utility of consuming low-quality services; V_i^H = the ith consumer's utility of consuming high-quality services; Q_L = the quantity of services in the low-quality-only market; Q_H = the quantity of services in the high-quality-only market; P_L = the price of services in the low-quality-only market; P_H = the price of services in the high-quality-only market; D_L = the demand curve for services in the low-quality-only market; D_H = the demand curve for services in the high-quality-only market (shown in mirror image).

change benefits some consumers, such as those with high preferences for quality, and harms others.

In some of the new models, licensing requirements take the form of unspecified fixed costs controlled by the licensing authority, broadly similar to typical licensing requirements such as payment of an annual licensing fee or maintenance of a surety bond. In one highly cited model (Shapiro 1986), skill affects the relative cost of producing high-quality services, and licensing takes the more specific form of a minimal human capital requirement, similar to actual requirements that entrants—and sometimes incumbents— take certain training programs or pass an exam. Apart from these special fixed costs, entry into and exit out of the occupation are unrestricted, which ensures that providers earn zero profits in equilibrium.

The basic idea is as illustrated in figure 6.2, which is loosely based on Shapiro (1986). The horizontal axis represents a fixed unit mass of consumers uniformly distributed from lowest preference for quality services, corresponding to zero, to highest, corresponding to one. Each consumer consumes one unit of service per period.[11] Consumers can choose among

11. Other models allow the total number of consumers and thus aggregate demand to vary; see Garcia-Fontes and Hopenhayn (2000).

three markets: a market for mature producers known to sell high-quality services, a market for mature producers known to produce low-quality services, and a market for young producers whose quality of service (low or high) is not known by the consumer at time of purchase. The figure shows the aggregate demand curve for services in the low-quality-only market relative to the left vertical axis (with number of units demanded measured to the right of the origin on the horizontal axis) and for services in the high-quality-only market in mirror-image form relative to the right vertical axis (with units of demand measured to the left of the point $[1,0]$ on the horizontal axis). In the initial steady-state equilibrium, a quantity Q_L is sold in the low-quality-only market for price P_L, a quantity Q_H is sold in the high-quality-only market for price P_H, and a quantity $1-Q_L-Q_H$ is sold in the mixed-quality market at the blended price $[Q_L/(Q_L + Q_H)] \cdot P_L + [Q_H/(Q_L + Q_H)] \cdot P_H$ (whose weights reflect the proportions of low- and high-quality producers in the economy, which also prevail among the new practitioners in the mixed market in steady state).

Suppose an increased fixed cost (which might be a human capital requirement) is imposed by the licensing authority. This makes low-quality production unprofitable at the initially prevailing prices. In the new steady state, there are fewer mature low-quality producers, represented by Q_L', and a higher price in the low-quality-only market, or P_L'. With no other changes, this would raise the blended price in the mixed-quality market and cause lifetime profits for high-quality producers to exceed zero. Hence more producers choose to be high quality, raising output in the high-quality-only market to Q_H' and lowering price there to P_H'. Consumers in the interval between Q_H and 1 are clearly better off in the new steady state, because they consume the same high-quality service as in the initial steady state but at a lower price. By similar logic, consumers in the interval between 0 and Q_L' are clearly worse off. This illustrates how, in asymmetric models, licensing tends to generate Pareto-noncomparable outcomes. However, the new models resemble the previous simple model in predicting, typically, that both the average quality and the average price of services within the regulated industry will rise as licensing requirements are tightened. Thus, compared to the simple model, the asymmetric-information models add more realistic assumptions about what licensing gatekeepers can see or control and yield deeper insights into the welfare effects of licensing, but their predictions regarding quality and price are similar.[12]

12. A possible effect not explicitly illustrated here is that the passage of tougher regulations not only raises providers' costs but also shifts out the demand for their services, by enhancing consumers' confidence that these services are of good quality. In the model underlying figure 6.2, this effect would operate in the market for young providers whose quality is not yet known. An outward shift in demand would accentuate the increase in the price of services, boosting provider incomes. In more general models where the total number of providers is endogenous, this effect can offset the direct effect of higher production costs, so that the overall effect of tighter regulation on the number of providers becomes ambiguous.

In applying any of these theories to mortgage broker licensing, it is important to consider what would be observed in the credit market if mortgage brokers provided higher-quality services. The nature of the service is to match a borrower and lender efficiently, so that loans are made with a favorable combination of greater gains from trade and/or lower search-plus-processing costs than if a broker had not been involved (Yavas 1994; Li 1998). However, because credit markets are also subject to information asymmetries, the credit market results of high-quality brokering are potentially counterintuitive. For example, higher quality might include that the broker provides the lender with more complete and accurate information about the borrower, so that loans are underwritten and priced more accurately. If so, it is conceivable that better brokers could be associated with a higher proportion of high-priced loans in the credit market, because lenders would be more willing to price risk rather than ration credit if they had more trust in the information brokers were submitting. In other words, the quality of mortgage brokering can affect the breadth of the credit market and thus the range of creditworthiness among loan applicants and recipients, and this can complicate the impact of higher-quality brokering on some credit market outcomes.

However, if we control for the creditworthiness of loan applicants, better brokering would presumably be associated with lower search- and processing-related costs, such as a lower percentage of loan applications being denied, a lower rate of bad matches that lead to delinquency or foreclosure, and a shorter time between loan application and loan closing or denial. The effects of better brokering on interest rates, controlling for creditworthiness, are less clear. Borrowers might be willing to accept higher interest rates in a brokered transaction, compared to a nonbrokered transaction, if there were more than offsetting reductions in search costs, just as lenders might be willing to accept lower interest rates if there were more than offsetting reductions in marketing and processing costs.

Previous Evaluations of the Effects of Occupational Licensing

Most studies of the influence of occupational licensing policies on the price of the occupation's service find a positive relationship (Cox and Foster 1990), sometimes with no improvement in quality. These studies cover policies ranging from restrictions on interstate mobility, such as by limiting reciprocity, to restrictions on advertising and other commercial practices (Shepard 1978; Feldman and Begun 1978; Bond et al. 1980; Kleiner, Gay, and Greene 1982). A review of empirical research on licensing found that licensing is associated with consumer prices that are 4 to 35 percent higher, depending on the type of commercial practice and location (Kleiner 2006). In cross-sectional studies, the overall impact of occupational licensing on wages in licensed relative to unlicensed occupations was found to be about 10 to 12 percent, with some estimates as high as 15 to 17 percent (Kleiner

2006; Kleiner and Krueger 2008). Kleiner and Kudrle (2000), for example, found that tougher state-level restrictions and more rigorous pass rates for dentists were associated with hourly wage rates that were 15 percent higher than in states with few restrictions, with no measurable increase in observable quality. Similarly, Barker (2007) found that higher state educational standards for real estate brokers "raise broker income without improving the quality of service."

Although some general patterns can be seen, the range of outcomes described in existing studies suggests that the effects of occupational licensing are sensitive to the form and strictness of regulations as well as to the nature of the occupation. Thus, the effects of mortgage broker licensing need to be directly measured. We are aware of only two studies that attempt to do this (El Anshasy, Elliehausen, and Shimazaki 2005; Backley et al. 2006), and both are inconclusive, in part due to limits in their data on mortgage broker licensing.

6.4   Measurement of Mortgage Broker Licensing

To associate mortgage broker licensing with market outcomes, we need measurements of the extent of mortgage broker licensing. We rely heavily on Pahl's (2007) compilation of these regulations in the fifty states and the District of Columbia for the period 1996 to 2006. Pahl shows that a wide range of licensing provisions may apply to mortgage brokerage firms (typically partnerships, LLCs, or corporations) and sole proprietors, such as:

1. The entity's *controlling individual(s)* may be required to be of minimum age; maintain in-state residency; meet minimums for professional pre-licensing education, experience, or examination results; provide evidence of ethical fitness and absence of criminal background; and/or complete required continuing education.

2. The entity may be required to name an individual as *managing principal,* and the managing principal may be subject to requirements similar to those for controlling individuals as well as to requirements to maintain a minimum net worth or surety bond or to obtain a license as an individual mortgage broker or loan officer.

3. The entity itself may be required to maintain a minimum net worth or a surety bond. Entities, sole proprietors, controlling individuals, and managing principals may be required to pay fees for licensing, application processing, application investigation, or license renewal.

4. Entities and sole proprietors may be required to meet minimum physical office requirements, such as maintaining a physical office in states where they operate. To open a branch office, entities and sole proprietors may be required to provide notification, obtain a license or certificate, pay various fees, maintain branch-specific amounts of net worth and/or surety bonds,

and/or name a branch manager who may be required to meet provisions similar to those discussed previously for managing principals. In some states, the loan officers who work for mortgage brokerage firms may also be required to meet standards of the same type as those listed earlier for managing principals, but often at a lower level. Additional provisions may specify that a loan officer can only work for one firm at a time. However, some states allow certain other professionals, such as real estate agents or attorneys, to engage in some aspects of mortgage brokering without obtaining a specific mortgage broker license; these exemptions may be subject to limits on the maximum number or volume of loans brokered.

For each state and the District of Columbia for each year from 1996 through 2006, Pahl assigns an integer value for the intensity of each of twenty-four regulatory components. Most of the components deal with human capital requirements. For example, regarding the controlling individuals in mortgage broker firms, Pahl codes separate intensities for prelicensing education, prelicensing experience, prelicensing examinations, and continuing education requirements. She codes the same four variables for managing principals, branch managers, and the firms' employees, for a total of sixteen human capital components. Three components reflect, respectively, the degree of individual licensing required of managing principals, branch managers, and employees. At the firm level, Pahl codes the intensity of both net worth and surety bonding requirements and separately codes the intensity of surety bonding required for branches. Finally, she codes whether an in-state office is required and the extent of exemptions that allow other professions to engage in mortgage brokering activities.

We use two overall indices of the intensity of mortgage broker regulation in a state: a simple sum of all twenty-four of Pahl's individual intensity values (the *summated rating scale*) and a statistically weighted index (*Rasch index*).[13] In a reduced-form sense, we can capture the major regulatory provisions affecting the occupation using both linear (summated rating scale) and nonlinear (Rasch index) measures of the system.

In addition to these composite indices, we also examine subsets of Pahl's twenty-four regulatory components.[14] Much of our analysis includes a dollar-valued measure of the bonding and net worth regulations, which we

13. This index is from a Rasch-type model (Andrich 1988) that places each of the variables within a logical structure based on frequency of outcome and an integer scale. The empirical measure of the Rasch model we use is known as a partial credit model, a nonlinear model that assigns weights that are consistent with an implicit structure to the regulatory system. This approach assumes that the distance between parameters is equal and that the categories are equal integers. The development of the Rasch scale uses maximum likelihood estimation to calculate a unique index for each state.

14. The anatomy of the regulatory system for brokers by state is generally consistent. Simple correlations among the individual items in our index were mostly positive, and a large number were statistically significant. None of the negative correlations among the components of the index were statistically significant.

Table 6.1   **Rankings of top and bottom five regulated states and changes using the summated rating scheme by state**

Top 5 regulated states 2004	
Florida	16
Montana	14
New Jersey	13
Ohio	12
Texas	12
North Carolina	12
Nevada	12
Bottom 5 regulated states 2004	
Colorado	0
Wyoming	0
Alaska	0
South Dakota	1
Maine	2
Top 5 states by change in regulation 1999–2004	
Montana	14
Texas	12
North Carolina	11
Oklahoma	8
Connecticut	7
Nevada	7
Utah	7

created by examining the details of each state's requirements and selecting what we judged to be the smallest dollar option by which new entrants could meet the bonding and net worth requirements.[15] We sometimes pair this measure with an index of all other requirements, constructed by subtracting the bonding and net worth indices from the composite indices. We have also examined other subindices and individual components, such as for the provisions regarding training and examinations, provisions that apply only to the management of brokerage firms, provisions that limit brokerage firm branches, and provisions that apply only to employees of brokerage firms. As discussed in appendix D, some of these other regulatory variables were significant in regressions with one or more of our labor and mortgage market dependent variables, and in a few cases their presence materially weakened the significance of the bonding and net worth variable. Further research on some of them seems warranted, but we focus on the bonding and net worth provisions because we judged them to show the broadest and most consistent pattern of significant relationships with market outcomes.

Table 6.1 shows the top and bottom five states ranked by the restrictiveness of their summated scale of mortgage broker licensing. Florida has the

15. The values we chose are listed in appendix A. Our focus on the barriers facing small entrants aligns with the evidence noted earlier that during most of our study period the industry grew on the extensive margin while the average mortgage brokerage remained small.

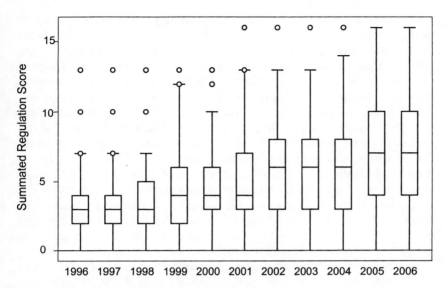

Fig. 6.3   Growth and variation of occupational regulation by state over time

Notes: This box-and-whisker plot shows annual values of the median, interquartile range, and outliers of the summated rating scale derived from Pahl's (2007) catalogue of state (and District of Columbia) mortgage broker regulations. The line in the middle of the box represents the median. The bottom and top edges of the box are the first and third quartile, respectively. The whiskers extending from the box represent the most extreme point within the range of one-and-a-half times the interquartile range (the difference between the third and first quartile). The remaining points represent outliers that do not fall within the range of the whiskers.

most statutory provisions regulating mortgage brokers. The five states with the least restrictive statutes in 2004, such as Alaska and Wyoming, are less populous. Texas and Montana had the greatest increase in the regulation of mortgage brokers during the period 1999 to 2004. In general, larger industrial states were more likely to impose regulatory provisions on mortgage brokers.

Figure 6.3 shows the more general growth and variation of regulation over time from 1996 to 2006, using a box-and-whisker plot. The mean value of the summated rating scale for all states was 3.2 in 1996 and increased to almost 8 by 2005. The variations in state practices also rose. As the membership in the occupation expanded in response to growth in the demand for broker services, more states began regulating the members of the occupation. This may have occurred because members in the occupation sought regulation or because of public concern about brokers allegedly charging excessive fees or leading customers into overly risky loans.

Because of their significance for our analysis, it is important to understand the nature of bonding requirements.[16] When brokers are required to have a

16. For background on the market for surety bonds in general and mortgage broker surety bonds in particular, see www.jwsuretybonds.com.

bond of, say, $50,000, this typically means that they pay an annual premium, ranging from several hundred to a few thousand dollars, to a surety bond company. It does not mean that the broker must own and place in trust a fixed-income security with a market value of $50,000. Under specified conditions of broker nonperformance of duties spelled out in the governing laws and regulations, third parties, such as the broker's customers, may collect up to the amount of the bond from the surety company. The role of the surety company is to ensure that a valid claim will be promptly paid.[17] If this occurs, the surety company will seek full compensation from the broker for the amount it paid out to the third party, plus expenses. The broker's annual premium is thus a fee paid to guarantee a line of contingent credit up to a legally required amount. In setting the annual premium it charges a broker, a surety company considers both the expected value of claims against the broker and the probability of collecting from the broker for any amounts paid out. Consequently, the bond company may conduct detailed screening of applicants, similar to credit underwriting, before issuing the bond.

We speculate that this screening could make bonding one of the most significant barriers to entry in states requiring bonds of $50,000 and more, especially given that the educational requirements for mortgage brokers may not be very demanding. Some support for this view comes from Barker's (2007) finding that state bonding requirements mattered in a related occupation—real estate brokerage—where they were associated with higher-quality service, as measured by a lower rate of consumer complaints. An industry expert, David Olson (2007), provides additional support. He notes that one factor that kept mortgage brokers from originating many Federal Housing Administration (FHA) mortgages was FHA's requirement that originators provide a formal audit, costing about $5,000 each year.[18] He suggests that more mortgage brokers would originate FHA loans if this audit requirement were dropped in favor of having brokers maintain a $75,000 surety bond. For established mortgage brokers with good credit, the cost of this bond would be about $750, but Olson notes that "Brokers with low net worth and fewer years in the business will have a more difficult time getting a bond at all." In such cases, the broker could seek a more costly bond from a surety company that specializes in serving higher-risk clients, but their premiums often reach 10 to 15 percent of the amount of the bond,

17. Surety companies investigate the validity of claims before paying out. We are referring here to claims they consider valid.

18. The FHA's audit requirement may, in part, illustrate Milton Friedman's point, discussed previously, that occupational regulations affect not only consumers within the regulated sector but also those who turn to substitute products as a result of the regulations. During this decade's housing boom, the FHA lost market share to less regulated subprime mortgage lenders. This occurred for many reasons, but one reason was that many brokers chose not to meet the FHA's standards and thus did not market FHA loans to their clients. We are not saying that the FHA should have lowered its requirements for brokers. We are simply noting that the FHA's unilateral maintenance of a relatively high audit requirement may have contributed to consumers being served by non-FHA brokers, and that this seems to illustrate Friedman's point that occupational licensing can shift demand toward less regulated providers.

compared to 1 to 2 percent for low-risk mortgage brokers. Thus, on just a $50,000 bond, a high-risk premium could match or exceed the $5,000 audit cost that Olson judged to be prohibitive for most brokers.

6.5   Methods

We fit multivariate statistical models of mortgage broker labor market variables and consumer mortgage market variables. These two classes of dependent variables are regressed on measures of state mortgage broker regulations and variables intended to control for other factors affecting these markets. Our analysis takes two main forms: panel data analyses using repeated annual cross sections of labor and mortgage market data, and cross-sectional analyses of hundreds to thousands of individual mortgages issued in 2005. Most of the panel data regressions utilize just state-level average data, but for mortgage broker earnings we combine observations on individual mortgage professionals with state-averaged data. The panel data regressions allow for fixed effects in each state as well as time trends. State-level fixed effects cannot be included in our cross-sectional regressions, due to collinearity with our regulatory variables. As a check on our results, we reestimate our cross-sectional regressions on a sample restricted to mortgages just in metropolitan statistical areas (MSAs) that cross state boundaries, so that we can include MSA fixed effects.

6.6   Results

6.6.1   Panel Data Results for Labor Market Variables

Table 6.2 provides descriptive statistics for key labor market variables as well as other mortgage market and regulatory variables used in our analysis. The table shows the growth in occupational regulation and a measure (from the annual American Community Survey [ACS]) of hourly wages and earnings of mortgage brokers and related lending professionals.[19] We take advantage of the variation across both space and time to analyze relationships between the intensity of licensing and key labor market variables such as mortgage brokers' employment (relative to the population) and earnings. These relationships could be either positive or negative, based on the theories discussed pre-

---

19. The ACS is conducted annually by the Census Bureau and replicates the long form on the decennial Census. It provides large samples of individuals, even for relatively detailed occupational classifications such as loan officers and brokers. As a check on the results using the ACS, we also use the Occupation Employment Survey (OES), which produces employment and wage estimates for over 800 occupations by state on a biennial basis from 1999 on. The OES also includes a category for loan officers and brokers. In both the ACS and OES, the data we use include mortgage loan officers and agents, collection analysts, loan servicing officers, and loan underwriters. These state OES figures are highly correlated ($r = .81$) with the National Mortgage Broker Association's count of membership by state. Similar high correlations were found between National Mortgage Broker Association memberships and the ACS figures we use.

Table 6.2   Summary statistics for the labor market, service market, and legal and bonding provisions

State-level and individual variables	2000 Mean (Standard deviation)	2005 Mean (Standard deviation)
Broker/loan officer hourly wage	20.12	25.15
	(12.74)	(16.87)
Annual broker/loan officer earnings	40,973.43	52,748.68
	(26,177.80)	(41,526.24)
Employment (loan officers and brokers/ population, %)	.15	.17
	(.06)	(.17)
Years of experience	18.49	19.51
	(10.54)	(11.51)
Years of schooling	14.54	14.69
	(1.79)	(1.80)
Mean number of loans	537,109.57	736,032.00
	(679,999.52)	(880,192.82)
Mean number of subprime loans	13,995.13	95,726.69
	(15,213.93)	(129,101.6)
Mean number of loans in foreclosure	6,214.27	8,580.52
	(8,883.82)	(9,444.91)
Mean state population	5,471,375.84	5,757,977.29
	(6,101,905.36)	(6,498,035.30)
Median household income	$58,574.57	$63,504.76
	(7,641.51)	(10,326.91)
Licensing index (1996)	2.33	
	(1.96)	
Licensing index (2005)	6.84	
	(3.68)	
Bonding/net worth index (2000)	1.70	
	(1.37)	
Bonding/net worth index (2005)	1.88	
	(1.35)	
Real bonding/net worth requirement (1996) **base year 2000	$15,825.12	
	(18,963.83)	
Real bonding/net worth requirement (2005) **base year 2000	$27,479.08	
	(25,928.68)	

viously. An additional complication, not reflected in the theoretical models, is that brokers may accelerate entry into the occupation before the standards become fully effective, leading to a spurious positive relationship between subsequent regulation and the number of practitioners in the short run.[20]

We begin by relating regulation to the employment of brokers and related

20. This was the case in accounting, where anticipated new regulations resulted in a surge of applicants just before more stringent education requirements took effect (Cummings and Rankin 1999).

Table 6.3   Fixed-effects models of loan officer employment/population by state
                   (ACS data)

	(1)	(2)
Summated regulation index lagged once	0.068	0.058
(no net worth/bonding)/100	(0.206)	(0.173)
Real net worth/bonding requirement lagged once/1,000,000	−0.545	−0.795
	(0.431)	(0.350)**
Summated regulation index lagged twice	−0.026	
(no net worth/bonding)/100	(0.235)	
Real net worth/bonding requirement lagged twice/1,000,000	−0.418	
	(0.403)	
Mean experience by state	−0.004	−0.004
	(0.003)	(0.003)
Mean experience by state squared/10,000	0.993	0.994
	(0.659)	(0.658)
Mean years of school by state	−0.001	−0.001
	(0.005)	(0.005)
Lag median state household income/100,000	0.218	0.211
	(0.162)	(0.161)
Lag state unemployment rate	0.010	0.010
	(0.006)*	(0.006)*
Lag state home ownership percentage	−0.001	−0.002
	(0.002)	(0.002)
Constant	0.172	0.187
	(0.176)	(0.175)
Year dummy controls (2001–2005) base 2000	Yes	Yes
Observations	300	300
Number of states	50	50
R^2	0.12	0.11
F-Test on one- and two-period lags of summated index	0.06	—
F-Test for one- and two-period lags of bonding/net worth	3.16**	—

Notes: Standard errors in parentheses.
***Significant at the 1 percent level.
**Significant at the 5 percent level.
*Significant at the 10 percent level.

lending professionals. Table 6.3 shows the relationship between bonding and net worth requirements and state-level employment from 2000 to 2005. Our measure of employment based on the ACS is the number of mortgage brokers and related lending professionals per capita by state. We use pooled time series and cross-sectional data that allow us to estimate fixed-effects models with a set of human capital, labor market, and service market state controls.[21] Our results show that the bonding/net worth requirement is sig-

21. We find that neither the linear summated rating scale nor the Rasch index is significantly related to mortgage broker employment at the state level. We also estimate random effects for our models (available from the authors). The basic findings hold whether the specification is fixed or random effects.

nificant and negatively associated with employment. Using the values at the mean of the distribution, we find that doubling the bonding requirement is associated with an 8 to 10 percent decrease in the number of brokers and related lending professionals in the state relative to the population.

The bonding requirement may have a stronger relationship to employment than the other licensing components, for several reasons. It may be both relatively onerous and easily enforced up front and thus may reduce entry into the occupation. We also find that states with older mortgage brokers and related lending professionals were the ones with lower per capita levels of employment within the occupation. This may simply reflect the fact that most new entrants are younger, so that impeding entry tends both to age the profession and reduce employment. It could also be that, as the occupation matures and public policies on regulation evolve, the political clout of mortgage brokers will grow, possibly leading to adoption of more rigorous educational and experience requirements that will complement those on bonding.[22]

Restricting entry could have direct effects on earnings. To examine this relationship, we estimate the association between the bonding requirements and annual earnings, using individual-level data in the ACS. Table 6.4 presents estimates of the relationship between regulation and annual earnings from 2000 to 2005, using the individual practitioner data for each year. The basic earnings equation can be stated as follows:

$$(1) \qquad Ln(Earnings_{it}) = a + b_1 R_{it} + b_2 \mathbf{X}_{it} + u_{it},$$

where $Earnings_{it}$ are the annual earnings of person i in time period t; R_{it} is the tightness of mortgage broker licensing through bonding and net worth requirements in person i's state in time period t; the vector $\mathbf{X}_{it}$ includes covariates measuring characteristics of each person and state, along with year time trends; u_{it} is the error term; and a, b_1, and b_2 are the coefficients we estimate.

We find a positive relationship between mortgage broker licensing and mortgage broker earnings, ranging from an imprecisely estimated 7–8 percent to a marginally significant 6 percent.[23] As shown in the table, the coefficients on the nonregulatory explanatory variables were consistent

22. We also estimated a quasi-DID model to analyze mortgage broker employment changes in states that adopted a mortgage broker licensing law or substantially increased the restrictiveness of the law (e.g., a change of three using our summated rating scale). We found no statistically significant relationships for the summated index or the bonding variable. We think that the noise relative to signal in these change results influenced the lack of precision in these estimates, which are available from the authors.

23. Estimates for hourly earnings showed generally similar results. We use total earnings in our estimates because of the variable nature of compensation for brokers that are commission-based. In addition, since many brokers are in small offices where profits are shared, the earnings variable would capture this form of compensation. Further, as an additional test for robustness of our results, we estimated the logarithm of earnings as a dependent variable and the logarithm

Table 6.4 **Pooled OLS models of log annual earnings using ACS, 2000–2005**

	(1)	(2)
Summated regulation index lagged once (no net worth/bonding)/100	0.290 (0.520)	−0.485 (0.204)**
Real bonding/net worth requirement lagged once/100,000	−0.076 (0.099)	0.060 (0.033)*
Summated regulation index lagged twice (no net worth/bonding)	−0.009 (0.006)	
Real bonding/net worth requirement lagged twice/100,000	0.148 (0.113)	
Experience	0.057 (0.004)***	0.057 (0.004)***
Experience squared/1,000	−1.018 (0.089)***	−1.020 (0.090)***
Log years of school	1.262 (0.059)***	1.263 (0.059)***
Lag median household income/1,000,000	10.823 (1.677)***	10.786 (1.668)***
Lag state population/1,000,000	4.950 (1.721)***	4.653 (1.702)***
Lag state unemployment rate/100	−0.231 (1.465)	−0.046 (1.453)
State homeownership percentage/100	−0.088 (0.226)	−0.070 (0.222)
Constant	6.430 (0.262)***	6.407 (0.262)***
Year dummy controls (2001–2004) base 2000	Yes	Yes
Observations	6,699	6,699
R^2	0.13	0.13
F-Test on one- and two-period lags of summated index	3.54**	—
F-Test for one- and two-period lags of bonding/net worth	1.97	—

Notes: Robust standard errors in parentheses.
***Significant at the 1 percent level.
**Significant at the 5 percent level.
*Significant at the 10 percent level.

with the labor economics and human capital literature. In column (2), we present a standard human capital model with experience and education included, and find that the coefficient values for bonding/net worth sum to 0.06 but are not significant. Alternatively, the bonding requirements could

---

of the ACS measure of state population as an independent variable and found results similar to those shown in table 6.3. These estimates are also available from the authors.

Estimates for changes in licensing and changes in wages also showed no statistically significant impact. In none of the earnings or wage estimates were the licensing index variables significant when we used state-level controls. We also estimated nonlinear models of the licensing variables, and they were also not significant. Further, tests using the OES found significance for the licensing variables only when the $\mathbf{X}_{it}$ controls are omitted. The estimates also are available from the authors.

affect selection into the occupation, potentially restricting entry to more educated and experienced brokers. In this case, education and experience of brokers could be outcomes of regulation that should not be controlled in the earnings regression. With this specification, the bonding/net worth coefficient is statistically significant at the .10 level with a value of 0.06. This suggests that bonding requirements also may influence the level of education and experience and that may be, in part, impacting the earnings of brokers.

In the following, we find that tighter bonding/net worth requirements also are associated with lower volumes of loans processed and a higher percentage of high-priced loans originated. One interpretation of this set of results is that the demand for mortgage broker services is approximately of unit elasticity, so that as the numbers of brokers and loans processed contract, brokers' fees per loan processed rise by enough to just offset the lower loan volume and higher operating costs that result from tighter licensing, leaving the average broker's net earnings only slightly higher.

6.6.2   Panel Data Results for Mortgage Market Variables

We also investigated the relationship between mortgage broker licensing and the volume of subprime lending and rate of mortgage foreclosures. As discussed previously, stricter licensing could reduce the number of subprime loans, for example, by restricting the number or work effort of mortgage brokers. Alternatively, stricter licensing could boost effective loan demand by enhancing the quality of broker services and thereby increasing the willingness of marginal borrowers to step forward. To probe these potential outcomes, we estimated the following model:

$$(2) \qquad \text{Ln(sp-loans originated}_{it}) = \alpha + \beta_1 R_{it} + \beta_2 \mathbf{X}_{it} + \mu_{it},$$

where sp-loans originated$_{it}$ is the number of new subprime mortgages in state i over period t; R_{it} are the state-level mortgage broker licensing indices in time period t; the vector $\mathbf{X}_{it}$ includes covariates measuring the characteristics of each state, along with year time trends; μ_{it} is the error term; and α, β_1, and β_2 are the coefficients we estimate. Subprime loans originated were measured as the number of all originations in a state for a given year that were made by lenders on the U.S. Department of Housing and Urban Development's list for that year, or for the most recent prior year available, of institutions whose mortgage activity is primarily in the subprime market.

The state fixed-effects results estimated over 2001 to 2005 with the bonding/net worth requirements are presented in table 6.5. The results show that the two-lag specification of bonding requirements is associated with fewer loans originated. These estimates are consistent with those on employment. We find that imposing bonding requirements correlates with fewer brokers and fewer subprime loans originated in the state. Quantitatively, our coefficients imply that a doubling of the mean bonding requirement

Table 6.5   **Fixed effects estimates of the log of state subprime loan originations**

	(1)	(2)
Summated regulatory index lagged once	−0.023	−0.020
(no net worth/bonding)	(0.011)**	(0.010)*
Real net worth/bonding requirement lagged once/100,000	0.104	−0.321
	(0.253)	(0.223)
Summated regulatory index lagged twice	−0.002	
(no net worth/bonding)	(0.012)	
Real net worth/bonding requirement lagged twice/100,000	−0.741	
	(0.219)***	
Lag state unemployment rate	−0.017	−0.014
	(0.034)	(0.035)
Lag state population/100,000	0.024	0.022
	(0.010)**	(0.010)**
Lag median state household income/100,000	0.622	0.511
	(0.938)	(0.965)
State home ownership percentage	0.050	0.049
	(0.012)***	(0.012)***
Constant	4.661	4.823
	(1.048)***	(1.076)***
Year dummy controls (2002–2005) base 2001	Yes	Yes
Observations	254	254
Number of states (including D.C.)	51	51
R^2	0.76	0.74
F-Test on one- and two-period lags of summated index	2.78*	—
F-Test for one- and two-period lags of bonding/net worth	6.91***	—

Notes: Standard errors in parentheses.
***Significant at the 1 percent level.
**Significant at the 5 percent level.
*Significant at the 10 percent level.

to approximately $54,000 would be associated with a cut in the number of subprime loans originated by about 220,000 per year in 2004, or approximately 9 percent.

If there are fewer loans with stricter licensing, does the quality of those loans, as measured by fewer negative outcomes—such as foreclosures—also vary with licensing requirements? If state licensing improves the quality of broker services, the effects might include more appropriate loan selection and more accurate loan underwriting, resulting in fewer foreclosures. Alternatively, foreclosures could be positively correlated with tighter licensing, perhaps because a reduced availability of brokers leads to less accurate underwriting or because states that have higher foreclosure rates for other reasons (e.g., low or volatile incomes) are more likely to enact tighter restrictions. To assess these possibilities, we estimate two versions of the following model with regard to owner-occupied properties, one for just subprime mortgages and one for all mortgages:

(3) $$\text{Home Foreclosures}_{it} = \alpha + \beta_1 R_{it} + \beta_2 X_{it} + \mu_{it},$$

where Home Foreclosures$_{it}$ is the percentage of mortgages (on owner-occupied properties) in foreclosure for state i over period t (as measured in the National Delinquency Survey of the Mortgage Bankers Association of America, 1979 to 2005); R_{it} are the state-level measures of mortgage broker bonding/net worth requirements in time period t; the vector X_{it} includes covariates measuring characteristics of each state, along with year time trends; μ_{it} is the error term; and α, β_1, and β_2 are the coefficients we estimate.

As shown in table 6.6 for the estimation period January 1999 through 2004, we find a significant positive relationship between bonding/net worth requirements and foreclosure rates for both subprime and all mortgages

Table 6.6   **Fixed-effects models of the percentage of loans (subprime and all loans) in foreclosure**

	(1) Subprime	(2) Subprime	(3) All loans	(4) All loans
Summated reg. index lagged once (no net worth/bonding)	0.022 (0.093)	0.004 (0.078)	0.016 (0.016)	0.021 (0.014)
Real net worth/bonding requirement lagged once/100,000	1.357 (1.585)	3.186 (1.245)**	0.217 (0.280)	0.540 (0.226)**
Summated reg. index lagged twice (no net worth/bonding)	−0.100 (0.104)		0.013 (0.018)	
Real net worth/bonding requirement lagged twice/100,000	3.659 (1.598)**		0.476 (0.283)*	
Lag state unemployment rate	0.873 (0.224)***	0.970 (0.196)***	0.222 (0.040)***	0.251 (0.036)***
Lag state population/100,000	−0.005 (0.069)	−0.059 (0.055)	−0.032 (0.012)***	−0.033 (0.010)***
Lag median state household income/100,000	−5.080 (6.709)	−7.396 (6.059)	−1.560 (1.187)	−3.003 (1.100)***
State home ownership percentage	−0.292 (0.087)***	−0.319 (0.080)***	−0.057 (0.015)***	−0.057 (0.014)***
Constant	27.444 (7.197)***	28.629 (6.168)***	6.617 (1.273)***	6.673 (1.120)***
Year dummy controls (2000–2004) base 1999	Yes	Yes	Yes	Yes
Observations	255	306	255	306
Number of States (including D.C.)	51	51	51	51
R^2	0.66	0.63	0.42	0.43
F-Test on one- and two-period lags of summated index	0.50	—	1.46	—
F-Test for one- and two-period lags of bonding/net worth	5.51***	—	3.29**	—

Notes: Standard errors in parentheses.
***Significant at the 1 percent level.
**Significant at the 5 percent level.
*Significant at the 10 percent level.

Table 6.7   **Hazard model estimates of time to adoption of a net worth or bonding bill
1998–2005 (Using a Weibull distribution of duration)**

	(1)	(2)	(3)	(4)
Avg. percent of subprime loans in foreclosure1998–2000	0.17 (0.19)	0.15 (0.26)		
Avg. percent of all loans in foreclosure 1998–2000			0.53 (0.75)	0.98 (1.25)
Avg. state unemployment rate 1998–2000		0.186 (0.386)		0.185 (0.390)
Avg. state population 1998–2000/1,000,000		−0.030 (0.062)		−0.050 (0.072)
Avg. state median household income 1998–2000/1,000		−0.047 (0.062)		−0.042 (0.064)
Avg. state homeownership percentage 1998–2000		−0.005 (0.085)		0.003 (0.089)
Constant	−3.742 (1.274)***	−2.029 (7.921)	−3.422 (1.113)***	−2.858 (8.308)
Observations	17	17	17	17

Notes: Standard errors in parentheses.
***Significant at the 1 percent level.
**Significant at the 5 percent level.
*Significant at the 10 percent level.

when state-level labor market and service market factors are also controlled for. The estimates are consistent with the view, discussed previously, that occupational regulation reduces the quality of an occupation's output. However, our results do not clarify the mechanism by which mortgage broker bonding would lead to higher foreclosures.

We have noted that the positive relationship between bonding and foreclosures could arise because states enact bonding or net worth requirements in response to previous periods of high foreclosure. As a check on this possibility (Autor 2003), we estimated the relationship between lagged subprime and lagged overall foreclosures and subsequent passage of a bonding or net worth requirement. Table 6.7, using a Weibull hazard model with similar covariates to those in tables 6.5 and 6.6, shows that the relationship is not statistically significant, indicating an absence of this form of simultaneity bias.[24]

One final issue we address in this section is presented in table 6.8, which shows the relationship of bonding/net worth requirements to home ownership. Using the same type of model as table 6.6, we estimate the relationship

24. Appendix B discusses evidence that the political initiatives leading to higher mortgage broker bonding requirements are often led by industry associations or state regulators rather than consumer groups, although consumer issues and competing consumer regulatory proposals sometimes serve to motivate mortgage broker associations to put forward their own bonding proposals. Causality may involve complicated feedback chains and substantial time delays.

Table 6.8   Fixed-effects models of state home ownership percentage

	(1)	(2)
Real bonding/net worth requirement lagged once/100,000	0.881	1.206
	(1.154)	(0.943)
Real bonding/net worth requirement lagged twice/100,000	0.582	
	(1.188)	
Lag state unemployment rate	−0.194	−0.191
	(0.155)	(0.155)
Lag state population/100,000	0.066	0.066
	(0.043)	(0.043)
Lag median state household income/100,000	10.896	11.029
	(4.778)**	(4.763)**
Constant	61.428	61.415
	(3.004)***	(2.999)***
Year dummy controls (2000–2004) base 1999	Yes	Yes
Observations	306	306
Number of states (including D.C.)	51	51
R^2	0.26	0.26
F-Test for one- and two-period lags of net worth/bonding requirements	0.94	—

Notes: Standard errors in parentheses.
***Significant at the 1 percent level.
**Significant at the 5 percent level.
*Significant at the 10 percent level.

of mortgage broker bonding/net worth requirements and home ownership. We find that income is positively related to home ownership, but that there is no statistically significant relationship between our measures of regulation and home ownership. Although bonding may matter for the quantity and quality of subprime mortgages, it does not seem to vary with the overall rate of state home ownership. This might reflect the fact that mortgage originations are flow variables and hence can change more from year to year than a stock variable like home ownership.

6.6.3   Cross-Sectional Data Results for Mortgage Market Variables

Brokers have short-term incentives to sell high-priced loans to consumers. The federal banking regulators track high-priced loans through the Home Mortgage Disclosure Act (HMDA) data collection, which records most home mortgage applications and originations in the United States. We focus on first-lien mortgages in our analysis. A high-priced first-lien mortgage is defined as one whose annual percentage rate (APR) is 3 or more percentage points above the contemporaneous thirty-year Treasury bond yield. The APR is defined essentially as an internal rate of return, taking into account initial fees and introductory rates and setting any index variables

Mortgage Broker Regulations that Matter

in the contract at current market values, assuming they remain constant for the scheduled maturity of the loan.

If mortgage broker licensing succeeds in protecting consumers, high-priced loans may be reduced.[25] However, as discussed in our theory section, this is not the only possible outcome, and the theoretical effects of licensing regulations are ambiguous.

We assess the empirical relationship between mortgage broker regulation and the probability that a mortgage will be high priced. We primarily consider broker-originated loans. We could, in addition, assess how broker regulation affects the chance that any mortgage, brokered or not, is high priced. This also would be plausible, since mortgage brokers compete strongly with other mortgage origination providers. However, looking at the entire mortgage market could weaken our ability to detect the direct effects of mortgage broker regulation, so we prefer to focus as closely as we can on broker-originated mortgages.

Focusing on brokered mortgages, however, confronts us with the problem that the HMDA data do not indicate whether a mortgage was brokered. We use two strategies to proxy for this missing information. For federally regulated banks and thrifts, we use the borrowers' location (available at the Census tract level from the HMDA data) to condition on whether the loan was made outside the lender's Community Reinvestment Act (CRA) assessment area. Under the CRA, federally regulated banks and thrifts must declare an assessment area where the degree of services they provide will be evaluated for compliance with the CRA. Typically these areas include the lender's principal retail offices, and lenders generally have fewer offices outside their assessment area. Federally regulated lenders are presumed to rely on their retail offices to originate the majority of their mortgages within their assessment areas but to rely much more on brokers to reach mortgage customers outside their assessment areas (Avery, Brevoort, and Canner 2006; Apgar, Bendimerad, and Essene 2007). Accordingly, for federally regulated banks and thrifts, we focus on mortgages originated outside each reporting lender's CRA assessment area.[26]

For mortgage banks not subject to the CRA, we rely on reports from industry publications and industry experts to identify a set of lenders known to rely almost exclusively on mortgage brokers for loan applications. For one lender, Option One, we have confirmed with a senior employee that in 2005, the year we study, the firm obtained almost all of its mortgage applica-

---

25. Two separate studies, based on proprietary data from selected major lenders' mortgages originated in 2002, suggest that, on average, consumers using brokers did get lower-priced loans than other borrowers, when other factors were controlled for. See El Anshasy, Elliehausen, and Shimazaki (2005) and LaCour-Little (2007b). Results to the contrary were found by LaCour-Little (2007c).

26. To keep the size of the data set manageable, we used a 50 percent random sample of the 2005 HMDA data from CRA-regulated mortgage originators.

tions through brokers. An industry expert, Thomas LaMalfa of Wholesale Access, helped us identify nine other "broker-dependent" mortgage originators in 2005: Taylor, Bean, and Whitaker Mortgage Co.; First Magnus Financial Corporation; American Mortgage Network; Loan City; Green Point Mortgage Funding; Argent Mortgage Company; New Century Mortgage Corporation; Nova Star Home Mortgage; and Résumé.[27]

In tables 6.9 and 6.10, we estimate linear probability models for whether a loan is high-priced using four different data sets.[28] We cluster observations by states to compute robust standard errors that allow for less than full independence among the observations in each state. We control for the state regulatory environment, borrower's income and racial/ethnic identity, the loan amount, and several economic and demographic properties of the Census tract where the property is located (the distribution of credit scores, unemployment rate, median age, median age of housing stock, percent minority population, median income, and the percentage of owner-occupied and vacant housing units).

For mortgage refinancing, the results are fairly consistent. However, there is a clear difference in the size of the constant term, which is low for the CRA lenders outside their assessment areas (0.10) and higher for the ten broker-dependent lenders (0.38). The 2005 national average was 0.26 for first-lien refinance mortgages. Although this gives a very different starting point to the two refinancing regressions, the marginal effects of many of the explanatory variables are similar. The coefficients on the mortgage broker regulatory variables for 2004 are of primary interest here. In tables 6.9 and 6.10, the coefficient on the bonding/net worth requirement is positive and significant, indicating that a $100,000 increase in this requirement is associated with, respectively, a 5.4 or a 3.5 percentage point increase in the probability that a refinancing is high priced. The coefficient on the index of other mortgage broker regulations is not significant in table 6.9 but is marginally significant at a 10 percent level, with a negative coefficient, in table 6.10.

Our results for two other regulatory variables—an index of state antipredatory lending laws and an indicator of states that prohibit deficiency judgments—are also consistent across the refinancing regressions in tables 6.9 and 6.10. The coefficient on the index of anti-predatory lending laws is negative but not significant at a 10 percent level. The coefficient on the indicator of no deficiency judgments is significant but with an unexpected negative sign, suggesting that high-priced loans are less likely in states that do not allow creditors to pursue deficiency judgments. A possible explanation

27. Their respective HMDA respondent ID numbers are 7499100008; 7979400002; 1788100000; 7428900001; 13-3210378; 1917700009; 7900200006; both 1512400000 and 1707500002 for Nova Star; and 1991500005. To make the data more manageable, we again took a 50 percent random sample.

28. We have estimated probit models for each of these regressions and obtained very similar results.

Table 6.9   **Linear probability of a high-priced loan in a cross section of ten broker-dependent lenders mortgages**

	Mortgage refinance ($N = 273{,}365$)	Home-purchase mortgage ($N = 185{,}773$)
State broker bonding/net worth requirement ($100,000)	0.054 (0.021)**	0.050 (0.028)*
Index of other state broker licensing requirements	0.002 (0.003)	0.002 (0.003)
Index of state anti-predatory lending laws	−0.012 (0.008)	0.004 (0.009)
State prohibition of deficiency judgments (dummy variable)	−0.130 (0.029)***	−0.098 (0.027)***
Borrower's income ($1,000)	−0.505 (0.077)***	−0.280 (0.068)***
Borrower's income squared ($1,000,000)	0.093 (0.020)***	0.035 (0.011)***
Adults in Census tract with very low credit score (%)	0.005 (0.001)***	0.006 (0.001)***
African-American borrower (dummy variable)	0.146 (0.018)***	0.173 (0.011)***
Asian-American borrower (dummy variable)	−0.060 (0.019)***	−0.032 (0.023)
Hispanic borrower (dummy variable)	0.074 (0.013)***	0.119 (0.019)***
Female borrower (dummy variable)	0.039 (0.006)***	0.163 (0.006)***
Constant	0.382 (0.073)***	0.537 (0.069)***
Number of state clusters for standard errors (D.C. included)	51	51
R^2	0.095	0.107

Notes: Standard errors in parentheses. Ordinary least-squares estimate of the probability that a mortgage is high-priced, using a 50 percent random sample of HMDA data on first-lien conventional mortgages originated in 2005 by ten broker-dependent lenders. The sample is further restricted to HMDA loan records in which the primary applicants' ethnicity, sex, and race are available and applicable to a person (not a business) and in which the property is an owner-occupied, one to four family nonmanufactured unit. Additional explanatory variables not presented include loan size; loan size squared; dummy variables indicating if the borrower is Hawaiian/Pacific Islander or American Indian/Alaska Native; percentage of credit files in the Census tract that lack a credit score; tract-level Census variables for the unemployment rate, median age of persons, median age of housing units, percent minority population, median income, percentage of housing units that are owner-occupied, and percentage of housing units that are vacant. Full results are available upon request. See appendix C for more detailed definitions of the variables.

***Significant at the 1 percent level.
**Significant at the 5 percent level.
*Significant at the 10 percent level.

Table 6.10 **Linear probability of a high-priced loan in a cross section of CRA-regulated lenders' mortgages made outside their CRA assessment areas in 2005**

	Mortgage refinance ($N = 625,573$)	Home-purchase mortgage ($N = 523,464$)
State broker bonding/net worth requirement ($100,000)	0.035 (0.014)**	−0.011 (0.016)
Index of other state broker licensing requirements	−0.0029 (0.0017)*	−0.0008 (0.0015)
Index of state anti-predatory lending laws	−0.006 (0.004)	0.0005 (0.0046)
State prohibition of deficiency judgments (dummy variable)	−0.060 (0.024)**	0.016 (0.017)
Borrower's income ($1,000)	−0.272 (0.022)***	−0.183 (0.035)***
Borrower's income squared ($1,000,000)	0.034 (0.004)***	0.035 (0.006)***
Adults in Census tract with very low credit score (%)	0.0058 (0.0005)***	0.0062 (0.0004)***
African-American borrower (dummy variable)	0.211 (0.015)***	0.344 (0.015)***
Asian-American borrower (dummy variable)	0.002 (0.010)	−0.012 (0.012)
Hispanic borrower (dummy variable)	0.093 (0.013)***	0.197 (0.013)***
Female borrower (dummy variable)	0.044 (0.002)***	0.028 (0.002)***
Constant	0.103 (0.032)***	0.010 (0.040)
Number of state clusters for standard errors (D.C. included)	51	51
R^2	0.093	0.141

Notes: Standard errors in parentheses. Ordinary least-squares estimate of the probability that a mortgage is high priced, using a 50 percent random sample of HMDA data on first-lien conventional mortgages originated in 2005 by lenders subject to the Community Reinvestment Act. The sample is further restricted to HMDA loan records in which the primary applicants' ethnicity, sex, and race are available and applicable to a person (not a business) and in which the property is an owner-occupied, one- to four-family nonmanufactured unit. Additional explanatory variables not presented include loan size; loan size squared; dummy variables indicating if the borrower is Hawaiian/Pacific Islander or American Indian/Alaska Native; percentage of credit files in the Census tract that lack a credit score; tract-level Census variables for the unemployment rate, median age of persons, median age of housing units, percent minority population, median income, percentage of housing units that are owner occupied, and percentage of housing units that are vacant. Full results are available upon request. See appendix C for more detailed definitions of the variables.

***Significant at the 1 percent level.
**Significant at the 5 percent level.
*Significant at the 10 percent level.

is that lenders ration credit more strictly in states that rule out deficiency judgments but use risk-based pricing to lend to a wider selection of applicants where they have the right to pursue a deficiency judgment.[29]

The coefficient on the percentage of adults in the Census tract of the mortgaged property who have very low credit scores is consistently positive and significant in tables 6.9 and 6.10. A 10 percentage point increase in the percentage of adults in the tract with a very low score is associated with about a 5 to 6 percentage point increase in the probability that a mortgage refinance loan in that tract will be high priced.[30]

African-American, Hispanic, and female borrowers are significantly more likely to get a high-priced mortgage refinancing than are non-Hispanic white male borrowers. The largest effect is for African-American borrowers. For example, for mortgage refinance loans by federally regulated banks and thrifts lending outside their CRA assessment areas, the probability of a high-priced loan increases by 21 percentage points for an African-American borrower, compared to increases of 9 percentage points for Hispanics and 4 percentage points for women. For other racial groups we find no significant effects, except that Asian-Americans refinancing with the ten broker-dependent lenders are about 6 percentage points less likely to get a high-priced loan.

Our results for the regulatory variables are not as strong or as consistent with home-purchase mortgages as with mortgage refinance loans. We again start with very different constant terms. However, the bonding/net worth variable is positive and significant at a 10 percent level for the ten broker-dependent lenders but has an insignificant and small negative coefficient for the CRA-regulated lenders on loans outside their assessment areas. The index of the remaining mortgage broker regulations is insignificant in the home-purchase regressions, as is the index of anti-predatory lending laws. The indicator of no deficiency judgments is again negative and significant for the broker-dependent lenders, but it is now insignificant for the CRA-regulated lenders' loans outside their assessment areas. Apparently, the process for making home-purchase loans differs in important ways from the process for making mortgage refinance loans, at least at the CRA-regulated institutions.[31]

In results not shown, but available from the authors, we repeated the estimates in table 6.10 for mortgages made within the CRA assessment areas of

29. We thank Karen Pence for bringing this possibility to our attention.
30. In the full regression results underlying tables 6.9 and 6.10, the coefficient on another credit score variable—the percentage of adults with a credit file who lack a credit score—is significantly positive but smaller for the CRA-regulated lenders but not significant for the ten broker-dependent lenders.
31. For the home-purchase mortgages examined in table 6.10, the coefficients on the credit score and racial/ethnic variables have a pattern of statistical significance not too different than for the mortgage refinance loans in table 6.9, although the size of the coefficients often differs substantially.

CRA-regulated lenders. None of the regulatory variables were statistically significant, except the coefficient on the indicator of no deficiency judgments was significant and positive for home-purchase mortgages. The insignificance of the mortgage broker regulation variables in these regressions is consistent with our presumption that loans within a CRA assessment area are much less likely to involve a mortgage broker. We have no clear explanation yet for why the results for the indicator of no deficiency judgments change. As Avery, Brevoort, and Canner (2006) note, CRA-regulated lenders' mortgage underwriting appears to be quite different inside, compared to outside, their assessment areas. They speculate that one explanation may be the use of differing marketing channels, including greater use of brokers outside assessment areas.

To limit the potential effects of unmeasured location-specific effects, we reestimate with a sample restricted to only observations in MSAs that straddle state borders, similar to the methods in Holmes (1998) and Bostic et al. (2007). We have data on fifty-one MSAs that cross state boundaries, touching parts of thirty-nine states.[32] We estimate the same equations as in tables 6.9 and 6.10 but with fixed effects for each MSA, which has the advantage of controlling for location-specific factors not measured by our other variables, such as the percentage of loans with adjustable rates or the level or rate of change in housing prices (LaCour-Little 2007a). This is useful, because the nature of our interest rate data (a single cross section) precludes controlling for these factors by means of state fixed effects (because they would be collinear with our state-level policy variables).

For the data from the broker-dependent lenders, the results on the sample from multistate MSAs for the bonding variable (and most of the other variables) are similar to those in table 6.9.[33] In particular, for mortgage refinancing loans by the broker-dependent lenders, the coefficient on the state broker bonding variable has a t-statistic of 2.05 and a coefficient of 0.048, compared to 0.054 in table 6.9. For home-purchase mortgages from the same lenders, the coefficient on the bonding variable has a 1.96 t-statistic and a coefficient of 0.041, compared to 0.050 in table 6.9. By contrast, for the sample from multistate MSAs, the results (with fixed effects) for refinanced mortgages by the CRA lenders outside their assessment areas include an insignificant coefficient of just 0.01 on the bonding variable, in contrast to the significant coefficient of 0.035 in table 6.10. For home-purchase loans by CRA lenders outside their assessment areas, the coefficient on the bonding variable is

32. Alabama, Arkansas, Delaware, District of Columbia, Georgia, Idaho, Illinois, Indiana, Iowa, Kansas, Kentucky, Louisiana, Maryland, Massachusetts, Michigan, Minnesota, Mississippi, Missouri, Nebraska, New Hampshire, New Jersey, New York, North Carolina, North Dakota, Ohio, Oklahoma, Oregon, Pennsylvania, Rhode Island, South Carolina, South Dakota, Tennessee, Utah, Vermont, Virginia, Washington, West Virginia, Wisconsin, and Wyoming.

33. The parallels are even closer if we estimate on just the split MSAs but without fixed effects.

–0.004 and insignificant for the multistate MSA sample with fixed effects, very similar to the results in table 6.10.

Thus the results for table 6.9, with data almost exclusively on broker-originated loans, are reasonably robust to location-specific effects not explicitly controlled for in our model. These results are also robust to the omission of data from the twelve states without multistate MSAs, including California. However, the same is not true of our results for mortgage refinance loans by CRA lenders outside their assessment areas, which probably consist of a mixture of broker-originated and other loans. The coefficient on the bonding variable for those loans becomes marginally insignificant when observations from the twelve states without border-crossing MSAs are dropped from the full sample or when estimated on the multistate MSA sample without fixed effects. With fixed effects on the multistate MSA sample, the coefficient becomes clearly insignificant.

6.7   Conclusions

Mortgage brokers are an emerging regulated occupation in the United States. About thirty years ago, there were almost no mortgage brokers, because individuals who wanted a loan to buy or refinance a house went to a bank or savings and loan. With deregulation of financial services and technology improvements that allowed easy development and dissemination of credit scores, this picture began to change, and in 2004 as much as two-thirds of all housing finance was initiated through a mortgage broker.

We examine the relationships between state regulation of mortgage brokers and outcomes in the labor and mortgage markets. We find that the relationship between mortgage broker licensing and market outcomes differs among the types of licensing requirements; in particular, financial bonding or net worth requirements are associated with somewhat higher earnings, modest reductions in the number of mortgage brokers, and the number of subprime loans originated as well as with somewhat higher foreclosure rates and higher interest rates on brokered loans.

Further analysis is needed to more clearly establish whether these relationships are robust and whether they reflect a causal link between broker regulation and market outcomes. However, we would draw attention to a few features of the results presented previously. First, the overall pattern of our results suggests that requiring mortgage brokers to maintain a surety bond or a minimum net worth may affect market outcomes, and that the net effects may not benefit consumers. Without a deeper understanding of the causal linkages underlying our statistical associations, we cannot say that bonding requirements are a bad idea, but we think our results underscore the need for both more research on this topic and a cautious approach to imposing additional restrictions on entry into the mortgage broker business and occupation.

Our study period ends in 2006, just as U.S. foreclosure rates on nonprime adjustable rate mortgages began to surge. Financial markets have reacted by raising the cost and cutting the availability of funding for both subprime and mortgage-broker-originated mortgages. State regulators have tightened regulations on mortgage contracts, mortgage origination, and mortgage broker licensing as well, and the Housing and Economic Recovery Act of 2008 brings federal oversight to mortgage broker licensing. Anecdotal and industry sources indicate that the number of mortgage brokers and their market share have fallen substantially as a result. We speculate that these developments could be part of a broader process by which the linkages between mortgage broker regulation and market outcomes may well strengthen over time. Such a result would be consistent with the findings of Law and Kim (2005) that showed that during the early periods of occupational regulation in the United States, the monopoly impacts were modest. As in other occupations that have evolved with near universal licensing in the states, surviving mortgage brokers could also eventually benefit through higher earnings and the ability to control entry. We anticipate that further analysis of the issue, with updated statutes, statistical techniques, and better measures of monitoring of the occupation, may help policymakers assess the quality impacts and monopoly implications of state regulations and whether federal regulation would provide a better solution for consumers as well as the emerging occupation of mortgage brokers.

Appendix A

Table 6A.1   Minimum bond plus net worth requirements (current dollars)

	1996	1997	1998	1999	2000	2001	2002	2003	2004	2005	2006
AL	0	0	0	0	0	0	25,000	25,000	25,000	25,000	25,000
AK	0	0	0	0	0	0	0	0	0	0	0
AZ	10,000	10,000	10,000	10,000	10,000	10,000	10,000	10,000	10,000	10,000	10,000
AR	50,000	50,000	50,000	50,000	60,000	60,000	60,000	60,000	75,000	75,000	75,000
CA	0	0	0	0	0	0	0	0	0	0	0
CO	0	0	0	0	0	0	0	0	0	0	0
CT	40,000	40,000	40,000	40,000	40,000	40,000	65,000	65,000	65,000	65,000	65,000
DE	25,000	25,000	25,000	25,000	25,000	25,000	25,000	25,000	25,000	25,000	25,000
DC	22,500	22,500	22,500	22,500	22,500	22,500	22,500	22,500	22,500	22,500	22,500
FL	0	0	0	0	0	0	0	0	0	0	0
GA	25,000	25,000	25,000	25,000	25,000	25,000	25,000	50,000	50,000	50,000	50,000
HA	15,000	15,000	15,000	15,000	15,000	15,000	15,000	15,000	15,000	15,000	15,000
ID	20,000	20,000	20,000	20,000	20,000	20,000	20,000	10,000	25,000	25,000	25,000
IL	55,000	55,000	55,000	55,000	55,000	55,000	55,000	55,000	70,000	70,000	70,000
IN	25,000	25,000	25,000	50,000	50,000	50,000	50,000	50,000	50,000	50,000	50,000
IA	15,000	15,000	15,000	15,000	15,000	15,000	15,000	15,000	15,000	15,000	15,000
KS	0	0	0	25,000	25,000	25,000	50,000	50,000	50,000	50,000	50,000
KY	25,000	25,000	50,000	50,000	50,000	50,000	50,000	50,000	50,000	50,000	50,000
LA	0	25,000	25,000	25,000	50,000	50,000	50,000	50,000	50,000	50,000	50,000
ME	10,000	10,000	10,000	10,000	10,000	10,000	10,000	10,000	10,000	10,000	10,000
MD	12,500	15,000	15,000	15,000	15,000	15,000	15,000	15,000	15,000	15,000	15,000
MS	0	0	0	0	0	0	0	0	0	0	0
MI	25,000	25,000	25,000	25,000	25,000	25,000	25,000	25,000	25,000	25,000	25,000
MN	0	0	0	0	0	0	0	0	0	0	0

(continued)

Table 6A.1 (continued)

	1996	1997	1998	1999	2000	2001	2002	2003	2004	2005	2006
MS	25,000	25,000	25,000	25,000	25,000	25,000	25,000	25,000	25,000	25,000	25,000
MO	20,000	20,000	45,000	45,000	45,000	45,000	45,000	45,000	45,000	45,000	45,000
MT	0	0	0	0	0	0	0	0	25,000	25,000	25,000
NE	50,000	50,000	50,000	50,000	50,000	50,000	50,000	50,000	50,000	50,000	100,000
NV	0	0	0	25,000	25,000	25,000	25,000	25,000	25,000	25,000	25,000
NH	20,000	20,000	20,000	20,000	20,000	20,000	20,000	20,000	20,000	20,000	20,000
NJ	75,000	100,000	100,000	100,000	100,000	100,000	150,000	150,000	150,000	150,000	150,000
NM	25,000	25,000	25,000	25,000	25,000	25,000	25,000	25,000	25,000	25,000	25,000
NY	0	0	0	0	0	0	0	0	10,000	10,000	10,000
NC	0	0	0	0	0	0	50,000	50,000	50,000	50,000	50,000
ND	25,000	25,000	25,000	25,000	25,000	25,000	25,000	25,000	25,000	25,000	25,000
OH	25,000	25,000	25,000	25,000	25,000	25,000	50,000	50,000	50,000	50,000	50,000
OK	0	0	0	0	0	0	0	0	0	0	0
OR	10,000	10,000	10,000	25,000	25,000	25,000	25,000	25,000	25,000	25,000	25,000
PA	0	0	0	0	0	0	0	0	0	0	0
RI	20,000	20,000	20,000	20,000	20,000	20,000	20,000	20,000	20,000	20,000	20,000
SC	10,000	10,000	10,000	10,000	10,000	10,000	10,000	10,000	10,000	10,000	10,000
SD	0	0	0	0	0	0	0	0	0	0	0
TN	50,000	50,000	50,000	50,000	50,000	115,000	115,000	115,000	115,000	115,000	115,000
TX	0	0	0	0	25,000	25,000	25,000	25,000	25,000	25,000	25,000
UT	0	0	0	0	0	0	0	0	0	0	0
VT	0	10,000	10,000	10,000	10,000	10,000	10,000	10,000	10,000	10,000	25,000
VA	5,000	5,000	5,000	5,000	5,000	25,000	25,000	25,000	25,000	25,000	25,000
WA	20,000	20,000	20,000	20,000	20,000	20,000	20,000	20,000	20,000	20,000	20,000
WV	0	0	0	0	25,000	25,000	50,000	50,000	50,000	50,000	50,000
WI	0	0	10,000	10,000	10,000	10,000	10,000	10,000	10,000	10,000	10,000
WY	0	0	0	0	0	0	0	0	0	25,000	25,000

Appendix B

Some Evidence on the Politics of Enacting Higher Bonding Requirements

To examine the potential endogeneity of mortgage broker regulations, we gathered some legislative history information from industry sources and regulators in eight states that have raised their bonding requirements at least once. Overall, these conversations suggest a somewhat long and complicated chain of legislative causality. Successful efforts to raise bonding requirements tend to originate from the mortgage broker industry or from state regulators rather than directly from consumer groups. However, consumer advocacy and issues still can motivate the industry or regulatory proposals, and there are also some signs of grass-roots industry opposition to proposals made by state mortgage broker associations. In addition, the gestation time between an initial legislative proposal and final passage and implementation may span several years, so that any market outcomes that may have initiated the legislative process may have changed by the time of implementation. Consumer issues seem to serve as the background from which industry and regulatory agency-initiated bonding requirements emerge, often via a multiyear process.

Of the nine increases we discussed, five were described as first proposed or drafted by the state's mortgage broker association (Ohio 1999; Texas 1999; North Carolina 2002; Idaho 2004; Montana 2004), and four were described as initiated by the state regulatory authority (New Jersey 2001; Tennessee 2001; Ohio 2002; Minnesota 2007). The distinction is somewhat blurred by the industry's frequent practice of vetting its proposals with state regulators, which often yields at least technical drafting suggestions but sometimes yields more affirmative legislative support from the regulator. No successful bonding proposal was said to have been opposed by state regulators. Sometimes earlier proposals that had not been vetted with the regulator had failed. As a result, regulators have been involved, actively or passively, in most of the successful bonding bills we examined.

The stated motivations of the industry and the regulators differed. Industry proposals were described as attempts to make the occupation more professional and to provide a degree of consumer protection by inhibiting some forms of fraud, thereby enhancing the occupation's reputation. However, industry-supported increases to bonding requirements were sometimes (e.g., North Carolina 2002) motivated on narrow grounds, such as to ensure that consumers could be compensated if a broker absconded with the relatively small amount of cash the customer had entrusted to the broker, but not to help the consumer collect on larger judgments for less narrow forms of fraud or negligence. By contrast, proposals initiated by the regulatory authorities tended to have bonding requirements that were higher and broader in scope, with the apparent intentions of providing both more resources to compensate consumers and more incentives for appropriate broker behavior.

None of our sources (which did not include consumer groups) suggested that the bonding requirement that passed had been either first proposed or subsequently opposed by consumer advocates. However, the industry's proposal in Texas was in part a response to a much higher bonding proposal previously introduced by a legislator on the grounds of consumer protection, and in at least two other cases (North Carolina 2002; Ohio 1999) the industry's proposal was said to be motivated in part by competing regulatory proposals (not including bonding) from consumer groups. Opposition to the bonding bills that passed was said to be limited and mainly from legislators who were concerned that it might be onerous enough to hurt their constituents in the business. In some cases, this was thought to reflect, in part, grass-roots lobbying by mortgage brokers at odds with their own industry association's position.

Appendix C
Data for High-Priced Lending Regressions

Sources: The data for the high-priced lending regressions come from multiple sources. The dependent variable and several explanatory variables are from data on individual first-lien mortgages originated in 2005 and reported per the requirements of the Home Mortgage Disclosure Act (HMDA)(2007). The HMDA data include the Census tract of the property securing the mortgage. Using this information, each loan record has also been associated with Census data for the loan's census tract. In addition, staff of the Board of Governors of the Federal Reserve System allowed us to link the loan records to data on the distribution of credit scores in each Census tract as of December 2004. Three types of "state" (including District of Columbia) regulatory variables are also used: an index of anti-predatory lending laws developed by Bostic et al. (2007), an indicator from Pence (2003) on whether the state's standard foreclosure process (as of the late 1990s) allows for deficiency judgments, and indicators of state regulations on mortgage brokers taken from Pahl (2007). All state variables are set according to the state in which the property securing the mortgage is located.

Dependent Variable

High-Priced Loan Indicator: Using the HMDA records, it is set to 1 if the mortgage meets the HMDA definition of a "high-priced" mortgage and zero otherwise. In 2005, a first-lien mortgage was high-priced if its annual percentage rate (APR, or basically the internal rate of return on scheduled mortgage payments over the full term of the loan, assuming all market interest rates referenced in the contract are unchanged) exceeds by 3 percentage points or more the average rate on a thirty-year Treasury bond for the month in which the mortgage was originated (as determined by a reference rate published by the federal banking regulatory agencies).

Explanatory Variables Shown in Tables 6.9 and 6.10

State broker bonding/net worth requirement: Constructed by the authors from information in Pahl (2007), this is the monetary value of the minimum bond or net worth required, in 2004, to enter the mortgage broker business, converted to units of hundreds of thousands of dollars for our statistical analysis. Because some states' requirements differ by characteristics of the firm or individual being licensed, the choice of the minimum amount needed to enter is subject to judgment. The dollar values we selected for this variable for each state (before conversion to units of hundreds of thousands of dollars) are listed in appendix B.

Index of other state broker licensing requirements: This is an index of the strictness of a state's mortgage broker regulations in 2004 that sums all of Pahl's individual regulatory components except those dealing with net worth or bonding.

Index of state anti-predatory lending laws: An index of the overall strictness of a state's anti-predatory lending laws, designed for use with 2004 and 2005 HMDA data (Bostic et al. 2007).

State prohibition of deficiency judgments: From Pence, an indicator variable set to 1 if a state's standard foreclosure procedure bars creditors from pursuing deficiency judgments when sale of a foreclosed property yields less than the amount owed by the borrower, and zero otherwise.

Borrower's income: The borrower's income, as stated in the HMDA loan record, in $1,000.

Adults in Census tract with very low credit score: In the loan's Census tract, a measure of the percentage of adults with a very low credit score. Specifically, 100 times the number of such adults divided by all adults with a credit score.

African-American, Asian-American, Hispanic, or female borrower: Dummy variables set to 1 if, respectively, the borrower's race is African-American, the borrower's race is Asian-American, the borrower's ethnicity is Hispanic, or the borrower is female, as indicated by the HMDA loan record's information on the lead applicant for the loan. (Information on coapplicants is ignored; loan records with missing or "not applicable" ethnicity information are omitted.)

Additional Explanatory Variables in the Regressions

Loan size: The amount borrowed, as stated in the HMDA loan record, in $1,000.

Adults with a missing credit score: In the loan's Census tract, a measure of the percentage of adults without a credit score. Specifically, 100 times the number of adults whose credit file lacks a credit score divided by the number of adults with a credit file.

Unemployment rate: From Census 2000, the unemployment rate in the loan's Census tract.

Median age: From Census 2000, the median age of all persons in the loan's Census tract.

Median age of housing units: From Census 2000, the median age of all structures in the loan's Census tract.

Minority percentage: From Census 2000, the percentage of minority population in the loan's Census tract. (Minority signifies all but those who identify as only non-Hispanic white.)

Median income: From Census 2000, median family income in the loan's Census tract, in $1,000.

Owner-occupied percentage: From Census 2000, owner-occupied housing units as a percentage of all housing units in the loan's Census tract.

Vacant-unit percentage: From Census 2000 records, vacant housing units as a percentage of all housing units in the loan's Census tract.

Appendix D

Results with Alternative Measurements of Mortgage Broker Regulation

In this chapter, we have focused on the relationship between mortgage broker bonding or net worth requirements and market outcomes, largely because we think that these relationships are relatively consistent and statistically significant, compared to the relationships between market outcomes and the other components of mortgage broker regulation. In tables 6.3, 6.4, 6.5, 6.6, 6.9, and 6.10, for example, the variable for licensing requirements other than bonding/net worth performs inconsistently. It is significant (and different in sign from the bonding variable) in tables 6.4 and 6.5, and the mortgage refinancing column of table 6.10, but not significant in tables 6.3, 6.6, and 6.9, and the home purchase column of table 6.10. However, using this index to summarize all of the mortgage broker regulations besides bonding or net worth requirements might obscure some strong, consistent relationships between individual components and market outcomes, just as our overall index of mortgage broker regulation obscured the results we have presented on bonding and net worth. To assess this possibility, we have reestimated a core set of our regression specifications, consisting of the one-lag versions of tables 6.3, 6.4, 6.6, and 6.9 and the two-lag version of table

6.5. We modify these regressions to include twenty other mortgage broker regulatory components, using the following specification of the mortgage broker variables:

1. The same bonding/net worth variable as in tables 6.3, 6.4, 6.5, 6.6, and 6.9.

2. Pahl's index for individual mortgage broker regulation component *j*, where *j* ranges over twenty regulatory components other than bonding and net worth.

3. A summated index of all the mortgage broker regulatory components not included in 1 and 2.

At the firm level, the components assessed are entry requirements for education, experience, or knowledge (via an examination) of the firm's principals as well as ongoing requirements for continuing education of the principals. For firms' managers, we assess similar requirements and an over-all dummy variable indicating whether any requirements apply to managers. Requirements assessed for branch managers and for employees parallel those for managers, and we also assess the requirement to maintain an in-state office location.

We find that these specifications generally have little effect on the size or significance of the coefficient on our bonding/net worth variable. That is, the results we have presented on the relationship between bonding or net worth requirements and market outcomes are nearly always robust to the alternative specifications described previously. Most of the individual components are significant for at least one of the seven labor and mortgage market relationships tested. (Tables 6.6 and 6.9 include two market outcomes each, with both subprime and all foreclosures in table 6.6 and both refinance and home purchase mortgages in table 6.9.) However, only six of the twenty components are significantly related to three or more outcomes, and only employee regulation provisions matter for most labor and mortgage market outcomes. We will briefly summarize some of the relationships that seem of potential interest for further research.

The relationships between our bonding/net worth variable and market outcomes were generally robust. The coefficient on this variable retained its sign and at least a 10 percent significance level in all of the new specifications for tables 6.3 (number of brokers), 6.5 (subprime originations), and 6.6 (fore-closures). In table 6.4 (broker earnings), the bonding/net worth variable was only marginally significant. Not surprisingly, the *p*-value for its coefficient rose from below 10 percent in table 6.4 to between 10 and 20 percent in nine of the twenty alternative regressions. Its coefficient changed little in most of these cases and never fell below 0.43, compared to 0.60 in table 6.4.

In the alternative regressions for table 6.9 (high-priced loans in 2005), the bonding/net worth variable retained its positive sign and at least a 10 percent significance level except when the alternative variable was either the overall dummy for presence of employee regulation or the requirement for continuing education for branch managers. The effect of the employee regulation dummy in the refinance mortgage regression was somewhat marginal; it lowered the coefficient for bonding/net worth from 0.054 to 0.047 and raised its p-value to 15 percent. It had a stronger effect in the purchase mortgage equation, cutting the coefficient in half and raising its p-value to 50 percent. The employee regulation dummy seems to parallel the bonding/net worth variable in equation 9, in that its coefficient is also positive. For purchase mortgages it is also significant, with a p-value of 7.2 percent. The requirement for branch manager continuing education had similar effects on the size and significance of the bonding/net worth coefficient and also became significant itself (p-value of 5.5 percent) in the purchase mortgage equation. However, its relationship to high-price loans was negative, −0.08. One possible explanation for the significance of the branch manager continuing-education variable is that it is nonzero for only four states. Because table 6.9 is a cross-sectional regression where we cannot estimate state fixed effects, the branch manager continuing-education variable may be reflecting general fixed effects for those four states. Data for additional years are needed to better resolve this question. These two exceptions in table 6.9 and the unsurprising sensitivity of the marginally significant results from table 6.4 show the need for further research on the relationship of bonding or net worth and market outcomes. We nonetheless consider our main results on these relationships to be relatively robust, in light of the many alternative specifications we tested.

Are other components of mortgage broker regulation also related to our labor and mortgage market outcomes? Not to the same degree, with the possible exception of the overall dummy variable for employee regulation. This regulatory indicator is significant at a 10 percent level or better in six of the seven alternative regressions, excluding only the one for higher-priced refinance mortgages from table 6.9. In five of the six cases, where its coefficient was significant its coefficient was of the same sign as the coefficient on the bonding/net worth variable. Only for brokers' earnings did it differ, with a coefficient of −0.05 (p-value 4.3 percent). This component of mortgage broker regulation merits further research, although its statistical relationships with market outcomes (fewer brokers, fewer subprime mortgages, and more foreclosures) suggest caution about regarding it as a pro-consumer measure. Some of the individual components of employee regulation, such as the entry requirements for education, experience, or passage of an examination, paralleled the overall employee regulation dummy in many cases but were not as consistently significant across the seven regression estimates.

Only one other regulatory component was individually significant for both a labor market outcome and a mortgage market outcome. This component, the educational background of new branch managers, was significantly associated with fewer brokers, more subprime originations, and fewer

2005 high-priced home purchase mortgages. We are inclined to discount the importance of these results because this regulatory indicator was nonzero in only two states, Florida and Nevada, as of 2004.

The other individual regulatory components with significant effects mainly affected the mortgage market but not the labor market. The human capital entry requirements for firm managers (education, experience, examinations) are perhaps the most interesting in this group. Nineteen states imposed at least one of these requirements in 2004, and the experience requirement was significant in the alternative regressions for subprime originations, subprime and total foreclosures, and 2005 high-priced home-purchase mortgages. In all four cases, the coefficient on the manager experience requirement was opposite to the coefficient on the bonding/net worth variable, or at least superficially more pro-consumer. The overall dummy for the presence of manager requirements parallels the manager experience requirement in the two foreclosure regressions. Likewise, the requirement that the brokerage firm maintain an in-state office was associated with fewer subprime originations and more subprime and total foreclosures. These regulatory factors also seem to be candidates for further research.

Two other human capital requirements for branch managers—experience and continuing education—were significant (and opposite in sign to the bonding/net worth coefficient) in the alternative mortgage market regressions for subprime originations, foreclosures, and 2005 high-priced home-purchase mortgages. We have already noted that branch manager continuing education requirements prevailed in only four states as of 2004, but the branch manager experience variable was nonzero in eight states and may thus be of some interest for future research.

We omit a full discussion of the results for the third mortgage variable in each regression, the index of the remaining mortgage broker regulation requirements.[34] For the table 6.3 alternative regressions, it was significant in only two cases. For table 6.4, it was often significant (nine of seventeen cases) when it directly or indirectly (via the overall employee regulation dummy) included the employee education and examination indicators but not when these moved from the index to become the individual component. In both tables 6.3 and 6.4, when the index was significant, its coefficient was opposite in sign to the bonding/net worth coefficient. In table 6.5 alternative regressions, the first lag of the index was significant in thirteen of fifteen cases when an employee regulation was not the individual variable but in only one of the five cases when an employee requirement became the individual component. (Its second lag was never significant.) In all cases, the coefficient on the index agreed in sign with the bonding/net worth coefficient. In the table 6.6 alternative regressions, the index was significant in three cases for subprime

---

34. These and other detailed results from our alternative regressions are available from the authors.

foreclosures (with a coefficient of opposite sign for the in-state office and overall employee regulation variables) and in seven cases for total foreclosures (with a coefficient of opposite sign for the overall employee regulation variable). In the alternative regressions for table 6.9, the index was generally insignificant, except in some of the home-purchase mortgage regressions with a managerial human capital variable as the individual component.

The results in this appendix show that our chapter has far from exhausted the information in our data. We highlight, in particular, that opportunity for other researchers to create and analyze alternative indices and subindices of mortgage broker regulation from the extensive regulatory history in Pahl (2007).

References

Akerlof, G. 1970. The market for lemons: Qualitative uncertainty and the market mechanism. *Quarterly Journal of Economics* 84 (August): 488–500.

Alexander, W. P., S. D. Grimshaw, G. R. McQueen, and B. A. Slade. 2002. Some loans are more equal than others: Third-party originations and defaults in the subprime mortgage industry. *Real Estate Economics* 30 (4): 667–97.

Andrich, D. 1988. *Rasch models for measurement.* Newbury Park, CA: Sage.

Apgar, W., A. Bendimerad, and R. S. Essene. 2007. Mortgage market channels and fair lending: An analysis of HMDA data. Harvard University, Joint Center for Housing Studies Working Paper MM07-2, April 25.

Apgar, W. C., M. Duda, and R. N. Gorey. 2005. *The municipal cost of foreclosures: A Chicago case study.* Homeownership Preservation Foundation Housing Finance Policy Research Paper 2005-1, February.

Autor, D. 2003. Outsourcing at will: The contribution of unjust dismissal doctrine to the growth of employment outsourcing. *Journal of Labor Economics* 21 (1): 1–42.

Avery, R. B., K. P. Brevoort, and G. B. Canner. 2006. Higher-priced home lending and the 2005 HMDA data. *Federal Reserve Bulletin,* September.

Backley, C., J. M. Niblack, C. J. Pahl, T. C. Risbey, and J. Vockrodt. 2006. License to deal: Regulation in the mortgage broker industry. Federal Reserve Bank of Minneapolis, *Community Dividend,* Issue no. 3.

Barker, D. 2007. Ethics and lobbying: The case of real estate brokerage. *Journal of Business Ethics* 80 (1): 23–35.

Bond, R. S., J. E. Kwoka Jr., J. J. Phelan, and I. T. Whitten. 1980. Effects of restrictions on advertising and commercial practice in the professions: The case of optometry. Staff Report, Bureau of Economics, Federal Trade Commission, Washington, D.C.

Bostic, R. W., K. C. Engel, P. A. McCoy, A. Pennington-Cross, and S. M. Wachter. 2007. State and local anti-predatory lending laws: The effect of legal enforcement mechanisms. Paper presented at the Federal Reserve System Community Affairs Research Conference. 29–30 March, Washington, D.C.

Conference of State Bank Supervisors. 2007. 40 state agencies commit to participate in nationwide mortgage licensing system. Available at: http://www.csbs.org/AM/

Template.cfm?Section=Press_Releases&TEMPLATE=/CM/ContentDisplay
.cfm&CONTENTID=12840.

Cox, C., and S. Foster. 1990. *The costs and benefits of occupational regulation.* Washington, D.C.: U.S. Federal Trade Commission, Bureau of Economics.

Cummings, J., and L. J. Rankin. 1999. 150 hours: A look back. *Journal of Accountancy* 187 (4): 53–58.

El Anshasy, A., G. Elliehausen, and Y. Shimazaki. 2005. The pricing of subprime mortgages by mortgage brokers and lenders. In *Promises and pitfalls: As consumer finance options multiply, who is being served, and at what cost?* Papers from the 2005 Federal Reserve System Community Affairs Research Conference. Available at: www.chicagofed.org/cedric/files/2005_conf_paper_session1_elliehausen.pdf.

Engel, K. C., and P. A. McCoy. 2002. A tale of three markets: The law and economics of predatory lending. *Texas Law Review* 80 (6): 1255–1367.

Ernst, K., D. Bocian, and W. Li. 2008. Steered wrong: Brokers, borrowers, and subprime loans. Center for Responsible Lending report, April 8.

Essene, R. S., and W. Apgar. 2007. Understanding mortgage market behavior: Creating good mortgage options for all Americans. Harvard University, Joint Center for Housing Studies Working Paper MM07-1, April 25.

Feldman, R., and J. W. Begun. 1978. The effects of advertising: Lessons from optometry. *Journal of Human Resources* 13 (Supplement): 247–62.

Friedman, M. 1962. *Capitalism and freedom.* Chicago: University of Chicago Press.

Garcia-Fontes, W., and H. Hopenhayn. 2000. Entry restrictions and the determination of quality. *Spanish Economic Review* 2 (2): 105–27.

Gerardi, K., H. S. Rosen, and P. Willen. 2007. Do households benefit from financial deregulation and innovation? The case of the mortgage market. NBER Working Paper no. 12967. Cambridge, MA: The National Bureau of Economic Research, March.

Gramlich, E. M. 2007. *Subprime mortgages: America's latest boom and bust.* Washington, D.C.: The Urban Institute Press.

Guttentag, J. 2000. Another view of predatory lending. University of Pennsylvania, The Wharton School, Financial Institutions Center Working Paper 01-23-B, August 21.

Holmes, T. 1998. The effect of state policies on the location of manufacturing: Evidence from state borders. *Journal of Political Economy* 106 (4): 667–705.

Home Mortgage Disclosure Act. 2007. Available at: http://www.ffiec.gov/hmda/online_rpts.htm.

Jackson, H. E., and L. Burlingame. 2007. Kickbacks or compensation: The case of yield spread premiums. *Stanford Journal of Law, Business, and Finance* 12 (2): 289–361.

Jacobides, M. G. 2005. Industry change through vertical disintegration: How and why markets emerged in mortgage banking. *Academy of Management Journal* 48 (3): 465–98.

Kandel, E., and E. Lazear. 1992. Peer pressure and partnerships. *Journal of Political Economy* 100 (4): 801–17.

Kim-Sung, K., and S. Hermanson. 2003. Experiences of older refinance mortgage loan borrowers: Broker- and lender-originated loans. AARP Public Policy Institute Research Report, January.

Kleiner, M. M. 2006. *Licensing occupations: Enhancing quality or restricting competition.* Kalamazoo, MI: Upjohn Institute for Employment Research.

Kleiner, M., R. Gay, and K. Greene. 1982. Barriers to labor migration: The case of occupational licensing. *Industrial Relations* 21 (3): 383–91.

Kleiner, M. M., and A. B. Krueger. 2008. The prevalence and effects of occupational licensing. NBER Working Paper no. 14308. Cambridge, MA: National Bureau of Economic Research, September.

Kleiner, M. M., and R. T. Kudrle. 2000. Does regulation affect economic outcomes? The case of dentistry. *Journal of Law and Economics* 43 (2): 547–82.

Kroszner, R. S. 2007. Legislative proposals on reforming mortgage practices. Testimony before the Committee on Financial Services, U.S. House of Representatives, October 24.

LaCour-Little, M. 2007a. Economic factors affecting home mortgage disclosure act reporting. Unpublished document, Department of Finance, College of Business and Economics, California State University Fullerton, July 28.

———. 2007b. The home purchase mortgage preferences of low-and-moderate income households. *Real Estate Economics* 35 (4): 265–90.

———. 2007c. The pricing of mortgages by brokers: An agency problem? Preliminary Working Paper, Department of Finance, College of Business and Economics, California State University Fullerton, February 5.

LaCour-Little, M., and G. H. Chun. 1999. Third-party originators and mortgage prepayment risk: An agency problem? *Journal of Real Estate Research* 17 (1/2): 55–70.

Law, M. T., and S. Kim. 2005. Specialization and regulation: The rise of professionals and the emergence of occupational licensing regulation. *Journal of Economic History* 65 (3): 723–56.

Li, Y. 1998. Middlemen and private information. *Journal of Monetary Economics* 42 (1): 131–59.

McGarity, M. 2001. A broker's market. *Mortgage Banking* 61 (6): 32.

Mortgage Bankers Association of America. 2007. National Delinquency Survey, 1979–2005.

Olson, D. 2007. FHA: An alternative to nonprime. Available at: www.Scotsman guide.com.

Pahl, C. 2007. A compilation of state mortgage broker laws and regulations, 1996–2006. Federal Reserve Bank of Minneapolis, Community Affairs Report no. 2007-2, August. Available at: www.minneapolisfed.org/community/pubs.

Pappalardo, J. K., and J. M. Lacko. 2007. Improving consumer mortgage disclosures: An empirical assessment of current and prototype disclosure forms. Federal Trade Commission Bureau of Economics Staff Report, June.

Pence, K. M. 2003. Foreclosing on opportunity? State laws and mortgage credit. Federal Reserve Board Finance and Economics Discussion Series no. 2003-16.

Rogerson, W. P. 1983. Reputation and product quality. *The Bell Journal of Economics* 14 (2): 508–16.

Schloemer, E., W. Li, K. Ernst, and K. Keest. 2006. Losing ground: Foreclosures in the subprime market and their cost to homeowners. Center for Responsible Lending, December.

Shapiro, C. 1986. Investment, moral hazard and occupational licensing. *Review of Economic Studies* 53 (5): 843–62.

Shepard, L. 1978. Licensing restrictions and the cost of dental care. *Journal of Law and Economics* 21 (1): 187–201.

Shumer, C. 2007. Sheltering neighborhoods from the subprime foreclosure storm. Joint Economic Committee, U.S. Congress, April 13.

Sichelman, L. 2003. Brokers dominate lending. *Realty Times,* July 2. Available at: http://realtytimes.com/rtpages/20030702_lending.htm.

U.S. Department of Housing and Urban Development. 2002. Economic analysis and initial regulatory flexibility analysis for RESPA proposed rule to simplify and improve the process of obtaining mortgages to reduce settlement costs to consumers. Office of Policy Development and Research, July.

Wholesale Access. 2005. New research about mortgage brokers published. Press release, July 28. Available at: www.wholesaleaccess.com/7_28_mbkr.shtml.

———. 2007. New broker research published. Press release, August 17. Available at: www.wholesaleaccess.com/8-17-07-prs.shtml.

Woodward, S. E. 2003. Consumer confusion in the mortgage market. Typescript, July 14. Available at: www.sandhillecon.com/pdf/consumer_confusion.pdf.

———. 2008. A study of closing costs for FHA mortgages. U.S. Department of Housing and Urban Development, Office of Policy Development and Research, May.

Yavas, A. 1994. Middlemen in bilateral search markets. *Journal of Labor Economics* 12 (3): 406–29.

III

Solving Collective Action Problems

The Effects of a Centralized
Clearinghouse on Job Placement,
Wages, and Hiring Practices

Muriel Niederle and Alvin E. Roth

7.1 Introduction

The market for almost all entry level positions (called residencies) for new doctors in the United States is mediated by a clearinghouse called the National Resident Matching Program (NRMP). Many other more advanced medical positions (called fellowships, which are the entry level positions for medical subspecialties) use similar clearinghouses, as do medical labor markets in Canada and Great Britain, and a number of other markets (e.g., for many nonmedical health care workers in the United States, for some new lawyers in Canada, and so on; see table 7.2).

These clearinghouses work as follows: applicants and employers make their own arrangements to interview each other, before submitting rank order lists representing their preferences, which are then used by the clearinghouse to centrally determine a matching that specifies which applicant will work for which employer. The algorithms used are generalized deferred acceptance algorithms (Gale and Shapley 1962; Roth 2002, 2008a), which we will describe in section 7.2.

These clearinghouses correct a set of market failures that often occur in entry level labor markets in which many people seek jobs that all begin at the

Muriel Niederle is an associate professor of economics at Stanford University and a research associate of the National Bureau of Economic Research. Alvin E. Roth is the George Gund Professor of Economics and Business Administration at Harvard University and in the Harvard Business School, and a research associate of the National Bureau of Economic Research.

Part of this work was supported by the National Science Foundation and the Sloan Foundation. We owe a special debt to Dr. Cody Webb, who first alerted us to the ongoing market failure in the labor market for gastroenterologists, and to our coauthor Dr. Deborah D. Proctor, who took the lead in reorganizing the gastroenterology match.

same time. One source of many problems is that these markets suffer from *congestion:* since making offers and considering them takes time, there may not be sufficient time for all offers that employers might like to make to, in fact, be made in a timely way. By the time a candidate has rejected an offer, the next-choice candidate may already have accepted an offer elsewhere. This often leads employers to make short-duration offers (or even exploding offers, which have to be accepted or rejected virtually immediately), and/or to try to make offers just a little bit earlier than their main competitors. It also means that employers may hesitate to make offers to their most preferred candidates if those offers have only a small chance of being accepted. That is, when choosing which offers to make, congestion forces firms to think not only about how much they like each candidate, but how much each candidate likes them, which can lead to coordination failures. Congestion makes it un*safe* for employers to make offers according to their preferences only.[1]

Once it becomes understood that positions in a market may reliably be filled through exploding offers, employers can use them strategically. By making an exploding offer, an employer can impose an ultimatum on a candidate, and make the candidate's effective market potentially very thin, limiting it, in the most extreme case, to this one employer. The use of exploding offers by some employers drives competitors to make offers with short deadlines themselves, even earlier, so as to not lose out on promising candidates. This prevents the market from being *thick* (see Niederle and Roth 2009).

To summarize, the problems many entry-level labor markets face are problems of (a) *thickness,* (b) *congestion,* and (c) *safety.*[2] (See table 7.1.)

In a number of markets these problems have become extreme: markets have unraveled, with candidates sometimes being hired several years before employment starts (see e.g., Avery et al. 2007 on lawyers; Niederle and Roth 2005; Niederle, Proctor, and Roth 2006 on gastroenterologists; and Roth and Xing 1994 on the labor market for Japanese university graduates, among many others). This, of course, may entail problems other than the lack of thickness. Information about candidates, and even the candidates' preferences over different employers, may not be as accurate long before employment as they will be nearer the time employment actually starts. As a result, many markets have institutions and organizations that aim to regulate the time and way in which offers are made and accepted; see table 7.1.

Entry-level medical markets, such as for residents and fellows, are prime examples of markets that experienced such problems, and also include many

---

1. In the market for junior economists, such hesitation can be seen as many departments shy away from interviewing candidates who have applied to them if the candidate seems too accomplished, because they do not know how much the candidate is *really* interested, as opposed to simply risk averse and applying widely.
2. See also Roth (2008), which expands on these themes in connection with a different set of markets.

Table 7.1 Some institutions to regulate offers, acceptances, and rejections

Market	Institution	Description
Graduate school admissions	Council of Graduate Schools (CGS)	Exploding offers discouraged, and acceptances before April 15 nonbinding (see text)
Undergraduate college admissions	National Association for College Admission Counseling (NACAC)	Binding early decision, nonbinding early action
U.S., Canadian, and British medical residencies	National Resident Matching Program (NRMP), Canadian Resident Matching Service (CaRMS), various regional matches in Britain.	Centralized clearinghouse
Medical fellowships	Specialty matching services (SMS)	Centralized clearinghouse
Clinical psychology	Association of Psychology Postdoctoral and Internship Centers (APPIC)	Centralized clearinghouse
Lawyers (particularly in large law firms)	National Association for Law Placement (NALP)	Principles and standards for law placement and recruitment activities
Federal judicial clerkships	Judicial Conference of the United States (and various ad hoc committees of judges)	Law Clerk Hiring Plan (http://www.cadc.uscourts.gov/lawclerk/)
Canadian lawyers (articling positions)	Regional law societies (e.g., Law Society of Upper Canada)	Articling Recruitment Procedures (centralized match abandoned for 2004 to 2005 articling term)
Japanese university graduates	The Japan Federation of Employers' Associations (Nikkeiren), Labor Ministry	Establishes guideline dates before which contracts should not be signed, and rules about interviewing
Recruitment of MBA graduates	Individual business school recruiting offices	Regulations of on-campus interviews, dates and duration of offers, etc.
US college graduates—on-campus recruiting	National Association of Colleges and Employers (NACE) www.naceweb.org/about/principl.html	Guidelines for good conduct that discourage reneging of acceptances by students and undue time pressure of acceptance and encouragement to renege on another offer
Postseason college football bowls	Bowl Championship Series (BCS)	Confederation of bowls and conferences
Sororities	National Panhellenic Conference	Regulates bidding procedure

examples of markets that fixed problems of timing by adopting centralized clearinghouses. In these markets, most applicants become available for work at a specific time; for example, residents take up work on graduating from medical school, and fellows upon completing their residency. In addition, these are markets in which the employers tend to share some forms of professional organization. Both of these things may facilitate the organization of a clearinghouse, to fix problems that may be common also to other markets.

In this chapter we discuss the effects of such a clearinghouse not only on hiring practices (namely the timing of the market, and the kinds of offers that are made), but also employment opportunities, job placement, and potential impact on salaries. A clearinghouse may affect more than just a market's timing. By making offers through a computerized algorithm, congestion problems can be solved, as algorithms operate very fast. Furthermore, as we will describe when we explain *deferred acceptance algorithms,* when applied to markets of this size, they make it safe for both employers and applicants to reveal their true preferences, no one is harmed by listing a first choice that they are unlikely to get. A deferred acceptance algorithm also allows consideration of any offer, no matter when it is made. Similarly, deferred acceptance algorithms allow applicants to safely wait for better offers, even if they receive an acceptable offer early on. Therefore if there is sufficient participation in the centralized clearinghouse, the market is thick, as employers and applicants are all available at the same time and the whole market can be considered at once.

The market for gastroenterology fellows provides a natural case study of the effects of a centralized clearinghouse, as this market was organized through a centralized fellowship match, the Medical Specialties Matching Program (MSMP, organized by the NRMP) from 1986 to the mid-nineties. The arrangement fell apart, and for the next decade the market operated in a decentralized way. It reestablished a match in 2006.

These events give us a unique opportunity to discern the effects of such a centralized clearinghouse. We find that, as the market moved from a centralized to a decentralized market, the national market broke up into a collection of more local markets (Niederle and Roth 2003b). Fellowship programs, particularly smaller ones, were more likely to hire their own residents than under a centralized match. Furthermore, the market without a centralized match again unraveled into a market in which, at any specific time, only a subset of hospitals were making offers, which means the market fragmented not only geographically, in space, but also in time (Niederle and Roth 2004; Niederle, Proctor, and Roth 2006). Candidates were once more subjected to very short duration offers, and the market, even after several years of operating without a centralized match, had still not settled down, in that interviews and offers were still made earlier from one year to the next. Finally, although a class action lawsuit (since dismissed) argued that a centralized match suppressed salaries, we did not find that the salaries of gastroenterology fellows, hired in a decentralized way, are any different from other internal medicine subspecialties, either those that use a match, or those that have not used a match for decades (Niederle and Roth 2003a). That is, we did not find any evidence that the match affected salaries.

Finally, we consider the obstacles to initiating a centralized match, especially in a market that had seen the breakdown of an earlier attempt. In the gastroenterology market, many employers who were themselves willing to delay hiring in order to participate in a match feared that their main competitors would not refrain from hiring candidates early, before a match. We employed some insights from decentralized markets (such as graduate school admissions), and from laboratory experiments, to help the gastroenterology professional organizations devise policies that helped to restart the match for gastroenterology fellows, in June of 2006 (Niederle and Roth 2009; Niederle, Proctor, and Roth 2006, 2008).

In the last section of the chapter we argue that medical labor markets are not special, many markets suffer from similar problems, namely problems establishing and maintaining (a) *thickness,* (b) *congestion,* and (e) *safety.* This can already be intuited from table 7.1, and we will present some examples in more detail. We also discuss decentralized alternatives to a centralized clearinghouse that some markets have adopted, such as the market for junior economists since 2006.

7.2   Deferred Acceptance Algorithms

In simple markets, in an *applicant-proposing deferred acceptance algorithm,* employers and applicants each submit rank order lists of potential matches; that is, each applicant lists which employer is his or her first choice, second choice, and so on, and each employer similarly ranks applicants. The algorithm uses these lists to conduct the following operations on behalf of applicants and employers. First, every applicant applies to his or her most preferred employer. Each employer collects all applications, and keeps those it has ranked highest—up to the number of positions it wishes to fill—and rejects all other applications. Applicants who had applications rejected apply to their next choice employer. Employers once more collect all applications (including applications kept from the last period), keep the ones they ranked the highest among the applications received so far, and so on, until no rejections are issued (because all applicants are either being held by an employer, or have run out of applications they wish to make; that is, reached the end of their rank order list). At this point the algorithm stops and every applicant is matched to the employer holding his or her application, and receives a contract from that employer. The outcome of such a matching is *stable;* that is, there exists no applicant-employer pair, not matched to each other, who prefer each other to their current match (given the submitted rank order lists).[3]

Furthermore, in simple environments it is a dominant strategy for applicants to submit their true preferences (Roth 1982, 1985). This is due in part to the fact that any employer remains available until the algorithm stops. That is, applicants incur no disadvantage from applying to employers in the order of their preferences, including applications to very desirable employers who are not likely to accept them. The centralized clearinghouse also makes the market safer for employers; they do not have to accept an applicant before they know that they cannot receive a better one (hence the term "deferred acceptance").

A centralized market solves the congestion problem by using an algorithm that produces a stable outcome, makes the market safe, and in turn, thick. Any employer can consider any applicant they interviewed, and vice versa.

The NRMP developed an algorithm in the early 1950s that is equivalent to a hospital proposing deferred acceptance algorithm (Roth 1984), and in 1998 adopted a redesigned algorithm, which among other things switched from an employer-proposing version of the deferred acceptance algorithm to one more like the applicant-proposing deferred acceptance algorithm described previously.[4] The more general Roth Peranson algorithm (Roth and Peranson 1999), now used by the NRMP and other stable centralized clearinghouses (see table 7.2), also allows for the possibility for couples to go through the match together, and for reversions or ordered contracts (in which employers can specify an increased demand for some positions in case other positions are not filled; see also Niederle 2007). In general, the stable outcome of a firm- and a worker-proposing deferred acceptance algorithm can be different. However, the same set of firms and positions are filled.[5] And, using rank order lists submitted to the medical residency match, Roth and Peranson (1999) show empirically that, given the submitted preferences, the outcomes were the same for all but about one in a thousand applicants (of which there are approximately 20,000/year). When the market is sufficiently large (Roth and Peranson 1999; Immorlica and Mahdian 2005; Kojima and

3. This is easy to see. Suppose applicant A prefers some employer E to his or her current match F. Then applicant A must already have applied to E before he or she applied to F, and been rejected, at a point in the algorithm at which E was holding a full set of applications that it preferred to A. Hence if A prefers E to F, E does not return the favor, so no blocking pair exists (Gale and Shapley 1962).

4. In general, the outcome of the applicant-proposing algorithm is the stable match that every applicant prefers over any other stable match (Gale and Shapley 1962; see Roth and Sotomayor 1990 for a survey of the related theory.)

5. Consider the case of two firms and two workers, where firm 1 prefers worker 1 over worker 2, while firm 2 prefers worker 2 over worker 1. Workers have just the opposite preferences, with each worker preferring the firm with the opposite index. Firm 1 will be matched to worker 1 (and firm 2 to worker 2) if we use the agents preferences and a firm-proposing algorithm, while the opposite matching is achieved with an applicant-proposing algorithm.

Table 7.2   **Stable two-sided centralized clearinghouses that have been studied (and verified to use an algorithm that produces a stable outcome)**

Matches now using the Roth Peranson algorithm

Organized by the NRMP
Medical Residencies in the United States (NRMP) (1952)
Abdominal Transplant Surgery (2005)
Child and Adolescent Psychiatry (1995)
Colon and Rectal Surgery (1984)
Combined Musculoskeletal Matching Program (CMMP)
• Hand Surgery (1990)
Medical Specialties Matching Program (MSMP)
• Cardiovascular Disease (1986)
• Gastroenterology (1986–1999; rejoined in 2006)
• Hematology (2006)
• Hematology/Oncology (2006)
• Infectious Disease (1986–1990; rejoined in 1994)
• Oncology (2006)
• Pulmonary and Critical Medicine (1986)
• Rheumatology (2005)
Minimally Invasive and Gastrointestinal Surgery (2003)
Obstetrics/Gynecology
• Reproductive Endocrinology (1991)
• Gynecologic Oncology (1993)
• Maternal-Fetal Medicine (1994)
• Female Pelvic Medicine and Reconstructive Surgery (2001)
Ophthalmic Plastic and Reconstructive Surgery (1991)
Pediatric Cardiology (1999)
Pediatric Critical Care Medicine (2000)
Pediatric Emergency Medicine (1994)

Pediatric Rheumatology (2004)
Pediatric Surgery (1992)
Primary care sports medicine (1994)
Radiology
• Interventional Radiology (2002)
• Neuroradiology (2001)
• Pediatric Radiology (2003)
Surgical Critical Care (2004)
Thoracic Surgery (1988)
Vascular Surgery (1988)

Organized or supported by NMS (National Matching Services)
Postdoctoral Dental Residencies in the United States
• Oral and Maxillofacial Surgery (1985)
• General Practice Residency (1986)
• Advanced Education in General Dentistry (1986)
• Pediatric Dentistry (1989)
• Orthodontics (1996)
Psychology Internships in the United States and Canada (1999)
Neuropsychology Residencies in the United States and Canada (2001)
Osteopathic Internships in the United States (before 1995)
Pharmacy Practice Residencies in the United States (1994)
Articling Positions with Law Firms in Alberta, CA (1993)
Medical Residencies in Canada (CaRMS) (before 1970)

Matches using other generalized stable algorithms

British (medical) house officer positions
• Edinburgh (1969)
• Cardiff (197x)

Reform rabbis (1998)
New York City high schools (2003)
Boston public schools (2006)

Note: Year of first use in parentheses.

Pathak forthcoming), it is almost a dominant strategy for all participants, both employers and applicants, to submit their true preferences.

7.3   The History of the Market for Gastroenterology Fellows

Gastroenterologists typically begin work in their subspecialty three years after graduating from medical school, after having completed a residency in internal medicine (IM). Three additional years as a gastroenterology (GI)[6] fellow qualifies them for gastroenterology board certification (before 1996, only two years of fellowship were required). Internal medicine residents who consider becoming gastroenterologists have many other possible career choices, including practicing as an internist or pursuing other internal medicine subspecialties, of which gastroenterology is but one.

While the number of GI fellowship positions each hospital can offer has been regulated by the gastroenterology organizations for a long time, prior to 1986 the market for fellows was decentralized. In the 1970s and 1980s, hospitals announced positions, received applications, interviewed candidates, and made offers at their own pace. The market experienced problems very similar to those experienced by the market of medical interns several decades earlier (Roth 1984, 2003), including the gradual unraveling of appointment dates. Offers for positions came to be made years before employment as a GI fellow would start. In an attempt to halt unraveling, guidelines for the time at which offers could be made were proposed, unsuccessfully. Eventually a centralized labor market clearinghouse was adopted, of the kind used for matching medical students to internal medicine and other residencies.

In 1986, the MSMP (Medical Specialties Matching Program) initiated a centralized match for gastroenterology and other internal medicine subspecialties, conducted one year before employment would start, and so two years into the IM residency. The MSMP uses the same algorithm to match applicants to programs such as the NRMP (National Residency Matching Program), which matches medical students to residencies (and since 1998 this is the Roth and Peranson [1999] algorithm). The match for GI fellows operated well, with most nonmilitary programs participating, and over 90 percent of participating positions being filled. However, after 1996, participation of GI fellows and programs rapidly declined, and the match was formally abandoned in 2000.

The collapse of the centralized market allows us to study how a labor market that operated in an organized way, in which interviews were conducted without time pressure, in which offers were made mostly all at once through the centralized match, adapted to the loss of the clearinghouse. Because the lack of the clearinghouse is recent (and because gastroenterology programs

---

6. The abbreviation "GI" stems from the older name for the specialty, gastrointestinal disease.

were interested in understanding how the new market worked), we were able to survey market participants and observe how the market changed, and how the decentralized market functioned in comparison to when the clearinghouse was in operation. We will also describe the process by which a new clearinghouse was organized and put into operation in 2006.

7.4 The Effects of a Centralized Match

We first study how the market for gastroenterology fellows operated after the match broke down. We describe when interviews were conducted and offers made, what kind of offers applicants received, and the thickness of the market—that is, how many programs were actively hiring at any given time.

We then address whether the decentralized organization of the market produced different outcomes than the centralized clearinghouse, apart from the timing and organization. We will investigate who got matched to whom under the different market organizations and whether salaries were affected. This latter point received some prominence due to an antitrust lawsuit against the match that was dismissed following the passage of new legislation.

7.4.1 The Decentralized Market for GI Fellows: What Kind of Offers When?

In the late nineties, the market moved from a centralized clearinghouse to a decentralized market: programs started to match to applicants outside of the match, more specifically, *before* the match. We will provide an overview of the reasons for the collapse of the match in section 7.4, but first we describe this new decentralized market.

From the outset, we were faced with a common problem when studying and describing decentralized markets. By their very nature, there are not a lot of data collected on the way the market works. We use two sources of data: the first is Fellowship and Residency Electronic Interactive Database (FREIDA) online (http://www.ama-assn.org/ama/pub/category/2997 .html), on which many programs announce the time at which they plan to interview.[7] Second, together with our colleague Dr. Deborah Proctor, and with the sponsorship of the American Gastroenterology Association (AGA), we administered a survey on hiring procedures of gastroenterol-

---

7. We accessed FREIDA in 2003 to retrieve data concerning fellowship positions in internal medicine subspecialties starting in 2005, and in the spring of 2002 for GI fellowship positions starting in 2003. We used data from programs whose end date of the interviews occurred after the deadline of the application period. The number of data points we have for the start date of the interview period (end date in parentheses) for positions starting in 2005 is forty-five (forty-four) of the 155 GI programs, of the match specialties we have eighty-three of the 174 cardiovascular disease programs, sixty-four of the 139 infectious disease programs, ten of the thirty pulmonary disease programs, and fifty-two of the 122 pulmonary disease and critical care programs.

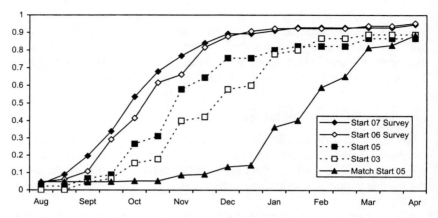

Fig. 7.1   Cumulative distribution of GI and Match programs that started interviewing by the time of any given two-week period

Source: Match Start 05: interview dates of internal medicine subspecialties that participated in the MSMP for positions starting in 2005. Start 03 and Start 05: Start dates of interviews for GI fellowship positions starting in 2003 and 2005, respectively, from FREIDA (Niederle and Roth 2004). Start 06 Survey: The replies from the survey of GI program directors to the question of when they started interviewing for 2006 positions. Start 07 Survey: the answers to the question of when GI program directors expected to start interviewing for 2007 positions (without a centralized match; see Niederle, Proctor, and Roth 2006).

ogy programs, in January 2005 (see Niederle, Proctor, and Roth 2006). A link to an online questionnaire was sent to the 154 GI fellowship programs accredited by the Accreditation Council for Graduate Medical Education and eligible to participate in a match. We obtained (partial) data from sixty-four U.S.-based programs, a response rate slightly higher than 40 percent, with larger and more prestigious programs somewhat overrepresented. The survey focused on the mechanics of how fellows were hired.

We asked when program directors conducted their first and last interview for positions beginning in the summer of 2006. We also asked when they expected to start interviewing for positions beginning in 2007 (at the time of the survey no decision had yet been made to reintroduce the GI fellowship match).

Using data from FREIDA and the survey on interview schedules, figure 7.1 shows the timing of interviews for GI fellowship positions, compared to the time of interviews of other internal medicine subspecialties that maintained participation in the match (Niederle, Proctor, and Roth 2006). We show the cumulative distribution of programs that started interviewing at any given two-week period.[8] Not only were GI programs interviewing earlier

---

8. Programs that started their interviews, for example, from December 23 to January 6 are coded as starting in January, and those that interviewed from January 7 to January 22 as mid-January. This way, programs that start interviewing on the last day of a month, or the first day in the next month—both prominent start times—are coded as starting at the same time.

than subspecialties that still used a match, but they were also interviewing earlier from year to year, even many years after the match collapsed in the late nineties.

The fifty-one programs that in the survey provided both a start date for interviews for 2006 positions and an anticipated start date for 2007 positions and did not start interviewing before August planned to interview significantly earlier for 2007 positions ($p < .01$, using a Wilcoxon matched-pairs signed rank test). Of these fifty-one programs, the programs that planned to interview earlier for 2007 positions are the programs that started interviewing later for 2006 positions.[9] This is consistent with the view that programs that interview later find that many of the applicants they would have liked to interview have already accepted positions. Furthermore, regression analysis shows that the timing of interviews is not correlated with the size of the program (which is a decent proxy for "desirability," with larger programs being more prestigious).

In the survey, Niederle, Proctor, and Roth (2006) not only asked about timing of interviews, but also about the timing and kinds of offers that were extended. For each of the forty-four fellowship programs that answered the questions in the survey, figure 7.2, panel A shows when the first offer was made, and the last offer expired, where (to be very conservative) we assumed that the last offer made was also the one with the longest deadline. Thus the figure shows, for each responding program, a line that begins on the day when the first offer was made and ends when the last offer made would have expired if it was the offer with the longest duration. This provides an upper bound for the time during which the program was actively on the market. Figure 7.2, panel B provides the proportion of programs that are actively on the market at any given time.

Figure 7.2, panel A shows that by November 15, eleven programs (27 percent) had already finished making offers, twelve (25 percent) had not yet started, and twenty-one (48 percent) were in the middle. Figure 7.2, panel B presents the same data another way by showing how many programs had outstanding offers at any point in time. At no point did even 60 percent of programs have outstanding offers. So offers were dispersed in time, with programs that made offers early, often requiring answers before many other programs had begun to make offers.

The hiring process resulted in quite intricate scheduling of interviews and offers. Most programs (53/61) had interviews cancelled, and about half (29/64) made offers before they finished interviewing (of these, almost half reported that they did so because of pressure from the market). Forty-three

---

9. A regression on the amount of time the program wants to move its interviews ahead (i.e., predicted interview begin next year minus interview begin this year), as a function of when the program started to interview, yields a coefficient of -0.17 (s.e. 0.07, $p = .02$). The relationship holds even when we control for the number of positions the program is trying to fill or the length of the interview period.

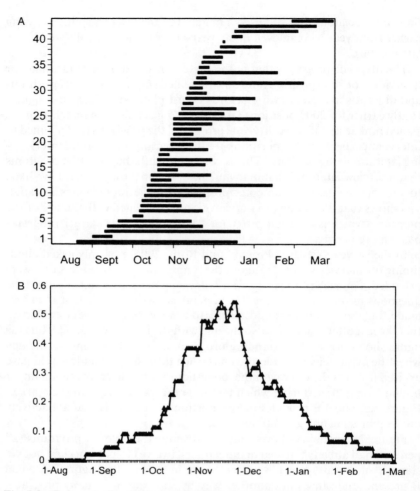

Fig. 7.2   Dates of offers by forty-four fellowship programs: *A*, **Each program is represented by a horizontal line, indicating the dates during which it had outstanding offers;** *B*, **The proportion of programs that have an outstanding offer on any given day**

percent of the respondents (twenty-eight programs) reported that they speeded up offers because the candidate had another offer, and many other programs reported that in such cases they provided feedback to the candidate about their chance of receiving an offer. Furthermore, 33 percent of programs (i.e., twenty-one) considered how likely it was that an applicant would accept their offer when deciding whether to extend an offer. Programs not only decided strategically when and to whom to make an offer, but also on the deadline of offers. More than half the programs (60 percent made at least one offer that required a reply in one week or less, and 95 percent required a reply to some offer in two weeks or less. And in fact, 21 percent of programs indicated that the longest time a candidate took to respond to an offer was one hour, 60 percent report one week at most, and 90 percent two weeks at most. Thus, the market moved fast. It was not a market in which program directors could interview all the candidates they might wish to before making offers, nor one in which they could safely extend offers to risky candidates, because meanwhile more attainable candidates might take other offers.

That is, the decentralized GI fellowship market made it unsafe to act straightforwardly according to preferences over candidates or employers only. It was a congested, thin market, even though there were (and are) many GI programs and potential GI fellows. As such, the GI market was less competitive than when there was a match, in that competition for each fellow was reduced to a thin slice of employers, and direct competition among fellows for programs was reduced as fellows were hired quickly and could only be considered by very few programs.

7.4.2 Does a Centralized Match Change the Final Outcome of the Market?

There were several reasons to think that the thin, early decentralized market that followed the loss of the match might produce different outcomes than the centralized match.

First, the centralized match yields a stable outcome—that is, there does not exist a program and resident that mutually prefer each other to their match outcome. (That is, every program could make an offer to any fellow it prefers to its current fellow, only to learn that this new fellow would turn them down, as he or she prefers the current match.) It seems unlikely that the decentralized market as operated by GI programs and fellows can achieve stability, when programs make exploding offers, strategically decide on the candidates to whom to make an offer, and markets are thin. Indeed, theoretical results by Niederle and Yariv (2009) suggest that, in general, a decentralized market like the market for GI fellows will not result in a stable outcome.

A second reason the decentralized market may yield a different matching is that offers in the decentralized market were made about six months to a year earlier than those in the centralized match. Instead of hiring internal medicine residents near the end of their second year, they came to be hired at the beginning of their second year. This means there was less information about residents available when programs decided to whom to make offers.

Finally, there is anecdotal evidence that markets that unravel rely more on informal networks. This can have several reasons: the first is that because candidates are hired earlier, interviews may be less informative, which means program directors have to rely more on recommendation letters and other sources of information. Clearly, if an internal medicine resident is from the same hospital, and has had a rotation in the GI unit, this unit will have more information on this applicant than on more distant applicants (and more information than other GI programs), and this difference increases as the information on outsiders becomes more noisy. Another reason why markets that unravel may rely more on networks is that the unraveled GI market had more candidates reneging on their acceptance, as internal medicine residents faced offers even earlier than before (and it may be harder to plan two years instead of one year in advance). Hiring fellows within a network may help reduce the enforcement problem and reduce the likelihood that a candidate reneges on his or her acceptance.

To address whether the market for GI fellows yields a different outcome when it used a centralized match than before or after, we purchased data from the AMA that includes the career path of every living U.S. physician who has completed or is currently completing a GI fellowship, is a board-certified gastroenterologist, or claims gastroenterology as a specialty (see Niederle and Roth 2003b). The data consist of the year in which each physician graduated from medical school and finished each residency, the location of each residency, and the medical school attended. Of the 15,187 entries we have a total of 9,180 fellows who completed a residency and a subsequent GI fellowship in the United States after 1977. They do their fellowship in 433 different hospital codes and come from 680 residencies.

Figure 7.3 shows the mobility of those fellows before, during, and after the fellowship match (i.e., whether they move to a different program, a different city, or a different state between their residency and the fellowship). We view 1997 as the first year in which the market was no longer effectively organized via the match. That is, gastroenterology fellows who got hired in

Share of mobility of GI fellows for each year

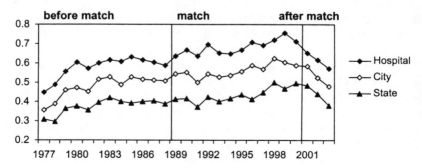

Fig. 7.3   Share of mobility of GI fellows for each year
Note: The vertical lines indicate the beginning and the end of the use of the centralized match, measured in year of fellowship *completion.*

Table 7.3   **Differences across mobility**

	Prematch— Match	Match 1— Prematch	Match 2— Match 1	Postmatch— Match 2	Postmatch— Match	Postmatch— Prematch
Hospital	.079	.052	.053	−.096	−.069	.009
	(.00)	(.00)	(.02)	(.02)	(.04)	(.52)
City	.059	.032	.054	−.058	−.031	.028
	(.00)	(.02)	(.00)	(.07)	(.19)	(.41)
State	.041	.014	.053	−.026	0	.041
	(.00)	(.099)	(.03)	(.44)	(.89)	(.23)

Notes: Prematch: 1980–88; match: 1989–2000; match 1: 1989–1994; match 2: 1995–2000; and Postmatch: 2001–2003; Differences in mobility, with *p*-values in parentheses.

1997, started employment in 1998, and finished in 2001 will have obtained their job after the match had started to break down. Note that the figure shows each fellow by the date when he or she ended the fellowship. Since fellowships were required to be two years before 1996, but three years since then—and the match operates a year before employment starts—gastroenterologists ending their fellowship in 1989 were the first ones who could have gone through a match, while those ending in 2001 were those who had no functioning match anymore.

Before the match, and after the collapse of the match, fellows were much more likely to perform their GI fellowship at the same hospital at which they performed their internal medicine residency. There is a statistically significant increase in mobility with the introduction of the match, and for the hospital and the city level there is a significant decrease in mobility since the demise of the match compared with the six years when the match was well established. Table 7.3 provides the differences across mobility with *p*-values, where we use a two-sided Mann-Whitney *U* test, with the proportion of mobility in each year as our data points.

Furthermore, we divided our sample into large and small GI fellowship programs. We found that larger programs hired a smaller proportion of local fellows than small programs (at the hospital, city, and state level). The effects of the match are larger and more significant for large programs than for small ones.[10]

Note that the increase in mobility is gradual, as measured over the first and second six-year periods of the match. This conforms to experimental

---

10. We also controlled for various other possible impacts, such as the fact that because of the consolidation of hospitals, some hospitals may have changed their name, introducing a spurious mobility at the hospital level. To control for this source of bias we eliminated for each hospital the first three years of observation (and hence eliminated fellows who may have finished their internal medicine residency in the same hospital when it had a different name). Note that the proportion of GI fellows who finished their GI fellowship by three years after their previous residency was always at least 70 percent. The qualitative results do not change.

evidence (Kagel and Roth 2000; McKinney, Niederle, and Roth 2005) in which the centralized match only gradually becomes fully used by participants.

An alternative explanation for the increase in mobility during the use of the centralized match is not that the match affects the process, but rather changes the self-selection of interns who aim for a GI fellowship. Specifically, it could be that physicians who are more mobile choose to do a GI fellowship whenever the market operates through a centralized match. To account for that, we can compute for each GI fellow a measure of "mobility" that corresponds to a change in city or state between finishing medical school and the residency they completed just before entering their GI fellowship (this reduces the sample to 6,789 physicians, as we discard all foreign medical graduates). While physicians become less mobile as their career advances, we do not find any evidence that the mobility of GI fellows during the match is driven by an increase in mobile physicians who choose to become gastroenterologists.

Therefore, the decentralized GI fellowship market was not only congested and thin, it also produced different outcomes than when it was organized through a match. With the loss of the centralized clearinghouse, the market broke down into more localized markets (the market became not only thin in time, but also in space).

7.4.3   Did the Clearinghouse Affect Salaries?

Another aspect of the matching of fellows to GI programs is not only who works where, but also under what conditions—specifically, at which salary. This question drew a lot of attention after, in May 2002, sixteen law firms filed a class action lawsuit on behalf of three former residents, seeking to represent the class of all residents and fellows, arguing that the National Resident Matching Program (NRMP) violated antitrust laws and was a conspiracy to depress salaries. The lawsuit was against a class of defendants, including the NRMP (which also operates the Medical Specialties Matching Program [MSMP]), other medical organizations, and the class of all hospitals that employ residents. (*Jung et al. v. Ass'n of Am. Med. C., et al.,* Class Action Complaint, No. 02-CV-00873, D.D.C. May 5, 2002).[11]

One way to investigate whether a match affects salaries of medical fellows is to examine comparable medical subspecialties, only some of which use a match (see table 7.4). Niederle and Roth (2003a) and (2004) compare

---

11. Another aspect that received considerable attention is the number of hours residents and fellows have to work each week, prompting demand for legislation to limit the hours per week to eighty. There are two reasons we did not focus on hours worked. First, the limitation to eighty hours is in general not binding for fellows, and more importantly, hours come in very different flavors and are not readily comparable across fellowship programs: some hours are spent on research, patient care, and educational activities, and may have considerable positive value, while others spent on clerical activities may be a cost.

Table 7.4   **Salaries in Internal Medicine Subspecialties**

Specialty	Match	No. of programs	Mean salary	Standard deviation	Min	Max
PUD	MSMP	26	45,418	5,859	37,185	58,536
CCM	No	31	43,460	3,376	36,966	50,422
IMG	No	90	43,266	4,989	28,200	58,536
HEM	No	17	42,952	4,739	36,000	51,853
ON	No	24	42,650	4,922	28,200	51,853
HO	No	110	42,526	4,415	32,000	58,328
NEP	No	118	42,426	4,357	30,733	58,328
ID	MSMP	124	42,352	4,863	30,000	58,328
CD	MSMP	153	42,288	4,246	26,749	54,450
PCC	MSMP	111	41,973	4,268	26,916	53,463
GE	No	142	41,800	4,638	26,000	58,328
END	No	103	41,656	4,000	33,700	53,463
ISM	No	2	41,390	1,259	40,500	42,280
RHU	No	97	41,182	4,743	28,824	58,328

Notes: For each specialty the number of programs reporting a positive salary, the mean salary, the standard deviation, the minimum and the maximum salary. The specialties are: PUD: pulmonary disease, CCM: critical care medicine; IMG: geriatric medicine; HEM: hematology; ON: oncology; HO: hematology and oncology; NEP: nephrology; ID: infectious disease; CD: cardiovascular disease; PCC: pulmonary disease and critical care medicine; GE: gastroenterology; END: endocrinology; ISM: internal sports medicine; RHU: rheumatology. We use the data from the Graduate Medical Education Library 2003–2004. We use all internal medicine subspecialties that require three years of prior residency, and all nonmilitary programs that record a positive wage and are not in Puerto Rico.

salaries of nonmilitary U.S. fellowship programs in all internal medicine subspecialties that require three years of prior residency. The data are from the Graduate Medical Education Library 2002 to 2003 and 2003 to 2004, respectively.

Using the 1148 salary data for 2003, a simple regression of the salary on a match dummy yields a constant of \$42,210.76 (s.e. 168.04, $p = 0.00$) and a coefficient on the match dummy of \$208.33 (s.e. 279.82, $p = 0.46$). That is, specialties that use a match do not have significantly lower salaries.[12]

To account for possible effects of hospital size (since match specialties tend to be larger), we want to determine whether, within hospitals, salaries for specialties that use the match are different than for specialties that do not. In the next regression we therefore include a dummy variable for each hospital when regressing the salary on a match dummy (there are 201 different hospitals, of which 165 have both match specialties and specialties that do not use the match). The regression yields a constant of \$42,650

12. The salaries of GI fellows, while somewhat on the low side, are not significantly different (at any conventional level of significance: lowest is 0.16) from either the specialties that participate in a match, or the specialties that do not.

(s.e. 2372.30, $p = 0.00$), and a coefficient on the match dummy of \$343.86 (s.e. 152.60 and $p = 0.024$). That is, within hospitals, the salaries of fellows whose specialty uses a match are higher than those that do not use a match, but the differences are not economically relevant; they are on the order of 1 percent of the salary.[13]

That is, while salaries may not be very high, empirically it does not appear that using a match affects the salary level in any way.

The lawsuit spurred a number of theoretical papers. Bulow and Levin (2006) provide some support for the lawsuit in a simple theoretical model. They compare a market with impersonal pay (that is, a market in which pay is attached to *positions* rather than depending on which applicant is hired for the position) to a market with perfectly competitive salaries at which each worker is paid his or her marginal product. They find that in their model, a market with impersonal salaries leads to lower average salaries and a more compressed pay schedule.[14]

Subsequent theoretical work has shown that these conclusions about pay compression do not necessarily follow if the model is expanded to include the possibility of firms hiring more than one worker (Kojima 2007).

There are centralized algorithms that allow for pay to be flexible, and whose outcomes can yield a competitive equilibrium (Kelso and Crawford 1982). The preferences firms and workers submit to a centralized match in such an algorithm consist of a ranking of each other for any possible pay. For example, a worker would indicate that his or her first choice is to work for a certain firm at a certain salary, his or her second choice may be to work for the same firm at a lower salary, and his or her third choice could be to work for another firm at the higher initial salary, and so on. While the centralized clearinghouse does not use exactly this algorithm, it uses the Roth and Peranson (1999) algorithm, which allows firms to list alternative positions at different salaries, and to express preferences for some workers in only some positions. This algorithm, in the environment studied by Bulow and Levin (2006), can yield competitive outcomes (Niederle 2007). A centralized clearinghouse using the Roth and Peranson (1999) algorithm therefore, does not reduce price competition per se.

How would a *decentralized* market yield competitive wages? In general, the assumption is that if a wage is below the competitive level, either the worker or some other firm becomes aware of an arbitrage opportunity, which would

13. However, within hospitals, GI fellows earn somewhat less than both the average fellow in a specialty that has a match, and the average fellow in a specialty without a match. While the results are statistically significant, they are not economically significant—they are very small (less than \$1,000), no more than 2 percent of the salary. Using Graduate Medical Education Library 2002 to 2003, the salary difference for gastroenterology fellows is only 268.64 and the difference is not significant. Otherwise, the results are similar when we use data from the Graduate Medical Education Library 2002 to 2003 (see Niederle and Roth 2004).

14. Bulow and Levin note that the empirical evidence in Niederle and Roth (2003a) does not bear this out in the actual market data.

eventually lead to a competitive outcome. This was implicitly the motivation for the lawsuit: the notion was that without a match, residents would receive many offers, and bargain until they receive their competitive outcome. We already showed that in the market for internal medicine residents seeking GI fellowships, the decentralized market is far from one in which residents can safely wait for multiple offers. Instead, the market is characterized by exploding offers made at very dispersed times that do not allow residents to seek out multiple offers simultaneously.

We studied empirically whether the limited offers that can be obtained simultaneously lead to bargaining (Niederle, Proctor, and Roth 2006). We asked gastroenterology program directors in the survey whether they offered different terms to different fellows, and whether wages were adjustable. Out of sixty-three program directors, all but four, (i.e., 94 percent) offered the same salary to all their fellows. Furthermore, all but four (although not all the same four programs) offered the same hours on call. While eighteen of the sixty-three programs (29 percent) offered different fellows different amounts of time for research, all but three of these programs formally differentiated the kinds of fellows doing different jobs (i.e., they had at least two kinds of fellows). That is, not many program directors offered different contracts to different fellows they hired in the same year (and remember that we oversampled the larger programs, which have more than one fellowship per year). All program directors responded that offers were not adjusted in response to outside offers and terms were not negotiable.

In general, markets with impersonal pay may be more common than standard models would suggest.[15] Thus, while different programs offer different salaries and terms, and while program directors respond in many other ways to the contingencies that arise in the course of the hiring process (such as adapting the timing and length of their offers), it does not appear that they adjust the terms of their offers to the situations of individual candidates. Rather, as the market for GI fellows abandoned the match it seems to have become less competitive, in the sense that at each point in time, residents did not face the whole market, but only the smaller set of programs that made offers at that time. And indeed, some fellows lamenting the loss of the match did so for that reason.[16]

A centralized match halted unraveling and solved congestion, allowing for a thick GI fellowship market, in which programs and fellows could safely

15. Wages seem to be also rather inflexible when it comes to junior hiring of professors. Assistant professors who start in the same department and the same year often receive almost the same salary, and some departments make that a policy.

16. Gastroenterology fellows Bauer et al. (1999) commented on the effects of the loss of the match. "Of recent concern is the deterioration of the match process for candidates applying for fellowship positions over the past two years. Our junior colleagues are concerned that they may not be able to wait safely to interview with the institution of their choice while a position is offered elsewhere early in the decision process. The absence of the match benefits the programs a great deal more than their applicants."

make and consider their offers. This led to a more national market with increased mobility of GI fellows. Furthermore, there is no theoretical or empirical evidence that a clearinghouse using the Roth and Peranson (1999) algorithm adversely affects the terms of the contracts.

Reflecting these considerations, President George W. Bush signed into law, as an addendum to the Pension Funding Equity Act of 2004, legislation that included a Congressional finding that "Antitrust lawsuits challenging the matching process, regardless of their merit or lack thereof, have the potential to undermine this highly efficient, procompetitive, and longstanding process. . . ." The legislation goes on to "confirm that the antitrust laws do not prohibit sponsoring, conducting, or participating in a graduate medical education residency matching program, or agreeing to do so. . . ." Following this legislation, the antitrust suit was dismissed.

7.5   Changing the Market Organization

The market for GI fellows raises two kinds of questions about the organization of a market. The first is why this match broke down (and why failures of centralized clearinghouses that produce stable matchings are so rare). The second is how can an unraveled, decentralized market be reorganized through a clearinghouse.

7.5.1   Why Did the GI Match Fail, and Why Are These Failures So Rare?

The market for GI fellows is among many markets that introduced a centralized match to overcome problems of unraveling and congestion. Empirically, markets that use a centralized algorithm that produces a stable outcome are more successful in remaining in use than those that do not. Of particular interest in this regard are the centralized clearinghouses used in various regions in the British National Health Service (NHS). In the 1960s, these markets suffered from the same problems as the American market for medical interns in the 1940s (successfully solved by the centralized match, the NRMP). A Royal Commission recommended that each region of the NHS use a centralized clearinghouse, and the various regions in Britain each invented their own algorithm, of which only some were stable.[17] Clearinghouses that produced

---

17. An example of unstable algorithms, are "priority algorithms" that use the exact place in which firms and workers rank each other. For example, Roth (1990, 1991) observed clearinghouses in Newcastle and Birmingham that first matched all firms (medical practices) and workers that listed each other first. After all such "1-1" pairs, 1-2 pairs were matched; that is, pairs in which the workers list the firm first, and the firm lists the worker second, followed by 2-1 pairs, and so forth. At each step, matched firms and workers are removed and the order of removal is given by the product of the worker-firm ranking, where in case of the same products priority is given to workers. This can create unstable outcomes. Consider a firm F and a worker A that both list each other 4th, which gives them priority 16. Now assume some other worker B lists firm F first, and the firm F lists him or her 15th. Nonetheless, this gives them priority 15, and hence firm F will be matched to worker B over worker A, who may receive some other lower-ranked firm that lists him or her highly, in which case worker A and firm F would be a blocking pair, in that they would rather be together than with their current matches.

stable matches succeeded, while others mostly did not (Roth 1991). However, considering all markets that use centralized clearinghouses, this correlation is not perfect—some matches with algorithms that do not provide stable matches survive, and some stable match algorithms fail. Furthermore, there are more differences between markets than simply the algorithms they use. Thus, controlled experiments can help clarify what is going on.

Kagel and Roth (2000) report an experiment that compares two small unraveled markets in the laboratory. In one, the stable matching mechanism observed in Edinburgh was introduced, while in the other the unstable mechanism used in Newcastle was used. In these otherwise identical sets of markets, the markets that used a stable algorithm adopted the clearinghouse successfully, and continued to use it. The markets that used the Newcastle mechanism that does not produce stable outcomes did not adopt the clearinghouse successfully, and the markets continued to experience offers and acceptances before the operation of the centralized clearinghouse.

Having a stable algorithm thus seems to be an important factor for a centralized clearinghouse to perform well, and continue to be used, and, as table 7.2 shows, most of these have been successfully in operation for years. The market for GI fellows is unusual, in that it used a centralized clearinghouse with a stable algorithm, and then, in the late nineties, started to unravel.

These events seem to have been set in motion in 1993 to 1994, when, in the middle of general discussions of health care reform, gastroenterology subjected itself to a manpower analysis. The resulting study was published in 1996 (Meyer et al. 1996). Its main conclusions were that the U.S. health care system and gastroenterologists would benefit from a reduction in gastroenterology fellowship programs. The Gastroenterology Leadership Council endorsed a goal of 25 to 50 percent reduction in the number of GI fellows over five years. Furthermore, an additional year of training was mandated: starting in the summer of 1996, three years of training were required to be eligible for board certification as a gastroenterologist, instead of two.

That is, in 1996 the *supply* of gastroenterology fellowships was sharply reduced, and the time needed to become a gastroenterologist was increased by a year (i.e., the cost of becoming a gastroenterologist was increased, although some three-year fellowship programs had already existed before 1996).

However, the announced (and hence expected) reduction in supply was accompanied by an *even larger reduction* in the number of residents who applied for GI fellowship positions. This seems to have been the start of the demise of the match. In 1996, for the first time, and despite the reduction in the number of positions offered, there were fewer applicants for GI fellowship positions than there were positions offered in the match. This resulted in a record low fill rate: only 74.8 percent of the positions in the match were filled through the match that year.

The next year, 1997, saw a sharp decline in the percentage of positions in the match. In particular, table 7.5 (Niederle and Roth 2003b) describes how withdrawal of positions from the match (as programs and applicants

Table 7.5   Participation in the gastroenterology match

Yr.	Positions advertised	Percent withdrawn	Positions in match	Percent matched	Number of programs	Number of applicants	Applicants per position in match
1992	—	—	377	96.6	160	658	1.75
1993	374	−6.7	399	94	173	642	1.6
1994	—	—	369	93	169	591	1.6
1995	351	4	337	88.7	171	433	1.3
1996	313	4.8	298	74.8	164	277	0.9
1997	254	16.1	213	85	128	240	1.1
1998	178	44.3	99	77.8	60	148	1.5
1999	35	60	14	—	11	—	—

Notes: For each year, Positions advertised is the number of positions whose availability in the match was announced in late March. Until late May, the programs may add or withdraw positions (Percent withdrawn), which leaves the final number of positions in the match (Positions in match). Percent matched is the percentage of positions in the match that are filled by the match. Number of applicants is the total number of applicants who listed at least one GI program in their rank order list.

reached agreements outside of the match) preceded the formal demise of that match. Withdrawals went from about 5 percent in 1996 to 16 percent in 1997, to 44 percent in 1998, to 60 percent in 1999, in each case followed by a sharp reduction the following year in the number of positions even advertised in the match, and after 1999 the match was formally abandoned, having already become moribund, as almost all positions were filled outside of the match.[18]

If a simple shift in supply or demand were enough to cause a match to collapse once it had become successfully established, many other markets, including other internal medicine subspecialties, would also have failed matches, since these shifts turn out not to be so rare. What was unusual about the change that the gastroenterology match experienced in 1996 was that it temporarily *reversed* the traditional excess supply of applicants (in table 7.5, the ratio of applicants to positions in the match dropped below 1 in 1996). None of the other internal medicine subspecialty matches (cardiovascular disease, pulmonary disease, and infectious disease) experienced such a shift. Infectious disease successfully operates a match in which there are persistently fewer applicants than positions.[19]

18. Dr. David Brenner, quoted in Gerson (1999), described that demise in part as follows: "Many applicants and a large percentage of the fellowship programs stopped using the match, which made choices more difficult for the remaining applicants and programs and created a vicious circle. Many training directors were very disappointed a few years ago when they didn't fill their slots because the applicants they thought were interested accepted positions before the match."

19. From 1990 to 1998 the ratio of applicants to positions offered in the cardiovascular match varied from a high of 1.6 to a low of 1.3. For pulmonary disease those ratios varied from a high of 1.5 to a low of 1.1, and for infectious disease (from 1994 to 1998) those ratios varied from a low of .68 to a high of .92. Thus, unlike in the gastroenterology market, the short side of these markets did not change, although in infectious diseases the *applicants* were in short supply, and in the other matches the *positions* were in short supply (Niederle and Roth 2004).

There are limits to the confidence with which one can draw conclusions simply by studying the circumstances in which rare events (like the collapse of a stable match) occur. So, one way to gather more evidence is to create small artificial markets in the laboratory and subject them to controlled changes in supply and demand. McKinney, Niederle, and Roth (2005) find in the laboratory that *anticipated* shifts in supply in demand, visible to both sides of the market, do not cause declines in match participation anywhere near the magnitude caused by unanticipated shocks, particularly when these are more visible to one side of the market than to the other. In particular, they consider shifts in demand for positions that are either visible to both firms and workers, or only to firms (as when an unexpected change in demand becomes visible to firms when they receive few applications, but not to workers). They find that demand reductions of both kinds cause firms to try to make more early hires, but that when workers know that they are on the short side of the market they are more likely to decline such offers than when they are unaware of the shift in demand. It is the combination of firms making early offers outside of the match, and workers not feeling safe to reject them and wait for the match that causes the market to unravel in the experiment. That is, the experiment shows that this combination of events can by itself be sufficient to cause the breakdown of a match. The results are thus suggestive that the same combination of events in the late 1990s caused the breakdown of the GI match.

On the basis of these results, McKinney, Niederle, and Roth (2005) conjecture that the breakdown in the GI market in 1996 was due to the unusual shock that caused an unanticipated reversal in the short side of the market, with many fewer high-quality residents wishing to start a GI fellowship. This increased incentives for programs to try to capture those GI fellows early. And because the shock was unusual, and not predicted, remaining residents may not have felt safe to reject early offers. The evidence supported the conjecture that now that market conditions had stabilized, a match could once more be successful.

7.5.2   Beyond Centralized Matching: Why Do Some Markets Work Well, while Others Do Not? How to Restart the GI Match?

The market for GI fellows seems to have broken down due to an unusual event, and then once more experienced unraveling and congestion. Clearinghouses solve both problems: they bring participants to the market at the same time and they overcome congestion. This helps to make it safe for participants to act according to their preferences over other participants, without additional constraints on behavior imposed by inferior market organization. The supply and demand for GI fellowships had stabilized in the interim, and many participants on both sides of the market wanted to have a match once again, so all seemed favorable for a successful restart.

To assess the demand by fellowship programs for a restart of the match, the questionnaire we administered to GI program directors in January 2005 (Niederle, Proctor, and Roth 2006) also asked "Do you think a match would be better than the current system if most programs would adhere to it?" Of the sixty responses, fifty said yes, and many of those who said no indicated that "most" would not be enough for them to have confidence in the match.

Following the announcement of the new GI match, communications from program directors confirmed that this was a lively concern, with some expressing concern about specific programs they regard as competitors.[20]

Program directors who wished to participate in the match worried that if their competitors made early offers, then applicants would lose confidence that the match would work and consequently would accept those early offers, because that had been the practice in the decentralized market. That is, in the first year of a match, applicants might not yet feel that it is safe to reject an early offer to wait for the match. Program directors who worried about their competitors might thus be more inclined to make early offers themselves. Recall that, before the reintroduction of the match, many program directors sped up offers because they felt pressured by applicants who were disappearing from the market in response to the early offers of other programs.

This raises the more general question as to why some markets unravel and experience congestion problems in the first place (and hence are good candidates for introducing a centralized match), and what are good policies to make markets operate at a later time.

Empirically, most markets that have been observed unraveling are markets in which employers make short-duration offers, and in which the acceptance of an offer is binding (see Niederle and Roth [2009]; for a description of the market for law graduates seeking employment as appellate court clerks see Avery et al. [2001, 2007], and for college admissions see Avery, Fairbanks, and Zeckhauser [2003]).[21]

On the other hand, there are markets that do not unravel, such as the market for graduate school admission. In this market, a policy (adopted by the large majority of universities) states that offers of admission and financial support to graduate students should remain open until April 15.

Students are under no obligation to respond to offers of financial support prior to April 15; earlier deadlines for acceptance of such offers violate

---

20. In June 2005, our colleague Debbie Proctor, the gastroenterologist who took the lead in reorganizing the match, sent us an e-mail saying, in part "I'm answering 3–4 emails per day especially on this issue. 'I want to make sure MY competition is in the match and that they don't cheat.' Well, this is another way of saying that if they cheat, then I will too! . . . Have you ever seen this before? The distrust amongst program directors? I find it hard to believe that we are unique. Maybe this is [a] social science phenomenon?"

21. Since 2003, the market for law clerks has succeeded in moving hiring new graduates nearer (by a year) to the date of graduation (and the beginning of employment). But exploding offers with binding agreements have kept the market very thin (Avery et al. 2007; Haruvy, Roth, and Ünver 2006).

the intent of this Resolution. In those instances in which a student accepts an offer before April 15, and subsequently desires to withdraw that acceptance, the student may submit in writing a resignation of the appointment at any time through April 15. However, an acceptance given or left in force after April 15 commits the student not to accept another offer without first obtaining a written release from the institution to which a commitment has been made. Similarly, an offer by an institution after April 15 is conditional on presentation by the student of the written release from any previously accepted offer. It is further agreed by the institutions and organizations subscribing to the above Resolution that a copy of this Resolution should accompany every scholarship, fellowship, traineeship, and assistantship offer.

This, of course, makes early exploding offers much less profitable. A program that might be inclined to insist on an against-the-rules early response is discouraged from doing so in two ways. First, the chance of actually enrolling a student who is pressured in this way is diminished, because the student is not prevented from later receiving and accepting a more preferred offer. Second, a program that has pressured a student to accept an early offer cannot offer that position to another student until after the early acceptance has been declined, at which point most of the students in the market may have made binding agreements.

Niederle and Roth (2009) study in the laboratory the impact of the rules that govern the types of offers that can be made (with or without a very short deadline) and the commitment of applicants upon accepting an offer. Firms decide when and to whom to make offers, while information about the quality of applicants is only revealed over time. In these small environments, designed so they are not prone to congestion, either eliminating the possibility of making exploding offers or making early acceptances nonbinding helps prevent markets from operating inefficiently early.

In practice, it is very hard to enforce the time at which programs make offers and how long offers are left open. The policy of making acceptances nonbinding instead helps the applicants themselves deal with such early and short offers. Because applicants can accept these offers without compromising their availability for subsequent offers from programs they prefer, no program need feel pressured to make an early offer itself just because another program is doing so.

We proposed a similar policy, adapted to the situation of the upcoming GI match (Niederle, Proctor, and Roth 2006). Ideally, such a policy would remove any temptation for fellowship programs to extend early offers and ask for a response before the match, by allowing applicants who had accepted early offers nevertheless to participate in the match. Under such a policy, an applicant who had accepted a prematch offer would be able to enter the match, listing only programs he or she preferred to the early offer. The match result would be binding, and if the applicant were successfully matched, he or she would then be freed from his or her pre-match commitment and able to fulfill his or her commitment to the match. Under such a policy, programs would have little incentive to ask for pre-match agreements, because doing so would give them no advantage in "capturing" candidates who would have preferred to consider all the options available in the match and await the match outcome. Note that programs would not lose in any way the ability to attract candidates who genuinely regarded them as their first choice, because any program and applicant who list each other first in the match are guaranteed to be matched to one another.

A modified version of this policy was adopted by all four major gastro-enterology professional organizations, the American Gastroenterological Association (AGA), the American College of Gastroenterology (ACG), the American Society for Gastrointestinal Endoscopy (ASGE), and the American Association for the Study of Liver Diseases (AASLD), regarding offers made before the (new) match. While it does not allow applicants who have accepted early offers to participate in the match before declining those offers, it does allow them to decline early offers and then participate in the match. It states, in part:

> The general spirit of this resolution is that each applicant should have an opportunity to consider all programs before making a decision and be able to participate in the Match. . . . It therefore seeks to create rules that give both programs and applicants the confidence that applicants and positions will remain available to be filled through the Match and not withdrawn in advance of it.
>
> This resolution addresses the issue that some applicants may be persuaded or coerced to make commitments prior to, or outside of, the Match. . . . Any applicant may participate in the matching process . . . by . . . resigning the accepted position if he/she wishes to submit a rank order list of programs . . . The spirit of this resolution is to make it unprofitable for program directors to press applicants to accept early offers, and to give applicants an opportunity to consider all offers.[22]

The gastroenterology match for 2007 fellows was held June 21, 2006, and succeeded in attracting 121 of the 154 eligible fellowship programs (79 percent). Ninety-eight percent of the positions offered in the match were filled through the match. Niederle, Proctor, and Roth (2008) show that in the second year of the new centralized match the interview dates were successfully pushed back and are now comparable to those of other internal medicine specialties that have used a centralized match for many years. Furthermore, there is considerable enthusiasm for the new match.

---

22. http://www.gastro.org/user-assets/Documents/04_Education_Training/Match/Match_Resolution_Nov_5_05_final.pdf.

7.5.3   Other Effects of the GI Match

There is an additional unexpected advantage of the match. It changed not only the timing but also the nature of interviews between candidates and fellowship programs (Niederle, Proctor, and Roth 2008). Interviews conducted prior to the match were more informative than those that had been conducted as part of the decentralized hiring process, and not only because they are now conducted later in applicants' careers, and hence with more information. The early impression is that the fact that interviews no longer lead immediately to offers changes the interaction: candidates are more relaxed, less anxious to please, and the discussion is more focused on the fellowship and the candidate, that is, on the transfer of information relevant to evaluating the quality of the match between that candidate and that position.

A further advantage of using a centralized match, briefly mentioned previously, is that a match also allows for programs to flexibly fill different kinds of positions. The GI fellowship match has been set up through the NRMP/SMS so that programs may offer four different tracks or categories through the match: (a) clinical, (b) clinical investigator research, (c) basic science research, and (d) research. Each track in every program is given a unique identifying code number by the NRMP/Specialty Matching Services (SMS). For each track, a program will submit a separate rank order list of applicants in preferred order. Furthermore, the program can specify that if it does not fill all of its available positions for one of its tracks, the position(s) can be *reverted* (i.e., reassigned) to one of the other tracks. In particular, by using the flexibility of the reversion algorithm, the match removes the pressure on programs to fill research positions early because, if a research position cannot be filled, it can automatically be converted into a clinical position.

Note that the move to a match does not appear to be a Pareto improvement: not all prospective GI fellows and GI program directors benefit from a match compared to a decentralized market. Recall that a decentralized market is a very local market, in which GI fellows were often internal medicine residents at the same hospital. In a more national market mediated by the match, therefore, some lower-prestige programs that were accustomed to recruiting talented local residents may find that these residents can now go to more prestigious programs elsewhere. Indeed, there are GI fellowship programs that were not pressing for gastroenterology to rejoin the match, and preferred the market to operate in a decentralized way, for this reason (Ehrinpreis 2004).[23]

---

23. This was seen very clearly in the experimental results of McKinney, Niederle, and Roth (2005). In the lab, unraveled markets were less efficient, and so there was less assortative matching. But this meant that some low-productivity employers were matched with some frequency to higher productivity workers than they could attract at a stable match, and such employers do less well under a stable matching mechanism operated at an efficient time (see also Niederle and Roth 2009).

7.6   Gastroenterology as a Case Study of Some General Phenomena

The market for gastroenterology fellows provides a case study for the effects of a centralized match and illustrates some challenges facing decentralized markets. As we have discussed, in periods in which it was decentralized, the market for gastroenterology fellows unraveled, but a centralized clearinghouse helped the market maintain thickness, avoided congestion, and with appropriate supporting rules about offers and acceptances, made it safe for applicants and employers to participate.

Which of the lessons learned from the GI market have relevance for other markets? And what makes markets prone to the problems faced by gastroenterologists—namely, lack of thickness, congestion, and lack of safety for market participants to act straightforwardly according to their preferences? While we were able to study the gastroenterology fellowship market in unusual detail, we observe many pieces of the pattern in other markets (cf. Roth and Xing 1994, 1997). Most recently we studied the market for orthopedic surgery fellows, which shows patterns very much like the market for GI fellows (Harner et al. 2008).

Another market recently studied in detail is the market for law clerkships. A prestigious and valuable career step for lawyers, after they finish the three years of law school, is to clerk for a senior federal judge. Over the past decades, the market moved from hiring students at the end of the third year to the beginning or middle of the second year of law school. The past two decades have been characterized by a multitude of reforms that try to regulate the timing and nature of the hiring process. These lasted, on average, three years, and share the fact that they all failed, apart from the most recent attempt, which is still ongoing (Avery et al. 2007).

While most of the market is now officially coordinated to make offers only after a specific point in time (most recently, this was Monday two weeks after Labor Day), the market is still thin. Most offers are exploding offers, which are often accepted instantly (even when they are not from the most preferred judge who offered an interview), resulting in a market that moves very fast. Because congestion has not been solved and exploding offers are still ubiquitous, a large proportion of applicants only receive one offer, and many judges do not make multiple rounds of offers. This is not a marketplace in which applicants can safely wait for more desirable offers, or judges can wait to make offers until they interview all candidates.

Hence, moving a market to an agreed-upon time window is not sufficient to solve problems of thickness, congestion, and safety. Indeed, the market appears to once more be experiencing some unraveling. Many judges have made offers shortly before the allowed time. Those who do so have access to a large applicant pool, and no information on applicants is lost by moving only a few days early.

Another well-studied market that experienced problems similar to those in gastroenterology is the very small market of post-season college football games, called "bowls" (Roth and Xing 1994; Fréchette, Roth, and Ünver 2007). In the early 1990s, the determination of which teams would play each other in which bowls was often made when several games still remained to play in the regular fall season. Most bowls had long-term contracts with football conferences, at least for one of the two teams that would play in their post-season bowl game, and had to recruit the other team. The National Collegiate Athletic Association (NCAA) tried for years to prevent the unraveling of the dates at which bowls and teams finalized agreements about which teams would play in which bowls. However, it gave up in failure following the 1990 to 1991 football season, in which early matching—when there were still four games left to play in the regular season—(once again) led to poorly matched teams. (A team that looks like a champion with four games still left to play will not look as good at the end of the season if it has lost some of those games.) Starting in 1992, a series of reforms eventually led to a reorganization through the Bowl Championship Series (BCS), in which a consortium of four bowls (Rose, Fiesta, Orange, and Sugar) and six athletic conferences agreed to do the matching of teams to bowls only after the conclusion of all regular season games, and always allow for a matchup in one of the participating bowls between the two highest-ranked teams in the BCS rankings. Fréchette, Roth, and Ünver (2007) show that the missed championship matchups (i.e., the number one team playing against the number two team according to the Associated Press [AP] Sportswriters' end of regular season rankings) in the precoalition era were due not only to precommitments of conferences to bowls, but largely also due to in-season unraveling that led to the selection of teams while games were still to be played.[24] Matchups between top-ranked teams has significantly increased in the coalition era, which has led to more viewers as measured by Nielsen ratings of the televised games. To the extent that the number of viewers is a measure of the output of this industry, this means that the changes in market organization that led to later and improved matchings substantially increased output and efficiency.

7.6.1   Do Problems of Congestion, Thickness, and Safety Afflict Only Special Markets?

How special is the market for GI fellows? Given the variety of markets that have experienced at least some of the failures that afflicted the GI fellows market, we consider some features of the market that we know are *not* special.

---

24. Four weeks prior to the end of the season, the top two teams have only a 35 percent chance to remain the top two teams at the end of the season, while it is 69 percent one week prior to the end of the season (and 100 percent if the teams are picked after the conclusion of the regular season [Fréchette, Roth, and Ünver 2007]).

The Size of the Market

The GI fellows market has about 300 fellows a year. The market for post-season college football bowls is substantially smaller, while the market for medical residents is much larger, with over 20,000 positions a year. An even larger market that has experienced significant unraveling is the market for college admission. In the late nineties, many highly ranked universities filled 40 to 60 percent of their slots through "early admission" (Avery, Fairbanks, and Zeckhauser 2003). In early admission, as opposed to regular admission, students submit their applications around October or November, as opposed to January; that is, without information about their fall semester of their last year in high school. Most early admissions programs allow students to only apply early to one program, and some (called "binding early decision") require students to agree to attend if accepted early. In this respect, early college admissions is not only unraveled in time, but it also becomes a thin market in which at least some students can entertain no more than one offer of admission.

Entry-Level Labor Markets Only?

The market for college football bowls has suffered from problems of thickness, congestion, and safety.[25] So has the market for college admissions (although it shares some of the property of an entry level labor market).

Price-Regulated Markets Only?

The market for college football bowls is a market in which prices are not regulated but which also suffered from unraveling. Similarly, in the late 1980s, the market for new law associates at large law firms substantially unraveled as summer associate positions increasingly became the channel through which new lawyers were hired, in a market that also showed active yearly wage competition (see Roth and Xing 1994).

7.6.2   Discussion

It is worth spending a little time reflecting on why unraveled, congested markets fail to produce competitive, stable outcomes; that is, why standard arbitrage and recontracting arguments fail. Suppose there is an outcome that is not competitive—why would a firm and a worker who would both prefer to be matched to each other not act on this, and match to each other, as opposed to his or her current partner? There are (at least) two constraints commonly observed in naturally occurring markets. The worker may have

25. Li and Rosen (1998), Li and Suen (2000), and Suen (2000) show how unraveling can occur as a form of insurance in competitive markets. In their models, markets clear early but remain competitive. In the markets we study, the decentralized markets do not appear to be well modeled as perfectly competitive markets. See also Halaburda (2007), who models unraveling as a function of how correlated are the preferences of firms for workers.

agreed to some prior commitment and may not be free to change his or her mind. Alternatively, if firms have a limited number of positions, the firm may have already hired another worker, who it cannot fire at will, or easily, or without loss of reputation. Then why did the firm and the worker make these prior commitments in the first place? For firms and workers to realize their best possible outcomes, the market has to transmit sufficient information to allow firms and workers to determine their stable match partner without first engaging in binding commitments. Much of the benefit of a market has to do with bringing together many buyers and sellers at the same time, so that they can consider a wide range of possible transactions. This is, however, not what happens in unraveled markets that experience exploding offers: in such markets, participants are not able to gather information about multiple options and then act on that information to seek out their most preferred alternatives. Choices must be made from a very small set of alternatives and in a short period of time. Decisions are reached on the basis of very limited information.

While there are not many detailed models of congested decentralized markets, Niederle and Yariv (2009) show theoretically how exploding offers, even in markets in which no other frictions are present, in general do not allow participants to reach a stable outcome. The problem is that the transmission of information is reduced compared to markets in which offers are tendered without a binding deadline.[26]

This description of obstacles to a stable outcome suggests that markets that are especially prone to unraveling are markets in which frictions are important, such as high costs of making an offer, or a long time required to make an offer (or a high cost of waiting for some participants). It may also be that markets in which employers are not very flexible in the number of workers they can hire are especially vulnerable to the difficulties caused by congestion. Recall, for example, the college football bowls: in a market in which transactions are made early, there are costs to waiting too long to try to engage a team, as good teams may become committed to other bowls. Neither can a bowl simply add a third team to its game because it turns out that a good team was overlooked early in the market. That is, a bowl needs to field exactly two teams. Similarly, medical residency and fellowship programs have inelastic demand for residents and fellows because of the way that funding and sometimes accreditation of those programs are determined by their ratio of doctors to patients.

In contrast to markets in which the number of contract partners is strictly limited, in the market for graduate students most departments are somewhat flexible as to the number of students in their incoming class. This may be the main reason that they can successfully use the Council of Graduate Schools

---

26. See also Segal (2007) on the information needed to determine if an outcome is stable.

policy that promotes open offers to regulate the timing of their market (see section 7.5.2).

In the market for GI fellows, a similar policy was successful *in combination* with a centralized clearinghouse to solve the congestion problem. Since fellowship programs have quite inelastic demand for fellows, it is likely that, in the absence of a clearinghouse, a policy promoting open offers would have been insufficient. Before adopting a centralized match, the market for residents tried a policy of advocating open offers, but failed, because of the congestion that resulted when many offers all had deadlines at roughly the same time, so that employers whose offers were rejected found that most applicants had already accepted positions (Roth 1984, 2003).

In addition to markets in which the number of positions is very inflexible, many markets that experience unraveling are also markets in which there is important heterogeneity. Consider once more the market for college football bowls: there is a very important difference between the best team and the third best team, not to mention the seventeenth best. If all teams were the same, the problem of finding a good match of bowls and teams would be much more tractable. But because viewership is driven most by the chance to see the number one ranked team play the number two ranked team, bowls were willing to tolerate considerable risk to sign up early teams that might be number one or two when the season ended.

It appears therefore that markets in which there is not a high degree of flexibility in the number of positions, and in which heterogeneity is important, are markets that may be particularly susceptible to problems associated with thickness, congestion, and safety. Entry-level labor markets for elite professionals often seem to fit this profile, particularly when the simultaneous entry of many new workers (e.g., upon graduation from medical or law school) exacerbates potential congestion since many workers have to be matched at the same time.

Do Centralized Markets Increase Efficiency?

There are several levels of efficiency that can be considered. Simple Pareto efficiency is hard to violate: for example, in a market in which all sides agree on which are the good jobs and the good candidates, a matching that assigns the worst candidates to the best jobs is still Pareto efficient, as an assortative match would make low-quality candidates worse off. It is very hard to gather data on narrower notions of efficiency; for example, to measure if an unraveled market lowers the total welfare or productivity of gastroenterologists compared to a centralized match. It is, however, the case that the majority of fellows and program directors welcomed the new system.

This is why it was useful to study college football bowls, in which the coalition era led to an increase in viewership, a reasonable proxy for output. In laboratory experiments, too, total welfare (sum of earnings) is in general lower for unraveled markets, due to the costs imposed by unraveling (either direct costs, or costs due to inefficient matchups, when hiring occurs before the final quality of applicants is known [Niederle and Roth 2009]).

Thus, although we often cannot measure efficiency loss due to unraveling, we have found inefficiency when we can measure it.

Why Do Only Some Markets Organize through a Centralized Clearinghouse?

Most markets that are organized through a centralized clearinghouse are markets that both (a) experienced very severe unraveling or congestion, in which the resulting inefficiencies were very widely felt, and (b) have a strong set of market organizations and institutions that were able to effectively coordinate market participants. This is certainly true for many medical labor markets that use a centralized match.[27]

While the sizable number of markets that use a centralized clearinghouse is still only a small proportion among all entry-level labor markets, many markets do experience problems of thickness, congestion, and safety. This means that employers, when making offers, not only have to assess how much they like each worker, but also how likely it is that the worker will accept an offer. This is because offers often have opportunity costs, because there are only a fixed number of positions, and the market moves ahead—that is, the pool of applicants for future offers becomes smaller over time, sometimes very rapidly. That is, there are costs to making offers that get rejected, since, in the meantime, other desirable candidates may have accepted commitments elsewhere.

Some markets that experience congestion and unraveling sometimes seek relief through other means than a centralized clearinghouse: they try to facilitate the process of transmitting information about how much candidates are interested in potential employers (see e.g., Roth and Xing 1997; Coles and Niederle 2007). In the economics junior market (for new PhDs), congestion is an issue when deciding which subset of about thirty applicants to interview at the ASSA meetings. Many departments face real constraints, as they have too many outstanding candidates they could interview, but need to make sure they also interview candidates that they would have a chance to hire later on. In this market it has been common that letters from advisors often would transmit specific interest for a place, or maybe even a country or continent. Last year, the AEA[28] instituted a centralized signaling facility,

---

27. The absence of a single strong professional society is presently making it somewhat difficult to change the market organization in the currently unraveled market for orthopedic surgery fellows. There are multiple orthopedic subspecialties that hire similar fellows. This is in contrast to the gastroenterologists, in which the American Gastroenterology Association had the largest number of members, and managed to coordinate with three other professional organizations on adopting a match, and appropriate policies to foster it.

28. Through its Ad Hoc Committee on the Job Market (Alvin E. Roth [chair], John Cawley, Philip Levine, Muriel Niederle, and John Siegfried). See http://www.aeaweb.org/joe/signal/signaling.pdf.

which applicants could use to credibly transmit signs of interest to employers, by allowing each job candidate to send a signal to at most two potential
employers. This was used extensively; about 1,000 job candidates used the
service in the year 2006 to 2007 (see Roth 2008b).

Market Failure and Market Design

Markets of all sorts need to provide thickness, deal with congestion, and
make participation safe. Market failures often involve the failure to accom-
plish one or more of these things. How such failures can be fixed, however,
often depends on the details of the particular market in question.

Consider again the problem of coordinating a market around a centralized clearinghouse, as opposed to having employers make early offers in a
decentralized way. In the gastroenterology fellows market, the four relevant
professional associations did not feel they could prevent program directors
from making early exploding offers, but they did believe that they could
effectively empower applicants to deal with such offers by allowing them to
change their minds later. This was effective in moving the market from early
exploding offers at dispersed times to wide participation in a clearinghouse.

Orthopedic surgery fellows face a very similarly unraveled market, with
early offers at dispersed times (Harner et al. 2008). There is considerable
doubt in that community, however, whether a policy allowing applicants to
change their minds about accepted early offers would be as effective as it has
been in gastroenterology. (Among other things, there is doubt that junior
surgeons would feel able to break promises to senior surgeons, even if this
was sanctioned by the professional societies.) However, unlike the case in the
gastroenterology market, a number of the orthopedic surgery professional
organizations feel that they could police the behavior of program directors
and effectively prevent them from making early offers by imposing sanctions
on offenders. Thus it is possible that the path to a labor clearinghouse in the
orthopedic surgery market may be different from the one in gastroenterology. (This transition may also be complicated by the fact that there are fifteen
professional organizations involved, rather than just four.)

The problems faced by federal judges who wish to reform the perenni-
ally chaotic market for clerks is made more difficult by the fact that they
face a combination of the problems that confront gastroenterologists and
orthopedic surgeons. Like the gastroenterologists, judges have no professional organization that is able to prevent early offers by judges. Like the
orthopedic surgeons, judges may not be able to adopt any policies that would
effectively allow law students to change their minds after having accepted
an early offer. (In fact, in that market, not only do law students not feel free
to change their minds about accepted offers, often they do not feel free to
decline the first offer they receive; cf. Avery et al. [2001, 2007]; Haruvy, Roth,
and Unver [2006].)

Sometimes, policies that might promote a centralized clearinghouse face objections having nothing to do with feasibility. In the market for clinical neuropsychologists, a policy empowering applicants to change their minds after accepting an early offer seems feasible in principle. However, there are strong feelings on the part of some involved that such a policy would be repugnant. The current president of the relevant professional organization said in an e-mail "I have said it once, and I will say it again: Two wrongs do not make a right. To state it another way: The end does not justify the means. I will be strongly opposed to any attempt at [a] . . . policy that allows candidates to accept an offer outside of the match, participate in the match anyway, and then renege on their earlier 'acceptance.'" Constraints imposed by repugnance toward certain kinds of transactions may be as powerful as constraints imposed by the nature of the market, and have to be taken seriously by market designers (see Roth 2007).

While the underlying problems are similar in the four markets discussed previously, namely to ensure that offers and acceptances are made in a late, centralized market, the possible solutions and policies to achieve that depend on the details of the market, including constraints given by the structure of the market as well as its social norms.

7.7   Conclusions

The market for gastroenterology fellows provides a case study of market failure and of the ways in which centralized clearinghouses can sometimes fix them. It appears that labor markets and other heterogeneous markets can suffer from congestion, which can in turn lead to strategic behavior that can result in lack of thickness and add risk to straightforward participation in the market. Consequently these markets may not always function efficiently when left to their own devices, but may need market institutions to facilitate commerce. Professional organizations can sometimes play a useful intermediary role in establishing and maintaining such institutions. More research is needed to try to understand how labor markets work in detail, so that we can better understand when they work well, and can fix them when they are broken.

References

Avery, C., A. Fairbanks, and R. Zeckhauser. 2003. *The early admissions game: Joining the elite.* Cambridge, MA: Harvard University Press.
Avery, C., C. Jolls, R. A. Posner, and A. E. Roth. 2001. The market for federal judicial law clerks. *University of Chicago Law Review* 68:793–902.
———. 2007. The new market for federal judicial law clerks. *University of Chicago Law Review* 74 (Spring): 447–86.
Bauer, W. T., W. Fackler, K. Kongara, C. Matteoni, B. Shen, and M. Vaezi, 1999.

Comment to "It's Time to Bring the Best and Brightest Back to Gastroenterology." *Gastroenterology* 116 (4): 1014.

Bulow, J., and J. Levin. 2006. Matching and price competition. *American Economic Review* 96 (3): 652–68.

Coles, P., and M. Niederle. 2007. Signaling in matching markets. Preliminary Working Paper, May.

Ehrinpreis, M. N. 2004. Con: The gastroenterology fellowship match: R.I.P. *American Journal of Gastroenterology* 99:7.

Fréchette, G., A. E. Roth, and M. U. Ünver. 2007. Unraveling yields inefficient matchings: Evidence from post-season college football bowls. *Rand Journal of Economics* 38 (4): 967–82.

Gale, D., and L. S. Shapley. 1962. College admissions and the stability of marriage. *American Mathematical Monthly* 69 (1): 9–15.

Gerson, L. 1999. To match or not to match. In *Gastroenterology: An interview with David Brenner, MD, Chair of AGA's Manpower and Training Committee. AGA Trainee & Young GI News* 5 (1). Avaialble at: http://www.gastro.org/trainee/trainee6.html.

Halaburda, H. W. 2007. Unravelling in two-sided matching markets and similarity of preferences. Harvard Business School Working Paper no. 09-068. Cambridge, MA: Harvard University.

Harner, C. D., A. S. Ranawat, M. Niederle, A. E. Roth, G. P. DeRosa, P. J. Stern, S. R. Hurwitz, W. Levine, and D. Hu. 2008. Current state of fellowship employment: Is a match necessary? Is it possible? *Journal of Bone and Joint Surgery* 90:1375–84.

Haruvy, E., A. E. Roth, and M. U. Ünver. 2006. The dynamics of law clerk matching: An experimental and computational investigation of proposals for reform of the market. *Journal of Economic Dynamics and Control* 30 (3): 457–86.

Immorlica, N., and M. Mahdian. 2005. Marriage, honesty, and stability. *SODA 2005:* 53–62.

Kagel, J. H., and A. E. Roth. 2000. The dynamics of reorganization in matching markets: A laboratory experiment motivated by a natural experiment. *Quarterly Journal of Economics* 115 (1): 201–35.

Kelso, A. S., and V. P. Crawford. 1982. Job matching, coalition formation, and gross substitutes. *Econometrica* 50 (6): 1483–1504.

Kojima, F. 2007. Matching and price competition: Comment. *American Economic Review* 97 (3): 1027–31.

Kojima, F., and P. A. Pathak. Forthcoming. Incentives and stability in large two-sided matching markets. *American Economic Review.*

Li, H., and S. Rosen. 1998. Unraveling in matching markets. *American Economic Review* 88 (June): 371–87.

Li, H., and W. Suen. 2000. Risk sharing, sorting, and early contracting. *Journal of Political Economy* 108 (October): 1058–91.

McKinney, C. N., M. Niederle, and A. E. Roth. 2005. The collapse of a medical labor clearinghouse (and why such failures are rare). *American Economic Review* 95 (3): 878–89.

Meyer, G. S., I. Jacoby, H. Krakauer, D. W. Powell, J. Aurand, and P. McCardle. 1996. Gastroenterology workforce modeling. *Journal of the American Medical Association* 276 (September): 689–94.

Niederle, M. 2007. Competitive wages in a match with ordered contracts. *American Economic Review* 97 (5):1957–69. Available at: http://www.stanford.edu/~niederle/Niederle.OrderedContracts.pdf.

Niederle, M., D. D. Proctor, and A. E. Roth. 2006. What will be needed for the new GI fellowship match to succeed? *Gastroenterology* 130 (January): 218–24.

———. 2008. The gastroenterology fellowship match: The first two years. *Gastroenterology* 135 (2): 344–46.

Niederle, M., and A. E. Roth. 2003a. Relationship between wages and presence of a match in medical fellowships. *Journal of the American Medical Association* 290 (9): 1153–54.

———. 2003b. Unraveling reduces mobility in a labor market: Gastroenterology with and without a centralized match. *Journal of Political Economy* 111 (6): 1342–52.

———. 2004. The gastroenterology fellowship match: How it failed, and why it could succeed once again. *Gastroenterology* 127:658–66.

———. 2005. The gastroenterology fellowship market: Should there be a match? *American Economic Review Papers and Proceedings* 95 (2): 372–75.

———. 2009. Market Culture: How Rules Governing Exploding Offers Affect Market Performance. *American Economic Journal: Microeconomics* 1, 2 (August), forthcoming.

Niederle, M., and L. Yariv. 2009. Decentralized matching with aligned preferences. NBER working paper, 14840.

Roth, A. E. 1982. The economics of matching: Stability and incentives. *Mathematics of Operations Research* 7 (4): 617–28.

———. 1984. The evolution of the labor market for medical interns and residents: A case study in game theory. *Journal of Political Economy* 92 (6): 991–1016.

———. 1985. The college admissions problem is not equivalent to the marriage problem. *Journal of Economic Theory* 36 (2): 277–88.

———. 1990. New physicians: A natural experiment in market organization. *Science* 250 (4987): 1524–28.

———. 1991. A natural experiment in the organization of entry level labor markets: Regional markets for new physicians and surgeons in the U.K. *American Economic Review* 81 (June): 415–40.

———. 2002. The economist as engineer: Game theory, experimental economics and computation as tools of design economics. *Econometrica* 70 (4): 1341–78.

———. 2003. The origins, history, and design of the resident match. *Journal of the American Medical Association* 289 (7): 909–12.

———. 2007. Repugnance as a constraint on markets. *Journal of Economic Perspectives* 21 (3): 37–58.

———. 2008a. Deferred acceptance algorithms: History, theory, practice, and open questions. *International Journal of Game Theory* (Special issue in honor of David Gale's eighty-fifth birthday) 36 (March): 537–69.

———. 2008b. What have we learned from market design? Hahn Lecture, *Economic Journal* 118 (March): 285–310.

Roth, A. E., and E. Peranson. 1999. The redesign of the matching market for American physicians: Some engineering aspects of economic design. *American Economic Review* 89 (4): 748–79.

Roth, A. E., and M. Sotomayor. 1990. *Two-sided matching: A study in game-theoretic modeling and analysis.* Cambridge, MA: Econometric Society Monograph Series, Cambridge University Press.

Roth, A. E., and X. Xing. 1994. Jumping the gun: Imperfections and institutions related to the timing of market transactions. *American Economic Review* 84 (September): 992–1044.

———. 1997. Turnaround Time and Bottlenecks in Market Clearing: Decentralized Matching in the Market for Clinical Psychologists. *Journal of Political Economy,* 105:284–329.

Segal, I. 2007. The communication requirements of social choice rules and supporting budget sets. *Journal of Economic Theory* 136 (1): 341–78.

Suen, W. 2000. A competitive theory of equilibrium and disequilibrium unravelling in two-sided matching. *Rand Journal of Economics* 31 (Spring): 101–20.

8

Helping Workers Online and Offline
Innovations in Union and Worker Organization Using the Internet

Richard B. Freeman and M. Marit Rehavi

Trade unions have been the major labor market intermediary for workers in market economies. Unions provide workers with information about the workplace and job market, represent workers in work-related grievances, and are workers' voice in dealing with collective goods at the workplace. In addition, unions are the key labor market intermediary that monitors business compliance with contracts, labor laws and regulations, and that lobbies on behalf of workers. Historically unions have depended on collective bargaining with employers to improve compensation and workplace conditions and have financed their activities with dues from members in collective bargaining sites.

In the United States, the role of unions as providers of services to workers has diminished as union density and collective bargaining coverage have shrunk. Despite survey evidence that large and increasing proportions of nonunionized workers desire union representation (Freeman and Rogers 2006), the number of workers in unions has fallen relative to the number of wage and salary workers in the private sector. Labor and community activists, nongovernmental organizations, and firms' own human resource departments have tried to provide some of the services that unions his-

Richard B. Freeman holds the Herbert Ascherman Chair in Economics at Harvard University and is director of the Labor Studies Program at the National Bureau of Economic Research. M. Marit Rehavi is an assistant professor of economics at the University of Michigan.

We are grateful to Paul Nowak and John Wood of the TUC for their helping us obtain data and carrying out the survey of www.unionreps.org.uk. Our discussion of Working America benefited from the Labor and Worklife Program at Harvard Law School Workshop on Working America, November 13–14, 2007, and in particular from the presentation by Robert Fox on the organization's online activities. Jason Abaluck, Rishi Patel, Morgan Freeman, and David Owen provided excellent research assistance. Peter Cappelli and David Autor gave valuable comments.

torically delivered to workers, with limited success (Freeman, Hersch, and Mishel 2005).

In the United Kingdom union density has stabilized at higher rates than in the United States, but the range of issues subject to collective bargaining has narrowed and union ability to affect outcomes has weakened. With unions helping workers only modestly through collective bargaining, an increasing proportion of workers in organized workplaces free ride on unions, while those in firms without a recognized union show no great desire for unionization.

Can unions in the United States and United Kingdom (and in other countries where unions face problems) resurrect their role in delivering services to workers and reestablish their bargaining power? Or, is unionism headed for obsolescence?

Some analysts argue that the innovative use of the Internet and other computer-related technologies will enable unions to resurrect their role (Shostak 1999; Darlington 2000; Freeman and Rogers 2002b; Diamond and Freeman 2002). In these analyses, modern information-communication technology is a tool to revolutionize the way unions provide services to workers that will allow them to reinvent their role in market capitalism and regain lost ground. Freeman and Rogers (2002b), in particular, argue that the Internet creates the opportunity for unions to develop a new union form, labeled open source (OS) unionism, which operates over the Internet and in communities as well as at work sites.

Columns (1) and (2) of table 8.1 provide a capsule summary of the differences between Freeman and Rogers' OS form and traditional unionism. As the name suggests, the OS union enlists members and delivers services online. It creates a virtual union hall through its website. It offers expert information on workplace issues and establishes a place for members to exchange views on work-related issues. Rather than having a one-size-fits-all membership structure, the OS union charges members based on the services they obtain. Freeman and Rogers argue that because OS unions will have less power at workplaces than traditional collective bargaining based unions, "Open source unions would not be able to turn inward when they faced struggle, but would have to look outward. They would be pressured to develop a more coherent and attractive public face and become a more visible source of stewardship and moral value in the broader economy. Open source unions would gain the political clout and social influence that would come of its playing a broader public role" (Freeman and Rogers 2002b, 22–23).

Absent bargaining clout and the potential for workplace actions such as strikes, what tools could an OS union have to pressure an employer and intercede on the behalf of workers? It would use online and area-based offline activities to pressure employees. The experience of www.greedyassociates. com, a website for young attorneys whose main feature is a message board

Table 8.1   **The open source union form versus traditional collective bargaining**

	Traditional	Open Source form
	Membership	
By location	Workplace-based	Independent of workplace; recruited over Internet; local areas outside workplace
Employer role	Dependent on employer recognition and collective bargaining contract	No veto of representation by employer
Level of dues	High, check-off by employer	Modest/nominal
Free-riders	Incentive to free ride: U.S. agency shop fees	Customized services to members only or by fee
	Activities	
Primary business	Collective bargaining	Political action on broad worker issues; support workers at individual employers
Delivery of services	Workplace or economic sector depending on locus of collective bargaining	Internet; local area
Service providers	Paid union staffers	Volunteers at local level; Internet and activist volunteers; Expert bots
Budget	High, based on substantial dues check-off	Modest, with potential support from traditional unions, grants from other groups
Main weakness	Depends on getting employer to agree to collective bargaining	Depends on getting workers/community to assist in workplace disputes
	Source of power	
Workplace	Industrial action, strikes	Information
Outside workplace	Political pressure	Members at other work sites; Political pressure; local community

Source: Derived and altered from Freeman and Rogers (2002a).

about employment opportunities, shows how effective online pressures can be. In the late 1990s, when major law firms paid newly hired associates more in Silicon Valley than elsewhere, complaints from associates working outside Silicon Valley forced the firms to raise pay in New York and other major cities, for fear that bad publicity would reduce their chances of recruiting top law students in the future. Taras and Gesser (2003) view the message boards as potentially "the beginning of a new area of Internet organization marked by effortless and instant dissemination of information between similarly situated employees"—a virtual union hall. They speculate that other non-union workers such as bank tellers, software designers, and lab technicians, especially those who like lawyers, find themselves in high demand could benefit from a similar site, but argue that this "is not a union. It is something else" (Taras and Gesser 2003, 26–27).

The 2002 success of the American Federation of Labor and Congress of Industrial Organizations (AFL-CIO) in gaining severance pay for the non-union workers who lost their jobs at Enron provides another example. The AFL-CIO combined a website on the plight of these workers (http://www.aflcio.org/enron/connections.htm) and an e-mail campaign using its Family Network database to bombard creditor committees and Enron executives with faxes, telephone calls, and e-mails on the workers' behalf with offline activity in the form of legal action and campaigns against Enron directors. It eventually won the workers thirty-two million dollars.

Whether unions can create a viable worker-based organization outside of collective bargaining and carry out campaigns like these on a regular basis is unclear. These nascent online efforts might develop into a new form for mediating between workers and employers or they may turn out to be a digital form of public relations in support of traditional collective bargaining-based unions and their political goals. Simply adopting Internet and related technologies, as many unions have done (Diamond and Freeman 2002; Freeman 2005; Newman 2005; Stevens and Greer 2005) is not sufficient. For a new union form to succeed it has to find packages of services for workers outside of collective bargaining at costs that workers will pay, outperform competitor suppliers of those services, and overcome employer and anti-union consultant use of online as well as offline access to workers.

The history of the Knights of Labor, who organized huge numbers of workers outside of collective bargaining in the United States in the 1880s, is a warning from labor history that noncollective bargaining organizations can prove unstable. Between 1885 and 1886, the Knights grew from about 100,000 members to 700,000 members by admitting all workers (except for lawyers, bankers, liquor dealers, and gamblers) regardless of whether the workers were part of an organization that attained a collective contract. Some chapters of the Knights bargained collectively, but the Knights grew as a social movement. Faced with employer pressure, however, the Knights lost membership in the late 1880s and were defunct by the end of the century (Voss 1993; Weir 1996). The lesson that Samuel Gompers and other founders of the American Federation of Labor drew from the Knights' experience was that business unionism, in which skilled craft workers gain collective bargaining contracts with employers, was the sole viable union form. The industrial unionism of the 1930s and 1940s seemed to confirm the view that unionism was essentially synonymous with collective bargaining contracts with employers.

This study examines two union innovations in the United States and United Kingdom that challenge this orthodoxy in different ways:[1] Working America (WA), the AFL-CIO's "community affiliate" that enrolls members by canvassing them at their homes and over the Internet (www

---

1. Freeman (2005) describes other ways unions have used the Internet.

.workingamerica.org); and www.unionreps.org.uk, the Trade Union Congress' discussion board for worker representatives that enables representatives to communicate about workplace issues directly without going through union staff or employers. It considers whether combining these and other innovations could produce an open-source union form that would prosper in the Internet era and avoid the fate of the Knights.

8.1 Working America

The problem facing U.S. unionism is that private sector density and collective bargaining coverage have been falling steadily. In 2007, 7.5 percent of private-sector wage and salary workers and 12.1 percent of all wage and salary workers were union members (see http://www.bls.gov/news .release/union2.nr0.htm), which put private-sector density 13 percentage points below the density in 1980 and put overall density 10.5 points lower than in 1980. Density did, however, roughly stabilize between 2006 and 2007, suggesting that the greater allocation of resources to organizing that the AFL-CIO encouraged among its affiliates and the formation of the Change-to-Win coalition (http://www.changetowin.org/) may have helped arrest the downward trend in unionization. But perhaps this is a just a blip of stability before union density continues on its long trend downward.

As far as we can tell from public opinion surveys, the downward trend in density does not reflect workers' loss of interest in union services. To the contrary, opinion surveys show that over half of U.S. nonmanagerial nonunion workers wanted trade unions to represent them in dealing with employers in the mid-2000s—an increase over the 40 or so percent of nonunion workers who said they wanted unions in the 1990s and the roughly 30 percent who so reported in the 1980s. An even larger proportion of workers—upward of three quarters—say that they want some workplace organization exclusive of a collective bargaining union to represent them to their employer (Freeman and Rogers 2006, chapter 1).

The adversarial nature of organizing contests has contributed to the erosion of U.S. union density. Unionization drives are typically hard-fought battles that pit workers who desire to unionize against managements who do not want unions because union-induced increases in compensation reduce profits and union work rules limit managers' power at workplaces. Firms typically spend large sums of money to counter organizing campaigns and some engage in questionable or illegal actions to deter workers' efforts to unionize.

For readers unfamiliar with tactics employed to counter union organizing campaigns, the 2007 independent arbitrator's report on Yale University Hospital's efforts to thwart an organizing drive is illustrative. The hospital agreed with the city of New Haven and the Service Employees International Union to remain neutral in the campaign. However, the arbitrator found that, the agreement notwithstanding, the hospital and its labor relation consultant broke federal labor law, violated its own agreement, and regularly lied to subvert the election process (Kern 2007). Finding that the company's actions made it impossible for workers to choose to unionize in an election setting, the arbitrator ordered Yale Hospital to pay 2.3 million dollars to the union for its organizing expenses and to pay 2.2 million dollars to workers—the amount the hospital had spent on the consultants fighting worker efforts to organize—on the grounds that this represented the minimal amount the employer thought workers might have gained from unionization.[2]

American unions have pursued three strategies to counter their eroding density and management opposition to unions that engage in collective bargaining. First, unions have pressed Congress to enact laws to restrict management's ability to contest organizing efforts and avoid collective agreement when unions gain majority status. The mid-2000s vehicle for this is the Employee Free Choice Act (EFCA) (see http://araw.org/takeaction/efca/index.cfm). It requires firms to recognize a union when a majority of workers sign cards for the union. Card check removes the option for management to campaign against the union in a National Labor Relations Board election and lowers the length and cost of organizing campaigns. Employee Free Choice Act also requires firms and unions to seek first contract mediation and arbitration when employers cannot reach a contract with a newly formed union. Finally, the proposed law raises the penalties on employers for unfair labor practices against workers seeking to unionize.

Second, unions have sought recognition from employers outside the framework of the National Labor Relations Act's electoral process. They pressure management to be neutral in organizing campaigns. Unions with collective bargaining contracts bargain that the firm remain neutral in organizing drives in other plants. The successes from these activities have been too limited to affect the trend decline in union density.

Third is the strategy that we study: organizing workers outside of collective bargaining. Some unions—teachers, firefighters, and police in some states in the public sector—have organized locals for workers even though state law does not allow for collective bargaining. These unions lobby legislatures and other government officials on behalf of members. In the private sector, the Communication Workers (Nack and Tarlau 2005) has a local in IBM (www.allianceibm.org), even though it has little chance of gaining a collective con-

---

2. U.S. labor law also makes it difficult for noncollective bargaining institutions to operate at the workplace. Section 8a2 of the Taft-Hartley Act makes it illegal for firms to set up or help workers set up nonunion groups within an enterprise to confer with management over issues relating to worker concerns for fear that such groups would be "company unions." In principle, labor law protects minority unionism as much (or as little) as majority unionism but unions have generally eschewed providing services to groups who can obtain only minority union status on the grounds that without collective bargaining they could not raise sufficient dues to pay for the services.

tract, and has locals for other workers in the IT sector. These unions use the Internet to connect to members and marshal information and publicity. But the biggest and arguably most successful effort to sign up workers outside of collective bargaining is the AFL-CIO's Working America.

8.1.1   What Is Working America?

The AFL-CIO describes Working America (WA) as a membership-based "community affiliate" for the millions of workers who say they want unions but cannot get union recognition at their workplace. Working America canvasses people in their homes and over the Internet to join the affiliate, so that the employer has no power to affect their decision. In summer 2004, WA hired staff in ten cities in five states to recruit members in urban neighborhoods with many union members, on the notion that people in those areas would have favorable views of unions (Greenhouse 2004). In contrast to the associate membership schemes that AFL-CIO affiliates tried in the 1980s and 1990s to attract workers for whom they could not gain collective contracts, WA stresses participation in a social movement as the prime reason to join. To avoid any conflict with affiliate unions, it only enrolls persons who are not otherwise members of a union. In addition to communicating with members through telephone calls and mailings, WA uses its website (www.workingamerica.org) to connect with workers and regularly e-mails members. It conducts Internet polls of preferences to ascertain the issues on which members want it to campaign and organizes online actions that ask members to e-mail Congress or other decision-makers on particular issues and to pass messages to others, and organizes offline activities where it asks members to contact decision-makers as well. It has an active get-out-the-vote drive.

The leadership of WA are AFL-CIO staffers. In this respect WA resembles a Nongovernmental Organization (NGO) rather than a union, whose members elect their leadership. Perhaps the closest comparable organization is the American Association for Retired Persons, which has established itself as a key group in issues relating to retirees, enlisting millions of members at low dues ($12.50 for a person and his or her spouse in 2007) and raising most of its budget in other ways.

When WA first sent canvassers to ask workers to join a noncollective bargaining union affiliate, the organization was uncertain of the response they would get. The survey data that showed a latent demand for unionism did not ask about a nonworkplace-based union affiliate with the attributes of Working America. Perhaps workers wanted collective bargaining—or nothing at all—and would reject a nonworkplace-based organization. Perhaps their responses to hypothetical questions on unionism would prove to be a bad indicator of future behavior (McClennan 2007).

The responses to the canvassing effort were striking. Two-thirds of the people WA contacted joined the organization. By fall 2004 WA had 400,000 members. In 2007 it had 2,000,000 members, making it one of the fastest-growing groups in U.S. labor history. Targeting urban areas in likely swing states in national politics, WA amassed 700,000 members in Ohio, over one-quarter of a million in Pennsylvania, and over 90,000 in Kentucky, Virginia, Minnesota, and Michigan. It also obtained sizable numbers in Florida, Missouri, Washington, and Oregon, among other states. Some 89 percent of participants gave phone numbers so they could be contacted, and one-third provided e-mail addresses, an increase over the proportion that had provided e-mails to canvassers when WA first began signing up members. As of mid-2007 WA had 250 to 300 organizers making approximately 250,000 contacts per month. If it maintained the two-thirds success rate that it had earlier, this would translate into 170,000 new members per month, or about two million recruits per year. Additionally, the organization recruited 135,000 members through online efforts, giving it members in New York, California, Massachusetts, and other states where it did not canvass people in their homes.

Given the geographic mobility of Americans and changes in interest, some WA members invariably lose their connection to the organization over time, producing a natural rate of depreciation in the stock of members. This means that to maintain a constant stock the organization must continually recruit new members. We do not have adequate data to estimate the rate of depreciation, which likely varies across areas, demographic groups, and with the method of recruitment, political events, and the business cycle. But with WA making roughly three million contacts at the door in 2007 to 2008, membership will continue to grow at any plausible depreciation rate. The estimated cost of signing up new members is about eight dollars per member, which compares to the $2,000 or so that it costs a union to obtain a new member in collective bargaining (Freeman 2004). At this writing, WA does not require that its members pay dues. Rather, it relies on outside funding, mostly from the AFL-CIO, for its budget. It also asks for voluntary contributions of $25, which it has obtained from about 10 percent of new members.

8.1.2   Who Joins Working America?

Table 8.2 shows that the demographics of WA's membership closely mimics the demographics of the U.S. population: 37 percent of members have at least a two-year college degree, 41 percent say that they attend church at least weekly, about one third report themselves as "born again," and one in three own a gun or supports the National Rifle Association. Most members describe themselves as moderate and conservative, and about half say they are neither strong Democrats nor Republicans.

With its limited budget, WA needs an "activist" core of members to volunteer to take action on its behalf. As a way to identify potential activists, WA canvassers ask new members to write to their Congressperson or some other official about an issue that matters to them. The canvassers promise

Table 8.2 **Attributes of working America**

1. Organizing activity as of winter 2007
   Budget ~$7.5 million (per year)
   Organizers 250–300
   Cost per recruit $11.00
   Members recruited online in 2007 134,796

2. Demographics of membership | WA | U.S. adults

	WA	U.S. adults
Two-year college degree or more	37%	36%
Attend church at least weekly	41%	40%
Own a gun	32%	35%
Had parents in union	39%	

3. Online attributes of members
   Members who provide e-mail 263,000
   Percentage who join online 18%
   Actions online 59,058
   Percentage from members who join online 60%

Source: Participant presentations, Harvard seminar on Working America, November 13–14, 2007.

to pick up and mail the letter later that day. Approximately 20 to 25 percent of new members undertake this action. In 2007 WA asked its members who had provided e-mail addresses (approximately 263,000 at mid-year) to undertake online activities such as sending e-mail protests to public officials or sending e-mail messages to friends or relatives about the issue. Members who joined online were more active and committed than those who joined through the canvass and provided their e-mail: although just 18 percent of WA's e-mail database comes from those who joined on the Internet, those persons accounted for 60 percent of the online advocacy actions. To see whether online activists would assist WA outside of cyberspace, four field offices asked the online activists in their area to attend meetings on local issues and found that about 80 percent did so.

8.1.3 What Does Working America Do?

Working America's website offers members and others who join in its campaigns involvement in a social movement that it markets as having "the priorities that matter most to working people . . . (and that can) . . . make a difference for your community, for America and for your working family." While from Mancur Olson (1965) on, economists have stressed the need for some personal incentives to get people involved in organizations, studies of volunteering and charitable activity suggest that by itself the "warm glow" of participation (Andreoni 1990) can motivate behavior. Behavioral and neuro-economics demonstrate that concern for fairness is deeply rooted in the human psyche (Kahneman, Knetsch, and Thaler 1986). Experiments show that consumers are willing to pay more for goods made under good labor practices (Hiscox and Smyth 2006). Working America canvassers report that people say that they join at the doorstep because they believe that being part of a group gives them influence in local or national policies that they would never have as individuals.

Working America also offers considerable information to workers on its website on such issues as health care benefits, the subprime mortgage crisis, and rights at work. Figure 8.1 illustrates four features of the website. "Ask a Lawyer" uses volunteer lawyers from unions or associated law firms to answer questions about legal issues that arise at workplaces. In 2007, visitors to the website asked over 200 questions per month, with most of the questions coming from persons new to WA. The site also solicits information from its members. Working America's most popular feature in 2007 was a contest called "My Bad Boss," where people reported on horrid work situations. It is unclear whether reading these stories made the typical worker feel better about his or her situation or added to the desire to seek some workplace organization. The "Health Care Hustle" was a similar feature focused on problems with health care. "Word on the Street" is a blog where canvassers report their experiences. Members of Working America get access to benefits through the AFL-CIO and its Union Plus programs. The benefits include health care via Union Plus Health Savings; a half hour of free legal advice and reduced fees from participating lawyers (Union Plus Legal Service); and an inexpensive Mastercard (Working America credit card). But these are treated as minor add-ons rather than selling points of membership.

Membership gives persons the right to vote on the website for the issues of greatest importance to them. In 2007 about 40,000 members voted that health care was the number one issue for which they wanted the organization to campaign. Local chapters have lobbied for minimum wages in Oregon and Pennsylvania, funding for health care in Seattle and for school spending in other areas. The focus of WA on societal issues rather than problems at particular firms has led WA to assess its success in part by the extent to which its members turn out in elections and vote for candidates favored by the AFL-CIO. Working America's internal assessments suggest that the organization succeeds in doing this to a similar extent as collective bargaining unions do for their members.[3]

While WA is the largest U.S. union innovation that operates outside of collective bargaining, it falls short of the Open Source model in several ways. It does not offer members assistance in dealing with their employer. In fact, while the organization asks members about their industry and occupation, it does not ask for their place of employment. It does not offer a forum for discussion among members that might help create leadership and new actions from members independently of the national or local leadership. Working

3. These assessments fall short of an ideal methodology for testing the effects of WA on voting. They do not, for instance, compare the voting of WA members to that of people with similar initial views in the same area or to that of persons with similar views in areas that do not have WA chapters.

Volunteer lawyers respond to questions submitted by workers. In 2007, the site received an average of 206 questions per month; 70% of which came from persons new to Working America; the leading area of concern was about overtime pay and firing/termination

This is most popular feature: 3.2 million page views, people stayed 9.2 minutes; 4,000 bad boss stories submitted, 20,000 votes for "worst"; enrolled 6,500 new members

Generated 20,267 "actions" against hustlers; 830 stories, 65% from new members

Canvassers blog about their experiences going door to door to enroll members

Fig. 8.1   Features of the Working America website

America's Washington-based leaders determine its activities, which makes it more like a nongovernmental organization, such as AARP, than a member-driven union.

8.1.4   Can WA Maintain/Increase Membership and Achieve Financial Independence if It Remains Focused on Broad Social Issues and Political Action?

There is historic precedence and arguments on both sides of this question. The collapse of the Knights of Labor shows that labor organizations that are primarily social movements can decline quickly under pressure. The success of the AARP shows that an organization that charges minimal dues and lobbies on behalf of retired workers is viable in the United States. Models of group formation in which persons join because their neighbors join predict that such organizations should be less stable than organizations in which persons join solely for personal gain (Centola 2007). To the extent that WA's spurt in membership benefited from two terms of a Republican presidential administration aligned with business, the election of an administration more attuned to workers' interests could dampen the desire for WA, since the government would be undertaking desired actions in any case. On the other hand, a favorable national government might increase desire to participate in the organization. We suspect that the organization will eventually have to find ways to support workers at their place of employment to become a viable form. With a large membership in different parts of the country, WA has the potential to experiment with alternative ways to do this and find the best mix of services and dues for its survival.

8.2   www.unionreps.org.uk.

British unions face a different problem than U.S. unions. Union density in the United Kingdom fell in the 1980s and 1990s, then stabilized in the 2000s at about 29 percent of the workforce. In 2006 private-sector unionism was 18 percent—two-and-a-half times the density in the United States. United Kingdom employers do not fight vehemently against unionism, presumably because collective bargaining does not cost firms much—the estimated union wage premium is close to zero (Blanchflower and Bryson 2004). Government-funded national health care removes one of the major cost items associated with collective bargaining in the United States. The challenge for unions in the United Kingdom is to attract workers even though it is unable to win a sizeable union premium for them, rather than to circumvent employer opposition. About 40 percent of workers in workplaces with collective bargaining see no need to join the organization. Unions have modest budgets and staffs and rely on voluntary workers or union representatives to deliver services at the workplace and to sign up new workers as well. Voluntary union representatives at worksites are the face of unions to most workers. Representatives work a median of two to five hours per week with their employer, typically paying for the time they spend as reps at the workplace but not paying for time spent outside the workplace. Providing services through volunteers limits the amount of direct control that the unions have over the quality and types of services provided. Reps spend much of their time on health and safety issues and in dealing with employee problems with the way management treats workers, and smaller amounts of time making sure workers are paid the wages and benefits in the contract and protecting the security of employment (see appendix).

Pondering the problem of U.K. unions enrolling members at organized worksites, Darlington (2001) and Diamond and Freeman (2002) argue that unions need to improve and personalize their services to members. One plausible way to improve services is to raise the knowledge and skills of union reps. The greater the tenure and intensity of reps' efforts, the less costly is the union investment in their knowledge and skills relative to the services delivered. In the OS model, unions would use the Internet to give greater services to dues-payers in organized sites and less service to visitors at union websites. Our U.K. innovation www.unionreps.org.uk is designed to harness the knowledge of the voluntary reps to improve services to workers at low cost to union staff.

8.2.1 What Is unionreps.org?

It is a website restricted to unique representatives who receive a unique password when they sign up that seeks to create an online community for them to discuss issues that arise as part of their representative duties. The Trade Unions Congress (TUC) launched unionreps.org in 2003. In February 2006, the site had 8,400 subscribers—3.4 percent of the approximately 250,000 representatives in the United Kingdom—and had 16,818 hits per month. The users come from a range of unions, industries, and geographic regions that is representative of the U.K. union movement.[4]

The main feature of the site is a set of topical bulletin boards on which reps pose questions that other representatives can answer. In principle, this harnesses the collective wisdom of union reps to deal with workplace problems (Surowiecki 2003). By enabling all representatives to benefit from questions and answers between two or more reps and providing an archive of previous questions and answers, the site harnesses economies of scale in its provision of information. It permits asynchronous communication, since

---

4. Forty-seven percent are in the public sector, 36 percent worked in industry, and 17 percent from the service sector. By comparison, 57 percent of union members are in the public sector, 23 percent in industry, and 19 percent in service sector jobs. Thirty-five percent of unionreps.org users live in the Southern/Eastern region, 12 percent in Scotland, and 9 percent live in Wales. These figures compare to 35 percent of union members residing in the Southern/Eastern region, 10 percent in Scotland, and 6 percent in Wales. Department of Trade and Industry (DTI), Employment Market Analysis and Research, April 2005, Trade Union Membership 2004, tables 3, 7, 27.

users can post questions and answers whenever they have time. The site also provides resources directly to the reps, sends a weekly newsletter to subscribers to inform them of the latest TUC news, events, and training opportunities, and contains links to union-related news stories and to other websites and materials that may be of use to reps. It polls reps about such things as the usefulness of online training. Because content on the site comes mainly from the voluntary efforts of reps, the site requires limited maintenance by TUC staff and costs little to run.

The TUC site resembles peer-to-peer Internet information sharing sites, such as the gnutella network for sharing music, where 70 percent of members free ride and small groups provide the bulk of the material (Adar and Huberman 2000), and usenet news groups, where anonymous users post information and answer questions (Resnick et al. 2000). Because such sites can be destroyed by maliciously given or erroneous information, their success requires that the vast majority of users act in a trustworthy way. This has produced an extensive information sciences and sociology literature on trust and online cooperation in virtual communities (Rheingold 1993; Kollak 1999; Jones, Ravid, and Rafaeli 2004; Bishop 2007). The site www.unionreps.org.uk has some advantages in this respect over other information-sharing websites. Only genuine reps using their regular union e-mails and full names have access to the sites. Moreover, the union community is a connected world, so that these worker reps may encounter each other (or common acquaintances) in the union hall or at union conferences. Individuals can build reputations for giving accurate responses and their online actions can follow them into the offline world.

8.2.2   How Does www.unionreps.org.uk Work?

To answer this question and find out whether the site helped union reps deal with workplace issues, raised their morale, and created an online community of union activists, working with the TUC staffers who developed the site, we gathered three types of data on potential and actual users.

First, we surveyed two types of union reps: reps undergoing TUC training between November 2003 and April 2004,[5] who were introduced to the site and encouraged to use it (herein the TUC training sample); and online union reps who used the website independent of TUC training. We obtained 857 usable responses from the training sample and 411 usable responses from the online sample, which gave us the largest sample of union reps in the United Kingdom.

Second, we created a data set that follows *postings* that reps placed on the

---

5. To improve the skills of workplace representatives, the TUC runs short training sessions around the country. Each year some 37,000 reps—or 15 percent of the total—are involved in a TUC training program. Our sample of trainees comes from two sources: in fall 2003, instructors at TUC training centers gave surveys to the worker representatives who passed through the centers; additionally, the TUC mailed copies of the survey directly to 1,000 previous TUC worker-representative training participants.

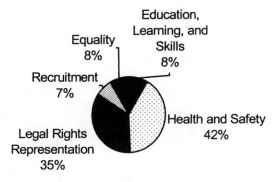

Fig. 8.2   Main areas of bulletin board discussion

website from June to December 2003. At the time of our study, unionreps
.org.uk had five bulletin boards: education, equality, health and safety, law
and representation, and organization and recruitment.[6] Figure 8.2 shows
the distribution of postings across the areas. We took all postings from the
bulletin board save for the health and safety area. We categorized the questions and responses by the individual who posted the comment, the time it
was posted, and the thread (query) to which it belonged. This meant that
we coded the data as X_{fit}, where X is a variable reflecting the content of the
question or response, f identifies the thread to which it belongs; i relates to
the person making the posting; and t is the time of the response. The X variables included the content of the query/response, whether it gave or asked
for off-site contact, whether it referred to official data (from the union or the
government), its relevance to the initial question, and so on. We use these
data to analyze the dynamics of the online discussion.

Third, we conducted a longitudinal survey of persons in our initial cross-
sectional survey. This follow-up survey was conducted in 2005 to 2006. We
obtained 266 responses from the group who received TUC training and 129
responses from the group of reps who were initially users of the site. This
enabled us to examine whether the trainees who were introduced to the site
as part of their training used the site in the future and whether use of the
site influenced users over time.

When we began the research, it was debatable whether the typical union
reps were Internet ready to make a website part of their representative activities. As table 8.3 shows, we found that most representatives were so ready: 45
percent of reps surveyed at TUC training centers reported using the Internet
daily; another 21 percent said they used it at least twice a week. Most had
access to the Internet at home. The table also shows that subscribers to
unionreps.org use the Internet more frequently. There was little difference in

6. In November 2004, the TUC added a pensions bulletin board to www.unionreps.org.uk.

Table 8.3   Union reps Internet use

	Regular trainees (%)	Unionreps.org (OS) (%)
Use Internet daily	45	87
Use Internet often		
For rep duties	32	63
Other union activities	24	50
Regular job	30	43
Use source often or very often		
Training material	42	43
Union staff	34	29
Internet	31	66
Older/exp workers	31	22
TUC	5	5
Use Internet as part of rep work to find out about		
Training possibilities	61	78
Worker rights and legislation	82	96
Pay/working conditions elsewhere	43	60
To inform workers of union/activities	60	76
To communicate with workers		69
To keep in touch/exchange information with		
Union officials	56	72
Other union reps	59	80
Other unions/worker orgs	38	60
Visit website often		
Own union site	9	19
TUC site	6	11
Unionreps site	3	15

Source: Unionreps.org data files.

use of the Internet between men and women, and across age groups.[7] Most important, many union reps report that they used the Internet in the course of their representative duties for a wide spectrum of activities.

The sample of subscribers made greater use of the Internet for representative duties than did the TUC trainees, but even the trainees (who had not yet been introduced to the site) used the Internet regularly for their representative duties—indeed, more so than for other union activity or on their jobs. Both groups used the Internet to learn about employment regulations and training opportunities, to communicate with the workers they represent, with other worker representatives, and with union officials. Given these rates of Internet access and usage it is clear that a web-based resource can reach most union representatives.[8] Indicative of how users view the site,

7. Those aged sixty and older are slightly less likely to use the Internet daily, but even 75 percent of those aged sixty and older report using the Internet more than once a week.

8. In the United States this could be more complicated. The NLRB's December 2007 ruling that firms in the United States may prohibit workers from using their work e-mail systems to send union-related e-mails could complicate efforts to use e-mail to reach those who mainly use the Internet at work.

over three quarters of those in our online survey report that they recommended the site to a friend. This, plus the growing number of subscribers to the site, suggest that many users find the site valuable.

8.2.3 What Does Analysis of Threads Tell Us?

The bulletin board at unionreps.org depends on questions posed by union reps, who post their question because they expect someone else on the site can help answer it in a reasonable time period. Whether this in fact occurs should depend on the number of persons on the site who could answer the question relative to the number of other questions on the site. The more persons on the site, the greater will be the chance of getting a useful response and the higher the value of posting a question. Contrarily, if the site is loaded with questions and has few people giving answers, the chance of getting an answer is likely to be small, which should discourage reps from posting their problem. A simple difference equation captures this relation. Let Q_t = the number of new questions on the site in time t; R_{t-1} be the number of responses to questions in the previous period; and Q_{t-1} be the number of questions in the previous period, Q_{t-1}. Then we have a supply-of-questions equation:

(1) $Q_t = f(R_{t-1}, Q_{t-1})$ with partial derivatives $f_1 > 0, f_2 < 0, f_{11} < 0, f_{22} > 0$.

From the threads on the site for 2004, we calculated the number of new questions in our sample per month—the arrival rate of questions—at approximately 100 per month.

Replies to question are the other side of the market for threads. Assuming that subscribers arrive and check questions on the site randomly, we hypothesize that the decision to answer a question depends on the number of questions on the site, the individuals' expertise, and their assessment of whether someone else might answer the question, which depends on the number of replies on the site. While it is possible that subscribers could compete over replies, which would generate lots of replies, we expect that free-riding behavior will create a negative feedback, so that persons are less likely to answer if they believe many other reps will do so (letting Nigel answer the posts). Formally, we write the number of replies to questions in period t, R_t, depends positively on the number of questions in the previous period and negatively on the number of responses in the previous period, R_{t-1}:

(2) $R_t = g(Q_{t-1}, R_{t-1})$ with partial derivatives $g_1 > 0, g_2 < 0, g_{11} < 0, g_{22} > 0$.

In this equation, replies fall when there are many replies, consistent with the finding by Jones, Ravid, and Rafaeli (2004) that persons on usenet sites tend to end active participation when mass interaction increases.

To examine the supply of replies in our sample, we tabulated the distribution of responses to threads. Column (1) of table 8.4 shows that just 11 percent of the questions received no answers. On average, a question obtained 3.1 responses—though the average masks the fact that there is considerable

Table 8.4   Distribution of responses to threads

Number of responses	Our sample (%) (350)	Total (%) (1,090)
0	39 (11)	126 (12)
1	63 (18)	187 (17)
2	79 (23)	233 (21)
3	52 (15)	173 (16)
4	37 (11)	126 (12)
5	35 (10)	87 (8)
6	14 (4)	47 (4)
7	8 (2)	40 (4)
8	7 (2)	18 (2)
9	4 (1)	18 (2)
10	4 (1)	11 (1)
>10	8 (2)	24 (2)

Source: Sample data, from sampled threads, July 2003 to December 2003. Total subscriber data, courtesy site (December 8, 2004).

dispersion in the number of responses per answer. Over 12 percent of threads received more than five responses and one obtained thirty-six replies. This distribution differs greatly from what one would expect if responses were randomly assigned to questions. Column (2) gives the distribution of *all* threads on the site in 2004. In the population, 12 percent of threads received no answers, essentially the same rate as in our sample. The general shape of the distribution of responses per thread is similar. The average number of responses per question was 3.5 and 15 percent of threads generated more than five responses.

The timing of replies to questions is important. If a posted question does not get a reply quickly, representatives are likely to be discouraged from posting questions. Fast responses should increase the number of questions. In our data the median number of days before a first response was one day: 35 percent of questions received a response the same day it was posted, and 22 percent received a response by the next day. Nearly two-thirds of all questions received a response within two days, and over 80 percent within a week.

To see if the responses helped resolve the issue that the question raised, we read all of the responses and coded them as to whether they "moved the thread toward answering the initial post." Table 8.5 shows that three-quarters of the responses did that. One-fourth did not. The one-fourth of responses that did not move toward answering the initial post were often at the end of a thread, suggesting that the thread drifted off target as persons responded to previous responses as opposed to the initial inquiry. Such patterns have been found in the telephone game, where people repeat a message along a line, inadvertently altering it (see http://en.wikipedia.org/wiki/Telephone_(game)). To verify this interpretation, we regressed the per-

Table 8.5   **Responses that moved toward answering the question posed (broken out by position of the response on the thread)**

Response number (1 = question poster)	Fraction that move toward answering question	Number of observations
All	0.74	786
2	0.79	304
3	0.64	242
4	0.75	163
5	0.69	110
6	0.71	79
7	0.67	45
8	0.48	31
9	0.70	23
10	0.50	16
11	0.67	12
12	0.38	8
13	0.50	4
14	0.25	4
15 or more	0.41	29

Source: Subscriber data, courtesy site (December 8, 2004).

centage of responses that help move the question along on the position of the response in the thread (number 2 being the first response to the question, number 3 for the next response, and so on). The regression gave a statistically significant coefficient of -0.028[9] on the number of the response, indicating that the proportion of responses that helped to answer the initial post fell by 0.28 points as the number on a response increased by ten.

We also examined whether responses that gave factual answers referenced a source of information for their response. One-third of responses gave a source. In an additional 30 percent, personal experience was the source. When there was more than one response to a question, a large proportion concurred or expanded on the previous thread, while just 4 percent of replies disagreed with an earlier posting, suggesting a general concordance in views about particular situations. In short, the site succeeds through most questions obtaining responses quickly in ways that resolve the issue.

Bulletin boards do not rely on prices to equilibrate supply and demand. Absent a price mechanism, the model of equations (1) and (2) makes the number of questions and replies themselves the mechanism that brings the market into equilibrium. By relating the supply of questions positively to responses and negatively to past questions and relating responses positively to questions and negatively to past responses, the model essentially makes

---

9. The equation regresses the dependent variable, percentage of responses that help move the question along, P, on the number of responses in the thread (N). The resultant estimated equation is $P = 0.82 - .028 \ (.006) \ N$, with $n = 14$ and an R^2 of 0.62.

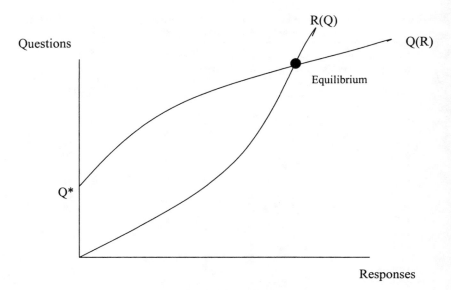

Fig. 8.3   Equilibrium in the market for threads
Notes: The question curve starts at some positive value Q^* and rises at a declining rate. The response curve starts at zero and rises at an increasing rate.

replies per question operate as a pseudo-price. Examining the likely shapes of the supply of questions and responses in figure 8.3, we see that the equations can produce a stable equilibrium with a fixed ratio of replies to questions. Starting the process with a given number of questions (Q^*), the negative second partial derivative of the supply of questions to the number of responses implies that increases in responses have an increasingly small effect on the supply of questions. Similarly, the second derivative of the supply of responses to the number of questions is also negative, so that increases in questions have an increasingly small effect on the supply of responses. This generates a fixed ratio of replies to questions in equilibrium.

8.2.4   Do Users of the Site Divide between Those Who Pose Questions and Those Who Answer Them, or Do Users Work "Both Sides of the Market," Depending on the Situation?

To answer this question, we divided our sample into three groups: those who only posted questions, those who only posted answers, and those who did both. The largest group only post answers (48 percent), the smallest group only posts questions (22 percent), while the remaining 30 percent operated on both sides of the market. This means that of those who give answers, 38 percent (= 30/78) also ask questions, while of those who ask questions 58 percent (= 30/52) also give answers, so that among both posers of questions and responders to queries a substantial number of persons work both sides of the market.

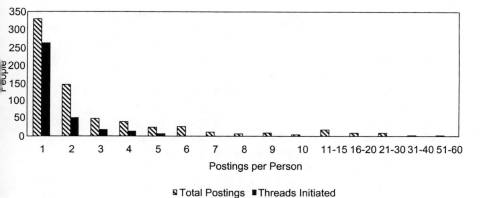

Total Postings   ■ Threads Initiated

Fig. 8.4   Postings per person follows a power law
Note: The power law regression: ln number of people who post N times = 5.27 – 1.58 (0.08) ln N R^2 is 0.95.

Figure 8.4 displays the frequency of posting (questions and responses) by individuals. The data follow a power law, with many people posting a small number of times and a few persons posting many times. Regressing the natural log of the number of individuals posting a given number of posts (ln freq) on the natural log of the number of posts (ln number) gives the following relation:

(3)   ln(freq) = 5.27 – 1.58 · (0.08) ln(number),

where the number in parenthesis is the standard error of the estimate.[10]

Dividing postings between questions posed and replies, the data (not given in the figure) show that the questions are less concentrated among a small number of persons than are replies. The top 5 percent of persons in terms of the number of questions posed asked 29 percent of all the questions, whereas the top 5 percent of persons who answered questions gave 35 percent of the total number of answers. But both distributions diverge from the distributions that would arise if the number of postings were determined "randomly," in the sense that each representative had a similar probability of making a posting per time unit in a period of n independent time units. In that case, the distribution of postings would be binomial and the variance of the number of postings would be smaller than the mean number of postings.[11] The data show the opposite: higher variances than means. Put differently, the actual distribution of questions per person (responses per person) is less concentrated around the mean number of questions per person (responses per person) than under the random model. This implies

10. The sample size is 22 and the R^2 is 0.95 in this regression.
11. If X is the number of postings and X is generated by a binomial process where in each of n periods a person has the probability p of making a posting, then the expected value of X is np and the variance of X is $np(1 – p)$, so that the variance is smaller than the mean.

considerable heterogeneity in posing and answering questions. Some representatives are more willing to pose questions or have more problems at their workplace than others, while some other representatives are either more willing to answer questions or have greater experience and knowledge to share than other representatives.

Finally, we examined the extent to which online interactions led to offline linkages. Seven percent of responses, covering 17 percent of threads, advised the person who posed the question to contact a union or TUC official, which would take them off the site. Although less than 3 percent of questions included offsite contact info and only 7 percent of responses did, even a modest listing of contact information could produce substantial offsite contacts, since many persons are on the site often and may only list their contact information once. On some of the boards, moreover, there was more direction to offsite contacts. Roughly a third of the threads on the "Education, Learning and Skills" bulletin board contain such offsite contact information, for example. Over time, the percentage of threads with offsite information rose from 25 percent in 2003 to 40 percent in 2004.

That some discussions go offsite suggests that analyses of the threads on the board understate the impact of the site in developing communication among representatives. Even though contact information *per question* or response is modest, it is sufficient to generate the considerable offsite links *per site user* found in our survey. Consistent with this in our longitudinal follow-up survey, a sizable number of respondents (40 percent) reported meeting people as a result of online contact. Moving discussions offline could also signify that members view the site as too public a forum for discussion of detailed, incident-specific or sensitive topics as the membership and volume grow. As responses move offsite they lose their public good nature and the answers cease to be part of the archive.

8.3   Longitudinal Analysis

Workers in the training sample were introduced to unionreps.org.uk as part of their TUC training program. We model the effect of the introduction and/or ensuing use of the site on their behavior and attitudes as representatives using a before-after treatment-control design. While some TUC trainees had seen or visited the unionreps.org.uk site before training, the vast majority had not done so. Their responses on our cross-sectional survey thus reflect a "before treatment" measure. Using the lingo of analyses of job training/other interventions, trainees who use the site are a "treatment" group, while the entire group of trainees are "the intention to treat" group. We then examine whether introduction to the site during training affected ensuing use of the site and whether that was associated with changes in attitudes or behavior as a rep. Whether persons in the training sample use the site (i.e., "take-up") is of course not random. As we lack a traditional control

Table 8.6   **Take-up of site use by trainees introduced to Unionreps.org during training**

	Training sample (Treatment group)		Online survey (Control group)	
Site use	Before (%)	After (%)	Before (%)	After (%)
Once a week or more	18	29	72	47
Once a month or less	14	38	26	51
Never	68	32	2	2

Source: Tabulated for the group that responded to follow-up survey as well as the initial survey; $n = 214$ for the trainees and 130 for the online survey group.

group that is not exposed to treatment, we will instead use the persons surveyed through the site and already using it as the control group. The key assumption here is that there are no preexisting differences in trend between them and the trainees.

Table 8.6 shows that introduction to the site during training increased ensuing use of it by trainees. The table records the percentage of persons reporting for whom we have responses on both the initial and follow-up surveys. At the time of the cross-sectional survey 68 percent of trainees had never used the site. Afterward that proportion was 32 percent. At the other end of the spectrum, just 18 percent used the site weekly before training while 29 percent used it weekly afterward. By contrast, among the respondents from the sample of users on the site, there is a drop in those who use it weekly or more from 72 to 47 percent, possibly reflecting a decline in their need to use the site regularly.

Respondents from the online sample of users of the site answered some questions about their representative work and attitudes toward unionism differently than did those in the TUC training sample. Table 8.7 gives the key questions that our cross-sectional survey used to assess how worker reps viewed their activity as reps and union activity in general. The online sample is more likely to report that their work is taxing and stressful (24 percent agree with the statement fully by giving a 1 score, while 29 percent give it a 2 score, compared to 14 percent and 22 percent for persons in the TUC training sample); that they are well prepared and trained to be a union representative (22 percent with complete agreement and 43 percent with agreement compared to 15 percent and 26 percent in the training sample); and that workers at their workplace benefit from the union (58 percent and 25 percent compared to 46 percent and 27 percent for the training sample). By contrast, there is little difference between the samples in views of the extent to which workers or their unions appreciate what they are doing.

To assess whether trainees who began to use the site changed their relative responses to questions about attitudes or behavior relative to previous users, we estimated the following equation:

Table 8.7   **Union representatives' views of their work activity**

On a scale from 1 to 5, where 1 means that you agree completely with the statement and 5 means that you disagree completely, how much do you agree or disagree with the following statements?

	1	2	3	4	5
Panel A: TUC training sample (%)					
a. My work as union representative is taxing and stressful	14	22	39	17	7
b. I am well-prepared and trained to be a union representative	15	26	37	16	7
c. The workers I represent fully appreciate my activities as workers' rep	10	23	35	25	7
d. My union fully appreciates my work as a union representative	27	31	24	12	6
e. The workers at my workplace benefit greatly from having a union	46	27	17	6	4
f. The union movement is on the right track for regaining influence on society	16	28	41	12	4
Panel B: Online sample (%)					
a. My work as union representative is taxing and stressful	24	29	28	13	6
b. I am well-prepared and trained to be a union representative	22	43	24	9	2
c. The workers I represent fully appreciate my activities as workers' rep	10	28	38	17	7
d. My union fully appreciates my work as a union representative	24	35	24	13	4
e. The workers at my workplace benefit greatly from having a union	58	25	10	4	2
f. The union movement is on the right track for regaining influence on society	16	33	33	13	5

Source: CEP, LSE survey of union representatives.

$$(4) \qquad Y_{it} = a + b\text{TREAT}_i + c\text{TREAT}_i \cdot \text{AFTER}_t,$$

where TREAT measures whether the respondents were a part of the group introduced to the unionreps.org.uk site through the TUC's training program and AFTER is a dummy variable that takes the value 1 for the follow-up survey. The coefficient c measures the change in the dependent variable between those who began to use the site after training compared to the control group of those who were already using the site when the first survey was conducted.

Table 8.8 shows the results of this analysis for three variables for which there was a significant difference in the first round of the survey between the training sample and the online sample. Column (a) under each statement record estimated differences in responses in the *first round* of the survey between persons introduced to the site in the training center and the online sample and in parentheses a *t*-statistic for the differences between the two samples. Recalling that higher responses mean greater disagreement with the statement, the coefficient 0.49, for example, shows that the trainees were less likely to say that they were well prepared and trained to be a representative than persons who always used the site. Column (a) also gives an estimate of the difference between the two samples in the rate of completing the second survey. The differences are modest. If they were large, we would have a serious sample attrition and selectivity problem.

The estimated coefficients and *t*-statistics for the coefficients of the variables in equation (4) are given under each statement in column (b) of the

Table 8.8   Coefficient estimates and *t*-statistics for the effect of being introduced to unionreps.org at TUC training on responses to questions about work as Union representatives

Variable/condition	I am well prepared and trained to be a union representative		Workers at my work place benefit greatly from the union		Work as a union representative is taxing and stressful	
	(a)	(b)	(a)	(b)	(a)	(b)
Training sample	0.49	0.31	0.29	0.28	0.34	0.49
Dummy (estimated difference between trainees and online sample of always users)	(7.7)	(3.1)	(4.6)	(3.0)	(5.1)	(4.3)
Training sample after site introduction (estimated effect of use of site on trainees)		−0.49 (4.4)		−0.29 (4.4)		−0.49 (3.8)
Estimated difference in rate of completing both surveys between trainees and online sample	−0.12 (1.9)		−0.05 (0.8)		0.02 (0.35)	
Sample	First survey	Completed both surveys	First survey	Completed both surveys	First survey	Completed both surveys
Number of observations	1,268	562	1,267	565	1,265	560

Source: CEP, LSE survey of union representatives.

Note: Respondents indicated their agreement with each statement on a 1–5 scale; 1 indicates complete agreement and 5 complete disagreement.

table. The coefficients on the dummy for being in the training sample are of similar magnitude to the comparable statistics in column (a). The estimates differ between the samples because the sample in column (b) is limited to persons who completed both surveys. The new information in column (b) is in the estimates of the effect of introducing the site to trainees. For each statement these estimates are significantly negative, indicating that the trainees introduced to the site *became more like* persons already using the site.[12] The implication is that use of the site influenced trainees: they regard themselves as better prepared and trained to be a union rep and believe more strongly that workers at their workplace benefit from unions. All of these effects are presumably due to their being involved with the unionreps.org.uk site and community. At the same time, they also found their work as a representative more taxing and stressful, which is surprising. We imagined that the additional support network of the online community and the resources it provides would diminish the perceived burden of being a union representative. One potential explanation for the result is that it reflects a natural decline in the enthusiasm of new recruits over time. To test this explanation, we reproduced the estimates in table 8.8 with the sample broken out by the tenure of the representatives, and found that the coefficients of interest are virtually unchanged, which rejects this explanation.[13] However, with only two time periods, it is still possible that there are differential trends across the groups that we cannot identify. Another possible explanation is that the exposure to the reps on the site increases the perceived burden by emphasizing the importance of the role and raising expectations about their duties, for example, through peer pressure or broader exposure to what is possible. But we have no evidence on this point.

8.4   Conclusion: Where Will These Innovations Lead?

Given the difficulties that U.S. unions have with organizing workers for traditional collective bargaining, unions must find ways to gain new members if they are to survive. The rapid expansion of Working America shows that a movement-based organization that campaigns for worker interests in society online and offline can attract large numbers at low cost. The greater activism of members who join online suggests further that the Internet may

---

12. Those who ultimately participated in both rounds of the survey do not appear to significantly differ, at least initially, on any measure except preparedness. Those who chose to participate in both rounds of the survey initially felt more prepared for their representative duties than those who only participated in the first round. While there may be some selective attrition between the rounds it does not appear to be substantial, at least with respect to the initial values of the variables of interest.

13. The sample was divided into those with six or more years of tenure and those with less experience (this demarcation was chosen to create roughly equal sample sizes). For those with six or more years of experience the estimates of B_{treat} and $B_{treat.Xafter}$ of 0.49 and −0.52, respectively, compared with estimates of 0.53 and −0.49 for those with less experience.

be a particularly good way to find highly committed persons. What we do not know is whether Working America's long-run stability will necessitate that it finds ways to deliver union services to workplaces in addition to campaigning and lobbying for workers in society and, if so, whether it will find the right mix of services at the level of dues members will be willing to pay.

Given the difficulties that British unions have in organizing workers in workplaces with traditional collective bargaining, it is critical for them to improve and personalize services to members. The success of www.unionreps .org.uk in building a community of voluntary worker representatives who exchange information suggests that unions can tap the wisdom of their members to advance this goal at low cost. The greater activism of reps that join the site suggests that it offers a way to increase the commitment and effort by reps. Whether the transmission of knowledge among reps improves services to workers by enough to attract more members or whether the TUC or constituent unions must go further and use their computer database on members to personalize services remain to be seen.

A service provision model that relies on the Internet may alleviate concerns of employer opposition, but it has challenges of its own. In collective bargaining, unions are essentially awarded a monopoly after winning recognition. On the Internet and outside the workplace, nonunion groups offer information and services to workers that compete with union services.[14] Unions will therefore have to compete not only to attract new members, but to keep the members they enroll through this venue. Unions have, however, some advantages in providing services over the Internet to workers. As member-based organizations that are democratically accountable to workers, they should be more responsive and trustworthy agents than other organizations. And unions can mobilize many more members and activists on a volunteer basis to provide services to fellow workers than can smaller nonmember-based organizations.

We suspect that Working America and the U.S. unions broadly will have to undertake other innovations to create a viable organization for workers outside of collective bargaining. Studies of high-performance workplaces find that single policies rarely transform a workplace. What is needed are complementary policies that make the sum of the package exceed the sum of its parts introduced singly. Given its mass membership and activists, Working America could potentially benefit from developing Internet bulletin boards

14. Internet recruitment sites such as Monster.com or Careerbuilder.com give information and advice to workers to attract more job applicants. Labor law firms advertise assistance to workers. Human resource divisions of major firms use the company's internal e-mail system and computer records to connect with workers. Internet aside, public interest legal organizations defend the interests of particular types of workers (Jolls 2005); community groups have formed to help immigrants and various ethnic groups (Osterman 2002; Fine 2006; Lynch 2005), often led by persons with union experience; NGOs have sought to provide portable benefits to workers outside of collective bargaining (Hersch 2005). The U.K.'s Citizens Advice Bureau offers government protections and assistance to workers more broadly.

of the www.unionreps.org type to stimulate local members and activists to find new directions for the organization. British unions are also likely to need innovations beyond unionreps.org.uk to improve services and attract free riders at organized workplaces and to expand to other workplaces. What our analysis has shown is that the U.S. and U.K. central union federations have begun the difficult process of changing how they conduct business and have some successes on which to build further.

Assuming that the online and noncollective bargaining-based activities become a permanent part of the labor scene, will they substitute for traditional union modes of intermediation or will they complement and strengthen collective bargaining representation at workplaces? If online union activities come to resemble those of other service providers or websites that give no collective backup for workers, online unions would be unions in name only. They would have lost the fundamental features of traditional unions as democratic workplace organizations that provided a collective voice to workers. Similarly, if the noncollective bargaining-based activities of Working America or related organizations come to resemble those that represent other groups in the political scene, such as the American Association of Retired People, they would also be unions in name only. They might help their constituents, but they would have lost the fundamental features of traditional unions.

The unionreps.org case demonstrates a way these sites can complement unions' traditional role. It strengthens the ability of unions to meet their traditional role as representing workers at their workplace. By pooling the information of representatives across areas, the unionreps.org site recognizes that the problems faced by workers extend beyond any one location in the modern labor market, and that information is an important tool in local representation and bargaining.

The Working America experiment has more of the flavor of an AARP-style substitute, but it is too early to know whether the organization will try to go beyond representing and organizing people for broad social purposes. To the extent that it helps collective bargaining unions augment their power with firms or in the political sphere by providing a larger base of support and information broking on particular measures, it may shore up unions' traditional intermediary role in the labor market. It is possible that WA will be able to maintain loyalty and support over a long period of time without giving members concrete support at their workplaces. But it is also possible that WA or some other union group will build on its noncollective bargaining members to develop an open source model that provides value at workplaces beyond collective bargaining.

What makes these union activities exciting is that they are not grandma's or grandpa's unions doing the same old thing in the same old way. They represent unionism in an innovative mode, trying to shore up its traditional roles and trying to find new ways to provide intermediary services in the modern labor market.

Appendix
Cross-Section 21 Survey UNIONREPS.ORG.UK Union Representatives Survey (TUC Training Sample: Response counts below)

1. How long have you been a union rep?

< 1 year	1–2 years	2–5 years	5–10 years	10+ years
323	149	182	86	110

2. In the last 12 months, how much time have you spent as a union representative on these issues?

	Lots of time	Some time	No time
a. Maintaining the wages and benefits of employees	137	327	336
b. Security of employment[a]	104	315	367
c. Treatment of employees by management[b]	241	408	159
d. Health and safety of employees[c]	330	377	132
e. Resolving conflicts between employees[d]	90	341	361
f. Finding ways to improve worker skills	58	355	383
g. Recruitment and organization	102	462	252

3. On average, how many hours per week do you usually spend on representative activities, including time spent at the workplace and at home?

< 1 hr	1–2 hrs	2–5 hrs	5–10 hrs	10+ hrs
100	216	246	147	138

4. Does your employer pay for the time spent on representative activities while at work?

Yes	No
817	36

5. In which of the following occupations are the bulk of the workers that you represent?[e]

Highly skilled professional	Craft and skilled labor	Less skilled/unskilled
278	286	215

6. On a scale from 1 to 5, where 1 means that you agree completely with the statement and 5 means that you disagree completely, how much do you agree or disagree with the following statements?

Coding	1	2	3	4	5
a. My work as union representative is taxing and stressful	118	191	334	147	63
b. I am well prepared and trained to be a union representative	124	223	317	137	56
c. The workers I represent fully appreciate my activities as workers' rep	88	200	296	213	60
d. My union fully appreciates my work as a union representative	232	265	208	100	47
e. The workers at my workplace benefit greatly from having a union	391	230	145	53	36
f. The union movement is on the right track for regaining influence on society	129	238	350	102	32

7. How often do you use the following sources to obtain information for your representative duties?

	Often	Sometimes	Rarely	Never
a. From union representative training materials and events	359	395	80	20
b. From full-time union staff by calling or writing to them	286	337	164	57
c. From TUC by calling or writing to them	44	192	305	297
d. From older/experienced workers	266	398	125	56
e. From the Internet	258	291	145	151

8. How often do you currently use the Internet (www, e-mail)?

Daily	2–5 times/week	Once a week	Once a month	Never (go to 11)
387	181	97	68	126

9. Where do you usually use the Internet (www, e-mail)?

At work	At home	Other
182	311	23
205		
	4	
13		

10. How often do you use the Internet for purposes related to:

	Often	Sometimes	Rarely	Never
a. Current job, excluding union rep duties	221	206	148	170
b. Union rep duties	235	317	121	73
c. Other union activities	180	255	183	120

11. If you have never used the Internet for union rep duties, are you interested in using it?

Yes	No
364	34

12. If you use the Internet to support your union rep duties, specify how (tick all that apply)

	Yes	No
a. To find out about training possibilities	431	273
b. To inform workers in your workplace about your union and its activities	422	280
c. To find out about worker rights and employment legislation	588	128
d. To find out about pay levels and working conditions elsewhere	298	397
e. To keep in touch and/or exchange information with your union officials	393	305
f. To keep in touch and/or exchange information with other union representatives	412	285
g. To keep in touch and/or make contacts with other unions or worker organizations	264	424

13. How often have you visited these websites?

	> 3 times/wk	2–3 times/wk	Once a wk	Once a month	never
a. Your union's website	75	77	194	264	192
b. TUC website	49	65	131	244	308
c. UNIONREPS.ORG.UK website	22	39	74	121	539

14. On a scale of 1 to 5, where 1 means that you agree completely with the statement and 5 means that you disagree completely. Answer only if you have used the relevant websites.

Coding	1	2	3	4	5
a. My union website is very useful	145	222	197	57	33
b. The TUC website is very useful	157	183	159	33	30
c. The UNIONREPS.ORG.UK website is very useful	77	99	124	35	45
d. Online training can be effective for union reps	115	157	193	57	40

15. How much loyalty do you have toward

	A lot	Some	A little	None
a. The TUC/wider union movement?	412	341	68	19
b. Your local union?	638	178	28	2
c. Your national union?	441	317	66	12
d. Your employer?	204	378	170	92

16. Age (average)

43.2

17. Gender

Male	Female
603	251

[a]Two responded 1.5
[b]Four responded 1.5 and 1 responded 2.5.
[c]Three responded 1.5.
[d]One chose 1.5 and 2 with 2.5.
[e]Some representatives reported that they represent multiple types of workers. Eleven represent both "highly skilled professional" and "craft and skilled labor"; twenty-eight represent "craft and skilled labor" and "less skilled/unskilled" labor; and eleven represent workers from all three categories. The aforementioned responses are *not* included in counts presented in the table.

References

Adar, E., and B. A. Huberman. 2000. Free riding on gnutella. Technical report, Xerox PARC. Available at: http://citeseer.ist.psu.edu/adar00free.html. Also, online at *First Monday* 5(10).

Andreoni, J. 1990. Impure altruism and donations to public goods: A theory of warm-glow. *Economic Journal* 100 (401): 464–77.

Bishop, J. 2007. Increasing participation in online communities: A framework for human-computer interaction. *Computers in Human Behavior* 23:1881–93. Available at: http://www.jonathanbishop.com/publications/display.aspx?Item=17.

Blanchflower, D. G., and A. Bryson. 2004. The union wage premium in the U.S. and the U.K. Centre for Economic Performance Discussion Paper Number 612. London: CEPD.

Centola, D. 2007. The strength of weak incentives. Harvard University.

Darlington, R. 2000. The creation of the e-union: The use of ICT by British unions. Internet Economy Conference, Centre for Economic Performance, LSE, November 7. Available at: http://members.tripod.co.uk/rogerdarlington/E-union.html.

Diamond, W., and R. B. Freeman. 2002. Will unionism prosper in cyber-space? The promise of the internet for employee organization. *British Journal of Industrial Relations* 40 (September): 569–96.

Fine, J. 2006. *Worker centers organizing communities at the edge of the dream.* Ithaca, NY: Cornell University Press.

Freeman, R. B. 2004. The road to union renaissance in the United States. In *The changing role of Unions,* ed. P. V. Wunnava, 3–21. London: ME Sharpe.

———. 2005. From the Webbs to the Web: The contribution of the Internet to reviving union fortunes. NBER Working Paper no. W11298. Cambridge, MA: National Bureau of Economic Research, May.

Freeman, R. B., J. Hersch, and L. Mishel. 2005. *Emerging labor market institutions for the twenty-first century.* Chicago: University of Chicago Press.

Freeman, R. B., and J. Rogers. 2002a. A proposal to American labor. *The Nation* 274:18–24.

———. 2002b. Open source unionism. *WorkingUSA* 5 (4): 8–40.

———. 2006. *What workers want,* 2nd ed. Ithaca, NY: Cornell University Press.

Greenhouse, S. 2004. Labor federation looks beyond unions. *New York Times,* July 11.

Hersch, J. 2007. A workers' lobby to provide portable benefits. In *Emerging labor market institutions for the 21st century,* ed. R. Freeman, J. Hersch, and L. Mishel, 207–230. Chicago: University of Chicago Press.

Hiscox, M., and N. Smyth. 2007. Is there consumer demand for improved labor standards? Evidence from field experiments in social labeling. Available at: http://www.courses.fas.harvard.edu:9095/~gov3009/Calendar/SocialLabeling_2.pdf.

Hurd, R., and J. Bunge. 2007. Unionization of Professional and Technical Workers: the labor market and institutional transformation. In *Emerging Labor Market Institutions for the 21st Century,* ed. R. B. Freeman, J. Hersch, and L. Mishel. Chicago: University of Chicago Press.

Ichniowski, C., K. Shaw, and G. Prennushi. 1997. The effects of human resource management practices on productivity: A study of steel finishing lines. *American Economic Review, American Economic Association* 87 (3): 291–313.

Jolls, C. 2007. The role and functioning of public-interest legal organizations in the enforcement of the employment laws. In *Emerging labor market institutions for the 21st century,* ed. R. Freeman, J. Hersch, and L. Mishel, 141–178. Chicago: University of Chicago Press.

Jones, Q., G. Ravid, and S. Rafaeli. 2004. Information overload and the message dynamics of online interaction spaces: A theoretical model and empirical exploration. *Information Systems Research* 15 (2): 194–210.

Kahneman, D., J. L. Knetsch, and R. H. Thaler. 1986. Fairness as a constraint on profit seeking: Entitlements in the market. *The American Economic Review* 76:728–41.

Kern, M. 2007. Arbitration proceeding before Margaret M. Kern. Yale-New Haven Hospital and Index Nos. 054 061(a) 061(d) 068 New England Health Care Employees, district 1199, SEIU, Oct 23.

Kollock, P. 1999. The economies of online cooperation: Gifts and public goods in cyberspace. In *Communities in cyberspace,* ed. P. M. Smith and P. Kollock, 3–28. London: Rutledge.

Lynch, L. 2005. Development intermediaries and the training of low-wage workers. In *Emerging labor market institutions for the 21st century,* ed. R. Freeman, J. Hersch, and L. Mishel, 293–314. Chicago: University of Chicago Press.

McLennan, K. 2007. What do unions do? A management perspective. In *What do unions do? A twenty year perspective,* ed. J. Bennett and B. Kauffman, 563–88. New Brunswick, NJ: Transactions.

Nack, D., and J. Tarlau. 2005. The Communications Workers of America experience with "open source unionism." *Working USA* 8 (December): 721–34.

Newman, N. 2005. Is labor missing the Internet third wave? *Working USA* 8 (December): 383–94.

Olson, M. 1971. *The logic of collective action: Public goods and the theory of groups,* 2nd ed. Boston, MA: Harvard University Press.

Osterman, P. 2002. Community organizing and employee representation. Available at: http://web.mit.edu/osterman/www/Community-Org-EE-Rep.pdf.

Resnick, P., K. Kuwabara, R. Zeckhauser, and E. Friedman. 2000. Reputation systems. *Communications of the ACM* 43 (12):45–48.

Rheingold, H. 1993. *The virtual community: Homesteading on the electronic frontier.* New York: Addison-Wesley.

Shostak, A. 1999. *Empowering labor through computer technology.* Armonk, NY: ME Sharpe.

Stevens, C. D., and C. R. Greer. 2005. E-voice, the Internet, and life within unions: Riding the learning curve. *Working USA* 8 (December): 439–55.

Surowiecki, J. 2003. *The wisdom of crowds.* New York: Anchor.

Taras, D., and A. Gesser. 2003. How new lawyers use E-Voice to drive firm compensation: The "greedy associates" phenomenon. *Journal of Labor Research* 23 (4): 9–29.

Voss, K. 1993. *The making of American exceptionalism: the Knights of Labor and class formation in the nineteenth century.* Ithaca, NY: Cornell University Press.

Weir, R. E. 1996. *Beyond labor's veil: The culture of the Knights of Labor.* University Park, PA: Pennsylvania State University Press.

IV

**Solving Information Problems:
The Special Case of Temporary
Help Agencies**

Temporary Help Services Employment in Portugal, 1995–2000

René Böheim and Ana Rute Cardoso

9.1 Introduction

There is much anecdotal evidence of poor working conditions in agency work, but much less hard evidence. None of the research referred to can differentiate between factors related to agency work per se (as a form of employment) and those related to the job or the worker. (Storrie 2002, 56)

Employment in temporary help service (THS) firms has increased throughout Europe over the last decade. This development has prompted the European Commission (EC) to propose a directive to safeguard THS workers' working conditions. In 2002 it issued a proposal for a European Parliament and Council Directive on working conditions for THS workers (EIRO 2002; European Commission 2002), which aims to ensure that temporary workers are not discriminated against, receiving at least as favorable a treatment as a regular comparable worker in the firm where she or he is posted. The relevant dimensions are the basic working and employment conditions, including duration of working time, rest and holiday periods, time of work, and seniority.

This concern comes from widespread evidence that workers in THS firms

René Böheim is an associate professor of economics at the Johannes Kepler University, Linz, and a research fellow with the Austrian Institute of Economic Research and the IZA Bonn. Ana Rute Cardoso is a research scientist at the Institute for Economic Analysis, Spanish National Research Council (IAE-CSIC), an Affiliated Professor at the Barcelona Graduate School of Economics (Barcelona GSE), and Research Fellow at the Institute for the Study of Labor (IZA Bonn). This chapter was prepared for the NBER Conference on Labor Market Intermediation, May 17–18, 2007. We thank David Autor, Jeff Smith, participants at the NBER conference, and participants in a seminar held at IZA Bonn for most helpful comments. We are grateful to the Ministry of Employment, Statistics Department, Portugal, for access to the data. René Böheim acknowledges financial support from the Austrian National Bank, grant no. 11090.

face worse working conditions than comparable workers in the placement firm. Evidence from Houseman (2001) suggests that THS may be used to save on worker benefit costs, such as health insurance and pension contributions. These concerns extend to wage rates, as there seems to be evidence of lower wages for THS workers.

Concern about workers in THS has also focused on whether they remain in low-paying, dead-end jobs or if they find, should they so desire, employment in a standard working career. High turnover involves a loss of firm-specific human capital, a decrease in productivity if production depends on continuous cooperation of workers, and possibly less coverage by trade unions, factors that may contribute to poorer career prospects. On the contrary, THS could serve as a screening method (Autor 2001; Houseman 2001) at little cost for the firm; that is, without a commitment about a future employment contract. Since THS work typically matches a worker with several firms, it can be seen as a job-matching mechanism.

The discussion has thus concentrated on whether workers in THS employment earn lower wages and whether THS employment enables workers to start a better career. There are numerous studies for the United States that find that THS workers receive lower wages than other workers; for example, Segal and Sullivan (1997), who report an average wage difference of about 28 percent, which is reduced to about 3 percent when observable and time-invariant unobservable characteristics are considered. (See also, among others, Blank [1998] or Nollen [1996].)

Workers may accept lower wages in THS firms because the employment in these firms allows a subsequent job match with better pay or more stable careers. Autor and Houseman (2005), using random placement assignments, do not find that THS work is associated with stable careers in post-THS employment. For welfare recipients, however, Heinrich, Mueser, and Troske (2005) find that work in THS is associated with better outcomes than not working at all.

The evidence for European countries is mixed. For example, Forde and Slater (2005) report a wage penalty of about 11 percent for men and 6 percent for women in THS in contrast to comparable workers in the United Kingdom. Zijl, van den Berg, and Heyma (2004) find for the Netherlands that THS work is associated with subsequent stable employment spells. Similarly, Amuedo-Dorantes, Malo, and Muñoz-Bullón (2006), for Spain, Booth, Francesconi, and Frank (2002), for the United Kingdom, and Ichino, Mealli, and Nannicini (2006), for Italy, find that THS work is associated with subsequent stable employment. However, Kvasnicka (2005) finds for Germany that THS work does not improve the subsequent careers of such workers, and Antoni and Jahn (2006) find that THS workers in Germany are increasingly found in repeated spells of THS work.

We use linked employer-employee data, obtained from the Ministry of Employment in Portugal, to analyze wages of workers in THS. These administrative data cover the universe of Portuguese workers in the private sector for the period 1995 to 2000. The panel dimension of these data allow us to control for worker and industry specific effects.

The purpose of the chapter is twofold. We analyze, first of all, if THS workers earn lower wages than comparable workers in other sectors, by estimating wage regressions. Because participation in THS work is not random, we control for workers' fixed effects in our estimations, taking advantage of the longitudinal nature of the data. We perform the analysis separately for men and women as well as for younger and older workers, since these groups tend to fare differently in the labor market. (We also perform the analyses on the pooled sample.) Secondly, we analyze workers' wages before and after spells of THS. On the one hand, we want to assess if THS work leads to lower wages in subsequent employment—that is, evidence of a stigma effect. On the other hand, we want to investigate if workers experienced a particular wage development before entering THS. For example, their wages could be deteriorating relative to similar workers, in which case the adverse labor market conditions would provide the motivation to search for a THS job.

Our empirical results suggest that THS workers earn about 1 percent less than similar workers in other firms, once their observable and unobservable attributes are controlled for. However, disaggregation of the sample by age and gender reveals interesting differences across groups of workers. Younger workers, both men and women, earn higher wages in THS firms than their peers in other firms. Prime-age workers, in particular men, earn a lower wage in THS firms than similar workers in other firms. Also interestingly, for young workers, THS is not associated with a stigma that slows their wage progression after they start to work in the THS sector. In contrast, for prime-age and older workers, in particular males, wage progression after entering THS is slower than for similar workers not engaged in THS. Before entering THS firms, prime-age workers, both men and women, see their wages deteriorate relative to their peers, suggesting that adverse labor market conditions might motivate them to search for a THS job. For young workers, we do not detect any pre-THS wage trend.

9.2 Background

9.2.1 The Association between THS Work and Wages

The distinguishing feature of work for a THS firm is the tripartite nature of the relationship and the commercial nature of the contract signed between the THS firm and the placement firm, which sets it apart from a traditional labor contract between a worker and a firm. Even though a particular assignment of a worker is temporary, it is not the duration of the contract that characterizes this sector.

While there is widespread belief that THS workers earn lower wages than comparable workers, in particular in countries where labor legislation is not stringent or trade union coverage is low, there are also reasons, and evidence, that point to the opposite direction. Temporary help service workers may earn a higher wage, which would compensate for the risk of a more variable income stream than comparable workers. It is also sometimes stressed that THS firms have difficulty recruiting workers and need to offer favorable conditions to attract them. Storrie (2002) reports that at the upper end of the pay scale, for instance in the health sector, THS workers seem to enjoy better pay and possibly better working conditions than regular workers. The wages in THS firms is thus an empirical issue that we will address in more detail in the following.

Some THS firms may choose to offer free general training instead of higher wages to attract more workers and to identify better-quality workers (Autor 2001). In general, the need to attract workers and the existence of economies of scale in the provision of some types of training have been pointed out as reasons why THS firms may provide more training than legally required. Such training could result in higher wages in post-THS employment.

On the contrary, Storrie (2002) reports evidence of circumvention of employment standards for THS workers, especially in terms of pay and working time regulations, and also evidence of other, illegal abuse. The short employment spells, possibly combined with low investment in human capital, and fewer workers' rights due to lower coverage by trade unions, are typically factors that characterize poor career prospects.

9.2.2   Legal Setting in Portugal

The market for THS is tightly regulated in Portugal.[1] Permission to operate as a THS firm is granted by the Ministry of Employment and Social Security. Candidates must show proof of a clean criminal record, previous compliance with labor law and tax and social security duties, technical capacity (i.e., a qualified director with experience of running human resources and supporting administrative staff), as well as a sound financial situation.[2] Temporary help service firms are allowed a wide range of activities, which include recruitment and selection of personnel, vocational orientation, training, consulting, and human resources management. The operation of the firm is regularly monitored by the Bureau of Labor Inspection and it must present records of workers hired out to using firms every six months.

The work contract is signed between the THS firm and the worker. The formal employer is thus the THS, and not the user firm, and it is responsible in particular for paying the workers, fulfilling the employer's Social Security obligations, providing insurance against work-related accidents, and allocating a minimum of 1 percent of the total turnover to training. (The

---

1. Decree-Law 358/89, Law 39/96, and Law 146/99.
2. A fund linked to the national minimum wage must be deposited, or a bank or insurance company guarantee presented, which is used for wage payments if the company does not pay its workers.

THS firm is legally forbidden to charge the worker for training provided.) The user firm is responsible for fulfilling regulations on health and security at the workplace.

The work contract between the worker and the THS can be open ended or of limited duration. If open ended, the worker is entitled to pay, even in periods when she or he is not actually assigned to a using firm. The amount is specified by collective bargaining or, if the worker is not covered, two-thirds of the national minimum wage.

Firms have to justify the need for temporary workers and a narrow set of reasons is permitted: to replace workers on leave, for seasonal work, in case of a temporary increase in product demand, or to bridge recruitment gaps, while the process to fill a vacancy is taking place.

The contract between the THS firm and the using firm must also specify, among other things, the duration of the assignment (which depends on the reason for use of temporary work, with a maximum limit of six months to two years), the description of tasks to be performed, the wage the using firm pays its workers who perform similar tasks, and the amount paid to the THS firm. A THS worker is entitled to the wage set by collective bargaining for THS work or the wage paid by the user firm to similar workers, whichever is higher. Because these rules aim at providing equal treatment for regular and THS workers, we would expect to see no, or a moderate, pay differential between THS and regular workers. Over 90 percent of the THS workers are covered by a collective bargaining contract, signed between trade unions and employer representatives.[3]

The regulations are monitored and enforced by the Bureau of Labor Inspection. However, situations of noncompliance with the law are frequently discussed in the press, where THS owners associations demand stricter controls by the Bureau, arguing that law-obeying firms are subject to unfair competition by firms that do not fulfill the law, especially the payment of taxes and Social Security contributions. Trade unions, on the other hand, claim that workers' rights are not always respected and also demand stricter monitoring. Finally, the Bureau of Labor Inspection claims that the firms in the sector are subject to close scrutiny and argues for higher legal sanctions to increase compliance.

Although the legalization and regulation of this type of work took place relatively early in comparison to other European countries, the use of THS is not as widespread in Portugal as in other European countries. In 1999, it comprised about 1 percent of total employment, below the European Union average of about 1.4 percent. In terms of growth, although employment in the sector more than doubled between 1995 and 1999, its growth has been modest when compared to most other European countries (Storrie 2002, 23).

---

3. In Portugal, a contract signed between workers' and employers' representatives is often extended to all workers in a sector or firm, irrespective of their union membership status.

9.3   Data

The study is based on linked employer-employee data collected annually by the Ministry of Employment in Portugal. The data cover all firms with wage earners in manufacturing and services in the private sector; because data provision is compulsory only for companies with wage earners, the coverage of the agricultural sector is low. Public administration and domestic work are not covered. Reported data include the firm's industry, location, employment, ownership (foreign, private, or public) and sales, and the worker's gender, age, occupation, schooling, date of admission into the company, monthly earnings, and duration of work. We use data from 1995 to 2000, since identification of THS work was not possible for earlier years.

The Portuguese Classification of Industries reports, under code 74500, firms in "labor recruitment and provision of personnel."[4] This is the definition we use to identify temporary help service firms and their workers.[5] Given the relevance of the distinction between stocks and flows for this activity (with high worker turnover), it should be stressed that the data refer to the stock of workers at a reference week in October each year.[6] Wage earners aged sixteen to sixty-five years were selected for analysis. We consider only the worker's main job, defined as the job where the most hours were worked per month. Extensive checks have been performed to guarantee the accuracy of the data, using gender, date of birth, highest educational level, and starting date in a company (details on the procedures followed to clean the panel can be found in Cardoso [2005]).

The administrative nature of the data and the legal requirement for the firm to post the data in a space public to its workers contribute to its reliability. Workers are identified by a personal identifier, based on a transformation of the social security number, and it is thus possible to track them over time, as long as they work in the private sector. If they are missing from the database, the workers could be, among other situations, unemployed, inactive, employed in the public administration, or self-employed without dependent workers, and we cannot ascertain the employment status.

In the analyses that follow, we will keep the whole population of workers who ever had a THS job, while limiting the data on workers who never had a THS job to a 10 percent sample, so as to keep computations manageable. For each worker sampled, all the available observations on his or her work history were kept for analysis. We report results on the overall sample, as well as separately for women and men of sixteen to twenty-five years of age and for women and men of twenty-six to sixty-five years of age.

---

4. This classification closely follows NACE, the Classification of Economic Activities in the European Community. Before 1995, a different industry classification, which did not assign a specific code to this activity, was used.

5. This definition has the disadvantage that we cannot distinguish between managers and clerical staff that operate the THS and the workers who are hired out to using firms.

6. Because of the timing of observations, we do not analyze the job tenure with THS firms because not all jobs of short duration are captured in the data.

Gross hourly wages were computed and were deflated using the Consumer Price Index (with the year 2000 as the base period). Wage outliers, that is, hourly wages of less than half the first percentile or above twenty times percentile 99, have been dropped from the analysis.

9.4 Descriptive Evidence on the Labor Force of THS Firms and Their Career Prospects

The number of firms and workers in the THS sector increased from 1995 to 2000, and we observe a rising share in overall employment, from 0.5 to 1 percent. (These figures are a lower bound on the overall number of THS workers, as short spells are underrepresented because of how the data are collected.) The number of firms, although increasing in absolute numbers, had a share of about 0.1 percent of all firms in the private sector. (A tabulation of the development over time is given in the appendix, table 9A.1.)

Table 9.1 provides the descriptive statistics of our estimating sample, by THS status. On average, THS workers had a wage lower than other workers, with a mean hourly wage difference of about 23 percent. We also see that the dispersion of wages is lower for THS workers, a finding also evident in figure 9.1, where we plot the two wage distributions, pooling the observations from the six years. The graph shows that the distribution of wages for THS workers is more concentrated, with a higher peak and a thinner upper tail.

We observe a similar percentage of women in THS firms as in other firms in the private sector (about 42 percent). Temporary help service workers are, on average, four years younger than workers in the rest of the private sector, who are, on average, thirty-six years old. Temporary help service workers are, on average, slightly better educated than other workers (about 50 percent of THS workers have six school years or less, compared to 61 percent in other sectors; nevertheless, there are fewer workers with a higher-education diploma in THS firms than in other firms; i.e., 4 versus 6 percent). There are also more low-skilled and administrative workers in THS than in other firms. We see that workers in THS have short tenures with their firms, with 68 percent of THS workers having tenures of less than one year; in contrast, for all other workers the fraction of workers who have tenures of less than one year is 18 percent. The incidence of part time is higher in THS firms than in the rest of the economy (25 percent versus 9 percent).

Temporary help services firms are concentrated in the Lisbon region (78 percent, as opposed to 42 percent for the remaining sectors).[7]

For 2000 only, data on the type of contract are available, indicating that

---

7. The agencies in Lisbon have, on average, a larger volume of business than companies in the rest of the economy, and the share of the market held by the five largest firms, either in terms of employment or sales volume, has remained stable at about 33 percent (not shown in the table). These figures are consistent with those reported in Storrie (2002) and they show Portugal as one of the countries where THS is least concentrated in Europe; only the United Kingdom and Germany have a lower market concentration.

Table 9.1   **Descriptive statistics**

| | THS workers | | Regular workers | |
Variable	Mean	Standard deviation	Mean	Standard deviation
Hourly wage (log)	6.416	(0.390)	6.519	(0.563)
Hourly wage (PTE)	673.784	(458.229)	831.341	(829.515)
Female	0.416		0.421	
Lisbon	0.777		0.418	
Education				
Four years	0.304		0.378	
Six years	0.207		0.232	
Nine years	0.185		0.148	
Twelve years	0.253		0.161	
Sixteen years	0.040		0.061	
Age	31.514	(10.383)	35.879	(11.142)
Occupation				
Profes., scientists	0.009		0.031	
Middle manag.	0.044		0.097	
Administrative workers	0.257		0.159	
Service and sales workers	0.104		0.134	
Farmers	0.005		0.003	
Skilled workers and craftsmen	0.275		0.266	
Machine operators, assembly workers	0.100		0.132	
Unskilled workers	0.198		0.153	
Tenure				
< 1 year	0.680		0.177	
1 ≤ tenure < 2 years	0.125		0.115	
2 ≤ tenure < 3 years	0.052		0.083	
Part-time	0.246		0.085	
Available for 2000 only:				
Fixed-term contract	0.736		0.145	
N	83,022		1,074,162	

74 percent of THS workers have a fixed-term contract, which compares to 15 percent of the workers in the rest of the private sector.

9.5   Lower Pay in THS Firms?

The comparison of mean wages points to a substantial and significant wage difference between THS and regular workers, despite the stringent legal requirements. In this section, we investigate in more detail if such wage differences are still evident once we control for the firm and worker characteristics.

Table 9.2 reports the estimated coefficients (and robust standard errors) of wage regressions where we estimate the hourly wages of workers in the private sector. We use several empirical specifications for men and women who are sixteen to twenty-five years of age and for men and women of

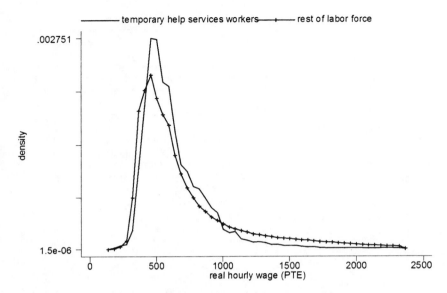

Fig. 9.1   Wage distribution for THS and other workers, 1995–2000
Source: Own computations based on Portugal (1995 to 2000).
Note: The graph plots the wage distribution of workers in the THS sector and in the rest of the economy, pooling observations from 1995 to 2000. Wages above the 99th percentile are not plotted. Wages are deflated to 2000 values using the Consumer Price Index.

ages twenty-six to sixty-five. (The full estimation results are provided in the appendix, where we also report estimation results for the complete sample.)

Specification 1 controls for location of the firm and age and education of the workers (and indicators for the year of observation). Specification 2 controls in addition for the workers' occupation, which is one of the following categories: senior managers, professionals or scientists: junior managers; administrative workers; service and sales workers; farmers; skilled workers and craftsmen; machine operators, assembly workers; and unskilled workers.

Because workers do not randomly choose to work for a THS firm, any observed wage difference between THS and other workers may be caused by personal characteristics not observed by us. We therefore estimate wage regressions where we control for worker unobservable quality by introducing worker fixed effects.[8] The estimated coefficients from these estimations are presented in columns (3) and (4) of table 9.2, where specification 3 (specification 4) has the same set of controls as specification 1 (specification 2).

---

8. Identification in this regressions of the impact of education on wages is feasible given that a share of the workforce is observed changing—increasing—its education level. These shares are 2 percent, 2 percent, 2 percent, and 1 percent, respectively, for workers initially observed with four, six, nine, and twelve years of education.

Table 9.2   Estimated wage differences for THS and regular workers

	OLS		Fixed-effects	
	Coefficient (Standard error) (1)	Coefficient (Standard error) (2)	Coefficient (Standard error) (3)	Coefficient (Standard error) (4)
Sixteen to twenty-five years of age				
Women	.077	.052	.050	.039
	(.003)***	(.003)***	(.005)***	(.006)***
Obs.	118,914	103,076	118,914	103,076
Men	.027	.021	.019	.013
	(.003)***	(.003)***	(.005)***	(.006)**
Obs.	134,774	112,916	134,774	112,916
Twenty-six to sixty-five years of age				
Women	−.135	−.118	−.006	−.010
	.003***	(.003)***	(.004)*	(.004)**
Obs.	367,492	346,779	367,492	346,779
Men	−.226	−.164	−.058	−.054
	(.003)***	(.003)***	(.004)***	(.004)***
Obs.	536,004	512,917	536,004	512,917

Note: The independent variable is (log) real hourly wages. Specifications 1 and 2 are based on pooled ordinary least squares (OLS) wage regressions and specifications 3 and 4 are fixed-effects panel wage regressions. All specifications control for location of the firm, age, and education of the workers, and the year of observation. Specifications 2 and 4 control in addition for the workers' occupation. The full set of estimation results are provided in the appendix, tables 9A.3 to 9A.6. Robust standard errors. Estimations based on Portugal (1995 to 2000).
***Significant at the 1 percent level.
**Significant at the 5 percent level.
*Significant at the 10 percent level.

The ordinary least squares (OLS) estimations show that younger women who work for a THS firm receive a higher wage than women who work for other firms. We estimate that they receive a wage that is about 5 to 7 percent greater than similar workers in other firms. See columns (1) and (2) in table 9.2. The results from the fixed-effects regressions indicate that younger women who start to work in THS firms have a higher wage than they would earn in the regular sector. This difference in wage development is estimated to be around 4 to 5 percent. See columns (3) and (4) in table 9.2.

For younger men—while they earn, on average, a wage that is some 2 percent greater in THS firms than in other firms—these differences are not as pronounced as for young women. Young men's wages are estimated to increase by about 1 to 2 percent if they start to work in a THS firm. All these estimated wage differences are statistically significant at an error level of 5 percent or less.

Prime-age women working in THS firms earn about 12 to 13 percent less than similar women in other firms. According to our fixed-effects estimates, their wages are estimated to decrease on starting to work with a THS firm.

Although the penalty for starting in a THS firm is statistically significant at conventional confidence levels, the point estimate is at about 1 percent and thus not overly important from an economic perspective.

For prime-age male workers, we obtain coefficients from the pooled OLS regression that indicate a remarkably lower average wage in THS than in the regular sector. The wage penalty is estimated to be between 16 and 23 percent. In addition, controlling for fixed characteristics, these workers experience a wage decrease of about 5 percent upon starting with the THS firm.

9.6   Wages Before and After Working in THS Firms

We proceed placing the spells of THS employment in the context of the workers' careers. The wages of those workers who chose to work for a THS firm could have been deteriorating relative to similar workers prior to entering a THS firm. This relative wage loss could have been their motivation to start a THS job. A second issue concerns the workers' careers once they start working for a THS firm and their wage progression thereafter. Two different hypotheses on the wage development on entering the sector may be formulated. Temporary help service firms typically place workers in several firms—this improves their position to finding a good job match, possibly leading to being formally hired by a firm that already hired them through the THS firm. As such, a worker would have already accumulated some firm-specific human capital, and we then expect the worker to have a comparable, if not faster, wage progression than other workers on leaving the THS firm. Alternatively, working for a THS might be interpreted as a signal of lower ability by employers and would result in fewer and/or worse job offers than other workers would receive. This kind of mechanism would lead to poorer employment prospects for former THS workers and their wages would be lower than those of otherwise similar workers.

In the vein of Segal and Sullivan (1998) and Jacobson, LaLonde, and Sullivan (1993), we construct a set of dummy variables to capture the number of years before or after the start of the THS spell. For each worker, the dummy variable D_t^k is 1 if the worker at time t is k years away from the start of the THS spell. Because our data cover six years, we have allowed k to range between -2 and 2, with a negative (positive) k indicating the time before (after) the start of a spell of THS employment. If the worker works for a THS firm at time t, the dummy variable D_t^0 is equivalent to a dummy variable on THS work, similar to the one used in the previous specifications.[9] We report results including controls for location, age, education, and worker-fixed effects, and the year of observation (with and without occupation included). For this part of the analysis, we dropped workers who

9. We have also used dummy variables for the post-THS wages that indicate the time since the end of the THS employment. However, since most THS spells are of short duration, the interpretation of our findings changes little. These results are available at request from the authors.

had more than one spell of THS, which led to an exclusion of 7 percent of workers who ever had a THS spell.

Table 9.3 reports the estimated coefficients for the indicator variables that control for employment episodes before and after the start of the THS spell. Focusing on the estimated coefficient on THS, the estimations confirm the previous results—that is, young workers earn a higher wage than in regular contracts. In contrast, older workers earn lower wages in THS firms than in other firms, with the difference being smaller for women than for men.

Before entering THS, we observe that there are no differences in terms of wages for young workers between those who started to work for a THS firm and those who did not. The motivation to enter THS seems to be different for younger than for older workers, because we estimate that older workers, both men and women, see their wages deteriorate relative to similar workers before starting to work in a THS firm, suggesting that adverse labor market conditions may motivate prime-age workers to search for a THS job.

After the start of the THS spell, we estimate that young female workers enjoy higher wages than their peers, at least for the two years we are able to investigate, a wage difference of some 2 to 4 percent. We do not find this pattern for young male THS workers. For them, post-THS wages are not significantly different from similar workers in other sectors, after accounting for worker-unobservable quality. Older female workers are estimated to have about 1 percent lower wages than women who did not work for a THS firm, but the difference is smaller than in the years before the THS spell, where it amounted to some 3 percent. Older male THS workers receive about 4 percent less than comparable workers before and after their THS spell.

9.7   Conclusion

Using unique, linked employer-employee data from Portugal that cover the entire private sector, we investigate whether workers in THS firms receive a lower wage than workers who work for other firms. Despite the extensive legal protection of THS workers, we observe a wage difference of about 23 percent for THS workers in the raw data. Once we control for standard human capital indicators, the differential is estimated to be 9 percent. The available data allow a more careful analysis in that we are able to control for unobservable workers' characteristics by using workers' fixed effects in our estimations. Controlling for this type of factors, the wage penalty of THS workers is reduced to 1 to 2 percent for the overall labor force.

However, interesting differences emerge across groups of workers: young and older, males and females. For young workers, working for a THS firm results in wages that are higher than other sectors. The difference is particularly high for women who earn about 4 to 5 percent higher wages in THS than elsewhere; for young men the difference is about 1 percent. In contrast, for older workers THS work is associated with a wage penalty, which is larger for males than for females.

Table 9.3   Estimated wage differences before and after start of THS work

	Age: sixteen to twenty-five				Age: twenty-six to sixty-five			
	Women		Men		Women		Men	
	Coefficient (Standard error)	Coefficient (Standard error)	Coefficient (Standard error)	Coefficient (Standard error)	Coefficient (Standard error)	Coefficient (Standard error)	Coefficient (Standard error)	Coefficient (Standard error)
Two yrs before start THS spell	−.008 (.011)	−.005 (.013)	.001 (.010)	.005 (.012)	−.032 (.008)***	−.031 (.008)***	−.008 (.007)	−.006 (.007)
One yr before start THS spell	−.017 (.011)	−.013 (.013)	−.013 (.011)	−.010 (.012)	−.037 (.008)***	−.029 (.009)***	−.038 (.008)***	−.037 (.008)***
THS work	.059 (.008)***	.053 (.009)***	.028 (.008)***	.022 (.009)**	−.014 (.005)***	−.014 (.005)***	−.065 (.005)***	−.059 (.005)***
One yr after start of THS spell	.034 (.009)***	.036 (.010)***	.023 (.009)***	.012 (.010)	−.009 (.005)*	−.007 (.005)	−.035 (.005)***	−.036 (.006)***
Two yrs after start of THS spell	.015 (.010)	.017 (.010)*	−.001 (.009)	−.005 (.010)	−.013 (.005)**	−.013 (.006)**	−.037 (.006)***	−.037 (.006)***
Occupation	—	yes	—	yes	—	yes	—	yes
Obs.	117,732	102,058	133,097	111,502	364,573	344,148	530,175	507,626
Adjusted R^2	.675	.683	.646	.655	.873	.876	.873	.874

Note: The independent variable is (log) real hourly wages. All specifications control for location of the firm, age, education, and worker-fixed effects, and the year of observation. The full set of estimation results are provided in the appendix, tables 9A.8 to 9A.11. Robust standard errors. Estimations based on Portugal (1995 to 2000).

***Significant at the 1 percent level.

**Significant at the 5 percent level.

*Significant at the 10 percent level.

The wage developments before starting to work for THS are clearly different for young and older workers, which may result in a different motivation to start working for a THS firm. Before entering a THS firm, prime-age workers see their wages deteriorate relative to similar workers, suggesting that adverse labor market conditions motivate them to search for a THS job. For younger workers, we cannot detect any pre-TWA wage trend.

The impact of THS employment on the subsequent career is different for young and older workers, too. For young females, wages are higher one and two years after starting to work for THS than for comparable women in other firms. For them, the training, networking, or other skills provided by THS firms lead to a faster wage growth than for similar workers elsewhere in the economy. For young males, the results do not differ significantly between those who worked for a THS firm and those who did not. For older workers, we identify once again a detrimental impact of THS work, since after the start of the THS spell, their wages remain significantly below those of similar workers not in THS, particularly for males.

The evidence collected lends support to attempts (namely by the European Commission) to safeguard the workers in THS firms and their subsequent career progression, in particular for prime-age and older workers. For young workers, the evidence suggests that working for a THS firm can be an entry gate and stepping stone in the labor market.

Appendix

Table 9A.1   **THS firms and workers in Portugal, 1995–2000**

	Firms	Workers
1995	148	7,637
	(0.10)	(0.46)
1996	158	9,415
	(0.10)	(0.57)
1997	184	13,072
	(0.11)	(0.74)
1998	203	15,634
	(0.11)	(0.86)
1999	223	17,179
	(0.11)	(0.89)
2000	243	20,085
	(0.11)	(1.00)

Note: Own calculations based on MTSS, 1995–2000, Portugal. Values in parentheses indicate percentage of all private sector.

Table 9A.2   **Wage regressions, all workers**

	Coefficient (Standard error) (1)	Coefficient (Standard error) (2)	Coefficient (Standard error) (3)	Coefficient (Standard error) (4)
THS work	−.122	−.097	−.012	−.016
	(.001)***	(.002)***	(.002)***	(.002)***
Lisbon	.164	.165	.039	.040
	(.0008)***	(.0008)***	(.002)***	(.002)***
Female	−.241	−.207		
	(.0008)***	(.0008)***		
Educ: four years	.115	.073	−.035	−.039
	(.002)***	(.002)***	(.010)***	(.010)***
Educ: six years	.281	.190	−.035	−.043
	(.003)***	(.003)***	(.010)***	(.011)***
Educ: nine years	.478	.313	−.019	−.031
	(.003)***	(.003)***	(.011)*	(.011)***
Educ: twelve years	.650	.398	.006	−.004
	(.003)***	(.003)***	(.011)	(.011)
Educ: sixteen years	1.272	.766	.156	.132
	(.003)***	(.004)***	(.013)***	(.014)***
Age	.050	.039	.080	.072
	(.0002)***	(.0002)***	(.0006)***	(.0006)***
Age sq.	−.0004	−.0003	−.0005	−.0005
	(2.97e-06)***	(2.96e-06)***	(7.30e-06)***	(7.70e-06)***
Const.	4.999	5.927	4.410	4.678
	(.005)***	(.007)***	(.015)***	(.017)***
Occupation (eight dummies)	—	yes	—	yes
Worker-fixed effects	—	—	yes	yes
Obs.	1,157,184	1,075,688	1,157,184	1,075,688
R^2	.457	.516	.858	.862

Note: Adjusted R^2 reported for the fixed-effects regressions. Robust standard errors in parentheses. All regressions control for year of observation. Estimations based on MTSS, 1995–2000, Portugal.

***Significant at the 1 percent level.

**Significant at the 5 percent level.

*Significant at the 10 percent level.

Table 9A.3 **Wage regressions, women sixteen to twenty-five**

	Coefficient (Standard error) (1)	Coefficient (Standard error) (2)	Coefficient (Standard error) (3)	Coefficient (Standard error) (4)
THS work	.077	.052	.050	.039
	(.003)***	(.003)***	(.005)***	(.006)***
Lisbon	.108	.109	.019	.022
	(.002)***	(.002)***	(.007)***	(.008)***
Educ: four years	−.00008	−.010	−.167	−.226
	(.016)	(.018)	(.110)	(.122)*
Educ: six years	.052	.036	−.153	−.220
	(.016)***	(.018)**	(.108)	(.120)*
Educ: nine years	.129	.095	−.146	−.217
	(.016)***	(.018)***	(.107)	(.120)*
Educ: twelve years	.263	.190	−.118	−.185
	(.016)***	(.018)***	(.108)	(.120)
Educ: sixteen years	.718	.508	.036	−.057
	(.017)***	(.019)***	(.109)	(.122)
Age	.053	.012	.141	.075
	(.007)***	(.008)	(.009)***	(.011)***
Age sq.	−.0006	.0002	−.002	−.0005
	(.0002)***	(.0002)	(.0002)***	(.0003)**
Const.	5.096	5.965	4.165	5.129
	(.074)***	(.089)***	(.150)***	(.179)***
Occupation (eight dummies)	—	yes	—	yes
Worker-fixed effects	—	—	yes	yes
Obs.	118,914	103,076	118,914	103,076
R^2	.34	.374	.673	.681

Note: Adjusted R^2 reported for the fixed-effects regressions. Robust standard errors in parentheses. All regressions control for year of observation. Estimations based on MTSS, 1995–2000, Portugal.

***Significant at the 1 percent level.
**Significant at the 5 percent level.
*Significant at the 10 percent level.

Table 9A.4   **Wage regressions, men sixteen to twenty-five**

	Coefficient (Standard error) (1)	Coefficient (Standard error) (2)	Coefficient (Standard error) (3)	Coefficient (Standard error) (4)
THS work	.027	.021	.019	.013
	(.003)***	(.003)***	(.005)***	(.006)**
Lisbon	.124	.123	.046	.050
	(.002)***	(.002)***	(.007)***	(.008)***
Educ: four years	.020	.015	−.009	−.018
	(.011)*	(.012)	(.034)	(.041)
Educ: six years	.069	.059	−.004	−.017
	(.010)***	(.011)***	(.034)	(.041)
Educ: nine years	.140	.120	.021	.013
	(.011)***	(.012)***	(.034)	(.042)
Educ: twelve years	.254	.199	.044	.038
	(.011)***	(.012)***	(.035)	(.043)
Educ: sixteen years	.728	.512	.190	.158
	(.013)***	(.015)***	(.042)***	(.049)***
Age	.131	.079	.220	.142
	(.007)***	(.008)***	(.009)***	(.012)***
Age sq.	−.002	−.001	−.003	−.002
	(.0002)***	(.0002)***	(.0002)***	(.0003)***
Const.	4.213	5.152	3.057	4.141
	(.074)***	(.090)***	(.108)***	(.145)***
Occupation (eight dummies)	—	yes	—	yes
Worker-fixed effects	—	—	yes	yes
Obs.	134,774	112,916	134,774	112,916
R^2	.28	.301	.642	.652

Note: Adjusted R^2 reported for the fixed-effects regressions. Robust standard errors in parentheses. All regressions control for year of observation. Estimations based on MTSS, 1995–2000, Portugal.

***Significant at the 1 percent level.

**Significant at the 5 percent level.

*Significant at the 10 percent level.

Table 9A.5   Wage regression, women twenty-six to sixty-five

	Coefficient (Standard error) (1)	Coefficient (Standard error) (2)	Coefficient (Standard error) (3)	Coefficient (Standard error) (4)
THS work	−.135	−.118	−.006	−.010
	(.003)***	(.003)***	(.004)*	(.004)**
Lisbon	.153	.149	.032	.031
	(.001)***	(.001)***	(.004)***	(.004)***
Educ: four years	.054	.025	−.021	−.021
	(.004)***	(.004)***	(.015)	(.015)
Educ: six years	.205	.125	−.022	−.025
	(.004)***	(.004)***	(.016)	(.016)
Educ: nine years	.454	.263	−.020	−.020
	(.004)***	(.004)***	(.016)	(.017)
Educ: twelve years	.638	.348	.003	.007
	(.004)***	(.005)***	(.017)	(.018)
Educ: sixteen years	1.250	.703	.100	.097
	(.005)***	(.006)***	(.022)***	(.023)***
Age	.049	.039	.058	.057
	(.0006)***	(.0006)***	(.001)***	(.001)***
Age sq.	−.0005	−.0004	−.0003	−.0003
	(7.44e-06)***	(7.15e-06)***	(.00002)***	(.00002)***
Const.	4.837	5.784	4.682	4.810
	(.013)***	(.015)***	(.029)***	(.031)***
Occupation (eight dummies)	—	yes	—	yes
Worker-fixed effects	—	—	yes	yes
Obs.	367,492	346,779	367,492	346,779
R^2	.451	.528	.872	.875

Note: Adjusted R^2 reported for the fixed-effects regressions. Robust standard errors in parentheses. All regressions control for year of observation. Estimations based on MTSS, 1995–2000, Portugal.

***Significant at the 1 percent level.

**Significant at the 5 percent level.

*Significant at the 10 percent level.

Table 9A.6   **Wage regression, men twenty-six to sixty-five**

	Coefficient (Standard error) (1)	Coefficient (Standard error) (2)	Coefficient (Standard error) (3)	Coefficient (Standard error) (4)
THS work	−.226	−.164	−.058	−.054
	(.003)***	(.003)***	(.004)***	(.004)***
Lisbon	.191	.188	.035	.040
	(.001)***	(.001)***	(.004)***	(.004)***
Educ: four years	.147	.087	−.039	−.043
	(.003)***	(.003)***	(.014)***	(.014)***
Educ: six years	.319	.206	−.044	−.048
	(.004)***	(.004)***	(.014)***	(.015)***
Educ: nine years	.561	.348	−.041	−.048
	(.004)***	(.004)***	(.015)***	(.016)***
Educ: twelve years	.759	.459	−.022	−.028
	(.004)***	(.004)***	(.016)	(.017)*
Educ: sixteen years	1.369	.849	.123	.105
	(.005)***	(.006)***	(.021)***	(.022)***
Age	.066	.054	.068	.065
	(.0005)***	(.0005)***	(.001)***	(.001)***
Age sq.	−.0006	−.0005	−.0004	−.0004
	(6.21e-06)***	(5.94e-06)***	(1.00e-05)***	(1.00e-05)***
Const.	4.591	5.546	4.635	4.783
	(.011)***	(.012)***	(.026)***	(.028)***
Occupation (eight dummies)	—	yes	—	yes
Worker fixed effects	—	—	yes	yes
Obs.	536,004	512,917	536,004	512,917
R^2	.422	.488	.870	.872

Note: Adjusted R^2 reported for the fixed-effects regressions. Robust standard errors in parentheses. All regressions control for year of observation. Estimations based on MTSS, 1995–2000, Portugal.

***Significant at the 1 percent level.

**Significant at the 5 percent level.

*Significant at the 10 percent level.

Table 9A.7   **Wage regression with additional regressors, all workers**

	Coefficient (Standard error) (1)	Coefficient (Standard error) (2)
Two yrs before start THS spell	−.018	−.014
	(.004)***	(.004)***
One yr before start THS spell	−.038	−.034
	(.004)***	(.004)***
Year of start of THS spell	−.017	−.019
	(.003)***	(.003)***
One yr after start of THS spell	−.008	−.010
	(.003)***	(.003)***
Two yrs after start of THS spell	−.016	−.016
	(.003)***	(.003)***
Lisbon	.039	.040
	(.002)***	(.003)***
Educ: four years	−.034	−.036
	(.010)***	(.010)***
Educ: six years	−.035	−.042
	(.010)***	(.011)***
Educ: nine years	−.018	−.029
	(.011)*	(.011)***
Educ: twelve years	.007	−.001
	(.011)	(.011)
Educ: sixteen years	.158	.135
	(.013)***	(.014)***
Age	.080	.073
	(.0006)***	(.0006)***
Age sq.	−.0005	−.0005
	(7.32e-06)***	(7.72e-06)***
Const.	4.407	4.669
	(.015)***	(.017)***
Occupation (eight dummies)	—	yes
Obs.	1,145,577	1,065,334
Adjusted R^2	.860	.864

Note: Robust standard errors in parentheses. All regressions control for year of observation and worker-fixed effects. Estimations based on MTSS, 1995–2000, Portugal.

***Significant at the 1 percent level.

**Significant at the 5 percent level.

*Significant at the 10 percent level.

Table 9A.8   **Wage regression with additional regressors, women sixteen to twenty-five**

	Coefficient (Standard error) (1)	Coefficient (Standard error) (2)
Two yrs before start THS spell	−.008	−.005
	(.011)	(.013)
One yr before start THS spell	−.017	−.013
	(.011)	(.013)
Year of start of THS spell	.059	.053
	(.008)***	(.009)***
One yr after start of THS spell	.034	.036
	(.009)***	(.010)***
Two yrs after start of THS spell	.015	.017
	(.010)	(.010)*
Lisbon	.019	.022
	(.007)***	(.008)***
Educ: four years	−.169	−.227
	(.111)	(.123)*
Educ: six years	−.157	−.224
	(.108)	(.120)*
Educ: nine years	−.152	−.222
	(.108)	(.120)*
Educ: twelve years	−.124	−.189
	(.108)	(.121)
Educ: sixteen years	.030	−.059
	(.109)	(.122)
Age	.141	.074
	(.009)***	(.011)***
Age sq.	−.002	−.0005
	(.0002)***	(.0003)*
Const.	4.171	5.138
	(.150)***	(.179)***
Occupation (eight dummies)	—	yes
Obs.	117,732	102,058
Adjusted R^2	.675	.683

Note: Robust standard errors in parentheses. All regressions control for year of observation and worker-fixed effects. Estimations based on MTSS, 1995–2000, Portugal.

***Significant at the 1 percent level.
**Significant at the 5 percent level.
*Significant at the 10 percent level.

Table 9A.9	Wage regression with additional regressors, men sixteen to twenty-five	
	Coefficient (Standard error) (1)	Coefficient (Standard error) (2)
2 yrs before start THS spell	.001 (.010)	.005 (.012)
One yr before start THS spell	−.013 (.011)	−.010 (.012)
Year of start of THS spell	.028 (.008)***	.022 (.009)**
One yr after start of THS spell	.023 (.009)***	.012 (.010)
Two yrs after start of THS spell	−.001 (.009)	−.005 (.010)
Lisbon	.047 (.007)***	.050 (.008)***
Educ: four years	−.009 (.034)	−.018 (.042)
Educ: six years	−.006 (.034)	−.019 (.042)
Educ: nine years	.019 (.035)	.013 (.042)
Educ: twelve years	.043 (.036)	.038 (.043)
Educ: sixteen years	.189 (.043)***	.160 (.050)***
Age	.219 (.010)***	.141 (.012)***
Age sq.	−.003 (.0002)***	−.002 (.0003)***
Const.	3.069 (.109)***	4.151 (.146)***
Occupation (eight dummies)	—	yes
Obs.	133,097	111,502
Adjusted R^2	.646	.655

Note: Robust standard errors in parentheses. All regressions control for year of observation and worker-fixed effects. Estimations based on MTSS, 1995–2000, Portugal.

***Significant at the 1 percent level.

**Significant at the 5 percent level.

*Significant at the 10 percent level.

Table 9A.10 **Wage regression with additional regressors, women twenty-six to sixty-five**

	Coefficient (Standard error) (1)	Coefficient (Standard error) (2)
Two yrs before start THS spell	−.032	−.031
	(.008)***	(.008)***
One yr before start THS spell	−.037	−.029
	(.008)***	(.009)***
Year of start of THS spell	−.014	−.014
	(.005)***	(.005)***
One yr after start of THS spell	−.009	−.007
	(.005)*	(.005)
Two yrs after start of THS spell	−.013	−.013
	(.005)**	(.006)**
Lisbon	.031	.029
	(.004)***	(.004)***
Educ: four years	−.020	−.021
	(.015)	(.015)
Educ: six years	−.022	−.025
	(.016)	(.016)
Educ: nine years	−.022	−.022
	(.016)	(.017)
Educ: twelve years	.001	.005
	(.017)	(.018)
Educ: sixteen years	.098	.094
	(.022)***	(.023)***
Age	.058	.057
	(.001)***	(.001)***
Age sq.	−.0003	−.0003
	(.00002)***	(.00002)***
Const.	4.695	4.815
	(.029)***	(.031)***
Occupation (eight dummies)	—	yes
Obs.	364573	344148
Adjusted R^2	.873	.876

Note: Robust standard errors in parentheses. All regressions control for year of observation and worker-fixed effects. Estimations based on MTSS, 1995–2000, Portugal.

***Significant at the 1 percent level.
**Significant at the 5 percent level.
*Significant at the 10 percent level.

Table 9A.11   Wage regression with additional regressors, men twenty-six to sixty-five

	Coefficient (Standard error) (1)	Coefficient (Standard error) (2)
Two yrs before start THS spell	−.008	−.006
	(.007)	(.007)
One yr before start THS spell	−.038	−.037
	(.008)***	(.008)***
Year of start of THS spell	−.065	−.059
	(.005)***	(.005)***
One yr after start of THS spell	−.035	−.036
	(.005)***	(.006)***
Two yrs after start of THS spell	−.037	−.037
	(.006)***	(.006)***
Lisbon	.035	.040
	(.004)***	(.004)***
Educ: four years	−.041	−.042
	(.014)***	(.014)***
Educ: six years	−.046	−.047
	(.014)***	(.015)***
Educ: nine years	−.040	−.045
	(.015)***	(.016)***
Educ: twelve years	−.021	−.025
	(.016)	(.017)
Educ: sixteen years	.126	.110
	(.022)***	(.022)***
Age	.068	.066
	(.001)***	(.001)***
Age sq.	−.0004	−.0004
	(1.00e-05)***	(1.00e-05)***
Const.	4.629	4.772
	(.026)***	(.028)***
Occupation (eight dummies)	—	yes
Obs.	530,175	507,626
Adjusted R^2	.873	.874

Note: Robust standard errors in parentheses. All regressions control for year of observation and worker fixed-effects. Estimations based on MTSS, 1995–2000, Portugal.

***Significant at the 1 percent level.

**Significant at the 5 percent level.

*Significant at the 10 percent level.

References

Amuedo-Dorantes, C., M. Malo, and F. Muñoz-Bullón. 2006. The role of temporary help agencies in facilitating temp-to-perm transitions. IZA Discussion Papers no. 2177. Bonn, IZA. Available at: http://ftp.iza.org/dp2177.pdf.

Antoni, M., and E. J. Jahn. 2006. Do changes in regulation affect employment duration in temporary work agencies. IZA Discussion Papers no. 2343. Bonn, IZA. http://ftp.iza.org/dp2343.pdf.

Autor, D. H. 2001. Why do temporary help firms provide free general skills training? *Quarterly Journal of Economics* 116 (4): 1409–48.

Autor, D. H., and S. N. Houseman. 2005. Do temporary help jobs improve labor market outcomes for low-skilled workers? Evidence from random assignments. Staff Working Paper no. 05-124. Kalamazoo, MI: W. E. Upjohn Institute for Employment Research.

Blank, R. M. 1998. Contingent work in a changing labor market. In *Generating jobs: How to increase demand for less-skilled workers,* ed. R. B. Freeman and P. Gottschalk, 258–94. New York: Russell Sage Foundation.

Booth, A., M. Francesconi, and J. Frank. 2002. Temporary jobs: Stepping stones or dead ends. *The Economic Journal* 112:F189–F213.

Cardoso, A. R. 2005. Big fish in small pond, or small fish in big pond? An analysis of job mobility. IZA Discussion Paper 1900. Bonn, Germany: Institute for the Study of Labor. Available at: http://ftp.iza.org/dp1900.pdf.

European Commission. 2002. Proposal for a directive of the European Parliament and the Council on working conditions for temporary workers. COM/2002/0149 final–COD 2002/0072.

European Parliament and Council Directive (EIRO). 2002. Commission proposes directive on temporary agency workers. European industrial relations observatory. Available at: http://www.eiro.eurofound.eu.int/2002/04/feature/eu0204205f.html.

Forde, C., and G. Slater. 2005. Agency working in Britain: Character, consequences and regulation, *British Journal of Industrial Relations* 43:249–71.

Heinrich, C. J., P. R. Mueser, and K. R. Troske. 2005. Welfare to temporary work: Implications for labor market outcomes. *Review of Economics and Statistics* 87 (1): 154–73.

Houseman, S. N. 2001. Why employers use flexible staffing arrangements: Evidence from an establishment survey. *Industrial and Labor Relations Review* 55 (1): 149–70.

Ichino, A., F. Mealli, and T. Nannicini. 2006. From temporary help jobs to permanent employment: What can we learn from matching estimators and their sensitivity? IZA Discussion Paper no. 2149. Bonn, Germany: IZA. Available at: http://ftp.iza.org/dp2149.pdf.

Jacobson, L. S., R. J. LaLonde, and D. G. Sullivan. 1993. Earnings losses of displaced workers. *American Economic Review* 83 (4): 685–709.

Kvasnicka, M. 2005. Does temporary agency work provide a stepping stone to regular employment? Discussion Papers 2005-031. Collaborative Research Center 649. Berlin: Humboldt University.

Nollen, S. D. 1996. Negative aspects of temporary employment. *Journal of Labor Research* 17 (4): 567–81.

Portugal. 1995 to 2000. Quadros de Pessoal, Ministério do Trabalho e da Segurança Social. Data on magnetic media.

Segal, L. M., and D. G. Sullivan. 1997. The growth of temporary services work. *Journal of Economic Perspectives* 11 (2): 117–36.

———. 1998. Wage differentials for temporary service work: Evidence from administrative data, Working Paper WP-98-23. Chicago: Federal Reserve Bank of Chicago.

Storrie, D. 2002. Temporary agency work in the European Union. Technical report, Office for Official Publications of the European Communities. Luxembourg.

Zijl, M., G. J. van den Berg, and A. Heyma. 2004. Stepping stones for the unemployed: The effect of temporary jobs on the duration until regular work. IZA Discussion Paper no. 1241. Bonn, Germany: IZA. Available at: http://ftp.iza.org/dp1241.pdf.

Does Temporary Help Work Provide a Stepping Stone to Regular Employment?

Michael Kvasnicka

10.1 Introduction

Temporary help work has expanded rapidly across Europe over the last decade. While concerns have been raised about this trend expansion, because of the perceived inferior quality of jobs created in this submarket, growing attention is being paid to the potential longer-term effects of temporary help service (THS) employment on the labor market prospects of workers. Labor turnover in this industry is exceedingly high, and THS employment spells generally constitute but a short transitory period in the labor market histories of workers. Policymakers throughout Europe, in fact, have taken an increasingly active stance over the last years in further promoting THS work by dismantling existing national regulations on temporary help work that circumscribed the operation of temporary help agencies and the use of THS workers by client firms.

The German case constitutes a prime example of this trend. Because of the strong employment record of the THS industry in Germany and the acclaimed stepping-stone function of THS work to regular employment for the jobless, restrictive provisions of the Law on Placement Activity (LoPA),

Michael Kvasnicka is an economist at RWI Essen. This paper has benefited from valuable comments by David Autor, Ronald Bachmann, Stefan Bender, Michael C. Burda, Andrea Ichino, Elke Jahn, Barbara Sianesi, Axel Werwatz, and participants of the 2004 EALE conference in Lisbon, the 2004 meeting of the Verein für Socialpolitik in Dresden, a CEPR workshop on temporary agency work in Berlin in 2005, the 2005 EEA conference in Amsterdam, the 2005 ESPE conference in Paris, and the 2007 NBER Conference on Labor Market Intermediation. I would like to thank the Institute of Employment Research (IAB) of the Federal Employment Agency, who has made the data for this project available. Financial support by the German Research Foundation, the EU-funded CEPR research network "A dynamic approach to Europe's unemployment problem," and the Collaborative Research Center 649 on Economic Risk at Humboldt University, Berlin, is gratefully acknowledged. All remaining errors are my own.

which governs the operation of the German THS submarket since 1972, were increasingly relaxed during the 1990s, a process that culminated in the large-scale labor market reform legislated in late 2002.[1] Among other measures, the latter initiated a near complete dismantling of hitherto existing regulations imposed on temporary help work in Germany (for details, see Burda and Kvasnicka 2006). With stubbornly high rates of unemployment putting a drain on public resources and the efficiency of the federal employment service increasingly being questioned, policymakers in Germany saw THS work as a cost-effective and complementary means to get the unemployed back into work. Apart from the deregulation of the Law on Placement Activity (LoPA), this is evinced by the large-scale creation following the 2002 reform of subsidized temporary help agencies, or personnel-service-agencies (PSA), in all of Germany's 181 employment office districts. These PSA operate as ordinary THS agencies for the sole purpose of providing unemployed workers ports of entry to the labor market and, above all, subsequent springboards to social security employment ("temp-to-perm") by way of temporary work assignments with different firms. What is surprising about these initiatives is that solid empirical evidence for the existence of such a stepping-stone function of THS work for unemployed job seekers was in fact lacking for Germany, and internationally sparse at best.

Using statistical matching techniques, this chapter investigates the validity of the stepping-stone hypothesis of THS work in Germany. We confine the empirical analysis to an investigation of the stepping-stone function of THS employment for unemployed job-seekers only. This restriction in focus is inspired by the fact that the most recent reform of the law on placement activity in Germany has been enacted largely for the acclaimed bridging function of THS work for this particular group of workers. With about every second worker entering THS work in Germany from unemployment, the population of interest chosen does, however, represent a significant share of all inflows into THS work. Conditioning the analysis on prior unemployment experience has the additional advantage of providing some sort of initial condition among the sample chosen—excluding, for instance, students and pupils who only perform vacation work in a THS agency, without seeking any steady employment. Focusing on the first unemployment spell of individuals who register as unemployed in 1994 to 1996, we are able to follow these workers for up to a minimum of five years and hence are in a position to study both the short-term and long-term effects of THS work experience on their subsequent employment trajectories. The matching approach employed in this study is based on the methodology applied by Barbara Sianesi in her studies on the short- and long-term effects of worker participation in Swedish labor market programs (Sianesi 2001, 2004).

Our results show that unemployed workers who enter THS employment

1. Details of the LoPA are provided in section 10.5.2 (subsection 2).

within twelve months of unemployment registration benefit from both higher monthly employment (THS or non-THS) and THS employment chances, as well as from significantly reduced monthly risks of unemployment throughout the four-year period these workers are followed post-entry compared to similar workers who did not join THS work at the same elapsed unemployment duration. Temporary help service workers, however, do not appear to enjoy greater chances of future non-THS employment. While our results, therefore, do not lend empirical support to the stepping-stone hypothesis of THS work for unemployed job-seekers, they neither confirm the existence of adverse effects of agency work on the future chances of workers to find employment outside agency work nor to return to unemployment. If anything, THS work seems to provide an access-to-work function for unemployed workers that leaves them with a higher probability of employment and a lower probability of unemployment for the entire four years their subsequent labor market states are followed.

In the remainder of this chapter, we will, as is commonly done, refer to social-security employment outside the THS industry as "regular employment." This is understood, at least in part, as a terminological convention. For apart from the irregular triangular setup of the THS submarket, workers in the German THS industry do in fact enjoy the same employment protection and worker rights as other workers under the provisions of general labor and social security law (Klös 2000). Temporary help service workers are regular employees of their agencies, for which the two bodies of law regulate and provide minimum standards regarding health and safety in the workplace, worktime, paid annual leave, sick pay, and periods of notice and dismissal protection more generally. Temporary help service workers are covered by the public pension and unemployment insurance system and must have health insurance. To all three of these, the agency and THS worker contribute equally. The distinction between regular and THS employment is hence not grounded in a generally inferior legal position of THS workers. In practice, of course, working conditions encountered may differ, sometimes considerably so. Until recently, wages and working conditions of most THS workers in Germany were not determined by collective bargaining to the effect that workers in agency work tended to be paid less and enjoyed less fringe benefits, such as extra holiday pay or on-the-job training, than workers employed outside agency work (a large fraction of such wage differences, however, as shown by Kvasnicka and Werwatz [2002], can be attributed to earnings-related productivity differences between agency and nonagency workers). Furthermore, employment spells in THS work often fall short of probationary periods granted by law in which layoffs are permitted at significantly shorter notice.

The chapter is structured as follows. Section 10.2 surveys arguments for and against the existence of a stepping-stone function of THS work, section 10.3 reviews the existing literature on the subject, and section 10.4 describes the data. Section 10.5 addresses the evaluation problem encountered in estimating the stepping-stone function of THS work and proposes an appropriate framework for empirical evaluation. Section 10.6 contains the empirical results, and section 10.7 concludes.

10.2   Preliminary Considerations

A number of reasons have been cited in the literature as to why THS work may provide a bridge to regular employment for the unemployed. First, THS workers are frequently recruited among the un- or nonemployed and are hence given access to paid work or entry-level jobs (see, for example, Mangum, Mayall, and Nelson [1985]), otherwise potentially denied to them on the general labor market. Surveys of THS workers show that one of the main reasons for taking up a job in the THS industry is the inability to find a regular job (see, for example, CIETT [2000] for Europe, Cohany [1998] for the United States, or IWG [1995] for Germany). Second, unemployed workers may acquire skills and gain work experience in THS jobs that increase their productivity and hence improve their future labor market prospects (Autor, Levy, and Murnane 1999; Paoli and Merrlié 2001; Kvasnicka and Werwatz 2003), which puts to a halt the depreciation of human capital that would take place in continued unemployment. Third, the search for regular employment may be more effective on a THS job than in unemployment, as work assignments with client firms provide opportunities for workers to get to know different potential employers (Storrie 2002), and to signal their ability (Ichino, Mealli, and Nannicini 2005). Fourth, employers may, in turn, deliberately utilize temporary help work as a riskless screening device to prospect and recruit workers for permanent positions (Segal and Sullivan 1997a; Houseman 1997; Abraham and Taylor 1996; Autor 2001). As client firms are in no way contractually bound to THS workers during a work assignment, on-the-job screening is possible without subjecting oneself to any firing restrictions or direct monetary firing costs. Finally, THS workers are prescreened by the agency, both in terms of general marketable skills when recruiting the worker, and in terms of the specific requirements of client firms for a particular work assignment (Autor 2001; Burda and Kvasnicka 2006). Increased screening may in turn also lead to better and therefore more stable employment relationships, as match quality is improved by prior extensive on-the-job screening (Katz and Krueger 1999).

However, there have also been dissenting voices, pointing out that THS workers often cycle between short employment spells in the industry and extended periods of unemployment (Bronstein 1991), leading to potential labor market segmentation into low wage, less stable THS jobs with little opportunities for career advancement and highly paid permanent jobs (Mangum, Mayall, and Nelson 1985; Segal and Sullivan 1997a). In particular, THS agencies are likely to provide less formal training on the job (Ferber and Waldfogel 1998), as investment in general and therefore marketable skills, by definition the only skills traded on this submarket, increase the risk of the worker being poached before the agency can recoup its outlays through temporary work assignments. Temporary help service employment, especially when full time, may also crowd out productive direct-hire job search. Finally, THS employment may stigmatize workers in the eyes of potential employers under incomplete information, as their inability to obtain regular work may be perceived by the latter as a signal of low productivity.

10.3   Previous Research

Lack of adequate longitudinal data on the individual employment histories of temporary help workers has tended to circumscribe empirical research on the stepping-stone function of THS work. However, a number of studies exist for different countries that have investigated the effect of agency work on the future labor market prospects of workers. These studies, as will be seen, differ markedly in their respective methodologies employed, institutional settings investigated, and populations of workers considered, a heterogeneity that makes it difficult to draw general conclusions. With the notable exception of the quasi-experimental study by Autor and Houseman (2005), however, work in this area has tended to find that THS employment improves rather than harms the subsequent labor market outcomes for workers.

While existing studies for Europe are in the majority descriptive in nature (see Storrie [2002] for a recent survey), they are exclusively so for Germany. Based on administrative data from the German federal employment service, Rudolph and Schröder (1997), for instance, calculate that a third of all THS jobs that were dissolved between 1980 and 1990 in Germany led to subsequent transitions of workers into non-THS employment within one month of job termination. Similarly, using retrospectively collected survey data on THS workers who left a major THS company in the second half of 1986, Brose, Schulze-Böing, and Mayer (1990) find that after their THS employment spell, more workers are employed outside agency work and less are unemployed than before their engagement in agency work. Lacking a comparison group of workers in their respective analyses, however, both studies do not permit any causal interpretation of their findings.[2]

Different types of flexible employment forms, such as fixed-term contract, casual, THS, or part-time employment, have also been frequently subsumed under the ambiguous catch-all term "temporary employment" to then estimate their impact on the future labor market prospects of those holding

---

2. The same applies to other studies that have documented transitions out of agency work without any reference to a suitably chosen control group of workers who did not join agency work. Examples include the studies by Finegold, Levenson, and van Buren (2003), and Segal and Sullivan (1997b) for the United States.

these jobs. Marked differences in their respective contractual arrangements, employment compositions, and economic roles, however, raise the question to what extent results obtained from such analyses do in fact apply to each and every of these heterogeneous employment forms considered. For the United Kingdom, for instance, Booth, Francesconi, and Frank (2002) study the effects on subsequent employment of temporary work, which in their study includes agency and fixed-term contract work. Similarly, Zijl, Heyma, and van den Berg (2004) subsume workers on fixed-term employment contracts, in THS work, on on-call contracts, and in subsidised temporary jobs. They estimate a multistage duration model using longitudinal survey data for the Netherlands. Their findings support a stepping-stone function for these contingent employment forms, as the latter tend to shorten unemployment durations and significantly increase the future chances of workers to be in standard employment.

Positive employment effects have also been found in the majority of studies that focus exclusively on the consequences of THS employment. Using Spanish social security administrative data for 1995 to 2000, García-Pérez and Muñoz-Bullón (2005) estimate a switching regression model to control for self-selection into agency work so as to quantify the effects of THS work spells on occupational upgrading and the chances of workers to find permanent employment (defined as holding an open-ended work contract). The results show that especially high-skilled workers benefit in their subsequent chances of obtaining such employment from a work spell in THS employment. Almus et al. (1999), in turn, examined whether workers unemployed in late 1996 in the German state of Rhineland-Palatinate benefited in terms of their postagency work employment chances from working in nonprofit THS firms that received special subsidies under a program of the federal German government designed to assist the reintegration of unemployed job-seekers. Using data for three employment office districts, they find former agency workers to exhibit significantly higher chances of employment outside agency work than the control group of unemployed workers not previously working in nonprofit agency work. Ichino, Mealli, and Nannicini (2005), also applying propensity-score matching, estimate the effect of a THS work assignment with Manpower in two regions of Italy in early 2001 on the probability to find a permanent job after eighteen months. They find THS work to increase the chances of permanent employment for workers by as much as 19 percentage points in Tuscany and by 11 percentage points in Sicily, compared to baseline probabilities of matched controls of 31 and 23 percent, respectively. This estimated treatment effect, however, is barely significant for Sicily. Furthermore, it is highly heterogeneous with respect to observable characteristics such as age, education, and firm's sector. Finally, Autor and Houseman (2005) exploit the random assignment of welfare-to-work clients in 1999 to 2003 (Work First program) across several welfare service providers with substantially different placement rates at temporary help jobs in a major metropolitan area in the U.S. state of Michigan to study the effect of holding a THS job on the labor market advancement for low-skilled workers. They find THS jobs to boost the short-term earnings of welfare clients, but to reduce their earnings and employment chances one to two years later, and to increase their welfare recidivism over this period. Temporary help service jobs, the authors conclude, appear overall no more effective than providing no job placements at all for low-skilled workers.

As this literature review illustrates, there is great heterogeneity in the methodologies used by different studies (e.g., mere descriptive statistics, statistical matching, quasi-experiments), their respective settings investigated (e.g., entire countries, regions, or subpopulations such as welfare clients), and definitions of treatment used (e.g., THS work, or contingent work more generally, such as fixed-term contract employment and agency work). While the majority of studies tends to find positive effects of THS employment on the subsequent labor market outcomes of workers, the only quasi-experimental that exists does not, which makes it hard to draw any general conclusions regarding the existence and quantitative importance of the stepping-stone function of THS work. With this study on the German THS submarket, we hope to contribute to this actively researched area.

10.4 The Data

The analysis is based on an extended version of the public-use IAB Employment Sample (IABS) of the Institute for Employment Research (IAB) at the German Federal Employment Agency, a 2 percent random sample of all employees registered in the period 1975 to 2001 by the social security system in Germany (data on East German workers is included from 1992 onward). Employment information in the IABS is based on statutory notifications of employers on their workforces to the institutions of the social security system. Containing a host of worker, firm, and job-specific attributes, and with information on unemployment periods involving benefit payments added from the federal unemployment register, the IABS provides exact daily information on the employment and unemployment trajectories of more than one million individuals in the twenty-seven years sampled. Large sample sizes and detailed flow information are indispensable for analyses of the THS industry, as the latter still accounts for only a small employment share in the German economy and is characterized by very high rates of labor turnover. As administrative data, typical problems besetting longitudinal survey data, such as panel mortality due to nonresponses, or memory gaps in retrospective questions, are not encountered in the IABS (Bender, Haas, and Klose 2000).

However, the IABS also has a number of potential shortcomings for the present analysis. First, as THS employment is identified by the industry affiliation of an employer in the IABS, THS workers cannot be differentiated from the administrative staffing personnel of THS firms in the data set. This shortcoming, encountered also in other data sets that have been used for analyses of THS employment, such as the U.S. Current Population Survey, is, however, unlikely to be of major practical importance for our analysis, as the workforce share of staffing personnel is generally very small. Second, as the THS firm alone issues the statutory employment notifications, the IABS neither contains information on client firms nor on work assignments of THS workers (this shortcoming is also shared with all public-use administrative data sources, which by design are tailored to the standard bilateral employment relationship). Lack of information on client firms implies that we are unable to tell whether a successful transition to regular employment occurred to a former client firm or not. As a consequence, we may not directly test the relative importance of the screening and signalling hypotheses for the stepping-stone function of THS work. Our analysis, by necessity, will hence be a reduced form in kind, seeking to uncover a causal effect of THS work without explicitly analyzing its potential causal pathways (see section 10.5.1, Treatment and Nontreatment Status, for further discussion of this point). Complementary future research could fruitfully analyze these pathways and assess their respective quantitative importance for any stepping-stone function of THS work. Finally, covering only employment relationships that are subject to social security contributions, civil servants, the self-employed, and those in marginal dependent employment (until 1999) are not included in the IABS. We may therefore only investigate the employment trajectories of workers in such dependent employment.

In the next section, we discuss in detail the peculiar features of the present evaluation problem of the stepping-stone function of THS employment for the unemployed in comparison to an archetypical-administered social experiment. In doing so, we define key terms, such as treatment (THS employment) and nontreatment status (the counterfactual for the treated), as well as various outcome measures that describe workers' future employment prospects, so as to formulate testable causal questions about the stepping-stone function of THS work, subject to the restrictions imposed by the nature of the phenomenon under investigation and the data available. Sample selection issues will be addressed in the course of this discussion, so that a presentation of summary statistics on major variables recorded in the data is deferred until then.

10.5   The Evaluation Problem

10.5.1   Evaluating the Stepping-Stone Function of THS Work

The archetypical-administered social experiment is conducted only once, with a specific starting and ending date, clearly circumscribed in the nature and scope of the treatment provided therein (e.g., a particular one-time training program), and linked to specific formal eligibility requirements for participation (e.g., a certain skill level of workers, or a minimum elapsed unemployment duration). None of these features, however, applies to the present evaluation problem of the stepping-stone function of THS employment for the unemployed. As an ongoing program, unemployed workers may join THS work both at different calendar dates and at different individual-elapsed unemployment durations. In addition, employment spells in the THS industry vary endogenously in length. Temporary help service workers may also be assigned to different numbers of client firms for different durations and for different tasks, rendering THS employment heterogeneous across workers in several respects that are endogenously determined but post-entry. An unemployed worker may furthermore hold a THS job more than once, and thus be subject to multiple treatments with interspersed repeated spells of unemployment or regular employment. One and the same worker may therefore be counted as treated at one point in time (when in THS work) and as nontreated at another. Finally, formal requirements for participation are absent. General profitable employability, a function of both individual characteristics of the unemployed job-seeker and general labor market conditions encountered, is alone decisive for temporary help agencies in the recruitment process. Likewise, unemployed workers decide on whether to seek employment in THS work, based on factors that determine job search behavior in general, such as the likelihood of finding alternative employment opportunities, reservation wages, and the like.

The definition of outcomes is equally beset with difficulties. Above all, the question to be addressed is when one should start to measure outcomes, both for those treated and for those not treated. For the former, the more obvious choice is between the start of a THS employment spell and its end, depending on how THS employment is valued relative to regular employment or the specific causal question asked. For those workers not treated, the case is even more ambiguous, as neither entry date to nor exit date from THS work are observed. These specific features inevitably require choices to be made with respect to the timing, as well as the definition of potential treatment and control groups. This we do in the remainder of this section, beginning with the units (workers) to be analyzed—that is, the sample selected.

Sample Selection

For the ensuing analysis, we select all individuals who in 1994 to 1996 register as unemployed and consider only their first unemployment spell in this period.[3] This allows us to observe the subsequent employment histories of those workers for an extended period of time in the IABS (up to a minimum total of five years). Entries into unemployment are sampled over a three-

---

3. An unemployment spell is defined as consecutive unemployment notifications for an individual in which the time between these notifications does not exceed one week.

year period to increase the absolute number of subsequent transitions to THS work observed in the data. The years of entry chosen have the advantage to sufficiently predate the 1997 reform of the LoPA, which, among other things, introduced a one-time exemption to the general rehiring ban in the THS industry. We further restrict this inflow sample to individuals who are between eighteen and fifty-five years of age at the time of unemployment registration. The upper age limit is imposed to reduce the likelihood of sampling older workers who may be entitled to some form of early retirement scheme that permits them to exit unemployment straight into inactivity without having to search for a job or accept job offers by the public employment service while drawing benefits. Furthermore, we exclude workers who lack some prior employment experience. This measure is imperative, given the data collection process, for important worker attributes, in particular the educational-vocational qualifications obtained, are recorded in employment notifications issued by employers, but not in the information collected in and contributed to the IABS from the federal unemployment register.

These restrictions leave us with a raw total of 106,383 workers in the sample selected who enter unemployment between 1994 and 1996. Summary statistics on major variables for this sample recorded at the time of inflow into unemployment are provided in appendix table 10A.1. As documented in table 10.1 following, 0.4 percent of these unemployment spells are right-censored at the end of 2001, and 7.1 percent end with no subsequent transition recorded within the sampling period 1994 to 2001. Of all unemployed workers, 68.1 percent enter a regular job (non-THS employment), almost eight out of ten within one month of exiting unemployment. Another 2.3 percent of the unemployed leave for a THS job, the great majority (80.8 percent) again within one month.

It is noteworthy that a much larger fraction, or 8.0 percent of all entries into unemployment at some point until December 2001, do in fact take

Table 10.1   Transitions to THS and regular employment of unemployment inflows in 1994–1996

Group of workers	Absolute number	Share (%)
Total entries into unemployment	106,383	100
With right-censored unemployment spells in 2001	429	0.4
With no subsequent record in sampling period	7,531	7.1
Who subsequently enter THS work		
Within < 1 month of exiting unemployment	2,006	1.9
After ≥ 1 month of exiting unemployment	477	0.4
At some point within sampling period	8,529	8.0
Who subsequently enter regular work		
Within < 1 month of exiting unemployment	59,070	55.5
After ≥ 1 month of exiting unemployment	13,441	12.6

Source: IABS.

up a job in the THS sector. With close to one in ten unemployed workers joining THS work over this period, THS employment appears to be more dispersed in the working population than its still small employment share in the economy suggests. In addition, but not shown in table 10.1, 85.5 percent of all direct entries into THS work (those who enter within one month of exiting from unemployment), do eventually find regular employment within the sampling period. The latter statistic is especially important in the present context, for a high "frequency of transitions from temporary to permanent employment suggests that the size of any permanent 'underclass' of temporary workers must be small" (Segal and Sullivan 1997a, 123). No subsequent transitions out of THS work are observed for only 2.2 percent of direct entries into THS employment. Moreover, only four out of ten of these 2.2 percent are accounted for by right-censored THS employment spells at the end of the sampling period. The median duration of THS job spells is four months (124 days). Sixty percent of them last less than half a year, 79 percent less than one year, and 92 percent end within two years.

However, past work experience in the THS sector seems to affect the probability of renewed entry into THS work. As table 10.2 shows, 13.2 percent of workers with some prior THS work experience exit unemployment for a THS job, compared to only 1.7 percent of workers who never worked in the THS sector. An even larger fraction (24.0 percent) of workers who enter unemployment directly from THS work again take up a THS job within one month of exiting from unemployment, but only one in eight of these return to their previous THS agency. Thus a sizeable fraction of THS workers, at least in the short-to-medium run, indeed appears to cycle between unemployment and temporary help service work spells before eventually finding regular employment. The vast majority of THS workers, however, do not. Additional explorations, not shown in table 10.2, underscore the importance

Table 10.2   Subsequent transitions to THS and regular employment of unemployment inflows in
                  1994–1996 by prior THS work experience

| | | Subsequent direct transition to | | |
| | Regular work (%) | THS work | | |
THS work experience prior to entry into unemployment		Any agency (%)	Same as before (%)	No subsequent transition observed in the data (%)
Anytime in the past	56.2	13.2		4.9
Entered unemployment from THS work	47.6	24.0	3.2	4.4
None	68.8	1.7		7.6

Source: IABS.

Note: A direct transition is defined as the taking up of employment within thirty days of exiting from unemployment. Deviations of row totals from 100 percent are comprised of transitions to employment occurring later than this threshold period and of workers who reenter unemployment.

of the THS submarket for labor market flows, and of past THS work experience for the likelihood of unemployed workers to enter THS employment. Workers with prior THS work experience and workers who enter unemployment directly from a THS agency, respectively, account for 5.1 percent and 1.5 percent of all entries into unemployment and for 29.0 percent and 11.5 percent of all observed subsequent direct transitions from unemployment to temporary help work. Rehirings within the THS industry, however, occur far less frequently than on the general labor market. Six percent of all workers last employed at a THS agency, in fact, return to the same agency when leaving unemployment. In contrast, 11.8 percent of workers entering unemployment from a regular job again return to the same employer when leaving unemployment. The rehiring ban imposed by the LoPA at the time is likely to be in the main accountable for this discrepancy, for a significant share of former THS workers, as we have seen, do in fact return to THS work, albeit not to the same employer. An additional reason is that THS workers are likely to accumulate less firm-specific human capital when in temporary help work, which reduces their attachment to former THS employers.

In the following, we restrict the analysis to transitions of individual workers to other labor market states (regular or non-THS employment, and THS work) that occur within one month of leaving unemployment (direct transitions). Apart from workers with some prior unemployment experience, we also retain workers in the analysis who have been employed in the THS sector—that is, "treated," before entering unemployment in 1994 to 1996, because of the scale of reentry into THS work documented previously. Exclusion of either of these two groups of workers from the analysis would likely result in above-average productivity individuals being sampled. It would also restrict the treatment effect investigated to a significantly reduced subsample of THS inflows from unemployment, which, at least from a policy perspective, does not represent the group of unemployed workers mostly concerned with in the context of the stepping-stone function of THS work. For completeness, however, we consider the case of unemployed workers with no prior work experience in THS employment in section 10.6.2, where we investigate potential heterogeneities in the treatment effects of THS work on the future regular employment chances of individuals for different subgroups of workers.

Treatment and Nontreatment Status

With respect to the definition and the timing of the treatment, we consider the first entry of workers into THS employment after having registered as unemployed in 1994 to 1996. Any subsequent treatments are therefore viewed as outcomes of the initial treatment. More specifically, we define treatment as entry into THS employment. Assuming the causal effects of THS work to set in upon entry into the sector, we disregard differences in

THS employment experience across workers (e.g., in terms of employment duration, number of work assignments), and focus on the overall or average effects of joining THS work on the subsequent labor market prospects of workers. As noted, practical restrictions imposed by the data, in particular the complete lack of information on client assignments, in part dictate this approach. However, one may argue for the definition of treatment adopted also on purely methodological grounds. For, in contrast to the archetypical program discussed previously, virtually all aspects of individual THS employment relationships formed are ultimately determined endogenously, depending on the post-entry decisions of both the temporary help agency and the THS worker. Moreover, the available, albeit limited evidence for Germany on the distribution of client assignments across THS workers and on the transitions of THS workers to regular employment suggests that the ability of THS workers to sample many potential employers during temporary work assignments and the ability of client firms to screen THS workers during such work assignments for permanent positions may not, in fact, be of primary importance for the acclaimed stepping-stone function of THS work. As the case study by Kvasnicka (2003) has shown, most THS workers have but a singular client assignment, while first evidence on the recently created PSA in Germany reveals that, in fact, less than a fourth of all transitions out of THS work into regular employment occurred to a former client firm (Jahn and Windsheimer 2004).

Outcomes, yet to be defined, are consequently measured from the month of entry into THS work for those actually receiving treatment. This raises the question as to when one should start to measure outcomes for those not observed to enter THS work. Theory suggests that unemployed workers conduct their job search sequentially, accepting or declining a particular job offer depending on the respective net payoffs associated with either decision. There is, in addition, ample evidence that THS workers in the majority prefer regular employment to holding a job in the THS industry,[4] largely because of the higher pay and superior working conditions expected to accrue in the former. Moreover, surveys reveal that unemployed workers frequently enter THS work after a period of unsuccessful search for a regular job, and because they hope to thereby improve their chances to find regular employment (see, for example, IWG [1995]; CIETT [2000]; Cohany [1998]). In other words, unemployed workers are likely to decide sequentially whether to enter THS work in a given month of unemployment. This implies that for the construction of an adequate control group for those actually observed to enter THS work in a given month of elapsed unemployment duration (u^1), only those unemployed workers should be chosen as potential controls who have

4. See, for example, Storrie (2002) for the European evidence, Finegold, Levenson, and van Buren (2003) for the United States, Hegewish (2002) for the United Kingdom, or IWG (1995) for Germany.

been unemployed for at least $u^0 \geq u^1$ and are not treated in u^1. Note that these workers may well enter THS work and therefore be treated at a later month of elapsed unemployment duration. Thus while potential controls can be treated at a later stage, treated workers may never subsequently become controls for workers who enter THS work at longer unemployment durations.

As individual months of entry into THS work (treatment) differ across workers, we adopt a relative timescale in measuring subsequent outcomes (the effects of the treatment) for the treated. For a matched control person, outcomes are measured from the observed u^1 of the treated worker. However, as u^1, that is, elapsed unemployment duration before entry into THS work, is an unobserved counterfactual for nontreated unemployed workers, it cannot be included as a regressor in the estimation of the propensity score. We nevertheless condition the construction of matches on elapsed unemployment duration, by estimating separate propensity scores for every month (u), where each estimation is based on those treated in a particular u and those not treated in the same u. This approach is equivalent to estimating a discrete hazard-rate model, where all estimated parameters are allowed to be duration specific (Sianesi 2004, 140).

Choosing potential controls from such a duration-based flow sample has an inherent advantage in the present context over the primary alternative comparison group design employed in the evaluation literature—that is, the exclusive selection of potential controls from among those workers never observed to enter the particular program investigated. For in the latter case, the construction of a comparison group is, in fact, conditioning on the future, and hence the outcomes when the program starts are not restricted to a particular period (see on this point, for example, Fredriksson and Johansson [2003]). In the current application, such restriction would, in all likelihood, introduce a downward bias in the estimated treatment effects of THS work on the future regular employment probabilities of individuals, as unemployed workers who act as controls are likely to never be observed to enter THS work simply because they have instead made a successful transition to regular employment.

We next formalize these ideas in the form of the average treatment effect on the treated (ATT) to be estimated in the present context, deferring a discussion of the different outcome measures employed in this study to the subsequent subsection.

Formal Specification of the Evaluation Problem

We formalize the evaluation problem based on Sianesi's (2001/2004) exposition in her application of statistical matching techniques to the evaluation of the effectiveness of active labor market program in Sweden. The outcomes of interest are various labor market states of individuals over time, that is, $(Y_{jt}^{(u)})_{t=u+1}^{T}$, where j denotes the type of outcome, that is, the particular labor market status considered, and $t = u + 1, \ldots, T$ are the months these outcomes are measured post elapsed unemployment duration of at least u months. At time u, the population of interest comprises workers with elapsed unemployment duration of at least u months. Treatment assignment is denoted by $D^u = (1, 0)$, with $D^u = 1$ for unemployed workers who join THS work in u, and $D^u = 0$ for those unemployed job seekers who have elapsed unemployment duration of at least u and do not join THS work in u. We further denote the potential labor market states of an individual at time t, where $t > u$, which joins THS work in his or her u'th month of unemployment with $Y_{jt}^{1(u)}$, and with $Y_{jt}^{0(u)}$ if an individual has not joined THS work up to that month, respectively.

The average treatment effects on the treated (ATTs), Δ_{jt}^u, in the present application then correspond to the average effects of joining THS work in month u of elapsed unemployment duration ($Y_{jt}^{1(u)}$) compared to not joining THS work in that month ($Y_{jt}^{0(u)}$) for those unemployed workers who actually take up a THS job in that same month ($D^u = 1$), that is,

(1) $\quad \Delta_{jt}^u \equiv E(Y_{jt}^{1(u)} - Y_{jt}^{0(u)} \mid D^u = 1)$

$\quad\quad = E(Y_{jt}^{1(u)} \mid D^u = 1) - E(Y_{jt}^{0(u)} \mid D^u = 1)$ for $t = u + 1, \ldots, T$.

To identify the second term in equation (1), that is, the unobserved counterfactual, we have to assume stable unit treatment value and conditional independence. The conditional independence assumption (CIA) in formal terms requires that:

(2) $\quad\quad\quad\quad Y_{jt}^{0(u)} \perp D^u \mid X = x \quad$ for $t = u + 1, \ldots, T$,

that is, for observably similar individuals ($X = x$) having reached the same elapsed unemployment duration (u), the distribution of potential nonparticipation outcomes ($Y_{jt}^{0(u)}$) is the same for unemployed workers entering THS work ($D^u = 1$) and unemployed workers not entering THS work ($D^{(u)} = 0$) in month u. Common support in the present context amounts to the condition that:

(3) $\quad\quad\quad\quad\quad 0 < \Pr(D^u = 1 \mid X) < 1$.

In other words, conditional on elapsed unemployment duration and individual worker characteristics of interest, a potential control has to exist for each treated individual. In the empirical analysis, we set $U = 12$; that is, we investigate the effect of taking up a THS job within one year of registering as unemployed in the period 1994 to 1996. The period workers are followed while still in unemployment is restricted for two reasons. First, to have a sufficiently long period at one's disposal in which the subsequent labor market outcomes of these workers can be studied in the IABS: with data until December 2001, this restriction provides us with at least forty-eight months for each individual worker, irrespective of the particular calendar months he or she entered and exited his or her unemployment spell. Second, as

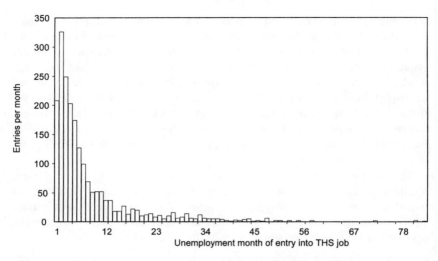

Fig. 10.1   Treated unemployed workers by month of entry into THS work
Source: IABS.
Note: Sample comprises inflows to unemployment in 1994–1996.

Table 10.3   Definition of outcome measures used in the empirical analysis

	Outcomes for each month up to four years post-treatment
Outcome 1	Monthly probability of regular employment
Outcome 2	Monthly probability of THS employment
Outcome 3	Monthly probability of employment (regular or THS)
Outcome 4	Monthly probability of unemployment

shown in figure 10.1, the total number of transitions from unemployment to THS work declines rapidly with elapsed months of unemployment duration. More than eight out of ten (82.1 percent), or 1,647 out of the 2,006 transitions to THS employment recorded in the sampling period 1994 to 2001 take place within the first year of unemployment.

Outcomes

To gain a comprehensive view of how the future labor market prospects of unemployed workers in Germany are affected by taking up a job in the THS industry, we employ a set of four different outcomes measures ($Y_{jt}^{(u)}$), described in table 10.3. These (respectively) forty-eight monthly post-treatment probabilities of regular employment (non-THS employment), THS employment, any type of employment (regular or THS), and unemployment allow us to study the dynamics of the effects that taking up THS employment exert on the individual likelihoods of observing these states over time.

It is important to note that these monthly outcome measures refer to the respective probabilities of observing workers in a particular labor market state at any point in time during a particular month. As workers may naturally spend time in more than one of these labor market states in a given month, outcomes 1, 2, and 4 are not mutually exclusive, and therefore, do not necessarily add up to 1 for a particular group of workers. Moreover, workers who return to education, or general inactivity—that is, states that are not recorded in the IABS, are retained in the respective monthly base groups from which the four outcome measures are calculated. For by virtue of the data generation process, we have complete information on the employment (regular and THS) and unemployment trajectories of workers over time who comprise our individual outcome measures of interest; that is, employment subject to social security contributions and unemployment periods that involve some kind of entitlement to financial support from the public authorities.

While Outcome 1 is of primary interest for the empirical assessment of the stepping-stone function of THS work, the remainder does provide important supportive evidence in this context. Outcome 2 provides information on the degree to which workers remain or tend to get stuck in the THS sector over time, whereas Outcome 3 conveys information on overall employment probabilities. The latter is of interest in its own right, for even if treated workers turn out not to benefit in their likelihood of obtaining regular work, or to suffer from increased risk of future unemployment (Outcome 4), they might still prove to enjoy relatively higher chances of employment in general.

10.5.2   Implementation of Propensity-Score Matching

Nearest-Neighbor Matching

We apply nearest-neighbor propensity score matching without replacement, but within caliper (Cochran and Rubin 1973).[5] In other words, conditional on elapsed unemployment duration u, each treated individual i in month u is matched to that nontreated individual z with the closest estimated propensity score $p(X)$ and used as a control C_i for individual i, subject to the condition that the absolute difference in the two estimated propensity scores, that is, the degree of residual mismatch, does not exceed a certain maximum Ψ, or caliper (see, for example, Heckman, LaLonde, and Smith [1999, 1954]):

(4) $$C_i = z \mid \Psi > \min_{z \in \{1, \dots, N^0\}} \| p_i(X) - p_z(X) \| .$$

In the empirical analysis, we set the caliper to $\Psi = 0.03$. From these pairs of treated and control individuals, the nearest-neighbor matching estimator

---

5. The matching estimator "psmatch2" by Leuven and Sianesi (2003) for STATA is used and adapted to the specific features of the present evaluation problem.

estimates the j times t ATTs (Δ_{jt}^u) for each entry month into THS work—
that is, u, as the difference in mean outcomes between the treated and their
matched controls:

$$(5) \qquad \Delta_{jt}^u = \frac{1}{N^{u1}} \sum_{i=1}^{N^{u1}} (y_{jt}^{1(u)} - y_{jt}^{0(u)}),$$

where N^{u1} is the number of matched treated workers with completed unemployment duration u. Assuming independent observations, homoskedastic-
ity of the outcome variables within the treatment and control groups, and
nondependence of the variance of the outcome on the propensity score
(Lechner 2001), the variances of the ATTs, Δ_{jt}^u can then be calculated as (see
Sianesi 2001, 28):[6]

$$(6) \quad \mathrm{Var}(\Delta_{jt}^u) = \frac{1}{N^{u1}} \, \mathrm{Var}(Y_{jt}^{1(u)} \mid D^u = 1) + \frac{\sum_{z=1}^{N^{u0}} \omega_z^2}{(N^{u1})^2} \mathrm{Var}(Y_{jt}^{0(u)} \mid D^u = 0),$$

where $D^u = 1$ and $D^u = 0$ denote matched treated and nontreated workers at
time u, respectively, and ω_z is the number of times individual z is being used
as a control, with $\sum_{z=1}^{N^{u0}} \omega_z = N^{u1}$. As matching is conducted without replace-
ment to reduce the standard errors of the estimated effects, however, $\omega_z = 1$ for all controls, so that $\sum_{z=1}^{N^{u0}} \omega_z^2 = N^{u1}$, too. As the true propensity score
is unknown, its estimate has to be used, which leads to reduced estimated
variances of the ATTs. Standard errors may be obtained by bootstrapping,
which, however, is not pursued here for the amount of computing time
required.

Estimating the Propensity Score

The plausibility of the CIA in equation (2) depends on the richness of
the available data with respect to the underlying mechanism that determines
treatment assignment and future outcomes—that is, the ability to control for
all factors that both determine selection into THS work and affect potential
outcomes in the two participation states. We discuss these factors in relation
to the two principal actors involved; that is, the THS and the unemployed
job-seeker, the potential restrictions imposed on their conduct by the LoPA,
as well as the general labor market conditions they are confronted with.

The Temporary Help Agency   As pointed out before, few formal requirements besides general "profitable employability," a function of both individual characteristics of the unemployed job-seeker and general labor market conditions, are relevant for temporary help agencies in the recruitment
process. Deferring a discussion of the latter for the time being, the former

---

6. Note, however, that unlike Sianesi (2001), we do not have to condition on treated workers being observed at individual outcome months, as we do not have any measurement error
in the labor market states of interest that underlie our outcome measures (see section 10.5.1
[subsection 4]).

necessitates the consideration of attributes related to the productivity of individuals in the estimation of the propensity score. Besides personal characteristics—that is, age, sex, foreign nationality, marital status, presence of children, as well as the highest educational and vocational attainment recorded for the worker, we control for the previous (recent and more distant) labor market history of individuals in the estimation of the propensity score. With respect to the last employment relationship, we control for employment tenure, real earnings, real average earnings in the last establishment, type of occupation held, part-time status, industrial sector, and whether the last job was a THS job. The latter in particular appeared quite significant in the descriptive explorations of observed transitions from unemployment to THS work in section 10.5.1 (sample selection). Information on the last sector the worker was employed, in turn, is likely to capture human capital and work experience that might be of use in the mainly manual, industrial tasks THS workers are usually assigned to at client firms. In addition, and by virtue of the data set, key summary statistics with respect to individuals' more distant labor market history are constructed. Attributes that are controlled for include whether the individual has ever worked in the THS sector before and whether the worker has ever been unemployed before. The latter acts as a proxy for past instability of employment, and possibly for the degree of labor market attachment of the worker, which itself may be related to unobserved individual characteristics related to worker productivity. Furthermore, a dummy for unemployment registration in the new German Lander is included, where THS agencies have only been able to operate from 1990 onward, and annual as well as seasonal indicators are used to capture cyclical and seasonal variations in the demand of THS agencies for manpower. By virtue of conditioning on elapsed unemployment durations in the estimation of the propensity score, we also implicitly control for unobservables correlated with the duration of unemployment, such as average time-invariant and time-variant differences in individual worker productivity not captured by our other covariates measured only at entry into unemployment.

The Unemployed Job-Seeker   The aforementioned factors are also likely to affect the participation decision and future labor market outcomes of unemployed job-seekers at a given time. Elapsed unemployment duration is of primary importance in this context. First, surveys, as noted, regularly find unsuccessful search for a regular job to be one of the most important motives for taking up work in the THS sector, thereby lending support to the notion of sequential decision-taking on the part of unemployed job-seekers of whether to join THS work. Second, benefit entitlement levels, and thus the reservation wage, decline with elapsed unemployed duration. As remuneration in the THS sector generally falls short of levels attainable in other industries, workers with prolonged unemployment spells, and hence a lower reservation wage, should be more likely to take up a THS job than workers who have just entered unemployment. Third, elapsed unemployment duration is likely to be correlated with individual unobserved ability, as more productive workers are, on average, more likely to exit unemployment quickly. And finally, job search activity and more generally "drive" are likely to decline with prolonged unemployment, as workers become discouraged. The latter raises the attractiveness of turning to THS agencies, who each manage a whole portfolio of potential job opportunities. Registering in the new German Lander and the local unemployment rate at entry are likely to have an effect on the employment opportunities of individual job-seekers, both in the THS sector and in other industries. We also control for the real gross daily earnings workers received at their last employer before entering into unemployment. These proxy individual worker productivity, and affect benefit entitlement levels as well as potential aspiration wages when searching for a new job in unemployment. As Kvasnicka and Werwatz (2002) have shown, relative earnings of workers who enter THS employment in Germany, on average, fall short of those of otherwise comparable workers even two to three years before actually entering temporary work. We in addition control for the type of entitlements received by a worker in a particular month of elapsed unemployment duration; that is, unemployment benefits, unemployment assistance, or unemployment support. The first is limited in duration and generally exceeds the latter two in financial terms. Eligibility for benefit entitlements is conditional on past employment, and its level depends on the last income earned.

Restrictions Imposed by the Law on Placement Activity (LoPA)   Before its large-scale deregulation in 2002, the LoPA contained a number of provisions that circumscribed the terms and conditions under which agencies could employ workers and place them with client firms for temporary work assignments (a detailed discussion of the LoPA is provided in Jahn and Rudolph [2002] and Burda and Kvasnicka [2006]). The most important of these provisions limited the maximum permissible duration of work assignments with client firms, banned the use of fixed-term employment contracts between agency and worker (special ban on fixed-term contracts), prohibited agencies to confine the term of an employment contract with a THS worker to the duration of his or her first client assignment (synchronization ban), and disallowed agencies to rehire a previously laid-off worker within three months of employment termination (rehiring ban).[7] All of these restrictive provisions served the same purpose of ensuring that agencies

---

7. As we have seen in section 10.5.1 (subsection 1), rehirings among our unemployment inflow sample in 1994 to 1996 indeed occurred much less frequently in the THS sector than in the economy at large.

indeed assumed employer responsibilities for their workforces. They prevented agencies from simply adjusting their stock of THS workers in line with the often volatile demand for staffing services by client firms. Initially set to three months, the maximum permissible duration of work assignments was raised by quarter of a year in 1985, 1994, and 1997, and was further extended to twenty-four months in 2002 before it was dropped altogether in the latest reform, which took effect in 2004. As to the three bans, agencies were permitted a respective one-time exemption for each worker from April 1997, before they, too, were dropped altogether in 2004. In the case of the rehiring ban—that is, the only restriction imposed by the LoPA in the observation period on the conduct of THS agencies in the recruitment process, this exemption implied that agencies were henceforth allowed to once dismiss a worker and rehire her or him again with three months. By virtue of sampling only inflows into unemployment between 1994 and 1996, however, the April 1997 reform of the rehiring ban is, in fact, immaterial for subsequent transitions of workers out of their spell of unemployment.

In our empirical analysis, we cannot directly account for the rehiring ban in its effect on the recruitment behavior of THS agencies in the estimation of the propensity scores by way of a dummy variable that takes the value 1 if less than three months have elapsed since a worker has been laid off by a THS, and zero otherwise. We run separate probit regressions for each elapsed month of unemployment. As a consequence, in months of unemployment greater than three, this indicator will always take the value zero—that is, we will have no variation in the data, as the rehiring ban ceases to be binding for all workers still unemployed after three months. In the context of our matching algorithm, however, we would expect immediately preceding employment in the THS sector to have less of a positive effect on the probability to reenter THS work in the first three months of unemployment than in the fourth, if the rehiring ban does indeed exert a material influence. We do, in fact, find such evidence (see appendix table A10.2).

General Labor Market Conditions   General labor market conditions influence both the search behavior and potential employment chances of unemployed job-seekers, as well as the recruitment decisions of THS agencies. Labor demand of THS firms is known to be both highly procyclical and subject to strong seasonal variations. We control for general labor market conditions along three dimensions: cyclical, seasonal, and regional. Cyclical and seasonal factors are controlled for by annual and quarterly indicator variables, measured at entry into unemployment. These indicator variables also account for differences in the inflow composition of workers into unemployment. The average annual unemployment rate in the employment office district where the worker registers as unemployed, in turn, is used to capture differences in local labor market imbalances. Finally, recorded unemployment registration in the new German Lander proxies for persistent structural differences between East and West Germany.

A note is in order on a problem that is commonly encountered in evaluation studies; that is, the presence of anticipatory effects of future treatment on the pretreatment behavior of workers and its likely pervasiveness in the current application. Anticipatory effects of unemployed job-seekers, leading to reduced job search prior to entry into THS work (akin to Ashenfelter's dip), are unlikely to be a major problem in the present evaluation problem of the stepping-stone function of THS work. Temporary help service agencies in Germany tend to hire workers predominantly on call, in line with current realizations of client demand (see Kvasnicka 2003), which is unlikely to be predictable with certainty even one or two weeks in advance. In addition, as already discussed, worker rehirings on the THS submarket at the time were prohibited within three months of prior employment termination, which effectively circumscribes the problem of anticipatory effects related to potential rehiring among workers who entered unemployment from THS work.

Matching Quality

The regression output of the probit estimations of the propensity scores for a number of treatment months are provided in appendix table 10A.2. All covariates except current entitlement status are measured at entry into unemployment. In particular, previous THS work experience and direct entry into unemployment from a THS job have a sizeable and statistically significant positive effect on the probability of transition to a THS job. Previous real earnings and the local unemployment rate, in contrast, surprisingly never exert any statistically significant effect on the likelihood of treatment assignment. The latter finding may be the product of two countervailing effects of local labor market conditions on the probability of treatment. While unemployed job-seekers may be more willing to accept a THS job, when other employment opportunities are scarce, THS agencies may only be inclined to recruit more workers when client demand for their services is high—that is, local labor market conditions are tight. Workers who spent less than one year in their last job, which proxies for past instability of employment, turn out to be at times more likely to enter THS work, potentially for the otherwise reduced chances to find employment and lack of sufficient occupation-specific skills acquired in their last job. Workers entering unemployment from training also appear to be more inclined to take up a THS job in the first months of their unemployment spells. Temporary help service work thus indeed appears to provide an access-to-work function for recent labor market entrants. It is important to keep in mind that all estimated probit regressions are conditional on treated and nontreated workers in the respective subsamples to have reached the same elapsed duration of unemployment. As the latter is likely to be correlated both with observable and unobservable worker characteristics, the respective monthly subsamples should already be more homogeneous than the full groups of treated and nontreated workers sampled for the entire first twelve months of elapsed unemployment duration. As a consequence, the estimated coefficients of the observable attributes controlled for in the individual probit regressions measure only the impact of these covariates on the probability of treatment assignment conditional on elapsed unemployment duration. Following Sianesi (2004), table 10.4 provides various summary statistics on covariate balancing and hence matching quality for all twelve probit regressions.

Given the very large groups of potential controls available for each unemployment month (column [3]), finding a suitable match partner for treated individuals is not a problem. Only one out of the 1,647 workers leaving unemployment for a THS job, as shown in column (10), are excluded for lack of common support.[8] The pseudo-R^2 from the individual probit regressions before matching (column [4]) indicate the extent to which the covariates explain the probability of treatment in a particular month of unemployment. The respective pseudo-R^2 from monthly probit regressions after matching (column [5]) show that, on average, over the twelve probits run, the covariates continue to explain only 8 percent of the variance in treatment assignment across the matched subsamples, and thus only about half the average respective figure obtained from the original samples of treated and nontreated workers. Associated probability values of likelihood ratio tests before and after matching are reported in columns (6) and (7). Whereas before matching, the null hypothesis of joint insignificance of the covariates is always rejected for any of our twelve probit regressions, it is always accepted after matching. Matching on the estimated propensity scores leads to significant improvements in the balancing of attributes between treated and (potential) control workers in the matched subsamples for each unemployment month u, as shown by the respective median absolute standardized biases before and after matching (columns [8] and [9]).[9]

---

8. In the treated/control group samples, the mean absolute distance in propensity scores between treated and control (neighbor) is very small: 0.00003 (standard deviation of 0.0003; max of 0.005). In terms of percentage differences in propensity scores between treated and controls, the mean difference is 0.04 percent (standard deviation of 0.17 percent; max 4.5 percent). So overall, distributions show very close overlap.

9. The median is taken over all regressors and calculated for each unemployment month u, following Rosenbaum and Rubin (1985) as: $Bias_{Before}(X) = (\overline{X}_1 - \overline{X}_0)/\sqrt{\{[V_1(X) + V_1(X)]/2\}} \times 100$ before matching and as $Bias_{After}(X) = (\overline{X}_1^M - \overline{X}_0^M)/\sqrt{\{[V_1(X) + V_1(X)]/2\}} \times 100$ after matching, where $\overline{X}_1$ and $\overline{X}_0$ are the respective sample means in the entire subsamples of treated and nontreated workers, $V_1(X)$ and $V_1(X)$ their associated variances, and $\overline{X}_1^M$ and $\overline{X}_0^M$ the respective sample means in the group of matched treated individuals within the common support and nontreated individuals—that is, controls (see Sianesi 2004, 154)

Table 10.4 Indicators of covariate balancing, before and after matching, by month

Month (u) (1)	Treated workers before (2)	Nontreated workers before (3)	Probit pseudo-R^2 before (4)	Probit pseudo-R^2 after (5)	$\Pr > \chi^2$ before (6)	$\Pr > \chi^2$ after (7)	Median bias before (8)	Median bias after (9)	Treated workers lost to CS after (10)
1	208	95,265	0.113	0.029	0.000	0.991	14.3	3.9	0
2	326	80,905	0.138	0.015	0.000	0.999	16.5	3.7	0
3	249	69,270	0.124	0.017	0.000	1.000	16.3	3.6	1
4	203	59,768	0.166	0.030	0.000	0.995	18.8	2.9	0
5	174	52,997	0.159	0.023	0.000	1.000	16.4	4.5	0
6	127	47,184	0.125	0.055	0.000	0.973	14.4	6.5	0
7	99	42,280	0.153	0.065	0.000	0.986	21.7	6.5	0
8	69	38,302	0.127	0.093	0.000	0.973	21.0	6.5	0
9	51	35,008	0.149	0.177	0.000	0.805	16.6	8.1	0
10	52	31,897	0.171	0.138	0.000	0.957	16.8	8.7	0
11	52	29,250	0.152	0.123	0.000	0.975	27.1	7.2	0
12	37	25,674	0.193	0.192	0.000	0.943	28.1	11.6	0

Source: IABS.

Note: Before = before matching, after = after matching; CS = common support. (1): Elapsed month u in unemployment; (2): Number of treated (i.e., joining THS work in month u of unemployment); (3): Number of potential controls (i.e., still unemployed in month u and not joining in u); (4), (5): Pseudo-R^2 from probit regressions for the monthly conditional treatment probability; (6), (7): P-value of likelihood ratio tests for the joint significance of regressors; (8), (9): Median absolute standardized biases taken over all regressors; (10): Number of treated workers outside the common support (using a caliper of 3 percent).

10.6　Empirical Findings

10.6.1　Summarizing Outcomes over Time

We begin with a graphical summary of the average time pattern of the different treatment effects, before presenting the results for the respective Δ_{jt}^u by month of entry into THS work in section 10.6.2; that is, the causal effects identified under the CIA in equation (2). Following Sianesi (2004, 140), an average effect on each outcome measure j in outcome month t may be derived for the entire group of workers treated in their first twelve months of unemployment as:

$$(7)\quad E_U(\Delta_{jt}^u \,|\, D = 1) = \sum_{u=1}^{U=12} [E(Y_{jt}^{1(u)} - Y_{jt}^{0(u)} \,|\, D^u = 1)\, P(D^u = 1 \,|\, D = 1)],$$

where $E(Y_{jt}^{1(u)} - Y_{jt}^{0(u)} \,|\, D^u = 1) = \Delta_{jt}^u$, which are weighted in the summation by the monthly entry distribution into THS work for those actually leaving unemployment for THS work—that is, $P(D^u = 1 \,|\, D = 1)$. The following subsections graph estimates of these average monthly effects on our four outcome measures together with 95 percent confidence intervals calculated on the basis of equation (6) for the entire population of individuals treated in their first twelve months of unemployment. These graphs summarize how unemployed job-seekers who take up THS work, on average, fared in their subsequent employment and unemployment trajectories by joining THS work relative to the counterfactual situation in which they would have continued their job search in registered unemployment.

Outcome 1: Probability of Regular Employment

Figure 10.2 shows that entering a THS job has no statistically significant effect for most of our four-year period that outcomes are measured on the monthly probabilities of regular employment. In other words, for the majority of months post treatment, neither a stepping-stone effect of THS employment nor an adverse effect on the future probabilities of regular employment is discernable.

In the first months, however, THS work appears to reduce the relative chances of being in a regular job, a differential effect that subsequently turns slightly positive, and then seems to increase in the fourth year post treatment. The estimated reduced probabilities of regular employment are in all likelihood the result of a lock-in effect of program participation, as THS employment spells of treated workers have a median duration of four months (and a mean duration of eight-and-a-half months), as pointed out before. The positive differentials observable in the fourth year post treatment, in turn, suggest that the potential advantages in terms of regular employment chances of taking up a THS job from unemployment tend to materialize rather late than early. It remains to be seen whether these posi-

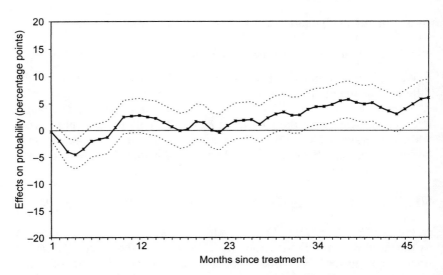

Fig. 10.2   Treatment effects over time on the probability of regular employment
Source: IABS.
Note: Dashed lines denote 95 percent confidence intervals.

tive differentials in our descriptive graphical analysis for all workers who enter within their first twelve months of unemployment registration remain when we explore the causal effects of THS work for each entry month into unemployment—that is, the treatment effects identified under the conditional independence assumption (equation [2]).

Some unemployed workers entering THS work might still be employed in their job at later outcome months, while others may also cycle between different THS jobs. While inspection of figure 10.2 provides little support for a stepping-stone function of THS work for most of the four-year post-treatment period, it does not give an answer as to whether, and if so, to what extent unemployed workers benefit in their overall future probability of employment, be it regular or temporary help work employment, from entering a THS job from unemployment. Having explored the former constituent part of this outcome measure in figure 10.2, we next turn to the latter component (Outcome 2), before considering both parts in combination—that is, Outcome 3.

Outcome 2: Probability of THS Employment

As is evident from figure 10.3, individuals who leave unemployment for THS work are significantly more likely throughout the four-year period that follows to be employed in the THS sector.

While the positive probability differential declines rapidly over the first eight to nine months, its declines become subsequently less marked and the differential roughly stabilizes at around 11 percent toward the end of

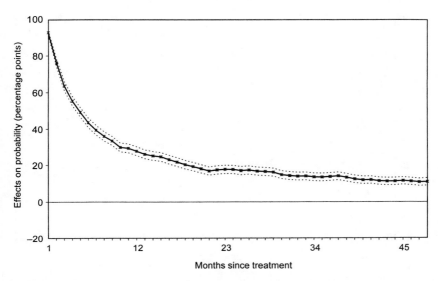

Fig. 10.3   Treatment effects over time on the probability of THS employment
Source: IABS.
Note: Dashed lines denote 95 percent confidence intervals.

the observation period. Prolonged program duration and repeated program participation may, in general, be a matter of concern if it keeps workers from obtaining regular work. This does not seem, however, to be the case in the present context. For, as we have seen in figure 10.2, unemployed workers entering THS work, on average, do not exhibit statistically significant lower monthly probabilities of regular employment than unemployed workers who chose not to join THS work as yet.

Outcome 3: Overall Probability of Employment

With respect to any social-security employment (THS or regular), figure 10.4 reveals that unemployed workers who take up a THS job exhibit a higher employment probability than those unemployed workers who do not join THS work in the same month of elapsed individual unemployment duration in each month following entry into the THS sector for the entire four-year period under investigation.

With Outcome 3 being a composite of outcomes 1 and 2, and the general time pattern of treatment effects discernable in figures 10.3 and 10.4, it is clear that the overall monthly employment probabilities quite closely resemble the levels and the trend of the increased likelihoods of THS employment for workers treated upon exit from unemployment. It remains to be seen how entry into THS work affects the risks of future unemployment over time. As noted, our outcome measures are neither mutually exclusive nor all

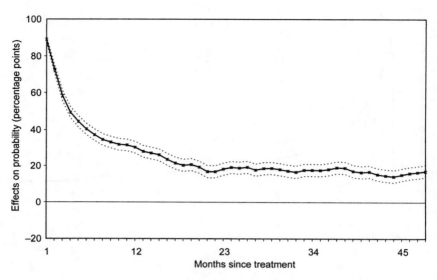

Fig. 10.4   Treatment effects over time on the probability of employment
Source: IABS.
Note: Dashed lines denote 95 percent confidence intervals.

inclusive (e.g., inactivity is not considered as an outcome), so that we cannot infer the treatment effects of THS work on a particular outcome from the treatment effects estimated for the other outcomes.

Outcome 4: Probability of Unemployment

Figure 10.5 documents that monthly probabilities of unemployment are significantly reduced for treated workers throughout the four-year observation period post-entry into THS work, but tend to converge to those experienced by workers who were not treated as of yet toward the end of the four-year observation period. Summarizing the four figures considered, it appears that unemployed workers seem to substantially improve (reduce) their overall future employment chances (risks of unemployment), while only benefiting potentially in terms of their future regular employment probabilities from their engagement in THS work toward the latter quarter of the four-year period that their subsequent labor market states are followed.

10.6.2   Treatment Effects by Month of Entry into THS Work

Having so far explored the average dynamics of the different treatment effects, table 10.5 reports the respective causal effects averaged over the forty-eight outcome months for different entry months into THS work, as well as for the entire population of workers entering THS work within their first twelve months of unemployment. The former only correspond to the causal effects identified under the CIA, equation (2), whereas the latter summarize

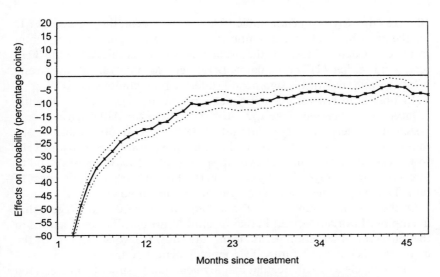

Fig. 10.5   Treatment effects over time on the probability of unemployment
Source: IABS.
Note: Dashed lines denote 95 percent confidence intervals.

Table 10.5   **Average treatment effects of THS work by unemployment month of entry into THS work**

	Effect (percentage points)[a]					
Outcomes	$u = 1-12$	$u = 1$	$u = 3$	$u = 6$	$u = 9$	$u = 12$
Reg. empl.	2.0	5.3	3.2	0.7	7.4	3.2
	(−1.3;5.3)	(−4.1;14.7)	(−5.3;11.8)	(−7.8;9.2)	(−11.0;25.7)	(−19.0;25.4)
THS empl.	24.0	24.7	25.1	26.6	27.8	20.1
	(21.6;26.3)	(18.1;31.4)	(19.0;31.1)	(18.4;34.8)	(13.9;41.6)	(5.9;34.4)
Any empl.	25.4	29.3	28.0	26.8	33.6	22.9
	(22.1;28.7)	(20.2;38.4)	(19.6;36.4)	(14.9;38.6)	(15.3;51.9)	(0.7;45.0)
Unemployment	−17.0	−20.6	−20.4	−12.5	−20.3	−12.6
	(−20.1;−14.0)	(−28.7;−12.5)	(−27.9;−12.8)	(−23.9;−1.2)	(−38.1;−2.5)	(−33.4;8.2)

Source: IABS.
Note: Ninety-five percent confidence intervals in parentheses; u = unemployment month of entry into THS work.
[a]Averaged over forty-eight months post-entry into THS work.

figures 10.2 to 10.5—that is, relates to the entire group of workers treated within their first year of unemployment and thus represent a benchmark against which to discuss the variations in ATTs by month of entry into THS work. Estimated baseline outcome probabilities for the respective control groups corresponding to the different groups of treated workers in table

10.5 are provided in appendix table 10A.3. As is evident, the averaged ATTs for the probability of regular employment are never significantly different from zero, whereas those for the probabilities to be employed in the THS sector, or in either THS or regular work (any employment) are always strong positively and statistically significantly affected if unemployment is left for a THS job. Future risks of unemployment, in turn, are in general significantly reduced for workers who take up a job in the THS sector. Although a marked systematic pattern by entry month into THS work is not observable for our four outcome measures, it appears that unemployed workers who join THS work very late in their unemployment spells (in the twelfth month) tend to fare worse, on average, than those workers who join earlier, with respect to both THS employment, any employment, and unemployment.

Overall, we may summarize the findings in table 10.5 to suggest that unemployed workers benefit in their overall future employment chances in the four-year observation period from entering THS work, because of the increased likelihood of future THS employment, but are neither, on average, more likely to obtain regular employment, nor to suffer from increased risks of future unemployment in the outcome period. Quite to the contrary, they appear to benefit substantially from reduced risks unemployment over the four-year post-treatment period considered. Sample sizes, however, are fairly small, which leads to large standard errors in the estimates of our ATTs obtained, as is evident from table 10.5. This is particularly a problem for our outcome measure of regular employment, for which all tabulated ATTs are insignificant, yet throughout positive. The estimated treatment effects on regular employment are, however, quite small for entries into THS work at the various months of unemployment duration considered in table 10.5 when compared to the baseline probabilities of regular employment for the respective matched control groups (see appendix table 10A.3).

The effects of THS employment on the future regular employment chances of unemployed workers, that is, our outcome of primary interest, may differ between subgroups of workers. In the following, a number of such groups are considered. Given the small sample size of unemployed workers that leave for a THS job and their rapidly declining numbers at longer-elapsed unemployment durations, however, we have to restrict the analysis to transitions to THS work that occur within the first six months of unemployment registration. Table 10.6 tabulates the causal effects for each subgroup on the probability of regular employment averaged over the forty-eight outcome months for different entry months into THS work, as well as, as a benchmark for the entire group of workers entering THS work within their first six months of unemployment, together with the estimated baseline probability of regular employment of their matched controls.

As is evident, average treatment effects over the four-year outcome period are in the majority positive, though at several instances also negative, never statistically significant for all entries months into THS work, and

Table 10.6   **Average treatment effects of THS work on probability of regular employment by unemployment month of entry into THS work for different subgroups of workers**

Groups of workers	Baseline probability[a]	Effect (percentage points)[a]			
		$u = 1–6$	$u = 1$	$u = 3$	$u = 6$
All workers ($N = 1,286$)	35.8	1.3	5.3	3.2	0.7
		(–2.5;5.0)	(–4.1;14.7)	(–5.3;11.8)	(–7.8;9.2)
Aged 18–40 at entry into u.	36.9	2.0	3.7	4.1	1.5
($N = 1,059$)		(–2.1;6.2)	(–7.0;14.3)	(–5.3;13.4)	(–11.6;14.6)
No prior THS experience	38.9	2.3	6.3	1.1	1.7
($N = 864$)		(–2.3;6.9)	(–5.6;18.1)	(–9.1;11.4)	(–12.1;15.4)
Unempl. in W. Germany	34.9	3.7	2.8	–3.0	5.2
($N = 874$)		(–0.8;8.2)	(–9.0;14.6)	(–13.5;7.5)	(–8.8;19.3)
Men ($N = 1,038$)	37.8	–2.4	1.2	–4.0	–1.7
		(–6.6;1.7)	(–9.5;11.9)	(–13.5;5.5)	(–14.1;10.8)

Source: IABS.

Note: Ninety-five percent confidence intervals are reported in parentheses; N = No. of treated in unemployment month of entry into THS work $u = 1–6$.

[a]Averaged over forty-eight months post-entry into THS work.

mostly modest in absolute value if compared to the baseline probabilities of matched controls for the entire entry period considered. It is notable that the reduction in the upper age limit of workers considered to forty years, and the sample restriction to workers without some prior THS experience do not result for each entry month into THS work in generally higher average treatment effects for regular employment probabilities than for all workers who enter THS work within the first six months of their unemployment spell. Furthermore, it appears that later entries into THS work ($u = 6$) once again appear to benefit less in their overall future regular employment chances than workers who enter THS employment earlier in their unemployment spell.

Finally, we want to look at the average treatment effects on the probability of regular employment for only the fourth year post-entry into THS work. For, as we have seen in figure 10.2, for the entire group of workers entering THS work within twelve months of unemployment registration, a positive differential in their monthly regular employment probabilities was discernable only in this fourth year of our observation period that outcomes are measured. Plotting the outcomes averaged over all entries into THS work within twelve months of their unemployment registration, this figure (like the other figures) did not have a causal interpretation, for the CIA, as noted, pertains only to treated workers and their matched controls who have identical elapsed unemployment durations at entry of the former into THS work. Considering only the averaged monthly regular employment differentials between treated and controls in the fourth year of our observation period, table 10.7 shows that neither for all workers that enter THS

Table 10.7   **Average treatment effects of THS work on probability of regular employment in the fourth year post-treatment by unemployment month of entry into THS work for different subgroups of workers**

Groups of workers	Effect (percentage points)[a]		
	$u = 1$	$u = 3$	$u = 6$
All workers ($N = 1,286$)	6.6	6.8	0.09
	(−3.0;16.2)	(−2.0;15.5)	(−11.0;12.9)
Aged 18 to 40 at entry into u. ($N = 1,059$)	7.9	8.3	−5.2
	(−2.8;18.6)	(−1.2;17.9)	(−18.9;8.5)
No prior THS experience ($N = 864$)	7.2	2.2	6.3
	(−4.7;19.0)	(−8.2;12.5)	(−7.9;20.5)
Unempl. in W. Germany ($N = 874$)	4.3	−2.3	−2.0
	(−7.6;16.2)	(−13.0;8.4)	(−16.6;12.7)
Men ($N = 1,038$)	3.2	0.9	−1.8
	(−7.6;14.1)	(−8.8;10.6)	(−14.9;11.4)

Source: IABS.

Note: Ninety-five percent confidence intervals are reported in parentheses; N = No. of treated in unemployment month of entry into THS work $u = 1$–6.

[a]Averaged over the fourth year post-entry into THS work.

work within six months of their unemployment registration, nor for any of the four subgroups already considered, are estimates statistically different from zero. Standard errors are, of course, once more very large due to the small sample sizes. Nevertheless, in the majority of cases, positive estimates are again small in magnitude, and in a quarter even negative, suggesting that workers do not significantly benefit in quantitative terms from generally higher chances of regular employment four years post-entry in THS work. Summing up the various analyses in this section, there is little evidence that suggests the existence of a general and significant stepping-stone function of THS work to regular employment for unemployed job-seekers in Germany in the time period considered.

10.7   Conclusion

Applying statistical matching techniques, this chapter has investigated the average effects of entering THS work on the future labor market outcomes over a four-year period of workers who registered as unemployed in 1994 to 1996 relative to the counterfactual, in which these workers would have continued their job search in registered unemployment.

Unemployed workers who entered THS employment within twelve months of unemployment registration turned out to benefit from both higher monthly chances of THS and overall employment (THS or regular employment) throughout the four-year period these workers were followed post-treatment. Workers who took up a job in the THS sector also appeared to enjoy significantly reduced future risks of unemployment. They did not, however, seem to enjoy generally greater chances of future regular employment. While our results, therefore, do not lend empirical support to the stepping-stone hypothesis of THS work for unemployed job-seekers in Germany, they also do not confirm concerns about potential adverse effects on the future regular employment and unemployment probabilities of THS workers. If anything, THS work appears to provide an access-to-work function for unemployed workers that leaves them with a higher probability of (THS) employment for the entire four years their subsequent labor market states have been analyzed than workers who did not join THS work, as of yet, in their unemployment spell.

Appendix

Table 10A.1   **Summary statistics of the sample at entry into unemployment**

Worker characteristics		Previous real daily gross wage (€)	49.5
Female	43.2	Ø real daily gross wage at employer (€)	54.9
Foreign	9.4	Duration of last job less than one year	48.7
Age (years)	34.5	Ever before in THS work	5.1
Married	48.6	Immediately before in THS work	1.5
Kids	38.2	Unemployment spell	
Educational/vocational degree		First time unemployed	50.4
Secondary	28.9	Registered in new German Lander	32.5
Secondary with vocational	66.3	Local unemployment rate	11.7
Polytechnic or university	4.8	Registration in	
Previous employment history		1994	38.7
Sector		1995	31.5
Farming and energy	2.7	1996	29.9
Manufacturing	26.8	1st quarter	32.1
Construction	15.9	2nd quarter	20.4
Trade	13.8	3rd quarter	24.2
Transport	5.0	4th quarter	23.2
Services	28.9	Entitlements	
State	6.0	Unemployment benefits	90.3
Other	0.8	Unemployment assistance	7.6
Type of last occupation		Unemployment support	2.1
In training	9.9		
Unskilled blue collar	24.3		
Skilled blue collar	28.6		
White collar	26.7		
Part-time	10.6		

Source: IABS.

Note: Number of workers = 106,383. All entries are in percent, unless stated otherwise.

Table 10A.2   Estimation of propensity scores by month of entry into THS work

	$u = 1$	$u = 4$	$u = 8$	$u = 12$
Personal characteristics				
Female	−.2582 (.0658)***	−.2038 (.0680)***	−.3076 (.1121)***	−.1689 (.1542)
Foreign	.0544 (.0762)	.0477 (.0778)	.0518 (.1151)	.2354 (.1656)
Age	.0084 (.0222)	−.0369 (.0241)	−.0183 (.0374)	−.0901 (.0546)*
Age²	−.0003 (.0003)	.0002 (.0003)	−.0000 (.0005)	.0008 (.0007)
Married	−.0218 (.0647)	.0296 (.0735)	−.0244 (.1108)	−.1095 (.1675)
Kids	−.0249 (.0660)	−.0961 (.0752)	−.1194 (.1136)	.0090 (.1665)
Education				
(ref.: secondary degree)				
Vocational degree	.2328 (.0776)***	.0690 (.0801)	−.0128 (.1237)	.2611 (.1810)
University	−.2668 (.2410)	−.4419 (.2972)		.6767 (.3159)**
Last employment spell				
Job tenure less than one year	.0896 (.0524)*	.0721 (.0588)	.2423 (.0949)**	.0987 (.1274)
Occupation:				
(ref.: unskilled blue collar)				
Training	.2229 (.1051)**	.3906 (.1024)***	.2356 (.1811)	.2981 (.2314)
Skilled blue collar	.0156 (.0737)	.0521 (.0833)	.2479 (.1283)*	.0602 (.1802)
White collar	.0664 (.0879)	.0668 (.0976)	.0752 (.1556)	−.3035 (.2312)
Part time	.0495 (.1223)	−.2019 (.1632)	−.0161 (.2066)	−.0566 (.2817)
Real gross daily income				
Of worker	−.0016 (.0010)	−.0006 (.0010)	−.0012 (.0016)	.0015 (.0018)
Average at employer	.0026 (.0015)*	.0031 (0.73)*	.0020 (.0026)	.0019 (.0034)
Sector				
(ref.: manufacturing)				
Agriculture / energy	.0854 (.1369)	.2471 (.1420)*	.1128 (.1289)	.1517 (.1764)
Construction	−.0463 (.0738)	.0645 (.0833)	−.0429 (.1622)	−.0189 (.2084)
Trade	−.1020 (.0881)	−.0270 (.0953)		

Transport	-.0595	(.1159)	-.1660	(.1510)	.1829	(.1775)	-.2767	(.3723)
Services	-.1413	(.0776)*	-.0984	(.0863)	.1042	(.1281)	-.0351	(.1794)
State	-.4917	(.2116)**	-.1126	(.1481)	-.3059	(.2996)		
Other	-.1465	(.3168)	.2503	(.2638)	.3850	(.3773)		
Previous THS work								
At some point in past	.6053	(.0776)***	.5850	(.0903)***	.4674	(.1306)***	.4801	(.1907)**
Last job was in THS sector	.6075	(.1134)***	.7466	(.1263)***	.2443	(.2019)	.3823	(.3015)
Unemployment characteristics								
First-time unemployed	.0657	(.0555)	.0055	(.0621)	-.0555	(.0973)	.0481	(.1405)
Registered in new Lander	.1188	(.0862)	.0742	(.0921)	.0479	(.1513)	-.4497	(.2256)**
Local unemployment rate	.0041	(.0099)	.0132	(.0106)	-.0107	(.0171)	.0244	(.0234)
Entitlements (ref.: benefits)								
Assistance payments	-.2045	(.0978)*	-.0884	(.0903)	-.0811	(.1125)	-.0027	(.1482)
Living supports			-.4684	(.1665)***	-.3018	(.1548)**	-.1329	(.1699)
Registration								
(ref.: 1994, 1st quarter)								
1995	.0625	(.0594)	-.0629	(.0648)	.0013	(.0982)	-.3129	(.1956)
1996	.1008	(.0591)*	-.0311	(.0634)	-.0916	(.1060)	.2421	(.1360)*
2nd quarter	.2172	(.0676)***	-.0896	(.0670)	-.1184	(.1330)	.4184	(.1806)**
3rd quarter	.2460	(.0656)***	-.2669	(.0735)***	-.0651	(.1214)	.3729	(.1798)**
4th quarter	.0658	(.0178)	-.4032	(.0796)***	.1751	(.1069)	.1331	(.2085)

Source: IABS.

Note: Standard errors in parentheses, u = unemployment month of entry into THS work.

***Significant at the 1 percent level.

**Significant at the 5 percent level.

*Significant at the 10 percent level.

Table 10A.3   Average probabilities of different labor market states for control workers by elapsed unemployment duration of their matched treated workers

Outcomes	Average probability (percent)[a]					
	$u = 1–12$	$u = 1$	$u = 3$	$u = 6$	$u = 9$	$u = 12$
Regular employment	34.8	37.7	36.2	31.6	30.6	37.3
	(32.6;37.0)	(31.1;44.3)	(30.3;42.1)	(24.0;39.3)	(19.1;42.0)	(24.3;50.3)
THS employment	3.9	3.8	3.5	2.0	4.0	2.2
	(3.0;4.8)	(1.2;6.4)	(1.2;5.7)	(–0.3;4.4)	(–0.9;9.0)	(–1.7;6.1)
Any employment	38.6	41.5	39.5	33.6	34.5	39.4
	(36.4;40.9)	(34.8;48.2)	(33.5;45.5)	(25.8;41.4)	(22.7;46.4)	(26.3;52.6)
Unemployment	37.6	35.6	36.9	37.9	43.1	36.8
	(35.4;39.9)	(29.1;42.1)	(30.1;42.8)	(29.9;45.9)	(30.7;55.4)	(23.8;49.8)

Source: IABS.

Note: Ninety-five percent confidence intervals are reported in parentheses; $u =$ unemployment month of entry into THS work of corresponding matched treated.

[a]Averaged over forty-eight months post entry into THS work of corresponding matched treated.

References

Abraham, K. G., and S. K. Taylor. 1996. Firms' use of outside contractors: Theory and evidence. *Journal of Labor Economics* 14 (3): 394–424.

Almus, M., J. Engeln, M. Lechner, F. Pfeiffer, and H. Spengler. 1999. Wirkungen gemeinnütziger Arbeitnehmerüberlassung in Rheinland-Pfalz. *Beiträge zur Arbeitsmarkt- und Berufsforschung* no. 225.

Autor, D. H. 2001. Why do temporary help firms provide free general skills training? *Quarterly Journal of Economics* 116 (4): 1409–48.

Autor, D. H., and S. N. Houseman. 2005. Do temporary help jobs improve labor market outcomes for low-skilled workers? Evidence from random assignments. NBER Working Paper no. 11743. Cambridge, MA: National Bureau of Economic Research.

Autor, D. H., F. Levy, and R. J. Murnane. 1999. *Skills training in the temporary help sector: Employer motivations and worker impacts.* Report to the U.S. Department of Labor Employment and Training Administration. Cambridge, MA: MIT Press.

Bender, S., A. Haas, and C. Klose. 2000. IAB employment subsample 1975–1995. Opportunities for analysis provided by the anonymised subsample. IZA Discussion Paper no. 117. Bonn, Germany: IZA.

Booth, A. L., M. Francesconi, and J. Frank. 2002. Temporary jobs: Stepping stones or dead ends? *The Economic Journal* 112 (127): 189–213.

Bronstein, A. S. 1991. Temporary work in Western Europe: Threat or complement to permanent employment? *International Labour Review* 130 (3): 29–35.

Brose, H. G., M. Schulze-Böing, and W. Meyer. 1990. *Arbeit auf Zeit—Zur Karriere eines "neuen" Beschäftigungsverhältnisses.* Opladen, Germany: Leske & Budrich.

Burda, M. C., and M. Kvasnicka. 2006. Zeitarbeit in Deutschland: Trends und perspektiven. *Perspektiven der Wirtschaftspolitik* 7 (2): 195–225.

CIETT. 2000. *Orchestrating the evolution of private employment agencies towards a stronger society.* Brussels: International Confederation of Private Employment Agencies.

Cochran, W., and D. B. Rubin. 1973. Controlling bias in observational studies: A review. *Sankyha* 35:417–46.

Cohany, S. R. 1998. Workers in alternative employment arrangements: A second look. *Monthly Labor Review* 121 (11): 3–21.

Ferber, M. A., and J. Waldfogel. 1998. The long-term consequences of nontraditional employment. *Monthly Labor Review* 121 (5): 3–12.

Finegold, D., A. Levenson, and M. van Buren. 2003. A temporary route to advancement? The career opportunities for low-skilled workers in temporary employment. In *Low-wage America: How employers are reshaping opportunity in the workplace,* ed. E. Appelbaum, A. D. Bernhardt, and R. J. Murnane, 317–67. New York: Russell Sage.

Fredriksson, P., and P. Johansson. 2003. Program evaluation and random program starts. IFAU Working Paper 2003:1. Uppsala: Institute for Labour Market Policy Evaluation.

García-Pérez, J. I., and F. Muñoz-Bullón. 2005. Temporary help agencies and occupational mobility. *Oxford Bulletin of Economics and Statistics* 67 (2): 163–80.

Heckman, J. J., R. LaLonde, and J. Smith. 1999. The economics and econometrics of active labor market programs. In *Handbook of labor economics,* vol. III, ed. O. Ashenfelter, and D. Card, 1865–2069. Amsterdam: Elsevier.

Hegewish, A. 2002. *Temporary agency work: National reports. United Kingdom.* Dublin: European Foundation for the Improvement of Living and Working Conditions.

Houseman, S. N. 1997. *Temporary, part-time and contract employment in the United States: New evidence from an employer survey.* Kalamazoo, MI: W. E. Upjohn Institute for Employment Research.

Ichino, A., F. Mealli, and T. Nannicini. 2005. Temporary work agencies in Italy: A springboard toward permanent employment? *Giornale degli Economisti* 64 (1): 1–27.

Institute for Economic and Social Research (IWG). 1995. *Die wirtschafts-und arbeitsmarktpolitische Bedeutung der Zeitarbeit in Deutschland.* Bonn: European Public Policy Advisers.

Jahn, E. J., and H. Rudolph. 2002. Zeitarbeit—Teil I. Auch für Arbeitslose ein Weg mit Perspektive. *IAB Kurzbericht* no. 20/28.8.2002.

Jahn, E. J., and A. Windsheimer. 2004. Personal-Service-Agenturen—Teil II. Erste Erfolge zeichnen sich ab. *IAB Kurzbericht* no. 2/15.1.2004.

Katz, L., and A. Krueger. 1999. The high-pressure U.S. labor market of the 1990s. *Brookings Papers on Economic Activity,* Issue no. 1:1–87.

Klös, H.-P. 2000. Zeitarbeit—Entwicklungstrends und arbeitsmarktpolitische Bedeutung. *iw-trends* 1/2000:5–20.

Kvasnicka, M. 2003. Inside the black box of temporary help agencies. SFB373 Discussion Paper 43/2003. Berlin: Humboldt University.

Kvasnicka, M., and A. Werwatz. 2002. On the wages of temporary help service workers in Germany. SFB 373 Discussion Paper, 70/2002, Humboldt University, Berlin.

———. 2003. Arbeitsbedingungen und Perspektiven von Zeitarbeitern. *DIW Wochenbericht* no. 46/2003, 717–25.

Lechner, M. 2001. Identification and estimation of causal effects of multiple treatments under the conditional independence assumption. In *Econometric evaluation of labour market policies,* ed. M. Lechner, and F. Pfeiffer, 43–58. Heidelberg: Physica/Springer.

Leuven, E., and B. Sianesi. 2003. PSMATCH2: Stata module to perform full Mahalanobis and propensity score matching, common support graphing, and covariate imbalance testing. Available at: http://ideas.repec.org/c/boc/bocode/s432001.html. Version 3.0.0.

Mangum, G., D. Mayall, and K. Nelson. 1985. The temporary help industry: A response to the dual internal labor market. *Industrial and Labor Relations Review* 38 (4): 599–611.

Paoli, P., and D. Merlié. 2001. *Third European survey on working conditions 2000.* Dublin: European Foundation for the Improvement of Living and Working Conditions.

Rosenbaum, P. R., and D. B. Rubin. 1985. Constructing a control group using multivariate matched sampling methods that incorporate the propensity score. *The American Statistician* 39 (1): 33–38.

Rudolph, H., and E. Schröder. 1997. Arbeitnehmerüberlassung: Trends und einsatzlogik. *Mitteilungen aus der Arbeitsmarkt und Berufsforschung* 1 (97): 102–26.

Segal, L. M., and D. G. Sullivan. 1997a. The growth of temporary services work. *Journal of Economic Perspectives* 11 (2): 117–36.

———. 1997b. Temporary services employment durations: Evidence from administrative data. Federal Reserve Bank of Chicago Working Paper, WP-97-23. Chicago: Federal Reserve Bank.

Sianesi, B. 2001. An evaluation of active labour market programmes in Sweden. IFAU Working Paper 2001:5. Uppsala: Institute for Labour Market Policy Evaluation.

———. 2004. An evaluation of the Swedish system of active labor market programs in the 1990s. *The Review of Economics and Statistics* 86 (1): 133–55.

Storrie, D. 2002. *Temporary agency work in the European Union.* Dublin: European Foundation for the Improvement of Living and Working Conditions.

Zijl, M., A. Heyma, and G. van den Berg. 2004. Stepping stones for the unemployed? The effect of temporary jobs on the duration until regular work. IZA Discussion Paper, no. 1241.

Temporary Help Agencies and the Advancement Prospects of Low Earners

Fredrik Andersson, Harry J. Holzer, and Julia Lane

11.1 Introduction

Do labor market intermediaries in general, and temp agencies in particular, help unskilled workers with limited work experience transition to more stable and higher-wage jobs? Earlier research on the impact of temporary help agencies for this population was generally positive. However, recent research by Autor and Houseman (2005, 2007), using data from a random assignment experiment, has raised questions about the robustness of the early research, and especially on whether any positive effects of temp agency employment persist over the longer run. Other researchers have continued to find positive effects for low earners of temp employment, among other efforts by a range of labor market intermediaries such as unions and various not-for-profit placement agencies.

In this chapter we contribute to the ongoing discussion about temp agencies and low-wage workers in a number of ways. We do this by using a very large-scale matched database on firms and employees that enables us to establish a broad set of facts about the workers who use temp agencies and the firms to which they transition. The data set has several key features that we use throughout the study. The first of these is that it is longitudinal in both firms and workers. A second key feature is that we estimated fixed personal characteristics that are unobserved in many studies. We also directly

Fredrik Andersson is a senior research associate of the ILR School at Cornell University. Harry J. Holzer is a professor of public policy at Georgetown University. Julia Lane is program director of Science of Science and Innovation Policy at the National Science Foundation.

This paper was prepared for the NBER Labor Market Intermediation Conference, May 17–18, 2007. We thank David Autor, Yukako Ono, and other conference participants for helpful comments.

estimate the premium (or discount) that different firms pay observationally equivalent workers.

Our analysis begins by estimating the impact of temp employment for initially low earners on their subsequent earnings. We then examine whether workers who work for temp agencies eventually transition to firms that pay higher wage premiums than do workers who find firms on their own. This is followed by a consideration of the extent to which these firm characteristics can account for any observed improvements in the earnings of these workers. Finally, we examine the long-term stability of the employment and earnings outcomes for low-wage workers engaged in temp work, relative to those who are not.

Our results show that temp earners clearly have lower earnings than others while working at these agencies, and even their subsequent earnings are somewhat mixed. But these earnings are generally higher if they manage to gain stable employment with other employers. In particular, we find that the effects of temp agency employment in the base period on subsequent earnings are uniformly positive for those reporting full-quarter earnings and for all earnings once we control for job tenure. Furthermore, the positive effects seem mostly to occur because those working for temp agencies subsequently work for higher-wage firms than do comparable low earners who do not work for temps.

11.2   Previous Literature

The fact that the temporary help industry generates substantial employment for workers in the low-wage labor market has been well documented (Autor and Houseman 2002). But its impact on the employment outcomes of these workers, however, is not clear a priori. On the one hand, temp agencies might provide a productive stepping stone on the path to more stable employment, both by reducing search time and imparting useful job skills. On the other hand, they might be seen as part of a "secondary" labor market in which low-wage workers churn from bad job to bad job.

Why might temp agencies have positive effects? A body of earlier work strongly suggests that the characteristics of *firms* and *jobs,* independently of worker skills, affect the labor market outcomes of less-skilled workers (Abowd et al. 2004; Holzer and Martinson 2004).[1] And various groups of less-skilled workers, especially minorities, might have less access on their own to stable employment and higher-wage jobs. For example, these workers might lack the informal networks and contacts that are often necessary to gain such employment (Holzer 1987; Ioannides and Loury 2004), or they

---

1. This notion, of course, has been heavily debated for decades in the labor economics literature—especially in discussions over "dual labor markets" and "efficiency wages." See Katz (1986) and Rebitzer (1993) for thoughtful reviews on these issues. For an earlier treatment of this topic see Dunlop (1957).

might lack the transportation and information needed to overcome spatial mismatch between their residential locations (particularly in inner-city neighborhoods or rural areas) and the more suburbanized locations of better jobs (Holzer 1991; Kain 1992; Ihlanfeldt and Sjoquist 1998). On the latter issue, Andersson, Holzer, and Lane (2005) also show that employers paying higher wage premiums tend to locate farther away from the residential areas inhabited by low-wage workers than do other employers, further suggesting some geographic mismatch between less-skilled workers and higher-wage job opportunities.

But do temp agencies help less-skilled workers overcome these geographic and informational gaps, thus improving their employment opportunities? Does the general skills training that they often provide these workers (Autor 2001) perhaps contribute to their opportunities as well?

Initial empirical research based on both survey and administrative data provided some evidence that temp agencies were providing pathways to more stable employment. Lane, Mikelson, and Summers (2003) applied matched propensity score techniques to data from the Survey of Income and Program Participation and concluded that spells in temp agency employment improved labor market outcomes relative to spells of unemployment. Heinrich, Mueser, and Troske (2005) came to similar conclusions.

In a more broad-ranging study using the same data set used in this chapter, Andersson, Holzer, and Lane (2005) found that low earners employed by temporary help services who subsequently changed firms were more likely to exit their low-earning status than were low earners not working for temps, while those who stayed with the temporary help firms had much lower chances of improving their earnings status. This was true even after controlling for person-fixed effects, and a variety of observable worker characteristics. Furthermore, the research suggested that the positive impacts of earlier temp employment were largely accounted for by the characteristics of the firms in which they were subsequently employed. This suggested that temp agencies seemed to offer low earners better access to other higher-wage firms rather than higher-wage employment while at the agency.

More recent work continues to show positive effects. For instance, Benner, Leete, and Pastor (2007) examined survey data on employers and workers in Milwaukee and Silicon Valley who used temp agencies, and a variety of not-for-profit intermediaries, to help fill job vacancies. Like Andersson, Holzer, and Lane, they find that workers who used temp agencies to find employment had higher earnings in subsequent jobs—though this seemed due more to higher hours worked than higher wages. Some other types of intermediaries—including community colleges, labor unions, and other not-for-profit agencies—seemed to generate higher wages as well as hours worked in subsequent jobs. A large number of European studies have similar positive findings (see Ichino, Mealli, and Nannicini [2006] for a review).

However, all of these studies relied on econometric techniques to identify the appropriate comparison groups, and concerns remain about selection on variables (including time-varying characteristics in studies that control for person-fixed effects) that are unobservable to the econometrician. In the only study to date that has used random assignment of Temporary Assistance to Needy Families (TANF) recipients to temporary help agencies, Autor and Houseman (2005, 2007) found that temp agencies increased the short-term earnings for workers—but their longer-term employment was characterized by lower earnings, less-frequent employment, and higher welfare recidivism.

Autor and Houseman also found that other intermediaries, which generated longer-term job placements for their clients, also generated some positive impacts over time. But some questions remain about the external validity of their results—especially since they are based only on TANF recipients, rather than a broader range of low-wage workers; and they use data from the "Work First" agency in only one city (Detroit) to generate their findings.[2]

11.3   Our Data

11.3.1   An Overview of the LEHD Data

The data used in this study are drawn from the Longitudinal Employer Household Dynamics (LEHD) program at the U.S. Census Bureau. The core of the data set is the universe of state-level quarterly Unemployment Insurance (UI) earnings records from forty-four states and the District of Columbia. The UI wage records cover data from the early 1990s to the third quarter of 2006 and have been merged with a variety of other household and employer survey data, including the 2000 Decennial Census of Population, the Current Population Survey (CPS), and the American Community Survey (ACS). This integration, which takes place under strict confidentiality protection protocols, is represented in figure 11.1.

The LEHD data have elsewhere been described in great detail (Andersson, Holzer, and Lane 2005; Abowd, Haltiwanger, and Lane 2004). Briefly, the UI wage records, which consist of quarterly reports filed by employers every quarter for each individual in covered employment, permit the construction of a database that provides longitudinal information on workers, firms, and the match between the two. The coverage is roughly 96 percent of private nonfarm wage and salary employment; the coverage of agricultural and federal government employment is less comprehensive. Self-employed individuals and independent contractors are also not covered. Although

---

2. Autor and Houseman note that their nonexperimental results are very similar to those of other researchers, perhaps implying that their results are more generalizable than might be expected on the basis of the particular sample on which they are based.

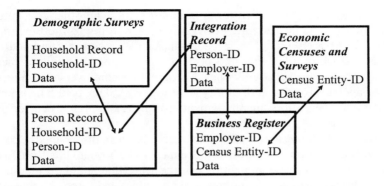

Fig. 11.1   LEHD data set used: Longitudinal employer-household dynamics

the administrative records themselves are subject to some error, staff at the LEHD program has invested substantial resources in cleaning the records and making them internally consistent.[3]

The Census Bureau information used in this study consists primarily of basic demographic information: date of birth, place of birth, sex, and a crude measure of race and ethnicity. These are available for almost all workers in the data set—the nonmatch rate is about 4 percent. The UI wage records have also been matched with the Current Population Survey, but since this is a cross-sectional match we simply use it as a consistency check in the research.

There are clearly many advantages associated with this integrated database—its enormous sample size, longitudinal structure, and information on employer-employee matches. There are also some disadvantages. One is that hours or weeks worked are typically not reported by employers. Another is that it is impossible to identify whether, when multiple jobs are held within a quarter, they are held sequentially or at the same time. We address both of these issues by creating, for each individual in the data, a measure of that person's annualized earnings at the primary employer in each year that they appear in the data. That is, for the entire year that an individual appears in a state, we identify his or her primary employer as the one that pays the highest earnings in that year.

There are two additional conceptual issues to be addressed. Although we typically refer to the employer as a "firm," the actual reporting unit in the data is an administrative rather than an economic entity; in other words, the filing unit reflects an "Employer Identification Number" rather than a specific firm. The distinction is immaterial for about 70 percent of workers, who work for a single establishment employer—but for those who work for a multiple-establishment employer, it is really not clear whether

3. The approach is described in Abowd and Vilhuber (2005).

they are working for the firm or an establishment. The other conceptual issue involves the measurement of earnings. According to the Bureau of Labor Statistics (1997), UI wage records measure "gross wages and salaries, bonuses, stock options, tips, and other gratuities, and the value of meals and lodging, where supplied." They do not include employer contributions to Old age, survivors, and disability insurance (OASDI), health insurance, workers' compensation, unemployment insurance, and private pension and welfare funds.

Given the sensitive nature of the data set, it is worth discussing the confidentiality protection in some detail. All data that are brought into the LEHD system have been made anonymous, in the sense that standard identifiers and names are stripped off and replaced by a unique "Protected Identification Key," or PIK. Only Census Bureau employees or individuals who have Special Sworn Status are permitted to work with the data, and they have not only been subject to an FBI check but also are subject to a $250,000 fine and/or five years in jail if the identity of an individual or business is disclosed. All projects have to be reviewed by the Census Bureau and other data custodians, and any tables or regression results that are released are subject to full disclosure review.

Standard measures of human capital include such variables as education and experience. Other measures, such as ability or family background, have rarely been able to be captured, yet work by Juhn, Murphy, and Pierce (1993), for example, demonstrates that a major contribution to increased earnings inequality in the 1980s was an increase in return to "unmeasured" characteristics—for example, interpersonal skills. Work by Holzer (1996), as well as the sociology literature, also finds that businesses increasingly value characteristics of the employee that have not traditionally been observable—again, interpersonal skills are frequently mentioned.

The newly developed longitudinal data set permits the quantification of the value of these measures, although not permitting a decomposition of the source.[4] This is achieved by capturing the portable component of individual earnings—that component that belongs to an individual as she or he moves from job to job in the labor market (and that is separate from the type of firm for which she or he works). In order to estimate this effect, the LEHD staff decomposed the log real annualized full-time, full-year wage rate (ln w) into *person* and *firm* effects:[5]

---

4. We interpret this person-fixed effect as a broad measure of human capital, though the source of the human capital—whether interpersonal skills, cognitive ability, family background, or some combination of these and other factors—cannot be determined.

5. This methodology is drawn from Abowd, Kramarz, and Margolis (1999) and further developed by Abowd, Creecy, and Kramarz (2002). A key assumption underlying this methodology is that worker mobility is (largely) exogenous. See Abowd, Kramarz, and Margolis (1999) for more discussion.

$$(1) \qquad \ln w_{it} = \theta_i + x_{it}\beta + \psi_{J(i,t)} + \varepsilon_{it}$$

$$\hat{h}_{ijt} = \hat{\theta}_i + x_{it}^{exp}\hat{\beta}^{exp}$$

$$\hat{z}_j = \hat{\psi}_j.$$

The definition of human capital we use here, h, is the part associated with the person-fixed effect—the unobservable individual heterogeneity—and the measurable personal characteristics (labor force experience, education). We are also interested in capturing and analyzing the role of the firm effect ψ. The firm effect literally captures the extent to which the firm the worker is attached to pays above or below average wages (after controlling for person effects).[6]

The firm-fixed effect similarly captures a variety of factors. Most simplistically, it captures the premium or discount that a given firm pays workers on average, controlling for their individual characteristics. This premium might be due to a higher level of capital in the firm, which would clearly increase the productivity of individual workers. Or, it might be due to unionization—the transportation equipment industry, for example, has a relatively high average firm-fixed effect. It might also be a compensating differential—the high average firm-fixed effect in the mining industry is presumably in order to compensate workers for the riskiness and unpleasantness of mine work. Finally, the firm effect will capture a range of human resource policies chosen by the firm, including the effects of training and promotion policies as well as compensation.

11.3.2 Sample Used Here and Definitions

Consistent with our earlier work (Andersson, Holzer, and Lane 2005), we use a sample of LEHD data for five states in this study: California, Florida, Illinois, Maryland, and North Carolina. These were the first five states for which long panels of microdata on both firms and workers were available to LEHD researchers. As we note in the following, we use data over the period 1993 to 2001 for workers who were prime-age adults in 1993 and who had at least minimal labor force attachment and earnings in each year. The result was a sample that included roughly eighteen million workers working in over 1 million firms per year.

The demographic characteristics of the workforce in the LEHD data, both overall and within these five states, are very similar to those of the decennial Census. There are, however, a few differences. The LEHD data

---

6. The individual fixed effects in our sample are estimates based on data through the year 1998. In our empirical work that follows, we report some earnings equations based on our own sample of data from 1996 to 1998 and also from 1999 to 2001. Clearly, our empirical work using the latter sample is not subject to any concerns about the use of fixed-effects wage measures that have been estimated over part of the time same period. Results over the two time periods are generally quite consistent with one another, as we note in the following.

used here have a high proportion of younger workers overall (about 20 percent), than do either the five-state Census sample or the full Census, which may be due to coverage and reporting differences. The five states that we are studying have a lower proportion of white workers than does the country at large—about 66 percent here rather than 78 percent for the nation. The industry distribution is, by and large, very similar—although the LEHD data show more workers in professional services, and fewer in educational, health, and social services. The earnings in the five states are typically slightly higher than for the country at large, but the LEHD earnings measures are, on average, slightly lower—probably primarily due to the coverage differences that were mentioned earlier.

As pointed out in our book, there are a variety of considerations associated with defining low earners on the basis of administrative data on quarterly and annual earnings only. It is important to try to separate out individuals who *voluntarily* work part time at high wage from those who work full time but at low wages, since UI wage records do not provide information on hours or weeks worked. Similarly, from a policy perspective, it is useful to separate those with *transitory* earnings difficulties—such as those returning to the labor market after a lengthy absence or those who have recently been displaced from a job—from those with *persistent* earnings difficulties over some number of years. Similarly, when studying the impacts of temp agencies, it is also important to measure impacts over a substantial period of time, so that transitory impacts can be separated from persistent ones in the labor market.

The practical way in which we address the first of these challenges is to limit the sample to one of prime-age workers (i.e., those aged twenty-five through fifty-four), at the beginning of our period of analysis (1993). This at least partially eliminates the largest groups who are most likely to work part time— such as students and the elderly (and near-elderly). While some groups of voluntary part-time workers—such as homemakers—will remain in the sample, the analysis will provide breakouts by gender (and also by race/ethnicity), thereby separating groups with many voluntary part-time workers (such as white females) from others where there presumably are fewer.

The second practical challenge is to identify people who are both attached to the labor market and persistently low earners. We address the attachment issue by only including in our sample of low earners those who have worked for at least one quarter in each year and earn at least $2,000 per year when doing so. These conditions are also applied for the subsequent six years of the sample, which tends to omit those who left the population of earners in a state for any number of reasons.[7]

---

7. Since each individual is required to appear in our data in each year of the analysis, we omit those who move out of state or who drop out of the labor force for other reasons.

We define *persistently low earners* as those who earn $12,000 per year or less for each of three years during a three-year base period of 1993 to 1995.[8] The three-year base period is long enough that we generally avoid those with strictly transitory problems, and focus instead on those with persistent low earnings. The implications for our sample sizes, and the characteristics of our sample (both in terms of employment outcomes, person-fixed effects, and temp agency employment) of these various sample restrictions are considered in the appendix. As expected, limiting the sample to persistently low earners in the base period clearer reduces outcomes and personal skills (while raising the incidence of temp agency employment, as we note later), but further limiting the sample in subsequent years beyond the base period has little effect on any of these measures.

In any event, after analyzing temp agency employment during the base period, we then examine labor market outcomes for low earners, and especially the impact of temp employment during the base period, in the six years *subsequent to the base period.* We also divide the six-year period into two three-year periods, 1996 to 1998 and 1999 to 2001. This enables us to examine the stability of these subsequent labor market outcomes for a lengthy period of time, and separate out transitory from more persistent impacts.

The $12,000 cutoff for low earnings may seem somewhat arbitrary, but we have an extended discussion in our earlier work (Andersson, Holzer, and Lane 2005) in which we discuss the basis for, and implications of, this cutoff.[9] The bottom line is that we find that the $12,000 cutoff generates a sample of workers whose personal and family characteristics approximate those in which we are most interested.[10] However, we also consider those in an intermediate category of earnings in the base period (whom we call "occasionally low earners"), who earn less than $12,000 a year for at least one but not all of the three years in the base period.

8. Earnings are measured in 1998 dollars. We have used the CPI-U to deflate earnings over time. Though this index is known to overstate the rate of inflation over time (e.g., Schultz 2003), this will have no effect on comparisons across groups in earnings or earnings growth in comparable time periods. We also have no data on the pecuniary values of fringe benefits for employees; however, these data are routinely omitted from calculations of poverty rates and the like. Inclusion of these measures would, if anything, exacerbate measured inequality across groups (Hamermesh 1999).

9. During this time period, a family relying on the earnings of a single worker earning $12,000 or less would clearly have income below the poverty line for a family of three, and even below the poverty line for a family of four if potential eligibility for the Earned Income Tax Credit were taken into account. Varying this cutoff in our earlier work never affected our qualitative results.

10. See the appendix to chapter 4 of our book, where we consider the educational characteristics and family incomes of workers from a smaller sample of LEHD workers who are matched to Current Population Survey (CPS) data and who are persistently low earners by our definition. The vast majority of these workers had education levels of high school or less and had family incomes below twice the poverty line.

Table 11.1   Use of temp agencies by workers in the base period (1993–1995)

Temp work	Non-low (%)	Occasionally low (%)	Persistently low (%)	All workers (%)
Any	4.0	16.0	16.3	8.0
Primary	0.6	2.4	3.8	1.3

Notes: Temp employment is considered "primary" if the agency was the worker's employer for the largest number of quarters in the three-year period. "Persistently low" earners are those who earned less than $12,000 per year (in 1998 dollars) for all three years between 1993 and 1995; "Occasionally low" had earnings less than $15,000 for at least some years, and "Non-low" earners had earnings above $15,000 for each of the three years.

11.4   Results

11.4.1   Summary Statistics

We begin with some data on the use of temp agencies by workers during our three-year base period (1993 to 1995). In table 11.1 we present summary data on the incidence of temp employment for all workers as well as separately by their earnings status in the base period—namely, for persistently low earners, occasionally low earners, and non-low earners.[11] We also present these results for individuals who had any employment through a temp agency over a three-year period, as well as for those who had temporary agencies as their primary source of employment over that period.

Our results show that, over a three-year period, roughly 8 percent of the sample's entire prime-age workforce has had some employment through a temporary agency—though only about 1 percent of the workforce had temp agencies as their primary employer over that period. However, when the sample is limited to include only persistently low earners, it is clear that temp agencies play a much greater role in securing employment for these workers than for the workforce overall—with 16 percent of all such low earners having some temp experience during those three years and about 4 percent having temp work as their primary source of employment. Temp employment for the "occasionally low earners" is very similar to that of workers whose earnings are "persistently low," but it is considerably lower for the "non-low earners," with 4 percent of this latter group having any temp experience and less than 1 percent working primarily for temps.

In table 11.2 we consider the personal characteristics of those who work for temp agencies during our base period. Once again, we consider these characteristics for all workers and for persistently low earners who have either worked for a temp agency or not, and we separately consider any work through a temp agency versus temp work as a primary source of employ-

11. "Persistently Low" earners are those who earned less than $12,000 per year (in 1998 dollars) for all three years between 1993 and 1995; "Occasionally Low" had earnings of less than $15,000 for at least some years, and "Non-Low" earners had earnings above $15,000 for each of the three years.

Table 11.2   **Personal characteristics of workers by temp agency employment in the base period**

Temp employment	Any (%)		Primary (%)	
	Yes	No	Yes	No
A. All workers				
Female	49.4	46.5	46.7	47.7
Age				
25–34	50.5	36.6	43.6	37.7
35–44	32.6	36.9	34.9	36.6
45–54	16.9	26.4	21.5	25.7
Race				
White	60.8	74.0	63.3	73.1
Black	21.5	11.1	20.0	11.8
Asian	4.8	4.3	4.4	4.4
Hispanic	13.0	10.6	12.4	10.8
Foreign born	18.1	17.6	18.0	17.6
Person-fixed effect	−0.06	0.08	−0.08	0.07
B. Persistently low earners in the base period				
Female	50.9	65.1	48.3	63.4
Age				
25–34	54.1	40.2	46.7	42.3
35–44	31.1	35.0	34.6	34.4
45–54	14.7	24.8	18.7	23.3
Race				
White	48.8	59.9	47.7	58.5
Black	30.1	13.1	32.0	15.3
Asian	4.8	2.9	2.9	4.5
Hispanic	18.2	22.2	17.4	21.7
Foreign born	20.3	29.7	19.7	28.4
Person-fixed effect	−0.41	−0.59	−0.47	−0.56

Notes: "Yes" and "No" under "Any" refer to those individuals who did and did not have any temp agency work experience respectively during the base period. "Yes" and "no" under "Primary" refer to those who did and did not have temp work as their primary form of employment. The latter category under "primary" includes those who have some nonprimary temp experience as well as those with no such experience at all.

ment. For all of these groups, we present data on the gender (female), age groups (twenty-five to thirty-four, thirty-five to forty-four, or forty-five to fifty-four), and race of such workers, as well as whether they are foreign-born. We also tabulate the mean person-fixed effects of workers in each category.[12]

A number of findings appear in table 11.2. Among workers of all earnings categories, those working at temp agencies are generally younger, more likely

12. Mean estimated person- (and firm-) fixed effects for the entire samples are both zero. Thus, positive and negative effects indicate those individuals with above-average and below-average skills, respectively.

to be minority (especially black), and more likely to have below-average personal earnings characteristics (i.e., fixed effects) than those not working at temp agencies.

Among those workers with persistently low earnings, those who work at temp agencies are still more likely to be young or black. But we also find that low earners who work for temp agencies are also more likely to be male, to be native-born, and to have above-average personal characteristics than those not working for temps. In other words, the self-selection mechanisms into temporary employment are somewhat different among low earners than among others, with *somewhat more positive self-selection into temp agencies occurring among low earners,* suggesting that it is important to control for such forms of selection in regression analysis, if possible.

Once these workers spend some time working for temp agencies during the three-year base period, how likely are they to continue with this form of employment in subsequent years? The answer to this question obviously has important implications for the issue of the extent to which temp agencies help workers—and especially low earners—transition to more stable and perhaps higher-wage employment later on.

Table 11.3 presents data on the extent to which those who worked for temp agencies during the base period—either with any amount of temp employment or as their primary form of work—continue to work for temp agencies during the subsequent three years or six years. These data thus constitute elements of *transition matrices* for those at temp agencies during the base period, which shed light on the persistence of such employment over long periods of time. Once again, the data appear for all workers at temp agencies and only for those who were persistently low earners during the base period.

The results of table 11.3 show some persistence over time in the attachment of workers to temp agencies, though large majorities of these workers

Table 11.3   Dynamics of temp agency employment across three-year time periods

	Temp work in	
Temp work in base period	1996–1998 (%)	1999–2001 (%)
A. All workers		
Any	40.2	26.4
Primary	61.2	36.9
B. Persistently low earners		
Any	49.2	34.4
Primary	63.9	41.5

Notes: Samples consist of all workers (Panel A) and persistently low earners (Panel B) in the base period who worked for temp agencies, either at any time or as their primary employer. The table thus indicates the fractions of these workers who still work for temp agencies in 1996 to 1998 and in 1999 to 2001.

no longer use temps by the period 1999 to 2001. For instance, among all workers who used temp agencies at any point in the base period, roughly 40 percent still use them at some point over the 1996 to 1998 period, and about a fourth still do so during 1999 to 2001. Among those for whom temp agencies constituted the primary employer in the base period, persistence is even greater—with about 61 and 37 percent, respectively, having some temp employment in the 1996 to 1998 and 1999 to 2001 periods. Also, those who were low earners in the base period and who used temp employment show modestly higher persistence in temp agency use than do workers overall, though qualitatively the pattern is quite similar for low earners.

In any event, the impacts of temp agencies on subsequent advancement for low earners will likely depend heavily on whether workers who used temps in the base period continue to do so subsequently, and this factor must be taken into account when we do our multivariate analysis of earnings gains for temp users over time in the following.

Having analyzed the personal characteristics of temp workers and the persistence of temp employment over time, we now consider a range of employment outcomes among these workers—both during the base period and in the subsequent three- and six-year periods. For here onward, we focus exclusively on those who were persistently low earners during the base period—as this is the group for whom temp agency might be considered a stepping stone to more stable and successful job opportunities.

In table 11.4 we present a set of employment outcomes for those who used temp agencies for employment during the base period and those who did not. We present the outcomes for the base period, and also for the two subsequent three-year periods. The outcomes we consider are: (a) the number of quarters during which the individual was employed over the three-year period—a rough measure of overall employment activity; (b) the number of full quarters worked with any employer during that time period, which measures employment instability; (c) the quarters of job tenure accumulated in their primary job during this period, or a measure of employment stability; (d) average quarterly earnings during the three-year period; (e) average quarterly earnings for full quarters worked with any employer during such a period; and (f) average annual earnings. Once again, these are presented separately for those with or without any temp employment in the base period, and for those with or without such employment as their primary source of work. And, in the two subsequent periods, we present results separately for the full samples of originally low earners (panels B and D) and for those omitting temp workers in the current period (panels C and E).

A number of findings appear in table 11.4. During the base period, those low earners who work at temp agencies work a bit less (in terms of quarters of employment), and are considerably less likely to work full quarters for their employers or to generate significant job tenure on these jobs. Their quarterly earnings in this time period are not greatly different from those

Table 11.4   **Employment outcomes in all periods of low earners during the base period: By temp agency employment during the base period**

	Any temp employment		Primary temp employment	
	Yes	No	Yes	No
A. Base period				
Quarters worked	10.09	10.39	9.99	10.34
Full quarters worked	5	7.85	5.15	7.48
Quarters of tenure	4.27	5.93	4.31	5.74
Quarterly earnings	$2,098	$2,021	$1,993	$2,089
Full quarter earnings	$2,365	$2,217	$2,221	$2,242
Annual earnings	$6,729	$7,110	$6,544	$7,068
B. 1996 to 1998				
Quarters worked	11.05	11.67	11.04	11.07
Full quarters worked	7.38	9.01	7.27	8.82
Quarters of tenure	7.12	12.22	6.73	11.66
Quarterly earnings	$3,275	$2,997	$3,265	$3,030
Full quarter earnings	$3,513	$3,076	$3,486	$3,129
Annual earnings	$12,510	$11,048	$12,093	$11,181
C. 1996 to 1998 excluding current temp workers				
Quarters worked	11.07	11.08	11.07	11.08
Full quarters worked	7.52	9.04	7.35	8.87
Quarters of tenure	7.09	12.29	5.72	11.78
Quarterly earnings	$3,356	$2,996	$3,498	$3,033
Full quarter earnings	$3,609	$3,074	$3,780	$3,130
Annual earnings	$12,476	$11,052	$13,305	$11,196
D. 1999 to 2001				
Quarters worked	11.1	11.15	11.07	11.14
Full quarters worked	7.48	8.57	7.43	8.44
Quarters of tenure	9.97	15.83	9.56	15.13
Quarterly earnings	$4,295	$4,038	$4,279	$4,070
Full quarter earnings	$4,473	$4,082	$4,452	$4,130
Annual earnings	$16,058	$15,107	$15,945	$15,225
E. 1999–2001 Excluding current temp workers				
Quarters worked	11.14	11.16	11.13	11.16
Full quarters worked	7.68	8.63	7.68	8.52
Quarters of tenure	10.20	16.03	9.39	15.39
Quarterly earnings	$4,420	$4,045	$4,553	$4,084
Full quarter earnings	$4,601	$4,087	$4,744	$4,141
Annual earnings	$16,590	$15,147	$17,054	$15,298

Notes: "Any temp employment" and "Primary temp employment" refer only to the base period; thus, outcomes for 1996 to 1998 and 1999 to 2001 are conditioned on temp employment during the base period (1993 to 1995). Results for the latter period are also presented with temp workers in those periods included (panels B and D) or excluded (panels C and E).

without such work, though their annual earnings are consistently lower (especially among those for whom such employment is their primary source of work over the base period).[13]

What happens to these low-earning workers over the subsequent three or six years in the labor market? Those who worked for temp agencies earlier on (of whom we now know that only a small fraction still work for temps) still work fewer full quarters for specific employers and therefore accumulate less tenure on any job. But *now their earnings are higher than those of low earners who did not work for temp agencies earlier.* Specifically, those with any temp agency employment in the base period now earn 8 to 9 percent more per quarter than those without such experience, and 9 to 14 percent more for full-quarter employment or annual employment. For those whose primary employment was through temp agencies in the base period, the positive earnings differentials relative to those without such work are fairly comparable (though just slightly smaller in most cases).

Among those who do not work in temp agencies in the subsequent periods, the earnings of earlier temp workers relative to nontemp workers are even larger.[14] And, in tabulations not included in table 11.4, we find these earnings gains among both women and men who were low earners in the base period, and among those of each racial/ethnic group—though the gains associated with earlier temp employment are somewhat larger for women than for men and for minorities than whites.[15]

Do these subsequent earnings advantages persist over time? During the second subsequent three-year period, those who had worked for temp agencies continue to have lower numbers of full quarters worked and less tenure accumulated, but they still earn more than those who did not—with differentials that are just a bit smaller than during the first subsequent period. Now we find quarterly earnings that are about 5 to 6 percent higher among temp workers than among nontemp workers, full quarter earnings that are about 8 to 10 percent higher, and annual earnings that are 5 to 6 percent higher. Thus, most of the earnings advantages associated with earlier temp work seem to persist over time.

13. Since we are truncating the earnings distribution at a fairly low level when generating this sample, it is not surprising that earnings differences between those working and not working at temp agencies during this period are modest.

14. Panels C and E show earnings that are 12 to 19 percent higher among those who had earlier worked in temp agencies during 1996 to 1998 and 9 to 15 percent higher in 1999 to 2001.

15. For instance, full quarterly earnings are 16 percent higher among women and 7 percent higher among men in 1996 to 1998 among low earners who worked in temp agencies in 1993 to 1995 (when their earnings were only 8 percent and 2 percent higher, respectively). Full quarterly earnings are 17 percent higher among whites, 12 percent higher among blacks, and 11 percent among Hispanics in 1996 to 1998, respectively, among those who worked for temp agencies in 1993 to 1995 (when their earnings were only 10 percent, 2 percent, and 2 percent higher, respectively). The gains associated with earlier temp work are thus higher for women than for men but higher for minorities than whites among low earners in the base period.

Of course, these summary statistics on earnings do not control for personal characteristics, and we observed earlier (in table 11.2) that there is positive self-selection into temporary employment among low earners in the labor market. We consider in the following whether the subsequently higher earnings among temp workers are still evident after controlling for observable differences in personal characteristics.

But, before we move to our regression analysis, we consider some data on the differences in job characteristics of low earners in the base period who work for temp agencies and those who do not—with the job characteristics presented for the base period and also for subsequent periods. In table 11.5 we present data on the industries and firm-fixed effects of employers of these different groups of workers. Once again, we present results for the base period and for the two subsequent periods, and separately for full samples and for those omitting current temp workers in the latter periods.

The results suggest that, during the base period, low earners working for temp agencies were much less likely to work in agriculture, retail trade, and other services. To a lesser extent, this remains true in the subsequent periods as well, because of the persistence of temp agency employment across these periods. But, in subsequent periods, those who worked for temp agencies in the base period are also now more heavily concentrated in a variety of higher-wage industries—notably durable manufacturing, but also to some extent in construction, nondurable manufacturing, transportation/utilities, and wholesale trade. This remains true even in the period 1999 to 2001, with the data showing relatively little erosion of this effect between the first and second subsequent periods. Indeed, by 1996 to 1998, 26 percent of previously low earners who had any temp work in the base period had jobs in these higher-wage industries, compared with only 18 percent of previously low earners who had no temp work in the base period. By 1999 to 2001 the proportions were roughly the same, at 28 percent versus 19 percent; the differences between those whose primary employment was in a temp agency and those for whom it was not are similar (though slightly smaller). And these differences are all considerably larger in the samples that exclude current temp workers than in those that include them.

Furthermore, *in the subsequent periods, those who worked for temp agencies in the base period now work for employers with higher firm-fixed effects than those who did not work for temp agencies.* This was true to a small extent during the base period, but in subsequent periods, the gaps between the firm-fixed effects of low earners who did and did not work for temp agencies in the base period, respectively, has grown. This is a critical finding, and suggests that temp agencies act as labor market intermediaries to link low earners to better employers than those whom they might be able to find on their own. And, once again, there is only modest evidence of erosion in the magnitude of this effect between 1996 to 1998 and 1999 to 2001.

Table 11.5   **Job characteristics of low earners by temp agency employment during the base period**

Industry	Any temp employment (%)		Primary temp employment (%)	
	Yes	No	Yes	No
A. Base period				
Agriculture	4.4	13.1	2.0	11.9
Construction	4.3	3.4	3.2	3.6
Durable mfg.	4.2	2.4	2.7	2.7
Nondurable mfg.	6.0	5.7	5.6	5.9
Trans., comm., and ut.	2.3	2.3	1.5	2.3
Wholesale trade	3.2	3.1	2.1	3.2
Retail trade	19.4	28.8	9.0	27.8
Fin., insur. and RE	2.1	3.0	1.2	2.9
Services				
Temp agency	28.8	0.0	60.6	3.0
Other	24.8	37.0	14.1	35.7
Public admin.	0.6	1.3	0.3	1.2
Firm-fixed effect	−0.30	−0.34	−0.35	−0.34
B. 1996 to 1998				
Industry				
Agriculture	3.7	12.0	2.1	10.9
Construction	4.7	3.6	3.8	3.8
Durable mfg.	6.2	2.8	6.3	3.2
Nondurable mfg.	6.1	5.4	5.6	5.5
Trans., comm., and ut.	3.3	2.6	2.7	2.7
Wholesale trade	3.9	3.2	3.4	3.3
Retail trade	19.0	25.5	12.7	24.8
Fin., insur., and RE	3.2	3.0	3.2	3.1
Services				
Temp agency	21.2	2.2	37.2	4.2
Other	28.0	38.3	22.2	37.1
Public admin.	0.9	1.5	0.8	1.4
Firm-fixed effect	−0.24	−0.3	−0.26	−0.29
C. 1996 to 1998 excluding current temp workers				
Industry				
Agriculture	3.70	10.90	2.20	10.20
Construction	5.40	3.30	5.30	3.50
Durable mfg.	10.00	3.20	12.80	3.90
Nondurable mfg.	9.90	6.50	10.70	6.80
Trans., comm., and ut.	4.60	2.70	5.00	2.90
Wholesale trade	5.90	3.50	7.50	3.70
Retail trade	21.20	25.60	18.80	25.20
Fin., insur., and RE	4.20	3.30	4.90	3.30
Services	33.50	39.30	38.80	31.00
Public admin.	1.70	1.70	1.90	1.70
Firm-fixed effect	−0.11	−0.26	−0.06	−0.25

(*continued*)

Table 11.5   (continued)

Industry	Any temp employment (%)		Primary temp employment (%)	
	Yes	No	Yes	No
	D. 1999 to 2001			
Industry				
Agriculture	3.1	11.2	1.6	10.2
Construction	5.5	4.1	4.2	4.3
Durable mfg.	7.1	3.6	7.7	4.1
Nondurable mfg.	6.6	5.1	6.4	5.4
Trans., comm., and ut.	4.1	2.9	3.8	3.1
Wholesale trade	4.4	3.6	5.1	3.7
Retail trade	17.9	24.0	13.0	23.3
Fin., insur., and RE	3.2	3.5	3.2	3.5
Services				
Temp agency	16.5	3.3	26.1	4.7
Other	30.2	37.2	36.3	27.6
Public admin.	1.3	1.6	1.5	1.3
Firm-fixed effect	−0.17	−0.25	−0.18	−0.24
	E. 1999–2001 excluding current temp workers			
Industry				
Agriculture	3.00	9.70	2.00	9.00
Construction	5.90	3.90	6.00	4.10
Durable mfg.	10.40	3.90	13.30	4.60
Nondurable mfg.	9.10	5.90	10.00	6.30
Trans., comm., and ut.	5.30	3.10	5.60	3.30
Wholesale trade	6.40	3.80	7.50	4.00
Retail trade	18.00	22.80	14.80	21.40
Fin., insur., and RE	4.20	3.70	5.30	3.80
Services	34.70	41.00	33.40	40.40
Public admin	2.40	2.20	2.50	2.20
Firm-fixed effect	−0.05	−0.2	−0.01	−0.19

Note: See table 11.4.

11.4.2   Regression Equations for Earnings in Subsequent Periods

The extent to which employment in these higher-wage industries and firms might account for the stronger employment outcomes in subsequent periods for low earners who initially worked at temp agencies, especially once we control for other personal characteristics, must now be ascertained.

In tables 11.6 and 11.7 we present the results of estimated regression equations of the following form for those who were low earners in the base period:

$$(2) \quad \ln(EARN)_{ij,t+1} = f(TEMP_{it}, TEMP_{i,t+1}, X_i, X_{i,t+1}, TEN_{ij,t+1}, TIME_{t+1}; X_j)$$
$$+ u_{ij,t+1},$$

Table 11.6   Estimated effects of temp agency employment during base period on earnings in subsequent periods: All low earners during the base period (*T*-statistics)

	Temp employment			
	All earnings		Full quarter earnings	
	Any	Primary	Any	Primary
1996 to 1998				
Controlling for				
Race/gender, foreign-born	−.193	−.168	.144	.120
	(22.18)	(10.13)	(17.98)	(7.69)
Race/gender, foreign-born, current	−.070	.062	.181	.192
temp	(7.74)	(3.64)	(21.86)	(11.69)
Person-fixed effect	−.103	.018	.156	.164
	(11.87)	(1.07)	(20.10)	(10.55)
Person-fixed effect, tenure	.036	.103	.112	.124
	(4.17)	(6.35)	(14.21)	(8.02)
Person-fixed effect, tenure, firm-	−.039	.032	.043	.049
fixed effect	(4.89)	(2.15)	(5.98)	(3.50)
1999 to 2001				
Controlling for				
Race/gender, foreign-born	−.129	−.136	.126	.090
	(12.66)	(6.95)	(13.90)	(5.12)
Race/gender, foreign-born, current	−.037	.018	.152	.135
temp	(3.61)	(10.94)	(16.56)	(7.55)
Person-fixed effect	−.074	−.021	.131	.118
	(7.43)	(1.10)	(14.92)	(6.84)
Person-fixed effect, tenure	.021	.035	.098	.083
	(2.17)	(1.88)	(11.03)	(4.85)
Person-fixed effect, tenure, firm-	−.056	−.033	.028	.014
fixed effect	(6.17)	(1.91)	(3.42)	(0.90)

Notes: The dependent variable in these regression equations is ln (quarterly earnings). Observations are person-quarters. The samples are restricted to those with full-quarter employment with any employer for results listed as "full-quarter." Each equation also includes controls for age and time dummies. Regressions are based on a 10 percent random sample of the relevant population (as described in the appendix).

where *EARN* represents quarterly earnings, *TEMP* represents employment at a temp agency, *TEN* represents job tenure, *TIME* represents quarter dummies, *X* represents a variety of characteristics; i, j, and t denote the person, firm, and time period, respectively, and l takes on the values of 1 or 2, depending on whether the observation is in the first or second of the three-year periods subsequent to the base period.

In other words, we have estimated earnings equations across person-quarters, separately for the periods 1996 to 1998 and 1999 to 2001. We are primarily interested in the coefficients (and *t*-statistics) on employment at

Table 11.7   Estimated effects of temp agency employment during base period on earnings in subsequent periods: Low earners during the base period who do not work for temp agencies in subsequent periods (*T*-statistics)

	Temp employment			
	All earnings		Full quarter earnings	
	Any	Primary	Any	Primary
1996 to 1998				
Controlling for				
Race/gender, foreign-born	−.075	.025	.203	.310
	(8.10)	(1.26)	(24.05)	(16.59)
Person-fixed effect	−.102	−.018	.180	.278
	(11.41)	(0.90)	(22.69)	(15.71)
Person-fixed effect, tenure	.065	.187	.132	.212
	(7.26)	(9.74)	(16.28)	(11.94)
Person-fixed effect, tenure, firm-fixed effect	−.027	.063	.055	.098
	(3.24)	(3.55)	(7.39)	(6.09)
1999 to 2001				
Controlling for				
Race/gender, foreign-born	−.004	.081	.180	.206
	(0.34)	(5.69)	(19.21)	(10.71)
Person-fixed effect	−.035	.041	.161	.186
	(3.40)	(1.91)	(18.00)	(10.01)
Person-fixed effect, tenure	.081	.149	.127	.144
	(8.00)	(7.14)	(14.00)	(7.75)
Person-fixed effect, tenure, firm-fixed effect	−.024	.017	.042	.036
	(2.57)	(0.89)	(5.08)	(2.15)

Note: Samples exclude workers who worked for temp agencies during the quarter observed in the periods 1996 to 1998 or 1999 to 2001. Other conditions from note in table 11.6 apply.

temp agencies during the base period, which is what we present in those tables. All other variables appear as controls.[16]

In table 11.6 we present five specifications of each equation. In the first, we control for observable fixed characteristics such as race/gender and foreign-born status, as well as age and time (quarter). In the second we add a control for current employment at a temp agency. In the third, we replace the fixed personal characteristics noted previously with a person-fixed effect. In the fourth we add a control for tenure in the current job. Finally, in the fifth, we add the firm-fixed effect. These different specifications shed light on how our results might be influenced by the omission or inclusion of all of these variables, since it seems that temp employment in the base period draws workers with different personal characteristics rather than the overall population

16. These regressions are based on random 10 percent samples of the full populations that meet our sampling criteria; sample sizes are thus about one-tenth of those that appear in the appendix for the two subsequent periods.

of low earners, and since temp employment may or may not causally affect not only subsequent job tenure and firm characteristics but also subsequent temp employment.

Separate equations have been estimated for all earnings and for full-quarter earnings (in the latter case, the sample is restricted only to individual workers' person-quarters of full-quarter employment with any particular firm). Separate estimates are also provided for those with any temp employment in the base period versus those whose primary employment was through the temp agency, and also for 1996 to 1998 versus 1999 to 2001. Also, table 11.6 presents results for all workers who were persistently low earners in the base period, while table 11.7 presents them only for nontemp workers in the subsequent three-year periods.[17]

Overall, the estimated effects of temp employment for low earners in the base period on their subsequent earnings are somewhat varied. The estimates for all earnings are quite mixed, with primary employment at a temp agency showing more positive effects than any temp employment, but the effects of temp employment on full-quarter earnings are uniformly positive—suggesting that those who manage to gain more stable employment after their temp experience benefit more from it than those who do not gain stable employment.

Without controlling for current temp employment, effects on all earnings are negative, though still positive for those with full-quarter earnings only. Controlling for current temp activity makes the results for all earnings considerably less negative, and even positive for those with primary temp employment in the base period. Controlling for person-fixed effects consistently makes the estimated effects of temp agencies less positive, by 2 to 4 log points; this is consistent with the notion of some positive self-selection into temp employment among low earners. Controlling for tenure has mixed effects, making the estimates more positive for all earnings (consistent with the shorter tenure among temp users that we observed in earlier tables) but less positive for those with full-quarter earnings (implying longer tenure among temp users who have full-quarter employment). Also, the estimated effects of current temp agency employment are large and negative in all equations (not shown in the tables), but controlling for these makes the effects of previous temp employment more positive as well.

Controlling for current temp status and also for job tenure, all of the estimated effects of temp agencies on either earnings measure are positive. Thus, both the estimates for full-quarter earnings and those controlling for tenure show that *temp agencies have positive effects on the earnings of low earners who manage to transition to stable non-temp employment afterward.* And while some—though not all—of the positive estimated effects of temp

---

17. Table 11.7 thus contains just four specifications, since the second one from table 11.6 is omitted.

employment diminish between the first and second three-year periods after the base period, at least some positive effects persist over time, suggesting that the positive effects are not purely short-term.

But all of the positive estimates become much smaller (or even negative) once we control for firm fixed effects. Indeed, controlling for firm characteristics consistently reduces the positive impacts of temp agencies by about seven log points. In other words, *most of the positive effects of temp agencies on subsequent earnings of low earners occur because they improve the access of these workers to higher-wage employers.* This is consistent with the results reported in Andersson, Holzer, and Lane (2005).

When we consider the effects of earlier temp employment on those not working as temps in the subsequent periods in table 11.7, we generally find much more positive effects of earlier temp employment than in table 11.6. As before, results for those with full-quarter earnings are positive and quite large—with earlier temp employment raising subsequent earnings by 20 to 30 log points in 1996 to 1998 and 16 to 20 log points in 1999 to 2001. For those with any earnings, the effects remain mixed but are clearly positive after controlling for job tenure. And controlling for firm-fixed effects now reduces the estimated effects of early temp employment by 9 to 13 log points.

To see more clearly the apparent positive impact of temp employment on the quality of firms to which workers get matched subsequently, we present estimates of early temp employment on the firm-fixed effects in 1996 to 1998 and 1999 to 2001 in table 11.8. As before, estimates appear for full-quarter earnings only and for all earnings, and for any earlier temp employment as well as primary employment during the base period. Results from two specifications are presented: the first, in which we control for observable personal characteristics (i.e., race/gender and foreign-born status), and the second controlling for person-fixed effects. As in table 11.7, those who still work with temp agencies in the subsequent periods are removed from the sample.

The results show quite substantial positive effects of early temp employment on the subsequent quality of firms to which low-earning workers are matched. For all earners, firm-fixed effects are 9 to 14 percentage points higher among those who earlier had worked for temp agencies; among those with full-quarter earnings, firm-fixed effects are 9 to 18 percentage points higher. Thus, for those making successful transitions to stable post-temp employment, access to higher-wage firms is improved by having worked for a time with a temp agency.

11.5   Conclusion

Using new longitudinal data from the Census Bureau on the universe of UI-covered workers and their employers in five states, we have estimated the

Table 11.8   **Estimated effects of temp agency employment during base period on firm fixed effect in subsequent periods: Low earners during the base period who do not work for temp agencies in subsequent periods**

	Temp employment			
	All earnings		Full quarter earnings	
	Any	Primary	Any	Primary
	1996 to 1998			
Controlling for				
Race/gender, foreign-born	.099	.131	.127	.178
	(31.15)	(19.00)	(29.31)	(18.63)
Person-fixed effect	.088	.118	.092	.135
	(28.26)	(17.67)	(22.65)	(15.16)
	1999 to 2001			
Controlling for				
Race/gender, foreign-born	.113	.139	.133	.163
	(30.46)	(18.10)	(28.39)	(16.93)
Person-fixed effect	.102	.128	.103	.130
	(28.16)	(17.09)	(23.02)	(14.20)

Notes: Samples exclude workers who worked for temp agencies during the quarter observed in the periods 1996 to 1998 or 1999 to 2001. Other conditions from the note to table 11.6 apply, except that the dependent variable is now the firm-fixed effect for that quarter.

effects of temp employment on the earnings of persistently low earners over a subsequent six-year period.

Our results show that temp earners clearly have lower earnings than others while working at these agencies, and even their subsequent earnings are somewhat mixed. But these earnings are generally higher if they manage to gain stable employment with other employers. In particular, we find that the effects of temp agency employment in the base period on subsequent earnings are uniformly positive for those reporting full-quarter earnings, and for all earnings once we control for job tenure.

While there is some positive self selection among low earners into temp employment, controlling for person-fixed effects does not completely eliminate the positive effects associated with temp employment. Furthermore, the positive effects seem mostly to occur because those working for temp agencies subsequently work for higher-wage firms than do comparable low earners who do not work for temps. And the positive effects we estimate seem to persist over time, for as much as six years beyond the base period during which the temp employment was observed.

Thus, our results are consistent with the notion that low earners, in addition to any deficiencies in skills that they bring to the labor market, sometimes have difficulty matching themselves to higher-wage employers in the labor market. This might reflect employer discrimination, their own limited information, and informal contacts in the labor market, transportation, and geographic mismatch, or other problems.

But temp agencies, and perhaps other labor market intermediaries, can help these workers overcome these problems and gain access to better employers across their regional labor markets. By providing the initial contact with employers, these intermediaries can perhaps overcome transportation and informational barriers that limit initial access (Giloth 2003), and by providing information about worker quality and previous performance that might be unobservable to employers on their own, they may overcome discriminatory behaviors among employers (Holzer, Raphael, and Stoll 2003). Indeed, the results suggest that such intermediaries may play a significant role in a strategy of helping the working poor advance in the labor market by moving them into better jobs over time, as long as such placements can be combined with appropriate job training and support services (Holzer 2004; Holzer and Martinson 2005).

Our results are thus consistent with much of the earlier literature on temp agencies that we reviewed previously, though somewhat less consistent with the recent work by Autor and Houseman in Detroit, which suggested that any positive effects are spurious or transitory. On the other hand, even in their work, contractors who placed TANF recipients into permanent jobs also generated positive impacts on earnings that persisted over time. In this broader sense, the results of Autor and Houseman are quite consistent with our results here, suggesting that temps and/or other intermediaries who manage to achieve more permanent job placements for their workers can have positive impacts.

Of course, we have not fully eliminated possible self-selection effects regarding temps, since person-fixed effects do not control for any time-varying characteristics of these individuals. But, combined with the clear evidence that temp agencies result in subsequent employment at higher-wage firms, our findings at least suggest that the positive effects of temp agencies or other intermediaries on the job-matching process for low earners might be real and persistent.

Appendix

Table 11A.1   **Effects of sample selection criteria on sample size, temp agency employment, earnings, and personal characteristics**

	N	Temp employment (%)	Quarterly earnings ($)	Person-fixed effect
Sample including:				
All workers aged 25 to 54 in 1995 with at least one quarter of work and $2,000 earned per year, 1993–1995	17,010	8.0	9,126	0.07
Only persistent low earners, 1993–1995	1,384	16.3	2,085	−0.56
At least one quarter of work and $2,000 earned per year, 1996–1998	880	14.8	2,118	−0.55
At least one quarter of work and $2,000 earned per year, 1999–2001	670	14.1	2,129	−0.55

Note: Sample size (N) is measured as person-quarters during the base period of 1993 to 1995. Temp Employment reflects the percentage of workers with at least one quarter of employment at a temp agency during the base period. Quarterly earnings reflects average quarterly earnings during the base period. Person-fixed effect is defined as in the text. The four conditions imposed on the sample are added sequentially.

References

Abowd, J. M., R. H. Creecy, and F. Kramarz. 2002. Computing person and firm effects using linked longitudinal employer-employee data. U.S. Census Bureau, LEHD Program Technical Paper TP-2002-06. Available at: http://lehd.dsd.census.gov/led/library/techpapers/tp-2002-06.pdf (cited March 4, 2007).

Abowd, J. M., J. Haltiwanger, and J. I. Lane. 2004. Integrated longitudinal employee-employer data for the United States. *American Economic Review Papers and Proceedings* 94 (2): 224–29.

Abowd, J. M., F. Kramarz, and D. Margolis. 1999. High-wage workers and high-wage firms. *Econometrica* 67 (2): 251–334.

Abowd, J. M., and L. Vilhuber. 2005. The sensitivity of economic statistics to coding errors in personal identifiers. *Journal of Business and Economic Statistics* 23 (2): 133–52.

Andersson, F., H. Holzer, and J. Lane. 2005. *Moving up or moving on: Workers, firms and advancement in the low-wage labor market.* New York: Russell Sage Foundation.

Autor, D. 2001. Why do temporary help firms provide free general skills training? *Quarterly Journal of Economics* 116 (4): 1409–48.

Autor, D., and S. Houseman. 2005. Do temporary help jobs improve labor market outcomes for low-skilled workers? Evidence from random assignments. NBER Working Paper no. 11743. Cambridge, MA: National Bureau of Economic Research, November.

———. 2007. Temporary agency employment: A way out of poverty? In *Working and poor: How economic and policy changes are affecting low-wage workers,* ed. R. Blank, S. Danziger, and R. Schoeni, 312–37. New York: Russell Sage Foundation.

Benner, C., L. Leete, and M. Pastor. 2007. *Staircases or treadmills? Labor market intermediaries and economic opportunity in a changing economy.* New York: Russell Sage Foundation.

Bureau of Labor Statistics (BLS). 1997. *BLS handbook of methods.* Washington, D.C.: Government Printing Office.

Doeringer, P., and M. Piore. 1971. *Internal labor markets and manpower analysis.* Lexington, MA: D. C. Heath.

Dunlop, J. 1957. *The theory of wage determination.* London: MacMillan.

Giloth, R. ed. 2003. *Workforce intermediaries for the twenty-first century.* Philadelphia: Temple University Press.

Hamermesh, D. 1999. Changing inequality in markets for workplace amenities. *Quarterly Journal of Economics* 114 (4): 1085–1124.

Heinrich, C. J., P. R. Mueser, and K. R. Troske. 2005. Welfare to temporary work: Implications for labor market outcomes. *Review of Economics and Statistics* 87 (1): 154–73.

Holzer, H. J. 1987. Informal job search and black youth unemployment. *American Economic Review* 77 (2): 446–52.

———. 1991. The spatial mismatch hypothesis: What does the evidence show? *Urban Studies* 28 (1): 105–22.

———. 1996. *What employers want: Job prospects for less-educated workers.* New York: Russell Sage Foundation.

———. 2004. Advancement for low-wage workers: A different approach. Policy Brief no. 30, *Welfare reform and beyond.* Washington, D.C.: Brookings Institution.

Holzer, H. J., and R. J. Lalonde. 1998. Job change and job stability among less-skilled young workers. In *Finding jobs,* ed. D. Card and R. Blank, 125–59. New York: Russell Sage Foundation.

Holzer, H. J., and K. Martinson. 2005. How can we improve the job retention and advancement prospects of low-income parents? Working Paper, The Urban Institute, Washington, D.C.

Holzer, H., S. Raphael, and M. Stoll. 2003. Employer demand for ex-offenders: Evidence from Los Angeles. Discussion Paper no. 1268-03, Institute for Research on Poverty, University of Wisconsin at Madison.

Ichino, A., F. Mealli, and T. Nannicini. 2006. From temporary help jobs to permanent employment: What can we learn from matching estimators and their sensitivity? IZA Discussion Paper no. 2149. Bonn: IZA.

Ihlanfeldt, K., and D. Sjoquist. 1998. The spatial mismatch hypothesis: A review of recent studies and their implications for welfare reform. *Housing Policy Debate* 9 (4): 849–92.

Ionnides, Y., and L. D. Loury. 2004. Job information networks, neighborhood effects, and inequality. *Journal of Economic Literature.* 42 (4): 1056–93.

Juhn, C., K. Murphy, and B. Pierce. 1993. Wage inequality and the rise in the return to skill. *Journal of Political Economy* 101 (June): 410–42.

Kain, J. 1992. The spatial mismatch hypothesis three decades later. *Housing Policy Debate* 3 (2): 371–469.

Lane, J., K. Mikelson, P. Sharkey, and D. Wissoker. 2003. Pathways to work for low income workers: The effect of work in the temporary help industry. *Journal of Policy Analysis and Management* 22 (4): 581–98.

Rebitzer, J. 1993. Radical political economy and the economics of labor markets. *Journal of Economic Literature* 31 (3): 1394–1471.

Schultz, C. 2003. The consumer price index: Conceptual issues and practical suggestions. *Journal of Economic Perspectives* 17 (1): 3–22.

The Role of Temporary Help Employment in Low-Wage Worker Advancement

Carolyn J. Heinrich, Peter R. Mueser, and
Kenneth R. Troske

12.1 Introduction

The large increase in temporary help service (THS) employment in recent years—from less than 0.5 percent in 1982 to approximately 2.5 percent by 2004 (U.S. Bureau of Labor Statistics 2005)—has been particularly dramatic for low-skilled, less-educated, and minority workers, who are now greatly overrepresented in the temporary help workforce (Autor and Houseman 2005; Heinrich, Mueser, and Troske 2005; DiNatale 2001). This disproportionate concentration of disadvantaged workers in THS employment, combined with the growing use of temporary help service firms as labor market intermediaries by both private firms and public social welfare programs, has engendered an active policy and research debate about the consequences of such mediated employment for workers' wages, job stability, access to fringe benefits, and labor market advancement. In addition, the literature on the effects of THS employment has more recently begun to address some of the more complex questions about the implications of temporary help

Carolyn J. Heinrich is director of the La Follette School of Public Affairs and a professor of public affairs at the University of Wisconsin-Madison. Peter R. Mueser is a professor of economics at the University of Missouri-Columbia. Kenneth R. Troske is the William B. Sturgill Professor of Economics and director of the Center for Business and Economic Research at the University of Kentucky.

This work was supported by a grant from the Rockefeller/Russell Sage Foundation Future of Work Program. We wish to acknowledge helpful comments from David Autor, Bernhard Broockman, John Fitzgerald, Gerald Oettinger, Jeffrey Smith, Daniel Sullivan, and participants in the NBER Conference on Labor Market Intermediation, the Third Conference on Evaluation Research (Mannheim), annual conferences of the Midwest Economics Association and the Society of Labor Economists, and seminars at the Bowdoin College and the Institute for the Study of Labor (IZA). Excellent research assistance was provided by Kyung-Seong Jeon and Chao Gu.

employment for workers' labor market outcomes, including these workers' subsequent labor market transitions, occupational mobility, and longer-term earnings trajectories.

In general, two competing arguments have been advanced about temporary help employment: (a) employment through THS firms may provide a path to permanent and stable employment for workers who might otherwise be excluded from such labor market opportunities, and (b) temporary help jobs supplant productive employment search and reduce access to better employment opportunities, ultimately depressing workers' wages and opportunities for advancement. The former argument is consistent with the basic premise underlying current U.S. public welfare and employment and training policies, which assumes that helping individuals to get jobs (even low-wage jobs) will give them the opportunity to gain on-the-job skills and experience and move up the career ladder to better positions (i.e., a foot in the door or a stepping stone). With this greater policy emphasis on short-term, work-oriented social services, the role of THS firms in facilitating job placements has naturally grown, particularly for disadvantaged workers served by such programs.

In order to examine whether employment in the temporary help industry helps or hurts workers relative to other employment in the long run, we explore the subsequent employment dynamics of workers in this industry and compare their experiences with those of workers who either do not have jobs or who take jobs in other industries (i.e., in end-user firms). We focus our analysis on individuals in the state of Missouri who sought job search assistance from employment exchange services funded under federal Wagner-Peyser legislation.

We draw on clients in this program in order to identify a diverse sample of individuals who are facing employment difficulties or who are entering the labor force.[1] Many clients of employment exchange services are facing an important juncture in their work lives or careers, as they are explicitly seeking services to support employment efforts. Our analysis allows us to consider the role that temporary employment and other industries play at such critical points in determining future labor market outcomes. This study does not consider the effects of employment exchange services.

We begin our analysis by examining whether there are other industries that serve a role similar to that of the temporary help industry. We observe that individuals in our sample are particularly likely to move into temporary help employment when they first seek employment exchange services, and we consider whether this pattern can be observed for any other industries. Next

---

1. An earlier version of this study considered participants in Missouri's job training program and in the Temporary Assistance for Needy Families program (Heinrich, Mueser, and Troske 2007). The results for participants in these programs are very similar to those presented here, suggesting that the findings are not an artifact of the particular experience of employment exchange service recipients.

we look at employment during the quarter following initial participation, examining how employment and wages two years later are influenced by the sector of employment, and, in particular, temporary help services. We limit the sample to those eighteen to sixty-four years of age and conduct analyses separately for men and women. We report analyses initially for those who obtain employment exchange services during calendar year 1997 and then consider analyses for an analogous sample in 2001. Our use of large and long panels of state-level administrative data allows us to extend previous research on the effect of employment in THS by examining the impact of THS over an extended period and at different points in the business cycle and by comparing individuals who obtain employment in various industries and who have very different demographic characteristics.

Our main findings are as follows. First, we find that THS is unique in serving as a general transitional industry. Second, we find that working in the THS sector has very little long-term negative impact on either earnings or employment for workers who access employment exchange services. If we believe that for workers in THS the next best opportunity is not having a job in a quarter, working in the THS sector imparts significant benefits. Third, we find that worker success is contingent on transitioning out of the THS sector; workers who remain in the THS sector have long-run earnings that are substantially below workers in other sectors. Finally, we find that our results are strikingly consistent across the business cycle, and that the experience of nonwhites in THS jobs is very similar to that of whites.

In the next section we review the literature on the temporary help service industry. In section 12.3 we discuss our data and in section 12.4 we consider the role of the temporary help service industry in providing transitional employment. We also examine the factors determining who takes a temporary help job. Section 12.5 presents estimates of the impact of temporary help employment on later earnings and employment, and section 12.6 considers the role that movements between jobs has in helping individuals achieve higher earnings and stable employment. In section 12.7, we consider the degree to which results are replicated for a similar sample of employment exchange participants in 2001 (a time when economic growth had slowed). Section 12.8 focuses on the experience of nonwhites in temporary help jobs. Section 12.9 turns to the issue of how robust our results are if the ordinary least squares (OLS) assumption of an independent error is violated. The final section concludes.

12.2   Literature

There is strong agreement among a large number of studies that temporary help services jobs pay lower wages, offer fewer work hours, are shorter in tenure, and are significantly less likely to provide health insurance coverage or other fringe benefits (Autor and Houseman 2005; Andersson, Holzer, and Lane 2002; Blank 1998; Booth, Francesconi, and Frank 2002; Cohany 1998; Heinrich, Mueser, and Troske 2005; Houseman and Polivka 1999; Houseman, Kalleberg, and Erickcek 2003; Lane et al. 2003; Nollen 1996; Pavetti et al. 2000; Pawasarat 1997; Segal and Sullivan 1997). A smaller number of studies go beyond descriptive statistics to examine the employment and earnings paths or trajectories of welfare recipients and other low-wage workers who enter temporary help services employment.

Using matched samples of "at-risk disadvantaged workers"[2] from the Survey of Income and Program Participation (SIPP), Lane et al. (2003) find that individuals who take temporary help services jobs have better employment and "job quality" outcomes than those who do not enter employment. Temporary help workers fare slightly worse than those who enter other employment sectors in terms of earnings and benefits, although differences are generally small and not statistically significant. In addition, they conclude that the effects of temporary help employment in reducing welfare receipt and poverty relative to no employment are substantial, and that there is no difference in these outcomes between those in temporary and conventional employment.

Despite different populations of study (welfare recipients in Missouri and North Carolina), the findings of Heinrich et al. (2005) mirror those of Lane et al. (2003). After following welfare recipients who go to work for temporary help services for two years, Heinrich et al. find very small differences (1 to 7 percent) in earnings between those who initially took temporary help jobs and those who entered jobs in other sectors, with measured characteristics explaining most of the differentials. The earnings of welfare recipients initially entering THS jobs increased faster over the two-year period, in part due to their movement from temporary help into higher-paying industries. In addition, temporary help workers were no more likely to be out of a job two years later and only slightly more likely to return to welfare than workers in end-user firms, and they were substantially more likely to be employed and off welfare two years later than recipients without a job.

Andersson, Holzer, and Lane (2002) use data from five states (California, Florida, Illinois, Maryland, and North Carolina) in the Longitudinal Employer Household Dynamics (LEHD) program at the U.S. Census Bureau to analyze a sample of workers with persistently low labor market earnings. Like Heinrich et al. (2005), they find that low-wage workers starting in THS employment earn lower pay while employed by the temporary agency but that subsequent job changes lead to higher wages and better job characteristics for these workers. Both Heinrich et al. and Anderson, Holzer, and Lane (2002) and observe that low-wage workers

---

2. Lane et al. (2003) use propensity-score matching to define comparison groups of "at-risk" workers (with incomes less than 200 percent of the poverty level) for their THS worker sample.

who begin work with THS firms are more likely to move to higher-paying industries, such as manufacturing, than those working in other sectors (or not working). Such mobility provides the primary path through which temporary help employment boosts later earnings; workers who do not leave the temporary help industry suffer an earnings shortfall. Andersson, Holzer, and Lane (chapter 11, this volume) also use this five-state LEHD sample, but consider a longer follow-up period and more sophisticated methods. Their results are substantively similar.

Autor and Houseman (2005) take advantage of random assignment of welfare recipients to welfare-to-work contractors, where contractors vary in their referrals to THS firms. Under the assumption that such referrals are not correlated with other contractor practices that influence client success, they estimate the effects of holding a THS job on low-skilled workers' labor market outcomes. Initial earnings increments among their THS workers do not persist, in part due to declines in rates of employment, and THS workers fare more poorly over the subsequent two years in terms of their earnings than "direct-hire" placements. Point estimates imply that THS workers also earn less than welfare recipients with no job placements, although these differences are not statistically significant. When they examine the impact of temporary help employment using OLS, they obtain results consistent with others—that is, implying a substantial benefit of temporary help employment—so their results differ from others because of their identification methods, not because of their sample.

There is also a growing literature examining temporary help firms in Europe.[3] Booth, Francesconi, and Frank (2002) study temporary help employment in Britain using data from the British Household Panel Survey and methods similar to Heinrich et al. and find temporary employment to be an effective stepping stone to permanent employment. Kvasnikca's (2005) study of temporary help workers in Germany does not produce evidence that these workers are more likely to move into permanent employment than unemployed workers, but neither does the analysis suggest that they suffer any adverse effects from temporary work. In their study of temporary help workers in Spain, Garcia-Perez and Munoz-Bullon (2005) find that temporary help workers in low-skill occupational groups had much lower probabilities of securing a permanent job than more skilled workers. They concluded that these workers would have fared better had they not worked through these intermediaries.

The findings of these and related studies speak to important, cross-national public policy questions about the role of labor market intermediaries as a solution to the problem of low-wage worker advancement (Poppe,

---

3. In the European literature, many studies examine jobs classified as "temporary" based on the contract under which an individual is hired. Such jobs account for over 10 percent of employment in France and Germany and over 30 percent of employment in Spain (Gagliarducci 2005). We limit our review to European studies that consider mediated employment corresponding to the temporary help services sector in the United States.

Strawn, and Martinson 2003). A recent study by Even and Macpherson (2003, 677) found that "switching jobs is vital to significant wage growth among minimum wage workers, particularly for young workers who find themselves in 'low-training' occupations." And Andersson, Holzer, and Lane (2005, 143) similarly concluded that "job changes account for the vast majority of 'complete' transitions out of low earnings and even for most partial changes." We expect the results of our study to contribute to these policy debates about the role of public and private intermediaries in helping workers connect with and advance in jobs.

The use of state-level administrative data allows us to expand the scope of our analyses beyond these existing studies in several ways. First, the long panel allows us to follow workers for an extended period after we first observe them in the temporary help industry. Our replication of the analysis over two time periods enables us to examine whether the effect of working in the temporary help industry varies across the business cycle. Second, because we have large sample sizes, we are able to compare the effects of working in a variety of industries. For example, we can compare the long-run impact of working in the temporary help industry with the impact of working in another service industry or in the retail trade industry, which may be the most relevant comparison for these workers.

It is important to emphasize that the only "treatment" we are considering in this analysis is the industry or employment sector of the firm into which individuals in our sample select after undertaking employment exchange activities. We have no information in our data about whether individuals who take temporary help services jobs are directed to these jobs by counselors in the employment exchange service. A 2001 survey of public assistance recipients who had engaged in temporary help services employment in North Carolina found that most (77 percent) did not learn about these jobs through program counselors, but rather through other channels, including word of mouth, newspaper ads, or by contacting the firm directly (Heinrich 2005).

12.3   Data

Employment exchange files from Missouri identify individuals in the state who register for services provided under federal Wagner-Peyser legislation.[4] Most individuals who receive Unemployment Insurance (UI) payments are required to register for these services, and a substantial portion of employment exchange registrants are UI recipients.[5] However, anyone in the state

4. Greater detail on the characteristics of individuals in our sample, including tabulations comparing employment exchange participants with participants in other programs, can be found in Heinrich, Mueser, and Troske (2007).
5. In 1997, the state's job exchange service was administered by Missouri's Division of Employment Security in the Department of Labor and Industrial Relations. In 1999, the program was transferred to the Division of Workforce Development in the Department of Economic Development.

is eligible to use these services, so registrants include employed individuals seeking better employment prospects as well as other job-seekers who are not receiving unemployment compensation. Information on program participation and demographic information about participants comes from data maintained by the state of Missouri to administer these programs.

Our basic sample consists of individuals who participated in the employment exchange service during 1997 or 2001 and who did not receive job exchange services in the prior quarter. An individual who obtained services during the first six months of the year, received no services for at least one quarter, and then again obtained services in a later quarter, will be included twice in the file for a given year. The number of such cases is very small.

Our data on earnings, employment history, and the industrial classification of the job come from the Unemployment Insurance (UI) programs in the states of Missouri and Kansas. Earnings for individuals in a quarter are reported by employers, and we are able to match these to employment exchange participants using Social Security numbers. Although these data exclude the self-employed, those in informal or illegal employment, and a small number of jobs exempt from UI reporting requirements, they include the overwhelming majority of employment in these states. These data allow us to identify all employers for an individual during a quarter, but we cannot determine whether jobs were held simultaneously or sequentially. A very small proportion of Missouri residents hold jobs in states other than Kansas.[6] All earnings in the analyses have been adjusted for inflation based on the consumer price index, using quarter 2 of 1997 as the base.

The industrial classification is taken from information about the employer on these files, and our identification of temporary help workers is based on the convention that individuals working on a temporary assignment from a THS firm are listed as employees of the THS firm. Although the THS firm's own direct employees (e.g., office staff) will also be included, the proportion of such cases is expected to be small, especially among participants in the program we are considering.[7]

Table 12.1 provides means and standard deviations for our samples of males and females receiving employment exchange services in 1997 and 2001. The samples are large and provide a substantial array of demographic measures, as well as prior labor market experience. The table also provides statistics about industry of employment in the quarter subsequent to program participation. We see that THS makes up 6 to 9 percent of employment at this point, but that, eight quarters later, THS is less important.

---

6. The largest concentration of Missouri residents holding jobs outside the state are those in Jackson County, Missouri, the central county for Kansas City, who cross the border to work in Kansas. The proportion of St. Louis residents with jobs in Illinois is much smaller, due to the depressed economy of East St. Louis, Illinois. No other significant concentrations of population are close to Missouri's borders.

7. Antoni and Jahn (2006) report that 7 percent of the employees in temporary help firms in Germany are permanent administrative staff.

Table 12.1 Means and standard deviations for employment exchange participants, 1997 and 2001

| | 1997 | | | | 2001 | | | |
| | Females | | Males | | Females | | Males | |
	Mean	SD	Mean	SD	Mean	SD	Mean	SD
Age	34.2	11.0	33.7	10.9	35.9	12.1	35.9	12.0
Age squared	1,293.9	825.0	1,255.1	812.9	1,433.4	923.2	1,432.1	921.5
Number of years of education	12.31	1.64	12.30	1.67	12.45	1.45	12.36	1.46
High school degree[a]	0.871	0.336	0.870	0.337	0.934	0.249	0.925	0.263
College degree	0.077	0.267	0.077	0.266	0.081	0.273	0.075	0.264
Nonwhite	0.267	0.442	0.234	0.424	0.238	0.426	0.225	0.418
Proportion of previous eight quarters working	0.628	0.395	0.632	0.395	0.700	0.376	0.690	0.381
Working all of previous eight qtrs	0.391	0.488	0.396	0.489	0.474	0.499	0.462	0.499
No work in any of previous eight qtrs	0.180	0.385	0.180	0.385	0.141	0.348	0.149	0.356
Total annual earnings in the prior year	8,944	10,319	12,747	15,349	13,792	15,203	19,302	29,751
Total annual earnings two years prior	7,847	10,197	11,355	15,330	12,489	14,730	17,663	23,801
St. Louis County and St. Louis City	0.218	0.413	0.205	0.404	0.205	0.403	0.188	0.391
Kansas City central area (Jackson County)	0.101	0.301	0.105	0.306	0.114	0.318	0.124	0.329
Suburban areas	0.126	0.332	0.141	0.348	0.172	0.377	0.170	0.375
Small metro	0.125	0.331	0.134	0.340	0.131	0.337	0.136	0.343
Outside metro	0.430	0.495	0.416	0.493	0.378	0.485	0.383	0.486
Earnings in quarter following program entry	1,845	3,002	2,591	3,903	2,213	3,354	3,041	6,541
Earnings eight quarters after reference quarter	2,430	2,841	3,353	4,035	2,691	3,321	3,476	4,568
Employment eight quarters after reference quarter	0.642	0.479	0.626	0.484	0.625	0.484	0.600	0.490

	Mean	SD	Mean	SD	Mean	SD	Mean	SD
Industry in reference quarter								
No job	0.334	0.471	0.325	0.468	0.358	0.479	0.360	0.480
THS	0.044	0.205	0.046	0.208	0.031	0.173	0.032	0.175
Manufacturing	0.086	0.281	0.131	0.337	0.086	0.280	0.145	0.352
Retail trade	0.127	0.333	0.098	0.297	0.125	0.330	0.100	0.300
Service (excluding THS)	0.192	0.394	0.089	0.285	0.196	0.397	0.096	0.294
Other	0.086	0.280	0.182	0.386	0.100	0.300	0.168	0.374
Multiple sectors: THS and any other	0.048	0.214	0.048	0.215	0.031	0.173	0.032	0.176
Multiple sectors: Any not THS	0.083	0.276	0.081	0.273	0.074	0.262	0.067	0.250
Industry eight quarters after reference quarter								
No job	0.358	0.479	0.374	0.484	0.375	0.484	0.400	0.490
THS	0.023	0.151	0.024	0.154	0.014	0.119	0.016	0.126
Manufacturing	0.086	0.281	0.135	0.342	0.077	0.267	0.135	0.341
Retail trade	0.113	0.317	0.085	0.279	0.112	0.315	0.092	0.290
Service (excluding THS)	0.220	0.414	0.096	0.294	0.223	0.416	0.104	0.305
Other	0.116	0.320	0.209	0.406	0.139	0.346	0.200	0.400
Multiple sectors: THS and any other	0.024	0.154	0.024	0.154	0.011	0.103	0.013	0.113
Multiple sectors: Any not THS	0.059	0.236	0.054	0.225	0.048	0.215	0.041	0.198
Number of observations	114,375		135,911		79,042		94,466	

Note: SD = Standard deviation.

[a]The high school degree dummy is coded 1 for those with at least a high school degree.

In the next three sections, we focus exclusively on individuals who obtain job exchange services in 1997. In section 12.7 we compare the experiences of entrants in 2001 with those who enter in 1997.

12.4   Temporary Help Services as Transitional Employment

Our analysis focuses on individuals who are likely to be at a juncture in their careers, either because they have lost a job or because they are making plans to pursue alternative employment or vocational training. Given its explicit temporary structure, it is natural to view THS as a transitional industry. In this section, we begin by looking at the patterns of job shift following program entry and examining the kinds of industries that may serve this kind of transitional role. Our conclusion is that THS appears to be unique among industries in filling this role. We then turn to an examination of the factors that are associated with employment in the THS industry.

Table 12.2 provides a comparison of the industry of employment four quarters prior to program entry and in the quarter subsequent to entry. The first row in the table shows the proportion of people without jobs. We see that employment increases in the first quarter after contact with the employment exchange system, presumably reflecting the fact that some individuals are seeking employment following a period out of the labor force. The

Table 12.2   Distribution of employment across industries prior and subsequent to program entry in 1997

	Females		Males	
	Four quarters before entry	One quarter after entry	Four quarters before entry	One quarter after entry
No job	36.26	33.39	35.25	32.05
Major industry group				
0 Agriculture, forestry, and fishing	1.16	0.59	1.88	1.50
1 Mining, construction	0.91	1.01	9.86	11.09
2, 3 Manufacturing	11.38	13.16	16.88	19.21
4 Transportation, communications, electric, gas, and sanitary services	2.72	3.09	5.00	5.56
5 Wholesale trade, retail trade	21.83	21.66	19.29	19.14
6 Finance, insurance, and real estate	3.60	3.97	1.52	1.58
7, 8 Services	29.01	35.58	16.81	22.15
9 Public administration	1.62	1.79	1.81	1.71
Four-digit industry				
5810 Eating and drinking places	8.71	8.18	6.42	6.15
7363 THS	3.87	8.73	4.08	8.78

Note: Counts include any job, so individuals who hold jobs in more than one industry are counted multiple times.

percentages in the table for each industry group identify the proportion of the sample that is employed in a job in the specified industry group in a given quarter. Individuals with jobs in more than one industry contribute multiple counts. We include all major industry categories in the upper panel. The lower panel provides the figures for THS and for eating and drinking establishments, the largest four-digit industry category in this sample.

The role that temporary help jobs play in this structure can be seen in the figures of THS and the comparison with other industries. Of the major industry groups, services display the largest increase, and this growth is largely due to growth in THS employment. The proportion of individuals in THS jobs more than doubles, increasing by nearly 5 percentage points, following contact with the job exchange system, reaching a level of about 9 percent. We undertook tabulations for all two-, three-, and four-digit industries to see if we could identify sets of industries that served the same function as THS employment. Where we identified specific industries that attracted increases in employment following enrollment, we found them to be of little quantitative importance. Both in terms of absolute size and proportional increase, THS is unique among industries that we can identify.

Table 12.3 provides information on factors associated with having jobs in THS in the quarter following initial program participation. Since we are concerned about the impact of industry of employment during this quarter, we refer to it as the "reference quarter." For ease of interpretation, we have divided employment into three categories: THS only, THS and some other industry, and other industry only. The table reports coefficients from a multinomial logit model predicting type of job, with the omitted category no employment during the quarter.[8] In every case, a likelihood ratio test rejected alternative models that combined these employment categories, and in every case we rejected models that combined THS with other employment.[9] Nonetheless, for many of the variables, coefficients for the three employment categories are similar, so that substantive differences in the determinants are small.

Those who are older are less likely to be working, but the relationship between age and employment is nonlinear, as indicated by the coefficient on the squared term that is negative and statistically significant.[10] This implies that as individuals get older, in those samples where older individuals are more likely to work, an additional year of age is associated with smaller

8. We also fitted models that controlled for industry of employment in the year prior to program entry. As expected, such controls reduce the impact of stable characteristics on industry choice, since such factors would partly affect industry choice through previous industry choices.

9. We tested models that constrained coefficients of all employment categories to be the same, as well as models that combined two of the three employment categories, performing a total of eight tests.

10. Inferences about the overall impact of age are based on evaluating the derivative of the quadratic of the age function at age 33.

Table 12.3   Multinomial logit estimation of job choice: Quarter following program entry in 1997

	Females			Males		
	Job in THS	Job in THS and other industry	Job, but none in THS	Job in THS	Job in THS and other industry	Job, but none in THS
Age	**0.054**	**0.018**	**−0.013**	**0.053**	**0.039**	**−0.026**
	(0.009)	(0.009)	(0.004)	(0.008)	(0.009)	(0.004)
Age squared · 100	**−0.092**	**−0.063**	−0.008	**−0.089**	**−0.095**	0.002
	(0.013)	(0.013)	(0.005)	(0.012)	(0.012)	(0.005)
Years of education	0.084	**0.117**	**0.041**	0.022	0.019	0.014
	(0.019)	(0.018)	(0.008)	(0.016)	(0.016)	(0.008)
High school degree	0.084	**0.149**	**0.206**	0.035	**0.204**	**0.371**
	(0.062)	(0.062)	(0.028)	(0.053)	(0.053)	(0.026)
College degree	−0.131	**−0.219**	**0.101**	−0.063	−0.079	**−0.093**
	(0.098)	(0.092)	(0.044)	(0.088)	(0.087)	(0.041)
Nonwhite	**0.445**	0.336	**−0.103**	**0.501**	**0.386**	**−0.169**
	(0.038)	(0.038)	(0.019)	(0.034)	(0.034)	(0.017)
Proportion of previous eight quarters working	**1.033**	1.383	1.152	**1.275**	**1.719**	**1.187**
	(0.089)	(0.091)	(0.041)	(0.079)	(0.081)	(0.038)
Working all of previous eight quarters	−0.045	**0.134**	**0.307**	**0.260**	**0.402**	**0.424**
	(0.054)	(0.051)	(0.025)	(0.049)	(0.047)	(0.023)
No work in any of previous eight quarters	**−0.396**	**−0.296**	**−0.451**	**−0.481**	**−0.269**	**−0.388**
	(0.063)	(0.069)	(0.028)	(0.055)	(0.059)	(0.026)
Total annual earnings in the prior year/1,000	**−0.008**	0.012	0.015	**−0.032**	**−0.015**	**0.020**
	(0.003)	(0.003)	(0.001)	(0.003)	(0.002)	(0.001)
Total annual earnings two years prior/1,000	**−0.021**	**−0.027**	**−0.015**	**−0.024**	**−0.035**	**−0.013**
	(0.003)	(0.003)	(0.001)	(0.003)	(0.003)	(0.001)
St. Louis central	**0.711**	**0.574**	**−0.159**	**0.555**	**0.356**	−0.040
	(0.046)	(0.046)	(0.021)	(0.041)	(0.042)	(0.019)
Kansas City central	**0.764**	**0.742**	**−0.223**	**0.689**	**0.827**	**0.138**
	(0.054)	(0.052)	(0.026)	(0.049)	(0.047)	(0.024)
Suburban metro	**0.679**	**0.755**	**−0.059**	**0.696**	**0.855**	**0.250**
	(0.054)	(0.050)	(0.023)	(0.050)	(0.046)	(0.022)
Small metro	**0.646**	**0.724**	**0.086**	**0.719**	**0.893**	**0.133**
	(0.055)	(0.051)	(0.023)	(0.046)	(0.043)	(0.021)
Unemployment rate in county at current quarter	**−4.664**	**−5.628**	**−2.822**	**−1.187**	**−2.017**	**−2.352**
	(0.725)	(0.744)	(0.243)	(0.597)	(0.638)	(0.247)

Notes: Coefficients for the dummy variables for each of the four quarters and the constant are not reported. Coefficient standard errors are in parentheses. Statistically significant estimates are in boldface.

increases in levels of employment, and in those samples where older individuals are less likely to work, this effect is stronger at higher ages.

Our specification controls for education using years of education and dummies for high school and bachelor's degrees. The dummy coefficients identify effects of degrees beyond the linear impacts of years of schooling. In general, greater schooling is associated with higher levels of employment;

those with high school degrees are more likely to be working than the simple linear model would imply.

As might be expected, prior employment is a strong predictor of employment in the reference quarter; we see that the three coefficients measuring employment in the prior eight quarters are substantial. Those who have no observed employment during the prior eight quarters are particularly unlikely to hold a job in the reference quarter. Prior earnings are related to employment in a complex way. The coefficients for earnings in the two prior years are in several cases negative. The coefficient in the immediately prior year is algebraically larger, implying that, controlling for the overall earnings level, growth in earnings is predictive of employment. In most cases, the sum of these coefficients is positive, as might be expected, so higher average earnings are associated with a greater chance of employment. Overall, prior earnings are less positively associated with temporary help work than with other employment, and those with higher prior earnings are *less* likely to be employed in temporary help than to be not employed at all. Note that this is after employment is controlled, so this implies that employed individuals with low incomes are likely to be in THS employment.

The coefficients for county unemployment rate confirm that those in depressed counties are less likely to be employed, and among women, they are particularly unlikely to combine a temporary help job with another job. There is no consistent relationship between the county unemployment rate and holding a temporary help job as compared with another job. In addition, those in metropolitan counties are much more likely to be in temporary help jobs than those in nonmetropolitan counties. Differences between large and small metropolitan areas are modest, as are differences between suburban and central metropolitan counties.

Overall, we can conclude that age, education, prior work experience, and the local economy predict who will be employed, but these variables contribute relatively little toward distinguishing temporary help employment from other employment. In contrast, race is among the most important predictors of temporary help employment, with nonwhites much more likely to be in temporary help employment.[11] This is particularly notable, since the relationship between other employment and race is generally small and inconsistent across our samples. Andersson, Holzer, and Lane (2002) and Heinrich, Mueser, and Troske (2005) similarly find that both black and other nonwhite minorities are more likely to be employed in the temporary help services sector. Andersson et al. also find that black males are more likely than any other group to escape a pattern of persistently low earnings through temporary help employment.

---

11. The overwhelming majority of nonwhites in the programs we are considering are African American.

These results suggest that explanations about selection into temporary help jobs that rest primarily on arguments about general levels of human capital miss the mark. What matters most is race and place. The explanation for the concentration of temporary help employment in metropolitan areas is undoubtedly the need for temporary help services to operate in an environment with a sufficient number of primary employers. We suspect that the large impact of race stems from employer difficulty judging worker productivity. If employers believe they are less able to judge the ability of nonwhite workers or that nonwhite workers are generally less productive, they may be less willing to hire nonwhite workers into regular jobs that imply long-term commitments. In the absence of effective legal prohibition against use of race by employers in hiring, temporary help jobs may provide valuable opportunities for nonwhites. In section 12.8 that follows, we return to the question of how the nonwhite experience may differ from that of whites in our sample.

12.5   Impacts of Temporary Help Experience on Earnings and Employment

To examine the impact of temporary help employment on ultimate earnings, we estimate a model that predicts earnings eight quarters after the reference quarter. Controls include basic human capital measures as well as indicators of prior employment experience, corresponding to the control variables in the logit equations reported in table 12.3. In addition, we control for industry prior to program entry, since we are interested in determining the impact of a temporary help job following program participation, not effects of prior experience.[12] Based on the same model, we also perform a difference-in-difference analysis, where the dependent variable is the difference in earnings between the outcome quarter and the quarter nine quarters prior to program entry.[13]

The program evaluation literature underscores the importance of taking account of the way in which program participants are selected (as reflected, for example, in the "Ashenfelter dip") in any attempt to identify program effects on the basis of comparisons between participants and others (Heckman, LaLonde, and Smith 1999). The analysis here differs from the standard evaluation in that all individuals in our sample receive the employment exchange services. Insofar as selection of such individuals per se is important

12. The measure of prior industry is based on industry of employment in all four quarters prior to program entry. Each industry dummy is coded 1 if there is any quarter in which the industry of employment falls in the specified category. Results are not sensitive to inclusion of these measures.

13. Such a symmetrical difference-in-difference specification controls for program selection by earnings if the time-varying component of earnings has a simple autoregressive structure (Ashenfelter and Card 1985).

in determining outcomes, our design controls for this selection. Nonetheless, prior employment experiences must be controlled, as we expect them to be related to job entry following program participation.[14] The difference-in-difference analysis allows us to control for stable differences across individuals that may lead them to take different kinds of jobs.

12.5.1   Estimated Effects on Earnings

Table 12.4 reports predicted quarterly earnings in the eighth quarter after the reference quarter based on linear regression equations as described previously, using the mean values of variables for the female and male samples.[15] For comparison, unadjusted earnings in the reference quarter and the outcome quarter are presented, along with predicted impacts of employment in various sectors relative to those not employed.[16] Focusing first on females, line 1 shows that mean earnings in the reference quarter of those with only a temporary help job are below those for individuals employed in all the other sectors and that, except for retail trade jobs, the difference is substantial. Controlling for individual characteristics (not shown) confirms that these patterns are not primarily due to differences in measured characteristics. Clearly, entering temporary help employment in the quarter after program entry is associated with a substantial immediate income decrement relative to most other kinds of employment. On the other hand, looking at those who hold jobs in multiple sectors, the role of temporary help employment is less clearly damaging, since those who hold THS jobs and other jobs have earnings closer to the level for those in most other sectors. Among those with jobs in a single major industry, those with manufacturing jobs usually have the highest earnings, although service and "other" jobs have similar or higher earnings in some cases.

Line 2 shows that, eight quarters later, the relative earnings of those initially in THS jobs have at least partly caught up with others. Earnings for temporary help workers increase by more than 50 percent in this period, an appreciably larger rate of growth than for any of our other industry categories.[17]

---

14. Dyke et al. (2006) evaluate job training for TANF participants using a similar design, although they control for prior labor market activity with a matching methodology.

15. For details of model specification and coefficient estimates, see Heinrich, Mueser, and Troske (2007).

16. Changes in the relative impacts of industries between lines 2 and 3 are equivalent to the explained portion of the Oaxaca-Blinder decomposition. Our use of a single equation constrains variable impact estimates to be the same for all industries, so the explained portion of the difference between industries i and j can be written as $(\overline{X}_i - \overline{X}_j)B$, where $\overline{X}_i$ and $\overline{X}_j$ are vectors of means for the industries and B is a vector of coefficients indicating variable effects.

17. Data from the Current Population Survey show that almost 40 percent of THS workers are working in service sector jobs, while 30 percent are working in manufacturing jobs (DiNatale 2001). Since many of these workers will transit into permanent jobs with the same employer where they are assigned as THS workers, and since manufacturing jobs in particular tend to pay above-average wages, such moves may be at least partly responsible for the rapid growth in wages for those initially in THS jobs. In the next section we explore more thoroughly the transition of THS workers into permanent jobs.

Table 12.4   Predicted earnings and impact by industry of employment in quarter following program entry in 1997 and impact eight quarters later

	One industry						Multiple industries	
	No job	THS	Manufacturing	Retail trade	Service[a]	Other	THS and any other industry	Any industry not THS
Panel A—Females								
1. Initial mean earnings	0	1,745	3,748	1,877	2,639	3,724	2,616	3,056
	(0)	(23)	(61)	(14)	(15)	(42)	(30)	(27)
2. Mean earnings eight quarters later	1,252	2,515	3,535	2,215	2,956	3,821	3,112	3,250
	(11)	(37)	(33)	(19)	(19)	(34)	(38)	(29)
3. Mean earnings eight quarters later controlling characteristics	1,578	2,605	3,186	2,449	2,783	3,192	2,986	3,020
	(13)	(35)	(28)	(21)	(17)	(26)	(33)	(25)
4. Impact on earnings, relative to no job category	0	**1,027**	**1,608**	**872**	**1,205**	**1,614**	**1,408**	**1,443**
	(0)	(37)	(31)	(25)	(22)	(30)	(36)	(29)
5. Difference-in-difference estimate of impact on earnings, relative to no job category	0	**1,333**	**1,853**	**943**	**1,306**	**1,486**	**1,424**	**1,569**
	(0)	(109)	(91)	(73)	(64)	(87)	(105)	(84)
Panel B—Males								
1. Initial mean earnings	0	1,716	5,119	2,628	3,369	4,519	2,667	4,133
	(0)	(25)	(33)	(24)	(30)	(31)	(25)	(51)
2. Mean earnings eight quarters later	1,575	2,393	5,218	3,161	3,706	4,954	3,082	4,434
	(14)	(37)	(35)	(29)	(35)	(29)	(39)	(38)
3. Mean earnings eight quarters later controlling characteristics	2,147	3,061	4,463	3,400	3,646	4,227	3,507	4,133
	(17)	(44)	(28)	(31)	(32)	(24)	(42)	(32)
4. Impact on earnings, relative to no job category	0	**915**	**2,316**	**1,254**	**1,499**	**2,081**	**1,360**	**1,986**
	(0)	(47)	(34)	(36)	(36)	(29)	(45)	(37)
5. Difference-in-difference estimate of impact on earnings, relative to no job category	0	**1,300**	**2,507**	**1,376**	**1,684**	**2,046**	**1,670**	**2,147**
	(0)	(113)	(81)	(86)	(88)	(71)	(110)	(90)

Note: Standard errors are in parentheses. Statistically significant impact estimates (shown in lines 4 and 5) are in boldface.
[a]Excluding THS.

Line 3 shows the impact of controls. Temporary help services workers are disadvantaged relative to other workers, so the relative benefits of having a manufacturing job are explained in part by observable differences among people.[18]

The largest categories of employment for females are retail trade and service, and the estimated impact on ultimate earnings of a retail trade job is close to that of a temporary help job. Service jobs produce incomes about 10 percent higher than temporary help jobs. Those with jobs in multiple sectors—whether they hold a THS job—have higher earnings than those with jobs in single sectors, except for manufacturing.

Line 4 indicates that the impact of holding any job—regardless of industry—is positive. Parallel (and very similar) estimates based on the difference-in-difference model are presented in line 5. If we aggregate all of the industries other than THS into a single category, this allows us to compare THS workers with the average alternative. Earnings in the outcome quarter for this category are about 10 percent higher than for THS workers, a difference that borders on statistical significance.[19]

Our conclusion is that temporary help employment has few deleterious effects on earnings relative to other industries for women eight quarters later. Earnings growth is greater than any other employment sector and ultimate earnings are only slightly below the average for other industries. Outcomes for those with any employment in the reference quarter are appreciably better than for those who do not obtain employment.

Patterns for males are similar to those for females. Earnings in the reference quarter for those in THS jobs alone are appreciably below earnings in all other industry categories, and less than half of earnings in manufacturing. However, earnings growth for those who begin in temporary help is much higher—about 50 percent over the two-year period, compared to less than 25 percent for other categories. As a result, the difference between temporary help and the highest-paid industries is substantially reduced in the outcome quarter. Line 3 indicates that more than half of the remaining difference is explained by individual characteristics and prior labor market measures.[20]

Those with any employment have appreciably higher earnings than those without jobs, but those in temporary help have earnings at least slightly below those in every other sector. Those with manufacturing jobs have ultimate earnings that are predicted to be 43 percent above observationally

18. Our earlier analysis (Heinrich, Mueser, and Troske 2007) shows that when we consider participants in TANF or job training programs, those who take THS work are not necessarily disadvantaged relative to others.

19. The direct estimate is statistically significant and the difference-in-difference estimate is not statistically significant.

20. Up to a fifth of the original difference is explained by the larger number of nonwhites and slightly lower level of education in the THS sample. The remainder is explained by the lower level of prior earnings we observe among THS workers.

similar individuals with temporary help jobs. If we aggregate all industries outside of THS, the increment is 31 percent. Finally, looking at predicted earnings of males who hold both a THS job and a job in another sector, we see that the predicted earnings are somewhat higher than for those with just THS jobs, and comparable to those for all industry groups except for manufacturing and "other."

12.5.2   Estimated Effects on Employment

We also estimated a linear probability model in which the dependent variable is employment eight quarters after the reference quarter. Control variables are identical to those used in the previous analysis. Table 12.5 provides measures of the impact on probability of employment (line 1) and the difference-in-difference estimate of the impact (line 2) relative to no job eight quarters later, based on sector of employment in the reference quarter.

The patterns of results parallel those for earnings fairly closely. The likelihood of employment eight quarters later is strongly associated with employment in any sector in the reference quarter. Differences between men and women are small. Although those in temporary help jobs are somewhat less likely to work in the outcome quarter than those in most other categories, the difference between temporary help workers and others in terms of ultimate employment is, as might be expected, substantially smaller than the difference in earnings. Those who combine jobs in more than one industry during the reference quarter generally have higher rates of later employment than other categories. As in the case of earnings, substantive conclusions for the difference-in-difference analyses are similar, although the impact of reference quarter employment is approximately half as large in the difference-in-difference estimates.

12.6   Transitions between Sectors

The pattern previously described, in which individuals in temporary help service jobs begin with lower earnings that increase faster over time, reflects in part their movement into more remunerative jobs outside the temporary help sector. In table 12.6 we examine movements between sectors over eight quarters. The tabs on the left of the table indicate the employment sector during the reference quarter, and row entries indicate the percentages of each group in the indicated industry categories eight quarters later. These tabulations show that those in THS jobs are much more likely to move into another major sector than are individuals in any other major sector.

Consider the proportion of individuals in temporary help service positions who remain in any service position. For women, some 28 percent of THS employees are in service positions (including THS) eight quarters later, whereas 52 percent of other service workers are in some kind of service

Table 12.5   Predicted probability of employment by industry in quarter following program entry in 1997

Impacts relative to no job	One industry					Multiple industries	
	THS	Manufacturing	Retail trade	Service[a]	Other	THS and any other industry	Any industry not THS
Panel A—Females							
1. Impact on probability of employment	**0.221**	**0.265**	**0.218**	**0.254**	**0.268**	**0.281**	**0.281**
	(0.007)	(0.006)	(0.005)	(0.004)	(0.005)	(0.006)	(0.005)
2. Difference-in-difference estimate of impact on probability of employment	**0.092**	**0.141**	**0.103**	**0.122**	**0.145**	**0.138**	**0.150**
	(0.005)	(0.004)	(0.004)	(0.003)	(0.004)	(0.005)	(0.004)
Panel B—Males							
1. Impact on probability of employment	**0.210**	**0.286**	**0.242**	**0.252**	**0.257**	**0.258**	**0.289**
	(0.006)	(0.004)	(0.005)	(0.005)	(0.004)	(0.006)	(0.005)
2. Difference-in-difference estimate of impact on probability of employment	**0.087**	**0.156**	**0.121**	**0.124**	**0.140**	**0.124**	**0.158**
	(0.005)	(0.003)	(0.004)	(0.004)	(0.003)	(0.005)	(0.004)

Note: Standard errors in parentheses. Statistically significant impact estimates are in boldface.

[a]Excluding THS.

Table 12.6   **Transition between sectors over eight quarters: Program entry in 1997**

	Employment eight quarters later (%)					
Reference quarter employment	No job	Service, including THS	Manufacturing	Retail trade	Other; multiple sectors	Total
Panel A—Females						
No job	58.3	17.7	4.0	8.5	11.5	100.0
THS	30.2	27.6	8.9	8.0	25.3	100.0
Manufacturing	22.5	9.6	49.6	5.3	13.1	100.0
Retail trade	29.2	15.1	4.0	35.0	16.7	100.0
Service excluding THS	25.1	51.5	2.8	5.9	14.7	100.0
Other; multiple sectors	20.9	21.2	7.2	9.6	41.2	100.0
Panel B—Males						
No job	62.3	9.2	6.0	5.9	16.6	100.0
THS	35.9	20.4	13.2	6.8	23.7	100.0
Manufacturing	21.6	4.6	53.3	3.3	17.3	100.0
Retail trade	27.5	10.3	6.0	34.1	22.1	100.0
Service excluding THS	27.9	39.9	5.4	6.1	20.7	100.0
Other; multiple sectors	24.0	9.3	9.3	6.3	51.0	100.0

position. We can also see that temporary help workers are more likely to move into manufacturing positions than are any other category of worker, with the exception of those in manufacturing. For example, for women in THS positions in the reference quarter, 8.9 percent are in manufacturing eight quarters later.[21] For those in retail trade, service or other industries, no more than 4 percent move to the manufacturing sector eight quarters later. Cross tabulations for males display the same patterns.

The importance of moves between industries is illustrated in table 12.7. Lines 1 and 2 are based on estimates from a model that controls for *both* reference quarter industry and outcome quarter industry. The estimates in line 1 confirm the view that once we have taken into account whether the individual is employed and the industry of employment in the outcome quarter, prior industry of employment is no longer important for predicting earnings. Among women, those with temporary help jobs are predicted to have earnings in the outcome quarter that are $1,027 higher than those with no jobs (line 4 of table 12.4); once industry in the outcome quarter is controlled, that increment declines to $283 (line 1 of table 12.7). Similarly, ultimate earnings are expected to be $581 higher for those with manufacturing jobs than for temporary help jobs, a difference in impacts that declines to $79 when ultimate industry is controlled. This basic pattern is the same for

---

21. Moves by THS workers to manufacturing may partly reflect reclassification of temporary help workers to permanent status within a firm. See footnote 17.

Table 12.7   Predicted earnings and impact by employment in reference and outcome quarter: 1997

Impacts relative to no job	One industry					Multiple industries	
	THS	Manufacturing	Retail trade	Service[a]	Other	THS and any other industry	Any industry not THS
Panel A—Females							
1. Impact of reference quarter industry, controlling outcome industry	**283**	**362**	**269**	**370**	**422**	**420**	**411**
	(29)	(25)	(20)	(17)	(24)	(28)	(22)
2. Impact of outcome quarter industry, controlling reference quarter industry	**2,011**	**4,301**	**2,686**	**3,291**	**4,187**	**2,706**	**3,520**
	(38)	(24)	(20)	(16)	(20)	(37)	(25)
Panel B—Males							
1. Impact of reference quarter industry, controlling outcome industry	70	**593**	**320**	**404**	**637**	**181**	**553**
	(36)	(27)	(28)	(29)	(23)	(35)	(29)
2. Impact of outcome quarter industry, controlling reference quarter industry	**2,451**	**5,718**	**3,855**	**4,366**	**5,390**	**3,175**	**4,692**
	(47)	(25)	(28)	(27)	(21)	(47)	(33)

Note: Standard errors in parentheses. Statistically significant impact estimates are in boldface.

[a]Excluding THS.

males; the primary way that reference quarter industry influences outcomes is through its impact on ultimate industry of employment.

Coefficients in line 2 show that movement into other employment is particularly valuable for those with reference quarter jobs in temporary help. Those who ultimately end up in temporary help jobs have the lowest earnings of any industry category, and the difference is substantial. This contrasts with estimates in table 12.4, which show that a temporary help job in the reference quarter provides ultimate earnings that are comparable to those of several other industry categories. Clearly, those who do not move out of temporary help jobs face substantially poorer prospects. This contrasts with individuals initially in retail trade jobs, who do less well than those in temporary help (table 12.4) but have higher earnings if they stay in retail trade than temporary help workers who stay in temporary help (line 2 of table 12.7).

12.7   Changes in the Role of Temporary Help Employment: Comparisons with 2001

Analyses to this point consider the impacts of temporary help employment for those facing employment difficulties in 1997, a period of extraordinary economic growth in Missouri and the nation as a whole. Missouri's unemployment rate was approximately 4 percent during 1997 and early 1998, when individuals obtained employment exchange services and started target quarter jobs, and it had declined further, to around 3 percent (eight quarters later), when we consider their employment outcomes. Over the three years 1997 to 1999, employment in Missouri grew by 4.4 percent.[22] It is possible that the role of temporary help may not be reproduced in a period of slower growth. Temporary help jobs may be harder to get when the economy is not growing, and those who take them may have a harder time moving onward from them.

We have therefore replicated our analysis for those entering employment exchange services in 2001. During 2001, the unemployment rate in Missouri increased from about 4 percent at the beginning of the year to about 5 percent at the end. Eight quarters later, unemployment had increased to over 5.5 percent, peaking at 6 percent around the middle of 2004. Missouri experienced an overall employment decline of 1.5 percent during the period.[23] Thus, although the recession in Missouri and the rest of the nation was mild by historical standards, the difference in labor market conditions between 1997 to 1999 and 2001 to 2003 was substantial.

The employment exchange system underwent changes between 1997 and 2001, and there is no certainty that the selection of individuals or the program impacts will be precisely the same. By 2001, most job exchange services

---

22. Employment growth was measured for January 1997 to January 2000.
23. Employment growth for January 2001 to January 2004.

were provided in one-stop centers offering a variety of job-related services (including job training under the Workforce Investment Act), replacing the stand-alone offices that previously supported the state's Unemployment Insurance program. Nonetheless, in both 1997 and 2001, a large share of clients consisted of individuals receiving Unemployment Insurance payments who were required to participate in the program. In both periods, program access remained open, so anyone could obtain services. The amount of time a client spent with a counselor or in job-related programs was generally quite limited.

Comparing table 12.8 with table 12.2, we see that in 2001 THS employment continues to play the transitional role that we observed in 1997, with increased temporary help employment immediately following employment exchange participation. We replicated our analysis, predicting industry of employment in the quarter following program entry. The similarities in the patterns of the coefficients were striking, with relative minor differences. Employment was more strongly associated with education—but not necessarily high school graduation—in 2001 than in 1997. The selection of nonwhites into THS employment was somewhat weaker in 2001, and THS employment was somewhat less strongly associated with the large metropolitan areas. Still, the conclusion that "race and place" are the two most important determinants of THS employment was clearly true in 2001.

Table 12.9 provides estimates based on program participants in 2001 of

Table 12.8　　Distribution of employment across industries prior and subsequent to program entry in 2001

	Females		Males	
	Four quarters before entry	One quarter after entry	Four quarters before entry	One quarter after entry
No job	33.47	38.61	34.77	39.03
Major industry group				
0 Agriculture, forestry, and fishing	0.60	0.58	0.87	1.09
1 Mining, construction	1.24	1.13	6.52	7.48
2, 3 Manufacturing	11.55	10.14	19.00	17.23
4 Transportation, communications, electric, gas, and sanitary services	4.04	2.94	5.82	4.82
5 Wholesale trade, retail trade	21.79	20.23	19.84	18.36
6 Finance, insurance, and real estate	4.95	4.46	1.99	1.70
7, 8 Services	28.34	31.45	16.64	19.46
9 Public administration	1.79	1.71	1.63	1.60
Four-digit industry				
5810 Eating and drinking places	7.35	6.95	5.76	5.60
7363 THS	3.11	5.94	3.19	6.39

Note: Counts include any job, so individuals who hold jobs in more than one industry are counted multiple times.

Table 12.9 Predicted earnings and impact by industry of employment in quarter following program entry in 2001 and impact eight quarters later

Impacts relative to no job	One industry					Multiple industries	
	THS	Manufacturing	Retail trade	Service[a]	Other	THS and any other industry	Any industry not THS
Panel A—Females							
1. Impact on earnings	**1,286**	**2,140**	**1,121**	**1,579**	**1,980**	**1,690**	**1,788**
	(60)	(45)	(35)	(30)	(38)	(60)	(41)
2. Difference-in-difference estimate of impact on earnings	**1,339**	**2,097**	**1,270**	**1,723**	**1,947**	**1,847**	**1,899**
	(79)	(59)	(46)	(39)	(50)	(79)	(54)
Panel B—Males							
1. Impact on earnings	**1,049**	**2,805**	**1,644**	**2,010**	**2,425**	**1,509**	**2,296**
	(76)	(47)	(49)	(49)	(41)	(76)	(55)
2. Difference-in-difference estimate of impact on earnings	**1,458**	**2,635**	**1,825**	**2,118**	**2,351**	**1,815**	**2,302**
	(117)	(72)	(76)	(76)	(63)	(117)	(85)

Note: Standard errors are in parentheses. Statistically significant impact estimates are in boldface.

[a]Excluding THS.

the effect of THS and other employment during the quarter following participation on earnings eight quarters later. The first and most important conclusion is that the pattern of results is very similar to that for 1997 participants. Yet there are a number of statistically significant differences. For females, earnings are initially higher in 2001, but they are also higher in the outcome quarter. For males, initial earnings are higher in 2001 than in 1997, but outcome earnings differences are inconsistent across initial occupation.

The patterns of effects for industries correspond closely. Perhaps most significant, if we examine the impact of a THS job as compared to no job (column [2], lines 1 and 2), the difference between the estimated effects for 1997 and 2001 is quite modest—and is not statistically significant in three out of four comparisons between these years.

Relative to other employment, the impact of THS employment is estimated to be slightly less beneficial in the later period. For example, for males in 1997, the benefit of having an initial THS job relative to no job was $915 (line 4, table 12.4). The additional increment of having a manufacturing job was $1,401. In 2001, the comparable benefit for a THS job was similar at $1,049 (panel B, line 1), but the additional increment for a manufacturing job had increased to $1,756. This is typical of the observed differences for both men and women. The differences over time are never more than a few hundred dollars, but they are consistent. Based on the two estimation approaches (lines 4 and 5 of table 12.4 and lines 1 and 2 of table 12.9), if we consider the four alterative industries, we have sixteen comparisons of the increment of an industry relative to THS. In eleven of these comparisons, the benefit of having an alternative job relative to a THS job increased between 1997 and 2001. We see the same pattern if we compare THS with an aggregated category of other industries.

We also examined the effect of initial THS employment for the 2001 samples on whether the individual is employed eight quarters later, corresponding with the estimates reported in table 12.5 for 1997.[24] Our findings for employment are similar to those for earnings. As is the case with earnings, for women the benefit of having a temporary help job relative to having no job remains unchanged, whereas the incremental benefit of other kinds of jobs has increased in 2001. In contrast, for men, the effects of THS employment relative to other industries are essentially the same for 1997 and 2001.

Taken together, the comparison of estimates of impact on earnings and employment for program participants in 2001 and 1997 confirms the view that, in a sluggish labor market, alternatives to temporary help employment provide greater relative benefits than when the economy is strong.

We performed analyses for program enrollees in 2001, looking at the transitions between sectors over the eight quarters following the reference

---

24. For details, see Heinrich, Mueser, and Troske (2007).

quarter and the relative importance of initial industry and ultimate industry in determining earnings. As might be expected, in the more recent period, individuals are more likely to find themselves without a job in the final quarter, but the pattern of results is very similar to the earlier results.

Notwithstanding the differences highlighted in this section, analyses for 2001 produce substantive conclusions that are identical to those for 1997. It is clear that whatever role the temporary help sector plays in the careers of individuals facing employment difficulties, this does not critically depend on economic growth.

12.8   Nonwhites

We have observed that nonwhites are appreciably more likely to work for THS firms than are whites and that this relationship remains strong even after controlling for demographic characteristics and metropolitan status. In order to provide insight into the role that THS employment may play for nonwhites, we have undertaken separate analyses for this group.

First, we have examined the pattern of THS employment prior to and immediately following program participation, considering nonwhites separately by gender. We observe that THS employment for nonwhites increases as it does for the full sample. Measured as a proportion of all nonwhite workers, the growth in THS employment is greater than that for whites, but as a proportion of prior THS employment, the increase is somewhat smaller. This suggests that the transitional role of THS employment is at least as important for nonwhites as for whites but that THS employment provides *non*transitional employment for a larger share of nonwhite workers.

Replicating the analysis predicting THS employment (three categories of employment contrasted to not employed) in the reference quarter, we found that the pattern of coefficients corresponded, in substance, to those reported previously in table 12.3. As in the full sample, we found no evidence that differences in human capital (as proxied by age and education) played an important role in allocating nonwhites to THS jobs. We conclude that it is unlikely that the overrepresentation of nonwhites in THS employment reflects differences in unmeasured levels of human capital. As expected, we found that metropolitan status was strongly related to THS employment, paralleling the results in the full sample.

If the returns for THS employment are greater for nonwhites, this may provide an explanation for their overrepresentation in THS jobs. On the other hand, if nonwhites face discrimination in hiring for direct-employment jobs, this could increase hiring rates of nonwhites by THS firms, causing nonwhites to gravitate toward such jobs even in the absence of greater benefits. Table 12.10 reports how estimates limited to the nonwhite sample differ from those for the full sample; thus, the numbers shown in table 12.10 are not the impact estimates (as in prior tables), but the difference in impacts

Table 12.10 Difference in impact of industry of employment in quarter following participation: Nonwhites versus full sample

Impacts relative to no job	One industry					Multiple industries	
	THS	Manufacturing	Retail trade	Service[a]	Other	THS and any other industry	Any industry not THS
Panel A—Females, 1997							
1. Impact on earnings	**−201**	64	**−194**	**−162**	**−188**	**−261**	−60
	−20%	4%	**−22%**	**−13%**	**−12%**	**−19%**	−4%
2. Difference-in-difference estimate of impact on earnings	**−431**	**−382**	**−192**	**−220**	**−165**	**−266**	**−255**
	−32%	**−21%**	**−20%**	**−17%**	**−11%**	**−19%**	**−16%**
Panel B—Males, 1997							
1. Impact on earnings	37	−187	**−349**	**−309**	**−417**	−157	−397
	4%	−8%	**−28%**	**−21%**	**−20%**	−12%	−20%
2. Difference-in-difference estimate of impact on earnings	**−243**	**−544**	**−361**	**−356**	**−421**	**−376**	**−479**
	−19%	**−22%**	**−26%**	**−21%**	**−21%**	**−23%**	**−22%**
Panel C—Females, 2001							
1. Impact on earnings	−77	**220**	**−224**	**−194**	−120	**−324**	−150
	−6%	**10%**	**−20%**	**−12%**	−6%	**−19%**	−8%
2. Difference-in-difference estimate of impact on earnings	−126	162	**−242**	**−222**	−138	**−414**	−220
	−9%	8%	**−19%**	**−13%**	−7%	**−22%**	−12%
Panel D—Males, 2001							
1. Impact on earnings	**−275**	36	**−448**	**−396**	**−367**	**−259**	**−218**
	−26%	1%	**−27%**	**−20%**	**−15%**	**−17%**	**−9%**
2. Difference-in-difference estimate of impact on earnings	**−380**	−216	**−628**	**−416**	**−402**	**−454**	**−357**
	−26%	−8%	**−34%**	**−20%**	**−17%**	**−25%**	**−15%**

Note: Significant differences are in boldface. Percentages use the full sample estimate as the base.

on earnings between nonwhites and the full sample for 1997 and 2001 and by gender.

Table 12.10 shows that effects for nonwhites are generally smaller than the full sample. Differences in estimated impacts are in the range of a few hundred dollars, with most between 15 and 25 percent. We are interested in whether there is any evidence that nonwhites may benefit more from THS employment, relative to other employment. This would reflect in smaller differences for the THS category than for the other industries. In fact, whether we look at percentages or absolute differences, we are unable to see any clear patterns of such differences between THS estimates and those for other industries.

When we look at mobility tables over the two years following employment exchange participation, we do find that nonwhites are more likely than whites to remain in THS positions in the two years following program participation. For example, among all men in the employment exchange sample who were in THS positions in 1997, only 20 percent remained in those jobs two years later (table 12.6). In contrast, among nonwhites, this proportion was 27 percent. It also appears that nonwhites are less likely to move from THS jobs into manufacturing jobs than are whites. Yet analyses that examine the importance of movement out of temporary help positions (corresponding to table 12.7) indicate that such movement is as important for nonwhites as whites. These results imply that although nonwhites experience lower levels of mobility toward high-paying jobs, the benefits of employment in particular industries are similar. Overall, analyses focusing on the nonwhite sample suggest that the mechanisms underlying THS employment for nonwhites operate much the same as for whites.

12.9   Robustness Tests of Industry Impact Estimates

Implicit in our estimates of the effect of current industry of employment on later earnings and employment is the assumption that no unmeasured individual characteristics affect both industry and ultimate earnings. We believe the approach taken here minimizes the importance of such factors. The previous analysis controls for a variety of measures reflecting pre-program labor market experience as well as standard demographic characteristics. Because we observe people in a period when they are experiencing employment distress, the randomness of the labor market may be of greater importance than at other times in their lives. The assumption that unmeasured factors do not seriously bias results is supported by our earlier results based on Temporary Assistance for Needy Families (TANF) recipients in Missouri and North Carolina (Heinrich, Mueser, and Troske 2005), which found no evidence that selection into initial jobs altered estimates.

Nonetheless, it is difficult to assure that the individuals who obtain jobs, or obtain jobs in various industries, are not different in unmeasured ways that influence ultimate employment. In a recent analysis of the effects of

Catholic school attendance on student outcomes, Altonji, Elder, and Taber (2005) suggest that information on the likely impact of unmeasured factors can be obtained by examining those variables used to control for measured differences. In particular, they argue that individual characteristics captured in measured variables may be expected to be similar to unmeasured factors influencing individual outcomes. Following an earlier analysis by Murphy and Topel (1990), they propose a statistical test to determine whether observed estimates of causal impacts are likely to be spurious.

12.9.1   Formal Structure[25]

Consider our estimation equation

(1)
$$Y = \mathbf{D}\alpha + \mathbf{X}\gamma + \varepsilon + u,$$

where Y is the outcome measure (quarterly earnings or employment), $\mathbf{D}$ is a vector of dummy variables identifying industry of employment in the reference quarter with no job the omitted category, $\mathbf{X}$ is a vector of control variables (including a constant), ε is the component of unmeasured determinants that reflects factors that may be associated with industry of employment in the reference quarter, and u is an independent error reflecting variation that is unstable from quarter to quarter. Vectors of coefficients α and γ have been estimated by OLS under the assumption that $(\varepsilon + u)$ is uncorrelated with $\mathbf{D}$ or $\mathbf{X}$. The methods presented here are designed to help in considering whether the correlation between $\mathbf{D}$ and ε may cause the estimated coefficients $\hat{\alpha}$ to be spurious.

We separately consider each of the seven industry categories that are used to identify employment during the reference quarter and focus on individuals in each industry category, comparing them with individuals with no jobs. For simplicity, our analysis assumes that there are no interaction effects between $\mathbf{D}$ and $\mathbf{X}$ in predicting earnings or employment. Consider now the relationship between the dummy identifying employment in a particular industry k and the other factors predicting the outcome variable—that is, $\mathbf{X}\gamma$ and ε. Focusing on the sample limited to those with no job ($\mathbf{D}_0 = 1$) or those with a job in industry k ($\mathbf{D}_k = 1$), we specify $\mathbf{D}_k^*$ as the linear projection of $\mathbf{D}_k$ onto $\mathbf{X}\gamma$ and ε,

(2)
$$\mathbf{D}_k^* = \phi_{0k} + \phi_{X\gamma,k}(\mathbf{X}\gamma) + \phi_{\varepsilon k}\varepsilon.$$

If $\phi_{\varepsilon k} \neq 0$, this implies that the estimate of α_k based on (1) will be biased. In particular, the standard formula for bias implies that

(3)
$$E(\hat{\alpha}_k) = \alpha_k + \phi_{\varepsilon k}\frac{Var(\varepsilon)}{Var(\tilde{\mathbf{D}}_k)},$$

---

25. For details of this approach, see Altonji, Elder, and Taber (2005), from which the following discussion is largely drawn.

where $\tilde{\mathbf{D}}_k$ is the industry dummy purged of its correlation with $\mathbf{X}$.[26] If unmeasured factors influencing earnings and employment are similar to measured factors, we might expect that $\phi_{X\gamma,k}$ and $\phi_{\varepsilon k}$ would be similar. Altonji, Elder, and Taber (2005) show that if there are a large enough number of variables predicting the outcome and if no small subset is disproportionately important in terms of explanatory power, we expect $\phi_{\varepsilon k} = \phi_{X\gamma,k}$. Since the error term is likely to contain some factors that are truly random, they argue that it is plausible to assume that $\phi_{\varepsilon k} = \rho\phi_{X\gamma,k}$ with $0 \leq \rho \leq 1$.

Using the bias estimate in (3), we can see that the true coefficient would be zero if $\phi_{\varepsilon k} = \phi_{\varepsilon k}^*$, with $\phi_{\varepsilon k}^*$ defined by

$$(4) \qquad\qquad \phi_{\varepsilon k}^* \equiv \hat{\alpha}_k \frac{Var(\tilde{\mathbf{D}}_k)}{Var(\varepsilon)},$$

where we have substituted the estimated value $\hat{\alpha}_k$ for $E(\hat{\alpha}_k)$. The ratio $\phi_{\varepsilon k}^*/\phi_{X\gamma,k}$ indicates how large the coefficient for the unobserved error term in (2) would have to be relative to the coefficient for observed determinants of the outcome in order for $\hat{\alpha}_k$ to be entirely spurious.

The extent of the bias is conditional on ρ, which is not observed. When $\phi_{\varepsilon k}^*/\phi_{X\gamma,k} > \rho$, the bias toward zero in α_k is less than the absolute value of $\hat{\alpha}_k$. If $0 \leq \phi_{\varepsilon k}^*/\phi_{X\gamma,k} \leq \rho$, this implies that the bias toward zero exceeds $\hat{\alpha}_k$, so that α_k is expected to have the opposite sign of $\hat{\alpha}_k$. When $\phi_{\varepsilon k}^*/\phi_{X\gamma,k} < 0$, the unbiased estimate of α_k will be greater in absolute value than $\hat{\alpha}_k$; that is, the bias is away from zero for any $\rho > 0$.[27]

Since there is no way to determine the exact size of ρ, we will interpret $\phi_{\varepsilon k}^*/\phi_{X\gamma,k}$ in terms of plausible possible values. If $\phi_{\varepsilon k}^*/\phi_{X\gamma,k}$ is larger than 1, this implies that in order for α_k to be zero (or of opposite sign of $\hat{\alpha}_k$), unmeasured determinants would have to be more strongly related to the industry than observed variables—that is, $\rho > 1$. Assuming this is implausible, we can take this as evidence that the estimate is not entirely spurious. A negative ratio suggests that unmeasured determinants would need to be qualitatively different than measured determinants to render the estimated coefficient entirely spurious—that is, it would require $\rho < 0$, which we again view as implausible. If the ratio $\phi_{\varepsilon k}^*/\phi_{X\gamma,k}$ is between zero and one, the estimated coefficient would be spurious for some ρ between zero and 1. Since this is a plausible range, implying that the unmeasured determinants were similar to the measured determinants, we conclude that the estimated coefficient could be entirely spurious, or even of opposite sign from the true value.[28] The details of the implementation of this test are provided in the appendix.

---

26. $\tilde{\mathbf{D}}_k = \mathbf{D}_k - \mathbf{X}\hat{\boldsymbol{\beta}}_k$, where $\hat{\boldsymbol{\beta}}_k$ is the vector of coefficients estimated from a regression of $\mathbf{D}_k$ on $\mathbf{X}$.

27. Estimating the exact size of the bias conditional on ρ is somewhat involved; see Altonji, Elder, and Taber (2005) for details.

28. Of course, in the absence of an independent measure of ρ, we have essentially no information on the true coefficient value.

12.9.2   Results

Table 12.11 provides diagnostics relevant to estimated effects of industry in the quarter following employment exchange participation on earnings eight quarters later, which are reported in table 12.4 (1997) and table 12.9 (2001). We focus on estimates of the impact relative to the no-employment category. The estimates in line 4 of table 12.4 and line 1 of table 12.9 are reproduced in line 2 of table 12.11; standard errors are reported in line 3. Line 1 of table 12.11 presents the simple difference in earnings between those with reference category jobs in a given industry and those with no jobs. The difference between estimates in lines 1 and 2 of table 12.11 indicates how controls affect the estimates. Where the difference is large, this implies that controls predicting earnings are strongly related to the industry, and in those cases we expect that our diagnostics will imply that the observed coefficient could be spurious. Line 4 lists the value of the implied ratio $\phi^*_{\varepsilon k}/\phi_{X\gamma,k}$, where $\phi_{X\gamma,k}$ is based on all variables taken together, as specified in the formal structure presented earlier. In lines 5 and 6, we have used an estimate that decomposes the factors predicting earnings into educational measures, labor force indicators, and other controls. In line 5, we use the education measures in constructing the ratio, and in line 6 labor market experience is used (further details are provided in the appendix). In the discussion that follows, if the implied ratio is between 0.0 and 1.2, we assume that the estimated coefficient could well be spurious; a ratio outside that range will be taken as an indicator that the estimated coefficient is not spurious.[29]

Looking across the calculated ratios in table 12.11, we see that there are substantial differences, although there are also some regularities. For THS, considering the results in line 4 (based on all variables), we see that all four ratios are outside the range (0.0 to 1.2), implying that the estimated coefficients are *not* spurious. If we use education as the comparison measure (line 5), we count three of four ratios outside that range, and if we examine prior market activity (line 6), all four are outside the range. In almost all cases, our tests therefore suggest that unmeasured determinants of earnings would have to differ quite dramatically from the measured variables—in terms of their relationship with THS employment—for the estimated impact of THS employment to be spurious.

If we look at other industries, retail trade and the multiple industries categories also yield ratios that are usually outside the 0 to 1.2 range, suggesting a robust underlying impact. In contrast, the implied ratios for coefficients of the three other industry categories support the robustness of these coefficients in only about a third of the cases.

29. Our choice of the 1.2 threshold is somewhat arbitrary, reflecting our view that a difference in the relationship between measured and unmeasured factors greater than 20 percent may be viewed as implausible if one believes that these should be "similar," as implied by the argument in Altonji, Elder, and Taber (2005).

Table 12.11 Robustness tests for estimated impact of industry on earnings: Employment exchange participants

Dependent variable	One industry					Multiple industries	
Earnings two years after reference quarter Industry in reference quarter	THS	Manufacturing	Retail trade	Service[a]	Other	THS and any other industry	Any industry not THS
Panel A—Females, 1997							
1. Simple difference between industry and no job	1,263	2,283	963	1,704	2,569	1,860	1,998
2. Estimated industry impact, all measured factors controlled	1,027	1,608	872	1,205	1,614	1,408	1,443
3. (Standard error)	(37)	(31)	(25)	(22)	(30)	(36)	(29)
4. Implied ratio: all measured to unmeasured determinants	1.36	0.62	1.91	0.80	0.56	1.03	0.82
5. Implied ratio: education to unmeasured determinants	1.63	−0.60	−1.13	0.60	0.71	1.49	1.37
6. Implied ratio: prior market activity to unmeasure determinants	2.24	0.53	1.68	0.85	0.58	1.24	0.80
Panel B—Males, 1997							
1. Simple difference between industry and no job	818	3,643	1,586	2,131	3,379	1,507	2,859
2. Estimated industry impact, all measured factors controlled	915	2,317	1,254	1,499	2,081	1,360	1,986
3. (Standard error)	(47)	(34)	(36)	(36)	(29)	(45)	(37)
4. Implied ratio: all measured to unmeasured determinants	−55.08	0.59	1.09	0.86	0.52	1.99	0.79
5. Implied ratio: education to unmeasured determinants	−1.60	−0.84	−59.07	0.26	4.68	−8.91	0.98
6. Implied ratio: prior market activity to unmeasure determinants	3.72	0.62	1.08	0.91	0.57	1.77	0.83

Panel C—Females, 2001

	1,411	918	1,976	2,913	1,919	2,159
1. Simple difference between industry and no job	1,411	918	1,976	2,913	1,919	2,159
2. Estimated industry impact, all measured factors controlled	1,286	1,121	1,579	1,980	1,690	1,788
3. (Standard error)	(60)	(35)	(30)	(38)	(60)	(41)
4. Implied ratio: all measured to unmeasured determinants	3.21	−2.94	1.35	0.71	2.40	1.57
5. Implied ratio: education to unmeasured determinants	1.04	−1.57	0.38	0.60	1.04	0.83
6. Implied ratio: prior market activity to unmeasure determinants	−48.84	−3.11	1.70	0.79	6.46	2.12

Panel D—Males, 2001

1. Simple difference between industry and no job	649	1,491	2,527	3,119	1,203	2,687
2. Estimated industry impact, all measured factors controlled	1,049	1,644	2,010	2,425	1,509	2,296
3. (Standard error)	(76)	(49)	(49)	(41)	(76)	(55)
4. Implied ratio: all measured to unmeasured determinants	−1.51	−7.72	1.50	0.90	−4.61	1.66
5. Implied ratio: education to unmeasured determinants	−0.72	−1.10	0.26	−2.02	−0.69	1.41
6. Implied ratio: prior market activity to unmeasure determinants	−2.71	15.03	1.64	0.99	−11.05	2.20

Notes: Line 4 indicates the ratio between the coefficient of the error term and the coefficient for measured variables in a regression predicting industry during the reference quarter that would be necessary in order for the estimated coefficient in line 2 to be spurious. Line 5 provides the implied ratio where the measured variable is a composite variable identifying educational attainment, and line 6 a composite variable identifying prior employment activity.

[a]Excluding THS.

The variation in these results reflects the fact that in some cases, the measured variables that predict earnings are more strongly associated with industry differences than in other cases. The variation across tests presented here underscores the point that these tests are not definitive. Not only is there no certainty that unmeasured factors will be related to industry as are measured determinants, but it is clear that there is no typical measured determinant. Nonetheless, the tests do allow us to reject the view that estimated coefficients can be fully explained by unmeasured factors that are similar to measured factors.[30]

Overall, our results support the view that estimated effects of reference-quarter industry on outcome earnings are very likely at least partly causal. Although one cannot reject the possibility that unmeasured factors both induce individuals to take certain kinds of jobs and affect earnings, the particular structure of the unmeasured correlates of industry would have to be quite different than measured factors, in most cases, to imply that estimated effects are zero.

12.10   Conclusion

Perhaps the most notable finding of this study is that the basic patterns of THS effects are very similar for women and for men and for individuals seeking employment in an economic boom (1997 to 1999) and in a period of relative stagnation (2001 to 2003).

There is little question that, on average, those who can obtain manufacturing jobs or jobs in selected other industries during the reference quarter have higher ultimate earnings than those who obtain THS jobs. This earnings advantage is larger in a recessionary period. But for many of these individuals, job choices are undoubtedly very limited, and difficulties obtaining desirable jobs are particularly severe during economic downturns. We see no other jobs filling a similar transitional role to that of temporary help employment for individuals facing employment difficulties. For many individuals, temporary help employment may well be available when other kinds of jobs are not. The concerns that individuals who make the choice to take

---

30. We also estimated ratios corresponding to those in table 12.11, using employment during the outcome quarter as the dependent variable. In this case, results are somewhat different. For every industry, the ratios were in the range 0 to 1.2 in most of the cases. For THS, in more than two-thirds of the tests, the ratio was in this range. Although individual industry results for specific samples differed depending on which ratio was considered, the overall pattern of results was the same. These results suggest that in the case of employment, it is much easier to argue that unmeasured factors may be responsible for inducing spurious coefficient estimates. Altonji, Elder, and Taber (2005) caution that where measured variables explain only a small portion of the variance in the dependent variable, making inferences about the structure of unmeasured factors is risky. In the case of earnings, in most cases, nearly half of the variation is explained by measured factors, whereas for employment, the proportion of variance explained is less than 30 percent. The test is therefore less likely to provide useful information in the latter case.

such a job will remain trapped in low-wage and unstable jobs appear to be unfounded; we see no evidence that a strategy of waiting for a better job yields any benefits at all.

In terms of the implications for workforce development policies, our results imply that both males and females, coming through the employment exchange, fare better in terms of earnings and earnings growth when they take jobs with temporary help service firms if the alternative is no employment. If temporary help service firms facilitate quicker access to jobs for those seeking employment assistance, then encouraging the use of these labor market intermediaries to expand access to employment networks for individuals seeking jobs should generate net benefits. And even if temporary help jobs do supplant some jobs, since many of these jobs are in the retail trade and service sectors, the costs are small. Nonetheless, it is clear that for most low-wage or disadvantaged workers, the key to labor market success via the path of a temporary help services firm is through a subsequent transition to a job in another sector. Those who do not move out of temporary help jobs face substantially poorer earnings prospects. If policymakers consider a greater role for temporary help services firms for those seeking employment assistance, tracking these firms' success in facilitating placements of workers into permanent jobs in other sectors may be important in evaluating and improving the effectiveness of such policies.

Appendix

Implementation of Robustness Tests of Industry Impact Estimates

We reproduce equations (1) and (4) for convenience:

(1) $$Y = \mathbf{D}\alpha + \mathbf{X}\gamma + \varepsilon + u$$

(4) $$\phi_{\varepsilon k}^{*} \equiv \hat{\alpha}_{k} \frac{Var(\tilde{\mathbf{D}}_{k})}{Var(\varepsilon)}$$

The estimate $\hat{\alpha}_{k}$ is based on (1); however, the other terms in $\phi_{\varepsilon k}^{*}$ are based on the null hypothesis that this coefficient is zero and so are estimated in a regression corresponding to (1) but omitting $\mathbf{D}$. Thus, $\phi_{X\gamma,k}$ is calculated using $\hat{\gamma}$ estimated in that same equation.

It is also necessary to identify ε, which is the component in earnings or employment that may be tied to individual characteristics or decisions made eight quarters earlier, which is in contrast to random variation in earnings due to variation in u. This is accomplished using earnings in adjacent quarters for a given individual. In particular, we rewrite the equation identifying the determinants of outcome earnings or employment to distinguish across quarters:[31]

(A1) $$Y_t = \mathbf{X}\gamma_t + [\pi'\varepsilon + u_t],$$

where we assume an autoregressive error structure of the form $u_t = ru_{t-1} + v_t$; v_t is an independent error term, and π and r are parameters. The variable t indexes quarters, and we take the outcome quarter (which is eight quarters after the reference quarter) as $t = 0$, so we have $\pi' = 1$ at $t = 0$. At $t = 0$, (A1) is equivalent to (1) with the industry dummies omitted. The term ε identifies the stable component of the unmeasured determinants of Y, and the term π allows for it to grow or decline in importance.

The expression in brackets, $[\pi'\varepsilon + u_t]$, can be estimated as the residual of a regression of earnings on $\mathbf{X}$ in a given quarter t. The variances and covariances of the residuals for three successive quarters (the outcome quarter, and quarters immediately prior and subsequent to the outcome quarter) can then be used to estimate π, r, and $Var(\varepsilon)$.[32]

The estimate of $\phi_{X\gamma,k}$ is obtained directly from the regression of the industry dummy for k in a regression limited to those in that industry and in no job during the reference quarter—that is,

$$\mathbf{D}_k = \phi_{0k} + \phi_{X\gamma,k}(\mathbf{X}\gamma) + v.$$

However, as Murphy and Topel (1990) note, it may be that we believe omitted determinants of income are more closely associated with certain observed measures than with others. We have grouped selected variables so that the relationship for each grouping can be considered. In particular, we estimate ϕ_{ik} in the equation

$$\mathbf{D}_k = \phi_{0k} + \sum_i \phi_{ik} Z_i + v',$$

where $Z_i = \sum_{X_j \in Gi} \hat{\gamma}_j X_j$, $\hat{\gamma}_j$ is the estimated coefficient of X_j in the regression predicting the outcome, and G_i is the set of variables in group i. The groups

---

31. Reference-quarter industry is omitted, given the null hypothesis that industry has no causal impact.

32. Denoting $\tilde{Y}_t \equiv [\pi'\varepsilon + u_t]$, the six equations defining the system are written as

$$Cov(\tilde{Y}_{-1}, \tilde{Y}_0) = \pi^{-1}Var(\varepsilon) + rVar(u_{-1})$$
$$Cov(\tilde{Y}_0, \tilde{Y}_1) = \pi Var(\varepsilon) + rVar(u_0)$$
$$Cov(\tilde{Y}_{-1}, \tilde{Y}_1) = Var(\varepsilon) + r^2 Var(u_{-1})$$
$$Var(\tilde{Y}_{-1}) = \pi^{-2}Var(\varepsilon) + Var(u_{-1})$$
$$Var(\tilde{Y}_0) = Var(\varepsilon) + Var(u_0)$$
$$Var(\tilde{Y}_1) = \pi^2 Var(\varepsilon) + Var(u_1).$$

These six equations can be solved for the six unknowns, π, r, $Var(\varepsilon)$, $Var(u_{-1})$, $Var(u_0)$, and $Var(u_1)$. Murphy and Topel (1990) use a related method to identify the stable and transient components of earnings.

are constructed to include all variables in **X**. If we believe that unmeasured determinants of earnings or employment are similar to a particular set of variables, the value of ϕ_{ik} associated with that group may provide a better comparison to the error term than the full set of variables. In addition to reporting $\phi_{ek}^*/\phi_{X\gamma,k}$ (based on all variables), we report the implied ratio ϕ_{ek}^*/ϕ_{ik} for education variables (years of education, high school degree, college degree) and for prior employment activities (five measures of work activity in the two years prior to program entry).

References

Altonji, J. G., T. E. Elder, and C. R. Taber. 2005. Selection on observed and unobserved variables: Assessing the effectiveness of Catholic schools. *Journal of Political Economy* 113 (1): 151–84.

Andersson, F., H. J. Holzer, and J. I. Lane. 2002. The interactions of firms and workers in the low-wage labor market. Report to the Assistant Secretary for Policy Evaluation, U.S. Department of Health and Human Services.

———. 2005. *Moving up or moving on: Who advances in the low-wage labor market?* New York: Russell Sage Foundation.

Antoni, M., and E. Jahn. 2006. Do changes in regulation affect employment duration in temporary work agencies? IZA Discussion Paper 2343. Bonn: Institute for the Study of Labor.

Ashenfelter, O., and D. Card. 1985. Using the longitudinal structure of earnings to estimate the effect of training programs. *Review of Economics and Statistics* 67 (4): 648–60.

Autor, D., and S. N. Houseman. 2005. Do temporary help jobs improve labor market outcomes for low-skilled workers? Evidence from "Work First." NBER Working Paper no. 11743. Cambridge, MA: National Bureau of Economic Research, November.

Blank, R. M. 1998. Contingent work in a changing labor market. In *Generating jobs: How to increase demand for less-skilled workers,* ed. R. B. Freeman and P. Gottschalk, 258–94. New York: Russell Sage Foundation.

Booth, A. L., M. Francesconi, and J. Frank. 2002. Temporary jobs: Stepping stones or dead ends? *The Economic Journal* 112 (127): 189–213.

Cohany, S. R. 1998. Workers in alternative employment arrangements: A second look. *Monthly Labor Review* 121 (11): 3–21.

DiNatale, M. 2001. Characteristics and preferences for alternative work arrangements, 1999. *Monthly Labor Review* 121 (5): 3–12.

Dyke, A., C. J. Heinrich, P. R. Mueser, K. R. Troske, and K. S. Jeon. 2006. The effects of welfare-to-work program activities on labor market outcomes. *Journal of Labor Economics* 24 (3): 567–608.

Even, W. E., and D. A. Macpherson. 2003. The wage and employment dynamics of minimum wage workers. *Southern Economic Journal* 69 (3): 676–90.

Gagliarducci, S. 2005. The dynamics of repeated temporary jobs. *Labour Economics* 12 (4): 429–48.

Garcia-Perez, J. I., and F. Munoz-Bullon. 2005. Temporary help agencies and occupational mobility. *Oxford Bulletin of Economics and Statistics* 67 (2): 163–80.

Heckman, J. J., R. J. LaLonde, and J. A. Smith. 1999. The economics and econometrics of active labor market programs. In *Handbook of labor economics*, ed. O. Ashenfelter and D. Card, 1865–2085. New York: Elsevier.

Heinrich, C. J. 2005. Temporary employment experiences of women on welfare. *Journal of Labor Research* 26 (2): 335–50.

Heinrich, C. J., P. R. Mueser, and K. R. Troske. 2005. Welfare to temporary work: Implications for labor market outcomes. *Review of Economics and Statistics* 87 (1): 154–70.

———. 2007. The role of temporary help employment in low-wage worker advancement. NBER Working Paper no. 13520. Cambridge, MA: National Bureau of Economic Research, October.

Houseman, S. N., A. L. Kalleberg, and G. A. Erickcek. 2003. The role of temporary agency employment in tight labor markets. *Industrial and Labor Relations Review* 57 (1): 105–27.

Houseman, S. N., and A. E. Polivka. 1999. The implications of flexible staffing arrangements for job stability. W. E. Upjohn Institute Working Paper no. 99-56. Kalamazoo, MI: W. E. Upjohn Institute.

Kvasnicka, M. 2005. Does temporary agency work provide a stepping stone to regular employment? SFB 649 Discussion Paper 2005-031, Sonderforschungsbereich 649. Berlin: Humboldt University.

Lane, J., K. S. Mikelson, P. Sharkey, and D. Wissoker. 2003. Pathways to work for low-income workers: The effect of work in the temporary help industry. *Journal of Policy Analysis and Management* 22 (4): 581–98.

Murphy, K. M., and R. H. Topel. 1990. Efficiency wages reconsidered: Theory and evidence. In *Advances in the theory and measurement of employment*, ed. Y. Weiss and R. H. Topel, 204–340. New York: St. Martin's Press.

Nollen, S. D. 1996. Negative aspects of temporary employment. *Journal of Labor Research* 17 (4): 567–81.

Pavetti, L. M., I. K. Derr, J. Anderson, C. Trippe, and S. Paschal. 2000. The role of intermediaries in linking TANF recipients with jobs. Paper presented at the Federal Reserve Bank of New York conference "Welfare Reform Four Years Later: Progress and Prospects," November.

Pawasarat, J. 1997. The employment perspective: Jobs held by the Milwaukee County AFDC single parent population (January 1996–March 1997). Working paper, Employment and Training Institute. Milwaukee, WI: Employment and Training Institute.

Poppe, N., J. Strawn, and K. Martinson. 2003. Whose job is it? Creating opportunities for advancement. In *Workforce intermediaries in the 21st century*, ed. R. P. Giloth, 31–72. Philadelphia: Temple University Press.

Segal, L. M., and D. G. Sullivan. 1997. The growth of temporary services work. *Journal of Economic Perspectives* 11 (2): 117–36.

U.S. Bureau of Labor Statistics. 2005. Discontinued CES data on SIC. Available at: http://www.bls.gov/ces/cesoldsic.htm.

Contributors

Fredrik Andersson
Cornell University, ILR School
Ives Hall East
Ithaca, NY 14853-3901

David H. Autor
Department of Economics
MIT, E52-371
50 Memorial Drive
Cambridge, MA 02142-1347

Manuel F. Bagues
Universidad Carlos III
Office 7.0.17
C/ Madrid 126
28903 Getafe
Madrid, Spain

René Böheim
Department of Economics
Johannes Kepler University
Altenberger Str. 69
A-4040 Linz-Auhof, Austria

Ana Rute Cardoso
IAE-CSIC
Institute for Economic Analysis
Spanish National Research Council
Campus UAB
08193 Bellaterra, Barcelona, Spain

Keith Finlay
Department of Economics
206 Tilton Hall
Tulane University
New Orleans, LA 70118

Richard B. Freeman
NBER
1050 Massachusetts Avenue
Cambridge, MA 02138

Carolyn J. Heinrich
Robert M. La Follette School of Public
    Affairs
University of Wisconsin—Madison
1225 Observatory Drive
Madison, WI 53706-1211

Harry J. Holzer
Georgetown Public Policy Institute
3520 Prospect Street NW, Suite 400
Washington, D.C. 20007

Morris M. Kleiner
University of Minnesota
Humphrey Institute
260 Humphrey Center
301 19th Street South
Minneapolis, MN 55455

Michael Kvasnicka
RWI Essen Büro Berlin
Hessische Straße 10
10115 Berlin, Germany

Julia Lane
National Science Foundation
4201 Wilson Boulevard
Arlington, VA 22230

Woong Lee
Department of Economics
University of California, Irvine
3151 Social Science Plaza
Irvine, CA 92697-5100

Peter R. Mueser
331 Professional Building
Department of Economics
University of Missouri
Columbia, MO 65211

Alice O. Nakamura
Department of Finance and
   Management Science
University of Alberta School of
   Business
Room 3-40B Business Building
Edmonton, AB T6G 2R6 Canada

Emi Nakamura
Columbia Business School
3022 Broadway, Uris Hall 820
New York, NY 10027

Muriel Niederle
Department of Economics
579 Serra Mall
Stanford University
Stanford, CA 94305-6072

Amanda Pyman
Kent Business School
The University of Kent
Canterbury
Kent CT2 7PE, England

M. Marit Rehavi
University of Michigan
109 Observatory
SPH-II, M2224
Ann Arbor, MI 48109-2029

Alvin E. Roth
Department of Economics
Littauer 308
Harvard University
Cambridge, MA 02138-3001

Kathryn L. Shaw
Graduate School of Business
Littlefield 339
Stanford University
Stanford, CA 94305-5015

Betsey Stevenson
The Wharton School
University of Pennsylvania
1454 Steinberg—Dietrich Hall
3620 Locust Walk
Philadelphia, PA 19104

Mauro Sylos Labini
IMT Lucca Institute for Advanced
   Studies
Piazza S. Ponziano, 6
55100 Lucca, Italy

Richard M. Todd
Federal Reserve Bank of Minneapolis
90 Hennepin Avenue
Minneapolis, MN 55401-1804

Kenneth R. Troske
Department of Economics
335BA Gatton Business and
   Economics Building
University of Kentucky
Lexington, KY 40506-0034

Author Index

Subject Index